Free Public Library of Sydney

Supplement to the catalogue of the Free Public Library Sydney

Free Public Library of Sydney

Supplement to the catalogue of the Free Public Library Sydney

ISBN/EAN: 9783337282325

Printed in Europe, USA, Canada, Australia, Japan

Cover: Foto ©Andreas Hilbeck / pixelio.de

More available books at **www.hansebooks.com**

SUPPLEMENT

TO THE

CATALOGUE

OF THE

FREE PUBLIC LIBRARY,

SYDNEY,

FOR THE YEARS

1888-92.

REFERENCE DEPARTMENT.

SYDNEY : CHARLES POTTER, GOVERNMENT PRINTER, PHILLIP STREET.

1895.

5) 33--95

SUPPLEMENTARY CATALOGUE—1888-1892.

A

A., E. One of Themselves. [*See* Our American Cousins.]

A B C RAILWAY GUIDE [of Great Britain], February, 1886. 8vo. Lond., 1886.   E

ABAILARD. Abailard et Héloïse: Essai Historique, par M. & Mme. Guizot. 12mo. Paris, 1876.   C 17 Q 29

ABBOT, Charles, First Baron Colchester. [*See* Colchester, Baron.]

ABBOTT, C. C. Upland and Meadow. 8vo. Lond., 1886.   D 18 R 19

ABBOTT, Edward. The English and Australian Cookery Book. Cookery for the many as well as for the Upper Ten Thousand; by "An Australian Aristologist." 8vo. Lond., 1864.   MA 1 V 67

ABBOTT, Rev. Edwin A. Philomythus; an antidote against Credulity: a discussion of Cardinal Newman's Essay on Ecclesiastical Miracles. 12mo. Lond., 1891.   G 13 U 39

The Anglican Career of Cardinal Newman. 2 vols. 8vo. Lond., 1892.   C 18 S 17, 18

Shakespearian Grammar. 12mo. Lond., 1869.   K 11 U 17

ABBOTT, Dr. Evelyn. History of Greece. 2 vols. 8vo. Lond., 1888-92.   B 27 Q 13, 14

Iliad of Homer. [*See* Homer.]

[*See* Duncker, Prof. M.]

ABBOTT, Rev. L., and HALLIDAY, Rev. S. B. Henry Ward Beecher: a Sketch of his Career. Roy. 8vo. Hartford, 1887.   C 12 T 28

ABBOTT, T. K. On Wells in Liverpool Plains. 8vo. Sydney, 1880.   MA 3 T 45

ABBOTT, W. E. Notes of a Journey on the Darling. [Read before the Royal Society of N.S.W., 1 June, 1881.] 8vo. Sydney, 1881.   MD 7 S 17

ABBOTT & Co. Victorian Post Office Almanac for 1860. 8vo. Melb., 1860.   ME 4 P

A'BECKET, Thomas. [*See* Becket, Thomas a'.]

A'BECKETT, G. A. Comic History of England. 2 vols. 8vo. Lond., 1863.   J 10 S 20, 21

A

A'BECKETT, Sir W. The Magistrates' Manual for the Colony of Victoria. 8vo. Melb., 1852.   MF 1 T 64

ABEL, Sir F. A. Professional Notes: Electricity applied to Explosive Purposes. 8vo. Lond. (n.d.)   A 21 S 31

ABERCROMBY, Hon. John. Trip through the Eastern Caucasus. 8vo. Lond., 1889.   D 18 U 10

ABERCROMBY, Hon. R. Seas and Skies in many latitudes; or, Wanderings in search of Weather. 8vo. Lond., 1888.   D 10 S 27

Weather : a Popular Exposition of the nature of Weather Changes. 8vo. Lond., 1887.   A 19 Q 25

ABINGTON, Mrs. F. (Miss F. Barton). Life of, including also Notes upon the History of the Irish Stage. 8vo. Lond., 1888.   C 3 R 50

ABNEY, Capt. W. de W. Pioneers of the Alps. [*See* Cunningham, C. D.]

Treatise on Photography. 12mo. Lond., 1888.   A 13 Q 4

ABOUT, E. Œuvres de. 25 vols. 8vo. Paris, 1864-87.   J 19 P 1-25

1. A B C du Travailleur.
2. Alsace en 1871-72.
3, 4. Causeries. 2 vols.
5. De Pontoise à Stamboul.—Le Grain de Plomb.—Dans les Ruines.—Les Œufs de Paques.—Le Jardin de Mon Grand' Père.—Au Petit Trianon.—Quatre Discours.
6. Germaine.
7. La Grèce Contemporaine.
8. Le Fellah.
9. Le Mari Imprévu.
10. Le Marquis de Lanrose.
11. Le Roi des Montagnes.
12. Le Roman d'un Brave Homme.
13. Les Mariages de Paris.
14. Les Mariages de Province.—La Fille du Chanoine.—Mainfroi.—L'Album du Régiment.—Etienne.
15. Les Vacances de la Comtesse.
16. Le Turco.—Le Bal des Artistes.—Le Poivre.—L'Ouverture au Château.—Tout Paris.—La Chambre d'Ami.—Chasse Allemande.—L'Inspection Générale.—Les Cinq Perles.
17. L'Homme à l'Oreille Cassée.
18. L'Infâme.
19. Madelon.
20. Maître Pierre.
21, 22. Salons de 1864 et 1866. 2 vols.
23. Théâtre Impossible.—Guillery.—L'Assassin.—L'Education d'un Prince.—Le Chapeau de Sainte Catherine.
24. Tolla.
25. Trente et quarante.—Sans Dot.—Les Parents de Bernard.

ABORIGINES. Aboriginal Tribes—North America, New South Wales, Van Diemen's Land, and British Guiana. Fol. Lond., 1834.   MF 8 P 11 †

Report from the Select Committee on Aborigines (British Settlements), with Minutes of Evidence, Appendix, and Index. Fol. Lond., 1837.   MF 8 P 10 †

Brief Account of the Natives of Western Australia, their character, manners, and customs; prepared to illustrate the collection of weapons, &c., sent to the Exhibition at Sydney, N.S.W., A.D. 1879. 8vo. Perth, 1879.   MA 3 T 41

Copies or Extracts of Despatches relative to the Massacre of various Aborigines of Australia in the year 1838, and respecting the Trial of their Murderers. Fol. Lond., 1839.   MF 8 P 12 †

Copies or Extracts from Despatches of Governors of the Australian Colonies, with Reports of Protectors of Aborigines, and other Correspondence to illustrate condition of Aboriginal Population of said Colonies from 1839. Fol. Lond., 1844.   MF 8 P 13 †

ABRAMOWITCH, I. An Essay on the Genealogy of Jesus of Nazareth, based upon the New Testament. 12mo. Sydney, 1891.   MG 2 P 37

ABUS (L') DES BOISSONS ALCOOLIQUES, Meeting International d'Anvers contre, 1885. 8vo. Bruxelles, 1886.   F 11 S 1

ACADÉMIE DES SCIENCES. Comptes rendus. Tomes 102–113. 4to. Paris, 1886–1891.   E

ACADÉMIE IMPÉRIALE DES SCIENCES, St. Pétersbourg. Comte-rendu de la Commission Impériale Archéologique. 21 vols. 8vo. and 2 vols. folio. St. Pétersbourg, 1860–1881.   E and E 8 R 15, 16 ‡

ACADEMY OF NATURAL SCIENCES, Philadelphia. Proceedings, 1841–91. 41 vols. roy. 8vo. Philad., 1843–92.   E

ACKROYD, W. History and the Science of Drunkenness. 8vo. Lond., 1883.   F 11 Q 1

ACLAND, A. H. D. Guide to the Choice of Books for Students and General Readers. 8vo. Lond., 1891.   K 7 R 50

ACLAND, A. H. D., and JONES, B. Working Men Co-operators: What they have done and what they are doing. 12mo. Lond., 1889.   F 14 P 41

ACLAND, A. H. D., and RANSOME, Prof. C. Handbook in Outline of the Political History of England to 1887. 3rd ed. 8vo. Lond., 1888.   B 4 P 6

ACTORS AND ACTRESSES of Great Britain and the United States, from the days of Garrick; edited by B. Matthews and L. Hutton. 5 vols. 8vo. New York, 1886.   C 12 Q 41–45

ACWORTH, W. M. The Railways of England. 2nd edition. 8vo. Lond., 1889.   A G T 27

The Railways and the Traders. 8vo. Lond., 1891.   F 6R 43

ADAM OF MIRIMUTH. [*See* Chronicles and Memorials of Gt. Brit., &c.]

ADAM, Sir C. E. View of Political State of Scotland; being the Political Opinions of 2,662 country voters in 1788. 8vo. Edinb., 1887.   B 31 Q 12

ADAM, G. M. Life and Career of Sir John A. Macdonald. 8vo. Lond., 1892.   C 18 S 6

ADAM, Wm. Speech of, in the House of Commons, on moving for the Production of certain Records and for an Address to the King to interpose the Royal Justice and Clemency in behalf of Thos. Muir and Rev. Thos. Fysho Palmer. 8vo. Lond., 1794.   F 2 V 3

ADAMS, C. K. Representative British Orations; printed in easy reporting style of phonography. 2 vols. 12mo. Lond., 1887.   F 1 P 34, 35

ADAMS, Sir F. O., and CUNNINGHAM, C. D. The Swiss Confederation. 8vo. Lond., 1889.   F 10 R 26

ADAMS, F. W. L. Madeline Brown's Murderer. 12mo. Melb., 1887.   MJ 1 T 54

Songs of the Army of the Night. 12mo. Sydney (n.d.)   MII 1 Q 39

ADAMS, Henry. Historical Essays. 8vo. Lond., 1891   B 17 P 29

ADAMS, Prof. H. B. College of William and Mary : a Contribution to the History of Higher Education, with Suggestions for its Natural Promotion. Roy. 8vo. Washington, 1887.   G 17 R 24

Study of History in American Colleges and Universities. Roy. 8vo. Washington, 1887.   G 17 R 24

[*See* Johns Hopkins University Studies.]

ADAMS, H. C. Public Debts : an Essay in the Science of Finance. 8vo. Lond., 1888.   F 12 Q 24

ADAMS, W. D. Book of Burlesque; Sketches of English Stage Travestie and Parody. 8vo. Lond., 1891.   J 1 U 43

ADAMSON, T. Acts and Ordinances in force in Victoria. 3 vols. roy. 8vo. Melb., 1855–57.   MF 2 S 51–53

ADDISON, G. R. [*See* Lee and Ross.]

ADDISON, J. Sir Roger de Coverley : Selections from the *Spectator*; edited, with an Introduction and Notes, by A. B. Piddington. 12mo. Sydney, 1892.   MJ 2 T 19

Cato : a Tragedy. [*See* British Drama, Modern.]

The Drummer : a Comedy. [*See* British Drama, Modern.]

ADDY, S. O. Sheffield Glossary. [*See* English Dialect Soc.]

ADELAIDE ALMANAC and Guide to South Australia. 8vo. Adelaide, 1864.   ME 4 P

ADELAIDE CIRCULATING LIBRARY, Catalogue of. 8vo. Adelaide, 1886.   MK 1 R 50

ADELAIDE JUBILEE INTERNATIONAL EXHIBITION, 1887–88. Official Catalogue of Exhibits from New South Wales. 8vo. Sydney, 1887.   MK 1 T 27

Another copy. 8vo. Sydney, 1887.   MK 1 R 46

Report of the Executive Commissioner for New South Wales. Roy. 8vo. Sydney, 1890.   MK 1 S 36

Report of the Royal Commission. 8vo. Lond., 1881.   ME

ADELAIDE UNIVERSITY. Calendars for the Years 1882, 1884, and 1892. 3 vols. 8vo. Adelaide, 1882-92.
ME 5 S

ADELINE, J. Adeline's Art Dictionary. 8vo. Lond., 1891.
K 18 P 32

ADINGTON, W. [*See* Apuleius, L.]

ADRIAN NORTH; by "Baroni." 12mo. Hobart, 1889.
MJ 2 T 4

ÆLFRIC. Lives of the Saints. [*See* Early Eng. Text Society.]

ÆSCHINES. Opera. 12mo. Lipsiæ, 1829.   J 15 Q 13

ÆSCHYLUS; by Rt. Rev. R. S. Copleston. (Ancient Classics for English Readers.) 8vo. Edinb., 1887.
J 14 P 1

Æschylus : The Seven Plays in English Verse; by Prof. L. Campbell. 8vo. Lond., 1890.
H 4 Q 33

Æschylus, Agamemnon of; freely translated into English on the occasion of the Performance of the Play by Students of the University of Sydney. 8vo. Sydney, 1886.
MH 1 S 47

Agamemnon : Introduction and Notes by A. Sidgwick. 3rd ed. 12mo. Oxford, 1887.
H 2 Q 47

Choephori : Introduction and Notes by A. Sidgwick. 12mo. Oxford, 1884.
H 2 Q 48

Eumenides : Introduction and Notes by A. Sidgwick. 12mo. Oxford, 1887.
H 2 Q 49

Tragedies of : New Translation by Very Rev. E. H. Plumptre. 12mo. Lond., 1890.
H 1 Q 39

The Seven against Thebes ; with Introduction, Commentary, and Translation, by A. W. Verrall. Roy. 8vo. Lond., 1887.
H 3 S 30

[Tragœdiæ] : recensuit J. Scholefield. 2nd ed. 8vo. Cantab., 1830.
H 9 S 4

Tragœdiæ : recensuit A. Wellauer. 2 vols. 8vo. Lipsiæ, 1823-24.
H 9 S 5, 6

ÆSOP. Æsop's Fables in words of one syllable, by Mary Godolphin. Printed in the learner's style of Phonography by I. Pitman. 12mo. Lond., 1888.
J 7 R 54

Fables of ; edited by J. Jacobs. 2 vols. 8vo. Lond., 1889.
J 11 S 36, 37

AFFILIATION OF CAPITAL AND LABOUR, by "Australis Ignotus." 8vo. Sydney, 1890. MF 1 T 36

AFFLECK, T. and GRAY, J. C. The *Border Post* (Albury) Almanac for 1877. 12mo. Albury, 1877.
ME 4 Q

AFTER TWENTY YEARS ; Our Distinguished Visitor, and Poems of the Post Office; by "A Local Letter Carrier." 8vo. Ballarat, 1884.
MJ 1 T 32

AGASSIZ, Prof. A. Embryology of the Ctenophoræ. 4to. Cambridge, Mass., 1874.
A 14 V 8

Three Cruises of the U. S. Coast and Geodetic Survey Steamer *Blake*, 1877-80, in the Gulf of Mexico : a Contribution to American Thalassography. 2 vols. roy. 8vo. Lond., 1888.
A 29 V 3, 4

AGASSIZ, A., FAXON, W., and MARK, E. L. Selections from Embryological Memoirs. Pt. 1, Crustacea. Pt. 2, Echinodermata. Pt. 3, Acalephs and Polyps. 4to. Camb., 1882-84.
A 36 S 1 ‡

AGASSIZ, Prof. Louis. Contributions to Natural History of the United States. Vols. 1 and 2, roy. 4to. Boston, 1857.
A 4 P 8, 9 †

Monographie des Poissons Fossiles du Vieux Grès Rouge, ou Système Dévonien (Old Red Sandstone) des Iles Britanniques et de Russie. Roy. 4to. Neuchatel, 1844.
A 34 P 12 ‡

Planches [to the above.] Ob. 4to. Neuchatel, 1844-45.
A 34 P 13 ‡

Recherches sur les Poissons fossiles. 5 vols. roy. 4to. Neuchatel, 1833-43.
A 34 P 5-9 ‡

Atlas [to the above.] 5 vols. (in 2) ob. 4to. Neuchatel, 1833-43.
A 34 P 10, 11 ‡

AGE, THE. 16 vols. fol. Melb., 1889-92.   ME

AGE ANNUAL, The : A Political and Statistical Register of Victoria for 1887. 8vo. Melb., 1887.   ME 2 R

AGNEW, Rev. D. C. A. Protestant Exiles from France ; or, the Huguenot Refugees and their Descendants in Great Britain and Ireland. 3rd ed. 2 vols. sm. fol. Edinb., 1866.
B 7 P 22, 23 †

AGRICULTURAL SOCIETY OF NEW SOUTH WALES. Journal. Vol. 1, No. 1—Vol. 3, No. 5. Sm. fol. Sydney, 1868-70.
ME 4 V

AGRICULTURE, Department of, New South Wales. Bulletin, No. 2. The Points of Stock and their relative Values, &c. 8vo. Sydney, 1891.
MA 1 Q 70

Bulletin No. 4. Report of the Conference of Fruit-Growers, together with Appendices. Roy. 8vo. Sydney, 1891.
MA 1 Q 70

Directions for Collecting, Packing, and Forwarding Specimens of Insects, Plants, and Fungi. Roy. 8vo. Sydney, 1890.
MA 3 R 3

AGRICULTURE, Department of, Queensland. Bulletins, Nos. 1-6. 8vo. Brisbane, 1890.
MA 3 S 4

Pig Raising and Pork Making ; by E. M. Shelton.
Report of Agricultural Conference, 1890.
Cultivation of Maize ; by E. M. Shelton.
Botany : Contributions to the Queensland Flora ; by F. M. Bailey.
Canning and otherwise preserving Fruits for the Home and Market ; by E. M. Shelton.
Tobacco : its cultivation in Northern Queensland ; by S. Lamb.

Papers for the People by Practical Men on Agriculture, Horticulture, and Pastoral Farming in Queensland. 12mo. Brisb., 1888-90.
MA 3 P 20

Arrowroot Cultivation and Manufacturing in Queensland ; by S. Grimes.
Butter, Cheese Making, and Co-operative Dairying.
Cheese Making simplified.
Cotton.
Flower Gardening ; by A. M. Cowan.
Forestry ; by C. A. Barton.
Fruit Culture.
Guide to the Culture of Broom Corn.
Ham and Bacon Industry ; by W. Watson.
Keeping the Dairy Cool.
Manufacture of Butter ; by W. Castles.
Notes on the Banana ; by W. Hill.

Papers for the People—*contd.*

Notes on the Mango.
Orange Cultivation in Queensland; by A. M. Cowan.
Pastoral Farming; by P. R. Gordon.
Pine Apple Cultivation.
Ramie or Fibre Industry.
Ramie or Rhoea.
Rice; by C. A. Collard.
Silos and Ensilage.
Sugar-cane; by G. Grimes.
The Apple in Queensland; by J. W. Cribb.
The Grape Vine and its Cultivation in Queensland.
The Olive.
Tobacco Cultivation in Queensland; by E. B. Greenup.
Vegetable Gardening in Queensland; by Wm. Soutter.
Wheat Growing.

AGRICULTURE, Department of, Victoria. Bulletins, June and October, 1888. 2 vols. 8vo. Melb., 1888.
MA 3 T 59, 60

AGRICULTURE IN NEW SOUTH WALES, The Present Condition and Future Prospects of, by "A Farmer." 8vo. Sydney, 1878.   MA 3 Q 8

AGRONOMES LATINS, Les. Caton, Varron, Columelle, Palladius. (Fr. et Lat.) Imp. 8vo. Paris, 1849.
A 18 V 8

AHN, Dr. F. Practical Grammar of the German Language. New ed., by D. W. Turner and F. W. Weinmann. 12mo. Lond., 1861.   K 16 P 32

AINGER, Rev. A. [Life of] Charles Lamb. 12mo. Lond., 1888.   C 2 R 5
Letters of C. Lamb.   [*See* Lamb, C.]

AINGER, A. C. Fives. [*See* Tennis, &c.]

AINSLIE, Gen. C. P. de. Historical Record of the First or the Royal Regiment of Dragoons. Roy. 8vo. Lond., 1887.   B 23 U 11

AINSWORTH, W. F. Personal Narrative of the Euphrates Expedition. 2 vols. 8vo. Lond., 1888.
D 16 U 3, 4
The River Karun, an opening to British Commerce. 8vo. Lond., 1890.   D 17 Q 8

AITKEN, G. A. Life and Works of Dr. J. Arbuthnot. 8vo. Oxford, 1892.   C 18 S 19
Satires of Andrew Marvell. [*See* Marvell, A.]

AITKEN, Sir W. On the Animal Alkaloids in their Pathological Relations. 12mo. Lond., 1887. A 26 P 1
On the Growth of the Recruit and Young Soldier. 2nd ed. 8vo. Lond., 1887.   A 26 Q 27
The Science and Practice of Medicine. 7th ed. 2 vols. roy. 8vo. Lond. 1880.   A 26 U 6, 7

AKBAR THE GREAT, Emperor of Hindostan. [Life of]; by Col. J. B. Malleson. (Rulers of India.) 12mo. Oxford, 1890.   C 12 P 37

AKERMAN, J. Y. Tradesmen's Tokens, current in London, 1648-1672. 4to. Lond., 1849. A 42 R 20 ‡

ALBANIAN LANGUAGE. Grammaire Albanaise; par P. W. 8vo. Lond., 1887.   K 20 Q 18

ALBERT, H.R.H. PRINCE. Life of H.R.H. the Prince Consort; by Charlotte M. Yonge. (Statesmen Series.) 8vo. Lond., 1890.   C 12 R 4C
[*See* Geffcken, Dr. F. H.]

ALBERT EDWARD, H.R.H. Prince of Wales. Speeches and Addresses of. Edited by James Macaulay. 8vo. Lond., 1889.   F 13 Q 26

ALBERUNI, 'Abû-Alraihân Muhammad Ibn 'Ahmad. Alberuni's India: an account of the Religion, Philosophy, Literature, Geography, Chronology, Astronomy, Customs, Laws and Astrology of India, about A.D. 1030. English edition by Prof. E. C. Sachau. 2 vols. 8vo. Lond., 1888.
B 29 S 1, 2

ALCAN, E. Les Cannibales et leur temps; Souvenirs de la Campagne de l'Oceanie. 12mo. Paris, 1887.
MD 2 W 30

ALCOHOL QUESTION, The; by Sir J. Paget and others. 8vo. Lond. (n.d.)   F 11 Q 7

ALCOHOLIC LIQUORS. The *Times'* Article on Alcoholic Liquors, examined in the light of Fact, Science, and Logic. 12mo. Lond., 1884.   F 11 P 66

ALCOOLISME EN BELGIQUE, 1er Rapport sur le Remède au Mal. 8vo. Bruxelles, 1884.   F 11 S 2

ALCOTT, Miss Louisa May. Her Life, Letters, and Journals; edited by [Mrs.] Ednah D. Cheney. 8vo. Lond., 1889.   C 12 P 1

ALCOTT, Ten. Nativity: its Facts and Fancies, Legends and Lore. Ob. roy. 8vo. New York, 1887. A 10 S 17 †

ALDERTON, G. E. Treatise and Hand-book of Orange Culture in Auckland, New Zealand. 8vo. Wellington, 1884.*   MA 1 Q 41

ALDIS, W. S. Text-book of Algebra. (Clar. Press.) 8vo. Oxford, 1887.   A 25 Q 28

ALDRICH, Rev. H. Artis Logicæ Compendium. 12mo. Lond., 1844.   G 13 Q 27
Artis Logicæ Rudimenta; with Notes by Rev. H. L. Mansel. 2nd. ed. 8vo. Oxford, 1852.   G 12 Q 30

ALEMAN, M. Aventuras y Nida de Guzman de Alfarache. 12mo. Madrid, 1829.   J 7 P 41

ALEXANDER THE GREAT. History of, being the Syriac version of the Pseudo-Callisthenes; edited with translation and notes, by E. A. W. Budge. 8vo. Camb., 1889.   C 14 T 15

ALEXANDER I. [*See* Czartoryski, Prince A.]

ALEXANDER OF BATTENBERG, Prince. Reminiscences of his Reign in Bulgaria; by A. Koch. 8vo. Lond., 1887.   C 12 T 1

ALEXANDER, Francesca. Christ's Folk in the Apennine: Reminiscences of her Friends among the Tuscan Peasantry; edited by J. Ruskin. 8vo. Orpington, 1887.   J 9 Q 42

ALEXANDER, S. Moral Order and Progress: an analysis of ethical conceptions. 8vo. Lond., 1889.   G 11 P 40

ALEXANDER, Stanley. Report on Proposed Railway from Tarago to Braidwood, New South Wales. Fol. Sydney, 1891. MA 11 Q 7 †

Report on Proposed Railways for Riverina, New South Wales. Fol. Sydney, 1891. MA 11 Q 8 †

ALEXANDER, W. D. A Brief History of the Hawaiian People. 8vo. New York, 1891. MB 1 R 38

ALEXANDROW, A. Complete English and Russian Dictionary. 2 vols. 8vo. Lond., 1890. K 12 U 24, 25

ALFIERI, Vittorio. Life of, with an Essay by W. D. Howells. 16mo. Boston, 1877. C 13 P 5

ALFORD, C. J. Geological Features of the Transvaal, South Africa. 8vo. Lond., 1891. A 24 U 10

ALFORD, Rev. H. New Testament. [*See* Bibles.]

ALGER, A. L. [*See* Hugo, V. M., Vicomte]

ALISON, Rev. A. Essay on Taste. [*See* Universal Library, The.]

ALKOHOLFRAGE. Botschaft des Bundesrathes an die Bundesversammlung, betreffend die auf die alkoholfrage bezüglichen Postulate und Petitionen. 8vo. Bern, 1884. F 11 R 2

Zur Alkoholfrage. 8vo. Bern, 1884. F 9 S 24

ALL THE YEAR ROUND. 13 vols. 8vo. Lond., 1886-92. E

ALLARDYCE, A. [*See* Sharpe, C. K., and Ramsay, J.]

ALLEN, C. F. R. [*See* Book of Chinese Poetry.]

ALLEN, Pastor D. The History of the Convent. 8vo. Sydney, 1878. MG 1 Q 60

ALLEN, F. H. The Great Cathedrals of the World. 4to. Boston, 1886. A 6 Q 11 ‡

ALLEN, G. B. [*See* Stephens, J. B.]

ALLEN, J. R. Early Christian Symbolism in Great Britain and Ireland before the 13th Century. Roy. 8vo. Lond., 1887. G 11 T 30

Monumental History of the Early British Church. 12mo. Lond., 1889. G 4 V 4

ALLEN, Rev. R. The Cry of the Curlew : a yarn from the Bush ; by "Guy Eden." 2nd ed. Lond., 1892. MJ 2 T 30

ALLEN, T. History and Antiquities of London, Westminster, and Southwark. 5 vols. 8vo. Lond., 1837-39. B 21 T 21-25

ALLEN, T. W. Notes on Greek Manuscripts in Italian Libraries. 12mo. Lond., 1890. K 20 Q 3

ALLEN, Rev. W. Random Rhymes. 2nd ed. 8vo. Melb., 1888. MH 1 S 46

ALLEN, W. Governor Chamberlain's Administration in South Carolina. 8vo. New York, 1888. F 12 Q 25

ALLEYNE, Sarah Frances. [*See* Duncker, Prof. M.]

ALLGEMEINE DEUTSCHE BIOGRAPHIE. Bande 23-33. Mün-Sem. Roy. 8vo. Leip., 1886-91. C 20 Q 1-11

ALLGEMEINES SCHWEIZER-LIEDERBUCH, eine sammlung von 725 der beliebtesten Gifänge, Rühreihen und Volkslieder. 5° auflage. 12mo. Uarau, 1851. H 6 P 48

ALLIBONE, S. A. Supplement to Allibone's Critical Dictionary of English Literature and British and American Authors ; by John Foster Kirk. 2 vols. Imp. 8vo. Philad., 1891. Librarian

ALLIONI, Carlo. Flora Pedemontana, sive enumeratio methodica stirpium indigenarum Pedemontii. 3 vols. fol. Augustae Taur., 1785. A 6 R 8-10 ‡

ALLMAN, Prof. G. J. Greek Geometry from Thales to Euclid. 8vo. Dublin, 1889. A 10 T 12

ALLOM, A. J. [*See* Sholl, M.]

ALLSOP, Robert Owen. The Turkish Bath. 8vo. Lond., 1890. A 26 T 9

ALMANACH DE GOTHA. 5 vols. 18mo. Gotha, 1888-92. E

ALTMAR, H. Reineke der Fuchs. Imp. 8vo. Leipzig, 1752. J 18 V 21

ALTON TOWERS, Catalogue of the Magnificent Contents of. Roy. 8vo. Lond., 1857. K 8 Q 41

AMATEUR MECHANICS ; by P. Hasluck. Vols 1, 2. 4to. Lond., 1883-84. E

AMERICAN AGRICULTURIST. Vols. 49, 50. Sm. fol. New York, 1890-91. E

AMERICAN ALMANAC AND TREASURY OF FACTS. 2 vols. 8vo. New York, 1887-89. E

AMERICAN ANTIQUARIAN AND ORIENTAL JOURNAL. Vols. 8-13. 8vo. Chicago, 1886-91. E

AMERICAN CATALOGUE, Annual, 1886-91. 6 vols. roy. 8vo. New York, 1887-92. Librarian

AMERICAN INEBRIATE ASSOCIATION. Minutes. 8vo. New York, 1870. F 11 S 9

AMERICAN INSTITUTE OF MINING ENGINEERS. Transactions. Vols. 1-19, 1873-91. 19 vols. roy. 8vo. Philad. and New York, 1873-91 E

Contents and Index for Vols. 1-14 [of the Transactions.] Roy. 8vo. New York, 1888 E

AMERICAN JOURNAL OF ARCHÆOLOGY. Vols. 2-7. Roy. 8vo. Boston, 1886-91. E

AMERICAN JOURNAL OF SCIENCE. 3rd Series. Vols. 23-42. 8vo. New Haven, 1887-91. E

AMERICAN TEMPERANCE SOCIETY. Permanent Temperance Documents. Vol. 1. roy. 8vo. Boston, 1835. F 11 R 1

AMEZAGA, Commandante C. de. Viaggio di Circumnavigazione della Regia Corvetta "Caracciolo" negli Anni 1881-84. 4 vols, roy. 8vo. Roma, 1885-86. D 9 U 30

AMICIS, E. de. Alle Porte d'Italia. 8vo. Milano, 1888.
       D 18 R·18

Sull' Oceano; con disegni di A. Ferraguti. 4to. Milano, 1890.   D 9 V 10

AMMIANUS MARCELLINUS. Œuvres de. [*See* Nisard, D.]

AMNEMA. [*See* Trials and Travels of a Dominie.]

AMPÈRE, J. J. La Grèce, Rome, et Dante: Études Littéraires d'après Nature. 8vo. Paris, 1880.   B 16 R 6

La Science et les Lettres en Orient. 8vo. Paris, 1865.   J 5 P 47

ANACREON. Carmina, Græce; e recensione G. Baxteri; ed. J. F. Fischerus. 8vo. Lipsiæ, 1793.   H 6 U 31

ANDERSON, Andrew. Scenes in Scotia; (Part first) Archibald Forbes and his Lecture "Kings and Princes I have met"; and Spring Flowers. 12mo. Adelaide, 1886.   MH 1 Q 60

Murmurs from the Ocean and Echoes from the Shore. 2nd ed. 12mo. Adelaide, 1881.   MH 1 Q 61

ANDERSON, Andrew. A. Twenty-five Years in a Waggon in the Gold Regions of Africa. 2 vols. 8vo. Lond., 1887.   D 14 R 1, 2

ANDERSON, D. "Scenes" in the Commons. 8vo. Lond., 1884.   F 5 T 31

ANDERSON, Dr. John. English Intercourse with Siam in the 17th Century. With map. 8vo. Lond., 1890.   B 29 S 3

ANDERSON, J. C. Croydon Inclosure. Plan and Award. Imp. 8vo. Croydon, 1889.   B 23 V 14

[*See* Hartley Library.]

ANDERSON, R. B. [*See* Rydberg, V.]

ANDERSON, W. J. Hysterical and Nervous Affections of Women. 12mo. Sydney, 1864.   MA 3 P 9

ANDREA, G. [*See* Ovidius Naso, P.]

ANDREWINA. [*See* Cox, Mrs. C.]

ANDREWS, C. C. Brazil, its Conditions and Prospects. 8vo. New York, 1887.   D 15 Q 6

ANDREWS, H. J. C. [*See* Chess Problem.]

ANDREWS, J. A. Temple Mystic, and other Poems. 12mo. Ballarat, 1888.   MH 1 Q 40

ANDREWS, Professor T. The Scientific Papers of; with a Memoir by Prof. P. G. Tait and Prof. A. C. Brown. 8vo. Lond., 1889.   A 5 T 21

ANDREWS, W. North Country Poets: Modern Section. Vol. 1. 8vo. Lond., 1888.   H 3 R 26

Old Church Lore. 8vo. Hull, 1891.   G 6 R 41

ANDREWS, W. A. Old-time Punishments. 8vo. Hull, 1890.   B 5 T 34

ANECDOTA OXONIENSIA. Classical Series. Vol. 1. Part 7. Sm. 4to. Oxford, 1891.   E

   1. Part 7. Collations from the Harleian M.S. of Cicero, 2682; by Albert C. Clark, M.A.

Mediæval and Modern Series. Vol. 1. Parts 2 and 5. 2 vols. sm. 4to. Oxford, 1887–90.   E

   1. Part 2. Alphita: a Medico-Botanical Glossary from the Bodleian M.S., Selden, B., 35; edited by J. L. G. Mowat, M.A.
   1. Part 5. Lives of Saints from the Book of Lismore; edited with a translation, &c. by Whitley Stokes, D.C.L.

Semetic Series. Vol. 1. Parts 3 and 4. 2 vols. sm. 4to. Oxford, 1887–89.   E

   1. Part 3. A Commentary on the Book of Daniel by Jephet Ibn Ali, the Karaite. (In Arabic); edited and translated by Prof. D. S. Margoliouth, M.A.
   1. Part 4. Mediæval Jewish Chronicles and Chronological Notes; edited by Ad. Neubauer.

ANGAS, George French. Description d'espèces nouvelles appartenant à plusieurs genres de Mollusques Nudibranches des environs de Port Jackson. 8vo. Paris (n.d.)   MA 2 U 48

Six Views of the Goldfield of Ophir. Ob. 4to. Sydney, 1851.   MD 3 P 8 ‡

ANGAS, George Fife. Father and Founder of South Australia, by Edwin Hodder. 8vo. Lond., 1891.   MC 1 T 6

ANGEL, A. C. Constitutional Limitations. [*See* Cooley, Dr. T. M.]

ANGLIN, S. Design of Structures: a practical treatise on the building of bridges, roofs, &c. 8vo. Lond., 1891.   A 22 Q 32

ANGLO-INDIAN GLOBE TROTTER, An. [*See* Sail, C. R.]

ANGLO-JEWISH HISTORICAL EXHIBITION.
Bibliotheca Anglo-Judaica: a Bibliographical Guide to Anglo-Jewish History; compiled by J. Jacobs and L. Wolf. 8vo. Lond., 1888.   K 19 P 3

Catalogue. 8vo. Lond., 1887.   K 7 R 43

Hebrew Deeds of English Jews before 1290; edited by M. D. Davis. 8vo. Lond., 1888.   B 21 R 20

Papers read at. 8vo. Lond., 1888.   G 13 T 42

ANGOULEME, Duchess of. [*See* Imbert de Saint-Amand, A.L., Baron.]

ANIMAL WORLD. Vols. 17-21. Fol. Lond., 1886–91.   E

ANNALES DES MINES. Memoires. 8me Série, Tomes 10–20. 9me Série, Tomes, 1, 2. 8vo. Paris, 1886–92   E

Lois, etc. 8me Série, Tomes, 5–10. 8vo. Paris, 1886–90.   E

ANNALS AND MAGAZINE OF NATURAL HIS-TORY. 5th Series, vols. 19, 20, and 6th Series, vols. 1–9. 8vo. Lond., 1887–92.   E

ANNUAIRE DES ÉTABLISSEMENTS FRANCAIS de L'Océanie pour l'an, 1865. 12mo. Papeete, 1865. ME 8 P

ANNUAL REGISTER, 1886-91. 6vols. 8vo. Lond., 1887-92.   E

ANSON, George, Lord. Supplement au Voyage à la Mer du Sud (Prévost, A. F., Suite de l' histoire générale des voyages, tome 17). 4to. Amst., 1761.   MD 11 P 16 †

ANSON, Sir W. R. The Law and Custom of the Constitution. Pt. 2 : The Crown. 8vo. Oxford, 1892.   F 10 S 9

ANSTED, Prof. D. T., TENNANT, Prof., and MITCHELL, Rev. W. Geology, Mineralogy, and Crystallography. 8vo. Lond., 1855.   A 24 R 4

ANSTIE, Dr. F. E. On the Uses of Wines in Health and Disease. Lond., 1877.   F 11 P 67
Stimulants and Narcotics, their mutual relations. 8vo. Lond., 1864.   F 11 S 8

ANTANANARIVO ANNUAL AND MADAGASCAR MAGAZINE. 6 vols. Antananarivo, 1886-92.   E

ANTHROPOLOGICAL INSTITUTE OF GREAT BRITAIN AND IRELAND. Journal : Vols. 16-21. 8vo. Lond., 1887-92.   E

ANTHROPOLOGICAL REVIEW, The. Nos. 1-29. 5 vols. 8vo. Lond., 1864-70.   E

ANTIQUAIRES DU NORD, Société des. Aarbøger for Nordisk Oldkyndighed og Historie. 6 vols. 8vo. Kjøbenhavn, 1886-91.   E
Islendinga Sögur. 8 vols. Kjøbenhavn, 1889.   E

ANTIQUARIAN MAGAZINE and Bibliographical Review. Vols. 11, 12. 8vo. Lond., 1887.   E

ANTIQUARIES OF LONDON, Society of. Archæologia. Vols. 50-52. 4to. Lond., 1887-90.   E
Index to Archæologia, vols. 1-50. 4to. Lond., 1889.   E

ANTIQUARY, The ; edited by E. Walford. Vols. 1-24. 4to. Lond., 1880-91.   E

ANVILLE, J. B. B. d'. Traité des Mesures itinéraires anciennes et modernes. 8vo. Paris, 1769.   A 22 R 28

APOLLODORUS. Bibliotheca ; ex recognitione I. Bekkeri. 8vo. Lipsiæ, 1854.   B 35 P 19

APOLLONIUS RHODIUS. Argonautica ; recensuit R. Merkel. 12mo. Lipsiæ, 1852.   H 10 P 23
The Argonautica of. Translated by E. P. Coleridge. 12mo. Lond., 1889.   H 7 P 46

APPIAN. Historia Romana ; ab I. Bekkero recognita. (Greek text.) 2 vols. (in 1.) 8vo. Lipsiæ, 1852-53.   B 30 Q 4

APPLETON, D., & Co. Appleton's Cyclopædia of American Biography ; edited by J. G. Wilson and J. Fiske. 6 vols. Imp. 8vo. New York, 1887-89.   C 12 V 1-6

APULEIUS, L. Opera. 2 vols. 8vo. Biponti, 1788.   G 16 T 35
The most pleasant and delectable Tale of the Marriage of Cupid and Psyche ; done in English by W. Adlington. 8vo. Lond., 1887.   J 5 P 38

AQUINAS, Saint T. Summa Theologica. Omnia hæc denuo recognoscente, &c., J. P. Migne. 4 vols. Imp. 8vo. Paris, 1860-61.   G 10 V 1-4

ARABIAN PRINCESS, An. Memoirs of. 8vo. Lond., 1888.   C 12 R 17

ARAGO, Jacques Etienne. Souvenirs d'un Aveugle : Voyage autour du Monde. 2 vols. Roy. 8vo. Paris (n.d.)   MD 7 R 35, 36
Another copy. 4 vols. 8vo. Paris, 1839.   MD 5 T 45, 48

ARBER, Prof. E. List of London Publishers, 1553-1640. 4to. Birm., 1890.   K 12 T 10 †

ARBUTHNOT, F. F. Arabic Authors ; a manual of Arabian History and Literature. 8vo. Lond., 1890.   B 36 S 1
Free Trade in Land ; or, a few Remarks on the English Land Question. 8vo. Lond., 1885.   F 5 U 34
Persian Portraits ; a sketch of Persian History, Literature, and Politics. 8vo. Lond., 1887.   B 16 S 1

ARBUTHNOT, Dr. J. Life and Works of ; by G. A. Aitken. 8vo. Oxford, 1892.   C 18 S 19

ARCANA FAIRFAXIANA MANUSCRIPTA. A Manuscript volume of Apothecaries' Lore and Housewifery, used and partly written by the Fairfax Family. Introduction by G. Weddell. Sm. 4to. Newcastle-on-Tyne, 1890.   A 26 U 19

ARCHÆOLOGIA. [*See* Antiquaries of London, Soc. of.]

ARCHÆOLOGIA CAMBRENSIS. [*See* Cambrian Archæological Association.]

ARCHÆOLOGIA CANTIANA. [*See* Kent Archæological Society.]

ARCHÆOLOGICAL INSTITUTE OF AMERICA. Papers, vol. 3. 8vo. Boston, 1888.   E
6th Annual Report, 1884-85. 8vo. Camb., Mass., 1885.   E
Bulletin. 8vo. Boston, 1883.   E
Preliminary Report of an Archæological Journey made through Asia Minor in 1884, by J. R. S. Sterrett. 8vo. Boston, 1885.   E
A Proto-Ionic Capital from the Site of Neandrein. 8vo. Baltimore, 1886.   E

ARCHÆOLOGICAL REVIEW. Vols. 1-4. Roy. 8vo. Lond., 1888-91.   E

ARCHER, F. How to write a good Play. 8vo. Lond., 1891.   J 11 W 12

ARCHER, Major J. H. Lawrence-. The British Army : its Regimental Records, Badges, Devices, &c. Roy. 8vo. Lond., 1888.   B 24 S 18
Orders of Chivalry ; from the original Statutes of the various Orders of Knighthood. Roy. 4to. Lond., 1887. K 11 Q 1 †

ARCHER, T. A. The Crusade of Richard I., 1189-92. (English History by Contemporary Writers.) 18mo. Lond., 1888.   B 22 P 4

ARCHER, William. William Charles Macready. (Eminent Actors). 12mo. Lond., 1890.   C 12 P 43

ARCHER-HIND, R. D.　[*See* Hind, R. D. Archer.-]

ARCHITECT, The.　Vols. 36-47.　Fol.　Lond., 1886-92.　　　　　　　　　　　　　　　　　E

ARCHITECTURAL PUBLICATION SOCIETY.　Detached Essays and Illustrations, 1848-52.　Fol.　Lond., 1853.　　　　　　　　　　　　　　A 37 P 22 ‡

ARCHITECTURAL SOCIETIES of Lincoln, Nottingham, York, &c., Reports and Papers.　8vo.　Lincoln, 1885-91.　　　　　　　　　　　　　　　　E

ARCHIV FÜR MIKROSKOPISCHE ANATOMIE.　Bande 28-39.　8vo.　Bonn, 1886-92.　　E

ARDEN, J.　Jos. Arden's Komic Monthly Papers.　No. 1.　12mo.　Sydney, 1882.　　　　MJ 1 R 44

ARGYLL, George Douglas Campbell, Duke of.　New British Constitution and its Master-Builders.　8vo.　Edinb., 1888.　　　　　　　　　　　　F 5 T 32
Scotland as it was and as it is.　2 vols.　8vo.　Edinb., 1887.　　　　　　　　　　　B 31 T 15, 16

ARISTEAS.　Historia LXXII. interpretum, accessere veterum testimonia de eorum versione. (Gr. et Lat.)　8vo.　Oxon., 1692.　　　　　　　　　　　　G 18 R 36

ARISTOPHANES ; by Rev. Canon Collins.　(Ancient Classics for English Readers).　8vo.　Edinb., 1880.　　　　　　　　　　　　　　　　J 14 P 2
Comœdiæ undecim ; (Gr. et Lat.) recensuit L. Kusterus.　Fol.　Amstelodami, 1710.　　　H 40 R 3 ‡
Notæ in Aristophanem.　3 vols.　8vo.　Lond., 1829.　　　　　　　　　　　　　　H 9 S 17-19

ARISTOTELES.　Aristotle on the Constitution of Athens : Fac-simile of Papyrus CXXXI. in the British Museum.　Fol.　Lond., 1891.　　　　　　　F 32 P 24 ‡
Aristotle on the Constitution of Athens ; edited by F. G. Kenyon.　8vo.　Lond., 1891.　　　F 8 Q 20
Aristotle ; by Sir A. Grant.　(Ancient Classics for English Readers.)　8vo.　Edinb., 1888.　J 14 P 3
Art of Poetry.　[*See* Prickard, A. V.]
Elementa Logices Aristotelæ ; excerpsit F. A. Trendelenburg.　8vo.　Berolini, 1845.　　　G 13 Q 35
Ethics of. (Greek text.)　Essays and Notes by Sir A. Grant.　2nd ed.　2 vols.　8vo.　Lond., 1866.　G 4 U 36, 37
The Nicomachean Ethics of.　Translated by Rev. D. P. Chase.　2nd ed.　8vo.　Oxford, 1861.　G 16 P 37
Ethicorum, sive de moribus, libri decem ; opera P. Victorii emendati. (Gr. text).　Sm. 4to.　Francof., 1584.　　　　　　　　　　　　　　　　G 16 T 16
Opera omnia : ed. C. H. Weise.　(Greek text.)　Imp. 8vo.　Lipsiæ, 1843.　　　　　　J 8 V 16
Organum.　(Gr. et Lat.)　12mo.　Francof., 1592.　G 13 Q 32
De Rhetorica.　(Gr. text.)　8vo.　Oxonii, 1833.　G 4 T 26
Ethicorum Nicomacheorum, libri decem ; notis illustrati a G. Wilkinson. (Gr. text.)　8vo.　Oxonii, 1716.　G 13 R 46
Politics of Aristotle ; with English Notes, by R. Congreve.　8vo.　Lond., 1855.　　　　　F 8 Q 19
Politics of. (Gr. text.)　English Notes, by J. R. T. Eaton.　8vo.　Oxford, 1855.　　　　　F 1 Q 19

ARISTOTELES—*contd.*
Politics of ; with an Introduction, Notes, &c., by W. L. Newman.　2 vols.　8vo.　Oxford, 1887.　F 12 R 9, 10
Politics of. (Gr. text.)　English Notes, by R. Congreve.　8vo.　Lond., 1855.　　　　　　F 3 P 13
On the Vital Principle ; translated by C. Collier.　8vo.　Camb., 1855.　　　　　　　　　A 26 Q 16

ARMSTRONG, A. S., and CAMPBELL, G. O.　Australian Sheep Husbandry : a Hand-book of Breeding and Treatment of Sheep and Station Management, &c.　8vo.　Melb., 1882.　　　　　　　　　MA 2 P 46

ARMSTRONG, Mrs. C. C., and TWOMEY, J.　The South Pacific Fern Album, New Zealand Section, containing Fronds of Ferns collected throughout the Islands.　Fol.　Melb. (n.d.)　　　　　　　　　MA 6 P 12 ‡

ARMSTRONG, E.　Elisabeth Farnese : "The Termagant of Spain."　8vo.　Lond., 1892.　　　C 18 S 7

ARMSTRONG, G.　Names and Places in the Old Testament and Apocrypha ; revised by Sir C. Wilson and Capt. Conder.　8vo.　Lond., 1887.　　　K 18 R 31
Another Copy.　8vo.　Lond., 1889.　　K 18 R 32

ARMSTRONG, H. J.　Treatise on the Law of Gold-mining in Victoria.　8vo.　Melb., 1891.　MF 3 T 24
A Handy Book on the Management of Mining Companies in Victoria.　8vo.　Melbourne, 1888.　MF 2 T 44

ARMSTRONG, Rev. R. A.　Is it reasonable to worship God ?　Verbatim Report of two nights' Debate between the Rev. R. A. Armstrong and C. Bradlaugh.　12mo.　Lond., 1887.　　　　　　　　　　G 2 V 27

ARMSTRONG, Walter.　Memoir of Peter de Wint.　Ob. fol.　Lond., 1888.　　　　　　　C 1 R 30 †
Scottish Painters : a Critical Study.　Sm. fol.　Lond., 1888.　　　　　　　　　　A 7 S 18 †
[*See* Bryan, M.]
Wrestling.　[*See* Fencing.]

ARMY AND NAVY CALENDAR, 1887-90.　4 vols.　8vo.　Lond., 1887-91.　　　　　　E

ARMY LIST.　85 vols. 12mo.　Lond., 1874-89.　E
[*See* Hart, H. G.]

ARNISTON MEMOIRS : Three Centuries of a Scottish House, 1571-1838 ; edited by G. W. T. Omond.　Roy. 8vo.　Edinb., 1887.　　　　　　　B 31 U 12

ARNOLD, Sir E.　Casket of Gems.—A Queen's Revenge, &c.　8vo.　Lond., 1887.　　　　　H 7 Q 38
Japonica ; with Illustrations, by R. Blum.　Roy. 8vo.　Lond., 1892.　　　　　　　　D 18 V 9
The Light of the World ; or, the Great Consummation.　8vo.　Lond., 1891.　　　　　　H 8 Q 19
Lotus and Jewel ; containing In an Indian Temple.—A Poems, National and Non-Oriental.　8vo.　Lond., 1888.　　　　　　　　　　　　H 7 Q 37
Seas and Lands.　8vo.　Lond., 1891.　　D 17 V 8

ARNOLD, E. L. L. Bird Life in England. 8vo. Lond., 1887.   A 14 Q 53

ARNOLD, Rev. F. Oxford and Cambridge: their Colleges, Memories, and Associations. Sm. 4to. Lond., 1873.   B 22 U 20

ARNOLD, Matthew. Biography of. [*See* Stuart, T. B.] Essays in Criticism. 2nd Series. 8vo. Lond., 1888. J 9 Q 3

On Translating Homer. 8vo. Lond., 1861. J 15 R 43

[*See* Robertson, J. M.]

ARNOLD, Theodor. Englisch-Deutsches Wörterbuch. [*See* Bailey, N.]

ARNOLD, Thomas. Life and Correspondence of ; by A. P. Stanley. 7th ed. 8vo. Lond., 1852.   C 14 U 16

[*See* Thucydides.]

ARNOLD-FORSTER, H. O. [*See* Forster, H. O. Arnold-].

ARNOLDSON, K. P. Pax Mundi ; a concise account of the Progress of the Movement for Peace by Means of Arbitration, &c. 12mo. Lond., 1892.   F 9 U 39

AROZ. [*See* Cambell, Z.]

ARRIAN. Anabasis et Indica ; emendavit F. Dübner. Imp. 8vo. Parisiis, 1846.   B 36 U 3.

De Expeditione Alexandri Magni historiarum libri 8. [Gr. et Lat.] Sm. fol. Lut. Paris, 1575. B 42 P 20‡

Expeditio Alexandri. 18mo. Lipsiæ, 1829. B 35 P 20

Scripta Minora ; recognovit R. Hercher. 12mo. Lipsiæ, 1854.   J 15 R 42

ARROM, Cecilia B. de F., "Fernan Caballero." National Pictures. 8vo. Lond., 1882.   J 9 Q 35

ART JOURNAL. 5 vols. 4to. Lond., 1887-91.   E

ART OF BOXING, SWIMMING, AND GYMNASTICS MADE EASY. 12mo. Sydney (n.d.)   MA 3 P 28

ART POUR TOUS, L'. Tomes 25-30, fol. Paris, 1886-91.   E

ARTHUR, Col. Sir G. A. Acts of Lieutenant-Governors of Tasmania. [*See* Tasmania.]

ARTHUR, J. C. Report on Botanical Work in Minnesota, 1886. (Geol. and Nat. Hist. Survey of Minn.) Roy. 8vo. St. Paul, 1887.   E

ARTHUR, W. Etymological Dictionary of Family and Christian Names. 12mo. New York, 1857. K 18 P 2

ASBOTH, J. de. An Official Tour through Bosnia and Herzegovina. Roy. 8vo. Lond., 1890.   D 18 V 5

ASHBEE, H. S. [*See* Graham, A.]

ASHBURNER, R. W. Shorthorn Herds of England, 1885-87. 8vo. Warwick, 1888.   A 1 T 36

ASHDY, Capt. W. New Zealand, the Land of Health, Wealth, and Prosperity; its present condition and future prospects. 8vo. Lond., 1889.   M D 1 R 27

ASHLEY, Lord. Moral and Religious Education of the Working Classes. 8vo. Lond., 1843.   G 15 R 27

B

ASHLEY, W. J. Edward III. and his Wars, 1327-60. (English History by Contemporary Writers.) 18mo. Lond., 1887.   B 22 P 3

English Economic History and Theory : The Middle Ages. 8vo. Lond., 1888.   F 5 T 33

[*See* Coulanges, F. de.]

ASHTON, John. Curious Creatures in Zoology. 8vo. Lond., 1890.   A 14 T 42

Drinks of the World. [*See* Mew, James.]

Social Life under the Regency. 2 vols. 8vo. Lond., 1890.   B 5 T 37, 38

Century of Ballads; collected, edited, and illustrated in Facsimile of the Originals. 4to. Lond., 1887. H 6 V 27

Eighteenth Century Waifs. 8vo. Lond., 1887. B 21 R 17

The Fleet : its River, Prison, and Marriages. 8vo. Lond., 1888.   B 22 U 7

Voiage and Travayle of Sir J. Mandeville, Knt. [*See* Maundeville, Sir J.]

[*See* Smith, Capt. J.]

ASHWORTH, P. A. [*See* Goltz, Lieut.-Col. Colmar, Baron von der.]

ASIATIC QUARTERLY REVIEW. 11 vols. 8vo. Lond., 1886-92.   E

ASIATIC SOCIETY, Royal. [*See* Royal Asiatic Society.]

ASIATIC SOCIETY OF BENGAL. Journal. Vols. 53-61. 4to. Calcutta, 1884-92.   E

ASSOCIATION BELGE CONTRE L'ABUS DES BOISSONS ALCOOLIQUES, Bulletin 1882-83. 5 vols. 8vo. Bruxelles, 1882-83.   F 11 S 3-7

ASTIUS, F. Lexicon Platonicum. 3 vols. (in 2). 8vo. Lipsiæ, 1835-38.   K 15 Q 36, 37

ASTLEY, Wm. Tales of the Convict System, by "Price Warung." 8vo. Sydney, 1892.   M J 3 Q 9

History of Bushranging in Australia. Illustrated. 8vo. Adelaide, 1891.   M B 2 Q 50

ATHENÆUM, The, 1828-29, 1836-92. 16 vols. 4to. Lond., 1828-92.   E

ATHENÆUS. Deipnosophistæ, e recognitione A. Meineke. 3 vols. (in 2). 12mo. Lipsiæ, 1858-59. J 19 R 30

A'THRAWLÆTH. Athrawiæth i'r Anwybodus. 12mo. (n.p. n.d.)   G 16 P 39

ATKINS, Rev. F. Reminiscences of Twelve Years' Residence in Tasmania and New South Wales, Norfolk Island and Moreton Bay, &c. 8vo. Malvern, 1869.   M D 6 P 21

ATKINS, J. The Coins and Tokens of the Possessions and Colonies of the British Empire. Roy. 8vo. Lond., 1889.   A 13 S 49

ATKINSON, D. H. Ralph Thoresby, the Topographer; his Town and Times. 2 vols. roy. 8vo. Lond., 1885-87.   C 12 T 15, 16

ATKINSON, Hon. Sir H. A. The Financial Condition of New Zealand, 1890. 4to. Wellington, 1890. M F 1 U 36

ATKINSON, Rev. J. C. The Coucher Book of Furness Abbey. [*See* Chetham Soc., N.S., 14.]
Forty Years in a Moorland Parish; Reminiscences in Danby in Cleveland. 8vo. Lond., 1891. D 18 R 20

ATKINSON, Miss. [*See* Calvert, Mrs. J. S.]

ATKINSON, P. Elements of Dynamic Electricity and Magnetism. 8vo. Lond., 1891. A 21 Q 30

ATTWELL, H. The Italian Masters, with special reference to the Italian Pictures in the National Gallery. 8vo. Lond., 1888. A 8 P 47

AUBERT, Sister. New and Complete Manual of Maori Conversation. 18mo. Wellington, 1885. M K 1 P 63

AUBERTIN, J. J. A Fight with Distances: the States, the Hawaiian Islands, Canada, British Columbia, Cuba, the Bahamas. 8vo. Lond., 1888. D 15 Q 4

AUBIGNÉ, J. H. Merle d'. [*See* Merle d' Aubigné, J. H.]

AUBONNE, Jean Baptiste Tavernier, Baron of. [*See* Tavernier, Jean.]

AUCKLAND, New Zealand. Hand-book for Emigrants to; with Particulars of the Free Grants of Land, &c. 8vo. Lond., 1860. MD 1 W 31

AUCKLAND ALMANAC. [*See* Brett, H.]

AUCKLAND FREE PUBLIC LIBRARY. General Catalogue of the Grey Collection, 1888. Roy. 8vo. Auckland, 1888. MK 1 R 54
Annual Supplements of the Catalogue of Sir George Grey's Collection. February, 1891. 8vo. Auckland, 1891. MK 1 R 55
Supplement to Catalogue. September, 1892. Roy. 8vo. Auckland, 1892. MK 1 R 56

AUCKLAND ISLANDS. Copies of Correspondence (if any) relating to the Absence of Mr. Enderby from the Auckland Islands; and of the Lease or Charter granted in respect of the Auckland Islands by the British Government. Fol. Lond., 1853. MF 11 Q 19 †
Copies or Extracts of Correspondence relating to Mr. Enderby, the late Lieut.-Governor of the Auckland Islands. Fol. Lond., 1855. MF 11 Q 19 †

AUDSLEY, G. A., and BOWES, J. L. Keramic Art of Japan. Imp. 8vo. Lond., 1891. A 8 U 31

AUGUSTINUS, A. De Civitate Dei, libri XXII. 2 vols. (in 1). 8vo. Lipsiæ, 1825. G 16 R 31

AULROY, Marie Catherine Junelle d'. Fairy Tales; newly done into English by Anne Thackeray Ritchie. Sm. 4to. Lond., 1892. J 3 T 17

AUSTAUT, J. L. Les Parnassiens de la Faune paléarctique. Sm. 4to. Leip., 1889. A 27 R 27

AUSTEN, Jane. [Life of]; by Mrs. Charles Malden. (Eminent Women Series). 8vo. Lond., 1889. C 12 Q 26

AUSTEN, Prof. W. C. Roberts. Introduction to the Study of Metallurgy. 8vo. Lond., 1891. A 24 Q 11

AUSTIN, A. Prince Lucifer. 8vo. Lond., 1887. H 9 Q 2

AUSTIN, R. Journal of, Commanding an Expedition sent by the Government to Explore the Interior of Western Australia. Fol. Perth, 1855. MD 11 Q 16 †

AUSTIN, Mrs. Sarah. Memoirs and Correspondence of. (Three Generations of Englishwomen); by Janet Ross. 2 vols. 8vo. Lond., 1888. C 14 R 5, 6

AUSTIN, T. Two Fifteenth-Century Books. [*See* Early Eng. Text Soc.]

AUSTRAL OBSERVER, The. 8vo. Melb., 1882. ME 6 R

AUSTRALASIAN ASSOCIATION FOR THE ADVANCEMENT OF SCIENCE. Reports of the First, Second and Third Meetings. 3 vols. 8vo. Sydney, 1889-91. ME 1 S

AUSTRALASIAN BUILDER AND CONTRACTOR'S NEWS. Sm. fol. Sydney, 1887-92. ME

AUSTRALASIAN CATHOLIC DIRECTORY, for 1889-90. 8vo. Sydney, 1888-89. ME 8 P

AUSTRALASIAN COLONIES. Return showing the date at which Responsible Government was proclaimed in each Australasian Colony; the Estimated Population, together with the area of each Colony, &c. Fol. Lond., 1890. MF 3 Q 33 †
Return showing for each of the Australian Colonies, the Expenditure incurred by assisting Emigration; the Revenue of the Colony raised by Taxation; the area of Land alienated from the Crown, and the Area of Land remaining. Fol. Lond., 1890. MF 3 Q 33 †
Correspondence relating to the Inspection of the Military Forces of the Australasian Colonies by Major-General J. B. Edwards. Fol. Lond., 1890. MF 3 Q 33 †
Papers relative to the Ambulance Transport of Civilian Sick and Wounded. Fol. Lond., 1890. MF 3 Q 33 †

AUSTRALASIAN COURSING CALENDAR. [*See* Haydon, T.]

AUSTRALASIAN FEDERAL DIRECTORY [*See* Rogers, J. W. F.]

AUSTRALASIAN FEDERATION CONFERENCE. Correspondence relating to the Federation Conference in Australia. Fol. Lond., 1890. M F 8 P 14 †
Official Record of Proceedings and Debates of the National Australasian Convention, Sydney, 1891. Fol. Sydney, 1891. MF 11 Q 1 †
Another Copy. Fol. Lond., 1891. MF 11 Q 2 †
Official Report of the National Australasian Convention Debates. Roy. 8vo. Sydney, 1891. MF 3 R 47
Official Record of Proceedings and Debates. 8vo. Melb., 1890. MF 1 T 15

AUSTRALASIAN INSURANCE AND BANKING RECORD. Vols. 9, and 11-13. 4to. Melb., 1885-89. ME

AUSTRALASIAN IRONMONGER, BUILDER, ENGINEER, AND METAL WORKER. Imp. 8vo. Melb., 1886. ME 8 T

AUSTRALASIAN MISSIONARY NEWS. Nov. and Dec., 1888. 8vo. Sydney, 1888. ME 6 R

AUSTRALASIAN NEWSPAPER DIRECTORY. 3rd ed., 1890. 8vo. Melb., 1892. ME 3 T

AUSTRALASIAN SUGAR COMPANY, Deed of Settlement. 8vo. Sydney, 1842. MF 1 T 63

Australasian Sugar Company for Refining Sugar in Australia. [Prospectus.] Fol. Sydney (n.d.) MF 11 Q 20 †

AUSTRALASIAN TURF REGISTER, 1876-1881. 6 vols. 12mo. Sydney, 1876-81. ME 3 S

AUSTRALASIAN WESLEYAN METHODIST CHURCH, Laws and Regulations. 8vo. Melb., 1885. MG 2 P 38

AUSTRALIA : an Appeal to the World on behalf of the younger branch of the Family of Shem. 8vo. Sydney, 1839. MG 1 R 35

Découvertes des Hollandois aux Terres Australes (Prévost, A. F. Suite de l'histoire générale des Voyages, tome 17). 4to. Amsterdam, 1761. MD 11 P 16 †

Examen de la Question s'il y a des Géans aux Terres Australes (Prévost, A. F. Suite de l'histoire générale des Voyages, tome 17). 4to. Amsterdam, 1761. MD 11 P 16 †

Guide to Australia, and the Gold Regions ; together with Advice to intending Emigrants ; by "A Liverpool Merchant." 12mo. Lond., 1852. MD 1 P 7

Papers relating to an Expedition for Exploring the Northern Portion of Australia. Fol. Lond., 1857. MD 11 Q 38 †

AUSTRALIA DIRECTORY, The. 3 vols. roy. 8vo. Lond., 1879-84. MD 5 V 38-40

1. South and East Coast, Bass Straits, and Tasmania.
2. East Coast, Torres Strait, and Coral Sea.
3. North, North-west, and West Coasts.

AUSTRALIAN, AN. [See Australian Gleanings.]

AUSTRALIAN, AN. [See Unfortunate Career of Johnson.]

AUSTRALIAN (THE) Christmas Number, 1880. 8vo. Sydney, 1880. ME 6 R

AUSTRALIAN ALMANAC. [See Howe, R.]

AUSTRALIAN ANGLICAN CHURCH DIRECTORY for 1891. 8vo. Sydney, 1891. ME 6 Q

AUSTRALIAN ARISTOLOGIST, An. [See Abbott, Hon. E.]

AUSTRALIAN AUCTION COMPANY : Report of Proceedings at a Meeting of Shareholders. 8vo. Sydney, 1841. ME 8 Q

AUSTRALIAN CLUB : Rules and Regulations for the Government of. 12mo. Sydney, 1838. MF 3 P 36

AUSTRALIAN COLONIES : an Act for the Better Government of Her Majesty's Australian Colonies. Fol. Lond., 1850. MF 11 Q 18

An Act intituled an Act for the Better Government of Her Majesty's Australian Colonies. 8 vo. Launceston, 1850. ME 1 T 62

AUSTRALIAN CRICKETERS' TOUR through Australia, New Zealand, and Great Britain ; by "Argus." 8vo. Sydney, 1878. MA 2 V 43

AUSTRALIAN CROCHET-BOOK. Ob. 12mo. Sydney, 1859. ME 4 Q

AUSTRALIAN ECONOMIC ASSOCIATION. [See Wise, B. R.]

AUSTRALIAN ETIQUETTE. [See Sempill, F.]

AUSTRALIAN FEDERATION. A Review of Mr. Forster's Paper "Fallacies of Federation." 8vo. Sydney, 1877. MF 1 T 16

AUSTRALIAN FREE RELIGIOUS PRESS. Vols. 1 and 2. February, 1870-January, 1872. 2 vols. 8vo. Sydney, 1871-72. ME 8 Q

AUSTRALIAN GLEANINGS : a Review ; by "An Australian." Parts 1 and 2. 12mo. Lond., 1865-66. MH 1 Q 62

AUSTRALIAN GOLD CALCULATOR and GOLD DEALER'S GUIDE. 12mo. Hobart, 1851. MA 3 P 18

AUSTRALIAN GOLD READY RECKONER. 18mo. Sydney, 1852. MA 3 P 21

AUSTRALIAN GRAPHIC, The. May-August, 1889. Fol. Sydney, 1889. ME

AUSTRALIAN HAND-BOOK. [See Gordon and Gotch.]

AUSTRALIAN HEROES AND ADVENTURERS. 12mo. Lond., 1889. MB 1 P 24

AUSTRALIAN ILLUSTRATED MAGAZINE. Vol. 1. No. 1. Roy. 8vo. Sydney, 1891. ME 7 R

AUSTRALIAN INTERNATIONAL EXHIBITION : Report of the Royal Commission. 8vo. Lond., 1882. MK 1 T 16

AUSTRALIAN JOINT-STOCK BANK : Deed of Settlement. Roy. 8vo. Sydney, 1853. MF 2 S 37

AUSTRALIAN JUVENILE INDUSTRIAL EXHIBITION, Ballarat, 1878. Official Record ; by C. J. Richardson. 8vo. Ballarat, 1879. MK 1 T 2

AUSTRALIAN JOURNAL OF EDUCATION. Vols. 1-3. 8vo. Sydney, 1868-70. ME 8 Q

AUSTRALIAN MEN of MARK. Illustrated with Authentic Portraits. 4to. Sydney, 1889. MC 12 P 1†
Another Copy. 2 vols. 4to. Sydney, 1889. MC 12 P 2, 3 †
Another Copy. 2 vols. 4to. Sydney, 1889. MC 12 P 4, 5 †
Another Copy. 2 vols. 4to. Sydney, 1889. MC 12 P 8, 9 †
Another Copy. 2 vols. 4to. Sydney, 1889. MC 12 P 6, 7 †

AUSTRALIAN MESSENGER AND PRESBYTERIAN RECORD. November, 1860. 8vo. Melb., 1860.
ME 8 Q

AUSTRALIAN MINING STANDARD. Vols 1 and 2. Fol. Sydney, 1889–90. ME

AUSTRALIAN MONTH, The. Vol. 1, Parts 1 to 6. *(All published.)* 8vo. Sydney, 1884. ME 6 R

AUSTRALIAN MUSEUM: Act of Incorporation, By-laws, Rules, and Regulations. 8vo. Sydney, 1892.
MF 2 T 42
Descriptive List of Australian Aboriginal Weapons, Implements, &c., from the Darling and Lachlan Rivers. 8vo. Sydney, 1887. MA 3 T 42
Guide to the Contents of. 8vo. Sydney, 1883. MA 3 T 51
Another copy [prepared and edited by S. Sinclair.] 8 vo. Sydney, 1890. MK 1 T 3
Memoirs, No. 2. Lord Howe Island : its Zoology, &c. Roy. 8vo. Sydney, 1889. MA 2 U 47
Plan of the Australian Museum and its Contents. Roy. 8vo. Sydney, 1887. MA 3 R 42
Records of. Vol. 1, Nos. 1 and 3. Roy. 8vo. Sydney, 1890. ME 8 R

AUSTRALIAN MUTUAL PROVIDENT SOCIETY, An Act to Incorporate ; also the Bylaws with Schedule of Tables. Roy. 8vo. Sydney, 1857. MF 1 S 70
Forty-first Annual Report, 1890. 4to. Sydney, 1890.
ME 7 Q
Quinquennial Report, 1874. 4to. Sydney, 1874.
ME 7 Q

AUSTRALIAN PRESENTATION ALBUM for 1855. [Music.] Fol. Sydney, 1855. MA 5 P 1 †

AUSTRALIAN PUBLIC OPINION, July–Oct., 1887. *(All published.)* Sm. fol. Sydney, 1887. ME

AUSTRALIAN PULPIT NEWS AND SUNDAY AT HOME. Vol. 1, No. 5, and Vol. 2, No. 36. [Bound with the "New South Wales Independent."] Fol. Sydney, 1871–72. ME 8 T

AUSTRALIAN RHYMES AND JINGLES ; by "Dogberry Dingo." 12mo. Fitzroy, 1871. MH 1 Q 45

AUSTRALIAN SCHOOL REVIEW. Vols. 1, 2. 8vo. Yass, 1873–74. ME 6 S

AUSTRALIAN SKETCHES ; by "Overlander." 8vo. Lond., 1887. MD 1 W 17

AUSTRALIAN STAR. 16 vols. Fol. Sydney, 1887–92.
ME

AUSTRALIE. [*See* Heron, Mrs. E. A.]

AUSTRALIE. [*See* King's Highway, The.]

AUSTRALIS IGNOTUS. [*See* Capital and Labour.]

AUTONNE, Léon. Sur la Théorie des Equations Différentielles du Premier Ordre et du Premier Degré. (Annales de l'Université de Lyon.) 8vo. Paris, 1892.
A 25 V 21

AVELING, Dr. E. B. Mechanics and Experimental Science as required for the Matriculation Examination of the University of London : Magnetism and Electricity. 8vo. Lond., 1889. A 21 Q 11
Mechanics and Experimental Science as required for the Matriculation Examination of the University of London : Mechanics. 8vo. Lond., 1888. A 25 Q 35
Key to [the above.] 8vo. Lond., 1888. A 25 Q 36
The Students' Marx : an Introduction to the Study of Karl Marx' *Capital.* 12mo. Lond., 1892. F 9 U 33
Mechanics and Experimental Science as required for the Matriculation Examination of the University of London : Chemistry. 8vo. Lond., 1888. A 21 Q 9
Key to [the above.] 8vo. Lond 1888. A 21 Q 10
[*See* Engels, F., and Tickhoonirov, F.]

AVELING, Dr. E. B. and Eleanor Marx. Working-class Movement in America. 8vo. Lond., 1888. F 14 P 21

AVIANUS, The Fables of ; edited by R. Ellis. 8vo. Oxford, 1887. J 3 V 17

AYRTON, Prof. W. E. Practical Electricity : a Laboratory and Lecture Course. 8vo. Lond., 1887. A 21 Q 4
The Execution of Montrose ; translated into Gaelic, by G. A. Murray. · 8vo. Sydney (n.d.) MH 1 S 57

B

B., C. E. [*See* Brontie's Diary.]

B.V. [*See* Thomson, J.]

BABELON, E. Manual of Oriental Antiquities, including the Architecture, Sculpture, and Industrial Arts of Chaldæa, &c.; translated and enlarged by B. T. A. Evetts. 8vo. Lond., 1889. B 28 R 4

BABYLONIAN AND ORIENTAL RECORD. Vols. 1–4. sm. 4to. Lond., 1887–90. E

BACH, A. B. The Art Ballad : Loewe and Schubert. 8vo. Edinb., 1890. C 14 R 32

BACHE, Dr. F. [*See* Wood, Dr. G. B.]

BACKHOUSE, E., and TYLOR, C. Witnesses for Christ, and Memorials of Church Life, from the 4th to the 13th Century : a "Sequel to Early Church History." 2 vols. 8vo. Lond., 1887. G 6 R 16, 17

BACKHOUSE, J. The Question, "Are Judicial Oaths Lawful," answered ; with some observations on the Moral Influence of Judicial Oaths. 12mo. Hobart, 1833.
MF 2 P 63
Memoir of ; by his Sister. 8vo. York, 1870. MC 1 Q 25

BACKHOUSE, J., and TYLOR, C. Life and Labours of G. W. Walker. 8vo. Lond., 1862. MC 1 R 35

BACON, Alice Mabel. Japanese Girls and Women. 12mo. Lond., 1891. D 17 P 1

BACON, Delia. A Biographical Sketch ; by Theodore Bacon. 8vo. Lond., 1888. C 14 S 2

BACON, Sir Francis. Essays, with annotations by Rev. R. Whately. 4th edition. 8vo. Lond., 1858. G 16 T 21

Essays. [*See* Universal Library.]

Francis Bacon, his Life and Philosophy ; by Prof. J. Nichol. 2 vols. 12mo. Edinb., 1888-89. C 12 P 50, 51

Novum Organum. 12mo. Glasguæ, 1803. G 8 P 30

Another copy. 8vo. Oxonii, 1813. G 16 T 17

The Columbus of Literature. [*See* Wigston, W. F. C.]

Bacon or Shakespeare. [*See* Martin, Sir T.]

[*See* Donnelly, I.]

BACON, Rev. J. H. Improvement of the Memory ; or, the Science of Memory Simplified. 12mo. Lond., 1890. G 4 V 6

BACON, Theodore. Delia Bacon: a biographical sketch. 8vo. Lond., 1888. C 14 S 2

BADDELEY, W. St. Clair. Tchay and Chianti ; or, Wanderings in Russia and Italy. 12mo. Lond., 1887. D 18 P 1

BÄDEKER, K. Rheinreise von Basel bis Düsseldorf. 12mo. Koblenz, 1849. D 19 P 2

Die Schweiz, die italienischen Seen, Mailand, Genua, Turin. 12mo. Coblenz, 1856. D 19 P 3

BADENOCH, J. G. Art of Letter Painting made easy. 4th ed. 12mo. Lond., 1888. A 23 Q 22

BADGER, Rev. G. P. English-Arabic Dictionary. 4to. Lond., 1881. K 33 P 17 ‡

BADGER, W. The Licensing Laws of Australasia. Roy. 8vo. Christchurch, 1888. MF 3 R 49

Land Transfer Laws of Australasia. Roy. 8vo. Christchurch, 1888. MF 3 R 48

BADHAM, Prof. Charles. Speeches and Lectures delivered in Australia. Roy. 8vo. Sydney, 1890. MC 1 T 7

[*See* Euripides, and Plato.]

BADHAM, W. A. Ablaut. [*See* English Dialect Soc.]

BAER, Dr. A. Die Trunksucht. 8vo. Berlin, 1881. F 11 R 5

Der Alcoholismus. 8vo. Berlin, 1878. F 11 S 10

BAER, Dr. K. G. V. Historische Fragen. 8vo. St. Petersburg, 1873. J 15 S 21

BAERNREITHER, Dr. J. M. English Associations of Working Men ; translated by Alice Taylor. 8vo. Lond., 1889. F 14 S 3

BAGEHOT, W. The English Constitution. 6 ed. 12mo. Lond., 1891. F 9 U 32

BAGNALL, J. E. The Flora of Warwickshire. 8vo. Lond., 1891. A 20 S 6

BAGWELL, R. Ireland under the Tudors. 3 vols. 8vo. Lond., 1885-90. B 29 T 18-20

BAILEY, F. M. Classified Index of First Supplement to the Indigenous and Naturalised Plants of Queensland. 8vo. Brisb., 1886. MA 1 U 34

Catalogue of Indigenous Queensland Woods in the Colonial and Indian Exhibition, 1886. 8vo. Brisbane, 1886. MK 1 P 10

Catalogue of Indigenous and Naturalised Plants of Queensland. 8vo. Brisb., 1890. MA 1 U 45

Contributions to the Queensland Flora. 8vo. Brisb., 1890. MA 3 S 4

A Few Queensland Grasses. 8vo. Brisb., 1888. MA 1 V 62

Fern World of Australia, with Homes of the Queensland Species. 8vo. Brisbane, 1881. MA 1 T 8

Flora of Queensland. [*See* Indian and Colonial Exhib., 1886.]

Index of Indigenous and Naturalised Plants of Queensland. 8vo. Brisbane, 1883. MA 1 U 35

Inquiry for Seeds of Grasses and other Fodder Plants, with a List of the Grasses of Queensland. 12mo. Brisbane, 1877. MA 2 P 69

Lithograms of the Ferns of Queensland. 8vo. Brisbane, 1892. MA 3 S 6

Occasional Papers on the Queensland Flora. No. 1. 8vo. Brisbane, 1886. MA 1 U 33

Queensland Woods, with a brief popular description of the Trees, their Distribution, Qualities, Uses of Timber, &c. (Melb. Cent. Int. Exhib., 1888.) 8vo. Brisbane, 1888. MA 3 Q 6

Sketch of the Economic Plants of Queensland. (Melb. Cent. Int. Exhib., 1888.) 8vo. Brisbane, 1888. MA 3 Q 7

Synopsis of the Queensland Flora, containing both the Phænogamous and Cryptogamous Plants. 1st—3rd Supplements. Brisbane, 1886-90. MA 1 U 31

BAILEY, F. M., and GORDON, P. R. Plants reputed Poisonous and Injurious to Stock. 8vo. Brisbane, 1887. MA 1 U 46

BAILEY, N., and ARNOLD, T. Compleat English Dictionary, Englisch-Deutsches Wörterbuch. 8vo. Leipzig, 1761. K 12 U 17

BAILEY, T. Life and Death of the renowned John Fisher, Bishop of Rochester. 12mo. Lond., 1739. C 13 P 1

BAILLIERE, F. F. Bailliere's Official Post Office Directory of New South Wales, 1867. 8vo. Sydney, 1867. ME 10 P

Bailliere's New South Wales Gazetteer and Road Guide. Second ed., with map. 8vo. Sydney, 1870. MD 2 S 37

BAILLON, H. Dictionnaire de Botanique. Tomes 1-4. 4to. Paris, 1876-92. K 14 R 15-18†

Natural History of Plants ; translated by M. M. Hartog. 8 vols. roy. 8vo. Lond., 1871-88. A 28 V 13-20

BAIN, A. On Teaching English ; with detailed Examples and an Enquiry into the definition of Poetry. 8vo. Lond., 1887. K 12 P 44

BAIN, E. Merchant and Craft Guilds of Aberdeen: a History of the Aberdeen Incorporated Trades. 8vo. Aberdeen, 1887.　　　　　　　　　　B 31 Q 17

BAINES, E. The History of the County Palatine and Duchy of Lancaster. The Biographical Department by W. R. Whatton, with additions of John Harland and the Rev. B. Herford ; edited by J. Croston. Vols. 1–4. 4to. Manch., 1888-91.　　　　　　B 23 V 8–11

BAIRD, R. Afholdenheds-Selskabornes. 12mo. Kjøbenhavn, 1841.　　　　　　　　　　　F 11 P 63

BAKER, E. B. Sport in Bengal, and how, when, and where to seek it. Roy. 8vo. Lond., 1887.　A 29 U 31

BAKER, H. B. The London Stage, its History and Traditions from 1576 to 1888. 2 vols. 8vo. Lond., 1889.　　　　　　　　　　　　　B 21 R 23, 24

BAKER, Hon. R. C. Manual of Reference to Authorities for the use of Members of the National Australasian Convention which will assemble at Sydney on March 2, 1891, for the purpose of Drafting a Constitution for the Dominion of Australia. 8vo. Adelaide, 1891.
　　　　　　　　　　　　　　　MF 1 T 65

BAKER, Sir S. W. Wild Beasts and their Ways : Reminiscences of Europe, Asia, Africa, and America. 2 vols. 8vo. Lond., 1890.　　A 14 T 44, 45

BAKER, W. R. Curse of Britain : an Essay on Intemperance. 12mo. Lond., 1855.　　F 11 P 16

BALCH, Elizabeth. Glimpses of Old English Homes. Roy. 8vo. Lond., 1890.　　　　　D 18 V 4

BALDWIN, Dr. James Mark. Handbook of Psychology. 2nd edition. 8vo. Lond., 1890.　　G 2 Q 38

BALDWIN, Joseph. Elementary Psychology and Education. 8vo. New York, 1888.　　　　F P 40

BALE, W. M. The Genera of the Plumulariidæ, with Observations on various Australian Hydroids. 8vo. Melb., 1886.　　　　　　　　M A 2 T 66

BALFOUR, A. Intemperance and the Licensing System. 12mo. Lond., 1879.　　　　　F 11 P 29

BALFOUR, Surg.-Gen. E. Agricultural Pests of India, &c., Vegetable and Animal, injurious to Man and his Products. 8vo. Lond., 1887.　　　A 14 Q 56

BALFOUR, F. H. Leaves from my Chinese Scrap-book. 8vo. Lond., 1887.　　　　　　B 20 S 1

BALFOUR, I. B. [*See* Bary, Prof. A. de.]

BALFOUR, Dr. J. H. Class-book of Botany. Roy. 8vo. Edinb., 1855.　　　　　　　　　A 20 T 7

Elements of Botany. 3rd ed. 12mo. Edinb., 1876.
　　　　　　　　　　　　　　　A 20 P 13

BALL, J. Notes of a Naturalist in South America. 8vo. Lond., 1887.　　　　　　　　D 15 R 1

BALL, Rt. Hon. J. T. Historical Review of the Legislative Systems operative in Ireland (1172–1800). 8vo. Lond., 1888.　　　　　　　　　F 12 Q 26

The Reformed Church of Ireland (1537–1886). 8vo. Lond., 1886.　　　　　　　　　G 12 T 35

BALL, Sir Robert. The Cause of an Ice Age. 8vo. Lond., 1891.　　　　　　　　　A 19 Q 28

BALL (V.) Travels in India by Jean Baptiste Tavernier. [*See* Tavernier, J. B.]

BALL, W. P. Are the effects of Use and Disuse Inherited? (Nature Series.) 12mo. Lond., 1890.　　A 27 V 26

BALL (W. W. Rouse.) Mathematical Recreations and Problems of Past and Present Times. 8vo. Lond., 1892.
　　　　　　　　　　　　　　　A 25 R 25

BALLANTYNE, A. Lord Carteret : a Political Biography, 1690–1763. 8vo. Lond., 1887.　　　C 13 U 3

BALLARAT SCHOOL OF MINES. Descriptive Papers relating to the Institution ; by "The Special Reporter of the *Ballarat Star*". 12mo. Ballarat, 1875.　MA 3 P 1 O

BALLIN, Ada S. The Science of Dress in Theory and Practice. 8vo. Lond., 1885.　　　　A 26 Q 11

BALLINGER, J. Free Libraries and the Photographic Survey of Counties. 8vo. Cardiff, 1891.　J 3 T 15

BALLOU, M. M. Under the Southern Cross; or, Travels in Australasia. 8vo. Lond., 1888.　　MD 3 R 35

BALMACEDA, J. M. Illegal Acts of. [*See* Montt, P.]

BALMAIN DIRECTORY for 1889. 8vo. Sydney, 1889.　　　　　　　　　　　　ME 8 Q

BALZAC, H. de. Œuvres de. 55 vols. 12mo. Paris, 1876-88.　　　　　　　　　J 19 Q 1–R 10
　1. Argow le Pirate.
　2. Béatrix.
　3. Dom Gigadas.
　4. Eugénie Grandet.
　5. Grandeur et décadence de César Birotteau.
　6. Histoire des Treize.—Ferragus.—La Duchesse de Langeais. La Fille aux Yeux d'Or.
　7. Honorine.—Le Colonel Chabert.—La Messe de l'Athée.— L'Interdiction.—Pierre Grassou.
　8, 9. Illusions Perdues. Les deux Poètes.—Un Grand Homme de Province à Paris.—Un Grand Homme de Province à Paris.—Eve et David.
　10. Jane la Pale.
　11. Jean-Louis.
　12. La Cousine Bette.
　13. La Dernière Fée.
　14. La Dernière Incarnation de Vautrin.—Un Prince de Bohème.—Un Homme d'Affaires.—Gandissart II.—Les Comédiens sans le Savoir.
　15. La Femme de Trente Ans.—La Femme Abandonnée.—La Grenadière.—Le Message.—Gobseck.
　16. La Maison du Chat-qui-Pelote.—Le Bal de Sceaux.—La Bourse. — La Vendetta. — Madame Firmiani. — Une Double Famille.
　17. La Maison Nucingen.—Les Secrets de la Princesse de Cadignan.—Les Employés.—Sarrazine.—Facino Cane.
　18. La Paix du Ménage.—La Fausse Maîtresse.—Etude de Femme.—Autre Etude de Femme.—La Grand Bretèche. —Albert Savarus.
　19. La Peau de Chagrin.
　20. La Recherche de l'Absolu.—Jésus-Christ en Flandre.— Melmoth Réconcilié.—Le Chef-d'Œuvre Inconnu.
　21. Le Centenaire.
　22. Le Contrat de Mariage.—Un Début dans la Vie.
　23. Le Cousin Pons.
　24. Le Curé de Village.
　25. Le Député d'Arcis.
　26. Le Lys dans la Vallée.
　27. Le Médecin de Campagne.
　28. L'Enfant Maudit.—Gambara.—Massimilla Doni.

BALZAC, H. de.—*contd.*
28. L'Envers de l'Histoire Contemporaine.—Z. Marcas.
30. Le Père Goriot.
31, 32. Les Célibataires. Pierrette.—Le Curé de Tours. 2. Un Ménage de Garçon.
33. Les Chouans ; ou, la Bretagne en 1799.—Une Passion dans le Désert.
34-36. Les Contes drolatiques colligez ez Abbayes de Touraine.
37. Les Marana.—Adieu.—Le Requisitionnaire.—El Verdugo. —Un Drame au Bord de la Mer.—L'Auberge Rouge.— L'Elixir de Longue Vie.—Maître Cornélius.
38. Les Parisiens en Province.—L'Illustre Gandissart.—La Muse du Département.
39. Les Paysans.
40. Les Rivalités.—La Vieille Fille.—Le Cabinet des Antiques.
41. Le Vicaire des Ardennes.
42. L'Excommunié.
43. L'Héritière de Birague.
44. L'Israélite.
45. Louis Lambert.—Les Proscrits.—Séraphita.
46. Mémoires de deux Jeunes Mariées.—Une Fille d'Eve.
47. Modeste Mignon.
48. Petites Misères de la Vie Conjugal.
49. Physiologie du Mariage ; ou, Méditations de Philosophie Eclectique sur le Bonheur et le Malheur Conjugal.
50. Splendeurs et Misères des Courtisanes.
51. Sur Catherine de Médicis.
52, 53. Théâtre. Les Ressources de Quinola.—Paméla Giraud. —Le Marâtre—Le Faiseur.
54. Une Ténébreuse Affaire.—Une Episode sous la Terreur.
55. Ursule Mirouët.

BALZANI, U. The Popes and the Hohenstaufen. 8vo. Lond., 1889.   B 12 P 43

BAMBER, E. F. [*See* Siemens, Sir C. W.]

BAMFORD, A. J. Turbans and Tails ; or, Sketches in the Unromantic East. 8vo. Lond., 1888.   D 17 Q 1

BANBURY, G. A. L. Sierra Leone ; or, the White Man's Grave. 8vo. Lond., 1888.   D 14 U 16

BANCROFT, G. Ancient Greece. [*See* Heeren, A. H. L.]

BANCROFT, H. H. The History of the Pacific States of North America. 27 vols. Roy. 8vo. San Francisco, 1882-89.   B 17 S—T
1-3. Central America, 1501-1887.
4-9. Mexico, 1516-1887.
10. North American States and Texas, 1531-1800.
11. Texas, 1801-1889.
12. Arizona and New Mexico, 1530-1888.
13-18. California, 1542-1859.
22, 23. The North-West Coast, 1543-1846.
24, 25. Oregon, 1834-88.
27. British Columbia, 1792-1887.
28. Alaska, 1730-1885.
29. California, Pastoral, 1769-1848.
30. California inter Pocula : a Review of some Classical Abnormities.
31. Popular Tribunals. Vol. 1.
Chronicles of the Builders : Historical Character Study, with index. 8 vols. 8vo. San Francisco, 1891-92.   B 19 T 5-12

BANCROFT, J., Dr. Contribution to Pharmacy from Queensland. [*See* Indian and Colonial Exhibition, 1886.]
On the Mode of Birth of the Kangaroo, communicated by the Hon. L. Hope, with Remarks on the Echidna and Platypus. 8vo. Brisbane, 1882.   MA 3 T 47

BANCROFT, S. B. and Marie E. Mr. and Mrs. Bancroft on and off the Stage ; written by themselves. 2nd. ed. 2 vols. 8vo. Lond., 1888.   C 12 S 9, 10

BANISTER, Prof. H. C. Lectures on Musical Analysis. 8vo. Lond., 1887.   A 8 P 50

BANISTER, T. Memoranda relating to the present Crisis as regards our Colonies, &c. 8vo. Lond., 1848.   MF 2 T 4

BANK OF AUSTRALASIA. Summary of the Deed of Settlement. 8vo. Sydney (n.d.)   MF 3 P 48

BANK OF NEW SOUTH WALES. Deed of Settlement. 8vo. Sydney, 1856.   MF 2 T 22

BANK OFFICIAL, A. [*See* Proshaw, G. O.]

BANKS, R. W. [*See* Beaufort, Duke of.]   •

BANNATYNE, D. J. Hand-book of Republican Institutions in the United States of America. 8vo. Edinb., 1887.   F 5 Q 37

BANNISTER, Saxe. Papers relating to the Case of. Fol. Lond., 1861-62.   MF 11 Q 24 †

BANNOW, W. Emigrant's Hand-book to the British Colonies. 8vo. Lond., 1887.   MD 3 Q 51
Guide to Emigration and Colonisation. 8vo. Lond., 1887.   MF 1 P 50

BARBÉ, L. A. Tragedy of Gowrie House : an Historical Study. Sm. 4to. Paisley, 1887.   B 31 T 21

BARBER, W. H. The Case of. 2nd. ed. Lond., 1849.   MF 1 T 17
Another Copy. 7th ed. Lond., 1849.   MF 1 T 18
Report from Select Committee on Petition of. Fol. Lond., 1858.   MF 7 Q 35 †

BARBOUR, J. The Bruce. [*See* Early Eng. Text Soc.]

BARBUT, Jas. Les Genres des Insectes de Linné. 4to. Lond., 1781.   A 15 T 14
The Genera Vermium exemplified by various Specimens of the Animals contained in the Orders of the Intestina et Mollusca Linnæi. [French and Eng.] 4to. Lond 1783.   A 36 P 27 ‡

BARCLAY, Rev. Dr. J. The Talmud. Roy. 8vo. Lond., 1878   G 6 Q 37

BARETTI, G. Dictionary of the Spanish and English Languages. [*See* Neuman, H., and Baretti, G.]

BARHAM, A. G. Foster. [*See* Nibelungen Lied, The.]

BARING-GOULD, S. Old Country Life. 8vo. Lond., 1890.   B 24 R 1
Historic Oddities and Strange Events. 2nd Series. 8vo. Lond., 1891.   B 36 T 11

BARKER, Edward Harrison. Wayfaring in France. 8vo. Lond., 1890.   D 18 U 9

BARKER, Rt. Rev. F., Bishop of Sydney. Episcopate of : a Memoir ; edited by W. M. Cowper, Dean of Sydney. 8vo. Lond., 1888.   MC 1 R 37
Correspondence respecting Orangemen in Public Schools. [*See* Reynolds, M.]

BARKER, Lady Mary A. Travelling about New and Old Ground. 8vo. Lond., 1883.   M D 7 T 1

BARKLEY, Henry C. Ride through Asia Minor and Armenia. 8vo. Lond., 1891.   D 17 R 6

BARLOW, E. D. Barlow's Profiles of the Natives. 8vo. Sydney (n.d.)   M A 1 R 55

BARLOW, Rev. F. The Complete English Peerage. 2 vols. 8vo. Lond., 1772-73.   K 12 V 29, 30

BARLOW, P. W. Kaipara, or Experiences of a Settler in North New Zealand. 8vo. Lond., 1888.   M D 4 Q 53

BARNARD, A. Whisky Distilleries of the United Kingdom. Roy. 8vo. Lond., 1887.   A 11 V 18

BARNARD, F. P. English History from Contemporary Writers: Strongbow's Conquest of Ireland. 12mo. Lond., 1888.   B 29 P 11

BARNEBY, W. H. The New Far West and the Old Far East, being notes of a tour in North America, Japan, China, Ceylon, &c. 8vo. Lond., 1889.   D 10 S 26

BARNES, W. Poems of Rural Life, in the Dorset Dialect, with Glossary. 2nd ed. 8vo. Lond., 1848.   H 10 Q 47
Poet and Philologist. Life of; by his daughter Mrs. L. E. Baxter ("Leader Scott"). 8vo. Lond., 1887.   C 12 R 27

BARNS, W. E. The Labor Problem, plain questions and practical answers. Edited by W. E. Barns. 12mo. New York, 1886.   F 14 P 22

BARON, Mich. L'homme à bonnes Fortunes. (Collection Jannet-Picard). 12mo. Paris (n.d.)   H 3 P 48

BARONI. [*See* Adrian North.]

BARRAUD, C. D. New Zealand, Graphic and Descriptive. Imp. 4to. Lond., 1877.   M D 1 P 9 †

BARRÈRE, A., and LELAND, C. G. Dictionary of Slang, Jargon, and Cant. 2 vols. Sm. 4to. Lond., 1889-90   K 12 U 14, 15

BARREY, Lodowick. Ram Alley or Merry Tricks: a comedy. [*See* British Drama, Ancient.]

BARRI, G. *Geraldus Cambrensis.* Opera. [*See* Chronicles and Memorials of Gt. Brit., &c.]

BARRINGTON, George. Memoirs of, with the whole of his celebrated speeches. 8vo. Lond. (n.d.)   M C 1 T 12
Voyage à Botany Bay, avec une description du Pays, des Mœurs, des Coutumes, et de la Religion des Natifs. 8vo Paris, 1797.   M D 1 R 29
Voyage to Botany Bay. 8vo. Lond., 1793.   M D 7 T 3

BARRINGTON, L. Tragedy of Druid's Glen : a Story of Irish and Australian Life. 8vo. Sydney, 1888. M J 1 Q 45

BARRON, C. C. N. Decisions of the Speakers of the House of Representatives, New Zealand, on points of Order, &c. 12mo. Wellington, 1889.   M F 2 P 74

BARROW, G. Lavengro, the scholar, the gypsy, the priest. 3 vols. 8vo. Lond., 1851.   J 5 Q 43-45

BARROWS, Wm. Oregon : the struggle for possession. (American Commonwealths.) 3rd ed. 12mo. Boston, 1885.   B 17 P 8
United States of Yesterday and of To-morrow. 12mo. Boston, 1888.   D 15 P 2

BARRY, Rt. Rev. A. Charge delivered at his Primary Visitation of the Diocese on July 10th, 1884. 8vo. Sydney, 1884.   M G 1 Q 56
Life and Works of Sir Charles Barry. Roy. 8vo. Lond., 1867.   C 11 P 41
Three Sermons on Religions' Education. 8vo. Sydney, 1884.   M G 1 Q 55

BARRY, Sir C. Life and Works of; by the Rev. A. Barry. Roy. 8vo. Lond., 1867.   C 11 P 41

BARRY, Very Rev. D. F. The Church and Science. The "Nemo" Letters. 8vo. Sydney, 1889.   M G 1 Q 62

BARRY, R. M. Bayreuth and Franconian Switzerland. 8vo. Lond., 1887.   D 19 Q 4

BARS AND BARMAIDS, or a Run round London and Melbourne by Night; by "The Two Obadias." 8vo. Melb. (n.d.)   M J 1 S 54

BARSANTI, P. O. I Selvaggi dell' Australia dinanzi alla Scienza e al Protestantismo. 8vo. Roma, 1868.   M A 1 R 24

BARTHOLOMEW, J. [*See* Philip, G.]

BARTLETT, T. New Holland ; its Colonization, Productions, &c. 8vo. Lond., 1843.   M D 4 S 44

BARTLEY, N. Opals and Agates ; or, Scenes under the Southern Cross and the Magelhans ; being Memories of Fifty Years of Australia and Polynesia. 8vo. Brisb., 1892.   M D 5 U 11

BARTON, C. H. [*See* Agriculture, Dept. of, Queensland.]

BARTON, Miss F. [*See* Abington, Mrs.]

BARTON, George Burnett. Draft Bill to Constitute the Commonwealth of Australia. 8vo. Sydney, 1891.   M F 2 T 23
Digest of the Law and Practice of Resident Magistrates and District Courts. 8vo. Dunedin, 1875. M F 1 T 77
History of New South Wales from the Records. Vol. 1. Governor Phillip, 1783-89. 8vo. Sydney, 1889.   M B 2 S 32

BARTON, George Burnett and Edmund. Excise Duty on Beer : Case and Opinion of Council. Sm. fol. Sydney, 1887.   M F 2 U 21

BARTON, J. A. G. The Modern World. 12mo. Edinb., 1870.   B 35 P 6

BARTON, W. Particulars of Joint Stock Institutions in New South Wales. 8vo. Sydney, 1838. M F 1 R 56
Report of a Trial upon an Indictment promoted by Capt. Sir W. E. Parry, Commissioner for Managing the Australian Agricultural Co. against the Accountant of that Company. 8vo. Lond., 1832.   M F 1 R 59

BARTTELOT, Brevet-Major E. M. Life of; by W. G. Barttelot. 2nd ed. 8vo. Lond., 1890.   C 12 S 8

BARTTELOT,W. G. Life of Edmund Musgrave Barttelot, Commander of the Rear Column of the Emin Pasha Relief Expedition. 2nd ed. 8vo. Lond., 1890.   C 12 S 6

BARUCHSON, A. Beetroot Sugar; being an Abridgment of the Pamphlet by A. Baruchson on the Advantages of the Growth and Manufacture of Beetroot Sugar. 8vo. Hobart, 1868.   MA 2 T 65

BARY, Prof. A. de. [*See* De Bary, Prof. A.*]*

BASCH and CO. Mineral Guide and Prospectors' Companion. 12mo. Sydney, 1872.   MA 2 P 57

BASHKIRTSEFF, Marie. Letters of; translated by Mary J. Serrano. 8vo. Lond., 1891.   C 14 R 20

BASSETT, A. B. Treatise on Hydrodynamics. Vol. 1. 8vo. Camb., 1888.   A 25 U 25

BASTABLE, C. F. Public Finance. 8vo. Lond., 1892.   F 9 S 13

BASTIAN, A. Inselgruppen in Oceanien. 8vo. Berlin, 1883.   MD 5 S 14

Message Sticks der Australier. Roy. 8vo. Berlin, 1880.   MA 3 R 21

Die Vorstellungen von der Seele. 8vo. Berlin, 1875.   F 13 P 41

BASTIAT, F. Popular Fallacies regarding Trade and Foreign Duties. 8vo. Lond., 1885.   F 5 Q 36

BASTON, l'Abbé G. A. R. Narrations d'Omai, Insulaire de la Mer du Sud. [*See* Omai.*]*

BASU, Prof. K. P. Students' Mathematical Companion; containing Problems in Arithmetic, Algebra, Geometry, and Mensuration. 8vo. Lond., 1887.   A 25 U 25

BATE, J. M. Silk Cultivation: Directions for Planting the Mulberry and Treatment of the Silkworm. 8vo. Sydney, 1864.   MA 1 P 86

BATES, E. Katharine. Kaleidoscope: Shifting Scenes from East to West. 8vo. Lond., 1889. MD 3 U 39

A Year in the Great Republic. 2 vols. 8vo. Lond., 1887.   D 3 Q 32, 33

BATES, H. W. Illustrated Travels. 6 vols. 4to. Lond. (n.d.)   D 39 P 8-13 ‡

BATHGATE, A. Far South Fancies. 12mo. Lond. (n.d.)   MH 1 Q 63

BATTERSHALL, J. P. Food Adulteration and its Detection. 8vo. New York, 1887.   A 26 S 4

BATTIE, Dr. W. [*See* Isocrates.*]*

BAUER, F. Prodromus Floræ Norfolkicæ, sive Catalogus Stirpium quae in Insula Norfolk, 1804-5. Vindobonæ, 1833.   MA 3 R 16

Exotick Plants cultivated in the Royal Garden, Kew. Fol. Lond., 1796.   A 8 R 11‡

BAUERLEN, W. Voyage of the *Bonito:* an Account of the Fly River Expedition to New Guinea. 8vo. Sydney, 1886.   MD 3 S 37

BAUERMAN, H. [*See* Phillips, J. A.*]*

BAUMEISTER, A. [*See* Homer.*]*

BAUR, Dr. F. C. Church History of the First Three Centuries. Translated from the German by Rev. A. Menzies. 3rd ed. 2 vols. 8vo. Lond., 1878-79.   G 4 U 28, 29

Paul, the Apostle of Jesus Christ, his Life and Work. 2 vols. 8vo. Lond., 1875-76.   G 4 U 30, 31

BAX, E. B. The Ethics of Socialism; being further Essays in Modern Socialist Criticism. 8vo. Lond., 1889.   F 6 R 36

Outlooks from the New Standpoint. 8vo. Lond, 1891.   F 14 P 2

The Religion of Socialism, being Essays in Modern Socialist Criticism. 8vo. Lond., 1889.   F 6 R 35

The Story of the French Revolution. 8vo. Lond., 1890.   B 26 Q 6

Will Socialism benefit the English People? A written debate between E. B. Bax and Charles Bradlaugh. 12mo. Lond., 1887.   F 5 Q 11

[*See* Schopenhauer, A., and Smith, A.*]*

BAXTER, A. B. Banking in Australasia from a London Official's point of view; with some remarks on Mortgage and Finance Companies. 8vo. Lond., 1883. MF 3 Q 8

BAXTER, Mrs. Lucy E. "Leader Scott." Life of William Barnes, Poet and Philologist. 8vo. Lond., 1887.   C 12 R 27

Tuscan Studies and Sketches. 8vo. Lond., 1888.   D 18 Q 5

Vincigliata and Maiano. Imp. 8vo. Lond., 1891. B 30 V 7

BAXTER, Rev. M. Louis Napoleon, the Destined Monarch of the World, and Future Personal Anti-Christ. 8vo. Melb., 1866.   MG 1 Q 6

BAXTER, Rt. Hon. W. E. Our Land Laws of the Past. 12mo. Lond., 1880.   F 5 Q 35

BAXTER, W. [*See* Anacreon.*]*

BAYLEY, Rev. Dr. C. Select Psalms. 2nd ed. 18mo. Manchester, 1794.   G 4 V 2

BAYLY, E. B. Alfreda Holme: a story of social life in Australia. 2nd ed. 8vo. Lond., 1889.   MJ 2 P 40

BAYLY, Capt. G. Sea Life Sixty Years Ago. 8vo. Lond., 1885.   MD 4 P 38

BAYNE, P. Martin Luther: his Life and Work. 2 vols. 8vo. Lond., 1887.   C 13 T 17, 18

BAZALGETTE, C. N., and HUMPHREYS, G. Law relating to Local and Municipal Government. Roy. 8vo. Lond., 1885.   F 12 V 1

c

BEACONSFIELD, Rt. Hon. Benjamin Disraeli, Earl of. [Life of]: by J. A. Froude. 8vo. Lond., 1890.
C 12 R 37

Life of; by T. E. Kebbel. (Statesmen Series.) 8vo. Lond., 1888.
C 3 R 19

Personal Reminiscences of; by H. Lake. 8vo. Lond., 1891.
C 12 R 38

Disraeli in Outline; by F. C. Brewster. 8vo. Lond., 1890.
C 12 T 12

Disraeli and his Day; by Sir W. Fraser. 8vo. Lond., 1891.
C 13 S 6

[*See* Geffcken, Dr. F. H.]

BEADON, R. J.   Uniform Imperial Postage : an enquiry and a proposal. 8vo. Lond., 1891.
F 8 Q 22

BEAL, Prof. S.   Life of Hiuen-Tsiang.   [*See* Hwui Li.] [*See* Muller, F. Max., Sacred Books, 19.]

BEALBY, J. T.   [*See* Hoffmann, E. T. W.]

BEALE, C. E.   History of the World's Progress, a general History of the Earth's Construction, &c.   Roy. 4to. Sydney, 1888.*
B 9 R 10†

BEALE, E. J.   English Tobacco Culture.   8vo. Lond., 1887.
A 1 U 2

BEALE, L. S.   How to Work with the Microscope.   5th ed. 8vo. Lond., 1880.
A 29 U 2

BEALE, T.   Natural History of the Sperm Whale.   8vo. Lond., 1839.
A 27 Q 43

BEALE, Thomas Willert.   "Walter Maynard." Light of Other Days seen through the wrong end of an Opera Glass.   2 vols.   8vo.   Lond., 1890.
C 14 T 3, 4

BEAMONT, W.   Account of the Ancient Town of Frodsham in Cheshire.   8vo.   Warrington, 1881.   B 23 T 6
Account of the Rolls of the Honour of Halton, part of Her Majesty the Queen's Duchy of Lancaster.   4to.   Warrington, 1879.
B 9 R 9 †
Annals of the Lords of Warrington and Bewsey, 1587–1833. Roy. 8vo.   Manchester, 1873.
C 8 Q 8
The Bull of Pope Innocent III, given at Rome, March 3rd, 1216 ; with a Translation, and a short Account of the Pope.   4to.   Warrington, 1886.
G 9 R 26 †
Hale, and Orford : an Account of Two Old Lancashire Houses.   8vo.   Warrington, 1886.
C 13 S 8
History of the Castle of Halton and the Priory of Norton. 4to.   Warrington, 1873.
B 9 P 30 †
Memoir of the late Thomas Robson, a Warrington Artist. 8vo.   Warrington, 1886.
C 5 U 29
Notes on some English Judges ; William Garnett.   8vo. Warrington, 1883.
F 5 U 33
On Three Dramas of Shakspere : Richard II.—Henry IV, part 1.—Henry IV, part 2.   8vo.   Warrington, 1879.
H 2 P 35
Retrospect of Warrington.   8vo.   Warrington, 1887.
B 23 T 8
Walks about Warrington towards the beginning of the Present Century.   8vo.   Warrington, 1887.   B 23 T 7
Winwick ; its History and Antiquities.   2nd ed.   8vo. Warrington (n.d)
B 23 T 5

BEAMONT, W., and RYLANDS, J. P.   Attempt to identify the Arms formerly existing in the Windows of the Parish Church and Austin Priory at Warrington.   Roy. 4to.   Warrington, 1878.
K 2 R 30 †

BEAN, E., and SLY, J. D.   High Schools *versus* Scholarships : an enquiry into the merits of the two systems. 8vo.   Bathurst, 1886.
MG 1 R 31

BEANEY, J. G.   The Generative System and its Functions in Health and Disease.   3rd edition.   8vo. Lond., 1876.
MA 2 S 14

BEAR, W. E.   The Relations of Landlord and Tenant in England and Scotland   12mo.   Lond., 1876.   F 12 S 2

BEATTY-KINGSTON, W.   [*See* Kingston, W. Beatty-.]

BEATON, David, Cardinal.   Priest and Politician ; by Rev. J. Herkless.   12mo.   Edinb., 1891.   C 12 P 45

BEATRICE, H.R.H., Princess.   [*See* Kraus. E.]

BEAUFORT, Duke of.   The Account of the Official Progress of His Grace Henry, the First Duke of Beaufort through Wales in 1684 ; from the original MS. of Thomas Dingley, or Dinely ; with preface by R. W. Banks.   4to.   Lond., 1888.
B 6 V 36

BEAUFORT, Sir Henry Chas. Fitzroy-Somerset, 8th Duke of.   Driving.   (Badminton Library.)   8vo.   Lond., 1889.
A 17 U 39

BEAUFORT, R. L. de.   [*See* Broglie, Duc de ; Napoleon I ; Napoleon, Prince J. ; and Talleyrand, Prince de.]

BEAUFOY, Henry Benjamin Hanbury.   Descriptive Catalogue of the London Traders, Tavern, and Coffeehouse Tokens current in the 17th Century.   2nd ed. 8vo.   Lond., 1855.
A 27 T 2

BEAULIEU, Prof. P. L.   Modern State in relation to Society and the Individual.   8vo.   Lond., 1891.   F 14 P 3

BEAUMONT, F., and FLETCHER, J.   Bonduca : a Tragedy.   [*See* British Drama, Modern.]
The False One : a Tragedy.   [*See* British Drama, Modern.]
A King and no King : a Tragedy.   [*See* British Drama, Modern.]
The Maid's Tragedy.   [*See* British Drama, Modern.]
Philaster : a Tragedy.   [*See* British Drama, Modern.]
Thierry and Theodoret : a Tragedy.   [*See* British Drama, Modern.]
Best Plays ; edited by J. S. L. Strachey.   (Mermaid Series.)   2 vols.   8vo.   Lond., 1887.   H 4 Q 20, 21
  1. The Maid's Tragedy.—Philaster.—The Wild-goose Chase.— Thierry and Theodoret.—The Knight of the Burning Pestle.
  2. Shirley's Address.—King and no King.—Bonduca.—The Spanish Curate.—The Faithful Shepherdess.—Valentinian.

BEAUMONT, Sir G., and Lady.   [*See* Knight, W.]

BEAUMONT, R.   Colour in Woven Design.   12mo. Lond., 1890.
A 25 Q 10
Woollen and Worsted Cloth Manufacture.   8vo.   Lond., 1888.
A 25 Q 3

BEAUVOIR, Ludovic, Marquis de.   Australie : Voyage autour du Monde.   4e éd.   12mo.   Paris, 1883.   MD 2 Q 11

BEAVAN, E. History of the Welsh Sunday Closing Act. 12mo. Cardiff, 1885. F 11 P 35

BEAVER, A. Memorials of Old Chelsea. Roy. 8vo. Lond., 1892. B 24 V 11

BECK, C. D. Index Græcitatis Euripideæ. 8vo. Cantab. 1829. K 17 Q 32

BECKER, Sarah C., and MORA, F. Spanish Idioms with their English Equivalents, embracing nearly 10,000 Phrases. 8vo. Boston, 1887. K 13 P 37

BECKET, Thomas a'., Martyr, Patriot; by R. A. Thompson. 8vo. Lond., 1889. C 12 R 10

Account of his Life and Fame, from the contemporary Biographers and other Chroniclers; selected by Rev. W. H. Hutton. 16mo. Lond., 1889. C 13 P 6

BEDDARD, F. E. Animal Coloration : Facts and Theories relating to the Colours and Markings of Animals. 8vo. Lond., 1892. A 27 U 23

BEDE,' Venerable. Ecclesiastical History of England; edited by Dr. J. A. Giles. 2nd ed. 12mo. Lond., 1849. G 7 U 26

BEDFORD, Rev. W. K. R. [*See* Sharpe, C. K.]

BEDSON, Prof. P. Phillips. Outlines of Theoretical Chemistry. [*See* Meyer, Prof. L.]

BEECHER, Rev. H. W. Biography of; by W. C. Beecher and Rev. S. Scoville, assisted by Mrs. H. W. Beecher. Roy. 8vo. Lond., 1888. C 12 U 6

A Sketch of his Career; by the Rev. L. Abbott and Rev. S. B. Halliday. Roy. 8vo. Hartford, 1887. C 12 T 28

BEECHER, W. C., SCOVILLE, Rev. S., and BEECHER, Mrs. H. W. Biography of Rev. Henry Ward Beecher. Roy. 8vo. Lond., 1888. C 12 U 6

BEESLY, E. S. [Life of] Queen Elizabeth. 12mo. Lond., 1892. C 17 Q 24

BEETHOVEN, Ludvig van. [Life of]; by H. A. Rudall. (Great Musicians.) 12mo. Lond., 1890. C 12 P. 39

BEGG, Rev. Dr. James. Memoirs of; by Prof. T. Smith. 2 vols. 8vo. Edinb., 1885. C 17 T 1, 2

BEHN, Mrs. Aphra. Plays, Histories, and Novels of. 6 vols. 8vo. Lond., 1871. H 3 S 31-36

BEHNKE, Emil. Voice, Song, and Speech. [*See* Browne, Lennox.]

BEHRENDS, Rev. Dr. A. J. F. Socialism and Christianity. 8vo. New York, 1886. F 14 P 4

BEITRÄGE ZUR GEOLOGIE VON NEIDERLÄNDISCH WEST-INDIEN. Band 1. Roy. 8vo. Leiden, 1887-89. E

BEKKER, I. Suidæ Lexicon. Roy. 8vo. Berolini, 1854. K 16 R 38

[*See* Apollodorus, Appian, Demosthenes, Heliodorus, Herodian, Sextus Empiricus, and Tacitus.]

BELCHER, Lady D., and her Friends; by the Rev. A. G. L'Estrange. 8vo. Lond., 1891. C 14 T 12

BELCHER, Capt. Sir E. The Last of the Arctic Voyages; being a Narrative of the Expedition in H.M.S. *Assistance* in search of Sir J. Franklin, 1852-54. [Illustrated.] 2 vols. Imp. 8vo. Lond., 1855. D 15 V 11, 12

BELGIUM. Guide de l'Etranger en Belgique. 12mo. Bruxelles, 1854. D 19 P 4

BELL, Sir C. The Hand. 8vo. Lond., 1834. A 26 U 15
Another Copy. 8vo. Lond., 1838. A 26 U 16

BELL, Clara. [*See* Jæger, H.]

BELL, C. F. M. From Pharaoh to Fellah. 4to. Lond., 1887. D 2 U 5

BELL, F. J. Comparative Anatomy. [*See* Gegenbaur, C.]
Comparative Anatomy and Physiology. 12mo. Lond., 1885. A 14 P 64

BELL, Henry Glassford. Life of Mary Queen of Scots. 2 vols. 12mo. Sydney, 1890. C 17 P 25, 26

BELL, H. T. M. A Forgotten Genius : C. Whitehead : a Critical Monograph. 8vo. Lond., 1884. C 14 S 11

BELL, S. S. Colonial Administration of Great Britain. 8vo. Lond., 1859. F 6 U 28

BELL, W. F. Irrigation for Farmers and Engineers. 8vo. Melb., 1890. M A 1 V 63

BELL, Major William Morrison. Other Countries. 2 vols. 8vo. Lond., 1872. D 10 S 33, 34

BELLESHEIM, Rev. Dr. A. History of the Catholic Church of Scotland; translated by Rev. D. O. H. Blair. 4 vols. 8vo. Lond., 1887-90. G 4 R 30-33

BELLEW, H. W. Short Practical Treatise on the Nature, Causes, and Treatment of Cholera. 8vo. Lond., 1887. A 26 T 1

BELLOC, L. S. Derniers Récits. 8vo. Paris, 1886. J 15 S 27
Les Leçons d'une jeune mère, contes et récits. 8vo. Paris, 1886. J 15 S 24

BELLORI, G. P. Le Pitture Antiche delle Grotte di Roma e del Sepolcro de' Nasoni. Fol. Roma, 1706. B 39 S 13 ‡

BELLOWS, Dr. A. J. The Philosophy of Eating. 16th ed. 12mo. Boston, 1887. A 26 Q 13

BELMORE, Earl of. Parliamentary Memoirs of Fermanagh, 1613-1885. 8vo. Dublin, 1885. B 11 Q 17
Parliamentary Memoirs of Fermanagh and Tyrone, 1613-1885. 8vo. Dublin, 1887. C 13 U 9

BELSHAM, Rev. T. Memoirs of the Late Rev. Theophilus Lindsey, M.A. 8vo. Lond., 1812. C 15 U 6

BENDALL, Prof. Cecil. A Journey of Literary and Archæological Research in Nepal and Northern India, 1884-85. 8vo. Cambridge, 1886. B 29 T 1

BENEDICT, St. The Rule of St. Benet. [*See* Early English Text Soc.]

BENEVOLENCE IN PUNISHMENT, or Transportation made Reformatory. 12mo. Lond., 1845. MF 2 P 54

BENEVOLENT SOCIETY OF NEW SOUTH WALES.
Abstract of the Proceedings for 1819. Sm. 4to.
Sydney, 1819.   MF 3 R 51

BENGEL, J. A. Gnomon Novi Testamenti. 3rd ed. Roy.
8vo. Lond., 1862.   G 15 T 21

BENHAM, Rev. W. Dictionary of Religion. Roy. 8vo.
Lond., 1887.   K 18 R 30
[*See* Davidson, Rev. R. T.]

BENJAMIN, S. G. W. Persia. (The Story of the
Nations.) 8vo. Lond., 1888.   B 16 Q 1

BENNET, Hon. H. G. Letter to Earl Bathurst, on the
Condition of the Colonies in New South Wales and Van
Diemen's Land. 8vo. Lond., 1820.   MF 1 T 76
Letter to Viscount Sidmouth on the Transportation Laws,
the State of the Hulks, and of the Colonies in New
South Wales. 8vo. Lond., 1819.   MF 2 T 19

BENNET, R. G., and WIJK, J. van. Verhandeling over
de Nederlandsche ontdekkingen in Amerika. Australie,
de Indiën en de Poollanden. 8vo. Utrecht, 1827.
                                         MD 7 S 44
Knarten [to the above]. Fol. Utrecht, 1827.
                                         MD 3 Q 8 ‡

BENNETT, A. W. Botany. [*See* Sachs, Prof. J.]

BENNETT, A. W., and MURRAY, G. Handbook of
Cryptogamic Botany. 8vo. Lond., 1889.   A 4 Q 12

BENNETT, E. T. The Gardens and Menagerie of the
Zoological Society delineated. 2 vols. 8vo. Chiswick,
1830.   A 27 T 32, 33

BENNETT, G., GIBSON, A., and SHERWIN, W. Reports on the Epidemic Catarrh or Influenza prevailing
among the Sheep in New South Wales, 1835. 8vo.
Sydney, 1835.   MA 3 P 30

BENNETT, S. The History of Australian Discovery and
Colonisation. Parts 1–5. 8vo. Sydney, 1865.
                                         MB 2 P 23

BENSON, A. C. William Laud, Archbishop of Canterbury : a Study. 8vo. Lond., 1887.   .   C 17 Q 5

BENSON, C. Rubrics and Canons of the Church of
England considered. 8vo. Lond., 1845.   G 15 R 27

BENTHAM, G. The Botany of the Voyage of H.M.S.
Sulphur, 1836–42. 4to. Lond., 1844.   A 36 P 22 ‡
Handbook of the British Flora. 12mo. Lond., 1868.
                                         A 20 P 14

BENTHAM, J. Panopticon ; or, the Inspection-house
(Text and Plates). 2 vols. 12mo. Lond., 1812.
                                         F 2 P 34, 35
Theory of Legislation. 12mo. Lond., 1891. F 9 U 31
Works of. 11 vols. 8vo. Edinb., 1843. F 14 V 3–13

BENTINCK, Lord G. C. Racing Life of ; by J. Kent.
8vo. Edinb., 1892.   C 18 Q 16

BENTINCK, Lord Wm. [Life of] ; by D. C. Boulger.
(Rulers of India.) 12mo. Oxford, 1892.   C 17 Q 26

BENTLEY, Dr. Richard. Life of ; by the Very Rev.
Dean Monk. 4to. Lond., 1830.   C 42 S 11‡
[*See* Horatius Flaccus, Q.]

BENTLEY, Prof. R. Manual of Botany. 4th ed.
12mo. Lond., 1882.   A 20 P 5
Another copy. 7th ed. 12mo. Lond., 1885. A 20 P 17
Text-book of Organic Materia Medica. 8vo. Lond.,
1887.   A 13 P 45

BENTLEY, Rev. W. H. Dictionary and Grammar of the
Kongo Language. 8vo. Lond., 1887.   K 12 U 5

BENTON, T. H. Life of ; by T. Roosevelt. (American
Statesmen.) 12mo. Boston, 1887.   C 13 Q 2

BENVENUTI, F. F. Episodes of the French Revolution
from 1789 to 1795. 8vo. Lond., 1880.   B 26 T 13

BEOWULF. The Deeds of Beowulf : an English Epic of
the Eighth Century done into modern Prose ; by Rev. J.
Earle. 8vo. Oxford, 1892.   J 12 Q 40

BERANGER, P. J. de. Dernières Chansons, 1834–51.
8vo. Paris, 1859.   H 7 P 43
Ma Biographie. 12mo. Paris, 1859.   C 12 Q 8
Œuvres de. 2 vols. 8vo. Paris, 1876.   H 6 P 41, 42

BÉRARD (—). Campagne de la Corvette *l'Alcmène* en
Océanie, 1850–51. 8vo. Paris, 1854.   MD 5 S 6

BERAUSCHUNG. Ueber die Künstliche Berauschung
pflanzen-, und fleischfressender Säugethiere. 8vo. (n.p.)
1834.   F 11 R 36

BERDOE, E. The Browning Cyclopædia. 8vo. Lond.,
1892.   K 7 S 34

BÉRENGIER, Théophile. La Nouvelle-Nursie, Histoire
d'une Colonie Bénédictine dans l'Australie Occidentale,
1846–78. Roy. 8vo. Paris, 1878.   MD 7 U 5

BERENS, Rev. E. History of the Prayer-Book of the
Church of England. New ed. 12mo. Lond., 1843.
                                         G 8 P 32

BERESFORD, G. W. D. [*See* South Australia.]

BERGERET, Dr. L. F. E. De l'Abus des Boissons
Alcooliques. 12mo. Paris, 1870.   F 11 P 70

BERGGRUEN, O. Cortège Historique de la Ville de
Vienne à l'occasion des Noces d'Argent de leurs Majestés
François-Joseph Ier. et Elisabeth. Fol. Paris, 1879.
                                         B 34 Q 17 ‡

BERGH, Dr. R. [*See* Semper, Dr. C.]

BERGK, T. [*See* Sophocles.]

BERICHT über die wissenschaftlichen Leistungen in der
Naturgeschichte der Niederen Thiere, 1876–79. 8vo.
Berlin, 1879.   E

BERKELEY, H. Wealth and Welfare ; or, Our National
Trade Policy and its Cost. 8vo. Lond., 1887. F 5 T 34

BERLESE, Dr. A. P. [*See* Saccardo, P. A.]

BERMINGHAM. Rev. P. [*See* St. Augustine's Literary
Institute.]

BERNARD, H. M. The Apodidæ: a Morphological Study. 8vo. Lond., 1892. A 28 Q 25

BERNAU, Rev. J. H. Missionary Labours in British Guiana. 8vo. Lond., 1847. D 15 R 5

BERNHARDT, Mme. Sarah. A Biographical and Critical Sketch; by Austin Brereton. Roy. 8vo. Sydney, 1891. MC 1 T 9

BERNIER, F. Travels in the Mogul Empire, 1656-68; revised by A. Constable. Vol. 1. 12mo. Lond., 1891. D 17 Q 17

BERNSTEIN, Dr. H. A. Dagboek van Dr. Bernstein's laatste Reis van Ternate naar Nieuw-Guinea, Salawati en Batanta, 1864-65. Roy. 8vo. s'Gravenhage, 1883. MD 7 U 6

BÉRON, P. Physique Céleste. 3 vols. 8vo. Paris, 1866-68. A 19 T 24-26

BERTI, Domenico. Giordano Bruno da Nola; sua Vita e sua Dottrina. 8vo. Torino, 1889. C 12 R 7

BERTIN, G. Abridged Grammars of the Languages of the Cuneiform Inscriptions. 8vo. Lond., 1888. K 20 Q 21

BERTKAU, Dr. P. Bericht über die wissenschaftlichen Leistungen im Gebiete der Entomologie. 8vo. Berlin, 1892. A 27 S 26

BESANT, Annie. The Queen v. C. Bradlaugh and Annie Besant. 12mo. Lond. (n.d.) F 9 U 51
Socialism. [*See* Bradlaugh, C.]

BESANT, W. Fifty Years Ago. 8vo. Lond., 1888. B 6 R 44
[Life of] Captain Cook. 8vo. Lond., 1890. MC 1 Q 39

BESANT, W., and PALMER, E. H. Jerusalem and City of Herod and Saladin. New ed. 8vo. Lond., 1889. B 28 R 7

BESANT, Dr. W. H. Conic Sections, treated Geometrically. 7th ed. 12mo. Camb., 1819. A 24 P 29

BESOMO, P. Nuts to Crack for Infidels and Materialists; No. 1 Lecture, The Alliance between Science and Religion. 8vo. Balmain, 1887. MG 1 Q 54

BESSON, Mgr. L. Frederick F. X. de Mérode, Archbishop of Melitinensis, his Life and Works. 8vo. Lond., 1887. C 15 Q 20

BETA. [*See* Burgess, Rev. H. T., and Milne, Rev. J.]

BETHAM-EDWARDS, M. [*See* Edwards, M. B.]

BETTANY, G. T. The World's Inhabitants; or, Mankind, Animals, and Plants. 2nd ed. 8vo. London, 1889. A 18 U 20
The World's Religions. Roy. 8vo. Lond., 1890. G 6 T 25
Botany. Illustrated. 12mo. Lond. (n.d.). A 20 P 9

BETTERTON, Thomas. [Life of]; by Robert W. Lowe. (Eminent Actors). 12mo. Lond., 1891. C 12 P 42
Life and Times of that excellent and renowned Actor. 8vo. Lond., 1888. C 15 Q 3

BETTS, B. W. Geometrical Psychology; or Science of Representation: an Abstract of the Theories and Diagrams of B. W. Betts: by L. S. Cooke. 8vo. Lond., 1887. G 12 T 41

BETTS, Rev. C. M. Eight Sermons, to which is prefixed a brief Memoir; by the Rev. J. Carter. Roy. 8vo. Canterbury, 1859. MG 1 T 22
Another copy. Roy. 8vo. Canterbury, 1859. MG 1 S 61

BÉULE, E. Causeries sur l'Art. 2ᵉ éd. 12mo. Paris, 1867. A 23 Q 8

BEUST, Count F. F. von. Memoirs of; with an Introduction by Baron H. de Worms. 2 vols. 8vo. Lond., 1887. C 12 S 24, 25

BEUVE, C. A. Sainte-. [*See* Sainte-Beuve, C.A.]

BEVAN, E. J. [*See* Cross, C. F.]

BEVAN, T. F. Toil, Travel, and Discovery in British New Guinea. 8vo. Lond., 1890. MD 5 Q 57
Fifth Expedition to British New Guinea: Preliminary Presentation Pamphlet. Roy. 8vo. Sydney, 1888. MD 5 V 35

BEVERIDGE, D. Between the Ochils and Forth: a Description of the Country between Stirling Bridge and Aberdour. 8vo. Edinb., 1888. D 19 Q 5
Culross and Tulliallan; or, Perthshire on Forth: its History and Antiquities. 2 vols. 8vo. Edinb., 1885. B 13 Q 22, 23

BEVERIDGE, H. Trial of Maharaja Nanda Kumar: a Narrative of a Judicial Murder. 8vo. Calcutta, 1886. F 12 Q 29

BEVERIDGE, P. Aborigines inhabiting Lower Murray, Lower Murrumbidgee, Lower Lachlan, and Lower Darling Districts. 8vo. Sydney, 1883. MA 1 S 19

BEVERIDGE, Rt. Rev. W. Private Thoughts upon Religion. 8vo. Lond., 1821. G 16 P 38

BEWICK, T. Memorial Edition of Thomas Bewick's Works. 5 vols. imp. 8vo. Lond., 1885-87. A 15 T 9-13
1. British Birds: Land Birds.
2. British Birds: Water Birds.
3. Quadrupeds.
4. Fables of Æsop and others.
5. Memoir of; written by himself.

BEWICK, T. and J. The Bewick Collector. [*See* Hugo, T.]

BEYERS and HOLTERMANN'S STAR OF HOPE GOLD-MINING COMPANY, Limited. Deed of Settlement. 8vo. Sydney, 1872. MF 2 T 47

BEYLE, M. H. "De Stendhal."
L'Abbesse de Castro. 12mo. Paris, 1891. J 18 P 31
Armance; précédé d'une notice biographique; par R. Colomb. 12mo. Paris, 1877. J 18 P 33
De l'Amour. 12mo. Paris, 1891. J 18 P 30
Le Chartreuse de Parme. 12mo. Paris, 1890. J 18 P 32
Histoire de la Peinture en Italie. 12mo. Paris, 1883. A 26 Q 33

BEYLE, H. M.—*contd.*

Mémoires d'un Touriste. 2 vols. 12mo. Paris, 1891.
D 18 P 19, 20
Promenades dans Rome. 2 vols. 12mo. Paris, 1883.
D 18 P 17, 18
Rome, Naples, et Florence. 12mo. Paris, 1887.
D 18 P 21
Le Rouge et le Noir. 2 vols. 12mo. Paris, 1889.
J 18 P 34, 35
Vie de Napoléon. 12mo. Paris, 1882. C 14 P 19
Vie de Rossini. 12mo. Paris, 1892. C 14 P 17
Vies de Haydn, de Mozart, et de Métastase. 12mo.
Paris, 1887. C 14 P 18

BEZA, T. Novum Testamentum. [*See* Bibles.]

BIBLES, TESTAMENTS, &c.

DUTCH.
Het nieuwe Testament. 8vo. Dordrecht, 1850.
G 15 P 22
ENGLISH.
The Apocryphal New Testament. 8vo. Lond., 1820.
G 12 Q 31
Books of Psalms, Proverbs, Ecclesiastes, and the Song of
Solomon. 12mo. Oxford, 1881. C 16 P 41
Comprehensive Bible, containing the Old and New
Testaments, Disquisitions on the Genuineness, Authen-
ticity, and Inspiration of the Holy Scriptures, various
divisions and marks of distinction in the sacred
writings, ancient versions, &c. 4to. Lond., 1827.
G 6 V 25
Holy Bible from the Latin Vulgate (Douay.) 9th ed.
Roy. 8vo. Belfast, 1857. G 15 T 19
Holy Bible. 12mo. Cambridge, 1661. G 19 P 19
Holy Bible. 18mo. Oxford, 1808. G 9 U 13
New Testament, after the Authorised Version: revised
by Rev. H. Alford. 18mo. Lond., 1871. G 9 U 7
New Testament in an Improved Version. 4th ed. Roy.
8vo. Lond., 1817. G 15 T 20
Select Psalms; by Rev. Dr. C. Bayley. 18mo. Man-
chester, 1794. G 4 V 2
EROMANGAN.
Matiyu : Ku nam navosavos ugi Jesu Kristo. (The Four
Gospels and Acts of the Apostles.) 8vo. Sydney,
1890. MG 2 R 33
FIJIAN.
A Lotu e na Sabegibogi e na Veisiga Tabu. 12mo.
(n.p.n.d.) MG 2 R 34
Ai Vola ni Veiyalayalato vou ni noda Turaga kei na
nodai Vakabula ko Jisu Kraisiti. 12mo. Viti, 1853.
MG 2 R 35
GAELIC.
New Testament, in Gaelic. 18mo. Lond., 1830. G 9 U 11
Sailm Dhaibhidh. Glasgow (n.d.) G 9 U 6
GERMAN.
Die Biebel. 8vo. Cöln, 1859. G 15 Q 28
GOTHIC.
Ulfilas : Veteris et Novi Testamenti Versionis Gothicæ.
Fragmenta quæ supersunt ediderunt H. C. de Gabe-
lentz et Dr. J Loebe. 3 vols. (in 1.) 4to. Lipsiæ,
1843–46. G 5 U 29

BIBLES, TESTAMENTS, &c.—*contd.*
GREEK.
New Testament in Modern Greek. 12mo. Lond., 1819.
G 19 P 20
Novi Testamenti libri omnes. 12mo. Lond., 1633.
G 8 P 33
Novum testamentum, Græce et Latine. C. Lachmannus
recensuit. 2 vols. (in 1.) 8vo. Berolini, 1842–50.
G 15 Q 27
Novum Testamentum Græce ; curavit Dr. I. M. A. Scholz.
2 vols. (in 1.) 4to. Lipsiæ, 1830. G 6 V 27
Novum Testamentum Græce ; recensuit P. Buttmann.
12mo. Lipsiæ, 1856. G 17 P 54
Vetus Testamentum Græce justa LXX Interpretes :
edidit C. Tischendorf. 2 vols. 8vo. Lipsiæ, 1850.
G 4 T 20, 21
Novum Testamentum sive Novum Fœdus ; interprete T.
Beza. 18mo. Dublin, 1767. G 9 U 12
Vetus Testamentum ex versione septuaginta interpretum,
edidit L. Bos. (Greek text.) 4to. Francequeræ, 1709.
G 6 V 26
HEBREW.
The Bible in Hebrew. 12 vols. 4to. Warszawie,
1859–64. G 39 Q 1–12 ‡
Biblia Hebraica, sine punctis. 12mo. Amstel., 1701.
G 9 U 14
HINDUSTANI.
Kitáb i Muqaddas. Imp. 8vo. Lond., 1860. G 3 V 22
New Testament, in Hinduwee. 8vo. Lond., 1863.
G 15 Q 26
ICELANDIC.
Biblia pad er Heirlög Ritning. 8vo. Lond., 1866.
G 15 S 17
LATIN.
Biblia Sacra Vulgatæ Editiones. Sm. 4to. Lyons, 1743.
G 2 T 30
Biblia Sacra. 12mo. Paris (n.d.) G 19 P 16
LUTHERAN.
Naujas Testamentas. 8vo. Berlyne, 1865. G 15 P 21
MAORI.
Ko te Kawenata Hou O To Tatou Ariki Te Kai Wakaora
A Ihu Karaiti. [Maori New Testament]. 8vo. Ranana,
1844. MG 2 R 10
NORWEGIAN.
Bibelen eller Den Hellige Skrift. 8vo. Christiania, 1848.
G 15 Q 25
PHONETIC.
Holi Bib'l. (Phonetic). 8vo. Lond., 1850. G 15 Q 30
The New Testament in Phonography. 12mo. Lond.,
1886. G 4 V 10
PORTUGUESE.
A Biblia-Sagrada. 8vo. Lond., 1850. G 15 Q 29
SAMOAN.
Koe Gaohi Kole moe Gaohi Hiva Katolika. I He Lea
Fakatoga. [Roman Catholic Prayer Book in Samoan.]
8vo. Fribourg, 1880. MG 2 R 8
SPANISH.
La Biblia. Lond. (n.d.) G 19 P 23
El Nuevo Testamento. 18mo. Lond., 1871. G 4 V 3

BIBLES, TESTAMENTS, &c.—*continued.*

SWEDISH.
Bibelen eller Den Heliga Skrift. 8vo. Stockholm
(n.d.) G 15 Q 31

TAHITIAN.
New Testament: Te Faufaa Api, A To Tatou Fatu E To
Ora A Jesu Mesia Ra : Iriti Hia Ei Parau Tahiti.
8vo. Lonedona, 1853. MG 2 P 43

TONGAN.
Ko Te Tohi-Lotu Katoliko Faka-Uvea. [Roman Catholic
Prayer Book in Tongan.] 8vo. Fribourg, 1878.
MG 2 R 9

WELSH.
Y Bibl Cyssegr-lan. 8vo. Llundain, 1841. G 17 P 55

BIBLIOTHECA POLYTECHNICA. [*See* Szczepanski,
F. von.]

BICE, Rev. C., and BRITTAIN, Rev. A. Journal of
Residence in the New Hebrides, S.W. Pacific Ocean.
8vo. Truro, 1887. MD 3 U 40

BICKERDYKE, J. Angling for Coarse Fish. 8vo.
Lond., 1888. A 29 Q 1

BICKERSTAFF, I. Love in a Village; a comic opera.
[*See* British Drama, Modern.]
The Maid of the Mill ; a comic opera. [*See* British Drama,
Modern.]
The Padlock : a comic opera. [*See* British Drama,
Modern.]
The Sultan ; a farce. [*See* British Drama, Modern.]

BICKERSTAFF, I., and FOOTE, S., Dr. Last in his
Chariot ; a comedy. [*See* British Drama, Modern.]

BICKERSTETH, Rev. E. Questions illustrating the
Thirty-nine Articles of the Church of England. 2nd ed.
8vo. Lond., 1846. G 16 R 32

BICKERSTETH, Rev. M. C. Sketch of the Life and
Episcopate of Robert Bickersteth, Bishop of Ripon.
1857–84. 8vo. Lond., 1887. C 13 T 21

BICKERSTETH, Rt. Rev. R. Sketch of the Life and
Episcopate of ; by his Son, the Rev. M. C. Bickersteth.
8vo. Lond., 1887. C 13 T 21

BICKFORD, J. Christian Work in Australasia, with
Notes on the Settlement and Progress of the Colonies.
8vo. Lond., 1878. MD 2 W 17

BIDDULPH, C. E. Afghan Poetry. [*See* Kushhal
Khan Khatah.]

BIDPAI. [*See* Pilpay.]

BIGELOW, John. [Life of] William Cullen Bryant.
(American Men of Letters.) 12mo. Boston, 1890.
C 12 P 21
France and the Confederate Navy, 1862–68: an Inter-
national Episode. 8vo. Lond., 1888. B 18 Q 1
[*See* Franklin, B.]

BIGELOW, Dr. M. M. Story's Commentaries. [*See*
Story, Dr. J.]

BIGGAR, E. B. Anecdotal Life of Sir John Macdonald.
8vo. Montreal, 1891. C 18 R 20

BIGGE, L. A. Selby. [*See* Hume, D.]

BIGMORE, E. C. [*See* Bouchot, H.]

BILBROUGH, E. E. [*See* Brett, H.]

BINET, A., and FÉRÉ, C. Animal Magnetism. 8vo.
Lond., 1887. A 21 Q 8

BING, S. Artistic Japan. 4to. Lond. (n.d.) A 40 S 11‡

BINGHAM, Hon. D. The Marriages of the Bourbons.
2 vols. 8vo. Lond., 1890. B 8 R 35, 36
The Bastille. 2 vols. roy. 8vo. Lond., 1888. B 26 U 10, 11

BINGLE, J. Review of the Treatment, by Government of
New South Wales, of. 8vo. Sydney, 1834. MF 3 P 47

BINGLEY, Rev. W. Biographical Conversations on the
most eminent Voyagers of Different Nations from Columbus to Cook. 8vo. Lond., 1819. MD 3 R 36

BINNEY, Thos. Conscientious Clerical Noncomformity ;
a discourse. 8vo. Adelaide, 1859. MG 2 Q 42

BIOLOGISCHES CENTRALBLATT. Vols. 6–11. 8vo.
Erlangen, 1886–91. E

BIRCH, W. de G. Cartularium Saxonicum : a Collection
of Charters relating to Anglo-Saxon History. Vols. 1–3.
Lond., 1885–93. B 25 U 2–4

BIRD, S. R. S. Guide to the Principal Classes of Docu-
ments in the Public Record Office. 8vo. Lond., 1891.
K 8 R 11
Domesday Book : a Popular Account of the Exchequer
Manuscript so called. 12mo. Lond., 1887. B 21 Q 25

BIRDWOOD, Sir George. Report on the Old Records of
the India Office. 2nd reprint. Roy. 8vo. Lond., 1891.
B 29 V 1

BIRKBECK, G. The Pioneer of Popular Education ; by
J. G. Godard. 12mo. Lond., 1888. C 16 P 26

BIRKMYRE, W. The Secretary of State for India in
Council. 2nd ed. Lond., 1886. F 5 Q 34

BIRMINGHAM FREE LIBRARIES. Catalogue of ;
by J. D. Mullins. 8vo. Birmingham, 1890. Libr.

BIRRELL, A. Res Judicatæ : Papers and Essays. 12mo.
Lond., 1892. J 11 W 2

BISHOP, G. The Beachcombers ; or, Slave Trading under
the Union Jack. Colonial edition. Sydney, 1889.
MJ 1 U 47

BISHOP, Mrs. I. L. Journeys in Persia and Kurdistan,
with portrait, maps, and illustrations. 2 vols. 8vo.
Lond., 1891. D 17 S 8, 9

BISMARCK, Schönhausen Otto Edward Leopold, Prince
von. Bismarck Intime ; by a Fellow Student. Translated by H. Hayward. 8vo. Lond., 1890. C 14 R 10

BLACK, J. [*See* Gerning, Baron J. J. von.]

BLACK, J. S. Notes on Dante. [*See* Dante Alighieri.]

BLACK, R. Horse-racing in France : a History. 8vo.
Lond., 1886. B 29 U 15

BLACK, W. G. Heligoland and the Islands of the North
Sea. 12mo. Edinb., 1888.　　　　　　　　　D 18 P 2

BLACKBURN, Prof. H. [*See* Newton, Sir I.]

BLACKBURN, H. Paris Universal Exhibition, 1889.
Complete Illustrated Catalogue of Paintings, &c., in the
British Fine Art Section. 8vo. Lond., 1889. A 23 T 5

New Gallery : an illustrated Catalogue. 4 vols. 8vo.
Lond., 1889-92.　　　　　　　　　　　　　　　　E

Grosvenor Gallery : an Illustrated Catalogue. 2 vols. 8vo.
Lond., 1889-90.　　　　　　　　　　　　　　　　E

Academy Notes : 6 vols. 8vo. Lond., 1887-92.　　　E

Academy Sketches. 6 vols. 8vo. Lond., 1887-92.　　E

BLACKIE, C. Dictionary of Place-Names, giving their
Derivations ; with an introduction by Prof. J. S. Blackie.
3rd ed. 8vo. Lond., 1887.　　　　　　　　　D 11 S 8

BLACKIE, Prof. J. S. On Self-culture, intellectual,
physical, and moral. (In phonetic shorthand.) 12mo.
Lond., 1882.　　　　　　　　　　　　　　　J 7 R 48

Scottish Song ; its wealth, wisdom, and social significance.
8vo. Edinb., 1889.　　　　　　　　　　　　H 10 Q 9
[*See* Blackie, C.]

BLACKLEY, Rev. W. L. [*See* Tegner, E.]

BLACKMORE, R. G. Decisions of the Rt. Hon. Sir H.
B. W. Brand on Points of Order, Rules of Debate, and
General Practice of the House. 12mo. Adelaide, 1883.
　　　　　　　　　　　　　　　　　　　　　MF 2 P 75

Decisions of the Rt. Hon. E. Denison, and of the Rt. Hon.
Sir H. B. W. Brand, 1857-1884. 8vo. Adelaide, 1892.
　　　　　　　　　　　　　　　　　　　　　MF 2 T 48

Manual of Practice, Procedure, and Usage of the Legislative Council of South Australia, 8vo. Adelaide, 1889.
　　　　　　　　　　　　　　　　　　　　　MF 3 P 44

Another copy. 2nd ed. 8vo. Adelaide, 1890.
　　　　　　　　　　　　　　　　　　　　　MF 3 P 45

BLACKWOOD, Alicia, Lady. Narrative of Personal Experiences and Impressions during a Residence on the
Bosphorus throughout the Crimean War. 8vo. Lond.,
1881.　　　　　　　　　　　　　　　　　　D 18 Q 3

BLACKWOOD'S EDINBURGH MAGAZINE. Vols.
141-151. Lond., 1887-92.　　　　　　　　　　　E

BLADES, W. The Enemies of Books. 12mo. Lond.,
1887.　　　　　　　　　　　　　　　　　　J 7 Q 46

Another Copy. 12mo. Lond., 1888　　　　　J 7 Q 47

The Pentateuch of Printing, with a Chapter on Judges.
4to. Lond., 1891.　　　　　　　　　　　　A 11 V 22

BLAGG, C. J. [*See* Mather, Rev. G.]

BLAGROVE, G. H. Marble Decoration, and the Termi-
nology of British and Foreign Marbles. 8vo. Lond.,
1888.　　　　　　　　　　　　　　　　　　A 2 R 45

Shoring and its Application : a Hand-book for the use of
Students. (Weale.) 12mo. Lond., 1887. A 17 R 16

BLAIR, D. Address on the Means of Fostering a National Literature. 8vo. Melb. (n.d.)　　　MJ 2 S 56

Cyclopædia of Australasia ; or Dictionary of Facts, Events,
Dates, Persons, &c. Imp. 8vo. Melb., 1881　MK 1 U 20

BLAIR, Rev. D. O. H. [*See* Bellesheim, Rev. Dr. A.]

BLAIR, J. Address [delivered before the Medical Society
of Victoria]. 8vo. Melb., 1873.　　　　　　MA 2 T 64

BLAIR, Rev. J. Chronological Tables ; revised and enlarged by J. W. Rosse.· 12mo. Lond., 1856. B 35 P 18

BLAIR, W. N. The Industries of New Zealand : an
Address. 8vo. W. Christchurch, 1887.　　　MF 2 T 46

BLAKE, Dr. A. Practical Essay on Delirium Tremens.
8vo. Lond., 1830.　　　　　　　　　　　　　F 11 R 7

BLAKE, F. C. Blake's Central Queensland Almanac and
Domestic Annual, 1891. 8vo. Rockhampton, 1891.
　　　　　　　　　　　　　　　　　　　　　ME 8 Q.

BLAKE, Mary Elizabeth. A Summer Holiday in Europe.
8vo. Dublin, 1890.　　　　　　　　　　　D 19 Q 12

BLAKE, W. A Critical Essay ; by A. C. Swinburne.
2nd ed. 8vo. Lond., 1868.　　　　　　　　　C 8 R 17

BLANC, L. Questions d'aujourd'hui et de demain.
4e. série ; Socialisme. 12mo. Paris, 1882.　　F 14 P 1

BLANCHE, J. F. The Prince's Visit and other Poems.
2nd ed. Melb., 1881.　　　　　　　　　　MH 1 S 44

BLAND, Dr. Wm. Account of the Duel between William
Bland and Robert Case ; from the Original MSS. to
which is appended a Report of the Trial Rex v. Bland,
Randall, and Fulton, 14th and 17th April, 1813. Sm.
4to. Sydney, 1862　　　　　　　　　　　MF 1 W 40

Services Rendered to New South Wales. 8vo. Sydney.
1862.　　　　　　　　　　　　　　　　　MC 1 Q 40

BLANNIM, Capt. A. Hasty Notes of a Flying Trip with
the Victorian Rifle Team to England and America in
1876. 8vo. Melb., 1877.　　　　　　　　MD 1 Q 51

BLEEK, Dr. F. Lectures on the Apocalypse. 8vo. Lond.,
1875.　　　　　　　　　　　　　　　　　　G 16 S 37

BLENNERHASSETT, Lady. Madame de Staël, her
Friends, and her Influence in Politics and Literature.
3 vols. 8vo. Lond., 1889.　　　　　　　C 13 U 16-18

BLIGH, Lieut. G. Voyage à la Mer du Sud, entrepris par
ordre de S. M. Britannique pour introduire, aux Indes
Occidentales, l'arbre à pain, et d'autres plantes utiles,
avec une relation de la révolte à bord de son vaisseau,
&c. Traduit de l'Anglais par F. Soulés. 8vo. Paris,
1792.　　　　　　　　　　　　　　　　　　MD 1 W 11

BLIN, C. Voyage en Oceanic, Nouvelle Caledonie, Tahiti,
&c. 12mo. Le Mans, 1881.　　　　　　　　MD 2 W 31

BLIND, Mathilde. Dramas in Miniature. 12mo. Lond.,
1891.　　　　　　　　　　　　　　　　　　H 9 P 10

BLOOMFIELD, C. J. [*See* Callimachus.]

BLOSSEVILLE, E. de. Histoire des Colonies Pénales de
l'Angleterre dans l'Australie. 8vo. Paris, 1831.
　　　　　　　　　　　　　　　　　　　　　MB 1 Q 41

BLOUET, P. "Max O'Rell." A Frenchman in America
12mo. Bristol (n.d.)　　　　　　　　　　　D 15 Q 17

BLOXAM, Prof. C. L. Chemistry, inorganic, and organic ;
with experiments. 6th ed. 8vo. Lond., 1888. A 5 U 41

BLUE MOUNTAIN GUIDE, The. Season 1892-93. 12mo. Katoomba, 1892. MD 7 T 2
[*See* Boyce, Rev. F. B.]

BLUEBELL. [*See* Browne, Lady Hester G.]

BLUM, R. Japonica. [*See* Arnold, Sir E.]

BLUME, C. L. Flora Javæ necnon Insularum Adjacentium. 3 vols. folio. Bruxelles, 1828. A 37 P 26–28 ‡

BLUNT, Rev. I. J. Sketch of the Reformation in England. 8th ed. 18mo. Lond., 1845. G 8 P 29

BLUNT, Rev. J. J. History of the Christian Church during the First Three Centuries. 8vo. Lond., 1856. G 16 T 23

BLYTH, A. W. Foods, their Composition and Analysis. 3rd ed. 8vo. Lond., 1888. A 21 Q 1

BLYTH, Dr. J. Chemistry. [*See* Liebig, J. von.]

BOARD OF HEALTH, England. [*See* Great Britain—Board of Health.]

BOASE, C. W. Historic Towns: Oxford. 8vo. Lond., 1887. B 22 Q 10

BOCCACCIO, G. The Decameron of, done into English by J. Payne. 3 vols. sm. 4to. Lond., 1886. J 6 Q 41–43

BÖCKH, A. [*See* Pindar.]

BÖCKING, E. [*See* Ulpianus.]

BODDINGTON, H. The Rodney Log. Roy. 8vo. Sydney, 1892. MH 1 T 19

BODMER, G. R. Hydraulic Motors: Turbines and Pressure Engines. 8vo. Lond., 1889. A 22 Q 25

BOECKER, Dr. F. W. Ueber eine Ursache des Branntweingenusses. 8vo. Braunsch., 1845. F 11 R 8

BOEHME, Jacob. Life and Doctrines of; by F. Hartmann. 8vo. Lond., 1891. G 13 S 44

BOEVEY, A. W. Crawley. Cartulary and Historical Notes of the Cistercian Abbey of Flaxley, otherwise called Dene Abbey. 4to. Exeter, 1887. B 4 R 28 †

BOGER, Mrs. E. Myths, Scenes, and Worthies of Somerset. 8vo. Lond., 1887. B 21 S 18

BOGUE, J. W. Country and Suburban Cottages and Villas; how to Plan and how to Build them. 4to. Edinb. 1888. A 36 S 3 ‡

BOHM-BAWERK, Prof. E. V. Capital and Interest: a critical history of economical theory; translated by W. Smart. 8vo. Lond., 1890. F 6 U 33
Positive Theory of Capital; translated by W. Smart. 8vo. Lond., 1891. F 8 Q 17

BOHN, H. G. Guide to the Knowledge of Pottery, Porcelain, and other objects of Vertu. 3rd ed. 8vo. Lond., 1887. A 23 Q 19

BOILEAU–DÉSPREAUX, N. Œuvres de. 2 vols. 18mo. Paris, 1800. J 15 Q 14, 15

D

BOIS, H. P. du. [*See* Du Bois, H. P.]

BOISSIER, G. [Life of] Madame de Sévigné. (Great French Writers.) 8vo. Lond., 1887. C 9 U 19

BOITO, Prof. C. The Basilica of St. Mark in Venice; translated by W. Scott. Imp. 8vo. Venice, 1888. A 36 P 16 ‡

BOLDREWOOD, Rolf. [*See* Browne, T. A.]

BOLINGBROKE, Henry St. John, Viscount. Life of; by A. Hassall. (Statesman Series.) 8vo. Lond., 1889. C 12 R 30

BOLTON, H. C. Counting-out Rhymes of Children, their Antiquity, Origin, and Wide Distribution; a Study in Folk-lore. 4to. Lond., 1888. C 14 P 11

BOLTON, Sarah Knowles. Famous English Statesmen of Queen Victoria's Reign. 12mo. New York (n.d.) C 14 P 11

BOMBAUGH, C. C. Gleanings for the Curious. 8vo. Lond., 1890. J 5 Q 46

BOMPAS, Rt. Rev. W. C. Diocese of Mackenzie River. (Colonial Church Histories.) 12mo. Lond., 1888. D 15 P 3

BONAPARTE, Madame. Life and Letters of; by E. L. Didier. 8vo. Lond., 1879. C 17 Q 15

BONAR, J. [*See* Ricardo, D.]

BONAVIA, Dr. E. The Cultivated Oranges and Lemons, &c., of India and Ceylon. (Text and plates.) 2 vols. 8vo. Lond., 1890. A 18 T 13, 14

BOND, H. S. S. Working Men's and Farmers' Victory over Freetrade. 8vo. Sydney, 1885. MF 1 T 20

BONNEY, F. A. Words of Light: Poems. 8vo. Sydney, 1889. MH 1 Q 41

BONNEY, G. E. Induction Coils: a practical manual for Amateur Coil-makers. 12mo. Lond., 1892. A 21 P 15

BONNEY, Rev. T. G. Abbeys and Churches of England and Wales, Descriptive, Historical, Pictorial. 4to. Lond., 1887. B 9 R 5 †

BONVALOT, G. Through the Heart of Asia, over the Pamir to India. Illustrations by A. Pépin. 2 vols. imp. 8vo. Lond., 1889. D 5 U 18, 19
Across Thibet; being a translation of "De Paris au Tonkin à travers le Tibet inconnu;" trans. by C. B. Pitman. With illustrations and map. 2 vols. roy. 8vo. Lond., 1891. D 16 V 7, 8

BONWICK, J. Early Struggles of the Australian Press. Roy. 8vo. Lond., 1890. M B 2 U 15
French Colonies and their Resources. 8vo. Lond., 1886.* MD 4 T 41
Geography of Australia and New Zealand. 3rd. ed. 12mo. Melb., 1856. MD 1 P 49
Orion and Sirius. 18mo. Lond., 1888. MA 2 P 20
Romance of the Wool Trade. 8vo. Lond., 1887. MF 1 P 46

BOOK-LORE. 6 vols. sm. 4to. Lond., 1884-88. E

BOOK OF CHINESE POETRY ; being the Shih Ching or Classic of Poetry, translated by C. F. R. Allen.   8vo. Lond., 1891.   H 9 S 26

BOOK OF COMMON-PRAYER, THE.   Facsimile of the original manuscript.   Fol.   Lond., 1891.
          G 38 Q 12 ‡
Book of Common-Prayer (Eng. and Irish).   8vo.   Lond. (n.d.)   G 13 R 45

BOOKWORM, THE.   Vols. 1-4.   8vo.   Lond., 1888-91.
          E

BOONE, Professor R. G.   Education in the United States, its History from the earliest settlements.   International Education Series.   12mo.   New York, 1889.
          G 17 P 43

BOOTH, A. J.   Robert Owen, the Founder of Socialism in England.   8vo.   Lond., 1869.   C 16 Q 20

BOOTH, C.   Labour and Life of the People.   Vols. I.-II., and Appendix.   3 vols.   8vo.   Lond., 1889-91.
          F 10 U 9-11

BOOTH, John.   The Battle of Waterloo.   Accounts, British and Foreign.   4th ed.   8vo.   Lond., 1815.
          B 26 V 4

BOOTH, William.   In Darkest England and the Way Out.   8vo.   Lond., 1890.   F 14 S 8

BOOTHBY, J.   Adelaide Almanack, Town and Country Directory and Guide to South Australia.   12mo.   Adelaide, 1864.   ME 4 P

BOPP, F.   Uber die Verwandtschaft der Malayisch-Polynesischen Sprachen mit den Indisch-Europäischen.   Sm. 4to.   Berlin, 1841.   MK 1 U 9

BORDER POST ALMANAC.   [*See* Affleck and Gray.]

BORGEN, Dr. C.   [*See* Neumayer, Dr.]

BORGESIUS, H. G.   Drankbestrijding en Drankwet. 8vo.   Haarlem, 1882.   F 11 S 13
Keinhandel in Sterken Drank.   8vo.   Sneek, 1881.
          F 11 Q 59

BORLAND, Rev. R.   Yarrow : its poets and poetry. 8vo.   Dalbattie, 1890.   H 8 V 40

BORLASE, J. S.   Australian Tales of Peril and Adventure in Town and Bush, told by an Officer of the Victorian Police.   8vo.   Melb. (n.d.)   MJ 2 T 20

BOS, L.   Vetus Testamentum.   [*See* Bibles, &c.—Greek.]

BOSANQUET, B.   Logic ; or, the Morphology of Knowledge.   2 vols.   8vo.   Oxford, 1888.   G 4 R 35, 36

BOSSOLI, C.   War in Italy.   Imp. 8vo.   Lond., 1859.
          B 36 S 16 ‡

BOSWELL, Jas.   An Account of Corsica and Memoirs of Pascal Paoli.   8vo.   Lond., 1769.   D 18 S 9
Life of Johnson ; including Boswell's Journal of a Tour to the Hebrides, and Johnson's Diary of a Journey into North Wales ; edited by G. B. Hill.   6 vols. roy. 8vo. Oxford, 1887.   C 12 U 7-12
Correspondence with Hon. A. Erskine.   [*See* Hill, G. B.]

BOSWELL, R. B.   [*See* Voltaire, F. M. A. de.]

BÖTTCHER, J. H.   Hunskorset, eller Hvad Man bör dömme om Brændevünsdrik.   8vo.   Kjöbenhavn, 1846.
          F 11 Q 25
Über den Branntwein-Genuss.   8vo.   Hannover, 1839.
          F 11 R 9

BOTTONE, S. R.   Electro-Motors, how made and how used.   12mo.   Lond., 1890.   A 21 P 8

BOUCHER, G.   Bibliothèque Universelle des Voyages.   6 vols.   8vo.   Paris, 1808.   K 19 R 11-16

BOUCHOT, H.   The Book, its printers, illustrators, and binders, from Guttenberg to the present time.   Roy. 8vo. Lond., 1890.   A 8 R 40
The Printed Book, its history, illustration, and adornment ; translated by E. C. Bigmore.   8vo.   Lond,, 1887.
          B 35 R 1

BOUDYCK-BASTIAANSE, J. H. de.   Voyages faits dans les Moluques à la Nouvelle-Guinée et à Célèbes. Roy. 8vo.   Paris, 1845.   MD 7 S 35

BOUGAINVILLE, L. A. de, Comte.   Voyage autour du Monde, en 1766-69.   2e ed.   2 vols.   8vo.   Paris, 1772.
          MD 4 S 7, 8

BOUILLET, N.   Atlas Universel d'Histoire et de Geographie.   Roy. 8vo.   Paris, 1865.   B 36 U 2
Dictionnaire Universel d'Histoire et de Geographie.   20 ed.   Roy. 8vo.   Paris, 1867.   K 11 P 21
Dictionnaire Universel des Sciences, des Lettres et des Arts.   8e ed.   Roy. 8vo.   Paris, 1867.   K 16 Q 29
[*See* Seneca, L.A.]

BOULANGER, E. D.   The European March.   Fol. Sydney (n.d.)   MA 11 Q 15†

BOULANGER, Gen. G. E. J. M.   a Biography ; by F. Turner.   8vo.   Lond., 1889.   C 15 U 5

BOULENGER, G. A.   The Fauna of British India, including Ceylon and India.   (Reptilia and Batrachia.)   8vo. Lond., 1890.   A 14 T 47

BOULGER, D. C.   [Life of] Lord William Bentinck (Rulers of India.)   12mo.   Oxford, 1892.   C 17 Q 26

BOURDILLON, F. W.   Aucassin and Nicolette : a Love Story ; edited in Old French, and rendered in Modern English.   12mo.   Lond., 1887.   J 9 P 37

BOURINOT, J. G.   Parliamentary Procedure and Practice, with an Account of Parliamentary Institutions in the Dominion of Canada.   8vo.   Montreal, 1884.   F 4 S 28
Local Government in Canada : an Historical Study.   Roy. 8vo.   Baltimore, 1887.   F 1 V 3
Canadian Studies in Comparative Politics.   Sm. fol.   Montreal, 1890.   F 13 P 12 †
Manual of the Constitutional History of Canada, from the Earliest Period to 1888.   12mo.   Montreal, 1888.
          B 19 Q 1

BOURKE, Capt. J. G.   On the Border with Crook.   Illustrated.   8vo.   Lond., 1892.   D 15 T 10
Scatalogic Rites of all Nations.   8vo.   Washington, 1891.
          A 18 V 24

BOURKE, Maj.-Gen. Sir R., and M'LEAY, A. Correspondence between. 8vo. Sydney, 1837.　MF 3 P 46

BOURKE, Richard Southwell. [*See* Mayo, Earl of.]

BOURNE, H. R. Fox. English Newspapers : Chapters in the History of Journalism. 2 vols. 8vo. Lond., 1887.
B 3 S 25, 26

The Story of our Colonies. 8vo. Lond., 1888.　MD 4 R 30

BOURNE, S. Extended Colonisation, a Necessity to the Mother Country. 8vo. Lond., 1879.　F 12 P 35

BOUSFIELD, C. [*See* Vicl Castel, Count H. de.]

BOUTCHER, W. Treatise on Forest Trees. 4to. Edin., 1775.　A 18 V 23

BOUTMY, E. The English Constitution ; translated by Isabel M. Eaden. 8vo. Lond., 1891.　B 24 Q 4

Studies in Constitutional Law—France—England—United States. 8vo. Lond., 1891.　F 6 P 44

BOUVERIE, E. O. P. Rackets. [*See* Tennis, &c.]

BOWDEN, H. S. [*See* Hettinger, Prof. F.]

BOWEN, Sir C. Virgil in English Verse. [*See* Virgilius Maro. P.]

BOWEN, Sir G. F. Thirty years of Colonial Government. Edited by Stanley Lane-Poole. 2 vols. 8vo. Lond., 1889.　MB 2 R 55, 56

BOWEN, W. [*See* Quin, J.]

BOWER, F. O. Course of Practical Instruction in Botany. 12mo. Lond., 1888.　A 20 P 11

BOWER, F. O., and VINES, S. H. Course of Practical Instruction in Botany. Part 1. Phanerogamæ—Pteridophyta. Part 2. Bryophyta—Thallophyta. 2 vols. 8vo. Lond., 1885-87.　A 4 P 31, 32

BOWES, James L. Japanese Pottery, with Notes, &c. Imp. 8vo. Liverpool, 1890.　A 23 V 1
[*See* Audsley, G. A.]

BOWKER, J. H. [*See* Trimen, R.]

BOWLES, Miss Emily. Madame de Maintenon. 8vo. Lond., 1888.　C 13 R 4

BOWLES, Capt. Thomas Gibson. The Log of the Nereid. 8vo. Lond., 1889.　D 18 T 6

BOWNE, Eliza S. A Girl's Life Eighty Years Ago ; Selections from the Letters of Eliza Southgate Browne ; with an Introduction by C. Cook. Lond., 1888.　C 13 S 2

BOWRON, W. Manufacture of Cheese, Butter and Bacon in New Zealand. 8vo. Wellington, 1883.　MA 1 Q 39

BOWYER, Dr. G. Commentaries on the Constitutional Law of England. 2nd ed. Roy. 8vo. Lond., 1846.
F 14 V 17

BOX, J. B. [*See* Victoria, Supreme Court.]

BOYCE, Rev. F. B. Blue Mountain Guide. 8vo. Sydney, 1887.　MD 3 P 48
Another copy. 8vo. Sydney, 1887.　MD 6 P 44

BOYCE, Rev. William B. The Higher Criticism and the Bible. 8vo. Lond., 1881.　G 19 P 4

Six Lectures on the Higher Criticism upon the Old Testament. Roy. 8vo. Sydney, 1878.　MG 1 T 30

BOYD, Dr. A. C. International Law. [*See* Wheaton, Dr. H.]

BOYD, A. J. Queensland ; an Introductory Essay. 8vo. Lond., 1886.　MD 7 Q 2

BOYD, B. Letter to Sir W. Denison on the expediency of transferring the unemployed Labor of Van Diemen's Land to New South Wales. 8vo. Sydney, 1847.　MF 2 T 4

BOYD, Hannah V. Voice from Australia, or an Inquiry into the probability of New Holland being connected with prophecies relating to New Jerusalem and the Spiritual Temple. 12mo. Sydney, 1851.　MG 2 P 9

BOYD, Mark. Reminiscences of Fifty Years. 8vo. Lond., 1871.　MC 1 S 1

BOYESEN, Prof. H. H. History of Norway from the earliest times to 1885. 8vo. New York, 1890.
B 20 R 15

BOYS, T. S. Picturesque Architecture in Paris, Ghent, Antwerp, and Rouen. Fol. Lond., 1839.　D 41 P 12‡

BRABANT, F. G. Elements of Plane and Solid Mensuration. 12mo. Lond., 1886.　A 25 P 25

BRABAZON, Lord, Earl of Meath. Some National and Board School Reforms. 8vo. Lond., 1887.　G 17 Q 31

BRACE, C. L. The Races of the Old World. 8vo. Lond., 1863.　A 18 Q 31

BRACKEN, T. Paddy Murphy's Annual. 8vo. Dunedin, 1886.　MH 1 S 45

Lays of the Land of the Maori and Moa. 12mo. Lond 1884.　MH 1 R 2

The New Zealand Tourist. 8vo. Dunedin, 1879.
MD 6 P 26

BRACKENBURY, G. The Campaign in the Crimea. [1st and] 2nd Series. 2 vols. Roy. 8vo. Lond., 1855-56.　B 24 V 13, 14

BRACKETT, Anna C. [*See* Rosencranz, Prof. J. K. F.]

BRACTON'S, H. de. Bracton's Note Book : a Collection of Cases decided in the King's Courts during the reign of Henry III ; edited by F. W. Maitland. 3 vols. 8vo Lond., 1887.　F 12 Q 26-28

BRADFORD, Andrew. Biographical Notice of. [*See* Smith, Jos.]

BRADFORD, William. Biographical Notice of. [*See* Smith, Jos.]

BRADLAUGH, C. A Cardinal's Broken Oath : a Letter to His Eminence Henry Edward, Cardinal-Archbishop of Westminster. 12mo. Lond., 1882.　F 7 V 21

A Few Words on the Christian's Creed. 8vo. Lond. (n.d.)　G 2 V 26

A Few Words about the Devil. 12mo. Lond., 1890.
G 2 V 26

BRADLAUGH, C.—*contd.*

A Plea for Atheism. 12mo. Lond., 1883.   G 2 V 26
Capital and Labor. 2nd ed. 12mo. Lond., 1888
                                                 F 5 Q 11
Compulsory Cultivation of Land; what it means, and
why it ought to be enforced. 12mo. Lond., 1887.
                                                 F 5 Q 11
Cromwell and Washington: a Contrast. 12mo. Lond.
1883.   F 7 V 21
Eight Hours' Movement: Verbatim Report of a Debate
between H. M. Hyndman and C. Bradlaugh. 12mo.
Lond., 1890.   F 5 Q 11
Employers' Liability Bill: Letter to T. Burt, M.P. 12mo.
Lond., 1888.   F 5 Q 11
Eternal Torment: a written debate between the Rev. J.
Lightfoot and C. Bradlaugh. 12mo. Lond., 1888.
                                                 G 2 V 27
Five Dead Men whom I knew when Living: Robert
Owen, Joseph Mazzini, Charles Sumner, J. S. Mill, and
Ledru Rollin. 12mo. Lond. (n.d.)   F 7 V 21
Genesis, its Authorship and Authenticity. 3rd ed. 12mo.
Lond., 1882.   G 2 V 25
Has Humanity gained from Unbelief? Two nights' Debate
between the Rev. M. Gibson and C. Bradlaugh. 12mo.
Lond., 1889.   G 2 V 27
Has Man a Soul? 12mo. Lond., 1888.   G 2 V 26
Has, or is, Man a Soul? Verbatim report of a two nights'
public debate between the Rev. W. M. Westerby and C.
Bradlaugh. 12mo. Lond. (n.d.)   G 2 V 27
Heresy, its Utility and Morality. 12mo. Lond., 1882.
                                                 G 2 V 26
Hints to Emigrants to the United States. 12mo. Lond.
(n.d.)   F 7 V 21
How are we to abolish the Lords? 2nd ed. 12mo. Lond.,
1891.   G 7 V 21
Humanity's Gain from Unbelief. 12mo. Lond., 1889.
                                                 G 2 V 26
Impeachment of the House of Brunswick. 9th edition.
12mo. Lond., 1883.   F 7 V 21
Is It Reasonable to Worship God? Verbatim report of
two nights' debate between the Rev. R. A. Armstrong
and C. Bradlaugh. 12mo. Lond., 1887.   G 2 V 27
Is there a God? 12mo. Lond., 1887.   G 2 V 26
John Churchill, Duke of Marlborough; the Mob, the
Scum, and the Dregs. 3rd ed. 12mo. Lond., 1884.
                                                 F 7 V 21
Labour and Law; with a Memoir and two Portraits [of
C. Bradlaugh]. 8vo. Lond., 1891.   F 10 Q 26
Labour's Prayer. 12mo. Lond. (n.d.)   F 5 Q 11
Letter to the Right Hon. Lord Randolph S. Churchill.
12mo. Lond., 1886.   F 7 V 21
May the House of Commons commit Treason? An Appeal
to the People. 12mo. Lond. (n.d.)   F 7 V 21
Mr. Gladstone in Reply to Col. Ingersoll on Christianity.
12mo. Lond., 1886.   G 2 V 26
Mr. Gladstone or Lord Salisbury: which? 12mo. Lond.,
1886.   F 7 V 21
New Life of Abraham. 12mo. Lond., 1895.   G 2 V 26

BRADLAUGH, C.—*contd.*

New Life of David. 12mo. Lond., 1884.   G 2 V 26
New Life of Moses. 12mo. Lond. (n.d.)   G 2 V 26
New Life of Jonah. 12mo. Lond. (n.d.)   G 2 V 26
New Life of Jacob. 12mo. Lond., 1885.   G 2 V 26
Notes on Christian Evidences. 12mo. Lond., 1887.
                                                 G 2 V 26
Parliament and the Poor. 12mo. Lond., 1889. F 5 Q 11
Poverty: its Effects on the Political Condition of the
People. 12mo. Lond., 1890.   F 5 Q 11
Secularism, Unphilosophical, Immoral, and Anti-Social:
Verbatim Report of a three nights' Debate between
the Rev. Dr. McCann and C. Bradlaugh. 12mo. Lond.,
1881.   G 2 V 27
Socialism: its Fallacies and Dangers. 12mo. Lond., 1887.
                                                 F 5 Q 11
Some Objections to Socialism. 12mo. Lond., 1887.
                                                 F 5 Q 11
Speeches. 8vo. Lond., 1890.   F 14 R 16
Supernatural and Rational Morality. 12mo. Lond., 1886.
                                                 G 2 V 26
Taxation; how it originated, how it is spent, and who
bears it. 12mo. Lond., 1887.   F 5 Q 11
The Atonement. 12mo. Lond., 1884.   G 2 V 26
The Autobiography of. 12mo. Lond., 1891. F 7 V 21
The Channel Tunnel: Ought the Democracy to oppose or
support it. 12mo. Lond., 1887.   F 7 V 21
The Civil List and Pensions and Grants to the Royal
Family. 12mo. Lond., 1888.   F 5 Q 11
The Eight Hours' Movement. 12mo. Lond., 1889.
                                                 F 5 Q 11
The Freethinker's Text-book. Part 1. 12mo. Lond.
(n.d.)   G 2 V 28
The Land, the People, and the Coming Struggle. 12mo.
Lond. (n.d.)   F 5 Q 11
The Queen versus C. Bradlaugh and Annie Besant. 12mo.
Lond. (n.d.)   F 9 U 51
The Radical Programme. 2nd. ed. 12mo. Lond., 1889.
                                                 F 5 Q 11
The Real Representation of the People. 2nd ed. 12mo.
Lond. (n.d.)   F 7 V 21
The True Story of my Parliamentary Struggle. 12mo.
Lond., 1882.   F 7 V 21
The Twelve Apostles. 12mo. Lond., 1884.   G 2 V 26
Were Adam and Eve our First Parents? 12mo. Lond.,
1888.   G 2 V 26
What does Christian Theism teach? Verbatim Report of
two nights' Discussion between the Rev. A. J. Harrison
and C. Bradlaugh. 2nd ed. 12mo. Lond., 1884. G 2 V 27
What did Jesus teach? 12mo. Lond., 1890.   G 2 V 26
What Freemasonry is, what it has been, and what it
ought to be. 12mo. Lond., 1885.   F 7 V 21
When were our Gospels written? 12mo. Lond., 1881.
                                                 G 2 V 26
Who was Jesus Christ? 12mo. Lond. (n.d.)   G 2 V 26
Why do men starve? 12mo. Lond., 1882.   F 5 Q 11

BRADLAUGH, C.—*contd.*
Will Socialism benefit the English People? Verbatim report of a debate between H. M. Hyndman and C. Bradlaugh. 12mo. Lond., 1884. F 5 Q 11
Will Socialism benefit the English people? A written debate between E. B. Bax and C. Bradlaugh. 12mo. Lond., 1887. F 5 Q 11

BRADLAUGH, Chas., and BESANT, Annie. Socialism, for and against. 12mo. Lond., 1887. F 5 Q 11

BRADLEY, E. T. Life of the Lady Arabella Stuart. 2 vols. 8vo. Lond., 1889. C 14 Q 17, 18

BRADLEY, H. The Goths, from the Earliest Times to the end of the Gothic Dominion in Spain. 8vo. Lond., 1888. B 7 S 53
[*See* Stratmann, F. H.]

BRADLEY, H. B. Life and Death: a Lecture. 8vo. Sydney, 1879. MA 2 S 8
House Poison: a Lecture. 8vo. Sydney (n.d.) MA 2 S 7
Twelve Lectures on the Subject of Health. 8vo. Sydney, 1881. MA 2 S 9

BRADLEY, J. W. Dictionary of Miniaturists, Illuminators, Calligraphers, and Copyists. 3 vols. 8vo. Lond., 1887-89. C 12 T 17-19
Life and Works of Giorgio Giulio Clovio, Miniaturist. 8vo. Lond., 1891. C 15 T 15

BRADSHAW, Henry. Collected Papers. 8vo. Camb., 1889. J 3 S 24
Memoir of; by G. W. Prothero. 8vo. Lond., 1888. C 15 U 3

BRADSHAW, J. New Zealand of To-day (1884-87). Roy. 8vo. Lond., 1888. M D 4 W 16

BRADSHAW'S ALMANAC. 8vo. Sydney, 1860. MF

BRADSHAW'S [Balmain] ALMANAC for 1880. 8vo. Sydney, 1880. ME 8 P

BRADSHAW'S NEW SOUTH WALES TOURIST'S COMPANION. 12mo. Sydney 1890. ME 3 P

BRADY, W. M. Anglo-Roman Papers. 8vo. Lond., 1890. B 36 T 3

BRAGG, J. Prison Life of a Notorious Character. 8vo. Sydney, 1886. MC 1 P 37

BRAHE, Tycho: a Picture of Scientific Life and Work in the 16th Century; by J. L. E. Dreyer. 8vo. Edinb., 1890. C 12 T 20

BRAHMS, J.: a Biographical Sketch, by Dr. H. Dieters; translated by Rosa Newmarch. 8vo. Lond., 1888. C 12 Q 30

BRAIM, T. H. Eutropii Historiæ Romanæ libri duo, Cornelii Nepotis selectæ vitæ excellentium Imperatorum, et Quædam Fabellæ ex Ovidio. 12mo. Sydneii, 1844. MB 2 P 49

BRAMWELL, Lord. Lord Bramwell as 'Drinker' and 'Thinker'; being a complete logical analysis of his case for drink. 12mo. Lond., 1885. F 11 P 41

BRAND, Rt. Hon. Sir H. B. W. [*See* Blackmore, E. G.]

BRANDES, L. J. Smaa Popularie Arbeider. No. 2. Om Brug og Misbrug at Spirituose Drikke. 12mo. Kjobenhavn, 1877. F 11 P 23

BRANDL, Prof. A. Samuel Taylor Coleridge and the English Romantic School. English edition by Lady Eastlake. 8vo. Lond., 1887. C 13 R 8

BRANNT, W. T. Practical Treatise on Animal and Vegetable Fats and Oils. Roy. 8vo. Philad., 1888. A 21 V 3
Practical Treatise on the Manufacture of Soap and Candles. Roy. 8vo. Philad., 1888. A 11 V 14

BRANTINGHAM, T. de. [*See* Devon, F.]

BRÄNVINSHANDTERINGEN i Sverige, 1531-1835; Historik öfver. 8vo. Stockholm, 1881. F 11 Q 24

BRASSEY, Lady A. The Last Voyage to India and Australia in the "Sunbeam." 8vo. Lond., 1889. MD 4 U 8

BRASSEY, T. A. Naval Annual. 2 vols. 8vo. Portsmouth, 1891-92. E
Sixteen Months' Travel, 1886-87. 8vo. Lond., 1888. MD 7 Q 8

BRASSINGTON, W. S. Historic Bindings in the Bodleian Library, Oxford. 4to. Lond., 1891. A 36 S 2 ‡

BRAUN, A. Neuere Untersuchungen über die Gattcingen Marsilia und Pilularia. 8vo. Berlin, 1870. MA 3 S 5

BRAY, J. S. Illustrations of Ethnology. 8vo. Sydney, 1887. MA 1 R 6

BRAYLEY, E. W. Londiniana; or Reminiscences of the British Metropolis. 4 vols. 12mo. Lond., 1829. B 24 P 5-8
[*See* Parkes, S.]

BRAZIL. Annaes da Bibliotheca Nacional, 1885-86. 4to. Rio de Janeiro, 1890. E

BREES, S. C. Guide and Description of the Panorama of New Zealand; illustrating the Country Habits of the Colonists, &c. 8vo. Lond., 1850. MD 7 S 19
Key to the Colonies; or, Advice to the Million upon Emigration. 18mo. Lond., 1851. MD 1 P 8

BRERETON, A. Sarah Bernhardt: a Biographical and Critical Sketch. Roy.8vo. Sydney, 1891. MC 1 T 9

BRERETON, Dr. J. Le Gay. Poems. 12mo. Lond., 1865. MH 1 Q 43
Goal of Time, a Poem. Melb., 1883. MH 1 Q 42
The Turkish Bath: a Lecture. 8vo. Hobart, 1869. MA 2 S 6
Genesis and the Beatitudes. Roy. 8vo. Lond., 1887. MG 1 T 23
The Travels of Prince Legion, and other Poems. 12mo. Lond., 1857. MH 1 Q 65

BRETON, Lieut. W. H. Excursions in New South Wales, Western Australia, and Van Dieman's Land, 1830-33. 3ed. 8vo. Lond., 1835 MD 3 T 37

BRETSCHNEIDER, E. Mediæval Researches from Eastern Asiatic Sources. 2 vols. 8vo. London, 1888.
　　　　　　　　D 16 T 2, 3

BRETT, H. Brett's Auckland Almanac, Provincial Handbook, &c., for 1878. 8vo. Auckland, 1878.　ME 3 T

Brett's Guide to Fiji : a Handbook for Residents, Tourists, &c. 8vo. Auckland, 1881.　　　　MD 2 S 38

Brett's Handy Guide to 'New Zealand ; edited by E. E. Bilbrough. 8vo. Auckland, 1890.　　MD 3 P 50

BRETT, Rev. W. H. Legends and Myths of the Aboriginal Indians of British Guiana. 8vo. Lond. (n.d.)　H 10 Q 15

"The Apostle of the Indians of Guiana ": a Memoir of the Life and Labours of the Rev. W. H. Brett; by the Rev. F. P. L. Josa. 8vo. Lond., 1887.　　C 3 R 4

BREVIARIUM ROMANUM. 8vo. Antverpiæ, 1685.
　　　　　　　　G 15 Q 24

BREWER, A. Lingua; or The Combat of the Tongue and the Five Senses for Superiority : a Serious Comedy. [*See* British Drama, Ancient.]

The Merry Devil of Edmonton : a Comedy. [*See* British Drama, Ancient.]

BREWER, Dr. E. C. The Historic Note-book. 8vo. Lond., 1891.　　　　　　B 35 Q 1

BREWER, Francis C. The Drama and Music in New South Wales. Roy. 8vo. Sydney, 1892.　MB 1 T 30

BREWSTER, Dr. F. Carroll. Disraeli in Outline. 8vo. Lond., 1890.　　　　　　C 12 T 12

BRIANO, Giorgio. Lettere di Silvio Pellico a. 12mo. Firenze, 1861.　　　　　　C 12 P 6

BRICE, A. Life of; by Dr. T. N. Brushfield. 4to. (n.p.) 1888.　　　　　　C 42 8 14‡

BRICE, S. Law, Practice, and Procedure relating to Patents, Designs, and Trade Marks ; with Rules and Forms, Notes and Comments. 8vo. Lond., 1885.
　　　　　　　　F 9 S 11

BRIDGEMAN, Rev. G. T. O. History of the Church and Manor of Wigan. [*See* Chetham Soc., n.s., 15–18.]

BRIDGER, A. E. The Demon of Dyspepsia; or, Digestion Perfect and Imperfect. 8vo. Lond., 1888.　A 26 Q 1

BRIDGES, Lieut.-Col. E. S. Round the World in Six Months. 8vo. Lond., 1879.　　　D 10 S 1

BRIDGETT, Rev. T. E. Life and Writings of Sir Thomas More. 8vo. Lond., 1891.　　　C 16 Q 16

BRIDGMAN, F. A. Winters in Algeria. Roy. 8vo. Lond., 1890.　　　　　　D 14 V 2

BRIGGS, R. A. Bungalows and Country Residences. 4to. Lond., 1891.　　　　　　A 40 S 5 ‡

BRIGHAM, W. T. Guatemala, the Land of the Quetzal. 8vo. Lond., 1887.　　　　D 3 U 29

BRIGHT, Chas. Are the Statements of Science and Genesis Contradictory ? Public Debate. Mr. C. Bright affirming, Rev. E. C. Spicer denying. 8vo. Melb., 1883.
　　　　　　　　MG 1 R 32

BRIGHT, John. Answer to the Internationa. Memorial on the Transvaal Question. (Folded sheet.) 8vo. Lond., 1881.　　　　　　F 8 S 26

Public Letters of ; edited by H. J. Leech. 8vo. Lond., 1885.　　　　　　C 16 Q 11

BRIGHT, Dr. J. F. History of England, 449–1880. 4 vols. 12mo. Lond., 1887–88.　　B 24 P 1–4

BRIGHTON, Dr. J. G. Admiral of the Fleet Sir Provo W. P. Wallis ; a Memoir. 8vo. Lond., 1892. C 18 S 5

BRIMMER, M., and CHAPMAN, Mrs. J. J. Egypt : three Essays on the History, Religion, and Art of Ancient Egypt. Roy. 8vo. Lond., 1892.　B 21 V 2

BRINDLEY, W., and WEATHERLEY, W. S. Ancient Sepulchral Monuments. 4to. Lond., 1887. B 34 Q 1 ‡

BRINTON, Prof. D. G. The American Race: a Linguistic Classification and Ethnographic Description of the Native Tribes of North and South America. 8vo. New York, 1891.　　　　　　A 18 Q 26

Rig Veda Americanus : Sacred Songs of the Ancient Mexicans with a Gloss in Nahuatl. 8vo. Philad., 1890.
　　　　　　　　G 4 S 40

Ancient Nahuatl Poetry, containing the Nahuatl Text of twenty-seven ancient Mexican Poems ; with Translation, Notes, &c. Roy. 8vo. Philad., 1887.　H 6 S 32

BRITANNIC CONFEDERATION. A Series of Papers. Edited by A. S. White ; with Map. 12mo. Lond., 1892.　　　　　　F 9 U 37

　White, A. S. Introduction by the Editor.
　Colomb, Admir. Sir J. Survey of Existing Conditions.
　Freeman, Prof. E. A. The Physical and Political Basis of National Unity.
　Chisholm, G. G. The Commerce of the British Empire.
　Nicholson, Prof. J. S. Tariffs and International Commerce.
　Hervey, M. H. Alternative Measures.
　Thring, Rt. Hon. Lord. The Consolidation of the British Empire.

BRITISH ALMANAC AND COMPANION. 6 vols. 8vo. Lond., 1887–92.　　　　　E

BRITISH ARCHÆOLOGICAL ASSOCIATION. Journal. Vols. 42–46. 8vo. Lond., 1886–90.　E

BRITISH ASSOCIATION FOR THE ADVANCEMENT OF SCIENCE. Reports of 56th–61st Meetings. 8vo. Lond., 1887–92.　　　　E

Reports 6th and 7th on the Migration of Birds in 1884–85. 2 vols. (in 1). 8vo. Lond., 1885–86.　　E

BRITISH AUSTRALASIAN. 7 vols. fol. Lond., 1886–91.
　　　　　　　　E

BRITISH CHESS ASSOCIATION. [*See* Löwenthal, J.]

BRITISH MUSEUM. Guide to the Gallery of Reptilia in the Department of Zoology. [*See* Günther, A.]

BRITISH DRAMA, ANCIENT. [Ed. by Sir W. Scott.] 3 vols. roy. 8vo. Lond., 1810.　　H 3 T 20–22
　Adventures of Five Hours, The ; A Tragi-Comedy. By Tuke. Vol. 3.
　Albumazar ; 'A Comedy. By Tomkis. Vol. 3.
　Alexander and Campaspe ; A Comedy. y Lyly. Vol. 1.
　All Fools ; A Comedy. By Chapman. Vol. 2.

BRITISH DRAMA, ANCIENT.—*contd.*

Andromana; or, The Merchant's Wife; A Tragedy. By Shirley. Vol. 3.
Antiquary, The ; A Comedy. By Marmion. Vol. 3.
Bird in a Cage, The ; A Comedy. By Shirley. Vol. 1.
City Match, The ; A Comedy. By Mayne. Vol. 2.
City Night Cap, The; A Tragi-Comedy. By Davenport. Vol. 3.
Damon and Pithias ; A Tragedy. By Edwards. Vol. 1.
Dumb Knight, The ; A Historical Comedy. By Markham and Machin. Vol. 2.
Dutchesse of Malfy, The ; A Tragedy. By Webster. Vol. 3.
Eastward Hoe; A Comedy. By Chapman and Marston Jonson. Vol. 2.
Edward II. ; A Tragedy. By Marlow. Vol. 1.
Elvira, or The Worst not always True ; A Comedy. By Digby. Vol. 3.
Ferrex and Porrex ; A Tragedy. By Sackville. Vol. 1.
Four P's, The : A Merry Interlude. By Heywood. Vol. 1.
Foure Prentises of London, with the Conquest of Jerusalem : au Historical Play. By Heywood. Vol. 3.
Gamester, The : A Comedy. By Shirley. Vol. 2.
Gammer Gurton's Needle : A Comedy. By Rt. Rev. John Still, Vol. 1.
George a Greene, the Pinner of Wakefield : A Comedy. By Greene. Vol. 1.
Greene's Tu Quoque ; or, The City Gallant : A Comedy. By Cooke. Vol. 2.
Grim, the Collier of Croydon. A Comedy. By J. T. Vol. 3.
Heir, The ; A Comedy. By May. Vol. 1.
Hog hath lost his Pearl, The : A Comedy. By Tailor. Vol. 3.
Honest Whore, The : A Comedy. By Dekkar. Vol. 1.
Honest Whore, The [Part the second] : A Comedy. By Dekkar. Vol. 1.
Jeronimo [Part the first] : A Tragedy. By Kyd. Vol. 1.
Jew of Malta, The : A Tragedy. By Marlowe. Vol. 1.
Jovial Crew ; or, The Merry Beggars : A Comedy. By Brome. Vol. 3.
Life and Death of Thomas, Lord Cromwell : A Tragedy. Vol. 1.
Lingua ; or, The Combat of the Tongue and the Five Senses for Superiority : A Serious Comedy. By Brewer. Vol. 2.
London Prodigal : A Comedy. Vol. 1.
Mad World, my Masters ; A Comedy. By Middleton. Vol. 2.
Malcontent, The : A Tragi-comic. By Marston. Vol. 2.
Match at Midnight ; A Comedy. By Rowley. Vol. 2.
Mayor of Quinborough, The : A Comedy. By Middleton. Vol. 3.
Merry Devil of Edmonton, The : A Comedy. By Brewer. Vol. 2.
Microcosmus : A Moral Masque. By Nabbes. Vol. 2.
Miseries of Inforced Marriage : A Comedy. By Wilkins. Vol. 2.
Muse's Looking-Glass, The : A Comedy. By Randolph. Vol. 2.
Old Couple, The : A Comedy. By May. Vol. 3.
Ordinary, The : A Comedy. By Cartwright. Vol. 3.
Parson's Wedding, The : A Comedy. By Killegrew. Vol. 3.
Puritan, The ; or, The Widow of Watling-street : A Comedy. By Smith. Vol. 1.
Ram Alley ; or, Merry Tricks : A Comedy. By Barrey. Vol. 2.
Rebellion, The ; A Tragedy. By Rawlins. Vol. 3.
Returne from Pernassus, The : A Comedy. Vol. 1.
Revenger's Tragedy, The : By Tourneur. Vol. 2.
Roaring Girl, The : or, Moll Cut-Purse. A comedy. By Middleton and Dekker. Vol. 2.
Sir John Oldcastle. [Part the first.] A tragedy. Vol. 1.
Spanish Tragedy, The : or, Hieronimo is mad again. A Comedy. By Kyd. Vol. 1.
White Devil, The ; or, Vittoria Corombona. A Tragedy. By Webster. Vol. 3.
Widow, The. A Comedy. By Jonson, Fletcher, and Middleton. Vol. 3.

BRITISH DRAMA, ANCIENT.—*contd.*

Witch, The. A Tragi-Comedy. By Middleton. Vol. 3.
Wits, The. A Comedy. By Davenant. Vol. 1.
Woman Killed with Kindness, A. A Tragedy. By Heywood. Vol. 2.
Yorkshire Tragedy. Vol. 1.

BRITISH DRAMA, MODERN. 5 vols. Roy. 8vo. Lond., 1811.   H 3 T 23-27

Alchemist, The. A Comedy. By Jonson. Vol. 3.
All for Love. A Tragedy. By Dryden. Vol. 1.
Apprentice, The. A Farce. By Murphy. Vol. 5.
Arden of Feversham. A Tragedy. By Lillo. Vol. 2.
Author, The. A Comedy. By Foote. Vol. 5.
Barbarossa. A Tragedy. By Brown. Vol. 2.
Beaux Stratagem, The. A Comedy. By Farquhar. Vol. 4.
Beggar's Opera, The. By Gay. Vol. 5.
Boadicea. A Tragedy. By Glover. Vol. 2.
Bold Stroke for a Wife, A. A Comedy. By Centlivre. Vol. 4.
Bon Ton. A Farce. By Garrick. Vol. 5.
Bondman, The. A Tragedy. By Massinger. Vol. 1.
Bonduca. A Tragedy. By Beaumont and Fletcher. Vol. 1.
Broken Heart, The. A Tragedy. By Ford. Vol. 1.
Brothers, The. A Comedy. By Cumberland. Vol. 4.
Brothers, The. A Tragedy. By Young. Vol. 2.
Busy Body, The. A Comedy. By Centlivre. Vol. 4.
Caractacus. A Tragedy. By Mason. Vol. 2.
Careless Husband, The. A Comedy. By Cibber. Vol. 3.
Cato. A Tragedy. By Addison. Vol. 1.
Chances, The. A Comedy. By Fletcher. Vol. 3.
Cheats of Scapin, The. A Farce. By Otway. Vol. 5.
Citizen, The. A Comedy. By Murphy. Vol. 5.
Clandestine Marriage, The. A Comedy. By Colman and Garrick. Vol. 4.
Cleone. A Tragedy. By Dodsley. Vol. 2.
Commissary, The. A Comedy. By Foote. Vol. 5.
Committee, The. A Comedy. By Howard. Vol. 3.
Comus. A Mask. By Milton. Vol. 2.
Comus. A Mask. Altered from Milton. By Colman. Vol. 5.
Confederacy, The. A Comedy. By Vanburgh. Vol. 3.
Conscious Lovers, The. A Comedy. By Steele. Vol. 4.
Constant Couple, The. A Comedy. By Farquhar. Vol. 4.
Contrivances, The. A Farce. By Carey. Vol. 5.
Countess of Salisbury, The. A Tragedy. By Hartson. Vol. 2.
Country Girl, The. A Comedy. By Wycherly. Vol. 3.
Critic, The. A Farce. By Sheridan. Vol. 5.
Crononhotonthologus. A Tragedy. By Carey. Vol. 5.
Deuce is in Him, The. A Farce. By Colman. Vol. 5.
Devil to Pay, The. A Ballad Farce. By Coffey. Vol. 5.
Devil Upon Two Sticks, The. A Comedy. By Foote. Vol. 5.
Distrest Mother, The. A Tragedy. By Philips. Vol. 1.
Dr. Last in His Chariot. A Comedy. By Bickerstaff and Foote. Vol. 5.
Don Sebastian. A Tragedy. By Dryden. Vol. 1.
Double Dealer, The. A Comedy. By Congreve. Vol. 3.
Douglas. A Tragedy. By Home. Vol. 2.
Drummer, The. A Comedy. By Addison. Vol. 4.
Earl of Essex, The. A Tragedy. By Jones. Vol. 2.
Earl of Warwick, The. A Tragedy. By Franklin. Vol. 2.
Elfrida. A Tragedy. By Mason. Vol. 2.
Englishman in Paris, The. A Comedy. By Foote. Vol. 5.
Englishman Returned from Paris, The. A Comedy. By Foote. Vol. 5.
Every Man in His Humour. A Comedy. By Jonson. Vol. 3.
Fair Apostate, The. A Tragedy. By Macdonald. Vol. 2.
Fair Penitent, The. A Tragedy. By Rowe. Vol. 1.
False One, The. A Tragedy. By Beaumont and Fletcher. Vol. 1.

BRITISH DRAMA, MODERN.—*contd.*

Falstaff's Wedding. A Comedy. By Kenrick. Vol. 4.
Fatal Curiosity. A Tragedy. By Lillo. Vol. 2.
Fatal Dowry, The. A Tragedy. By Massinger and Field. Vol. 1.
Funeral, The. A Comedy. By Steele. Vol. 4.
Gamester, The. A Tragedy. By Moore. Vol. 2.
George Barnwell. A Tragedy. By Lillo. Vol. 2.
Good-natured Man, The. A Comedy. By Goldsmith. Vol. 4.
Grecian Daughter, The. A Tragedy. By Murphy. Vol. 2.
Guardian, The. A Comedy. By Garrick. Vol. 5.
Gustavus Vasa. A Tragedy. By Brooke. Vol. 2.
High Life below Stairs. A Farce. By Garrick. Vol. 5.
Hypocrite, The. A Comedy. By Cibber. Vol. 4.
Inconstant, The. A Comedy. By Farquhar. Vol. 4.
Intriguing Chambermaid, The. A Ballad Farce. By Fielding. Vol. 5.
Irene. A Tragedy. By Johnson. Vol. 2.
Irish Widow, The. A Comedy. By Garrick. Vol. 5.
Isabella. A Tragedy. By Southern. Vol. 1.
Jane Shore. A Tragedy. By Rowe. Vol. 1.
Jealous Wife, The. A Comedy. By Colman. Vol. 4.
King and No King. A Tragedy. By Beaumont and Fletcher. Vol. 1.
King and the Miller of Mansfield, The. A Farce. By Dodsley. Vol. 5.
King Charles I. A Tragedy. By Havard. Vol. 2.
Knights, The. A Comedy. By Foote. Vol. 5.
Lady Jane Gray. A Tragedy. By Rowe. Vol. 1.
Lame Lover, The. A Comedy. By Foote. Vol. 5.
Lethe. A Dramatic Satire. By Garrick. Vol. 5.
Liar, The. A Comedy. By Foote. Vol 5.
Love a-la-Mode. A Farce. By Macklin. Vol. 5.
Love for Love. A Comedy. By Congreve. Vol. 3.
Love in a Village. A Comic Opera. By Bickerstaff. Vol. 5.
Love makes a Man. A Comedy. By Cibber. Vol. 3.
Lying Valet, The. A Comedy. By Garrick. Vol. 5.
Mahomet. A Tragedy By Miller. Vol. 2.
Maid of Bath, The. A Comedy. By Foote. Vol. 5.
Maid of the Mill, The. A Comic Opera. By Bickerstaff. Vol. 5.
Maid of the Oaks, The. A Dramatic Entertainment. By Burgoyne. Vol. 5.
Maid's Tragedy, The. By Beaumont and Fletcher. Vol. 1.
Male Coquette, The. A Farce. By Garrick. Vol. 5.
Mariamne. A Tragedy. By Fenton. Vol. 2.
Matilda. A Tragedy. By Franklin. Vol. 2.
Mayor of Garratt, The. A Comedy. By Foote. Vol. 5.
Midas. An English Burletta. By O'Hara. Vol. 5.
Minor, The. A Comedy. By Foote. Vol. 5.
Miser, The. A Comedy. By Fielding. Vol. 4.
Miss in Her Teens. A Farce. By Garrick. Vol. 5.
Mistake, The. A Comedy. By Vanbrugh. Vol. 3.
Mock Doctor, The. A Ballad-farce. By Fielding. Vol. 5.
Mourning Bride, The. A Tragedy. By Congreve. Vol. 1.
Mysterious Mother, The. A Tragedy. By Walpole. Vol. 2.
Neck or Nothing. A Farce. By Garrick. Vol. 5.
New Way to Pay Old Debts. A Comedy. By Massinger. Vol. 3.
Old Bachelor, The. A Comedy. By Congreve. Vol. 3.
Old Maid, The. A Comedy. By Murphy. Vol. 5.
Orators, The. A Comedy. By Foote. Vol. 5.
Orphan, The. A Tragedy. By Otway. Vol. 1.
Orphan of China, The. A Tragedy. By Murphy. Vol. 2.
Oroonoko. A Tragedy. By Southern. Vol. 1.
Padlock, The. A Comic Opera. By Bickerstaff. Vol. 5.
Patron, The. A Comedy. By Foote. Vol. 5.
Peep Behind the Curtain. A Farce. By Garrick. Vol. 5.

BRITISH DRAMA, MODERN.—*contd.*

Philaster. A Tragedy. By Beaumont and Fletcher. Vol. 1.
Plain Dealer, The. A Comedy. By Wycherly. Vol. 3.
Provoked Husband, The. A Comedy. By Vanbrugh and Cibber. Vol. 3.
Provoked Wife, The. A Comedy. By Vanbrugh. Vol. 3.
Recruiting Officer, The. A Comedy. By Farquhar. Vol. 4.
Rehearsal, The. A Comedy with Key. By Buckingham. Vol. 3.
Revenge, The. A Tragedy. By Young. Vol. 2.
Rival Queens, The. A Tragedy. By Lee. Vol. 1.
Rivals, The. A Comedy. By Sheridan. Vol. 4.
Roman Father, The. A Tragedy. By Whitehead. Vol. 2.
Rosina. A Musical Farce. By Mrs. Brooke. Vol. 5.
Rule a Wife and Have a Wife. A Comedy. By Fletcher. Vol. 3.
She Stoops to Conquer. A Comedy. By Goldsmith. Vol. 4.
She Would and She Would Not. A Comedy. By Cibber. Vol. 3.
Siege of Damascus, The. A Tragedy. By Hughes. Vol. 1.
Sir Harry Wildair. A Comedy. By Farquhar. Vol. 4.
Sir John Cockle at Court. A Farce. By Dodsley. Vol. 5.
Spanish Friar, The. A Comedy. By Dryden. Vol. 3.
Sultan, The. A Farce. By Bickerstaff. Vol. 5.
Suspicious Husband, The. A Comedy. By Hoadly. Vol. 4.
Tamerlane. A Tragedy. By Rowe. Vol. 1.
Tancred and Sigismunda. A Tragedy. By Thomson. Vol. 2.
Taste. A Comedy. By Foote. Vol. 5.
Tender Husband, The. A Comedy. By Steele. Vol. 4.
Theodosius. A Tragedy. By Lee. Vol. 1.
Thierry and Theodoret. A Tragedy. By Beaumont and Fletcher. Vol. 1.
Three Weeks after Marriage, A Comedy. By Murphy. Vol. 5.
Tom Thumb. A Burletta. By Fielding. Vol. 5.
Two Misers, The. A Musical Farce. By O'Hara. Vol. 5.
Two Noble Kinsmen, The. A Tragedy. By Shakespeare and Fletcher. Vol. 1.
Upholsterer, The. A Farce. By Murphy. Vol. 5.
Venice Preserved. A Tragedy. By Otway. Vol. 1.
Volpone. A Comedy. By Jonson. Vol. 3.
Way of the World, The. A Comedy. By Congreve. Vol. 3.
Way to Keep Him, The. A Comedy. By Murphy. Vol. 4.
West Indian, The. A Comedy. By Cumberland. Vol. 4.
Wonder, The : A Women Keeps a Secret. A Comedy. By Centlivre. Vol. 4.
Zara. A Tragedy. By Hill. Vol. 2.
Zenobia. A Tragedy. By Murphy. Vol. 2.

BRITISH MUSEUM. Guide to the Galleries of Mammalia. 2nd edition. 8vo. Lond., 1885.

Guide to the Gallery of Reptilia. 2nd edition. 8vo. Lond., 1886.

Guide to the Collection of Fossil Fishes. 8vo. Lond., 1885.

Guide to the Exhibition Galleries of the Department of Geology and Palæontology. 4th edition. 8vo. Lond., 1886.

Introduction to the Study of Minerals, with a Guide to Mineral Gallery. 8vo. Lond., 1887.

BRITISH QUARTERLY REVIEW. Vol. 165. 8vo. Lond., 1886. E

BRITISH RECORD SOCIETY (*with which is incorporated the Index Society.*) Publications. 8vo. Lond., 1891. E
　Index to the Biographical and Obituary Notices in the Gentleman's Magazine. 1731-80.

BRITTAIN, Rev. A. [*See* Bice, Rev. C.]

BRITTEN, Emma H. On the Road; or the Spiritual Investigator. 12mo. Melb., 1878. MG 2 P 10

Spiritualism: Is it a Savage Superstition? A Lecture. 8vo. Melb., 1878. MG 2 P 27

BRITTON, T. A. Treatise on the Origin, Progress, Prevention, and Cure of Dry Rot in Timber. 8vo. Lond., 1875. A 19 Q 2

BROAD, L. The Law of Innkeepers in New Zealand, and Licensing Committee's Guide. 8vo. Nelson, 1887. MF 2 T 17

BROADBENT, J. The Australian Botanic Guide; being a family hand-book of Botanic Treatment. 8vo. Melb., 1887. MA 3 P 29

BROADFOOT, Major George. Career of, in Afghanistan and the Punjab; by Major W. Broadfoot. 8vo. Lond., 1888. C 13 U 23.

BROADFOOT, Major W. Career of Major George Broadfoot in Afghanistan and the Punjab. 8vo. Lond., 1888. C 13 U 23

BRODRIBB, Rev. W. J. Demosthenes (Ancient Classics for English Readers). 8vo. Edinb., 1880. J 14 P 7 [*See* Church, Rev. A.]

BRODERICK, G. C. Different Principles on which the Chief Systems of Popular Representation have been based in Ancient and Modern Times: a Prize Essay. 8vo. Oxford, 1855. F 9 R 27

Promotion by Merit in relation to Government and Education. 8vo. Lond., 1858. F 9 R 28

BRODY, J. [*See* Epigrammatum Graecorum.]

BROGLIE, A., Duc de. Personal Recollections of the late, 1785-1820; edited by R. L. de Beaufort. 2 vols. 8vo. Lond., 1887. C 12 S 1, 2

Nouveaux Éloges Historiques. [*See* Mignet, F. A. M.] [*See* Talleyrand, Prince de.]

BROKEN HILL PROPRIETARY COMPANY. Reports and Statements of Accounts, 1889-92. 6 vols. 4to. Melb., 1889-92. ME 7 Q

BROMBY, J. E. Sermons on the Earlier Chapters of Genesis. 8vo. Melb., 1880. MG 2 P 12

BROME, R. A Jovial Crew, or the Merry Beggars: a Comedy. [*See* British Drama, Ancient.]

BRONN, Dr. H. G. Die Klassen und Ordnungen des Thier-Reichs. Spongien (Porifera).—Protozoa.—Reptilien.—Vogel. 8 vols. roy. 8vo. Leip., 1880-91. E

BRONSON, Mrs. A. [*See* Lawless, Hon.Emily.]

BRONTE ESTATE, Waverley. Particulars and Description, with Plan of the Property. Imp. 8vo. Sydney, 1882. MD 3 V 29

BROOKE, H. Gustavus Vasa: a Tragedy. [*See* British Drama, Modern.]

BROOKE, Mrs. Rosina: a Musical Farce. [*See* British Drama, Modern.]

BROOKER, A. [*See* Slingo, W.]

BROOKS, E. S. Historic Girls: Stories of Girls who have influenced the History of their Times. 8vo. New York, 1887. C 13 S 3

BROOM, H. A Selection of Legal Maxims. 3rd ed. 8vo. Lond., 1858. F 1 Q 26

BROTHERS, A. Photography: its History, Processes, Apparatus, and Materials. 8vo. Lond., 1892. A 23 T 9

BROTHERS, B. Materialism Vindicated [and on Electricity and Evolution, in MS.] by "Veni." 8vo. Sydney, 1890. MG 1 Q 57

BROUGH, B. H. Treatise on Mine-surveying. 8vo. Lond., 1888. A 25 Q 5

BROUGHAM, Lord. Nouveaux Éloges Historiques. [*See* Mignet, F. A. M.]

BROUGHTON, Mrs. V. D. [*See* Papendiek, Mrs. C. L. H.]

BROUGHTON, Rt. Rev. W. G. Farewell Address on the Eve of his Embarkation for England. "Let Brotherly Love Continue." 8vo. Sydney, 1853. MG 1 Q 61

The Righteousness of Faith: a Sermon. 8vo. Sydney, 1836. MG 2 R 2

BROUGHTON, W. R. Voyage of Discovery to the North Pacific Ocean in the years 1795-98. 4to. Lond., 1804. D 19 V 21

Another copy. 4to. Lond., 1804. MD 4 R 10 †

BROUN, Capt. T. Manual of New Zealand Coleoptera. Parts 1-4. 3 vols. roy. 8vo. Wellington, 1880-86. MA 2 U 26-28

BROWN, Prof. A. C. [*See* Andrews, Prof. T.]

BROWN, C. History of Nottinghamshire. (Popular County Histories.) 8vo. Lond., 1891. B 24 S 24

BROWN, D. Wealth and Wages in New South Wales. 8vo. Sydney, 1891. MF 2 P 62

BROWN, D. K. Almanac and Guide to New South Wales, 1885. 12mo. Sydney, 1885. ME

BROWN, E., and STRAUSS, A. Dictionary of American Politics. 8vo. New York, 1888. F 14 Q 1

BROWN, E. B. [*See* Pennefather, F. W.]

BROWN, G. A. "Bruni." Sheep Breeding in Australia. 8vo. Melb., 1890. MA 1 S 45

BROWN, G. L., and STEWART, C. G. Report of Trials for Murder by Poisoning. 8vo. Lond., 1883. F 9 S 23

BROWN, H. A. A Winter in Albania. 8vo. Lond., 1888. D 19 Q 9

BROWN, H. F. The Venetian Printing Press: an Historical Study. 4to. Lond., 1891. B 30 V 5

Venetian Studies. 8vo. Lond., 1887. B 12 Q 45

BROWN, J. A. Palæolithic Man in North West Middlesex. 8vo. Lond., 1887. A 24 U 2

E

BROWN, J. A. Harvic, and BUCKLEY, T. E. Vertebrate Fauna of Sutherland, Caithness, and West Cromarty. Roy. 8vo. Edinb., 1887. A 14 T 39

BROWN, John. Barbarossa; a tragedy. [*See* British Drama, Modern.]

BROWN, J. & A. The Australian Code, comprising a ready method of transmitting cable messages on business connected with the purchase and consignment of Australian Coals, and the employment and engagement of ships, &c. 8vo. Sydney (n.d.) MF 2 T 20

BROWN, J. C. Management of Crown Forests at the Cape of Good Hope under the Old Regime and the New. 8vo. Edinb., 1887. F 10 P 22

Schools of Forestry in Germany. 8vo. Edinb., 1887. A 1 U 26

BROWN, J. C. Plain and Practical Letters to Working People, concerning Australia, New Zealand, and California. 12mo. Lond., 1889.. MD 1 P 61

BROWN, J. E. Hints for the Collection and Preservation of Herbarium Specimens, Seeds and Samples for the Museum of Economic Forestry. Roy. 8vo. Sydney, 1891. MA 3 R 31

Forest Flora of South Australia. Parts 1–9. Fol. Adelaide, 1892. MA 3 Q 10 ‡

BROWN, J. M. Polo. [*See* Weir, Capt. R.]

BROWN, Prof. J. M. Student Life and the Fallacies which oftenest beset it. 8vo. Christchurch, 1881. MG 2 Q 40

BROWN, Marie A. The Icelandic Discoverers of America. 8vo. Lond., 1887. B 17 Q 3

BROWN, N. E. English Botany. [*See* Sowerby, J.]

BROWN, P. H. Early Travellers in Scotland. 8vo. Edinb., 1891. B 16 R 7

BROWN, R. General Remarks on the Botany of Terra Australis. 4to. Lond., 1814. MA 1 P 23 †

Prodromus Floræ Novæ-Hollandiæ et Insulæ Van Diemen. 4to. Lond., 1810. MA 1 T 53

Supplementum primum Prodomi Floræ Novæ-Hollandiæ. 8vo. Lond., 1830. MA 1 T 54

BROWN, R. Our Earth and its Story : a Popular Treatise on Physical Geography ; edited by R. Brown. Vol. 1. Imp. 8vo. Lond., 1887. A 9 V 27

BROWN, Dr. R. [*See* Pellow, T.]

BROWN, R. H. Vernacular Writings of Geo. Buchanan. [*See* Scottish Text Society.]

BROWN, Capt. T. Illustration of the Recent Conchology of Great Britain and Ireland. 2nd. ed. Fol. Lond. (n.d.) A 42 S 7 ‡

BROWN, W. Science and Practice of Butter Making in Australasia. 8vo. Melb., 1889. MA 1 R 52

BROWN, W. T. Notes of Travel : Extracts from Home Letters Written during a Two Years' Tour Round the World, 1879–81. 8vo. Lond., 1882. MD 2 W 16

BROWNE, A. J. Jukes. The Building of the British Isles : a Study in Geographical Evolution. 12mo. Lond., 1888. A 9 P 53

BROWNE, C. O. Armour and its Attack by Artillery. Roy. 8vo. Woolwich, 1887. A 19 V 3

BROWNE, Major E. C. The Coming of the Great Queen: a Narrative of the Acquisition of Burma. 8vo. Lond., 1888. B 10 U 36

BROWNE, G. L. Nelson : the Public and Private Life of Horatio, Viscount Nelson, as told by himself, his comrades and his friends. 8vo. Lond., 1891. C 15 U 13

Wellington ; or, the Public and Private Life of Arthur, first Duke of Wellington. 8vo. Lond., 1888. C 17 Q 4

BROWNE, Lady Hester G., and MIDDLEMASS, Miss Hume. The Bouquet, culled from Marylebone Gardens, by "Bluebell" and "Mignonette." 5th Collection. 12mo. Lond., 1854. MJ 2 T 53

BROWNE, Hugh J. The Religion of the Future ; or, the Higher Law of Truth and Right. 8vo. Melb., 1883. MG 2 P 39

BROWNE, I. Law and Lawyers in Literature. 8vo. Boston, 1883. J 12 Q 32

BROWNE, Lennox, and BEHNKE, Emil. Voice, Song, and Speech : a practical guide for singers and speakers. 3rd ed. 8vo. Lond., 1884. A 8 Q 39

BROWNE, Phillis. A Year's Cookery, giving Dishes for Breakfast, Luncheon, and Dinner for Every Day in the Year. 8vo. Lond., 1888. A 22 Q 2

BROWNE, T. Hydriotaphia, Urne-Buriall ; or, a Discourse of the Sepulchrall Urnes lately found in Norfolk, together with the Garden of Cyrus. Sm. 4to. Lond., 1658 B 23 T 2

BROWNE, T. A. "Rolf Boldrewood." A Sydney Side Saxon. 8vo. Lond., 1891. MJ 2 T 7

Robbery Under Arms. 8vo. Lond., 1889. MJ 1 U 15

BROWNE, T. F. de C. Mining Leaseholders' Guide. 5th ed. 12mo. Sydney, 1890. MF 2 P 64

BROWNE, T. M. Family Notes collected during many years. Roy. 8vo. Hobart, 1887. MK 1 S 8

BROWNE, Mrs. W. C. The Three Sisters. 18mo. Parramatta, 1892. MG 2 P 46

BROWNE, Mrs. W. D. Fragmenta : a Christmas Anthology ; by "Ecce Homo." 8vo. Sydney, 1881. MJ 1 T 55

BROWNE, W. H. Maryland : the History of a Palatinate. (American Commonwealths.) 4th ed. 12mo. Boston, 1888. B 17 P 11

BROWNING, Elizabeth Barrett. [Life of]; by J. H. Ingram. (Eminent Women Series.) 8vo. Lond., 1888. C 12 Q 27

BROWNING, O. England and Napoleon in 1803 ; being the Despatches of Lord Whitworth and others ; edited by O. Browning. 8vo. Lond., 1887. B 22 U 10

The Flight to Varennes, and other Historical Essays. 8vo. Lond., 1892. B 17 P 27

BROWNING, Robert. Asolando : fancies and facts. 5th ed. 12mo. Lond., 1890. H 10 P 17

Browning Cyclopædia. [*See* Berdoe, E.]

Criticism of Life. [*See* Revell, W. F.]

Four Great Teachers : Ruskin, Carlyle, Emerson, and Browning ; by J. Forster. 8vo. Orpington, 1890. C 12 Q 11

Life and Letters of ; by Mrs. S. Orr. 8vo. Lond., 1891. C 14 R 30

Parleyings with Certain People of Importance in their Day. 12mo. Lond., 1887. H 5 R 41

The Poetical Works of. 16 vols. 12mo. Lond., 1888-89. H 10 P 1-16

1. Pauline.—Sordello.
2. Paracelsus.—Strafford.
3. Pippa Passes.—King Victor and King Charles.—The Return of the Druses.—A Soul's Tragedy.
4. A Blot in the 'Scutcheon.—Colombe's Birthday.—Men and Women.
5. Dramatic Romances.—Christmas Eve and Easter Day.
6. Dramatic Lyrics.—Luria.
7. In a Balcony.—Dramatis Personæ.
8-10. The Ring and the Book.
11. Balaustion's Adventure.—Prince Hohenstiel-Schwangau.—Fifine at the Fair.
12. Red Cotton Night-cap Country.—The Inn Album.
13. Aristophane's Apology.—The Agamemnon of Æschylus.
14. Pacchiarotto, and How he Worked in Distemper ; with other Poems.
15. Dramatic Idyls.—Jocoseria.
16. Ferishtah's Fancies.—Parleyings with Certain People.

Robert Browning, Chief Poet of the Age : an essay ; by W. G. Kingsland. 12mo. Lond., 1887. C 13 P 3

[*See* Corson, H., Fotheringham, J., and Murray, Miss A.]

BROWNING, R. J. The Municipalities Act of 1867 and the Amending Acts ; with Notes of the principal Cases decided thereunder, &c. 8vo. Sydney, 1884. MF 2 T 18

[*See* Watkins, J. L.]

BROWNLEE, W. M. W. G. Grace : a Biography ; with a Treatise on Cricket by W. G. Grace. 8vo. Lond., 1887. C 3 R 2

BRUBERGER, W. J. Quædam de Ebrietate ejusque causis. 8vo. Berolini, 1827. F 11 Q 26

BRUCE, A. Report on Inoculation for Pleuro-Pneumonia in Cattle. Roy. 8vo. Sydney, 1869. MA 1 R 51

BRUCE, A., and LOIR, A. Les Maladies du Bétail en Australie. Roy. 8vo. Sceaux (n.d.) MA 3 R 14

BRUCE, J. R. La Sténographie Phonetique : Pitman's Phonography adapted to French. 12mo. Lond., 1888. K 20 P 18

BRUCK, L. Australasian Medical Directory and Handbook, 1883 and 1892. 2 vols. 8vo. Sydney, 1883-92. ME 3 S

Guide to the Health Resorts in Australia, Tasmania, and New Zealand. 8vo. Sydney, 1888.* MA 2 P 25

The Mineral Springs of Australia. 12mo. Sydney, 1891. MA 2 P 75

BRUDER, C. H. Concordantiæ omnium vocum Novi Testamenti Græci. 4to. Lipsiæ, 1853. K 18 T 25

BRUGMANN, Prof. K. Elements of the Comparative Grammar of the Indo-Germanic Languages. Vols. 1 and 2. 8vo. Lond., 1888-91. K 16 T 16, 17

BRUGSCH, H. History of Egypt under the Pharaohs ; translated from the German by H. D. Seymour. 2 vols. 8vo. Lond., 1879. B 21 T 1, 2

BRÜHL-CRAMER, Dr. C. von. Ueber die Trunksucht und eine rationelle Heilmethode derselben. 12mo. Berlin, 1819. F 11 P 19

BRUMFITT, G., and KIRBY, J. I. England v. Australia at the Wicket : a complete Record of all Cricket Matches played between English and Australian Elevens. 8vo. Ilkley, 1887. MB 1 Q 31

BRUNCK, R. F. P. [*See* Sophocles.]

BRUNETIÈRE, F. L' Évolution des Genres. Tome 1. 12mo. Paris, 1890. B 26 Q 23

BRUNNER, A. [*See* Desty, R.]

BRUNO, Giordano. Sua Vita e sua Dottrina, di D. Berti. 8vo. Torino, 1889. C 12 R 7

The Heroic Enthusiasts (Gli Eroici Furori) : an Ethical Poem. Part 1, translated by L. Williams. 8vo. Lond., 1887. H 8 S 43

Life of ; by I. Frith ; revised by Prof. M. Carriere. 8vo. Lond., 1887. C 13 S 5

BRUNTIE'S DIARY : a Tour round the World ; by "C.E.B." 12mo. Lond., 1889. MD 1 P 50

BRUSHFIELD, T. N. Life and Bibliography of Andrew Brice. 4to. Exeter, 1888. C 42 S 14 ‡

BRYAN, M. Dictionary of Painters and Engravers, biographical and critical ; revised and enlarged by W. Armstrong and R. E. Graves. 2 vols. Imp. 8vo. Lond., 1886-89. K 17 U 19, 20

BRYANT, William Cullen. [Life of.] By J. Bigelow. (American Men of Letters.) 12mo. Boston, 1890. C 12 P 21

BRYCE, Prof. G. Short History of the Canadian People. 8vo. Lond., 1887. B 17 Q 1

BRYCE, Jas. The American Commonwealth. 3 vols. 8vo. Lond., 1888. F 10 R 23-25

Transcaucasia and Ararat. 3rd ed. 8vo. Lond., 1878. D 17 Q 6

BRYDGES, Sir E. [*See* Milton, J.]

BUBB-DODINGTON, George. Lord Melcombe. [*See* Dodington, G. Bubb.]

BUCCANEERS AND MAROONERS OF AMERICA ; edited by H. Pyle. 8vo. Lond., 1891. B 19 S 3

BUCHAN, William P. Ventilation ; with a Supplementary Chapter upon Air Testing. (Weale.) 12mo. Lond., 1891. A 17 R 24

BUCHANAN, D. Donkey Worship *v.* Hero Worship; or Cricket and Boat-Pulling amongst Australians. 8vo. Sydney, 1882. MJ 1 T 31

The Heresy and Sham of all the Leading so-called Christian Sects: a Christmas Chant in Prose. 8vo. Sydney, 1875. MG 1 Q 58

BUCHANAN, George. Vernacular Writings of. [*See* Scottish Text Soc.]

BUCHANAN, J. The Indigenous Grasses of New Zealand. (Colonial Museum of New Zealand.) Imp. 4to. Wellington, 1878-80. MA 1 R 6 ‡

BUCHANAN, Robert. The Coming Terror, and other Essays and Letters. 8vo. Lond., 1891. J 5 Q 47

The Outcast, a rhyme for the time. 8vo. Lond., 1891. H 7 T 33

A Look round Literature. 8vo. Lond., 1887. J 5 P 40

The City of Dream: An Epic Poem. 12mo. Lond., 1888. H 6 Q 38

BUCHANAN, W. Observations on the Book of Revelation. 8vo. Sydney, 1874. MG 1 R 30

BUCHANAN, W. F. Australia to the Rescue: a Hundred Years' Progress in New South Wales. 8vo. Lond., 1890. MD 2 W 15

BUCHHEIM, Prof. C. A. Deutsche Lyrik. 12mo. Lond., 1875. H 6 P 46

BUCK, H. A. Ice-Sailing. [*See* Heathcote, J. M.]

BUCK, Dr. J. D. A Study of Man and the Way to Health. 8vo. Cincinnati, 1889. A 26 T 10

BUCKINGHAM, George Villiers, Duke of. Impeachment of. [*See* Camden Soc.]

The Rehearsal; a Comedy. [*See* British Drama, Modern.]

BUCKINGHAM, J. S. National Evils and Practical Remedies. 8vo. Lond., 1849. F 11 R 6

BUCKINGHAM, L. A. The Bible in the Middle Ages. 8vo. Lond., 1853. G 13 R 39

BUCKLAND, Rev. W. Geology and Mineralogy considered with reference to Natural Theology. 2 vols. 8vo. Lond., 1838. A 24 T 11, 12

BUCKLE, J. G. Theatre Construction and Maintenance. Roy. 8vo. Lond., 1888. A 19 V 2

BUCKLER, W. Larvæ of British Butterflies. [*See* Ray Soc.]

BUCKLEY, T. E. [*See* Brown, J. A. Harvie.]

BUCKLEY, W. Savage Life in Australia: the story of Wm. Buckley, the Runaway Convict. Illustrated. Roy. 8vo. Melb., 1889. MC 1 T 8

BUCKNALL, H. L. A Search for Fortune: the Autobiography of a Younger Son. 8vo. Lond., 1878. MC 1 T 10

BUCKNILL, Dr. J. C. Habitual Drunkenness and Insane Drunkards. 12mo. Lond., 1878 F 11 P 40

BUDDHA, Life of. [*See* Müller, F. Max, Sacred Books, 19].]

BUDGE, E. A. W. History of Alexander the Great. [*See* Alexander.]

BÜHLER, G. [*See* Burgess, J., and Müller, F. Max, Sacred Books, 1, 14, 25.]

BUILDER, The. Vols. 51-62. Fol. Lond., 1887-92. E

BUILDING AND ENGINEERING JOURNAL OF AUSTRALIA AND NEW ZEALAND. 2 vols. Fol. Sydney, 1889-90. ME

BUILDING CONSTRUCTION, Notes on. Parts 1-4. 4 vols. roy. 8vo. Lond., 1875-91. A 3 P 29-32

BUILDING NEWS. Vols. 50-62. Fol. Lond., 1886-92. E

BULKELEY, J., and CUMMINS, J. Voyage to the South Seas in the years 1740-41. 8vo. Lond., 1743. MD 1 R 28

Sequel to the above. [*See* Campbell, A.]

BULL, F. W. Sketch of the History of the Town of Kettering. 8vo. Kettering, 1891. B 21 V 18

BULL, Dr. H. G. Notes on the Birds of Herefordshire, contributed by Members of the Woolhope Club; collected and arranged by H. G. Bull. 8vo. Lond., 1888. A 14 T 36

BULLEN, A. H. Poems, chiefly lyrical, from romances and prose-tracts of the Elizabethan Age. 8vo. Lond., 1890. H 8 Q 16

England's Helicon: a Collection of Lyrical and Pastoral Poems, published in 1600; edited by A. H. Bullen. 8vo. Lond., 1887. H 8 8 40

More Lyrics from the Song-books of the Elizabethan Age; edited by A. H. Bullen. 8vo. Lond., 1888. H 8 S 41

Speculum Amantis: Love-Poems from rare Song-books and Miscellanies of the 17th Century; edited by A. H. Bullen. 8vo. Lond., 1889. H 8 S 39

Lyrics from the Dramatists of the Elizabethan Age. 8vo. Lond., 1889. H 8 Q 17

Musa Proterva: Love-Poems of the Restoration. 8vo. Lond., 1889. H 8 Q 18

[*See* Campion, Dr. T.; Davenport, R.; Nabbes, T.; and Poole, G.]

BULLER, Sir W. L. Classified List of Mr. S. W. Silver's Collection of New Zealand Birds. 8vo. Lond., 1888. MA 2 U 49

History of the Birds of New Zealand. 2 vols. 4to. Lond., 1888. MA 3 P 12, 13 †

BULLETIN, The. 25 vols. fol. Sydney, 1880-92. ME

BULLETIN MONUMENTAL. Tomes 1-56, et Tables. 8vo. Paris, 1834-90. E

BULLETINS OF THE CAMPAIGN, 1797. 18mo. Lond., 1797. B 19 P 2

BULLI COAL MINING COMPANY. Deed of Settlement. Roy. 8vo. Sydney, 1865. MF 3 T 2

BULU, J. Autobiography of a Native Minister in the South Seas; translated by "A Missionary." 12mo. Lond., 1887.   MC 1 P 64

BULWER, Sir E. L. [*See* Lytton, Lord.]

BUNCE, D. Language of the Aborigines of Victoria and other Australian Districts. 12mo. Melb., 1856.
                                                         MK 1 P 48

BUNDEY, W. H. Reminiscences of Twenty-five Years Yachting in Australia. 8vo. Adelaide, 1888.
                                                         MA 2 V 44

BUNNY, H. J. Spiritual Philosophy comprising Wise Words and Practical Teachings. 12mo. Melb., 1881.
                                                         MG 2 P 11

BUNYAN (John). Te Tere no te Tuitarere mei Teianei no ki te ao a Muri Atu; e Mea Akakitein Mai Mei te Mea. [Pilgrim's Progress in Rarotongan.] 12mo. Rarotonga, 1846.   MG 2 P 47

BUNYARD, George. Fruit-growing for Profit (up to date): a practical treatise on all the most profitable fruits. 3rd ed. 8vo. Maidstone, 1890.   A 18 T 12

BUONAROTTI, M. A. Life of, with Translations of his Poems and Letters; by J. S. Harford. 2 vols. 8vo. Lond., 1858.   C 14 V 9, 10

BURD, L. A. [*See* Machiavelli, N.]

BURDETT, H. C. Cottage Hospitals: their Progress, Management, and Work. 2nd ed. 8vo. Lond., 1880.
                                                         A 13 P 48

Prince, Princess, and People: an Account of the Social Progress and Development of our own Times, as illustrated by the public life and work of their Royal Highnesses, the Prince and Princess of Wales, 1863–89. 8vo. Lond., 1889.   C 12 S 6

BURDETT-COUTTS, W. The Brookfield Stud of Old English Breeds of Horses. 4to. Lond., 1891. A 32 U 21

BURDON-SANDERSON, J. [*See* Sanderson, J. Burdon.]

BURGE, C. O. Graphic Analysis applied to Structures under Anistathmic Stresses, as illustrated by the Trusses of the Hawkesbury Bridge, New South Wales. 8vo. Sydney, 1888.   MA 1 Q 6

BURGE, W. Commentaries on Colonial and Foreign Laws generally, and in their conflict with each other, and with the Law of England. 4 vols. roy. 8vo. Lond., 1838.   F 12 R 20–23

BÜRGER, G. A. Gedichte. 18mo. Leip. (n.d.)
                                                         H 6 P 49

BURGES, W. Architectural Designs of. Details of Stonework; edited by R. P. Pullan. Sm. fol. Lond., 1887.   A 7 Q 19 †

BURGESS, E. English and American Yachts. Illustrated; with a Treatise on Yachts and Yachting. Ob. fol. Lond., 1888.   A 1 R 31 †

BURGESS Rev. H. T., and MILNE, Rev. J. Frazer. Prize Essays on Agnosticism, from a moral and spiritual point of view; by "Veritas Vincit" and "Beta." 8vo. Sydney, 1888.   MG 1 R 37

BURGESS, J. Archæological Survey of Southern India. The Buddhist Stupas of Amaravati and Jaggayyapeta, in the Krishna District, Madras Presidency, surveyed in 1882; with Translations of the Asoka Inscriptions at Jaugada and Dhauli, by J. Bühler. Imp. 4to. Lond., 1887.   B 11 Q 2 †

BURGESS, Rev. Richard. The National Education Question practically considered. 8vo. Lond., 1842.
                                                         G 15 R 27

Letter to the Rev. Dr. W. F. Hook, on his proposed plan for the Education of the People. 8vo. Lond., 1846.
                                                         G 15 R 27

BURGH, N. P. Pocket-Book on Compound Engines. 2nd ed. Ob. 32mo. Lond., 1887.   A 22 P 25

BURGON, Very Rev. J. W. Dean of Chichester. A Biography, with extracts from his letters and journals; by the Rev. E. M. Goulburn, Dean of Norwich. 2 vols. 8vo. Lond., 1892.   C 14 R 28, 29

Lives of Twelve Good Men. 1, M. J. Routh; 2, H. J. Rose; 3, C. Marriott; 4, E. Hawkins; 5, S. Wilberforce; 6, R. C. Cotton; 7, R. Gresswell; 8, H. O. Cox; 9, H. L. Mansel; 10, W. Jacobson; 11, C. P. Eden; 12, C. L. Higgins. 2 vols. 8vo. Lond., 1888.
                                                      C 13 R 10, 11

Another Copy. New edition. 8vo. Lond., 1891.
                                                         C 18 T 6

BURGOYNE, J. The Maid of the Oaks: a Dramatic Entertainment. [*See* British Drama, Modern.]

BURILL, Dr. P. De l'Ivrognerie et des Moyens de la Combattre. 8vo. Paris, 1872.   F 11 S 12

BURKE, Sir J. B. Genealogical and Heraldic Dictionary of the Peerage and Baronetage, 1888–92. 5 vols. roy. 8vo. Lond., 1888–92.   E

Genealogical and Heraldic History of the Colonial Gentry. Vol. 1. Imp. 8vo. Lond., 1891.   MK 1 U 26

BURKE, H. F. [*See* Howard, J. J.]

BURKE, J. and Sir J. B. Heraldic Illustrations, with Explanatory Pedigrees. 3 vols. roy. 8vo. Lond., 1844–46.
                                                      K 10 T 21–23

BURKE, O. J. South Isles of Aran (County Galway). 8vo. Lond., 1887.   D 18 Q 4

BURKE, R. O'H., and WILLS, W. J. The Burke and Wills Exploring Expedition: an account of the crossing the Continent of Australia from Cooper's Creek to Carpentaria, with Biographical Sketches. 8vo. Melb., 1861.   MD 3 T 24

Copy of all Despatches from Sir Henry Barkly and other Colonial Governors on the Subject of the Australian Exploring Expedition. Fol. Lond., 1862. MF 11 Q 23 †

BURKE, U. R. Sancho Panza's Proverbs. [*See* Cervantes Saavedra, M. de.]

BURKITT, Rev. W. Expository Notes on the New Testament. 7th ed. Fol. Lond., 1719.   G 39 S 12 ‡

BURN, D. Plays, and Fugitive Pieces in Verse. 2 vols. (in 1). roy. 8vo. Hobart, 1842.   MH 1 S 52

BURN, Rev. R.   Roman Literature in relation to Roman
Art.   8vo.   Lond., 1888.   A 23 S 3

BURNE, Maj.-Gen. Sir O. T.   Clyde and Strathnairn
(Rulers of India.)   8vo.   Oxford, 1891.   C 17 Q 7

BURNETT, G.   [*See* Scotland.]

BURNEY, Fanny, and her Friends; select passages from
her Diary and other Writings; edited by L. B. Seeley.
2nd ed.   8vo.   Lond., 1890.   C 12 R 14

BURNHAM, S. M.   Precious Stones in Nature, Art, and
Literature.   Roy. 8vo.   Boston, 1886.   A 10 Q 25

BURNIE, R. W.   [*See* Thomas, S. G.]

BURNLEY, J.   The Romance of Life Preservation.   8vo.
Lond., 1888.   A 29 P 1
History of Wool and Wool-combing.   8vo.   Lond., 1889.
                                          A 11 S 26

BURNOUF, E.   The Science of Religions; translated by
Julie Liebe.   8vo.   Lond., 1888.   G 6 P 36

BURNS, Rev. D.   Drink, Drunkenness, and the Drink
Traffic.   12mo.   Leeds (n.d.)   F 11 P 14
Vital Statistics of Total Abstinence.   12mo. Lond. (n.d.)
                                          F 11 P 64
Statistics of the Liquor Traffic.   8vo.   Lond., 1872.
                                          F 11 R 3
Liquor Traffic and Legislative Action.   8vo.   (n.p.n.d.)
                                          F 11 R 37
Christendom and the Drink Curse.   8vo.   Lond., 1875.
                                          F 11 S 11
[*See* Caine, W. S.]

BURNS, J. F.   Financial Statement of the Hon. J. F.
Burns, Colonial Treasurer of New South Wales, made
31st October, 1888.   8vo.   Sydney, 1888.   MF 1 Q 27

BURNS, R : Concordance of [*See* Reid, J. B.]
Poetical Works.   3 vols.   12mo.   Lond., 1839.
                                        H 10 P 20–22
Burnsiana :   a Collection of Literary Odds and Ends;
by J. D. Ross.   Vol. 1.   sm. 4to.   Paisley, 1892.
                                          J 6 U 29

BURNS, PHILP & CO.   Queensland Hand-book of
Information ; issued by Burns, Philp & Co.   8vo.   Sydney, 1884.   MD 5 V 34

BURROWS, Prof. M.   Cinque Ports (Historic Towns.)
8vo.   Lond., 1888.   B 22 Q 27

BURROWS, Rev. R.   Extracts from a Diary during
Heke's War in the North.   8vo.   Auckland, 1886.
                                          MB 2 Q 21

BURT, F.   Letter to (on the Employers' Liability Bill.)
[*See* Bradlaugh, C.]

BURTON, J. H.   Emigrant's Manual :   Australia, New
Zealand, America, and South Africa.   8vo.   Edinb.,
1851.   MD 2 Q 33

BURTON, Sir Richard F. :   his Early, Private, and Public
Life ; with an Account of his Travels and Explorations,
by F. Hitchman.   2 vols.   8vo.   Lond., 1887.   C 13 U 24, 25

BURTON, Robert.   The Anatomy of Melancholy.   New
edition.   8vo.   Lond., 1849.   G 12 Q 34

BURTON, W. W.   Insolvent Law of New South Wales,
with Practical Directions and Forms.   8vo.   Sydney,
1842.   MF 2 T 21
Observations on the Constitution of the Government of
New South Wales.   8vo.   Lond., 1840.   MF 1 T 19

BURY, J. B.   History of the Later Roman Empire,
395–800.   2 vols. 8vo.   Lond., 1889.   B 30 U 13, 14

BURY, Rt. Rev. R. de.   The Philobiblon of Richard de
Bury, Bishop of Durham, Treasurer and Chancellor of
Edward III. ;   edited and translated by E. C. Thomas,
8vo.   Lond., 1888.   J 9 S 1

BURY, Viscount, and HILLIER, G. L.   Cycling.   8vo.
Lond., 1887.   A 17 U 37

BUSBY, J.   Manual of Directions for planting and cul-
tivating Vineyards, and for making Wine in New South
Wales.   12mo.   Sydney, 1830.   MA 1 P 16

BUSH, G. G.   Harvard, the first American University.
12mo.   Lond., 1886.   B 17 P 1

BUSTEED, H. E.   Echoes from Old Calcutta ; being
chiefly Reminiscences of the Days of Warren Hastings,
Francis, and Impey.   2nd ed.   8vo.   Calcutta, 1888.
                                          B 29 R 1

BUTCHER, Dr. S. H.   Some Aspects of the Greek Genius.
8vo.   Lond., 1891.   J 11 W 32

BUTLER, A. J.   Court Life in Egypt.   8vo.   Lond.,
1867.   D 14 R 3
Hell of Dante.   [*See* Dante Alighieri.]
[*See* Marbot, Baron de.]

BUTLER, Annie R.   Glimpses of Maoriland.   8vo.
Lond., 1886.   MD 4 S 45

BUTLER, George.   Codex Virgilianus.   [*See* Virgilius
Maro, P.]

BUTLER, J.   Works of.   2 vols. 8vo.   Oxford, 1849–50.
                                          G 4 U 44, 45
    1. Analogy of Religion.
    2. Sermons.

BUTLER, Robert.   Trial of, for the Dunedin Tragedy.
8vo.   Christchurch, 1880.   MF 2 T 45

BUTLER, Samuel.   Emigrants' Handbook of Facts concerning Canada, New Zealand, Australia, &c.   12mo.
Glasgow, 1843.   MD 1 P 59
Erewhon ;   or, over the Range.   5th ed.   8vo.   Lond.,
1873.   MJ 2 T 21

BUTLER, Col. Sir W. F.   Campaign of the Cataracts : the
Great Nile Expedition of 1884-85.   8vo.   Lond., 1887.
                                          D 14 U 19
Charles George Gordon.   (English Men of Action.)   8vo.
Lond., 1889.   C 12 Q 34
Sir Charles Napier.   (English Men of Action.)   8vo.
Lond., 1890.   C 12 Q 35

BUTT, W.   [*See* Ford, H.]

BUTTERWORTH, G. Deerhurst, a Parish of the Vale of Gloucester. 8vo. Tewkesbury, 1887. B 22 Q 2

BUTTMANN, Dr. P. Greek Grammar. 3rd ed. 8vo. Lond., 1848. K 12 V 20

Novum Testamentum Græce. [*See* Bibles.]

BUXTON, S. Finance and Politics: an Historical Study, 1783-1885. 2 vols. 8vo. Lond., 1888. F 7 Q 24, 25

Mr. Gladstone's Irish Bills : what they are and the Arguments for them. 8vo. Lond., 1886. F 5 U 36

BUXTORF, J. Epitome Grammaticæ Hebrææ ; emendata. J. Leusden. ed. 5a. 12mo. Lugd. Bat.,1761. K 16 P 23

BUZACOTT, Rev. A. Mission Life in the Islands of the Pacific. 8vo. Lond., 1866. MD 4 Q 24

BYNG, George. [*See* Torrington, Viscount.]

BYRNE, J. Origin of the Greek, Latin, and Gothic Roots. 8vo. Lond., 1888. K 12 U 4

BYRNE, J. C. Twelve Years' Wanderings in the British Colonies, 1835-47. 2 vols. 8vo. Lond., 1848. MD 2 V 37, 38

BYRNE, Mrs. W. P. De Omnibus Rebus : an Old Man's Discursive Ramblings on the Road of Every-day Life. 8vo. Lond., 1888. J 7 S 28

Gossip of the Century. 2 vols. roy. 8vo. Lond., 1892. C 17 S 4, 5

BYRON, J. [*See* Thistlewood, A.]

BYRON, Commodore J. Journal of a Voyage Round the World in His Majesty's ship "The Dolphin ;" by "A Midshipman on board the said ship." 12mo. Lond. (n.d.) MD 1 P 60

BYRON, George Gordon, Lord. The Beauties of Byron, consisting of Selections from the popular works of ; by A. Howard. 18mo. Lond., 1835. H 6 P 53

C

C., A. S. [*See* Lace-making.]

C., H. J. [*See* Lines written on first seeing the Comet.]

C., M. [*See* Explorers, The.]

C. et A. [*See* Sempill, F.]

CABALLERO, Fernan. [*See* Arrom, C. B. de F.]

CABRY. [*See* Dean, W. B.]

CADDY, Mrs. F. Through the Fields with Linnæus : a Chapter in Swedish History. 2 vols. 8vo. Lond., 1887. C 12 Q 14, 15

CÆSAR, C. J. Commentaries of Cæsar, by A. Trollope. (Ancient Classics for English Readers.) 12mo. Edinb., 1887. J 14 P 4

Cæsar : a Sketch ; by J. A. Froude. 8vo. Lond., 1879. C 15 U 7

Cæsar de Bello Gallico. Book I. Edited by A. H. Davis. 12mo. Melb., 1875. MB 2 P 45

CÆSAR, C. J., and HIRTIUS, A. Quæ exstant omnia' Sm. 4to. Cantab., 1727. B 30 R 1

CAGLIOSTRO, Comte De. [*See* Macmahon, P.]

CAINE, R. H. Love Songs of the English Poets, 1500-1800. 12mo. Lond., 1892. H 3 P 45

CAINE, Thomas Henry Hall. The Little Manx Nation. 8vo. Lond., 1891. B 23 R 2

CAINE, W. S. Picturesque India. Roy. 8vo. Lond., 1890. D 16 V 1

CAINE, W S., HOYLE, W., and BURNS, Rev. D. Local Option. 2nd ed. 12mo. Lond., 1885. F 11 P 45

CAIRD, J. Spinoza. 12mo. Edinb., 1888. G 8 P 25

CAITHNESS, Marie, Countess of. The Mystery of the Ages, contained in the Secret Doctrine of all Religions. 8vo. Lond., 1887. G 6 P 35

CALCUTTA INTERNATIONAL EXHIBITION, 1883-84. Official Report. 2 vols. roy. 8vo. Calcutta, 1885. K 8 R 7, 8

CALDECOTT, A. English Colonization and Empire. 12mo. Lond., 1891. B 23 Q 5

CALDECOTT, R. Complete Collection of his Contributions to the *Graphic* ; with a Preface by A. Locker. Imp. 4to. Lond., 1888. J 29 Q 8 ‡

CALDER, E. H. S. [*See* Meyer, Dr. H.]

CALDER, J. F. Oyster Culture ; a Compilation of Facts. 8vo. Hobart, 1868. MA 3 Q 27

CALDERON DE LA BARCA, Don P. Select Plays ; edited by N. Maccoll. 8vo. Lond., 1888. H 9 Q 3

El Principe Constante.—La Vida e Sueno.—El Alcalde de Zalamea.—El Escondido y la Tapada.

CALDWELL, W. H. Embryology of Monotremata and Marsupialia. Part I. 4to. Lond., 1887. A 39 P 23‡

CALENDAR OF PATENT ROLL, James I. Fol. Dublin (n.d.) B 44 P 9‡

CALENDAR OF THE PATENT AND CLOSE ROLLS OF CHANCERY IN IRELAND, in the reign of Charles I.; by J. Morrin. Roy. 8vo. Dublin, 1863. B 11 R 3

CALENDAR OF STATE PAPERS, Domestic Series of the Reign of Charles I, 1641-43 ; edited by W. D. Hamilton. Imp., 8vo. Lond., 1887. B 24 V 8

CALIFORNIA ACADEMY OF SCIENCES. Proceedings. 2nd Series, Vol. 2. 8vo. San Franc., 1890. E

CALLAGHAN, T. Acts and Ordinances of New South Wales. 2 vols., roy. 8vo. Sydney, 1844. MF 2 S 45, 46

Supplement to [the above.] Roy. 8vo. Sydney, 1846-52. MF 2 S 47

CALLEN, D. Rosalind Schottische. Fol. Sydney (n.d.) MA 11 Q 15 †

CALLIMACHUS. Quae Supersunt ; edidit C. J. Blomfield. 8vo. Lond., 1815. H 6 T 30

CALVERT, J. [Life of] or, from Dark to Dawn in Fiji, by R. Vernon. 8vo. Lond., 1890. M C 1 Q 41

CALVERT, Mrs. J. S., Miss Atkinson. Cowanda, the Veteran's Grant ; an Australian Story. 12mo. Sydney, 1859* MJ 1 R 4

CAMBELL, Z. Mrs. Button's Boarders : their adventures : a Sydney Romance, by "Aroz." 12mo. Sydney, 1890. MJ 2 T 6

CAMBRIAN ARCHÆOLOGICAL ASSOCIATION. Archæologia Cambrensis : a Record of the Antiquities of Wales and its Marches, and Journal of the Cambrian Archæological Association. 5th Series. Vols. 3–8. 8vo. Lond., 1886-91. E

CAMBRIDGE, Rev. O. P. Araneidea : Scientific Results of the Second Yarkand Mission, based upon the Notes of F. Stoliczka. Imp. 4to. Calcutta, 1885. A 22 P 17 ‡

CAMBRIDGE PRIZE POEMS. Complete Collection of the English Poems, which have obtained the Chancellor's Gold Medal in the University of Cambridge. 8vo. Camb., 1859. H 7 Q 43

CAMBRIDGE UNIVERSITY CALENDAR. 6 vols. 12mo. Camb., 1887-92. E

CAMDEN SOCIETY. Publications of. 11 vols. 8vo. Lond., 1887-92.

Custumals of Battle Abbey, 1283-1312.
Visitations of the Diocese of Norwich, 1492-1532.
Dr. R. Pococke's Travels.
Impeachment of the Duke of Buckingham, 1626.
Memoirs Relating to the Lord Torrington.
Essex Papers, 1672-79.
Visitations of Southwell Minster.
The Clarke Papers. Vol. 1.
Correspondence of Sir E. Nicholas. Vol. 2.
Accounts of the Obedientiars of Abingdon Abbey.

CAMERON, Alex. Australia Felix ; or, Sir Valiant Love ; a Drama. 8vo. Sydney, 1892. MH 1 S 56

CAMERON J. Soaps and Candles ; edited by J. Cameron. (Churchill's Technological Handbooks.) 8vo. Lond., 1888. A 25 Q 2

CAMERON, Lieut.-Gen. J. Facsimiles of Anglo-Saxon Manuscripts ; translations by M. B. Sanders. 3 vols. fol. Southampton, 1878-84. B 8 Q 6-8

CAMERON, Miss. Soups and Stews, and Choice Ragouts. 12mo. Lond., 1890. A 22 Q 6

CAMERON, Rev. J. Adelaide de la Thoreza : a Chequered Career. 12mo. Sydney, 1878. MC 1 P 62

CAMERON, P. British Phytophagous Hymenoptera. [*See* Ray Society.]

CAMERON, Commander V. L. [*See* Choyce, J.]

CAMM, A. B. Liberal Religion in the Higher Current Literature ; Lectures. 8vo. Sydney, 1883. MG 1 S 47

CAMP. W. American Football. 12mo. New York, 1891. C 29 P 43

CAMPANELLA, T. Œuvres Choisies. 8vo. Paris, 1844. J 1 W 49

CAMPBELL, A. The Sequel to Bulkeley and Cummins' Voyage to the South Seas. 8vo. Lond., 1747. MD 1 R 28

CAMPBELL, A. Letter to the Queensland Sheep Investment Company in reply to certain statements made by Mr. W. C. Wentworth. 8vo. Sydney, 1866. MF 1 T 25

CAMPBELL, A. J. Notes on Western Australian Oölogy with Descriptions of New Eggs. 8vo. Melb., 1890. MA 3 S 9

CAMPBELL, C. Marriage with Deceased Wife's Sister, 8vo. Sydney. 1873. MF 1 T 26

CAMPBELL, Sir Colin. [*See* Clyde, Lord.]

CAMPBELL, D. Lexicon of Freemasonry. [*See* Mackey, A. G.]

CAMPBELL, Rev. G. Christianity and Civilization : an address. 8vo. Sydney, 1884. MG 1 R 33

CAMPBELL, Sir G. The British Empire. 8vo. Lond., 1887, F 5 T 35

CAMPBELL, George Douglas, Duke of Argyll. [*See* Argyll, Duke of.]

CAMPBELL, G. O. Australian Sheep Husbandry. [*See* Armstrong, A. S.]

CAMPBELL, H. The Causation of Disease : an exposition of the ultimate factors which induce it. 8vo. Lond., 1889. A 26 S 3

CAMPBELL, J. Norfolk Island and its Inhabitants. 8vo. Sydney, 1879. MD 1 W 45

Physical and Political Geography of Australia, Tasmania, and New Zealand. 12mo. Sydney, 1876. MD 1 P 63

The Amateur Photographer's Primer. 12mo. Sydney, 1884. MA 2 P 70

CAMPBELL, Rev. John. The Martyr of Erromanga ; or the Philosophy of Missions ; Illustrated from the Labours, Death, and Character of the Late Rev. John Williams. 8vo. Lond., 1842. MG 1 R 64

CAMPBELL, Dr. John. Thirty Years' Experience of a Medical Officer in the English Convict Service. 12mo. Lond., 1884. F 5 S 46

CAMPBELL, Prof. J. The Hittites : their Inscriptions, and their History. 2 vols. 8vo. Lond., 1891. B 36 T 4, 5

CAMPBELL, J. F. Popular Tales of the West Highlands orally collected, with translation. 2 vols. 8vo. Paisley, 1890. J 5 P 5, 6

CAMPBELL, J. G. The Fians ; or, Stories, Poems, and Traditions of Fionn and his Warrior Band. (Waifs and Strays of Celtic Tradition, 4.) 8vo. Lond., 1891. B 32 T 14

CAMPBELL, Rev. Lewis. The Theætetus of Plato. [*See* Plato.]

[*See* Æschylus.]

CAMPBELL, Rev. T. R. C. Some of the Evidences of Christianity : a Lecture. 8vo. Sydney, 1878.
MG 1 S 48

CAMPBELL, W. [See Gipps, F. B.]

CAMPBELL, W. D. An Account of the Surveys of Australasia. Roy. 8vo. Sydney, 1887. MB 2 U 16

CAMPBELL, W. S. Extracts from Reports on certain Agricultural Districts of New South Wales. Roy. 8vo. Sydney, 1888. MA 1 Q 44

CAMPBELL-JOHNSTON, A. R. [See Johnston, A. R. Campbell-.]

CAMPBELLTOWN BOTANICAL COLLECTING SOCIETY. Third Annual Report. 8vo. Sydney, 1881.
ME 6 Q

CAMPEAU, F. R. E. [See Canada.]

CAMPION, Dr. T. The Works of. Edited by A. H. Bullen. 8vo. Lond., 1889. H 10 R 3

CAN, C. N. S. W. [See Great Statesman, A.]

CANADA. Act respecting the Sale of Intoxicating Liquors. 8vo. Halifax, 1886. F 11 S 14

Liquor License Act (Ontario), and Amending Acts of 1877, 1878, 1881, 1883, and 1884. 2 vols. 8vo. Toronto, 1884. F 11 S 15, 16

Canadian Archives, Report on. 8vo. Ottawa, 1889. E

Geological and Natural History Survey : Contributions to Canadian Palæontology ; by J. F. Whiteaves. 4 vols. Roy. 8vo. Montreal, 1889-91. E

Geological and Natural History Survey : Annual Reports, 1885-90. Roy. 8vo. Montreal, 1886-91. E

Illustrated Guide to the Senate and House of Commons of Canada ; by F. R. E. Campeau. 8vo. Ottawa, 1885.
C 17 Q 23

Acts of Parliament, 1877-78. Vol. 1. 8vo. Ottawa, 1878. F 11 T 1

Statistical Abstract and Record. 8vo. Ottawa, 1877.
E

Temperance Act of 1878, and amendments. (The Scott Act.) 8vo. Toronto, 1884. F 11 R 11

CANADIAN PATENT OFFICE RECORD, 1882-89. 8 vols. imp. 8vo. Ottawa, 1882-89. E

CANAL DE SUEZ. Le Bulletin décadaire. 4to. Paris, 1890-91. E

CANAWAY, A. P. The Crown Lands Acts now in force in New South Wales. Roy. 8vo. Sydney, 1891.
MF 3 R 45

CANDISH, E. Whispering Voices. 8vo. Sydney, 1888.
MH 1 Q 44

CANDISH, S. Candish's Defence ; a Review of Colonial Criticism, and Essay on Love. 4to. Sydney, 1887.
MH 1 T 4

Love : a Poetical Essay. 4to. Sydney, 1887.
MH 1 T 3

CANDISH, Thomas. Journalen van drie Voyagien te Weten. 1. Van Mr. Thomas Candish met drie schepen door de Magallaen straet rondom de Warelt, inden Jare 1586-88. 2. Vande Heer Francoys Drueck en de Heer Jan Haukeins, Ridderin, naer West Indien gepretendeert Panama, 1593 ; noch een Beschryvinge vande Zee vaert der geheeler Werelt. Nassauche Vloot, 3. Oste Beschryvinge vande Voyagie om den gantschen Aert-kloot door de Straet Lemaire onder 't beleydt vandem Admirel Jaques l'Heremite in de Jaren 1623-26. Sm. 4to. Amstelrodam, 1643. MD 1 R 41

CANDLER, C. The Prevention of Consumption ; a Mode of Prevention founded on a New Theory of the Nature of the Tubercle Bacillus. Roy. 8vo. Lond., 1887.
A 12 U 35

Another copy. Roy. 8vo. Lond., 1887. MA 2 S 29

CANDOLLE, A. and C. de. Monographiæ Phanerogamarum. Vols. 1-7. Roy. 8vo. Parisiis, 1878-91.
A 32 T 16-22

1. Smilaceæ, Restiaceæ, Meliaceæ, cum Tabulis IX.
2. Araceæ.
3. Philydraceæ, Alismaceæ, Butomaceæ, Juncaginceæ, Commelinaceæ, Cucurbitaceæ, cum Tabulis VIII.
4. Burseraceæ et Anacardiaceæ, Pontederiaceæ.
5. Cyrtandreæ, Ampellideæ.
6. Andropogoneæ.
7. Melastomaceæ.

CANDOLLE, A. P. de. Organographie Végétale. 2 vols. 8vo. Paris, 1827. A 20 R 1, 2

CANDY-MAKER, THE : a practical guide to the Manufacture of the various kinds of plain and fancy Candy. 12mo. New York (n.d.). A 22 Q 8

CANNING, G. Life of ; by F. H. Hill (Eng. Worthies). 12mo. Lond., 1887. C 12 P 27

Some Official Correspondence of : edited by E. J. Stapleton. 2 vols. 8vo. Lond., 1887. C 12 S 22, 23

CANNING, George, Earl. [Life of] ; by Sir H. S. Cunningham (Rulers of India). 12mo. Oxford, 1891.
C 16 P 24

CANNING, Stratford. [See Stratford de Redcliffe, Viscount.]

CANTERBURY, NEW ZEALAND. Map of the Province of, showing Freehold Selections and Pasturage Runs. 8vo. Lond., 1856. MD 7 R 16.

CANTERBURY ASSOCIATION, New Zealand. Copy of correspondence between the Colonial Office and the Canterbury Association since the date of the charter of Incorporation of that body. Fol. Lond., 1853.
MF 11 Q 34 †

CANTERBURY COLLEGE. Calendars 1888 and 1892. 8vo. Christchurch, 1888-92. ME 5 S

CANTERBURY PAPERS, New Zealand. Nos. 1-12. 8vo. Lond., 1850-52. MD 7 Q 59

CANTONI, G. Il Vino. 8vo. Milano, 1882. A 1 U 19

CAPITAL AND LABOUR, Affiliation of, by "Australis Ignotus." 8vo. Sydney, 1890. MF 1 T 38

CAPPER, J. Australia ; as a field for Capital, Skill, and Labour. 12mo. Lond. (n.d.) MD 1 P 62

F

CAPPI, Prof. G. [*See* Giusti, G.]

CAPRICORNUS. [*See* Ranken G.]

CAQUETS DE L'ACCOUCHÉE. Les recueil général; suivi de l'Anti-Caquet, des Essais de Mathurine et de la sentence par corps (Collection Jannet-Picard). 18mo. Paris. (n.d.).   J 15 Q 21

CAREY, H. Crononhotonthologos; a Tragedy. [*See* British Drama, Modern, 5.]

The Contrivances: a Farce. [*See* British Drama, Modern, 5.]

CAREY, J. The Kings of the Reefs: a Poem. Imp. 8vo. Melb., 1891.   MH 1 T 18

CARGILL, J. Information for the guidance of intending Emigrants: Otago, New Zealand. 8vo. Edinb., 1840.   MD 1 W 46

CARGIL, Mrs. M. Memoirs of, by Rev. D. Cargill. 2nd ed. 12mo. Lond., 1855.   MC 1 P 61

CARLES, W. R. Life in Corea. 8vo. Lond., 1888.   D 16 U 7

CARLETON, W. Farm Festivals. 12mo. Lond., 1888.   H 5 Q 26

Farm Legends. 3rd edition. 12mo. Lond, 1888.   H 5 Q 27

CARLISLE. Municipal Records of. [*See* Ferguson, R. S., and Nanson, W.]

CARLSEN, W. War as it is. 12mo. Lond., 1892.   J 11 W 20

CARLYLE, Mrs. Jane Welsh. Early Letters of, and some of Thomas Carlyle; edited by D. G. Ritchie. 8vo. Lond., 1889.   C 15 U 1

Life of; by Mrs. A. Ireland. 8vo. Lond., 1891.   C 13 R 3

CARLYLE, T. [Life of]; by J. Nicol. (Eng. Men of Letters.) 12mo. Lond., 1892.   C 1 U 41

History of Friedrick II. of Prussia, called Frederick the Great. 10 vols. 12mo. Lond., 1872-73.   B 25 Q 3-12

Carlyle, as seen in his Works: his Characteristics as a Writer and a Man; by J. Kerr. 8vo, Lond., 1887.   C 12 Q 10

Correspondence between Goethe and Carlyle; edited by C. E. Norton. 8vo. Lond., 1887.   C 12 Q 9

Four Great Teachers: Ruskin, Carlyle, Emerson and Browning; by J. Forster. 8vo. Orpington, 1890.   C 12 Q 11

Inaugural Address at Edinburgh, 1866. 12mo. Edinb., 1866.   G 18 P 32

Lectures on the History of Literature; edited by Prof. Greene. 8vo. Lond., 1892.   B 17 P 19

Letters of, 1826-36; edited by C. E. Norton. 8vo. Lond., 1888.   C 12 Q 7, 8

Reminiscences; edited by C. E. Norton. 2 vols. 8vo. Lond., 1887.   C 16 Q 1, 2

CARLYLE, T.—*contd.*

Shooting Niagara, and after ? 12mo. Lond., 1867.   J 1 W 43

Rescued Essays; edited by P. Newberry. 12mo. Lond., 1892.   J 11 W 8

Last Words of. 8vo. Lond., 1892.   J 11 W 25

[*See* Carlyle, Mrs. Jane W.]

[*See* Robertson, J.]

CARMEN, SYLVA. [*See* Elizabeth of Roumania, Queen.]

CARMICHAEL, C. H. E. English Constitutional History. [*See* Langmead, T. P. T.]

CARNAC, Col. E. S. Rivett-. The Presidential Armies of India. 8vo. Lond., 1890.   B 29 T 2

CARNARVON, Earl of. [*See* Chesterfield, Earl of.]

CARNELLEY, Prof. T. Physico-chemical Constants: Melting and Boiling Point Tables. Vol. 2. Roy. 4to. Lond., 1887.   A 2 Q 14 †

CARO, E. M. [Life of] "George Sand" [Madame Dudevant]; translated by G. Mason. (Great French Writers.) 8vo. Lond., 1888.   C 7 P 41

CARPENTER, Dr. A. Alcoholic Drinks: as Diet, as Medicines, and as Poisons. 12mo. Croydon, 1878.   A 26 P 3

Alcoholic Drinks not Necessaries of Life. 12mo. Lond. (n.d.)   F 11 P 60

CARPENTER, J. E. Memoir of W. B. Carpenter. [*See* Carpenter, Dr. W. B.]

CARPENTER, Mary. Juvenile Delinquents: their Condition and Treatment. 8vo. Lond., 1853.   F 6 T 31

Our Convicts. 2 vols. 8vo. Lond., 1864.   MF 3 R 10, 11

Reformatory Schools for the Children of the Perishing and Dangerous Classes, and Juvenile Offenders. 8vo. Lond., 1851.   F 6 T 32

CARPENTER, Dr. W. B. The Microscope and its Revelations. 12mo. Lond., 1856.   A 29 P 19

Another copy. 7th ed.; revised by W. H. Dallinger. 8vo. Lond., 1891.   A 30 T 5

Moderate Use of Intoxicating Drinks physiologically considered. 12mo. (n.p.n.d.)   F 11 P 12

Use and Abuse of Alcoholic Liquors in Health and Disease 2nd ed. 12mo. Lond., 1851.   F 11 P 24

Physiology of Temperance and Total Abstinence. 8vo. Lond., 1853.   F 11 Q 2

Nature and Man: Essays, scientific and philosophical; with an introductory Memoir, by J. E. Carpenter. 8vo. Lond., 1888.   A 29 S 1

Principles of Comparative Physiology. 4th ed. 8vo. Lond., 1854.   A 27 T 35

Principles of Human Physiology. 5th ed. 8vo. Lond., 1855.   A 26 U 18

Vegetable Physiology and Systematic Physiology. 12mo. Lond., 1865.   A 20 P 12

CARR, Rev. A. The Church and the Roman Empire. 12mo. Lond., 1887.   G 19 P 13

CARR, L. Missouri: a Bone of Contention. 12mo. Boston, 1888. B 17 P 4

CARRON, W. Narrative of an Expedition undertaken under the direction of the late Mr. E. B. Kennedy, for the Exploration of the Country lying between Rocking-ham Bay and Cape York; to which are added the Statements of the Aboriginal Native Jacky Jacky, Dr. A. Vallack, Captain Dobson, and Captain Simpson. 8vo. Sydney, 1849. MD 7 S 3

CARSON, H. L. The Supreme Court of the United States; its History. 4to. Philad., 1891. F 42 S 15 ‡

CARSTAIRS, R. British Work in India. 8vo. Edinb., 1891. F 6 R 43

CARTER, H. J. Mathematical Papers set in the Sydney University Junior Public Examination for 1883-87, with Complete Solutions, &c. 8vo. Sydney, 1888. MA 2 Q 49

Mathematical Papers set in the Sydney University Junior Public Examinations, 1884-91; with Complete Solutions, &c. 8vo. Sydney, 1892. MA 3 S 10

CARTER, Rev. J. [*See* Betts, Rev. C. M.]

CARTER, J., & Co. Carter's Tested Seeds for the Vegetable and Flower Garden. 4to. Lond., 1888. A 18 V 1

CARTERET, John, Lord. A Political Biography, 1690-1763; by A. Ballantyne. 8vo. Lond., 1887. C 13 U 3

CARTWRIGHT, W. The Ordinary: a Comedy. [*See* British Drama, Ancient.]

CARVALHO, Prof. F. R. P. de. Diccionario Grammatical, destinado a auxiliar aos estudantes nos exercicios de analyse etymologica e logica da Lingua Portugueza. 8vo. Rio de Janeiro, 1886. K 11 T 47

CARY, Henry. Collection of Statutes affecting New South Wales, containing all the Statutes of Practical Utility, to the Present time. 2 vols. sm. fol. Sydney, 1861. MF 12 Q 3, 4 †

[*See* New South Wales Statutes.]

CASATI, Capt. G. Ten Years in Equatoria and the Return with Emin Pasha; translated by Hon. Mrs. J. R. Clay and Mr. J. W. S. Landor. 2 vols. 8vo. Lond., 1891. D 14 U 10, 11

[*See* Jephson, A. J. Mounteney-.]

CASAUBON, I. [Life of] 1559-1614; by Mark Pattison. 2nd ed. 8vo. Oxford, 1892. C 18 Q 8

[*See* Suetonius Tranquillus, C.]

CASE, Robert. [*See* Bland, Dr. W.]

CASEY, Prof. J. Treatise on Plane Trigonometry. 8vo. Dublin, 1888. A 25 Q 27

CASEY, J. J., and DUFFY, F. G. Casey's Justice's Manual, with the Justices Statutes and Notes thereon. 2nd ed. 8vo. Melb., 1879. MF 3 T 12

CASH, Martin. Adventures of Martin Cash, in company with Kavanagh and Jones in the year 1843. 8vo. Hobart 1870. MC 1 Q 22

CASH, Martin—*contd.*
Martin Cash, the Bushranger of Van Diemen's Land in 1843: a Personal Narrative of His Exploits, &c. 8vo. Hobart (n.d.) MC 1 Q 53

CASS, Lewis. [Life of]; by Prof. A. C. McLaughlin. (American Statesmen.) 12mo. Boston, 1891. C 13 Q 8

CASSELL AND CO. Cassell's complete Book of Sports and Pastimes. 8vo. Lond., (n.d.) A 29 T 13

Cassell's Picturesque Australasia; edited by E. E. Morris. 4 vols. imp. 8vo. Lond., 1887-89.* M D 6 U 6-9

Cassell's Natural History. [*See* Duncan, P.M.]

CASSELLA, P. and O. Abbicci dell' Agricoltore. 8vo. Napoli, 1884. A 1 U 18

CASTEL, H. de Viel, Comte. [*See* Viel Castel, H. de, Comte.]

CASTLE, F. A. [*See* Wood, Dr. G. B.]

CASTLES, W. [*See* Agriculture, Dept. of, Queensland.]

CASTILLO, E. D. del. Remarques sur la Flore de la Polynésie et sur ses Rapports avec celle des Terres Voisines. 4to. Paris, 1890. M A 8 Q 21†

CASWALL, A. Hints from the Journal of an Australian Squatter. 8vo. Lond., 1843. M D 5 Q 29

CATANÆUS, J. M. [*See* Plinius Caecilius Secundus, C.]

CATES, F. "Gags": a Miscellany in prose and verse; forming the first issue of the Australian Dramatic and Musical Journal for 1889. 12mo. Melb., 1889. M J 2 T 22

CATES, W. L. R. Dictionary of General Biography. 4th ed. Roy. 8vo. Lond., 1885. C 13 V 2

CATHERINE OF ARAGON. Divorce of. [*See* Froude, J. A.]

CATHOLIC ALMANAC, The. 12mo. Sydney, 1854. M E 4 R

CATON, Marcus Porcius. [*See* Agronomes Latins, Les.]

CATULLUS, C. V., TIBULLUS, A., et PROPERTIUS, S. A. Opera. 18mo. Lond., 1816. H 11 P 5

Catullus, Tibullus, et Propertius; ex recensione J. G. Graevii, cum notis. Traj. ad Rhen., 1680. H 10 Q 21

Catullus, Tibullus, and Propertius; by Rev. J. Davies. (Ancient Classics for English Readers.) 12mo. Edinb., 1880. J 14 P 5

CAUDERLIER, E. Les Boissons Alcooliques et leurs effets sociaux en Belgique. 8vo. Bruxelles, 1883. F 11 S 17

Les Boissons Alcooliques en Belgique, et leur action sur l'appauvrissement du pays. 2ᵉ éd. 8vo. Bruxelles, 1884. F 11 S 18

CAUSES CÉLÈBRES, Recueil des. Rédigé par M. Méjan. 26 vols. 8vo. 2ᵉ éd. Paris, 1808-17. F 2 U 1 -26

CAUTLEY, Sir P. T. Report on the Ganges Canal Works; from their commencement until the opening of the Canal in 1854. 3 vols. roy. 8vo. and 4to. Lond., 1860. A 22 S 30, 31, and 5 P 14 †

Plans [to the above.] El. fol. Lond., 1860. A 23 P 19 ‡

CAVENDISH, Thomas. Life and Voyages of. [*See* Drake, Sir F.*]

CAXTON, Wm. Encydos. [*See* Early Eng. Text Soc.] Blanchardyn and Eglantine. [*See* Early Eng. Text Soc.]

CAYLUS, Martha Marguerite de Villette de Mursay, Marquise de. Souvenirs. 12mo. Paris (n.d.) C 19 P 7

CAZOTTE, J. Le Diable Amoureux. [*See* Contes Fantastiques.]

CEADDA or CHAD, Saint. Codex S. Ceaddae Latinus, in Ecclesia Cathedrali Lichfieldiensi Servatus. Prolegomena conscripsit F. H. A. Scrivener. 4to. Cantab., 1887. G 37 P 9 ‡

CECIL, C. Free Trade in Every Age; a Historical, Philosophical, and Statistical Review of the Subject. 12mo. Sydney, 1867. MF 2 P 65

CECIL, E. Notes of my Journey round the World. 8vo. Lond., 1889. D 10 S 25

CECIL, Sir Robert. The Secret Correspondence of Sir Robert Cecil with James VI., King of Scotland. 12mo. Edinb., 1766. C 2 P 4

CELLARIUS. Dr. Die künstliche Weinfabrication der neuern Zeit vom ärztlichen Standpunkt. 8vo. Maing, 1855. F 11 Q 60

CELLINI, B. The Life of; translated by J. A. Symonds. 2 vols. 8vo. Lond., 1888. C 12 U 13, 14

CELSUS, Aulus Cornelius. De medicina libri octo; ad fidem optimorum librorum denuo recensuit C. Daremberg. 12mo. Lipsiae, 1859. A 26 P 6

CENTLIVRE, Mrs. Susannah. A Bold Stroke for a Wife: a Comedy. [*See* British Drama, Modern.]

The Busy Body: a Comedy. [*See* British Drama, Modern.]

The Wonder; a Woman keeps a Secret: a Comedy. [*See* British Drama, Modern.]

CENTRAL BROKEN HILL SILVER-MINING COMPANY, LIMITED. Reports and Statement of Accounts for half year ending June 30th, 1890. 4to. Sydney, 1890. ME 7 Q

CENTURY DICTIONARY, The: an encyclopedic lexicon of the English language, prepared under the superintendence of Prof. W. D. Whitney. 6 vols. sm. fol. New York, 1889-91. K 18 U 1-6

CERILLO, E., and COTTRAY, C. G. Dipinti Murali di Pompei. Fol. Napoli (n.d.). A 8 R 4 ‡

CERVANTES SAAVEDRA, M. de. The Ingenious Gentleman Don Quixote of De La Mancha; done into English by H. E. Watts. 5 vols. sm. 4to. Lond., 1888. J 3 V 1-5

Sancho Panza's Proverbs; translated by U. R. Burke. 12mo. Lond., 1892. J 11 W 4

CHAD, St. [*See* Ceadda, St.]

CHADS, Mrs. E. A. Tracked by Bushrangers, and other Stories. 8vo. Melb., 1891. M J 2 T 5

CHADWICK, E. The Health of Nations: a Review of the Works of E. Chadwick; with a Biographical Dissertation by B. W. Richardson. 2 vols. 8vo. Lond., 1887. F 7 Q 26, 27

Supplementary Report on the Practice of Interment in Towns. 8vo. Lond., 1843. A 26 T 12

CHADWICK, Dr. J. Essay on the Use of Alcoholic Liquors in Health and Disease. 12mo. Lond., 1849. F 11 P 46

CHAFFERS, W. Marks and Monograms on European and Oriental Pottery and Porcelain. Roy. 4to. Lond., 1886. A 11 V 17

CHAFFEY BROS. Australian Irrigation Colonies. [*See* Vincent, J. E. M.]

CHAILLEY-BERT, Joseph. [*See* Cobden Club.]

CHALMERS, A. Life of Shakespeare. [*See* Shakespeare, W.]

CHALMERS, G. Opinions of Eminent Lawyers on Points of English Jurisprudence, chiefly concerning the Colonies, Fisheries, and Commerce of Great Britain. Roy. 8vo. Lond., 1858. F 14 V 18

Caledonia; or, a Historical and Topographical Account of North Britain. New edition. 6 vols. 4to. Paisley, 1887-90. B 31 V 12-17

CHALMERS' FREE CHURCH, HOBART TOWN, Trust Deed of. 8vo. Hobart, 1858. MF 1 T 66

CHALMERS, J. James Chalmers, Missionary and Explorer of Rarotonga and New Guinea; by W. Robson. 12mo. Lond., 1887. MC 1 P 45

Pioneering in New Guinea. 8vo. Lond., 1887. MD 6 T 4

CHALMERS, Rev. T. Power, Wisdom, and Goodness of God, as Manifested in the Adaptation of External Nature to the Moral and Intellectual Constitution of Man. 8vo. Lond., 1838. G 16 S 44

CHALMERS, Rev. William. [*See* Church History.]

CHAMBERLAIN, Prof. H. B. Handbook for Travellers in Japan. [*See* Murray, J.]

Simplified Grammar of the Japanese Language (modern written style). 8vo. Lond., 1886. K 20 Q 19

CHAMBERLAIN, D. H. Administration in South Carolina. [*See* Allen, W.]

CHAMBERLAIN, Rt. Hon. J. Home Rule and the Irish Question: Speeches delivered between 1881 and 1887. 8vo. Lond., 1887. F 5 T 36

CHAMBERS, C. H. [*See* Mennell, P.]

CHAMBERS, G. F. Handbook of Descriptive and Practical Astronomy. 4th ed. 3 vols. 8vo. Oxford, 1889-90.
A 19 T 21-23

CHAMBERS, R. Index to Heirs-at-Law, Next-of-kin, &c. ; by F. Preston. 4th ed. 8vo. Lond., 1887. K 10 S 32

Supplement to fourth edition of "Chambers's Index to Next-of-Kin"; by S. H. Preston. 8vo. Lond., 1888.
K 10 S 33

CHAMBERS, Sir W. The Decorative Part of Civil Architecture; with Illustrations, Notes, and an Examination of Grecian Architecture; by J. Gwilt. 4to. Lond., 1862. A 36 P 25‡

CHAMBERS, W. and R. Chambers's Encyclopædia, a Dictionary of Useful Knowledge. New edition. Vols. 1-9. 9 vols. imp. 8vo. Lond., 1888-92. K 4 T 1-9

English Dictionary, Pronouncing, Explanatory, and Etymological ; edited by J. Donald. Roy. 8vo. Lond., 1887.
K 16 Q 1

Political Economy. 12mo. Edinb., 1852. F 14 Q 8

Chamber's Historical and Miscellaneous Questions. 8vo. Lond., 1886. K 11 V 50

CHAMBERS'S JOURNAL. 6 vols. 8vo. Lond., 1886-91. E

CHAMISSO, L. C. A. de. Merveilleuse Histoire de P. Schlémihl. [*See* Contes Fantastiques].

CHANDLER, A. T. Songs of the Sunland. 12mo. Adelaide, 1889. MH 1 Q 64

CHANNING, W. E. Memoir of. 3 vols. 8vo. Lond., 1848. C 13 S 16-18

Works of. 5 vols. 8vo. Glasgow, 1840. J 10 Q 37-41

CHANNING, W. H. Memoir of ; by O. B. Frothingham. 8vo. Lond., 1887. C 13 R 13

CHANTER, Gratiana. Wanderings in North Devon. [*See* Chanter, Rev. J. M.]

CHANTER, Rev. J. M. Wanderings in North Devon ; edited by Gratiana Chanter. 8vo. Ilfracombe, 1887.
D 19 Q 8

CHAPMAN, Mrs. E. F. Sketches of some Distinguished Indian Women. 12mo. Lond., 1891. C 16 P 8

CHAPMAN, G. All Fools : a comedy. [*See* British Drama, Ancient.]

CHAPMAN, G., JONSON, B., AND MARSTON J. Eastward Hoe : a comedy. [*See* British Drama, Ancient.]

CHAPMAN, G. T. New Zealand Almanac for the Year 1861. 8vo. Auckland, 1861. ME 8 P

The Natural Wonders of New Zealand. 8vo. Auckland, 1881. MD 4 P 19

New Zealand Almanac and Directory for 1867. 8vo. Auckland, 1867. ME 4 S

CHAPMAN, H. S. New Zealand Portfolio, No. 2 ; on the advantages which would accrue from the establishment of a Loan Company for New Zealand. 8vo. Lond., 1842. MD 6 T 2

CHAPMAN, Mrs. J. J. Egypt. [*See* Brimmer, M.]

CHAPMAN, W. S. Is the Modern Scientific Doctrine of Evolution Consistent with Theism ? 8vo. Melb., 1889.
MG 1 S 52

CHAPPELL, W. Popular Music of the Olden Time ; a collection of ancient songs, ballads, and dance tunes, illustrative of the National Music of England. 2 vols. Imp. 8vo. Lond. (n.d.) A 7 V 23, 24

CHARENCEY, H. de. Recherches sur les Dialectes Tasmaniens. 8vo. Paris, 1880. MK 1 T 13

CHARITY ORGANISATION SOCIETY OF MELBOURNE : Proceedings of First Australasian Conference on Charity, held in Melbourne from 11th to 17th Nov., 1890. 8vo. Melb., 1891. ME 6 S

CHARLEMAGNE, Emperor of Germany. History of Charles the Great (Charlemagne) ; by J. I. Mombert. Roy. 8vo. Lond., 1888. B 32 U 4

CHARLES, Mrs. E. R. Cronicas de la Familia Schönberg-Cotta. 8vo. Valparaiso, 1876. J 7 S 31

Martyrs and Saints of the first Twelve Centuries. 8vo. Lond., 1887. G 16 R 28

CHARLOTTE, Queen. [*See* Papendick, Mrs. C. L. H.]

CHARNAY, D. Ancient Cities of the New World; being Travels in Mexico and Central America, 1857-82. Imp. 8vo. Lond., 1887. D 15 V 5

CHARNOCK, Dr. R. S. Prænomina ; or, the Etymology of the Principal Christian names of Great Britain and Ireland. 12mo. Lond., 1882. K 19 P 14

CHARTIER, Alain. The Curial. [*See* Early Eng. Text Soc.]

CHASE, Dr. A. W. Third, Last, and Complete Receipt Book and Household Physician. Memorial edition. Sq. 8vo. Dunedin, 1887. A 26 T 8

CHASE, Rev. D. P. [*See* Aristoteles.]

CHASSANG, A. Histoire du Roman. 8vo. Paris, 1862.
B 35 P 11

CHAUCER, G. The Chaucer Birthday Book, compiled by Harriet Waechter. 8vo. Lond., 1889. H 7 S 40

CHAUCER SOCIETY. Publications. 7 vols. 8vo. Lond., 1887-89. E

A One-text Print of Chaucer's Troilus and Criseyde.
The Tale of Beryn.
Early English Pronunciation, with special reference to Shakspere and Chaucer ; by A. J. Ellis. Pt. 5.
John Lane's continuation of Chaucer's " Squire's Tale."
Ryme Index : Chaucer's Minor Poems.
More odd texts of Chaucer's Minor Poems.

CHAUNCY, M. Historia aliquot Martyrum Anglorum maxime octodecim Cartusianorum sub rege Henrico Octavo. Reprint of the edition of 1550. 4to. Lond., 1888. G 9 R 27 †

CHAUVEAU, Prof. A. Comparative Anatomy of the Domesticated Animals. 2nd ed. Roy. 8vo. Lond., 1891.
A 15 Q 14

CHEMICAL SOCIETY. Catalogue of the Library. 8vo. Lond., 1886.
K 8 P 37

Journal. Vols. 49–60. Lond., 1886-91.
E

CHENEY, Ednah D. [*See* Alcott, L. M.]

CHÉNIER, A. Œuvres en Prose, 8vo. Paris, 1886.
F 5 Q 38

Poésies de. (Collection Jannet-Picard.) 12mo. Paris (n.d.)
H 1 P 45

Poésies de. 8vo. Paris, 1884.
H 7 Q 13

CHERUBINI, L. M. C. Z. S. [Life of ;] by F. J. Crowest. 8vo. Lond., 1890.
C 16 P 15

CHESHIRE, F. R. Bees and Bee-keeping, Scientific and Practical. 2 vols. 8vo. Lond., 1886–87. A 14 P 50, 51

CHESS PROBLEM, The. Text-book, with Illustrations, containing 400 Positions selected from the Works of Andrews, Frankenstein, Laws, and Planck. 8vo. Lond., 1887.
A 17 W 38

CHESTER, H. M. Narrative of Expeditions to New Guinea. 8vo. Brisbane, 1878.
MD 3 S 44

CHESTER, Col. J. L. London Marriage Licenses, 1521-1869; edited by J. Foster. Roy. 8vo. Lond., 1887. K 8 S 3

CHESTER. Views in Chester and its Vicinity. Ob. 12mo. Chester, (n.d.)
D 18 P 24

CHESTERFIELD, Philip Dormer, Fourth Earl of. Letters of, to his Godson and Successor ; edited by the Earl of Carnarvon. Roy. 8vo. Oxford, 1890. C 13 V 1

CHETHAM SOCIETY. Publications. New series Vols. 12–25. 14 vols. (in 11.) 4to. Manchester, 1887-91.
E

12. Crosby Records ; edited by T. E. Gibson.
13. Bibliography of Works by Dr. J. Worthington ; compiled by R. C. Christie.
14. The Coucher Book of Furness Abbey ; edited by Rev, J. C. Atkinson.
15, 16. History of the Church and Manor of Wigan ; by Rev. G. T. O. Bridgeman.
19. Correspondence of Edward, third Earl of Derby; edited by T. N. Toller.
20, 22, 24. Minutes of the Manchester Presbyterian Classis, 1646-00 ; edited by W. A. Shaw.
21, 23. Fellows of the Collegiate Church of Manchester ; by Rev. F. R. Raines.
25. History of St. Michaels-on-Wyre ; by H. Fishwick.

CHETWYND, Sir George. Racing Reminiscences and Experiences of the Turf. 2 vols. 8vo. Lond., 1891.
C 16 T 9, 10

CHEVRON, P. [*See* Schuster, Dr. J.]

CHEYNE, A. Sailing Directions from New South Wales to China and Japan. 2nd ed. Roy. 8vo. Lond., 1862.
MD 7 S 20

CHICAGO. [*See* United States—Illinois.]

CHICHESTER, H. M. [*See* Shipp, Lieut. John.]

CHILD, Rev. G. F. On Related Caustics of Reflection. 8vo. Cape Town, 1859.
A 25 T 34

Investigations in the Theory of Reflected Ray-Surfaces. 8vo. Cape Town, 1857.
A 25 T 33

CHINESE IMMIGRATION into the Australasian Colonies, Correspondence relating to. Sm. fol. Lond., 1888.
MF 1 U 22

CHIPIEZ, Charles. History of Art in Persia. [*See* Perrot, Prof. G.]

History of Art in Phrygia, Lydia, Caria, and Lycia. [*See* Perrot, Prof. G.]

CHISHOLM, G. G. Handbook of Commercial Geography. 8vo. Lond., 1889.
D 11 U 18

Longmans' School Geography for Australasia. 8vo. Lond., 1888.
MD 1 R 17

New Atlas. [*See* Longmans' New Atlas.]

CHITTY, J. Collection of Statutes of Practical Utility. 4th ed. ; by J. M. Lely. 6 vols. roy. 8vo. Lond., 1880.
F 11 T 16–21

CHIUSHINGURA ; or the Loyal League : a Japanese Romance; translated by F. V. Dickins. Roy. 8vo. Lond., 1880.
J 7 U 1

CHOLERA. Report on the Mortality of Cholera in England 1848-49. Roy. 8vo. Lond., 1852. A 26 V 6

CHOPIN, Frederick. As a Man and Musician ; by F. Niecks. 2 vols. Lond., 1888.
C 13 U 7, 8

CHOYCE, J. The Log of a Jack Tar, or the Life of James Choyce, with O'Brien's Captivity in France ; edited by Commander V. L. Cameron. 8vo. Lond., 1891.
C 13 S 15

CHRISTIAN, Princess. [*See* Wilhelmine, Margravine of Baireuth.]

CHRISTIAN, J. Behar Proverbs classified and arranged. 8vo. Lond., 1891.
K 20 T 4

CHRISTIE, R. C. Bibliography of Works by Dr. J. Worthington. [*See* Chetham Society, 13.]

CHRISTIE, Rev. W. Traditional Ballad Airs. 2 vols. roy. 4to. Edinb., 1876-81.
A 4 Q 13, 14 †

CHRISTINGER, J. Des Alkoholismus. 8vo. Zurich, 1885.
F 11 R 10

CHRISTY, M. Trade Signs of Essex : a Popular Account of the Origin and Meaning of Public-house and other Signs. 8vo. Chelmsford, 1887.
B 7 P 26

CHRISTY, R. Proverbs, Maxims, and Phrases of all ages. 2 vols. 8vo. Lond., 1888.   K 19 Q 16, 17

CHRONICLES AND MEMORIALS of Great Britain and Ireland. 18 vols. 8vo. Lond., 1888–92. E

Lestoric des Engles solum la translacion Geffrei Gaimar.
Chronica Rogeri de Wendover III.
Chronicon Henrici Knighton vel Cnitthon Monachi Lycestrensis.
Ade Murimuth Continuatio Chronicarum Robertus de Avesbury.
Year-books of the Reign of King Edward III.
Literæ Cantuarienses. Vol. 1.
Willelmi Monachi Malmesbiriensis de Regum Gestis Anglorum. Edited by Wm. Stubbs. Vol. 2.
Register of the Abbey of St. Thomas, Dublin.
Flores Historiarum. Vols. 1-3. Edited by H. R. Luard.
Chronicles of the Reigns of Stephen, Henry II., and Richard I. Vol. 4. The Chronicle of Robert of Torigni.
Memorials of St. Edmund's Abbey. Vol. 1.
Recueil des Chroniques de la Grant Bretaigne. Par J. de Waurin. Vol. 5.
Charters and Documents of Salisbury.
Giraldi Cambrensis Opera Vol. 8.
Collection of the Chronicles of England.
Year-books of the Reign of Edward III.

CHURCH, Rev. Alfred John. Ovid (Ancient Classics for English Readers.) 12mo. Edinb., 1880. J 14 P 19

Early Britain. (Story of the Nations.) 8vo. Lond., 1889. B 23 S 3

Henry the Fifth. (English Men of Action.) 8vo. Lond., 1889. C 12 Q 33

CHURCH, Rev. Alfred John, and BRODRIBB, Rev. W. J. Pliny's Letters. (Ancient Classics for English Readers.) 12mo. Edinb., 1888. J 14 P 23

CHURCH, Prof. Arthur Herbert. The Chemistry of Paints and Painting. 8vo. Lond., 1890. A 8 P 40

CHURCH, I. P. Mechanics of Materials: a Treatise on the Elasticity and Strength of Beams, Columns, Arches, &c., for Students of Engineering, Roy. 8vo. New York, 1887. A 6 U 19

CHURCH, Rev. R. W. The Oxford Movement, 1833–45. 8vo. Lond., 1891. G 12 S 42

CHURCH, W. C. Life of John Ericsson. 2 vols. 8vo. Lond., 1890. C 16 T 11, 12

CHURCH HISTORY, Four Lectures on ; by Rev. Canon Chalmers, Rev. W. C. Pritchard, Rev. J. F. Stretch, and Rev. Canon Potter. 8vo. Melb., 1888. MG 1 R 15

CHURCH OF ENGLAND. Colonial Church Legislation. Fol. Lond., 1852. MF 8 P 23 †

Digest of Acts and Resolutions passed in the Diocesan Synod of Tasmania. 8vo. Hobart, 1876. MG 1 Q 64

Diocese of Goulburn. Report of the Twenty-fifth Annual Meeting of the Church Society. 8vo. Goulburn, 1889. ME 6 Q

Diocese of Newcastle. Report of Proceedings of First Session of the Fourth Synod, 1874. 8vo. Sydney, 1874. ME 6 Q

Diocese of Newcastle. Short Account of Church Work, 1873. 8vo. Sydney, 1874. MG 1 R 49

Diocese of Sydney. Proceedings of the Synod, 1866–79. 4 vols. 8vo. Sydney, 1867-79. ME 6 Q

CHURCH OF ENGLAND—*contd.*

Diocese of Sydney. Reports of the Church Society, 1865–73, 1875, 1877–84, 1886-91. 24 vols. 8vo. Sydney, 1866–92. ME 6 Q

Papers read at the Church Congress held at Melbourne, 1882. 8vo. Melb., 1882. ME 6 Q

Papers read at the Church Congress held at Sydney, 1889. 8vo. Sydney, 1889. ME 6 Q

Proceedings of the Conference of Lay Delegates of the. 12mo. Hobart, 1852. MG 2 P 40

CHURCH OF ENGLAND TEMPERANCE MAGAZINE. 8vo. Lond., 1862–63. F 11 Q 58

CHURCH OF ROME : Acta et Decreta Concilii Plenarii Australasiae, habiti apud Sydney A.D. 1885, a Sancta Sede recognita. 8vo. Sydney, 1887. MG 1 R 61

CHURCH SOCIETY, SYDNEY. [*See* Church of England.]

CHURCH MISSIONARY SOCIETY. Missions of the Church Missionary Society at Kishnaghur, and in New Zealand. 12mo. Lond., 1840. MD 2 W 32

Statement of the Committee of the Church Missionary Society in reference to Land purchased by the Missionaries in New Zealand. 8vo. Lond., 1845. MF 1 T 78

CHURCHILL, Randolph Henry Spencer, Lord. Men, Mines, and Animals in South Africa. [Map and Illustrations.] 8vo. Lond., 1892. D 14 V 10

Lord Randolph Churchill : a Study of English Democracy ; by J. B. Crozier. 12mo. Lond., 1887. C 2 R 22

Speeches of. Collected by L. J. Jennings. 2 vols. 8vo. Lond., 1889. F 13 Q 27, 28

CHURCHWARD, W. B. "Blackbirding" in the South Pacific. 8vo. Lond., 1888. MD 3 S 49

My Consulate in Samoa : a Record of Four Years in the Navigators Islands. 8vo. Lond., 1887. MD 3 U 38

CHURTON, Rev. E. Memoir of Joshua Watson. 2 vols. 8vo. Oxford, 1861. C 16 R 5, 6

CHUTE, C. W. History of the Vyne in Hampshire ; being an Account of the Building and Antiquities of that House. 4to. Winchester, 1888. B 3 V 20

CIBBER, Colley. Apology for the Life of ; written by himself. New edition, with notes by R. W. Lowe. 2 vols. 8vo. Lond., 1889. C 12 S 14, 15

The Careless Husband : a Comedy. [*See* British Drama, Modern.]

The Hypocrite : a Comedy. [*See* British Drama, Modern.]

Love Makes a Man : a Comedy. [*See* British Drama, Modern.]

She Would and She Would not : a Comedy. [*See* British Drama, Modern.]

The Provoked Husband. [*See* Vanbrugh, Sir J.]

CICERO, M. T. Cicero; by the Rev. W. L. Collins. (Ancient Classics for English Readers.) 12mo. Edinb., 1886.   J 14 P 6

Collations from the Harleian MS. of. [*See* Anecdota Oxoniensia.]

Correspondence of; with a Revision of the Text, a Commentary and Introductory Essays, by Prof. R. Y. Tyrrell and L. C. Purser. Vols. 1–3. 8vo. Dublin, 1885–90.   C 14 U 6–8

La République de Cicéron; traduite par A. E. Villemaine. 12mo. Paris, 1878.   F 5 Q 7

Opera quae extant omnia, nunc denuo recognita. J. Gronovio. 2 vols. sm. 4to. Lugdun: Bat., 1692.   J 18 V 18

Scripta quae manserunt omnia; recognovit R. Klotz. 5 vols. 12mo. Lipsiæ, 1851–55.   J 19 R 31–35

Tusculanarum disputationum libri V,, cum commentario, J. Davisii. Ed. 4a. 8vo. Camb., 1738.   G 13 R 44

CINCINNATI PUBLIC LIBRARY. Bulletin of Books added during 1888–90. *3 vols. 4to. Cincinnati, 1882–92   Libr.

CINDERELLA : a Manual of Political Economy for Free Men; by "A Member of the Sydney School of Arts." 8vo. Sydney, 1890.   MF 1 T 24

CINNAMUS, J. De Rebus Gestis Imperat. Constantinop. Joannis et Manuelis, Comnenorum; C. Tollius, edidit. Sm. 4to. Trajecti ad Rhenum, 1652.   B 34 Q 13

CIVIL ENGINEERS. Institution of. [*See* Institution of Civil Engineers.]

CLARK, A. The Colleges of Oxford : their History and Traditions. 8vo. Lond,, 1891.   B 5 T 29

CLARK, A. C. Collations from the Harleian MS. of Cicero. [*See* Anecdota Oxoniensia.]

CLARK, D. K. [*See* Dempsey, G. D.]

CLARK, G. B. British Policy towards the Boers. 8vo. Lond., 1881.   F 8 S 26

CLARK, G. T. Limbus Patrum Morganiæ et Glamorganiæ; being the Genealogies of the Families of Morgan and Glamorgan. Roy. 8vo. Lond., 1886.   K 8 S 4

CLARK, H. J. Lucernariæ and their Allies; a Memoir on the Anatomy and Physiology of Haliclystus Auricula. 4to. Wash., 1878.   A 42 R 24‡

CLARK, J. W. Wood and Iron Work in Cambridge. [*See* Redfarn, W. B.]

CLARK, J. W., and HUGHES, Prof. T. M. Life and Letters of the Rev. A. Sedgwick. 2 vols. 8vo. Camb., 1890.   C 14 U 2, 3

CLARK, W. A. [*See* Shakespeare, W.]

CLARKE, Rev. G. Sunday Lectures on the Epistle to the Hebrews. 8vo. Hobart, 1884.   MG 2 R 4

CLARKE, Major G. S. Fortification : its past Achievements, recent Development, and future Progress. 8vo. Lond., 1890.   A 22 U 25

CLARKE, H. On the Languages of Australia in their connection with those of the Mozambique and of the South of Africa. 8vo. Sydney, 1880.   MK 1 T 9

CLARKE, Rev. H. W. History of Tithes. 8vo. Lond., 1887.   B 23 S 1

Another Copy. 8vo. Lond., 1891.   F 6 P 43

CLARKE, Rev. J. S. [*See* Falconer, W.]

CLARKE, Rev. J. S., and McARTHUR, T. Life and Services of Viscount Nelson. 3 vols. 8vo. Lond. (n.d.)   C 18 R 3–5

Life of Adm. Lord Nelson. 2 vols. 4to. Lond., 1809.   C 33 P 18, 19‡

CLARKE, Marcus A. H. Sensational Tales. 8vo. Sydney, 1886.   MJ 1 Q 55

The Marcus Clarke Memorial Volume, containing selections from the writings of. 8vo. Melb., 1884.   MJ 1 Q 54

CLARKE, Mrs. Mary Victoria Cowden. Complete Concordance to Shakespere. Roy. 8vo. Lond., 1874.   K 17 R 24

CLARKE, P. Australian Etchings. [Eleven Plates.] Ob. 8vo. (n.p.n.d).   MD 3 P 16

CLARKE, Dr. S. Historical Memoirs of the Life of ; by W. Whiston. 8vo. Lond., 1730.   C 4 T 3

CLARKE, W. [Life of] Walt. Whitman. 12mo. Lond., 1892.   C 17 P 2

CLARKE, Dr. W. B. Narrative of the Wreck of the *Favorite* on the Island of Desolation; detailing Adventures, Sufferings, and Privations of John Nunn ; with chart and engravings. 8vo. Lond., 1850.   D 20 S 5

CLARKE, Rev. W. B. Address Delivered to the Royal Society of New South Wales at the Anniversary Meeting, 1872. 8vo. , Sydney, 1872.   MA 2 T 55

Biographical Sketch of ; by Prof. J. Smith. (Anniversary Address, Royal Soc. of N.S.W., 1879.) 8vo. Sydney, 1879.   MA 2 T 52

Notes on Deep Sea Soundings. 8vo. Sydney, 1876.   MA 3 Q 28

Remarks on the Sedimentary Formations of New South Wales. 8vo. Sydney, 1867.   MA 2 T 37

On Marine Fossiliferous Secondary Formation in Australia. 8vo. Sydney, 1866.   MA 2 T 38

CLARSON, W. The Island of Lord Howe : the Madeira of the Pacific; by "Linnæus." 12mo. Sydney, 1882.   MD 1 W 47

CLASSICAL REVIEW. Vols. 1–5. roy. 8vo. Lond., 1887–91.   E

CLAUDIANUS, C. Opera Omnia. Sm. 4to. Amstel., 1760.   H 36 S 11‡

CLAVERHOUSE, John Graham of. [*See* Dundee, Viscount]

CLAY, H. Life of; by C. Schurz. (American Statesmen.) 2 vols. 12mo. Boston, 1887. C 12 P 48, 49

CLAY, Hon. Mrs. J. R. [*See* Casati, Capt. G.]

CLAY, Rev. W. F. Food as Connected with Public Health; a Lecture. 8vo. Sydney, 1878. MA 2 T 36

CLAYDEN, A. New Zealand : its History, Institutions, and Industries; by "A Resident". 8vo. Lond., 1884. MB 1 R 47

CLAYDEN, P. W. Early Life of Samuel Rogers. 8vo. Lond., 1887. C 4 V 38

England Under the Coalition : Political History of Great Britain and Ireland from the General Election of 1885 to May, 1892. 8vo. Lond., 1892. B 22 Q 26

Rogers and His Contemporaries. 2 vols. 8vo. Lond., 1889. C 13 R 20, 21

CLEMENS, Samuel Langhorne. "Mark Twain." Life on the Mississippi. 8vo. Lond., 1883. D 3 P 59

The Celebrated Jumping Frog of Calaveras County, and other Sketches; by "Mark Twain." Australian edition. 12mo. Melb., 1868. MJ 1 P 56

Mark Twain's Library of Humour. 8vo. Lond., 1888. J 5 Q 35

CLERGY LIST, THE. 8vo. Lond., 1890. E

CLERICUS ANGLICANUS. [*See* Devil, The.]

CLERKE, Miss Agnes Mary. Familiar Studies in Homer. 12mo. Lond., 1892. J 11 W 27

CLERY, Brig.-Gen. C. F. Minor Tactics. 11th ed. 8vo. Lond., 1891. A 29 Q 13

CLEVE, P. T., und GRUNNON, A. Beiträge zur Kenntniss der Arctischen Diatomeen. 4to. Stockholm, 1880. A 36 P 29‡

CLEVELAND, Catherine Lucy Wilhelmine, Duchess of. The Battle Abbey Roll, with some account of the Norman Lineages. 3 vols. sm. 4to. Lond., 1889. B 6 T 48-50

CLEWS, H. Twenty-eight years in Wall-street. 8vo. New York, 1888. F 7 S 26

CLIFFORD, F. C. Richmond River District of New South Wales; New Italy : a brief sketch of a new and thriving colony. Roy. 8vo. Sydney, 1889. MD 3 V 11

CLINTON, Sir H. The Campaign in Virginia, 1781 : a Reprint of Six Rare Pamphlets on the Clinton-Cornwallis Controversy; with Notes, &c.; edited by B. F. Stevens. 2 vols. roy. 8vo. Lond., 1888. B 1 V 14, 15

CLIVE, Mrs. C. Life of; with an Account of her Adventures on and off the Stage; by P. Fitzgerald. 8vo. Lond., 1888. C 3 R 18

CLIVE, Robert, Lord. [Life of]; by Col. Sir C. Wilson. (Eng. Men of Action). 12mo. Lond., 1890. C 12 P 33

Life of; [*See* Yonge, C. D.]

CLODD, E. The Childhood of the World : a simple account of Man in the Early Times. 9th ed. 12mo. Lond., 1890. A 18 P 26

Story of Creation; a Plain Account of Evolution. 8vo. Lond., 1888. A 24 Q 3

CLODE, C. M. Early History of the Guild of Merchant Taylors of the Fraternity of St. John the Baptist. Lond., 2 vols. Imp. 8vo. Lond., 1888. B 24 V 4, 5

CLOUGH, A. H. Prose Remains; with a Selection from his Letters and a Memoir; edited by his Wife. Lond., 1888. C 12 Q 25

CLOUSTON, Dr. T. S. Clinical Lectures on Mental Diseases. 3rd ed. 8vo. Lond., 1892. A 12 Q 47

CLOUSTON, W. A. Book of Noodles; Stories of Simpletons; or, Fools and their Follies. 12mo. Lond., 1888. J 1 S 48

Popular Tales and Fictions; their Migrations and Transformations. 2 vols. 8vo. Edinb., 1887. J 6 S 32, 33

CLOVIO, Giulio Giorgio. Life and Works of, with notices of his Contemporaries, &c.; by J. W. Bradley. 8vo. Lond., 1891 C 15 T 15

CLOWES, W. L. Black America : a study of the ex-slave and his late master. 8vo. Lond., 1891. F 6 Q 8

CLUTTERBUCK, W. J. About Ceylon and Borneo. Illustrated. 12mo. Lond., 1891. D 17 Q 15

CLYDE, Sir Colin Campbell, Lord. Clyde and Strathnairn; by Maj. Gen. Sir O. T. Burne. (Rulers of India.) 8vo. Oxford, 1891. C 17 Q 7

Life of; [*See* Yonge, C. D.]

CLYDE, J. Greek Syntax. 8vo. Edinb., 1856. K 16 P 35

COATES, D. Two Letters to Sir Robert H. Inglis, in reference to the New Zealand Company and the New Zealand Missionaries. 8vo. Lond., 1845. MF 2 P 3

COBBETT, J. P. [*See* Cobbett, W.]

COBBETT, W. French Grammar. 15th ed. revised, with Additions and Corrections; by J. P. Cobbett. 12mo. Lond., 1861. K 20 P 1

COBDEN, Richard. An English Hero: the Story of Richard Cobden, written for young people; by Francis E. Cooke. 12mo. Lond., 1889. C 14 P 5

Life of; by R. Gowing. (The World's Workers.) 12mo. Lond. 1889. C 14 P 6

Life of; by John Morley. 4to. Lond., 1882. C 17 U 20

The Three Panics. 12mo. Lond., 1884. F 9 U 28

Political Writings of. 12mo. Lond., 1886. F 5 Q 39

COBDEN CLUB. Presentation of an Address to Mr. Thomas Bayley Potter, M.P., on behalf of the Cobden Club, with the Great Free Trade Speech made in presenting the Address by the Right Hon. W. E. Gladstone. 12mo. Lond., 1890. F 14 P 50

COBDEN CLUB—*contd.*
The Cobden Club Dinner held at the Ship Hotel, Greenwich, on the 1st of July, 1893. The Right Hon. Lord Playfair, K.C.B., in the chair. The Speeches of the Chairman ; Mr. J. W. Probyn ; Mr. I. S. Leadam ; the Comte de Franqueville ; M. Chailley-Bert ; Herr F. C. Philippson ; Mr. Thomas G. Shearman ; Mr. Thomas Bayley Potter, M.P. 12mo. Lond., 1893.   F 7 V 27

COBLEY, E. H. Government House Waltz. Fol. Sydney (n.d.)   MA 11 Q 15 †

COBURN, F. D. Swine Husbandry : a practical manual for the breeding, rearing, and management of Swine. 12mo. New York, 1888.   A 18 Q 12

COCHRAN, W. Pen and Pencil in Asia Minor ; or, Notes from the Levant. 8vo. Lond., 1887.   D 16 U 10

COCHRAN, Dr. G. W. Revised Statutes of Illinois. [*See* United States–Illinois.]

COCHRAN-PATRICK, R. W. [*See* Patrick R. W. Cochran–.]

COCKBURN, H. T., Lord. An Examination of the Trials for Sedition which have hitherto occurred in Scotland. 5 vols. 8vo. Edinb. 1888.   F 7 Q 28, 29
Circuit Journeys [1837-54.] 8vo. Edinb., 1888.   C 12 R 43

COCKSHOTT, H. M. and LAMB, S. E. Digest of Cases decided in the Supreme Court of New South Wales from 1884 to 1891 inclusive. Roy. 8vo. Sydney, 1892.   MF 3 R 50

COCOA : all about it ; by "Historicus." 12mo. Lond., 1892.   A 1 U 31

COFFEY, C. The Devil to Pay : a Ballad Farce. [*See* British Drama, Modern.]

COFFEY, W. H. and Elles H. L. The District Courts Acts, 1858-1884 and the Small Debts Recovery Act, 1881. 8vo. Sydney, 1884.   MF 2 T 49

COGHLAN, T. A. Discharge of Streams in Relation to Rainfall, New South Wales. 8vo. Lond. (n.d.)   MA 1 V 35
Hand-books of New South Wales Statistics for 1887 and 1888. 2 vols. roy. 8vo. Sydney, 1888–89.   ME 8 R
Hand-book to the Statistical Register of New South Wales for 1886. Roy. 8vo. Sydney, 1887.   ME
Report on the Vital Statistics of Sydney and Suburbs for 1888. Roy. 8vo. Sydney, 1889.   ME 8 R
Statistical Account of the Seven Colonies of Australasia. 3 vols. 8vo. Sydney, 1890-92.   ME 8 Q
Statistics showing the Relative position and importance of each of the Australasian Colonies. 1888-90. 2 vols. 8vo. Sydney, 1889-91.   ME
Wealth and Progress of New South Wales, 1886-90. 4 vols. 8vo. Sydney, 1887-90.   ME 5 R

COGLIOLO, P., and MAJORANA, A. Codice Scolastico del Regno d' Italia. 12mo. Firenze, 1892.   F 12 S 1

COHEN, I. R. How will it end ? 8vo. Sydney, 1886.   MJ 1 U 14

COIGNET, Clarisse. Francis the First and his times ; translated by Fanny Twemlow. 8vo. Lond., 1888.   B 26 U 2
A Gentleman of the Olden Time : François de Scépeaux, Sire de Vieilleville, 1509–71. 2 vols. 8vo. Lond., 1887.   C 3 S 21, 22

COIT, S. Neighbourhood Guilds : an instrument of Social Reform. 8vo. Lond., 1891.   F 14 P 46

COLBECK, A. Summer's Cruise in the Waters of Greece, Turkey, and Russia. 8vo. Lond., 1887.   D 9 Q 9

COLBURN'S UNITED SERVICE MAGAZINE. 9 vols. 8vo. Lond., 1888-92.   E

COLBY, C. C. Parliamentary Government in Canada : a Lecture. 12mo. Montreal 1886.   F 1 P 33

COLCHESTER, Charles Abbot, First Baron. Letter to William Augustus Miles, Esq., on " A Description of the Deverel Barrow," dated 25th Nov., 1826. 4to. Lond. 1826.   B 23 V 3

COLE, A. C. Studies in Microscopical Science. 2 vols. 8vo. Lond., 1883-84.   A 29 U 5, 6

COLE, A. S. [*See* Lace-making.]

COLE, Prof. G. A. J. Aids to Practical Geology. 8vo. Lond., 1891.   A 24 R 1

COLE, H. Documents illustrative of English History in the 13th and 14th Centuries, selected from the Records. Fol. Lond. 1844.   B 36 S 12 ‡

COLE, Nathan. Royal Parks and Gardens of London, their history and mode of embellishment. 8vo. Lond. 1877.   A 18 T 2

COLEBROOK, Sir E. [*See* Elphinstone, Hon. M.]

COLEMAN, G. The Deuse is in him : a Farce. [*See* British Drama, Modern.]

COLEMAN, J. Cattle, Sheep, and Pigs of Great Britain ; edited by J. Coleman. Roy. 8vo. Lond., 1887. A 1 T 29

COLENSO, Rt. Rev. J. W., Bishop of Natal. Life of ; by the Rev. Sir G. W. Cox. 2 vols. 8vo. Lond., 1888.   C 12 T 5, 6

COLENSO, W. Ancient Tide-Lore and Tales of the Sea from two ends of the World. 8vo. Napier, 1889.   MB 2 Q 3
Fifty Years ago in New Zealand : a Plain and True Story. 8vo. Napier, 1888.   MB 2 Q 39
Authentic and Genuine History of the Signing of the Treaty of Waitangi. 8vo. Wellington, 1890.   MB 2 Q 40
In Memoriam : account of Visits to and Crossings over the Ruahaine Mountain Range. Roy. 8vo. Napier, 1884.*   MD 3 V 42

COLERIDGE, A. D. [*See* Hauptmann, M.]

COLERIDGE, E. P. [*See* Apollonius Rhodius.]

COLERIDGE, H. J. [*See* Fullerton, Lady G.]

COLERIDGE, H. N. Introduction to the Study of the Greek Classic Poets. 3rd ed. 12mo. Lond., 1846.   H 10 P 26

COLERIDGE, S. T., and the English Romantic School; by Prof. A. Brandl; English edition by Lady Eastlake. 8vo. Lond., 1887.   C 13 R 8
[*See* Knight, W.]

COLES, Dr. Abraham.. Biographical Sketch, Memorial Tributes, Selections from his Works; edited by Dr. J. A. Coles. 8vo. New York, 1892.   C 18 Q 1
A new Rendering of the Hebrew Psalms into English Verse with Notes, &c. 12mo. New York, 1888.   G 10 P 30
Life and Teachings of our Lord, in Verse. 2 vols. (in 1.) 8vo. New York, 1885.   H 10 R 19

COLES, Dr. J. A. [*See* Coles, Dr. A.]

COLET, Rev. J., Dean of St. Paul's. Life of; by J. H. Lupton. 8vo. Lond., 1887.   C 12 T 21

COLLARD, C. A. [*See* Agriculture, Dept. of, Queensland.]

COLLES, R. A Synopsis of the Laws relating to Sheriffs in the Execution of Writs. 8vo. Melb., 1883.   MF 2 T 50

COLLES, W. M. The Literature and the Pension List. 8vo. Lond., 1889.   F 6 T 35

COLLETTE, C. H. Life, Times, and Writings of Thomas Cranmer, Archbishop of Canterbury. 8vo. Lond., 1887.   C 10 T 22

COLLIER, C. [*See* Aristoteles.]

COLLIER, J. The Literature relating to New Zealand: a Bibliography. Roy. 8vo. Wellington, 1889. MK 1 S 37

COLLINGRIDGE, George. Early Discovery of Australia. [*See* Royal Geographical Society of Australasia.]

COLLINGWOOD, Cuthbert, Lord: Life of. By W. C. Russell. 8vo. Lond., 1891.   C 15 U 8

COLLINGWOOD, W. G. The Art Teaching of John Ruskin. 8vo. Lond., 1891.   A 23 Q 28

COLLINS, C. W. Plato (Ancient Classics for English Readers). 12mo. Edinb., 1886.   J 14 P 21
Sophocles (Ancient Classics for English Readers. 12mo. Edinb., 1886.   J 14 P 24

COLLINS, Capt. G. Great Britain's Coasting Pilot of England and Scotland. Fol. Lond., 1785. D 41 P 20‡

COLLINS, J. C. Illustrations of Tennyson. 12mo. Lond., 1891.   H 9 P 9

COLLINS, J. H. A First Book of Mining and Quarrying. (Weale.) 2nd ed. 12mo. Lond., 1888.   A 17 R 20

COLLINS, Wilkie. [*See* Dickens, C.]

COLLINS, Rev. W. L. Aristophanes. (Ancient Classics for English Readers). 12mo. Edinb., 1880.   J 14 P 2

Cicero. (Ancient Classics for English Readers.) 12mo. Edinb., 1886.   J 14 P 6

Homer—the Iliad. (Ancient Classics for English Readers.) 12mo. Edinb., 1886.   J 14 P 12

Homer—the Odyssey. (Ancient Classics for English Readers.) 12mo. Edinb., 1882.   J 14 P 13

Livy. (Ancient Classics for English Readers.) 12mo. Edinb., 1880,   J 14 P 16

Lucian. (Ancient Classics for English Readers.) 12mo. Edinb., 1880.   J 14 P 17

Plautus and Terence. (Ancient Classics for English Readers.) 12mo. Edinb., 1880.   J 14 P 22

Thucydides. (Ancient Classics for English Readers.) 12mo. Edinb., 1887.   J 14 P 26

Virgil. (Ancient Classics for English Readers.) 12mo. Edinb., 1882.   J 14 P 27

COLMAN, G. The Jealous Wife, a comedy. [*See* British Drama, Modern.]

COLMAN, G., and GARRICK, D. The Clandestine Marriage, a comedy. [*See* British Drama, Modern.]

COLMAN, R. J. Trifles from a Tourist in Letters from Abroad. 8vo. Norwich, 1886.   D 20 S 6

COLMAN, T. Comus a Mask, altered from Milton. [*See* Milton J.]

COLOMB, Capt. Sir John C. R. Colonial Defence and Colonial Opinion. 8vo. Dublin, 1877,   MF 1 P 51
A Survey of Existing Conditions. [*See* Britannic Confederation.]

COLOMB, Rear-Admiral P. H. Naval Warfare, its ruling principles and practice historically treated. Roy. 8vo. Lond., 1891.   A 29 V 8

COLOMB, R. Notice Biographique de H. Beyle. [*See* Beyle, H.]

COLOMBO MUSEUM. First Report on the Collection of Moths in the Colombo Museum. 8vo. Colombo, 1888.   A 27 T 27

First Report on the Exhibited Coins. 8vo. Colombo, 1889.   A 27 T 1

First Report on the Collection of Lizards in the Colombo Museum. 8vo. Colombo, 1886.   A 27 T.29

First Report on the Collection of Batrachia in the Colombo Museum. 8vo. Colombo, 1886.   A 27 T 28

First Report on the Collection of Snakes in the Colombo Museum. 8vo. Colombo, 1886.   A 27 T 30

List of Exhibited Minerals. 8vo. Colombo, 1888.   A 24 T 4

COLONIAL BRITON, A. [*See* Our River.]

COLONIAL CONFERENCE. Proceedings of the. 2 vols. sm. fol. Lond., 1887.   MF 1 U 19, 20

COLONIAL EXECUTIVES. Return showing the Constitution of the Executive in each Colony, and in the case of Colonies having Representative Assemblies, the Constitution of those Assemblies, the number of Members, the number of Electors, and the Qualifications requisite for Members and for Electors. Fol. Lond., 1889.   MF 12 Q 26†

COLONIAL LAND AND EMIGRATION COMMISSION. Copy of Instructions from the Secretary of State [and] First to Sixth General Reports, 1840–46. 4 vols. (in 1). 8vo. Lond., 1843–46.   MF 2 T 51

COLONIAL MAGAZINE, The. Vols. 1–18. 8vo. Lond. 1844–50.   ME 5 R

COLONIAL MILITARY EXPENDITURE. Reports from Select Committees on. Fol. Lond., 1834–35.   MF 11 Q 36 †

COLONIAL MINING JOURNAL of Victoria, Australia, and adjacent Colonies. Vol. 1. Fol. Melb., 1858-59.   ME

COLONIAL MUSEUM AND LABORATORY, NEW ZEALAND. Annual Reports. 2 vols. Roy. 8vo. Wellington, 1890–91.   ME 9 Q
Catalogue of the Library of. Roy. 8vo. Wellington, 1890.   MK 1 S 33

COLONIAL NAVAL FORCE. Copies or Extracts from Correspondence relative to the Formation and Maintenance of. Fol. Lond., 1885.   MF 11 Q 35 †

COLONIAL OFFICE LIST. 6 vols. 8vo. Lond., 1887–92.   E

COLONIAL POSSESSIONS. [See Great Britain.]

COLONIAL YEAR-BOOK, The. 2 vols. 8vo. Lond., 1890–91.   E

COLONISATION. Report from the Select Committee on. Fol. Lond., 1890.   MF 3 Q 34 †
Copy of Correspondence from Colonial Governments in answer to the Memorandum by the Parliamentary Colonisation Committee. Fol. Lond., 1889.   MF 3 Q 35 †
Report from Select Committee on Colonisation, with Proceedings of the Committee, &c. Fol. Lond., 1891.   MF 3 Q 35 †

COLONNA, Vittoria. Le Rime di; corrette su i testi a penna dal Cav. P. E. Visconti. Roy. 8vo. Roma, 1840.   H 7 V 29
Le Rime Spirituali. Sm. 4to. Vinegia, 1548.   H 9 S 23

COLONY OF AUSTRALIA, The. Views of Sir Alfred Stephen and Sir John Robertson, and Views of the Press. 8vo. Sydney, 1887.   D 16 V 5

COLQUHOUN, A. R., and HALLETT, H. S. Report on the Railway Connexion of Burmah and China. Sm. fol. Lond., 1879–85.   F 36 Q 9 ‡

COLTMAN, Dr. R. The Chinese: their Present and Future; Medical, Political, and Social. Illustrated. 8vo. Philad., 1891.   D 16 V 5

COLUMBUS, C., The Career of; by C. I. Elton. 8vo. Lond., 1892.   C 18 S 21
The Letter in Spanish of Christopher Columbus announcing the Discovery of the New World; reproduced in facsimile; with revised Spanish version and English translation. Sm. 4to. Lond., 1889.   D 15 V 4
The Spanish Letter of Columbus to Luis de Sant' Angel, 1493. Reprinted from the copy of the original edition. 4to. Lond., 1891.   B 40 Q 18 ‡

COLUMELLE, Lucius Junius Moderatus. [See Agronomes Latins, Les.]

COLVILLE, Col. H. E. History of the Sudan Campaign. 3 vols. 8vo. Lond., 1889.   B 2 S 20–22

COLVIN, S. The Drawings of Flaxman. Fol. Lond., 1876.   A 8 R 10 ‡
Keats. English Men of Letters. 8vo. Lond., 1887.   C 1 U 39
Letters of John Keats. [See Keats, J.]
[See Jenkin, F.]

COMBE, Dr. A. Observations on Mental Derangement; edited and abridged by A. Mitchell. 8vo. Edinb., 1887.   A 13 P 44

COMBES, E. The Material Progress of New South Wales. 8vo. Lond., 1886.   MF 1 T 23
Report on Technical Education. Fol. Sydney, 1887.   MG 3 Q 27 †

COMMELIN, P. Begin ende Voortgang vande Vereenigde Neederlandtsche, Geoctroyeerde Oost-Indische Compagnie. 2 vols. ob. 4to. Amst., 1846.   D 20 R 4, 5

COMETTANT, O. Au Pays des Kangourous et des Mines D'Or. 8vo. Paris, 1890.   MD 1 W 48

COMMERCIAL BANKING COMPANY OF SYDNEY. Deed of Settlement. 8vo. Sydney, 1834. MF 3 P 49
Deed of Settlement: Act of Incorporation and Amending Acts. 8vo. Sydney, 1859.   MF 3 Q 7

COMMISSION IMPÉRIALE ARCHÉOLOGIQUE. Comptes Rendus. 1859–81. 21 vols. 8vo. St. Petersb., 1860–83.   E
Atlas [to the above], 1859–81. 2 vols. fol. St. Petersb., 1860–83.   E

COMPAYRÉ, G. History of Pedagogy; translated by W. H. Payne. 8vo. Boston, 1886.   G 17 P 30

COMPTON, H. [See Eastwick, Capt. R. W. and Reid, E.]

COMTESSE, Mons. [See Roulet, Mons.]

CONDER, Maj. Claude Reignier. Tent Work in Palestine: a Record of Discovery and Adventure. 2 vols. 8vo. Lond., 1878.   D 16 U 15, 16
Survey of Eastern Palestine. Memoirs, vol. 1—The Adwân Country. 4to. Lond., 1889.   D 3 R 16,†
Altaic Hieroglyphs and Hittite Inscriptions. 8vo. Lond., 1887.   B 2 S 17
[See Armstrong, G.]

CONDER, J. The Flowers of Japan and the Art of Floral Arrangement. 4to. Tokio, 1892. A 40 Q 15 ‡

CONGRÈS INTERNATIONAL pour l'étude des questions relatives à l'alcoolisme, 1880. 8vo. Bruxelles, 1880.   F 11 T 3

CONINGTON, Prof. J. [*See* Virgilius Maro, P.]

CONGREVE, R. Politics of Aristotle. [*See* Aristoteles.]

CONGREVE, W. Best Plays ; edited by A. C. Ewald. (Mermaid Series.) 8vo. Lond., 1887.   II 4 Q 22

The Old Bachelor.—The Double Dealer.—Love for Love.—The Way of the World.—The Mourning Bride.

The Double Dealer : a Comedy. [*See* British Drama, Modern.]

Love for Love : a Comedy. [*See* British Drama, Modern.]

The Mourning Bride. [*See* British Drama, Modern.]

The Old Bachelor : a Comedy. [*See* British Drama, Modern.]

The Way of the World : a Comedy. [*See* British Drama, Modern.]

CONIGRAVE, J. F. Agriculture in South Australia ; a Description of the South Australian Seedsower, Stripper, and Winnower. 8vo. Adelaide, 1883.   MA 1 V 65

Technical Education in New South Wales. 8vo. Adelaide, 1886.   MG 1 R 34

CONINGTON, J. [*See* Horatius Flaccus, Q.]

CONN, W. Cow-boys and Colonels. [*See* Mandat-Grancey, Baron E. de.]

CONSTANT, B. Adolphe ; Anecdote trouvée dans les Papiers d'un Inconnu. 12mo. Paris, 1884. J 16 R 35

CONSTANTINUS VII. De Administrando Imperio ; J. Meursius vulgavit. 12mo. Lug. Bat., 1611.   B 34 P 13

CONSTANTINUS XIII. Emperor. [*See* Mijatovich, C.]

CONTEMPORARY REVIEW. Vols 51-61. Roy. 8vo. Lond., 1887-92.   E

CONTES FANTASTIQUES. Le Diable Amoureux ; par J. Cazotte. Le Démon Marié ; par N. Machiavel. Merveilleuse Histoire de P. Schlémihl; par A. de Chamisso. (Collection Jannet Picard.) 12mo. Paris (n.d.)
                                                        J 15 Q 29

CONVICTS. Copies or Extracts of any Correspondence with the Governor of Tasmania, connected with the institution of an Inquiry by a Committee of the Legislative Assembly into the working of the Convict Department. Fol. Lond., 1856.   MF 11 Q 30 †

Copies or Extracts of any Correspondence on the subject of Convict Discipline in Van Diemen's Land. Fol. Lond., 1846.   MF 11 Q 29 †

Annual Reports of the Convict Establishments at Western Australia and Tasmania. 5 vols. (in 1.) fol. Lond., 1865-69.   MF 11 Q 27 †

Return of Number of Persons who have been Transported as Criminals to New South Wales since the first establishment of the colony. Fol. Lond. 1810.
                                                        MF 11 Q 26 †

CONVICTS—*contd.*

Correspondence on the subject of Convict Discipline and Transportation. Fol. London, 1847.   MF 11 Q 25 †

Correspondence on the subject of Convict Discipline and Transportation. 6 vols. fol. Lond., 1847-69.
                                                        MF 8 P 15-20 †

Copies or Extracts of any Correspondence between the Secretary of State and the Governor of Van Diemen's Land, on the subject of Convict Discipline. Fol. Lond., 1843-46.   MF 8 P 21 †

Copies or Extracts of any Correspondence respecting the Convict System administered in Norfolk Island under the Superintendence of Captain Maconochie. Fol. Lond., 1846.   MF 8 P 22 †

Copy of a Despatch from Lieut.-Governor Sir J. Franklin to Lord Glenelg relative to the present System of Convict Discipline in Van Diemen's Land. Fol. Lond., 1838.
                                                        MF 3 U 46

Another Copy. Fol. Lond., 1838. Reprinted Hobart, 1838.   MF 3 U 47

CONWAY, Moncure Daniel. Omitted Chapters of History disclosed in the Life and Papers of Edmund Randolph. Roy. 8vo. New York, 1888.   C 12 U 3

Demonology and Devil-lore. 3rd ed. 2 vols. 8vo. Lond., 1889.   G 6 S 34, 35

COOK, Madame C. Lectures on Education. 8vo. Sydney, 1876.   MG 1 S 51

COOK, C. [*See* Browne, Eliza S.]

COOK, E. T. Studies in Ruskin : Some aspects of the work and teaching of John Ruskin. Imp. 8vo. Orpington, 1890.   A 8 T 33

Popular Hand-book to the National Gallery. 8vo. Lond., 1888.   A 23 R 1

COOK, H. The Scenery of Central Italy. Fol. Lond. (n.d.)
                                                        D 41 P 3 ‡

COOK, Capt. J. [Life of] by Walter Besant. 8vo. Lond., 1890.   MC 1 Q 39

Life of. Stereotype edition. 18mo. Belfast, 1835.
                                                        MC 1 P 63

Troisième Voyage de Cook, ou Journal d'une Expédition faite dans la Mer Pacifique du Sud et du Nord, 1776-80; traduit de l'Anglois. 8vo. Paris, 1782.   MD 1 R 40

Troisième Voyage de Cook, ou Voyage à l'Océan Pacifique, 1776-80 ; traduit de l'Anglois. 4 vols. 4to. Paris, 1785.   MD 11 P 25-28 †

Cartes et Figures [to the above.] 4to. Paris, 1785.
                                                        MD 11 P 21 †

Narrative of his Voyage round the World ; by A. Kippis. 12mo. Lond., 1839.   MD 1 T 44

Unveiling of the Captain Cook Statue, Hyde Park, Sydney, N.S.W. Imp. 8vo. Sydney, 1879.   MB 2 U 18

Vie du, traduite de l'Anglois du Docteur Kippis. 4to. Paris, 1789.   MC 11 P 18 †

Voyage dans l'Hémisphère Austral, et Autour du Monde, 1772-75 ; traduit de l'Anglois. 5 vols. 4to. Paris, 1778.   MD 11 P 19-23 †

COOK, Capt. J.—*contd.*
Cartes et Figures [to the above.] 4to. Paris, 1778.
MD 11 P 24 †
Voyages round the World during the years 1768-80 ; to which is added Governor Phillip's Voyage to Botany Bay. 3 vols. 8vo. Newcastle, 1790. MD 6 S 13-15
Voyage round the World, illustrated with Maps and numerous Engravings. 2 vols. imp. 8vo. Lond., (n.d.)
MD 12 Q 1; 2 †
Voyages of, with an Appendix giving an account of the Present Condition of the South Sea Islands. 2 vols. roy. 8vo. Lond.; 1842. MD 7 U 9, 10
[*See* Hamy, Dr. E. T.]

COOK, Rev. J. Advanced Thought in Europe, Asia, Australia, &c. 8vo. Lond., 1883. MG 1 S 50
Socialism, with Preludes on Current Events. 8vo. Lond., 1888. F 14 P 5

COOK, S. The Jenolan Caves : an Excursion in Australian Wonderland. Imp. 8vo. Lond., 1889.
M D 6 U 24

COOKE, C. K. [*See* Scratchley, Major-Gen. Sir P. H.]

COOKE, Capt. Edward. Voyage to the South Sea and Round the World, 1708-11. 2 vols. 8vo. Lond., 1712.
MD 7 T 28, 29

COOKE, Frances E. An English Hero : the Story of Richard Cobden, written for young people. 12mo. Lond., 1889. C 14 P 5

COOKE, John. Greene's Tu Quoque or the City Gallant : a Comedy. [*See* British Drama, Ancient.]

COOKE, J. E. Virginia : a History of the People. (American Commonwealths.) 12mo. Boston, 1890. B 17 P 15

COOKE, J. P. The New Chemistry. 8th ed. 12mo. Lond., 1884. A 21 Q 37

COOKE, Louisa S. [*See* Betts, B. W.]

COOKE, Dr. M. C. Introduction to Fresh-water Algæ, with an Enumeration of all the British Species. 8vo. Lond., 1890. A 20 Q 4
Handbook of British Fungi. 2nd ed. 8vo. Lond., 1883. A 20 S 5
Fungi Australiani (Supplementum ad Fragmentorum Phytographiæ Australiæ). 8vo. Melb., 1883. MA 1 T 77
British Desmids : a supplement to British Fresh-water Algæ. 8vo. Lond., 1887. A 20 S 2

COOKSON, C. [*See* King, J. E.]

COOLEY, A. J. Cooley's Cyclopædia of Practical Receipts. 7th ed. Revised by W. North. 2 vols. roy. 8vo. Lond., 1892. K 4 Q 19, 20

COOLEY, Dr. T. M. Treatise on the Constitutional Limitations which rest upon the Legislative Power of the States of the American Union. 6th ed. ; with additions by A. C. Angell. Roy. 8vo. Boston, 1890.
F 14 V 19
Michigan : a History of Governments. (American Commonwealths.) 4th ed. 12mo. Boston, 1889.
B 17 P 13

COOPER, A. Colonies of the United Kingdom. 8vo. Brighton, 1888. MF 2 P 46

COOPER, E. Forest Culture and Eucalyptus Trees. 8vo. San Francisco, 1876. MA 1 V 66

COOPER, H. S. Islands of the Pacific : their People and Products. 8vo. Lond., 1888. MD 1 Q 8
Our New Colony : Fiji, its History, Progress, and Resources. Roy. 8vo. Lond., 1882. MD 7 R 37

COOPER, T. Alderman Ralph ; or, the History of the Borough of Willowncre, &c.; by "A. Hornbrook." 2 vols. 8vo. Lond., 1893. J 9 Q 36, 37

COOPER, Thomas. Astbury Church, Cheshire : an impartial Inquiry respecting the Canopied Tomb, &c., in the Churchyard. 8vo. Lond., 1888. B 23 T 1

COOPER, T. Biographical Dictionary of Eminent Persons. 8vo. Lond., 1890. C 21 P 14 15

COOPER, T. S. My Life. 2 vols. 8vo. Lond., 1890.
C 15 T 11 12

COOPER, W. J. [*See* Wanklyn, J. A.]

CO-OPERATION. Reports by Her Majesty's Representatives Abroad, on the System of Co-operation in Foreign Countries. Roy. 8vo. Lond., 1886. F 14 V 1

CO-OPERATIVE INDEX TO PERIODICALS for 1888-91. 6 vols. Sm. 4to. New York, 1887-92. E

CO-OPERATIVE STORES, Report from Select Committee ; with Proceedings of Committee, Minutes of Evidence, and Appendix. Fol. Lond., 1879. F 42 P 18‡

COOTO, H. C. Practice of the High Court of Admiralty of England ; with Forms and Bills of Costs. 2nd edition. 8vo. Lond., 1860. F 9 S 12

COOTE, W. L'Océan Pacifique Occidental ; description des Groupes d'Isles au Nord et à l'Est du Continent Australien. 8vo. Paris, 1886. MD 7 R 39

COPE, C. W. Reminiscences of ; by C. H. Cope. 8vo. Lond., 1891. C 18 S 1

COPE, C. H. Reminiscences of C. W. Cope. 8vo. Lond., 1891. C 18 S 1

COPE, E. D. Origin of the Fittest : Essays on Evolution. Roy. 8vo. Lond., 1887. A 29 V 1

COPINGER, W. A. Incunabula Biblica ; or the First Half Century of the Latin Bible, 1450-1500. Fol. Lond., 1892. G 38 Q 18 ‡

COPLESTON, Rt. Rev. R. S. Æschylus. (Ancient Classics for English Readers.) 8vo. Edinb., 1887. J 14 P 1

COPLEY, F. S. Set of Alphabets of all the various Hands in Modern Use. Ob. 8vo. New York (n.d.) A 23 Q 21

COPLEY, W. Report on the Village Homestead Special Settlement System in New Zealand. Fol. Adelaide, 1891. MF 11 Q 37 †

CORBETT, E. An Old Coachman's Chatter, with some Practical Remarks on Driving. 8vo. Lond., 1890.
A 30 T 4

CORBETT, J. [Life of] Sir Francis Drake. (English Men of Action.) 8vo. Lond., 1890. C 15 Q 13

CORBETT, Julian. [Life of] Monk. (English Men of Action.) 12mo. Lond., 1889. C 12 P 32

CORBIN, Diana F. M. Life of M. F. Maury. 8vo. Lond., 1888. C 12 S 18

CORFIELD, W. H. Treatment and Utilization of Sewage. 3rd ed., revised and enlarged by the Author and L. C. Parkes. 8vo. Lond., 1887. A 6 U 14

CORLETTE, Rev. J C. The Law of Man at Variance with the Law of God : a Speech on the Marriage Question. 8vo. Sydney, 1876. MG 1 R 60

CORNEILLE, P. Corneille et son Temps : Étude Littéraire par M. Guizot. 8vo. Paris, 1889. C 17 Q 30

CORNHILL MAGAZINE. 8 vols. 8vo. Lond., 1887-92. E

CORNWALLIS, Charles, Marquess. [Life of] ; by W. S. Seton-Karr. (Rulers of India.) 8vo. Oxford, 1890. C 17 Q 9

[*See* Clinton, Sir H.]

CORRY, T. H. [*See* Stewart, S. A.]

CORSON, H. Introduction to the Study of R. Browning's Poetry. 8vo. Boston, 1886. H 5 R 40

CORTAMBERT, E. Dernières Explorations en Australie. 8vo. Paris (n.d.) MD 7 S 14

CORYN, H. A. W. Moral and Physical Advantages of Total Abstinence. 12mo. Lond., 1886. F 11 P 36

COSH, Rev. J. The Adaptability of the Church to the Times : a Sermon. 8vo. Sydney, 1883. MG 1 R 65

COSMOPOLITAN, A. [*See* Random Recollections.]

COSMOS. Vols. 8-10. 4to. Torino, 1883-91. E

COSTA, E. M. da. Historia Naturalis Testaceorum Britanniæ ; or, the British Conchology. [Eng. and Fr.] 4to. Lond., 1778. A 42 R 18 ‡

COTMAN, J. S. Engravings of Sepulchral Brasses in Norfolk and Suffolk. 2 vols. Fol. Lond., 1839. B 6 R 4, 5 ‡

COTTA, B. von. Der Altai : sein Geologischen Bau und seine Erzlagerstätten. Roy. 8vo. Leip., 1871. A 24 V 16

COTTEAU, E. En Océanie, Voyage autour du Monde en 365 Jours, 1884-85. 8vo. Paris, 1888. MD 1 Q 23

COTTERILL, J. H. Applied Mechanics : an elementary general Introduction to the Theory of Structures and Machines. 2nd ed. Roy. 8vo. Lond., 1890. A 22 T 26

COTTON, Sergt.-Major E. A Voice from Waterloo. 7th ed. 12mo. Mont-St.-Jean, 1877. B 26 P 3

COTTON, F. The Prophet of San Francisco. [Henry George] ; and other Sketches. 12mo. Bathurst, 1888. MF 3 P 39

COTTON, J. S. [Life of] Mountstuart Elphinstone. (Rulers of India). 12mo. Oxford, 1892. C 18 P 7

COTTON, Richard Lynch. Life of. [*See* Burgon, Very Rev. J. W.]

COTTON, Rev. S. G. Sons of Loyola. 8vo. Dublin, 1875. MJ 2 P 24

COTTRAV, C. G. [*See* Cerillo, F.]

COUCHE, C. Permanent Way ; Rolling Stock, and Technical Working of Railways ; translated by J. N. Shoolbred and J. E. Wilson. 3 vols. 8vo. Lond., 1877-78. A 42 S 1-3 ‡

Atlas [to the above] ; translated by J. E. Wilson. 3 vols. 4to. Lond., 1877-82. A 42 S 4-6 ‡

COUES, E. Birds of the Colorado Valley. Part I. Passeres to Laniidæ. 8vo. Washington, 1878. A 14 U 9

COULANGES, F. de. Origin of Property in Land ; with Introductory Chapter on the English Manor, by Prof. W. J. Ashley. 8vo. Lond., 1891. F 14 P 47

COUNSEL, E. The Last Glimpse of Erin ; Song. (Words by Moore.) Fol. Somerville (n.d.) MA 7 Q 31 †

Maxims ; Political, Philosophical, and Moral. 12mo. Melb., 1889. MG 2 P 14

Another Copy. 2nd ed. 8vo. Melb., 1892. MG 2 P 15

Melodies of Erin. [Music.] 4to. Somerville, 1890. MA 7 Q 31 †

COUPLAND, W. C. The Gain of Life and other essays. 8vo. Lond., 1890. G 16 R 48

COURTNEY, W. Taranaki : the Garden of New Zealand. 2nd ed. 8vo. Lond., 1889. MD 4 U 10

COURTNEY, W. L., LL.D., &c. Studies at Leisure. 12mo. Lond., 1892. J 11 W 28

Studies, New and Old. 8vo. Lond., 1888. J 5 Q 41

COUSIN, V. Life of ; by Jules Simon. (Great French Writers.) 8vo. Lond., 1888. C 7 P 40

Instruction Publique. 2 vols. 12mo. Paris, 1850. G 18 P 7, 8

Fragments Philosophiques, pour faire suite aux cours de l' Histoire de la Philosophie. 4ᵉ édition. 4 vols. 12mo. Paris, 1847. G 2 V 9-12

Cours de l' Histoire de la Philosophie moderne. 1ᵉ et 2ᵉ série. 8 vols. 12mo. Paris, 1846-47. G 2 V 13-20

Fragments de Philosophie Cartésienne. 12mo. Paris, 1845. G 2 V 21

Littérature. 3 vols. 12mo. Paris, 1849. J 16 R 28-30

Notice Historique sur la Vie et les Travaux de ; par F. A. M. Mignet. 8vo. Paris, 1869. C 21 R 8

Nouveaux Eloges Historiques. [*See* Mignet, F. A. M.]

The Philosophy of Kant. 8vo. Lond., 1854. G 13 S 38

COWAN, A. M. [*See* Agriculture, Dept. of, Queensland.]

COWIE, W. G. Our Last Year in New Zealand (1887). 8vo. Lond., 1888. MD 3 Q 52

COWLEY, Capt. William Ambrosia. Voyage autour du Monde, 1683–86. (Prévost, A. F. Suite de l'histoire générale des Voyages, tome 17) 4to. Amsterdam, 1761. MD 11·P 16 †

COWPER, W. Concordance of. [*See* Neve, J,]

COWPER, Very Rev. W. M. Two Sermons upon Marriage and Divorce. 12mo. Sydney, 1888. MG 2 R 3 [*See* Barker, Rt. Rev. F.]

COX, David. Life of; by G. R. Redgrave. (Great Artists.) 8vo. Lond., 1891. C 17 Q 6

COX, Mrs. E. Poems; by "Andrewina." 18mo. Sydney (n.d.) MH 1 P 32

COX, Rev. Sir G. W. Life of J. W. Colenso, Bishop of Natal. 2 vols. 8vo. Lond,, 1888. C 12 T 5, 6
Lives of Greek Statesmen. 1st series, Solon–Themistokles; 2nd series, Ephialtes–Hermokrates. 2 vols. 12mo. Lond., 1885–86. C 1 R 43, 44

COX, Dr. J. C. Exchange List of Land and Marine Shells from Australia and the adjacent Islands. 12mo. Sydney, 1868. MA 2 T 39
Distribution of Australasian Volutes. 8vo. Sydney, 1872. MA 2 T 35

COX, S. H. Development of Mining in Australasia. 8vo. Sydney, 1888. MA 3 T 50

COX, S.H., and RATTE, F. Mines and Minerals: a Guide for the Australian Miner. 12mo. Sydney, 1885. MA 2 P 58

COX AND CO. Australian Almanac for 1858. 8vo. Sydney, 1858. ME 4 R

COXE, Henry O. Life of. [*See* Burgon, Very Rev. J. W.]

COXE, Rev. W. Memoirs of the Administration of the Rt. Hon. H. Pelham. 2 vols. 4to. Lond., 1829. C 13 P 2, 3 †

COXHEAD, J. An Essay on the Secret Springs or Primary Principles of all Human Actions. 12mo. Sydney, 1869. MG 2 P 13

COXWELL, H. My Life and Balloon Experiences. 1st and 2nd Series. 2 vols. 8vo. Lond., 1887–89. C 14 Q 25, 26

CRAIB, A. America and the Americans. 12mo. Paisley, 1892. D 15 Q 18

CRAIG, J. E. Azimuth : a Treatise on this Subject ; with a Study of the Astronomical Triangle, &c. Roy. 4to. New York, 1887. A 4 P 20 †

CRAIG, John Stirling. Why the Shoe Pinches. [*See* Meyer, H.]

CRAIG, T. Treatise on Projections. 4to. Washington, 1882. A 36 S 5 ‡

CRAIK, Prof. G. L. The New Zealanders. 12mo. Lond., 1830. MB 2 P 17

CRAMER, Dr. C. von Brühl. [*See* Brühl-Cramer, Dr. C. v.]

CRAMP, W. B. Narrative of a Voyage to India ; of a Shipwreck on Board the Lady Castlereagh ; and a Description of New South Wales. 8vo. Lond., 1823. MD 7 R 38

CRANMER, T., Archbishop of Canterbury. Life, Times, and Writings of ; by C. H. Collette. 8vo. Lond., 1887. C 10 T 22

CRANSTOUN, J. Satirical Poems of the Reformation. [*See* Scottish Text Soc.]

CRAUFURD, Rev. A. H. General Craufurd and his Light Division. 8vo. Lond., 1891. C 18 S 2

CRAUFURD, General R., and his Light Division ; by the Rev. A. H. Craufurd. 8vo. Lond., 1891. C 18 S 2

CRAVEN, Mrs. A. Life of Lady Georgiana Fullerton. 8vo. Lond., 1888. C 15 Q 25

CRAWFORD, J. M. The Kalevala : the Epic Poem of Finland. 2 vols. 8vo. New York, 1889. H 10 R 1, 2

CRAWFORD, R. Reminiscences of Foreign Travel. 8vo. Lond., 1888. D 10 R 21

CRAWFORD AND BALCARRES, J. L. Lindsay, Earl of. Bibliotheca Lindesiana : Catalogue of a Collection of English Ballads of 17th and 18th Centuries. Roy. 8vo. Aberdeen, 1890. K 8 R 12

CRAWFURD, Oswald. Round the Calendar in Portugal. Sq. 8vo. London, 1890. D 18 U 8

CRAWLEY, C. Law of Life Insurance. 8vo. Lond., 1882. F 9 S 5

CRAWLEY–BOEVEY, A. W. [*See* Boevey, A. W. Crawley-.]

CREASY, Sir E. Rise and Progress of the English Constitution. 13th edition. 8vo. Lond., 1877. B 21 S 29
Imperial and Colonial Constitutions of the Britannic Empire. 8vo. Lond., 1872. F 9 T 8

CREHORE, J. D. Mechanics of the Girder : a Treatise on Bridges and Roofs. Roy. 8vo. New York, 1886. A 6 U 18

CREIGHTON, Charles, M.D., &c. History of Epidemics in Britain from A.D. 664 to the Extinction of Plague. [Vol. 1.] 8vo. Cambridge, 1891. A 26 T 19

CREIGHTON, Prof. M. Historic Towns : Carlisle. 8vo. Lond., 1889. B 22 Q 6
[Life of] Cardinal Wolsey. 8vo. Lond., 1888. C 3 R 1
History of the Papacy during the period of the Reformation, 1464–1518. Vols. 1-4. 4 vols. 8vo. Lond., 1882–87. G 14 T 17–20

CREMORNE WALTZES, The [Music]. . Fol. Sydney (n.d.) MA 11 Q 15 †

CREW, B. J. Practical Treatise on Petroleum, comprising its Origin, Geology, &c. Roy. 8vo. Philad., 1887. A 24 V 4

CRIBB, J. W. [*See* Agriculture, Dept. of, Queensland.]

CRICHTON, D. A. The History, Uses, and Culture of the Orange, and other species of the Citrus Family. 8vo. Melb. (n.d.). MA 1 T 78

CRICKET, Chronicles of : Fac-simile Reprints of Nyren's "Cricketer's Guide," Lillywhite's "Hand-book of Cricket," Denison's "Sketches of the Players." 8vo. Lond., 1888. A 16 Q 28

CRISP, F. A. Catholic Registers of the City of Worcester. Sm. fol. Lond., 1887. B 2 Q 27 ‡

Parish Registers of Onga, Essex. Sm. fol. Privately printed. Lond., 1886. B 36 P 6 †

Registers of the French Church at Dover, Kent. Sm. fol. Lond., 1888. B 9 R 29 †

Sepulchral Memorials of Bobbingworth, Essex ; with Genealogical Notes and Pedigrees. Imp. 8vo. Privately printed, Lond., 1888. B 11 P 26 †

CRISTIANI, R. S. Perfumery and Kindred Arts : a comprehensive Treatise on Perfumery. Roy. 8vo. Philad., 1877. A 25 V 3

CRITCHLY, F. A King of Shreds and Patches : a Society Story. 8vo. Melb., 1891. MJ 2 T 23

CROCKETT, Col. D. Life of. [*See* Roche, J. J.]

CROLY, Rev. G. The Holy Land. [*See* Roberts, D.]

CROMBIE, B. W. Modern Athenians : Original Portraits of Memorable Citizens of Edinburgh. 4to. Edinb., 1882. C 42 S 16 ‡

CROMWELL, Oliver. Oliver Cromwell, the Protector : an appreciation based on Contemporary Evidence ; by R. F. D. Palgrave. 8vo. Lond., 1890. C 12 R 45

Cromwell and Washington : a contrast ; by C. Bradlaugh. 12mo. Lond., 1883. F 7 V 21

Oliver Cromwell ; by F. Harrison. (Twelve English Statesmen.) 8vo. Lond., 1888. C 15 Q 23

CROMWELL, T. The Character and Times of ; by A. Galton. 8vo. Birmingham, 1887. C 4 S 35

CROOKES, W. Researches in the Phenomena of Spiritualism. Roy. 8vo. Lond. (n.d.) G 4 S 41

CROOKSHANK, Prof. E. M. Photography of Bacteria. 8vo. Lond., 1887. A 12 T 28

Manual of Bacteriology. 3rd edition. 8vo. Lond., 1890. A 12 T 27

History and Pathology of Vaccination. 2 vols. roy. 8vo. Lond., 1889. A 12 V 21, 22

CROSBY, E. E. The Persecutions in Tonga, as narrated by onlookers, and now taking place, 1886. 8vo. Lond., 1886. MB 1 R 46

CROSLAND, Mrs. N. [*See* Hugo, V.]

CROSS, C. Sailor Jack : a tale of the Southern Seas. 8vo. Lond. (n.d.) MJ 1 S 55

CROSS, C. F., and BEVAN, E. J. Text-book of Papermaking. 8vo. Lond., 1888. A 25 Q 4

H

CROSTON, J. History of Lancaster. [*See* Baines, E.]

County Families of Lancashire and Cheshire. Roy. 8vo. Lond., 1887. B 4 V 18

CROUCH, A. P. Glimpses of Feverland ; or, a Cruise in West African Waters. 8vo. Lond., 1889. D 14 Q 7

CROUCH, G. J. Epitome of News and Miscellaneous (Gleaner. Vol. 1. 8vo. Sydney, 1859. ME 8 Q

CROWE, P. W. An examination of various Schemes of Labour and Capital. 8vo. Brisb., 1891. MF 4 Q 3

CROWEST, F. J. [Life of] Cherubini. 8vo. Lond., 1890. C 16 P 15

CROWN LANDS, IN THE AUSTRALASIAN COLONIES. Papers relating to. Fol. Lond., 1870. MF 11 Q 31 †

CROZET ISLANDS. Correspondence between Lords of the Admiralty and the Committee of Lloyd's, with respect to Her Majesty's Ships calling at the Islands between the Cape of Good Hope and Australia, to Relieve those Shipwrecked upon them. Fol. Lond., 1876. MF 12 Q 12 †

Correspondence in Regard to Her Majesty's Ships Visiting Groups of Uninhabited Islands lying on the Tracks of Vessels between Great Britain and the Australasian Colonies. Fol. Lond., 1877. MF 12 Q 12 †

CROZIER, J. B. Lord Randolph Churchill : a Study of English Democracy. 12mo. Lond., 1887. C 2 R 22

CRUICKSHANK, W. D. Strength and Construction of Steam Boilers. 8vo. Sydney, 1882. MA 1 V 64

CRUIKSHANK, George, Memoir of,: by F. G. Stephens; and an Essay on the Genius of George Cruikshank, by W. M. Thackeray. 8vo. New York, 1891. C 16 Q 15 [*See* Humourist The.]

CRUIKSHANK, I. R., and G. The Cruikshankian Momus. Imp. 8vo. Lond., 1891. J 2 U 20

CRUISE, Dr. F. R. Thomas à Kempis : Notes of a Visit to Scenes in which his Life was spent ; with some Account of the Examination of his Relics. 8vo. Lond., 1887. G 14 T 1

CRUMP, A. An Investigation into the Causes of the Great Fall in Prices which took place coincidently with the Demonetisation of Silver by Germany. Roy. 8vo. Lond., 1889. F 12 R 12

CUDMORE, P. The Civil Government of the States, and the Constitutional History of the United States. 2nd edition. 8vo. New York, 1875. B 19 T 4

Poems and Songs, Satires and Political Rings. 4th edition. 8vo. New York, 1885. H 7 P 40

CUDWORTH, Rev. R. The True Intellectual System of the Universe. 3 vols. 8vo. Lond., 1845. G 4 T 17–19

CUDWORTH, William. Life and Correspondence of Abraham Sharp, with Memorials of his Family and Associated Families. Roy. 8vo. Lond., 1889. C 12 U 2

CULCHETH, W. W. The Drainage of Melbourne. 8vo. Melb., 1881.   MA 3 Q 26

CULIN, S. China in America : a Study in the Social Life of the Chinese in the Eastern Cities of the United States. Roy. 8vo. Philad., 1887.   F 12 R 18

CULLEN, W. P. Federal Systems and Australian Federation. 8vo. Sydney, 1891.   MF 1 T 67

CULLEY, W. T. [*See* Early English Text Society.]

CULLIMORE, Dr. D. H. The Book of Climates : Acclimatization ; Climatic Diseases ; Health Resorts and Mineral Springs ; Sea Sickness ; Sea Voyages ; and Sea Bathing. 12mo. Lond., 1890.   A 26 Q 6

CULLODEN PAPERS, comprising an extensive and interesting Correspondence, 1625–1748. 4to. Lond., 1815.   B 9 P 28 †

CUMBERLAND, C. The Guinea Pig, or Domestic Cavy, for Food, Fur, and Fancy. 12mo. Lond. (n.d.)   A 27 Q 27

CUMBERLAND, R. The Brothers : a Tragedy. [*See* British Drama, Modern.]

The West Indian : a Comedy. [*See* British Drama, Modern.]

CUMBERLAND, S. C. A Thought Reader's Thoughts ; being the Impressions and Confessions of S. Cumberland. 8vo. Lond., 1888.   G 7 R 38

The Queen's Highway, from Ocean to Ocean. 8vo. Lond., 1887.   D 15 T 1

CUMMING, Miss Constance F. Gordon. Fire Fountains : the Kingdom of Hawaii ; its Volcanoes, and the History of its Missions. 2 vols. 8vo. Edinb., 1883.   MD 7 S 36, 37

Two Happy Years in Ceylon. Illustrated. 2 vols. 8vo. Edinb., 1892.   D 17 T 4, 5

CUMMING, F. The Sydney Garden Palace : a Patriotic and Historical Poem. 8vo. Sydney, 1887.   MH 1 S 60

CUMMINS, C. Book-keeping ; the Science explained, with Improved Systems for Keeping Accounts. Roy. 8vo. Dublin, 1887.   A 25 V 25

CUNNINGHAM, C. D. [*See* Adams, Sir F. O.]

CUNNINGHAM, C. D., and ABNEY, W. de W. Pioneers of the Alps. Roy. 4to. Lond., 1887.   C 3 P 9 †

CUNNINGHAM, P., Review of Two Years in New South Wales. 8vo. Lond., 1828.   MD 7 S 4

CUNNINGHAM, Sir H. S. [Life of] Earl Canning : Rulers of India. 12mo. Oxford, 1891.   C 16 P 24

CUNNINGHAM, W. The Growth of English Industry and Commerce during the Early and Middle Ages. 8vo. Camb., 1890.   B 24 T 13

The Growth of English Industry and Commerce in Modern Times. 8vo. Camb., 1892.   B 24 T 14

CUNNINGHAM, Rev. W. [*See* Free Church of Scotland.]

CUPPARI, P. Lezioni di Agricoltura. 2 vols. 8vo. Firenze, 1882.   A 1 U 16, 17

CURR, E. Petitions of the District of Port Phillip (Australia Felix) for Separation from the Territory of New South Wales. 8vo. Melb., 1844.   MF 1 Q 16

CURR, E. M. The Australian Race ; its Origin, Languages, Customs, &c. 4 vols. 8vo. and fol. Melb., 1886–87.   MA 1 R 30–32, and 2 P 18 ‡

CURRAN, Rev. J. M. Contribution to the Geology and Petrography of Bathurst, New South Wales. 8vo. Sydney, 1891.   MA 3 S 11

CURTIN, J. Empire Hotel Visitors' Guide to Sydney. 8vo. Sydney (n.d.)   MD 2 W 11

CURTIN, J. Myths and Folk-Tales of the Russians, Western Slavs, and Magyars. 8vo. Lond., 1890.   B 17 Q 8

CURTIS, G. H. Bishop Selwyn of New Zealand and of Lichfield : a Sketch of his Life and Work. 8vo. Lond., 1889.   MC 1 Q 52

CURTIS, G. T. Constitutional History of the United States, from their Declaration of Independence to the close of their Civil War. Vol. 1. 8vo. New York, 1889.   B 19 S 8

Creation or Evolution ? a Philosophical Inquiry. 8vo. Lond., 1887.   G 8 R 24

CURTIS, G. W. [*See* Motley, J. L.]

CURTIS, J. Visitor's Guide-book to Ballarat. 8vo. Ballarat, 1875.   MD 1 W 49

CURTIS, R. Homœopathy and Allopathy. 12mo. Launceston, 1890.   MA 3 P 12

Capital and Labour and Occupation of the Land. 8vo. Launceston, 1890   MF 1 T 21

CURTIS, W. E. The Capitals of Spanish America. Roy. 8vo. New York, 1888.   D 3 U 39

CURTIS'S BOTANICAL MAGAZINE. Vols. 43–47. Roy. 8vo. Lond., 1887–91.   E

CURTIUS, G. [*See* Leipziger Studien.]

CURTIUS RUFUS, Q. Historia Alexandri Magni. 8vo. Amst., 1684.   B 27 Q 23

CURZON, Hon. G. N. Persia and the Persian Question. Maps and Illustrations. 2 vols. 8vo. Lond., 1892.   D 17 U 18, 19

Russia in Central Asia in 1889 and the Anglo-Russian Question. 8vo. Lond., 1889.   D 16 U 18

CUSHING, W. Initials and Pseudonyms : a Dictionary of Literary Disguises. 2nd series. Roy. 8vo. New York, 1888.   Libr.

Anonyms : a Dictionary of Revealed Authorship. 2 vols. roy. 8vo. Lond., 1893.   Libr.

CUST, R. Les Races et les Langues de L'Océanie. 12mo. Paris, 1888.   MA 3 P 11

CUST, R. N. Linguistic and Oriental Essays; written from 1846-78. 8vo. Lond., 1880. K 12 R 30
Linguistic and Oriental Essays; written from 1847-87. 2nd series. 8vo. Lond., 1887. K 12 R 31

CUSTER, Elizabeth B. Tenting on the Plains; or, General Custer in Kansas and Texas. Roy. 8vo. Lond., 1888. D 15 U 2

CUSTER, Gen. G. A. Tenting on the Plains. [*See* Custer, Elizabeth B.]

CUTLER, T. W. A Grammar of Japanese Ornament and Design. 4to. Lond., 1880. A 40 Q 2 ‡

CUTTS, Rev. E. L. Colchester. (Historic Towns.) 8vo. Lond., 1888. B 22 Q 8

CUVIER, G. C. L. D., Baron. The Animal Kingdom. Roy. 8vo. Lond., 1854. A 28 V 10

CUVIER, G. C. L. D., Baron, and VALENCIENNES, A. Histoire Naturelle des Poissons. 22 vols. 4to. Paris, 1828-49. A 12 P 1-22 †

CZARTORYSKI, A., Prince. Memoirs of and his Correspondence with Alexander I; edited by A. Gielgud. 2 vols. 8vo. Lond., 1888. C 12 S 20, 21

D

D., F. J. [*See* Donohue, F. J.]

DADANT, Chas., and Son. [See Langstroth, L. L.]

DADELSZEN, E. J. von. New Zealand Official Handbook, 1892. 8vo. Wellington, 1892. ME 6 S

DAHLGREN, Mrs. M. V. South Sea Sketches. 12mo. Boston, 1881. D 15 Q 15

DAILY TELEGRAPH, The [*formerly the Sydney Daily Telegraph*]. 22 vols. Fol. Sydney, 1887-92. ME

DAINTREE, R. Queensland, Australia: its Territory, Climate, Products, &c. 8vo. Lond. (n.d.) MD 7 S 21

D'ALBERT, C. Bo Peep Quadrilles. Fol. Sydney (n.d.). MA 11 Q 15 †
Star of the Night Waltz. Fol. Sydney (n.d.). MA 11 Q 15 †

D'ALBERTIS, L. M. La Nouvelle-Guinée, ce que j'y ai fait, ce que j'y ai vu. 12mo. Paris, 1883. MD 7 T 13

DALDY, F. R. Colonial Copyright Acts. 8vo. Lond., 1889. F 14 T 22

DALE, PHILIP. [*See* Haviland, Mrs. Cyril.]

DALE, R. W. Impressions of Australia. 8vo. Lond., 1889. MD 1 R 7

DALHOUSIE, James Andrew Broun Ramsay, Marquess of. [Life of]; by Sir W. W. Hunter. (Rulers of India.) 8vo. Oxford, 1890. C 12 Q 36
Life of; by Capt. L. I. Trotter. (Statesmen Series.) 8vo. Lond., 1889. C 12 Q 37

DALLEY, Rt. Hon.W. B. Speech delivered in Legislative Council of New South Wales on 22nd July, 1879, on certain resolutions submitted to that Chamber, by Hon. Joseph Docker, M.L.C. 12mo. Sydney, 1879. MF 3 P 40
Speech, delivered by, at the Masonic Hall, on 20th May, 1872. 8vo. Sydney, 1872. MF 1 T 29
The Doughty Dalley's Doubtful Device; by "An Obscure Sceptic." Roy. 8vo. Sydney, 1885. MF 3 T 3

DALLINGER, W. H. [*See* Carpenter, Dr. W. B.]

DALRYMPLE, Alexander. Voyage dans la Mer du Sud, par les Espagnols et les Hollandois. 8vo. Paris, 1774. MD 1 R 37

D'ALVIELLA, G., Count. Origin and Growth of the Conception of God as illustrated by Anthropology and History. (Hibbert Lectures, 1891.) 8vo. Lond., 1892. G 12 S 41

DALTON, C. History of the Wrays of Glentworth, 1523-1852. 2 vols. 8vo. Lond., 1880-81. C 10 U 35, 36

DALY, A. [Peg] Woffington: a Tribute to the Actress and the Woman. 2nd ed. 4to. New York, 1890. C 17 U 15

DALY, Mrs. D. D. Digging, Squatting, and Pioneering Life in the Northern Territory of South Australia. 8vo. Lond., 1887. MD 6 T 6

DALY, J. B. The Dawn of Radicalism. 12mo. Lond., 1892. F 9 U 34
Ireland in '98: Sketches of the Principal Men of the Time; based upon the works of Dr. R. R. Madden. 8vo. London., 1888. B 11 R 21
Ireland in the Days of Dean Swift. 8vo. Lond., 1887. B 29 Q 11

DALY, J. G. The South Australian Justices' Manual, compiled for the Information and Guidance of Magistrates, their Clerks, &c. 8vo. Adelaide, 1871. MF 2 T 58

DALY, Rt. Rev. R. Memoir of; by Mrs. H. Madden. 8vo. Lond., 1875. C 22 P 2

DALZIEL, H. British Dogs: History, Characteristics, Points, &c. 2nd ed. 2 vols. 8vo. Lond., 1888-89. A 14 T 40, 41

DAMM, C. T. Novum Lexicon Græcum; cura J. M. Duncan. 4to. Lond., 1827. K 16 U 22
Novum Lexicon Græcum. 2 vols. 8vo. Glasgow, 1833. K 16 T 27, 28

DAMPIER, Capt. William. Life and Voyages of. 12mo. Edinb., 1831. MC 1 S 7
[Life of]; by W. C. Russell. (English Men of Action.) 12mo. Lond., 1889. C 12 P 30

DANA; Prof. Jas. D. Characteristics of Volcanoes, with Contributions of Facts and Principles from the Hawaiian Islands. 8vo. Lond., 1890. MA 2 R 40
Manual of Geology, with Special Reference to American Geological History. 8vo. Philad., 1863. A 24 T 6
System of Mineralogy; aided by G. J. Brush. 5th ed. Roy. 8vo. Lond., 1883. A 24 V 17

Free Public Library, Sydney

DANCE (—). Dance's Veterinary Tablet; being a Synopsis of Diseases of Horses, Cattle, and Dogs; with their Cause, Symptoms, and Cure. [Folded] 12mo. (n.p.n.d.)
MA 2 P 77

DANGAR, H. Index and Directory to Map of the Country bordering upon the River Hunter; with ground-plan and allotments of King's Town, New South Wales: containing a detail of the annual Quit Rent, and amount of the redemption of the same; also, historical notes upon the tenure and principle of granting lands in the Colony since 1810. 8vo. Lond., 1828. MD 7 R 11

DANIELL, C. J. The Industrial Competition of Asia: an Inquiry into the Influence of Currency on the Empire in the East. 8vo. Lond., 1890. F 4 Q 19

DANIELL, G. W. [Life of] Bishop Wilberforce. 8vo. Lond., 1891. C 15 Q 9

DANIELSSEN, D. C [See Koren, J.]

DANSK TOTAL AFHOLDS BLADET BLAD. 4to. Fredagen, 1886. F 40 S 7 ‡

DANSON, J. T. Observations on the Speech of Sir W. Molesworth in the House of Commons, 25th July, 1848, on Colonial Expenditure and Government. 8vo. Lond., 1848. MF 2 T 3

DANTE ALIGHIERI. The Banquet (Il Convito): translated by Katharine Hillard. 8vo. Lond., 1889. G 13 R 41

La Commedia di; col commento inedito di S. Talice da Ricaldone. 4to. Torino, 1886. H 40 S 15 ‡

Commedia and Canzoniere; translated by Rev. E. H. Plumptre. 2 vols. 8vo. Lond., 1886-87. H 7 V 6, 7

Concordance of. [See Fay. E. A.]

Dante and his Early Biographers; by E. Moore. 8vo. Lond., 1890. C 12 R 8

Divina Commedia; translated by F. K. H. Haselfoot. 8vo. Lond., 1887. H 8 U 35

The Hell of; translated by A. T. Butler. 8vo. Lond., 1892. H 9 P 11

Illustrations and Notes; illustrations by Phœbe A. Traquair, notes by J. S. Black. 8vo. Edinb., 1890. H 9 S 25

Introduction to the Study of Dante; by J. A. Symonds. 8vo. Edinb., 1890. C 12 R 9

Readings on the Purgatorio of Dante; by Hon. W. W. Vernon. 2 vols. 8vo. Lond., 1889. H 8 Q 42, 43

Textual Criticism. [See Moore, Rev. E.]

[See Hettinger, F.]

DARE, Ishmael. [See Jose, A. W.]

DAREMBERG, C. [See Celsus, A. C.]

DARLEY, C. W. Notes on Drilling and Boring Artesian Wells, as practised in the United States of America. Roy. 8vo. Sydney, 1884. MA 3 R 20

DARMESTETER, A. De la Création actuelle de Mots Nouveaux dans la langue Française, et des lois qui la régissent. 8vo. Paris, 1877. K 16 Q 27

DARMESTETER, J. [See Müller, F. Max; Sacred Books, vols. 4, 23.]

DARWIN, C. Darwin and his Works: a Biological and Metaphysical Study; by H.A.S. 8vo. Lond., 1888. A 29 P 2

The Descent of Man. 2nd ed. 8vo. Lond., 1881. A 18 Q 30

Expression of the Emotions in Man and Animals. 2nd ed. 8vo. Lond., 1890. A 26 Q 3

Geological Observations on the Volcanic Islands and parts of South America visited during the Voyage of H.M.S. "Beagle." 2nd ed. 8vo. Lond., 1876. A 24 R 10

Life and Letters of; including an Autobiographical Chapter; edited by his son, F. Darwin. 2nd ed. 3 vols. 8vo. Lond., 1887. C 12 S 2-5

Structure and Distribution of Coral Reefs. 2nd ed. 8vo. Lond., 1874. A 24 R 5

Variation of Animals and Plants under Domestication. 2nd ed. 2 vols. 8vo. Lond., 1875. A 27 R 30, 31

DARWIN, F. [See Darwin, C.]

DARYL, P. Ireland's Disease: Notes and Impressions. 8vo. Lond., 1888. D 18 Q 1

DAS, D. N. Sketches of Hindoo Life. 8vo. Lond., 1887. D 17 Q 3

DASENT, G. W. Story of Burnt Njal, or Life in Iceland at the End of the Tenth Century. 2 vols. 8vo. Edinb., 1861. B 20 S 10, 11

Icelandic Grammar. [See Rask, E.]

D'ASSIER, A. Posthumous Humanity: a Study of Phantoms; translated and annotated by H. S. Olcott. 8vo. Lond., 1887. G 8 Q 31

D'AUBIGNE, J. H. Merle. [See Merle, D'Aubigné, J. H.]

DAUDET, A. Robert Helmont: Diary of a Recluse, 1870-71. 8vo. Lond., 1888. J 6 U 11

Sappho: Parisian Manners. 8vo. Paris, 1887. J 5 Q 40

Tartarin of Tarascon: Traveller, "Turk," and Lion-hunter. 8vo. Lond., 1887. J 5 V 39

Thirty Years of Paris, and of my Literary Life. 8vo. Lond., 1888. C 12 Q 4

D'AULNOY, Marie C. J. [See Aulnoy, Marie C. J. d'.]

DAVENANT, Sir W. The Wits: a Comedy. [See British Drama, Ancient. Vol. 1.]

DAVENPORT, Carrie. Toothsome Dishes: fish, flesh, and fowl; soups, sauces, and sweets. 2nd ed. 12mo. Lond. (n.d.) A 22 Q 7

DAVENPORT, I. E. and W. H. Davenport Brothers and Prof. W. M. M. Fay: a Short Sketch of the Lives, Travels, and Performances of the Brothers Davenport and Prof. Fay; by J. H. Jenkins. 8vo. Tamworth, 1877. MC 1 Q 44

DAVENPORT, Robert. Works of; edited by A. H. Bullen. (Old English Plays.) Sm. 4to. Lond., 1890. H 4 T 3

The City Night Cap: a Tragi-comedy. [*See* British Drama, Ancient.]

DAVEY, R. History of Mourning. 4to. Lond., 1889. B 42 S 13‡

DAVID, the Shepherd King: a Book for the Bush; by "Hippocampus." 12mo. Melb., 1867. MJ 1 U 11

DAVID, T. W. E. Geology of the Vegetable Creek Tin-mining Field. (Geol. Survey, N.S.W.) Roy. 4to. Sydney, 1887.* MA 2 Q 21 †

Origin of the Laterite in the New England District of New South Wales. 8vo. Sydney, 1888. MA 3 T 49

DAVIDS, T. W. R. Questions of King Milinda. [*See* Müller, F. M.]

[*See* Müller, F. Max; Sacred Books of the East, 11, 13, 17, 20.]

DAVIDSON, Dr. Andrew. Geographical Pathology: an inquiry into the Geographical Distribution of Infective and Climatic Diseases. 2 vols. roy. 8vo. Edinb., 1892. A 26 U 26, 27

Another Copy. 2 vols. roy. 8vo. Edinb., 1892. MA 3 R 18, 19

DAVIDSON, A. F. [*See* Dumas, A.]

DAVIDSON, J. [*See* Montesquieu, C. de S.]

DAVIDSON, Rev. R. T., and BENHAM, Rev. W. Life of Archibald Campbell Tait, Archbishop of Canterbury. 2 vols. 8vo. Lond., 1891. C 14 T 20, 21

DAVIDSON, S. The Canon of the Bible. 12mo. Lond., 1877. G 13 Q 33

The New Testament. 8vo. Lond., 1875. G 16 T 20

DAVIES, D. C. Treatise on Earthy and other Minerals and Mining. 2nd ed. 8vo. Lond., 1888. A 24 Q 13

Treatise on Metalliferous Minerals and Mining. 4th ed. 8vo. Lond., 1888. A 24 Q 14

DAVIES, H. [*See* Wise, B. R.]

DAVIES, Rev. J. Catullus, Tibullus, and Propertius. (Ancient Classics for English Readers.) 12mo. Edinb., 1880. J 14 P 5

Hesiod, and Theognis. (Ancient Classics for English Readers.) 12mo. Edinb., 1881. J 14 P 11

D'AVIGDON, E. H. Antipodean Notes, collection on a Nine Months' Tour round the World; by "Wanderer." 8vo. Lond., 1888. MD 5 Q 45

DAVIS, A. H. [*See* Cæsar, C. J.]

DAVIS, Elizabeth. Autobiography of; by Jane Williams. 2 vols. 8vo. Lond 1857. C 16 R 7, 8

DAVIS, G. B. Outlines of International Law. 8vo. Lond., 1888. F 5 U 39

DAVIS, G. E. Practical Microscopy. 8vo. Lond., 1889. A 29 U 3

DAVIS, H. F. A. Building Societies, their Theory, Practice, and Management. 12mo. Melb., 1887. MF 3 P 52

Guide to the Trade Disputes, Conciliation, and Arbitration Act, 1892. 12mo. Sydney, 1892. MF 3 P 53

Law and Practice of Friendly Societies, and Trade Unions; with Official Regulations, Rules and Forms. 8vo. Lond., 1876. F 9 S 8

DAVIS, Lieut.-Col. J. History of the Second, Queen's Royal Regiment, now the Queen's (Royal West Surrey) Regiment. Vol 1. The English Occupation of Tangiers, 1661-84. Roy. 8vo. Lond., 1887. B 5 V 38

DAVIS, John. Mormonism: or the Doctrines of the Self-Styled Latter-day Saints compared with itself, and the Bible. 12mo. Sydney, 1857. MG 2 P 48

DAVIS, J. [*See* Imbert de Saint-Amand, A. L., Baron.]

DAVIS, J. [*See* Cicero, M. T.]

DAVIS, J. D. Contributions towards a Bibliography of New Zealand. 12mo. Wellington, 1887. MK 1 P 41

DAVIS, J. R. A. Text-book of Biology; comprising Vegetable and Animal Morphology and Physiology. 8vo. Lond., 1888. A 14 Q 61

DAVIS, L. C. The Story of the Memorial Fountain to Shakspeare at Stratford-upon-Avon. 8vo. Lond., 1890. J 12 Q 33

DAVIS, M. D. [*See* Anglo-Jewish Historical Exhibition.]

DAVIS, N. D. The Cavaliers and Roundheads of Barbados, 1650-52. 8vo. Georgetown, 1887. B 1 S 51

Mr. Froude's Negrophobia; or, Don Quixote as a Cook's Tourist. 8vo. Demerara, 1888. D 15 S 7

DAVIS, Thomas. Memoirs of an Irish Patriot, 1840-46; by Sir C. G. Duffy. 8vo. Lond., 1890. C 14 T 19

DAVISON, C. F. Case of the Boers in the Transvaal. 2nd ed. 8vo. Lond., 1881. F 8 S 26

DAWHORN, F. W. State School Geography, arranged to suit the new programme of Instruction for State Schools in Victoria. 2nd ed. 8vo. Melb., 1890. MD 2 W 2

DAWE, W. Zantha. 12mo. Melb., 1886. MJ 1 P 62

Love and the World, and other poems. 12mo. Melb., 1886. MH 1 Q 49

DAWE, W. C. The Golden Lake; or, the Marvellous History of a Journey through the great Lone Land of Australia. 2nd thous. 12mo. Lond., 1890. MJ 2 T 8

DAWKINS, W. B. Cave-hunting: Researches on the evidence of Caves respecting the early inhabitants of Europe. 8vo. Lond., 1874. A 9 T 12

DAWSON, E. C. Last Journals of Bishop Hannington. [*See* Hannington, Rt. Rev. J.]

DAWSON, G. Shakespeare and other Lectures; edited by G. St. Clair. 8vo. Lond., 1888. J 5 R 36

DAWSON, G. M. Mineral Wealth of British Columbia, 8vo. Montreal, 1888. A 24 V 12

DAWSON, H. Life of H. Dawson, Landscape Painter, 1811–78 ; with Plates from some of his works. 4to. Lond., 1891.   C 40 Q 17 ‡

DAWSON, Sir J. W. Acadian Geology : An Account of the Geological Structure, and Mineral Resources of Nova Scotia. 8vo. Edinb., 1855.   A 24 P 9

Geological History of Plants. (Int. Science Series.) 8vo. Lond., 1888.   A 24 Q 4

DAWSON, W. H. German Socialism and Ferdinand Lassalle. 8vo. Lond., 1888.   F 14 P 6

Bismarck and State Socialism. 8vo. Lond., 1890.   F 14 P 7

DAY, A. Treatise on Harmony ; edited by Prof. G. A. Macfarran. Roy. 8vo. Lond., 1885.   A 8 R 37

DAY, Capt. C. R. Descriptive Catalogue of the Musical Instruments recently exhibited at the Royal Military Exhibition, London, 1890. Roy. 8vo. Lond., 1891.   A 8 R 39

DAY, F. British and Irish Salmonidæ. Imp. 8vo. Lond., 1887.   A 28 V 1

DAY, Lewis F. Text Books of Ornamental Design : Nature in Ornament. 8vo. Lond., 1892.   A 23 Q 30

The Anatomy of Pattern. 8vo. Lond., 1887.   A 23 Q 1

The Planning of Ornament. 8vo. Lond., 1887.   A 8 P 46

DAYTON, W. T. [*See* Stuart, Prof. T. P. A.]

DEACON'S BOOK OF DATES. [*See* Yonge, C. M.]

DEACON, Hon. A. [*See* Victoria.—Water Supply.]

DE AMICIS, E. Alle Porte d'Italia. 8vo. Milano, 1888.   D 18 R 18

DEAN, W. B. Notorious Bushrangers of Tasmania, by "Cabby." 12mo. Launceston, 1891.   MB 2 P 47

DEATH, J. The Beer of the Bible, one of the hitherto unknown Leavens of Exodus. 8vo. Lond., 1887.   G 8 T 25

DE BARY, Prof. A. Comparative Anatomy of the Vegetable Organs of the Phanerogams and Ferns. Roy. 8vo. Oxford, 1884.   A 20 V 19

Comparative Morphology and Biology of the Fungi, Mycetozoa and Bacteria ; revised by I. B. Balfour. Roy. 8vo. Oxford, 1887.   A 4 V 15

Lectures on Bacteria ; revised by I. B. Balfour. 2nd ed. 8vo. Oxford, 1887.   A 20 Q 1

DE BEAUVOIR, L. Marquis de. [*See* Beauvoir, L. Marquis de.]

DEBRETT'S Peerage, Baronetage, Knightage, &c., 2 vols. 8vo. Lond., 1891–92.   E

DE BROGLIE, A. Duc. [*See* Broglie, A. Duc de.]

DEBTS AND ASSETS OF AUSTRALASIA. Roy. 8vo. Sydney, 1884.   MF 1 S 2

DE BURY. R. [*See* Bury, Rt. Rev. R. de.]

DE CANDOLLE. [*See* Candolle.]

DE CAYLUS, Marquise. [*See* Caylus, Marquise de.]

DE CHAMISSO, L. C. A. [*See* Chamisso, L. C. A. de.]

DE COSSON, E. A. The Cradle of the Blue Nile. 2 vols. (in 1.) 8vo. Lond., 1877.   D 14 R 8

DEICHMANN, H. Baroness [*See* Stackelberg, Baroness.]

DETTERS, Dr. H. Johannes Brahms : a Biographical Sketch ; translated by Rosa Newmarch. 8vo. Lond., 1888.   C 12 Q 20

DEKKER, T. Best Plays ; edited by E. Rhys. (Mermaid Series ; edited by H. Ellis.) Lond., 1887.   H 4 Q 23

The Shoemaker's Holiday.—The Honest Whore.—Old Fortunatus.—The Witch of Edmonton.

The Honest Whore : a Comedy. [*See* British Drama, Ancient.]

The Roaring Girl : a Comedy. [*See* Middleton, T.]

DELABAUME, P. La Nouvelle-Calédonie devant la France. Roy. 8vo. Paris, 1886.   MD R 15

DELAFIELD, J. Origin of the Antiquities of America. 4to. New York, 1839.   B 13 P 6 †

DE LAGNY, G. The Knout and the Russians. 8vo. Lond., 1854.   D 7 Q 2

DE LAMARTINE, A. [*See* Lamartine, A. de.]

DELAMBRE, J. B. J. Astronomie, Théorique et Pratique. 3 vols. 4to. Paris, 1814.   A 19 V 10–12

DE LEON, Edwin. Thirty Years of my Life on Three Continents. 2 vols. 8vo. Lond., 1890.   C 16 T 4, 5

DE LISSA, A. Bankruptcy and Insolvent Law, Proposal of a New System, &c. 8vo. Sydney, 1881.   MF 2 T 24

DELOUIS, C. Les Saules, paroles de Marcel Delouis. [A song.] English words by Gerald Marr Thompson. Fol. Sydney, 1892.   MA 7 Q 31 †

DE MAISTRE, Xavier, Comte. [*See* Maistre, X. de, Comte.]

DE MARBOT, Baron. [*See* Marbot, Baron de.]

D'EMDEN, H. J. The Parliamentary Guide ; a Manual for the Electors of both Houses of the Parliament of Tasmania. 8vo. Hobart, 1856.   MF 1 T 27

DE MEISSAS, l'Abbé. [*See* Meissas, l'Abbé de.]

DEMON McGUIRE, The. [A Poem.] 4to. Sydney, (n.d.)   MH 1 T 17

DE MORNAY, A. A. A Grammar of the English Language, based on Organic Principles. 8vo. Melb., 1873.   MK 1 P 66

DEMOSTHENES ; by Rev. W. J. Brodribb. (Ancient Classics for English Readers.) 12mo. Edinb., 1880.   J 14 P 7

Demosthenis quae supersunt ; edidit J. J. Reiske ; curante G. H. Schaefero. 9 vols. 8vo. Lond., 1822–23.   F 3 P 17–25

DEMOSTHENES—*contd.*

Olynthiacs of ; edited by the Rev. H. M. Wilkins. 8vo. Lond., 1860. F 2 U 30

Opera ; recensuit Græce et Latine ; edidit Dr. J. T. Vœmelius. Imp. 8vo. Paris, 1849. F 9 V 1

Orationes ; edidit I. Bekker. 2 vols. 8vo. Lipsiæ, 1854. F 1 Q 29, 30

DEMPSEY, G. D. On the Drainage of Lands, Towns, and Buildings ; revised by D. K. Clark. 8vo. Lond., 1887. A 22 Q 29

DENDY, A., and LUCAS, A. H. S. Introduction to the Study of Botany, with a special chapter on some Australian Natural Orders. 8vo. Melb.. 1892. MA 3 P 34

DENISON, Rt. Hon. E, [*See* Blackmore, E. G.]

DENISON, W. Denison's "Sketches of the Players." [*See* Cricket, Chronicles of.]

DENISON, H. [*See* Shakespeare, W.]

DENISON, Leut.-Gen Sir W. T., K.C.B., &c. Remarks on "Essays and Reviews." 8vo. Madras, 1862. G 3 T 20

The Suez Canal ; edited by J. Forrest. 8vo. Lond., 1867. A 6 S 32

DENHAM, M. A. Slogans of the North of England. 12mo. Newcastle-upon-Tyne, 1851. B 22 Q 23

DENNETT, R. E. Seven Years among the Fjort ; being an English Trader's experiences in the Congo District. 8vo. Lond. 1887. D 14 P 1

DENNING, W. F. Telescopic Work for Starlight Evenings. 8vo. Lond., 1891. A 19 S 26

DENNIS, L. M. Methods of Gas Analysis. [*See* Hempel, Prof. W.]

DENNIS, R. Industrial Ireland : a Practical and Non-political View of "Ireland for the Irish." 8vo. Lond., 1887. F 5 Q 40

DENT, C. T. Mountaineering. (Badminton Lib.) 8vo. Lond., 1892. A 29 R 14

DENTON, S. F. Incidents of a Collector's Rambles in Australia, New Zealand, and New Guinea. 8vo. Boston, 1889. MD 1 R 8

DENTON, Rev. W. England in the 15th Century. 8vo. Lond., 1888. B 22 U 5

DENTON, W., and Elizabeth M. F. The Soul of Things ; or, Psychometric Researches and Discoveries. 3 vols. 8vo. Wellesley, 1884. G 7 R 31–33

DEPEW, C. M. Orations and After-dinner Speeches. 8vo. Lond., 1890. J 9 S 5

DEPLANCHE, E. [*See* Vieillard.]

DEPPE (—). Deppe's Principles of Pianoforte-Playing. [*See* Ehrenfichter, C. A.]

DE QUINCEY, Thomas. De Quincey Memorials, being letters and other records here first published ; edited by Dr. A. H. Japp. 2 vols. 8vo. Lond., 1891. C 16 T 6, 7

Suspiria de Profundis, with other essays. 8vo. Lond., 1891. J 5 P 2

DERBY, Edward, third Earl of. Correspondence of. [*See* Chetham Soc., 19.]

DERBY, E. G. G. Smith Stanley, fourteenth Earl of. Life of ; by T. E. Kebbel. (Statesmen Series.) 8vo. Lond., 1890. C 12 R 36

[Life of] ; by G. Saintsbury. 12mo. Lond., 1892. C 13 Q 22

DE RÉMUSAT, P. [*See* Rémusat, P. de.]

DE ROOS, Lieut., Hon. F. F. Personal Narrative of Travels in the United States and Canada in 1826. 8vo. Lond., 1827. D 15 T 6

DE SAINT-PIERRE. [*See* Saint-Pierre, de.]

DESAIX, Gén. L. C. A. Généraux des Vingt Ans. 8vo. Paris, 1891. C 18 S 14

DE SALIS, Mrs. Harriet A. Cakes and Confections à la mode. 12mo. Lond., 1889. A 22 Q 10

DESCARTES, R. Principia Philosophiæ. Sm. 4to. Amstelodami, 1677. A 29 S 7

Passiones Animæ. Sm. 4to. Amst., 1677. A 29 S 7

DESCENDANTS OF RUSSIAN CZARS in Wandsworth. 12mo. Lond., 1889. B 25 Q 5

DE SENANCOUR, E. P. [*See* Senancour, E. P. de.]

DE SÉVIGNÉ, Mme. [*See* Sévigné, Mme. de.]

DESGRAZ, C. [*See* Vincendon-Dumoulin, C. A.]

DESGUIN, Dr. V. De l'Abus des Boissons Alcooliques. 8vo. Anvers, 1878. F 11 R 14

DESPREAUX, Mons. [*See* Longinus.]

DESPREY, L. [*See* Horatius Flaccus, Q.]

DE STENDHAL. [*See* Stendhal, de.]

DESTY, R. Constitution of the United States. 2nd ed. ; with supplement and table of cases by A. Brunner. 12mo. San Francisco, 1887. F 2 P 36

DETHICK, H. Visitation of Middlesex. [*See* Foster, J.]

DETHLEFSEN, P. Den alkoholiske Eklampsi. 8vo. Kjöbenhavn, 1885. F 11 Q 53

DE TOCQUEVILLE. [*See* Tocqueville, de.]

DEVAS, C. S. Political Economy. (Manuals of Catholic Philosophy.) 12mo. Lond., 1892. F 9 U 35

DE VERE, A. Essays, chiefly on Poetry. 2 vols. 12mo. Lond., 1887. H 5 S 41; 42

DEVEY, Louisa. Life of Rosina, Lady Lytton ; with Extracts from her M.S. Autobiography. 8vo. Lond., 1887. C 12 S 19

DEVIL, The: who and what is he? or, the Origin of Evil; by "Clericus Anglicanus." 8vo. Melb., 1888.
M G 1 Q 43

DE VIT, Dr. V. [*See* Forcellini, A.]

DEVON, F. Issue Roll of Thomas de Brantingham, Lord High Treasurer, 1370. (Record Com. Pubs.) Roy. 8vo. Lond., 1835.
B 15 T 29

Issues of the Exchequer during the Reign of King James I. (Record Com. Pubs.) Roy. 8vo. Lond., 1836.
B 15 T 28

Issues of the Exchequer; being a Collection of Payments made out of His Majesty's Revenue, from Henry III. to Henry VI. inclusive. (Record Com. Pubs.) Roy. 8vo. Lond., 1837.
B 15 T 27

DEWAR, J. On the Application of Sulphurous Acid, Gaseous and Liquid, to the Prevention, Limitation, and Cure of Contagious Diseases. 8vo. Sydney. 1868.
MA 2 Q 67

D'EWES, J. China, Australia, and the Pacific Islands, in 1853–56. 8vo. Lond., 1857.
MD 2 W 1

DEWEY, M. Tables and Index of the Decimal Classification for Cataloging. 8vo. Boston, 1888.
Libr.

DE WINDT, H. [*See* Windt, H. de.]

DE WINT, P. Memoir of; by W. Armstrong. Ob. 4to. Lond., 1888.
C 1 R 30†

DE WITT, C. [*See* Witt, C. de.]

DIBBLE, S. History of the Sandwich Islands. 12mo. Lahainaluna, 1843.
MB 2 P 48

DIBDEN, J. C. Annals of the Edinburgh Stage, with an Account of the Rise and Progress of Dramatic Writing in Scotland. 4to. Edinb., 1888.
B 13 S 17

DICEY, Prof. A. V. The Privy Council. (The Arnold Prize Essay, 1860.) 8vo. Lond., 1887.
F 6 P 45

DICK, W. B. Encyclopedia of Practical Receipts and Processes. 5th ed. New York, 1892.
K 4 S 20

DICKENS, Charles. Childhood and Youth of; by R. Langton. 8vo. Lond., 1891.
C 15 Q 17

Charles Dickens and the Stage: a Record of his connection with the Drama as Playwright, Actor, and Critic; by T. E. Pemberton. 8vo. Lond., 1888.
C 12 R 41

Dickens' Dictionary. [*See* Pierce, G. A.]

Letters of, to Wilkie Collins, 1851–1870. 12mo. Lond., 1892.
C 17 Q 16

Pickwick Papers. (National Phonographic Library.) 2 vols. 12mo. Lond. (n.d.)
J 7 R 49, 50

[*See* Kitten, F. G. and Proctor, R. A.]

DICKERSON, E. N. Joseph Henry and the Magnetic Telegraph: an Address. 8vo. New York, 1885.
A 21 S 4

DICKINS, F. V. [*See* Chiushingura.]

DICKINSON, R. Summary of the Constitution and Procedure of Foreign Parliaments. 2nd ed. 8vo. Lond., 1890.
F 9 S 7

DICKSON, T. [*See* Scotland.]

DICKSON, W. G. Gleanings from Japan. 8vo. Edinb., 1889.
D 16 U 5

DICKSON, W. P. [*See* Mommsen, T.]

DICTIONNAIRE ABRÉGÉ TAHITIEN-FRANÇAIS. 12mo. (n.p. n.d.)
MK 2 P 1

DICTIONNAIRE TOGA-FRANÇAIS ET FRANÇAIS-TOGA-ANGLAIS précédé d'une Grammaire et de quelques Notes sur l'Archipel par les Missionnaires Maristes, revu et mis en ordre par le P. A. Colomb. 8vo. Paris, 1890.
MK 1 T 10

DIDEROT, D. Jaques le Fataliste et son maître. (Collection Jannet Picard.) 12mo. Paris (n.d.)
J 15 Q 30

La Religieuse Madame de la Carlière. (Collection Jannet Picard.) 12mo. Paris (n.d.)
J 15 Q 31

Le Neveu de Rameau. (Collection Jannet Picard.) 12mo. Paris (n.d.)
J 15 Q 32

Œuvres Philosophiques. 6 vols. 8vo. Amst., 1772.
J 16 R 1–6

  1. Essai sur le Mérite et la Vertu.—Code de la Nature, ou le Véritable Esprit de ses Loix.—Mémoire pour servir à la Béatification d'Abraham Chaumeix.
  2. Pensées Philosophiques.—Épitre philosophique à un Philosophe.—Pensées sur l'Interprétation de la Nature.—Lettre sur les Aveugles, à l'Usage de ceux qui voient.—Lettre sur les Sourds et Muets, à l'Usage de ceux qui entendent et qui parlent.
  3. Le Père de Famille: Comédie en cinq Actes.—De la Poésie dramatique.
  4. Le Fils Naturel: ou, les Epreuves de la Vertu: Comédie; avec l'Histoire véritable de la Pièce.
  5. Les Bijoux indiscrets.
  6. Traité du Beau.—De la Philosophie des Chinois.—Principes d'Acoustique.

Pensées Philosophiques. (Collection Jannet Picard.) 12mo. Paris (n.d.)
G 4 V 5

[*See* Scherer, E.]

DIDIER, E. L. Life and Letters of Madame Bonaparte. 8vo. Lond., 1879.
C 17 Q 15

DIDON, Rev. Father. Jesus Christ. 2 vols. 8vo. Lond., 1891.
G 12 S 32, 33

DIESING, Dr. K. M. Sechzehn Gattungen von Binnenwürmern und ihre arten. 4to. Wien, 1855.
A 42 R 12 ‡

Neunzehn Arten von Trematoden. 4to. Wien, 1856.
A 42 R 12 ‡

DIETERICH, U. W. Ausführliche Schwedische Grammatik. 8vo. Stockholm, 1840.
K 16 P 33

DIEZ, F. Grammatik der Romanischen Sprachen. 3 vols. 8vo. Bonn, 1856–60.
K 12 V 24–26

Etymologisches Wörterbuch der Romanischen Sprachen. 2 vols. 8vo. Bonn, 1861–62.
K 12 V 27, 28

DIGBY, G. Elvira: a Comedy. [*See* British Drama, Ancient.]

DIGBY, K. E. Introduction to the History of the Law of Real Property. 3rd ed. 8vo. Oxford, 1884.
F 9 S 17

DILKE, Sir C. W., Bart. The British Army. 8vo. Lond., 1888, F 9 S 6
The Present Position of European Politics ; or, Europe in 1887. 8vo. Lond., 1887. F 12 Q 31

DILKE, Sir C. W., Bart., and WILKINSON, S. Imperial Defence. 12mo. Lond., 1892. F 39 U 30

DILLENIUS, J. J. Horti Elthamenis Plantarum Rariorum Icones et Nomina. 2 vols. Fol. Lugd. Bat., 1774. A 40 P 3, 4 ‡

DILLON, Capt. P. Voyage aux Iles de la Mer du Sud, 1827-28. 2 vols. 8vo. Paris, 1830. MD 1 R 35, 36

DILLON, W. Life of John Mitchel. 2 vols. 8vo. Lond., 1888. C 12 T 1, 2

DINDORF, Ludovic. [*See* Sophocles, Dion Chrysostomus, Estienne, H., and Euripides.]

DINDORF, William. [*See* Estienne, H.]

DINGLEY, or DINELEY, T. [*See* Beaufort, Duke of.]

DIO. [*See* Morton, Mrs. A.]

DIODORUS SICULUS. Bibliothecæ Historicæ libri quindecim de quadraginta. [Greek text.] Fol. Augsburg, 1559. B 39 S 7 ‡

DIOGENES LAERTIUS. De Vitis clarorum Philosophorum, Libri X. 12mo. Vienna, 1616. G 16 P 4
De Vitis Dogmatis et Apophthegmatis eorum qui in Philosophia Claruerunt, libri X. Fol. Lond., 1664. G 39 S 2 ‡
De Vitis Philosophorum libri X. [Greek text, 2 in 1.] 12mo. Lipsiæ, 1833. G 9 U 3

DION CASSIUS. Historiæ Romanæ libri XLVI. [Gr. et Lat.] Fol. Hanoviæ, 1606. B 39 S 1 ‡
Romanarum Historiarum Libri 23. [Editio princeps. Greek Text.] Fol. Lutetiæ, 1548. B 39 S 5 ‡

DION CHRYSOSTOMUS. Orationes ; recognovit L. Dindorfius. 12mo. Lipsiæ, 1857. F 14 Q 12

DIONYSIUS HALICARNASSENSIS. Scripta quae exstant omnia. [Gr. et Lat.] Fol. Francofurti, 1586. B 39 S 10 ‡
[*See* Fortunatianus, C.]

DISTANT, W. L. A Naturalist in the Transvaal. 8vo. Lond., 1892. A 27 T 36

DITCHFIELD. P. H. Old English Sports, Pastimes, and Customs. A 29 P 17

DITTMAR, Prof. W. Exercises in Quantitative Chemical Analysis; with a short Treatise on Gas Analysis. Roy. 8vo. Lond., 1887. A 21 V 2

DIXON, C. Stray Feathers from Many Birds. 8vo. Lond., 1890. A 27 U 24

DIXON, Capt. George. Voyage Autour du Monde, et Principalement à la Côte Nord-Ouest de l'Amérique, 1785-88. 2 vols. 8vo. Paris, 1789. MD 1 R 38, 39

DIXON, J H. Gairloch ; its Records. Traditions, Inhabitants and Natural History ; with a Guide to Gairloch and Loch Maree. 8vo. Edinb., 1886. B 13 R 24

DIXON, R. Map of the Colony of New South Wales, exhibiting the Situation and Extent of the Appropriated Lands. [Folded.] 8vo. (n.p. n.d.) MD 7 S 23

DIXON, Rev. R. W. History of the Church of England, 1529-58. 4 vols. 8vo. Lond., 1878-91. G 2 R 23-26

DIXON, T. [*See* Schncideberg, Dr. O.]

DIXON, W. A. On Saltbush and Native Fodder Plants of New South Wales. 8vo. Sydney, 1880. MA 3 T 53

DJÉMAL-EDDIN-MOHAMMED. Alfiyya ; ou, la Quintessence de la Grammaire Arabe : Ouvrage de Djémaleddin-Mohammed, connu sous le nom d'Ebn-Malec ; publié en original, avec un Commentaire, par le Baron Silvestre de Sacy. Roy. 8vo. Paris, 1833. K 13 R 25

DOBELL, B. Memoir of James Thomson. [*See* Thomson, J.]

DOBSON, A. [*See* Fielding H.]

DOBSON, A. D. Timaru Water Supply. 8vo. Lond. (n.d.) MA 1 V 60

DOBSON, Capt. Statement of. [*See* Carron, W.]

DOBSON, George. Russia's Railway Advance into Central Asia. 8vo. Lond., 1890. D 17 Q 7

DOBSON, G. S. [*See* Lysias.]

DOBSON, W. T. History of the Bassandyne Bible, the first printed in Scotland ; with Notices of the Early Printers of Edinburgh. 8vo. Edinb., 1887. G 12 P 30

DOCKER, E. B. Hymns of the Kingdom. 12mo. Sydney, 1876. MH 1 U 22

DOD, C. R. Dod's Peerage, Baronetage, and Knightage of Great Britain and Ireland, 1841-92. 49 vols. 12mo. Lond., 1841-92. E

DODINGTON, George Bubb, Lord Melcombe. Diary of ; with an Appendix published by H. P. Wyndham. 8vo. Salisbury, 1784. C 16 T 28

DODD, Anna Bowman. Cathedral Days : a Tour through Southern England. 8vo. Lond., 1887. D 18 R 4

DODGE, Col. R. I. Our Wild Indians : Thirty-three Years' Personal Experience among the Red Men of the Great West. 8vo. Hartford, 1886. D 3 S 13

DODSLEY, R. Cleone : a Tragedy. [*See* British Drama, Modern, 2.]
The King and the Miller of Mansfield : a Farce. [*See* British Drama, Modern, 5.]
Sir John Cockle at Court : a Farce. [*See* British Drama, Modern, 5.]

DOEDERLEIN, L. Die Lateinische Wordbildung. 8vo. Lond., 1839. K 16 T 26

I

DOELTER, Dr. C. Die Bestimmung der Petrographisch Wichtigeren Mineralien durch das Mikroskop. 8vo. Wien, 1876. A 24 U 7

DOGBERRY DINGO. [*See* Australian Rhymes.]

DOLE, N. H, A Score of Famous Composers. 12mo. New York, 1891. C 16 P 25

DÖLLINGER, Dr. J. I. von. Declarations and Letters on the Vatican Decrees, 1869–1887. 8vo. Edinb., 1891. G 18 Q 9

Studies in European History, being Academical Addresses. 8vo. Lond., 1890. B 7 T 34

DOLLMAN, F. T. The Priory of St. Mary Overie, South-Wark. 4to. Lond., 1881. B 40 Q 20‡

DOMINIC. St. History of; by Augusta T. Drane; with illustrations. 8vo. Lond., 1891. C 18 T 7

DONALD, J. [*See* Chambers, W. and R.]

DOMVILE, Lady Margaret. Life of Lamartine. 8vo. Lond., 1888. C 5 Q 3

DONALDSON, J. W. The New Cratylus. 3rd ed. 8vo. Lond., 1859. K 12 V 14

Complete Greek Grammar. 2nd ed. 8vo. Camb., 1859. K 12 V 23

Ancient Greece. [*See* Müller, K. O.]

DONISTHORPE, W. Individualism: a System of Politics. 8vo. Lond., 1889. F 8 R 7

DONKIN, J. G. Trooper and Redskin in the Far North-West, 1884–88. 8vo. Lond., 1889. D 15 Q 12

DONNE, M. A. The Sandwich Islands and their People. 12mo, Lond., 1866. MD 2 W 33

DONNE, W. B. Euripides. (Ancient Classics for English Readers.) 12mo. Edinb., 1887. J 14 P 8

Tacitus. (Ancient Classics for English Readers.) 12mo. Edinb., 1889. J 14 P 25

DONNELLY, I. The Great Cryptogram: Francis Bacon's Cipher in the so-called Shakespeare Plays. 2 vols. roy. 8vo. Lond., 1888. J 4 U 9, 10

DONNELLY, R. Digest of the Acts of Council made and passed in New South Wales. Part 1. Roy. 8vo. Sydney, 1841. MF 3 R 44

DONOHUE, F. J. History of Botany Bay, by "Arthur Gayll." 4to. Sydney (n.d.) MB 2 V 11

A Sheaf of Stories for the Centennial Year; by F. J. D. 12mo. Sydney, 1888. MJ 2 T 10

DONOVAN, E. Epitome of the Natural History of the Insects of New Holland, New Zealand, &c. 4to. Lond. 1805. MA 11 P 17 †

DORAN, Dr. J. "Their Majesties' Servants": Annals of the English Stage, from Thomas Betterton to Edmund Kean; edited and revised by R. W. Lowe. 3 vols. 8vo. Lond., 1888. C 12 S 11–13

DOREN, J. B. J. van. Bijdragen tot de Kennis van Verschillende Overzeesche Landen, Volken, enz. 2 vols. 8vo. Amsterdam, 1860–64. MD 7 R 42

DORIEN, Dr. Zur Lehre von der Trunksucht. 8vo. Berlin, 1866. F 11 R 13

DOUARRE, Rt. Rev. Guillaume. Le Premier Vicaire Apostolique de la Nouvelle-Calédonie; ou Mgr. Guillaume Douarre, Evêque d'Amata et la Nouvelle-Calédonie, par "l'Auteur de la Vie du Capitaine Marceau." 12mo. Lyon, 1861. MC 1 8 5

DOUGHTY, C. M. Travels in Arabia Deserta. 2 vols. 8vo. Camb., 1888. D 16 U 1, 2

DOUGLAS, Prof. R. K. Chinese Manual, comprising a Condensed Grammar, with Idiomatic Phrases, and Dialogues. 12mo. Lond., 1889. K 16 P 11

DOUTRE, Jos. Constitution of Canada: British North America Act, 1867; its Interpretation, &c.; to which is added the Quebec Resolutions of 1864, and the Constitution of the United States. Roy. 8vo. Montreal, 1880. F 1 V 4

DOVE, P. E. Domesday Studies: Papers read at the Domesday Commemoration, 1886. Bibliography of Domesday Book, by H. B. Wheatley. 2 vols. roy. 8vo. Lond., 1889–91. B 4 V 19, 20

DOWDEN, Prof. Edward. Shakespere: a Critical Study of His Mind and Art. 9th edition. 8vo. Lond., 1889. C 16 R 1

Transcripts and Studies. 8vo. Lond., 1888. J 12 Q 31

[*See* Taylor, H.]

DOWIE, Ménie Muriel. A Girl in the Carpathians. 8vo. Lond., 1891. D 19 Q 14

DOWLING, H. The Western Railway: the Cost, Working Expenses, and Traffic Returns. 8vo. Launceston, 1863. MF 2 T 65

DOWLING, J. P. Dairying in Australasia. 8vo. Sydney, 1888. MA 1 P 43

DOWN, J. L. On some of the Mental Affections of Childhood and Youth. 8vo. Lond., 1887. A 26 R 1

DOWN, R. Ruminations and Reminiscences, being a Collection of Incidental Pieces and Poems. 12mo. Melb., 1878. MH 1 U 6

DRAGOMANOFF, M., "Stepniak." The Russian Peasantry; their Agrarian Condition, Social Life, and Religion. 2 vols. 8vo. Lond., 1888. B 12 U 32, 33

DRAKE, Sir Francis. Entertaining and Instructive Selections of Voyages and Travels. 8vo. Lond., 1822. D 10 S 32

[Life of]: by J. Corbett. (English Men of Action.) 8vo. Lond., 1890. C 15 Q 13

DRAKE, Sir Francis, CAVENDISH, Thomas, and DAMPIER, William. Lives and Voyages of; including an Introductory View of the Earlier Discoveries in the South Sea; and the History of the Buccaneers. 12mo, Edinb., 1831. MC 1 S 7

DRAKE DEL CASTILLO, E.   Illustrationes floræ Insularum Maria Pacifici. 4to. Parisiis, 1886-92.
MA 12 Q 5 †

DRAKENBORCH, A. [*See* Livius, T.*]*

DRAMATIC NOTES, 1886-91 ; edited by C. Howard. 8vo. Lond., 1887-92.
E

DRANE, Augusta T. History of St. Dominic. 8vo. Lond., 1891.
C 18 T 7

DRAPER, Rev. D. J. Life of, by the Rev. J. C. Symons. 8vo. Lond., 1870.
MC 1 Q 47

DRAPER, J. W. History of the Conflict between Religion and Science. 19th edition. Lond., 1885.
G 16 P 48

DRESDEN GALLERY. Hand-book of the Italian Schools in the Dresden Gallery ; by C. J. Ff. 8vo. Lond., 1888.
A 8 P 48

DREWE, A. J. Music for the Ceremonies of the Masonic Order. 4to. Sydney, 1891.
MA 11 P 6 †

DREYER, Dr. J. L. E. Tycho Brahe, a picture of scientific life and work in the 16th century. 8vo, Edinb., 1890.
C 12 T 20

DRIKFÆLDIGHEDS-FORHOLDENE I DANMARK, Beretning til Finansministeren om, 1882. 8vo. Kjöbenhavn, 1882.
F 11 S 19

DROUGHT, Rev. C. E. The Music of the Cross : Meditations on the Seven Last Words. 12mo. Lond., 1888.
G 8 P 27

DRUERY, C. T. Choice British Ferns ; their Varieties and Culture. 8vo. Lond., 1888.
A 20 Q 2

DRUMMOND, H. Tropical Africa. 8vo. Lond., 1888.
D 14 R 5

DRUMMOND, J. Philo Judæus ; or, the Jewish-Alexandrian Philosophy in its Development and Completion. 2 vols. 8vo. Lond., 1888.
G 12 P 31, 32

DRUMMOND, Thomas. Life and Letters ; by R. B. O'Brien. 8vo. Lond., 1889.
C 13 U 4

DRUMMOND, W. V. The Statute of Evidence, 1864 ; with Notes. 12mo. Melb., 1871.
MF 3 P 51

DRUNKENNESS. Evidence on Drunkenness, presented to the House of Commons. 8vo. Lond., 1834.
F 11 R 4

DRURY, R. Madagascar ; or Robert Drury's Journal during 15 years' captivity on that island ; and a further description of Madagascar by Abbé A. Rochon. [Reprint, 1829.] 8vo. New York, 1890.
D 14 S 4

DRYDEN, J. All for Love : a Tragedy. [*See* British Drama, Modern.]

Don Sebastian : a Tragedy. [*See* British Drama, Modern.]

The Spanish Friar : a Comedy. [*See* British Drama, Modern.]

Works of ; with notes, &c., by Sir W. Scott ; revised by G. Saintsbury. 14 vols. 8vo. Edinb., 1882-89.
II 4 U 1-14

DUBLIN REVIEW. 11 vols. 8vo. Lond., 1886-92.
E

DUBLIN UNIVERSITY CALENDAR. 6 vols. 12mo. Lond., 1887-92.
E

DÜBNER, F. Arriani Anabasis et Indica. [*See* Arrian.]

Theophrasti Characteres. [*See* Theophrastus.]

DU BOIS, H. P. Four Private Libraries of New York. 8vo. New York, 1892.
J 3 T 7

DU BOIS, J. P. I. Vies des Gouverneurs Généraux, avec l'Abrégé de l'Histoire des Etablissemens Hollandois aux Indes Orientales. 4to. La Haye, 1763.
C 17 U 17

DU CANGE, D. Glossarium Mediæ et Infimæ Latinatis. Vols. 8-10. 4to. Niort, 1887.
K 13 U 25-27

DU CHAILLU, P. B. The Viking Age : the early history, manners, and customs of the ancestors of the English-speaking nations. 2 vols. 8vo. Lond., 1889.
B 20 T 14, 15

DUCKETT, Sir G. F. Charters and Records among the Archives of the Ancient Abbey of Cluni, 1077-1534. 2 vols. roy. 8vo. Lewes, 1888.
B 26 V 2, 3

DUCKHAM, T. [*See* Herd Book.]

DUCKS AND GEESE, their characteristics, points, and management ; by various Breeders. 8vo. Lond. (n.d.)
A 18 R 4

DUCONDRAY, G. History of Modern Civilization. 8vo. Lond., 1891.
B 35 R 3

DUDEVANT, Mme., "George Sand" [Life of] ; by the late E. M. Caro ; translated by G. Masson. (Great French Writers.) 8vo. Lond., 1888.
C 7 P 41

Œuvres complètes. 110 vols. 12mo. Paris, 1865-88.
J 19 S 1-U 2

1. Adriani.	38, 39. La Confession d'une
2. André.	Jeune Fille.
3. Antonia.	40. La Coupe—Lupo Liverani.
4. Autour de la Table.	—Le Toast.—Garnier.—Le
5. Cadio	Contrebandier.—La Rêverie
6. Césarine Dietrich.	à Paris.
7. Constance Verrier.	41, 42. La Daniella.
8-10. Consuelo.	43. La Dernière Aldini.-Myrza.
11-16. Correspondance, 1812-	—Les Visions de la Nuit.—
76.	Georges de Guérin
17. Dernières Pages.	44. La Famille de Germandre.
18. Elle et Lui.	45. La Filleule.
19. Flamarande.	46. La Mare au Diable.
20. Flavie.	47. La Marquise.—Lavinia.—
21. Francia.—Un Bienfait n'est	Pauline.—Mattea.—Metella.
jamais perdu.	—Melchior.
22. François le Champi.	48. La Petite Fadette.
23-26. Histoire de ma Vie.	49. La Tour de Percemont.—
27. Horace.	Marianne.
28. Impressions et Souvenirs.	50. Laura.—Les Charmettes.—
29. Indiana.	Lettre d'un Voyageur.—Ce
30. Isidora.	que dit le Ruisseau.
31. Jacques.	51. La Ville Noire.
32. Jean de la Roche.	52. Le Beau Laurence.
33. Jean Ziska.—Gabriel.	53. Le Chateau de Pictordu.—
34. Jeanne.	La Reine Coax.—Le Nuage
35. Journal d'un Voyageur pendant la Guerre.	Rose.—Les Ailes de Courage.
36, 37. La Comtesse de Rudolstadt	Le Géant Yéous.
	54. Le Chateau des Désertes.

DUDEVANT, Mme.—*contd.*

55. Le Chêne l'arlant. — Le Chien et la Fleur Sacrée.— L'Orgue du Titan.—Ce que disent les Fleurs.—Le Marteau Rouge.—La Fée Poussière.—Le Gnome des Huitres. —La Fée aux Gros Yeux.
56, 57. Le Compagnon du Tour de France.
58. Le Dernier Amour.
59. Le Diable aux Champs.
60. Légendes Rustiques.—Fanchette.
61, 62. Lélia.
63. Le Marquis de Villemer.
64. Le Meunier d'Angibault.
65, 66. Le Péché de Monsieur Antoine.
67, 68. Le Piccinino.
69. Les Amours de l'Age d'Or. —Evenor et Leucippe.
70, 71. Les Beaux Messieurs de Bois-Doré.
72. Les Dames Vertes.
73. Les Deux Frères.
74. Le Secrétaire Intime.— Mattéa.—La Vallée Noire.
75. Les Maîtres Mosaïstes.
76. Les Maîtres Sonneurs.
77. Les Sept Cordes de la Lyre. —Let tres à Marcie.-Carl.— Le Dieu Inconnu. —La Fille d'Albano. — Cléopatre.— Fraguement d'une Lettre écrite de Fontainebleau.— Les Fleurs de Mai.—Coup d'œil général sur Paris.
78. Lettres d'un Voyageur.
79–81. L'Homme de Neige.
82. Lucrezia Floriani.-Lavinia.
83. L'Uscoque.-Sur la dernière publication de M. F. La Mennais.-Quelques reflexions sur J. J. Rousseau.
84. Mademoiselle la Quintinie.

85. Mademoiselle Merquem.
86. Malgré tout
87. Ma Sœur Jeanne.
88. Mauprat.
89. Monsieur Sylvestre.
90. Mont-Revêche.
91. Nanon.
92. Narcisse.
93. Nouvelles Lettres d'un Voyageur.
94. Pauline.
95. Pierre qui roule.
96. Promenades autour d'un Village.
97. Questions d'Art et de Littérature.
98. Questions Politiques et Sociales.
99. Simon.-La Marquise.-Monsieur Roussot.-Mouny-Robin. —Les Sauvages de Paris.
100. Souvenirs de 1848.
101. Tamaris.
102. Teverino.—Leone Leoni.
103-6. Théâtre complet.
1. Cosima.-Le Roi Attend. François le Champi.-Claudie. Molière.
2. Le Mariage de Victorine. —Les Vacances de Pandolphe.—Le Démon du Foyer. —Le Pressoir.
3. Mauprat. — Flaminio. — Maître Favilla.—Lucie.
4. Françoise.-Comme il vous plaira.-Marguerite de Sainte-Gemme. — Le Marquis de Villemer.
107. Théâtre de Nohant.—Le Drac.—l'Autus.—Le Pavé.— La Nuit de Noël.—Marielle.
108. Un Hiver à Majorque.— Spiridion.
109. Valentine.
110. Valvèdre.

DUFFERIN AND AVA, Harriet Georgina, Marchioness of. Our Vice-regal Life in India, 1884-88. 2nd thousand. 2 vols. 8vo. Lond., 1889. D 17 S 3, 4

DUFFERIN AND AVA, Marquis of. Speeches, delivered in India, 1884-8. 8vo. Lond., 1890. F 13 Q 31

Administration of the Earl of Dufferin. [*See* Leggo, Wm.]

DUFFIELD, A. J. Recollections of Travels Abroad. 8vo. Lond., 1889. D 20 S 1

DUFFY, Bella. Madame de Staël. (Eminent Women.) 8vo. Lond., 1887. C 12 Q 29

DUFFY, Sir C. G. Thomas Davis; the Memoirs of an Irish Patriot, 1840-46. 8vo. Lond., 1890. C 14 T 20

Guide to the Land Law of Victoria. 8vo. Melb., 1862. MF 1 Q 25

DUFFY, F. G. [*See* Casey, J. J.]

DUFFY, Frank G., and **IRVINE, W. H.** The Law relating to the Property of Married Women. Roy. 8vo. Melb., 1886. MF 3 T 25

DUKE OF CAMBRIDGE'S GALOP, The. Fol. Sydney, (n.d.) MA 11 Q 15 †

DUKES, C. Health at School, considered in its Mental, Moral, and Physical Aspects. 8vo. Lond., 1887. A 13 P 1

DUKERUS, C. A. [*See* Florus.]

DULEEP, Singh. [*See* Login, Lady L.]

DUMAS, Alexandre, Père. The Memoirs of; selected and translated by A. F. Davidson. 2 vols. 8vo. Lond., 1891. C 15 Q 18, 19

DUMAS, G. Sunshine and Showers. Australian Sketches. 12mo. Melb. (n.d.) MJ 2 T 9

DUNBAR, Wm. Poems of. [*See* Scottish Text Soc.]

DUNCAN, A. H. The Wakatipians; or Early Days in New Zealand. 12mo. Lond., 1888.* MD 1 P 13

DUNCAN, H. Colony of South Australia. 8vo. Lond., 1850. MD 6 T 3

DUNCAN, J. M. Lexicon Græcum. [*See* Damm, C. T.]

DUNCAN, P. M. Cassell's Natural History. [Illustrated.] 6 vols. Imp. 8vo. Lond. (n.d.) A 28 V 4-9

DUNCAN, Sara Jeannette. A Social Departure: how Orthodocia and I went round the World by Ourselves. 8vo. Lond., 1890. D 20 Q 6

DUNCAN, S. T. Journal of a Voyage to Australia, Six Months in Melbourne, and return to England. 8vo. Edinb., 1869. MD 2 R 3

Another Copy. New and enlarged edition. 8vo. Edinb., 1884. MD 1 Q 24

DUNCAN, W. A. [*See* Monnier, Rev. J.]

DUNCKLEY, Henry. Lord Melbourne. 8vo. Lond. 1890. C 16 Q 17

DUNCKER, Prof. M. History of Greece from the Earliest Times to the end of the Persian War; translated by Sarah Frances Alleyne and Evelyn Abbott. 2 vols. 8vo. Lond., 1883-86. B 10 P 16, 17

DUNDEE, John Graham of Claverhouse, Viscount Claverhouse; by M. Morris. 12mo. Lond., 1887. C 12 P 28

DUNLOP, J. Biographical Sketch of; by J. Service. 8vo. Edinb., 1890. MC 1 Q 48

DUNLOP, J. Philosophy of Artificial and Cumpulsory Drinking Usage in Great Britain and Ireland. 6th edition. 8vo. Lond., 1839. F 11 Q 3

DUNLOP, J. C. History of Prose Fiction; revised by H. Wilson. 2 vols. 8vo. Lond., 1888. B 35 P 9, 10

DUNLOP, Robert. Life of Henry Grattan. (Statesmen Series.) 8vo. Lond., 1889. C 12 R 31

DUNN, F. On delicate Ground : a Picture from Life, &c.; by "Kuz." 8vo. Sydney, 1889. MJ 1 R 45

DUNN, Capt. J. New Edition of the Lightning Timber Calculator. 18mo. Sydney, 1892. MA 2 P 76

DUNN, J. P., jun. Indiana: a Redemption from Slavery. (American Commonwealths.) 12mo. Boston, 1888.
B 17 P 10

DU NOYER, Madame Anne Marguerite Petit. Correspondence of. Translated and edited by Forence L. Layard. 2 vols. 8vo. Lond., 1890. C 14 T 10, 11

DUNOYER, C. Nouveaux Éloges Historiques. [*See* Mignet, F. A. M.]

DUPLEIX, Joseph Francis. [Life of]; by Col. G. B. Malleson. (Rulers of India.) 12mo. Oxford, 1890.
C 12 P 32

DU PREL, Dr. C. The Philosophy of Mysticism. Translated by C. C. Massey. 2 vols. 8vo. Lond., 1889.
G 8 T 26, 27

DURAND, l'Abbé E. J. Les Missions Catholiques Françaises. 12mo. Paris, 1874. M G 2 R 7

DURAND, T. Index Generum Phanerogamorum. Roy. 8vo. Brussels, 1888. K 7 Q 31

DURAND, Mme. La Générale. Napoleon and Marie-Louise, 1810-14: a Memoir. 8vo. Lond., 1886.
C 16 P 28

DUSK. [*See* Spirit of the Twilight Hour.]

DUTCH EAST-INDIA COMPANY. [*See* Commelin, P.]

DUTHIE, J. F. The Fodder Grasses of Northern India. Roy. 8vo. Roorkee, 1888. A 18 U 12
Illustrations of the Indigenous Fodder Grasses of the Plains of North-Western India. Roy. 4to. Roorkee, 1886. A 3 P 17 †

DUTT, R. C. History of Civilization in Ancient India. 3 vols. 8vo. Calcutta, 1889. B 28 Q 7–9

DUVAL, A. Monuments des Arts du Dessin. 4 vols. fol. Paris, 1829. A 41 P 5–8 ‡

DUVAR, John Hunter. The Stone, Bronze, and Iron Ages. 8vo. Lond., 1892. A 18 Q 27

DYER, J. The Fleece: a Poem. Sm. 4to. Lond., 1757.
H 9 S 21
Poems. 12mo. Lond., 1761. H 3 P 43

DYER, L. Studies of the Gods in Greece at certain Sanctuaries recently excavated. 8vo. Lond., 1891.
B 27 S 14

DYER, T. F. T. The Folk-lore of Plants. 8vo. Lond., 1889. A 20 P 1

DYER, W. T. T. Botany. [*See* Sachs, Prof. J.]

DYKE, H. Van. [*See* Van Dyke, H.]

DYMOND, J. Essays on the Principles of Morality, and the Private and Political Rights and Obligations of Mankind. 4th edition. Lond., 1852. G 4 T 25

DZIEWICKI, M. H. [*See* Wiclif, J.]

E

E. A. T. [*See* Mackouochie, A. H.]

EADEN, Isabel M. [*See* Boutmy, E.]

EARDLEY, Sir C. The Testimony to Christian Union of Australia, France, and Germany, in 1859. 8vo. Lond., 1859. MG 1 S 53

EARDLEY-WILMOT, S. [*See* Wilmot, Lieut. S. E–.]

EARLE, H. Commerce and Industries of Queensland. [*See* Indian and Colonial Exhibition, 1886.]

EARLE, Prof. J. Hand-book to the Land-Charters, and other Saxonic Documents. 8vo. Oxford, 1888.
B 21 S 17
Philology of the English Tongue. 12mo. Oxford, 1887. K 11 T 25
Another copy. 5th ed. 8vo. Oxford, 1892. K 11 T 50
The Deeds of Beowulf. [*See* Beowulf.]

EARLY ENGLISH TEXT SOCIETY. Publications. 13 vols. 8vo. Lond., 1886–91. E
Two 15th Century Cookery Books; edited by T. Austin.
The Rule of St. Benet; edited by Dr. H. Logeman.
The Curial made by Alain Charretier; edited by F. J. Furnival.
The Bruce; compiled by John Barbour. Pt. 4.
Defensor's Liber Scintillarum; edited by E. W. Rhodes.
On Early English Pronunciation, part 4; by A. J. Ellis.
The Book of Quinte Essence, or, the Fifth Being; edited by F. J. Furnival.
Religious Pieces in Prose and Verse.
Caxton's Eneydos, 1490; edited by W. T. Culley and F. J. Furnival.
Caxton's Blanchardyn and Eglantine; edited by Dr. L. Kellner.
Lydgate's Temple of Glas; edited by J. Schiick.
Ælfric's Lives of the Saints; edited by Rev. W. W. Skeat.
Early South-English Legendary, or, Lives of Saints; edited by Dr. C. Horstmann.

EARWAKER, J. P. The Recent Discoveries of Roman Remains found in Repairing the North Wall of the City of Chester: a Series of Papers edited by J. P. Earwaker. 8vo. Manchester, 1888. B 23 U 5

EASTERBY, W. History of the Law of Tithes in England. 8vo. Camb., 1888. F 12 Q 34

EASTLAKE, Lady. [*See* Brandl, Prof. A.]

EASTWICK, E. B. Hand-book of the Bengal Presidency, with an Account of Calcutta City. (Murray's Hand-book.) 12mo. Lond., 1882. D 12 S 7

EASTWICK, Capt. R. W. A Master Mariner: being the Life and Adventures of Capt. R. W. Eastwick. Edited by H. Compton. 8vo. Lond., 1891. C 14 S 10

EATON, J. R. T. · [*See* Aristoteles.]

EBBLEWHITE, E. A. Parish Registers of Great Hampden, Co. Bucks, 1557–1812; edited by E. A. Ebblewhite. Imp. 8vo. Lond., 1888. B 23 V 3

EBEL, F. A. De Spirituosorum Imprimis Immodice Haustorum Effectu. 8vo. Berolini, 1826. F 11 Q 4

EBN-MALEC. [*See* Djémal-eddin Mohammed.]

EBSWORTH, J. W. Cavalier Lyrics: "For Church and Crown." 8vo. Lond., 1887. H 6 S 33

ECHO, The. 20 vols. fol. Sydney, 1887–92. ME

ECKER, Prof. A. Anatomy of the Frog.. 8vo. Oxford, 1889. A 27 U 33

ÉCOLE PRATIQUE DES HAUTES ÉTUDES. Rap ports, 1868–77. 8vo. Paris, 1879. E

EDDIN, Djémal. [*See* Djémal-eddin Mohammed.]

EDEN, Charles Page. Life of; by Very Rev. J. W. Burgon. (Lives of Twelve Good Men.) 2 vols. 8vo. Lond., 1888. C 13 R 10, 11

EDEN, Guy. [*See* Allen, Rev. R.]

EDGAR, Lucy A. Among the Blackboys : History of an Attempt at Civilising some young Aborigines of Australia. 8vo. Lond., 1865. MA 1 R 3

EDGCUMBE, E. R. P. Zephyrus : a Holiday in Brazil, and on the River Plate. 12mo. Lond., 1887. D 15 P 4

EDGCUMBE, Lady E., and WOOD, Lady M. Four Months' Cruise in a Sailing Yacht. 8vo. Lond., 1888. D 10 Q 32

EDGELOW, Dr. G. Cancer and Simple Tumours dispersed by Electricity. 16mo. Lond., 1883. A 26 P 4

EDGER, S. Autobiographical Notes and Lectures. 8vo. Lond., 1886. C 13 T 26

EDGREN, Prof. H. Compendious Sanskrit Grammar. 8vo. Lond., 1885. K 20 Q 17

EDINBURGH ALMANAC. [*See* Oliver and Boyd.]

EDINBURGH INTERNATIONAL EXHIBITION, 1886. Memorial Catalogue of the French and Dutch Loan Collection. Imp. 4to. Edinb., 1888. A 3 Q 22 †

EDINBURGH REVIEW. Vols. 164–175. 8vo. Lond., 1886–92. E

EDINBURGH UNIVERSITY CALENDAR. 5 vols. 12mo. Edinb., 1887–92. E

EDMOND, John P. Last Notes on the Aberdeen Printers. 12mo. Lond., 1888. C 12 P 47

EDMONDS, Mrs. [*See* Kolokotronês, T.]

EDMONDS, Thomas. The Wishing Tree : a Poem. 8vo. Sydney, 1891. MH 1 S 66

EDMONDSON, F. W. [*See* Waterhouse, G. W.]

EDUCATION, Thirteen Essays on. 12mo. Lond., 1891. G 18 P 10

Statement explanatory of the System of Education ad ministered by the National Board of New South Wales. 8vo. Sydney, 1858. MG 1 T 24

EDUCATIONAL WORKS, Classified Catalogue of, in use in the United Kingdom and its Dependencies, 1887. 8vo. Lond., 1887. K 7 R 45

EDWARDES, Charles. Sardinia and the Sardes. 8vo. Lond., 1889. D 18 T 3

EDWARDS, Amelia B. Pharaohs, Fellahs, and Explorers. 8vo. Lond., 1892. B 21 T 5

[*See* Maspero, Prof. G.]

EDWARDS, A. T. Freemasonry in New South Wales from its Early History to the Installation of Lord Jersey as M.W.G.M. 8vo. Sydney (n.d.) MJ 2 R 29

EDWARDS, C. E. M. Gold Mines in Great Britain and the Law relating to them. 8vo. Lond., 1888. F 12 P 34

EDWARDS, D., and Co. General Directory of South Africa, 1890–91. Roy. 8vo. Cape Town, 1890. E

Gold Fields of South Africa. [Directory.] 2 vols. roy. 8vo. Cape Town, 1890–92. E

EDWARDS, H. Milne-. Manual of Zoology ; translated by R. Knox, M.D. 12mo. Lond., 1856. A 27 Q 31

EDWARDS, H. S. Idols of the French Stage. 2 vols. 8vo. Lond., 1889. C 13 S 10, 11

The Prima Donna : her History and Surroundings from the 17th to the 19th century. 2 vols. 8vo. Lond., 1888. C 12 S 16, 17

EDWARDS, H. T. Wales and the Welsh Church. 8vo. Lond., 1889. G 7 R 37

EDWARDS, Major-Gen. J. B. Correspondence relating to Inspection of the Australasian Colonies. Fol. Lond., 1890. MF 12 Q 18 †

[*See* Australasian Colonies.]

EDWARDS, M. B-. France of To-day ; a Survey Com parative and Retrospective. 2 vols. 8vo. Lond., 1892. D 18 R 21, 22

EDWARDS, R. Damon and Pithias : a Comedy. [*See* British Drama, Ancient, 1.]

EDWARDS, S. The Russians at Home. 8vo. Lond. (n.d.) D 8 Q 35

EDWARDS, Sydenham. The New Flora Britannica, illustrated. 2 vols. 4to. Lond., 1812. A 42 P 1, 2 ‡

EGAN, P. The Life of an Actor. Roy. 8vo. Lond., 1892. J 6 U 15

EGBERT, H. Pretty Cockey ; or, the Life and Death of a Terrible Flirt. 12mo. Newcastle, 1889. MJ 1 S 50

EGEDE, H. A Description of Greenland. 2nd edition. 8vo. Lond., 1818. D 16 S 2

EGGELING, J. [*See* Müller, F. Max : Sacred Books. vols. 12, 26.]

EGESON, C. Egeson's Weather Almanac for 1891. 8vo. Sydney, 1890. ME 8 Q

Egeson's Weather System of Sun Spot Causality. 8vo Sydney, 1889. MA 1 V 32

EGYPT. Correspondence Respecting the Egyptian Exiles in Ceylon. Fol. Lond., 1891. F 42 P 16 ‡

Correspondence Respecting Affairs at Suakim. Fol. Lond., 1889. F 42 P 15 ‡

Convention between the Governments of Great Britain, Germany, Austria-Hungary, &c., relative to the Finances of Egypt, March 18, 1885. Sm. fol. Lond., 1887. F 36 Q 18 ‡

Further Correspondence respecting the Affairs of. Sm. fol. Lond., 1886. F 36 Q 17 ‡

Description de l'Egypte, ou recueil des Observations et des Recherches qui ont été faites en Egypte pendant l'expédition de l'Armée Française. 23 vols. Fol. Paris, 1809–22. D 40 P 14–22 ‡, D 43 Q 1–11 ‡, and Board Room

Report on the Finances of, 1890. Fol. Lond., 1890. F 42 P 17 ‡

EGYPT EXPLORATION FUND. Bubastis (1887–89), by E. Naville. 8th Memoir. Fol. Lond., 1891. B 42 S 8 ‡

The Mound of the Jew and the City of Onias; by E. Naville. The Antiquities of Tel el Yahúdiyeh; by F. L. Griffith. 4to. Lond., 1890. B 42 R 27 ‡

Tanis. Pts. 1 and 2, by W. M. F. Petrie. 2 vols. 4to. Lond., 1885–88. B 39 P 20, 21 ‡

Two Hieroglyphic Papyri from Tanis. 4to. Lond., 1889. K 13 P 14 †
  1. The Sign Papyrus; by F. L. Griffith.
  2. The Geographical Papyrus; by W. M. F. Petrie.

EHRENFECHTER, C. A. Technical Study in the Art of Pianoforte Playing (Deppe's Principles). 2nd ed. 8vo. Lond., 1892. A 23 Q 29

EIMER, Dr. T. Die Medusen Physiologisch und Morphologisch auf ihr Nervensystem. 4to. Tübingen, 1878. A 36 P 28 ‡

EISSLER, M. The Metallurgy of Gold. 3rd edition. 12mo. Lond., 1891. A 24 Q 9

Hand-book of Modern Explosives. 12mo. Lond., 1890. A 25 Q 9

The Metallurgy of Silver : a Practical Treatise on the Amalgamation, Roasting, and Lixiviation of Silver Ores. 8vo. Lond., 1889. A 24 Q 6

ELGIN, Lord. Embassy to China. [*See* Loch, Sir H. B.]

ELIZABETH, Queen of England. Life of; by E. S. Beesly. 12mo. Lond., 1892. C 17 Q 24

ELIZABETH, Queen of Roumania. Life of Carmen Sylva ; by Baroness Stackelberg; translated by Baroness H. Deichmann. 8vo. Lond., 1890. C 15 U 15

Elisabeth of Roumania : a study ; with two Tales from the German of Carmen Sylva ; by Blanche Roosevelt. 8vo. Lond., 1891. C 15 U 16

ELIZABETH FARNESE, Queen of Spain. Life of ; by E. Armstrong. 8vo. Lond., 1892. C 18 S 7

ELLACOMBE, Rev. H. T. Practical Remarks on Belfries and Ringers, with an Appendix on Chiming. 5th edition. 8vo. Lond., 1884. A 24 T 6

ELLARD, F. The Australian Bird Waltz. Fol. Sydney (n.d.) MA 11 Q 15 †

Great Britain Polka. Fol. Sydney (n.d.) MA 11 Q 15 †

ELLENDT, F. Lexicon Sophocleum. 2 vols. 8vo. Regimontii Prussorum, 1835. K 15 P 37, 38

ELLES, R. L. [*See* Coffey, W. H.]

ELLIOT, Hon. Hugh. Life of Sidney, Earl of Godolphin, K.G., Lord High Treasurer of England, 1702–10. 8vo. Lond., 1888. C 9 U 23

ELLIOT, J. The Magistrate's Companion ; being a Guide to the Statutes of Queensland. 8vo. Brisb., 1871. MF 1 R 62

ELLIOT, Sir W. Memoir of Dr. T. C. Jerdon. [*See* Jerdon, T. C.]

ELLIOTT, H. The Australian Pastor ; a Record of the Remarkable Changes in Mind, &c., of H. Elliott ; by the Rev. E. Strickland. 12mo. Lond., 1862. MC 1 P 65

ELLIOTT, O. L. The Tariff Controversy, in the United States, 1789–1833. Roy. 8vo. Palo Alto, California, 1892. F 11 T 22

ELLIS, Major A. B. The Ewe-speaking Peoples of the Slave Coast of West Africa : their religion, manners, customs, laws, languages, &c. 8vo. Lond., 1890. A 18 T 27

South African Sketches. 8vo. Lond., 1887. D 10 Q 10

Tshi speaking Peoples of the Gold Coast of West Africa. Lond., 1887. D 14 U 17

ELLIS, A. J. Early English Pronunciation. [*See* Chaucer Society, and Early English Text Soc.]

English Dialects. [*See* English Dialect Soc.]

ELLIS, E. Pets of the Public : a Book of Beauty containing Twenty-five Portraits of Favourite Actresses of the Australian Stage. 8vo. Sydney, 1888. MC 1 T 1

ELLIS, F. S. Lexicon Concordance to the Poetical Works of P. B. Shelley. Imp. 8vo. Lond., 1892. K 17 S 20

ELLIS, Havelock. The Criminal. 8vo. Lond., 1890. A 18 Q 26

ELLIS, H. [*See* Ford, J. ; Middleton, T. ; Marlowe, C., and Nero and other Plays.]

ELLIS, John. Essay towards a National History of the Corallines. 4to. Lond., 1755. A 30 V 1

Natural History of many Curious and Uncommon Zoophytes ; arranged and described by Dr. D. Solander. 4to. Lond., 1786. A 15 T 16

ELLIS, John Eimeo. Life of William Ellis, Missionary to the South Seas and to Madagascar. Roy. 8vo. Lond., 1873. MC 1 T 2

ELLIS, Mary M. Memoir of ; by the Rev. W. Ellis. 12mo. Lond., 1838. M C 1 S 6

ELLIS, R. [*See* Avianus.]

ELLIS, Mrs. Sarah. The Island Queen; a poem. 8vo. Lond., 1846. 　　　　　　　　　　　MH 1 U 24

ELLIS, Wm. Life of William Ellis, Missionary to the South Seas and Madagascar; by his son, J. E. Ellis. Roy. 8vo. Lond., 1873. 　　　　　　　　　　　MC 1 T 2
Vindication of the South Sea Missions, from the Misrepresentations of Otto von Kotzebue. Roy. 8vo. Lond., 1831. 　　　　　　　　　　　MD 7 R 41

ELLISON, Rev. H. J. Local Option—Local Control. 8vo. Lond., 1882. 　　　　　　　　　　　F 11 R 15

ELLISON, T. Cotton Trade of Great Britain, including a History of the Liverpool Cotton Market, &c. 8vo. Lond., 1886. 　　　　　　　　　　　F 12 Q 33

ELPHINSTONE, Hon. Mountstuart. Rise of British Power in the East; edited by Sir E. Colebrooke. 8vo. Lond., 1887. 　　　　　　　　　　　B 10 S 36
[Life of]; by J. S. Cotton. (Rulers of India.) 12mo. Oxford, 1892. 　　　　　　　　　　　C 18 P 7

ELTON, Chas. I. Origins of English History. 2nd edition. Roy. 8vo. Lond., 1890. 　　　　　　　　　　　B 24 U 1
The Career of Columbus. 8vo. Lond., 1892.
　　　　　　　　　　　C 18 S 21

ELVIN, C. N. Hand-book of Mottoes, borne by the Nobility, Gentry, Cities, Public Companies, &c. 12mo. Lond., 1860. 　　　　　　　　　　　K 12 V 9

ELWES, A. Grammar of the Italian Language. 12mo. Lond., 1852. 　　　　　　　　　　　K 16 P 25

ELY, R. T. Labour Movement in America. 8vo. New York, 1886. 　　　　　　　　　　　F 5 T 38
Another Copy. 8vo. Lond., 1890. 　　　　　　F 14 P 23
Introduction to Political Economy. 8vo. Lond., 1891.
　　　　　　　　　　　F 14 Q 3

ELYARD, S. Scenery of Shoalhaven: Facsimiles in Photography of Eighteen Original Drawings. Fol. Nowra, 1892. 　　　　　　　　　　　MD 12 Q 6 †

ELZE, K. William Shakespeare: a Literary Biography; translated by L. Dora Schmitz. 8vo. Lond., 1888.
　　　　　　　　　　　C 12 P 8

EMDEN, A. Law relating to Building, Building Leases, and Contracts, &c. 2nd edition. 8vo. Lond., 1885.
　　　　　　　　　　　F 10 S 21

EMERSON, P. H. Wild Life on a Tidal Water: the Adventures of a House-boat and her Crew. Illustrated. 4to. Lond., 1890. 　　　　　　　　　　　D 13 P 13 †
Pictures of East Anglian Life. 4to. Lond., 1888.
　　　　　　　　　　　D 34 Q 2 ‡

EMERSON, Ralph Waldo. Essays and Orations. [*See* Universal Library, The.]
Talks with; by C. J. Woodbury. 12mo. Lond., 1890.
　　　　　　　　　　　C 12 P 24
Four Great Teachers: Ruskin, Carlyle, Emerson, and Browning; by J. Forster. 8vo. Orpington, 1890.
　　　　　　　　　　　C 12 Q 11
His Maternal Ancestors; with some Reminiscences of him; by D. G. Haskins. 12mo. Lond., 1886.　·　C 2 R 19
[*See* Robertson, J. M.]

EMIGRANT'S ALMANACK and Guide to the Goldfields, 1854. 8vo. Lond., 1854. 　　　　　　　　　　　ME 3 R

EMIGRATION. Copies or Extracts of Correspondence between the Secretary of State for the Colonies and Governors of the Australian Colonies, respecting Emigration, since 1836. 3 vols. Fol. Lond., 1837-48.
　　　　　　　　　　　MF 8 P 24-26 †
Correspondence respecting Emigration, with Map of New South Wales. Fol. Lond., 1871. 　　　MF 11 Q 28 †
Report on the Emigrants' Information Office for 1889. Fol. Lond., 1889. 　　　　　　　　MF 12 Q 26 †
Practical Suggestions for the formation of Emigration Mutual Aid Societies. 8vo. Dublin, 1849. MF 2 Q 8
Emigration to Queensland. [*See* Indian and Colonial Exhibition, 1886.]

EMIN PASHA. [*See* Schnitzer, Dr. E.]

EMMONS, S. F. [*See* U.S. Geological Exploration of 40th Parallel. Vol. 2.]

EMTAGE, W. T. A. Introduction to the Mathematical Theory of Electricity and Magnetism. 8vo. Oxford, 1891. 　　　　　　　　　　　A 21 Q 25

ENCYCLOPÆDIA AMERICANA, of Art, Science, and General Literature. 4to. New York, 1883-87.
　　　　　　　　　　　K 2 T 12-15

ENCYCLOPÆDIA BRITANNICA: a dictionary of Arts, Sciences, and General Literature. 9th edition. With Index. 24 vols. 4to. Edinb., 1875-89. K 2 S 5-T 10

ENCYKLOPÆDIE DER NATURWISSENSCHAFTEN. 11 vols. Roy. 8vo. Breslau, 1887-92. 　　　E
　　Botanik, Bande 3 und 4.
　　Chemie, Bande 5-9.
　　Mineralogie, Geologie, und Palæontologie, Band 3.
　　Physik, Band 1.
　　Zoologie, Anthropologie, und Ethnologie, Bande 5 und 6.

ENDEAN, J. R. The Public Education of Austria. 8vo. Lond., 1888. 　　　　　　　　　　　G 18 T 1

ENDERBEY, C. [*See* Auckland Islands.]

ENGEL, L. From Handel to Hallé: Biographical Sketches. 4to. Lond., 1890. 　　　　　　　　　　　C 42 S 12 ‡

ENGELS, F. Socialism, Utopian and Scientific; translated by E. Aveling. 12mo. Lond., 1892. 　F 9 U 10
The Condition of the Working Class in England in 1844; translated by Florence K. Wischnewetzky. 12mo. Lond., 1892. 　　　　　　　　　　　F 9 U 11
[*See* Marx, K.]

ENGELSKA SAMTALSÖFNINGAR. 12mo. Stockholm, 1871. 　　　　　　　　　　　K 16 P 28

ENGINEER, The. Vols. 63-73. Fol. Lond., 1887-92. E

ENGINEERING. Vols. 43-53. Roy. 4to. Lond., 1886-92. 　　　　　　　　　　　E

ENGINEERING AND MINING JOURNAL. From July, 1889. Sm. fol. New York, 1889-91. 　　　E

ENGINEERING ASSOCIATION OF NEW SOUTH WALES, Minutes of Proceedings. Vols. 1 and 5. 8vo. Sydney, 1886–1891.   ME 1 T

ENGINEERING RECORD, BUILDING RECORD, AND SANITARY ENGINEER. Vols. 14–25. Fol. New York, 1886–92.   E

ENGLAND AND HER COLONIES: Five best Essays on Imperial Federation, submitted to the London Chamber of Commerce for their Prize Competition. 8vo. Lond., 1887.   F 5 Q 41

ENGLISH DIALECT SOCIETY: Publications. 9 vols. 8vo. Lond., 1889–91.   E

  Glossary of Words used in the Wapentakes of Manley and Corringham, Lincolnshire; by E. Peacock. 2nd edition. 2 vols.
  English Dialects; by A. J. Ellis.
  Glossary of Dialect and Archaic Words used in Gloucester; by J. D. Robertson.
  Rutland Words; by Rev. C. Wordsworth.
  Ablaut in the Modern Dialects of the South of England; translated by W. A. Badham.
  Supplement to the Sheffield Glossary; by S. O. Addy.
  Dialect of Hartland, Devonshire.

ENGLISH HISTORICAL REVIEW. Vols. 1–6. Roy. 8vo. Lond., 1886–91.   E

ENGLISH HISTORY, An Epitome of the Leading Events in. 12mo. Sydney, 1868.   MB 2 P 50

ENGLISH ILLUSTRATED MAGAZINE. 10 vols. 8vo. Lond., 1883–93.   E

ENGLISH MECHANIC. Vols. 44–55. Sm. fol. Lond., 1887–92.   E

ENGLISHMAN in Paris, An. Notes and Recollections. 2 vols. 12mo. Lond., 1892.   J 11 W 13, 14

ENGLISHWOMAN'S REVIEW. 4 vols. 8vo. Lond., 1885–86, 1887–88.   E

ENSOR, Laura. [*See* Ligne, Princess H. de.]

ENTOMOLOGIST'S MONTHLY MAGAZINE. 6 vols. 8vo. Lond., 1886–91.   E

EPICTETUS. Dissertationum ab Arriano digestorum libri IV. 5 vols. 8vo. Lipsiæ, 1799–1800.   G 12 R 36–40

EPIGRAMMATUM GRÆCORUM: annotationibus J. Brodæi. [Gr. et Lat.] Fol. Francofurte, 1600.   J 39 S 4 ‡

EPPS, W. The People and the Land; an Essay. 8vo. Sydney, 1892.   MF 2 T 57

ERASMUS, D. Apophthegmes of; translated into English by N. Udall. [Reprint, 1564.] 8vo. Boston, 1877.   J 10 V 11

  Enchiridion Militis Christiani. 32mo. Lugd. Bat., 1641.   G 9 U 4

ERBACH, Count George Albert of. Adventures of; translated from the German of Emil Kraus, by H. R. H. Beatrice. 8vo. Lond., 1890.   C 16 Q 26

ERCKMAN-CHATRIAN, E. E. and A. C. Madame Thérèse; or, the Volunteers of '92. 12mo. Lond. (n.d.)   J 1 W 46

K

ERDMANN, J. E. History of Philosophy; translated by W. S. Hough. 3 vols. roy. 8vo. Lond., 1890.   G 4 T 27–29

ERICSSON, John. [Life of]; by W. C. Church. 2 vols. 8vo. Lond., 1890.   C 16 T 11, 12

ERMATINGER, C. O. Canadian Franchise and Election Laws. 8vo. Toronto, 1886.   F 9 S 28

ERNEST, J. A. [*See* Homer.]

ERNESTI, C. T. [*See* Silius Italicus.]

ERNST, H. R. De Spirituosorum et physiologico et pathologico effectu. 8vo. Berolini, 1861.   F 11 Q 27

ERSKINE, Hon. A. Boswell's Correspondence with. [*See* Hill, G. B.]

ESEGAR. [*See* Historical Review.]

ESHELBY, H. D. Genealogy of the Family of De Eskelby or Exelby of the North Riding of the County of York. 8vo. Birkenhead, 1891.   K 10 T 28

ESSAI sur l'isle d'Otahiti, et sur l'esprit et les Mœurs de ses Habitans. 12mo. Avignon, 1779.   MD 7 T 12

ESSAYS ON REFORM. 8vo. Lond., 1867.   F 9 S 26

ESTIENNE, Henri. Thesaurus Græcæ Linguæ. 4 vols. Fol. Paris et Geneva, 1572.   K 42 Q 10–13 ‡

  Thesaurus Græcæ Linguæ, ab Henrico Stephano constructus. Post editionem Anglicam novis additamentis auctum; ordineque alphabetico digestum tertio ediderunt C. B. Hase, Guilielmus Dindorfius et L. Dindorfius. 8 vols. (in 9) sm. fol. Paris, 1865.   K 7 Q 5–13 †

[*See* Memnon.]

ETHEREDGE, Sir G. Works of: Plays and Poems; edited by A. W. Verity. 8vo. Lond., 1888.   H 3 Q 25

  The Comical Revenge; or, Love in a Tub.—She would if she could.—The Man of Mode; or, Sir Fopling Flutter.—Poems.

ETHERIDGE, R. Geology. [*See* Phillips, J.]

ETHERIDGE, R., Jun. Invertebrate Fauna of the Hawkesbury—Wianamatta Series of New South Wales. (Geol. Survey of New South Wales.) Roy. 4to. Sydney, 1888.*   MA 1 Q 34 †

ETTINGSHAUSEN, Dr. C. F. von. Die Genetische Gliederung der Flora Australiens. Roy. 4to. Wien, 1875.   MA 1 Q 33 †

  Ueber die genetische Gliederung der Cap-Flora. Roy. 4to. Wien, 1875.   A 20 V 3

  Zur Entwicklungsgeschichte der Vegetation der Erde. Roy. 8vo. Wien, 1874.   A 20 V 2

[*See* New South Wales.]

EUGENE of Savoy, Prince. [Life of]; by Col. G. B. Malleson. 8vo. Lond., 1888.   C 13 R 9

EURIPIDES. Alcestis of, from the Text of Dindorf, with Notes by the Rev. J. Milner. 12mo. Sydney, 1853.   MH 1 Q 51

  Euripides; by W. B. Donne. (Ancient Classics for English Readers.) 12mo. Edinb., 1887.   J 14 P 8

EURIPIDES—contd.

Fabulæ cum annotationibus L. Dindorfii. (Gr. text.) 2 vols. 12mo. Lipsiæ (n.d.)   H 2 Q 41, 42

Fragmenta, collegit F. G. Wagner. Imp. 8vo. Parisiis, 1846.   J 18 V 22

Ion ; with Notes by Prof. C. Badham. 2nd ed. (Gr. text.) 8vo. Lond., 1867.   H 4 R 37

Tragœdiæ priores quatuor. Edidit R. Porson, recensuit J. Scholefield. 2nd ed. (Gr. text and Lat. notes.) 8vo. Cantab., 1829.   H 9 S 20

EUSEBIUS PAMPHILUS. Historiæ Ecclesiasticæ libri X. Recognovit A. Schwegler. 8vo. Tubingæ, 1852.   G 4 S 35

EUTROPIUS. Historiæ Romanæ libri duo. [*See* Braim, T. H.]

EVANS, Rev. A. C. Cruise of H.M.S. "Calliope" in China, Australian, and East African Waters, 1889-90. 8vo. Portsmouth, 1890.   MD 4 P 49

EVANS, G. E. Repentance of Magdalené Despar, and other Poems. 8vo. Lond., 1891.   MH 1 U 23

EVANS, G. W. Voyage à la terre de Van Dieman, by Description Historique, Géographique et Topographique de cette Ile. 8vo. Paris, 1823.   MD 7 S 42

EVANS, J. G. Facsimile of the Black Book of Carmarthen. Roy. 8vo. Oxford, 1888.   B 6 V 35

[*See* Mabinogion.]

EVANS, Marian. [*See* Feuerbach, L.]

EVANS, R. W. The Bishopric of Souls. 12mo. Lond., 1842.   G 16 P 44

Parochial Sermons. 12mo. Lond., 1844.   G 16 P 43

EVELYN, J. Captain Kangaroo : a Story of Australian Life. 8vo. Lond., 1889.   MJ 1 S 49

Life of Mrs. Godolphin ; edited by E. W. Harcourt. 8vo. Lond., 1888.   C 14 Q 27

EVENING NEWS. 26 vols. fol. Sydney, 1887-92. ME

EVERITT, G. Doctors and Doctors : some curious Chapters in Medical History and Quackery. 8vo. Lond., 1888.   A 13 P 43

EVETTS, B. T. A. [*See* Babelon, E.]

EWALD, A. C. Paper and Parchment: Historical Sketches. 8vo. Lond., 1890.   B 23 R 1

Studies Re-Studied. 8vo. Lond., 1885.   B 24 T 18

Life of Sir J. Napier, ex-Lord Chancellor of Ireland ; from his private Correspondence. 8vo. Lond., 1887.   C 13 T 3

Our Public Records : a brief Handbook to the National Archives. 8vo. Lond., 1873.   F 12 Q 35

[*See* Congreve, W., and Farquhar, G.]

EWALD, Dr. G. H. A. von. Commentary on the Psalms ; translated by Rev. E. Johnson. 2 vols. 8vo. Lond., 1880-81.   G 4 U 18, 19

Commentary on the Book of Job, with Translation ; translated from the German by J. F. Smith. 8vo. Lond., 1882.   G 4 U 46

Commentary on the Books of Yôêl, 'Amôs, Hosêa, and "Zakharya," with Translation ; translated from the German by J. F. Smith. 5 vols. 8vo. Lond., 1875-81.   G 4 U 20-24

EWAN, J. Geography of the Australian Colonies. 12mo. Sydney, 1851.   MD 1 P 51

EWART, Lieut. J. S. [*See* Mackenzie, Capt. T. A.]

EWING, Lt.-Col. A. [*See* Hoffmann, E. T. W.]

EWING, J. A. [*See* Jenkin, F.]

EX-M.L.A. [*See* Our Present Parliament.]

EXPLORERS, The, and other Poems ; by "M.C." 12mo. Melb., 1874.   MH 1 Q 47

EXPLORERS OF AUSTRALIA [from the Edinburgh Review, July, 1862]. 8vo. Lond., 1862.   MD 7 S 43

EXPRESS, The Illustrated. Fol. Sydney, 1887.   ME

EXTRAMURAL SEPULTURE, Report on a General Scheme for. 8vo. Lond., 1850.   A 26 T 11

EYRE, Rev. W. L. W. Brief History of the Parishes of Swarraton and Northington. 4to. Lond., 1890.   B 2 U 36

EYS, W. J. Van. [*See* Van Eys, W. J.]

EYTON, T. C. Synopsis on the Anatidæ, or Duck Tribe. 12mo. Wellington, Salop, 1869.   A 14 Q 6

Herd Book of Hereford Cattle. [*See* Herd Book.]

F.

FABERT, Abraham. [Life of ;] by G. Hooper. 8vo. Lond., 1892.   C 14 V 11

FABRI, T. [*See* Longinus, D. C.]

FACCIOLATI, J., and FORCELLINI, A. Totius Latinitatis Lexicon ; edidit J. Bailey. 2 vols. 4to. Lond., 1828.   K 42 P 21, 22 ‡

FACULTÉ des Lettres de Lyon. Annuaire. 8vo. Paris, 1883-85.   E

FAGAN, C. E. [*See* Tuer, A. W.]

FAGAN, L. Descriptive Catalogue of the Engraved Works of William Faithorne. Imp. 8vo. Lond., 1888. K 8 T 3

The Reform Club, its Founders and Architects, 1836-86. Imp. 4to. Lond., 1887.   B 7 P 7 †

FAIRFAX CORRESPONDENCE, The. Memoirs of the Reign of Charles I. 2 vols. 8vo. Lond., 1848.   B 24 S 6, 7

Memorials of the Civil War. 2 vols. 8vo. Lond., 1849.   B 24 S 8, 9

FAIRHOLT, F. W. Tobacco : its History and Associations. 12mo. Lond., 1876. A 18 R 35
Domestic Manners in England. [*See* Wright, T.]

FAITHORNE, W. [*See* Fagan, L.]

FALCONER, Hon. I Keith. Memorials of ; by the Rev. It. Sinker. 8vo. Camb., 1888. C 6 P 27

FALCONER, W. The Shipwreck, a poem ; with a life of the author ; by J. S. Clarke. 8vo. Lond., 1811. H 7 U 6

FALK, D. G. Riek ; or, the Récidiviste : a Romance of Australian Life. 8vo. Lond., 1891. MJ 2 T 29

FALKENER, E. Games, Ancient and Oriental, and How to Play Them. 8vo. Lond., 1892. A 29 T 29

FALLERSLEBEN, II. von. [*See* Reineke Vos.]

FALLON, James T. The "Murray Valley Vineyard," Albury, New South Wales, and Australian Vines and Wines. 8vo. Melb., 1874. MA 3 S 27

FANE, Violet. [*See* Marguerite Do Valois.]

FANFANI, P. Vocabolario della Lingua Italiana. Roy. 8vo. Firenzo, 1891. K 14 Q 5

FARADAY, M. Six Lectures on the Chemical History of a Candle, to which is added a Lecture on Platinum ; edited by W. Crookes. 12mo. Lond., 1865. A 21 P 16
Naturgeschichte einer Kerzo. 12mo. Berlin, 1871. A 21 P 14

FARIS, S. Decline of British Prestige in the East. 8vo. Lond., 1887. F 5 U 37

FARJEON, B. L. The Golden Land ; or, Links from Shore to Shore. 8vo. Lond., 1886. MJ 1 Q 31
[*See* Mennell, P.]

FARMER, A. [*See* Agriculture in New South Wales.]

FARMER, H. The Laughing Galop. Fol. Sydney (n.d.) MA 11 Q 15 †

FARMER, J. S. Americanisms, Old and New : a Dictionary of Words, Phrases, and Colloquialisms peculiar to the United States, &c. 4to. Lond., 1889. K 12 U 13
Slang and its Analogues, Past and Present. Vols. 1 and 2. Sm. 4to. Lond., 1890-91. K 12 V 29, 30

FARMER AND STOCKBREEDER, The. 7 vols. fol. Lond., 1886-91. E

FARNELL, G. S. Greek Lyric Poetry. 8vo. Lond., 1891. H 8 V 39

FARQUHAR, G. Dramatic Works of ; edited by A. C. Ewald. 2 vols. 8vo. Lond., 1892. H 2 T 28, 29
The Beaux Stratagem : a Comedy. [*See* British Drama, Modern, 4.]
The Constant Couple : a Comedy. [*See* British Drama, Modern, 4.]

FARQUHAR, G.—*contd.*
Sir Harry Wildair : a Comedy. [*See* British Drama, Modern, 4.]
The Inconstant : a Comedy. [*See* British Drama, Modern, 4.]
The Recruiting Officer : a Comedy. [*See* British Drama, Modern, 4.]

FARRAR, Ven. Archd. F. W. The Duty of Governments. 8vo. Manchester, 1884. F 11 R 16
Lives of the Fathers. Sketches of Church History in Biography. 2 vols. 8vo. Edinb., 1889. G 8 T 28, 29
The Use of Alcohol : an Address. 8vo. Sydney, 1878. MF 1 T 30

FARREN, R. Cathedral Cities : Peterborough, with the Abbeys of Crowland and Thorney. Fol. Camb., 1888. A 32 P 25 ‡

FARRER, Rev. E. Church Heraldry of Norfolk. 2 vols. 8vo. Norwich, 1887-89. B 22 U 16, 17

FARRER, J. A. Books condemned to be Burnt. 12mo. Lond., 1892. J 11 W 3

FAUCHER, L. Remarks on the Production of Precious Metals, and on the Demonetization of Gold. 8vo. Lond., 1852. MA 2 Q 52

FAVENC, E. History of Australian Exploration, 1788-1888. Imp. 8vo. Sydney, 1888.* MD 6 U 4

FAWCETT, Rt. Hon. H. Labour and Wages. 8vo. Lond., 1884. F 14 P 24

FAXON, H. H. Extracts from the Public Statutes of Massachusetts. 12mo. Boston, 1884. F 11 P 47

FAY, E. A. Concordance of the Divina Commedia. (Italian.) Roy. 8vo. Camb., 1888. K 17 R 23

FAY, Prof. W. M. [*See* Davenport, J. E. and W. H.]

FAYETTE, La. [*See* La Fayette.]

FEA, C. [*See* Horatius Flaccus, Q.]

FEARNLEY, W. Course of Elementary Practical Histology. 8vo. Lond., 1887. A 13 P 39

FEATHERMAN, A. Social History of the Races of Mankind. Div. 2. Oceano-Melanesians and Papuo- and Malayo-Melanesians. 2 vols. 8vo. Lond., 1887-88. MA 1 S 21, 22
Social History of the Races of Mankind. Div. 3 : Aoneo-Maranonians. 8vo. Lond., 1889. A 1 W 43
Social History of the Races of Mankind. Div. 3. Chiapo- and Guarano-Maranonians. Div. 4 Dravido-Turanians, Turco-Tatar-Turanians, Ugrio-Turanians. 2 vols. 8vo. Lond., 1890-91. A 18 T 20, 21

FEATON, Mr. and Mrs. E. H. Art Album of New Zealand Flora ; being a Systematic and Popular Description of Native Flowering Plants of New Zealand and adjacent Islands. 4to. Wellington, 1889. MA 8 Q 22 †

FEATON, J. The Waikato War, 1863-64. 8vo. Auckland, 1879. MB 2 R 42

FEDERAL ASSOCIATION OF THE AUSTRALIAN COLONIES. Copy of Correspondence on. Fol. Lond., 1857.   MF 11 Q 39 †

FEDERAL COUNCIL OF AUSTRALASIA. 3rd Session, 1889. Official Records of Debates. 8vo. Hobart, 1889.   ME 8 R

FEDERATION AND INTERCOLONIAL FREE-TRADE. Roy. 8vo. Adelaide, 1890.   MF 3 T 4

FÉE, A. L. A. Mémoire Physiologique et Organographique sur la Sensitive et les Plantes dites Sommeillantes. 4to. Strasbourg, 1849.   A 36 P 22 ‡

Mémoire sur l'Ergot du Seigle et sur quelques Agames qui vivent parasites sur les epis de cette céréale. 4to. Strasbourg, 1843.   A 36 P 22 ‡

FEHON, W. M. Fehon Inquiry Commission. Report of Royal Commission. Fol. Sydney, 1889.   MF 2 U 47

FEISTMANTEL, O. Notes on the Fossil Flora of Eastern Australia and Tasmania. 8vo. Sydney, 1880.   MA 3 Q 30

FELKIN, H. M., and Emmie. [See Herbart, Prof. J. F.]

FELIS, J. M. [See Garcke, E.]

FELS, Mme. D. The Fols' Lady Tailor System. Roy. 8vo. Sydney, 1890.   MA 3 R 7

FELTON, Myra. Eena Romney; or, Word-Pictures of Home-Life in New South Wales. 8vo. Sydney, 1887.
MJ 1 U 30

FENCING, &c. Fencing, by W. H. Pollock, F. C. Grove, and C. Prevost; Boxing, by E. B. Michell; Wrestling, by W. Armstrong. (Badminton Library.) 12mo. Lond., 1889.   A 17 U 42

FENN, C. Fenn's Compendium of the English and Foreign Funds, Debts, and Revenues of all Nations. 14th edition, re-written by R. L. Nash. 8vo. Lond., 1889.   F 4 Q 29

FENTON, E. Marianne: a Tragedy. [See British Drama, Modern, 2.]

FENTON, F. D. Important Judgments delivered in the Compensation Court, and Native Land Court, N.Z., 1866–79. 8vo. Auckland, 1879.   MF 2 P 24

New Zealand Thermal-Springs Districts. 4to. Wellington, 1882.   MD 7 P 22 †

Suggestions for a History of the Origin and Migrations of the Maori People. 8vo. Auckland, 1885.   MB 2 R 41

FENTON, J. [See Price, Rev. C.]

FÉRÉ, C. [See Binet, A.]

FERGUSON, A. M. and J. All about Spices; including practical instructions for planting, cultivation, and preparation for market. 8vo. Colombo, 1889. A 18 T 10
[See Tropical Agriculturist.]

FERGUSON, D. Vicissitudes of Bush Life in Australia and New Zealand. Roy. 8vo. Lond., 1891. MJ 2 R 30

FERGUSON, Capt. James, and Col. P. Ferguson. Two Scottish Soldiers; by James Ferguson. 8vo. Aberdeen, 1888.   C 14 T 1

FERGUSON, James. Two Scottish Soldiers: a Soldier of 1688 and Blenheim, a Soldier of the American Revolution, and a Jacobite Laird and his Forbears. 8vo. Aberdeen, 1888.   C 14 T 1

FERGUSON, M. C. The Story of the Irish before the Conquest. 12mo. Lond., 1868.   B 29 P 12

FERGUSON, Col. Patrick. [See Ferguson, Jas.]

FERGUSON, R. The Plotter; or, the Secret of the Rye-house Conspiracy, and the Story of a Strange Career; by J. Ferguson. 8vo. Edinb., 1887.   C 12 S 32

FERGUSON, R. S.   Carlisle.   (Diocesan Histories 12mo. Lond., 1889.   B 23 P 6

History of Cumberland. 8vo. Lond., 1890.   B 5 T 30

FERGUSON, R. S., and NANSON, W. Some Municipal Records of the City of Carlisle. 8vo. Carlisle, 1887.
B 22 U 6

FERGUSON, Sir S. Ogham Inscriptions in Ireland, Wales, and Scotland. 8vo. Edinb., 1887.   B 29 U 13

FERGUSSON, Lieut.-Col. A. Fraser's Manuscript. [See Fraser, Major J.]

FERGUSSON, Dr. Jas. History of the Modern Styles of Architecture. 3rd ed. 2 vols. Lond., 1891. A 19 T 3,4

FERNS which grow in New Zealand and the adjacent Islands, plainly described; by "H. E. S. L." 8vo. Auckland, 1875.   MA 3 T 54

FERRAGUTI, A. [See Amicis, E. de.]

FERRARIO, Dr. G. Monumenti Sacri e Profani dell' Imperiale e Reale Basilica di Sant' Ambrogio in Milano. Fol. Milano, 1824.   A 37 Q 11 ‡

FERREL, Wm. A Popular Treatise on the Winds. 8vo Lond., 1889.   A 19 U 31

FERRES, A. My Centennial Gift; or, Australian Stories for Children. 8vo. Sydney, 1887 *   MJ 2 P 25

FERRY, G. Vagabond Life in Mexico. 8vo. New York, 1856.   D 15 R 6

FESTUS, S. P. De Verborum Significatione quae supersunt; emandata C. O. Muellero. Fol. Lipsiæ, 1839.
K 42 S 9 ‡

FEUERBACH, L. Essence of Christianity; translated by Marian Evans. 8vo. Lond., 1854.   G 13 S 37

FEUILLET, O. Œuvres Complètes. 16 vols. 12mo. Paris, 1887–89.   J 11 Q 36–51

1. Les Amours de Philippe.	9. Un Mariage dans le Monde.
2. Bellah.	10. Monsieur de Camors.
3. Le Divorce de Juliette.	11. La Morte.
4. Histoire de Sibylle.	12. La Petite Comtesse.
5. Histoire d'une Parisienne.	13. Le Roman d'un Jeune Homme Pauvre.
6. Honneur d'Artiste.	14. Scènes et Comédies.
7. Le Journal d'une Femme.	15. Scènes et Proverbes.
8. Julia de Trécœur.	16. La Veuve.

FF., C. J. [See Dresden Gallery.]

FICHTE, J. G. Popular Works of; translated by Dr. W. Smith. 2 vols. 8vo. Lond., 1889. J 3 T 18, 19

The Science of Rights; translated by A. E. Kroeger. 8vo. Lond., 1889. G 11 P 38

The Science of Knowledge; translated by A. E. Kroeger. 8vo. Lond., 1889. G 11 P 39

FIDLER, T. C. Practical Treatise on Bridge Construction. Roy. 8vo. Lond., 1887. A 6 U 15

FIELD, H. C. The Ferns of New Zealand and its immediate Dependencies, with directions for their collection and cultivation. 4to. London, 1890. MA 11 P 5 †

FIELD, Henry M. Gibraltar Illustrated. 8vo. Lond., 1889. D 18 T 2

Old and New Spain. 8vo. Lond., 1888. D 18 T 1

FIELD, M. Sight and Song; a poetical description of some great pictures. 12mo. Lond., 1892. H 3 P 42

FIELD, N. The Fatal Dowry. [See British Drama, Modern, 1.]

FIELD, The. Vols. 68–79. Fol. Lond., 1886–92. E

FIELDING, H. Journal of a Voyage to Lisbon; notes by A. Dobson. 12mo. Lond., 1892. D 18 R 17

The Intriguing Chambermaid : a Ballad Farce. [See British Drama, Modern, 5.]

The Miser : a Comedy. [See British Drama, Modern, 4.]

The Mock Doctor : a Ballad Farce. [See British Drama, Modern, 5.]

Tom Thumb : a Burletta. [See British Drama, Modern, 5.]

FIENNES, Celia. Through England on a Side-saddle in the Time of William and Mary. 8vo. Lond., 1888. D 18 U 7

FIGUIER, L. L'Année Scientifique et Industrielle, 1888-91. 4 vols. 8vo. Paris, 1889-92. F

FIJI. Ordinances introduced to regulate the Treatment of Polynesian Labourers, and the Introduction of Indian Coolies into Fiji, and Correspondence relating to these Ordinances. Fol. Lond., 1878. MF 11 Q 52 †

Correspondence relating to the Native Population. Fol. Lond., 1887. MF 11 P 33 †

Correspondence relative to Fiji. Fol. Lond., 1862. MF 11 Q 40 †

Copies of Correspondence relating to the Fiji Islands, in so far as the same relate to their annexation to the Colonial Empire of this country, or otherwise affording protection to British subjects resident in those Islands. Fol. Lond., 1871. MF 11 Q 41 †

Copy of a Letter to Commodore Goodenough, R.N., and E. L. Layard, Esq., instructing them to report upon various questions connected with the Fiji Islands; with enclosures. Fol. Lond., 1874. MF 11 Q 42 †

Correspondence respecting the Session of Fiji and the Provisional Arrangements made for administering the Government. Fol. Lond., 1875. MF 11 Q 42 †

Correspondence respecting the Colony of Fiji, 1875. Fol. Lond., 1876. MF 11 Q 42 †

FIJI—contd.

Further Correspondence respecting the Colony of Fiji. 3 vols. (in 1.) Fol. Lond., 1876–77. MF 11 Q 43 †

Correspondence relative to Land Claims, 1883–85. 3 vols. (in 1.) Fol. Lond., 1883–85. MF 11 Q 44 †

Correspondence relating to the Native Population. Fol. Lond., 1885. MF 11 Q 45

FILIPPINI, Alessandro. The Table : How to Buy Food, How to Cook it, and How to Serve it. Revised edition, 8vo. New York, 1891. A 22 T 1

FINCK, H. T. The Pacific Coast Scenic Tour. 8vo. Lond., 1891. D 4 P 36

Romantic Love and Personal Beauty; their Development, Causal Relations, Historic and National Peculiarities. 2 vols. 8vo. Lond., 1887. G 8 Q 21, 22

FINDEN, E. W. The Royal Gallery of British Art. Fol. Lond. (n.d.) A 8 Q 11‡

FINDLAY, Lieut. C. [See Mackenzie, Capt. T. A.]

FINDLAY, Lieut.-Col. George. Working and Management of an English Railway. 3rd edition. 8vo. Lond., 1890. A 22 Q 31

FINLAY, Dr. G. Greece under the Romans, B.C. 146—A.D. 716. 2nd ed. Roy. 8vo. Edinb., 1857. B 27 U 25

History of the Byzantine Empire, 716–1057. 2nd ed. 8vo. Edinb., 1856. B 34 Q 12

History of the Greek Revolution. 2 vols. 8vo. Edinb., 1861. B 27 U 23, 24

History of Greece under Othoman and Venetian Domination. 8vo. Edinb., 1861. B 27 U 22

FINN, Edmund. Chronicles of Early Melbourne, 1835–52, Historical, Anecdotal, and Personal; by "Garryowen." 2 vols. 4to. Melb., 1888. MB 11 P 30, 31 †

The Hordern Mystery. 8vo. Melb., 1889. MJ 1 S 56

A Priest's Secret, "Under Seal of Confession." 8vo. Melb., 1888. MJ 1 S 57

FINNAMORE, J. Carpio : a tragedy in five acts. Roy. 8vo. Melb., 1875. MH 1 S 61

Handy Book of Insolvency Law; with introductory remarks and a Copious Index. Roy. 8vo. Melb., 1871. MF 1 Q 63

FINNISS, B. T. Constitutional History of South Australia, 1836–57. 12mo. Adelaide, 1886. MB 1 P 16

FINSCH, Dr. O. Samoafahrten. Reisen in Kaiser Wilhelms-Land und Englisch-New-Guinea in den jahren 1884–85 an bord des Deutscher Dampfers "Samoa." Roy. 8vo. Leipzig, 1888. MD 2 V 1

FIRBANK, J. Life and Work of; by F. McDermott. 8vo. Lond., 1887. C 7 T 10

FIRE UNDERWRITERS' ASSOCIATION OF NEW SOUTH WALES. Fire Clauses and Stipulations. 12mo. Sydney (n.d.) MF 2 P 66

FIRTH, J. C. Nation Making : a story of New Zealand ; Savagism v. Civilization. 8vo. Lond., 1890.
MD 2 W 3
Our Kin across the Sea ; with a Preface by J. A. Froude. 12mo. Lond., 1888. D 15 P 1

FIRTH, J. F. B. Reform of London Government, and of City Guilds. 8vo. Lond., 1888. F 5 T 39

FISCHER, J. F. [See Anacreon.]

FISCHER, Prof. K. A Critique of Kant. 8vo. Lond., 1888. G 16 S 33
History of Modern Philosophy : Descartes and his School. Roy. 8vo. Lond., 1887. G 12 T 36

FISCHER, W. Wagner's Letters to. [See Wagner, R.]

FISCHERN, Dr. T. Praktische Alkoholometrie. 8vo. Dresden, 1872. F 11 Q 51

FISHER, J. C. Hang out the Banner : Australian Patriotic Song and Chorus. Fol. Sydney (n.d.)
MA 11 Q 15 †

FISHER, John, Bishop of Rochester. Life and Death of ; by T. Bailey. 12mo. Lond., 1739. C 13 P 1

FISHWICK, H. History of St. Michael's-on-Wyre. [See Chetham Soc., N.S. 25.]
History of the Parish of Rockdale in the County of Lancaster. 4to. Rockdale, 1889. B 6 V 26
The Registers of the Parish Church of Rockdale, 1582-1641. Edited by H. Fishwick. 2 vols. 8vo. Rockdale, 1888-89. B 22 U 13, 14

FISKE, John. The American Revolution. 2 vols. 8vo. Lond., 1891. B 18 Q 2, 3
Darwinism, and other essays. 8vo. Lond., 1879.
J 11 S 33
The Discovery of America. 2 vols. 8vo. Lond., 1892. B 18 Q 5, 6
[See Appleton, D., and Co.]

FISON, Rev. L. Land Tenure in Fiji. 8vo. Lond., 1881. MF 1 R 43
The Nanga, or Sacred Stone Enclosure of Wainimala, Fiji. 8vo. Lond., 1884. MD 4 V 8

FITCH, Dr. J. G. Notes on American Schools and Training Colleges. 12mo. Lond., 1890. G 18 Q 7

FITZGERALD, E. Letters and Literary Remains of. Edited by W. A. Wright. 3 vols. 8vo. Lond., 1889.
C 16 Q 12-14
Works of. 2 vols. roy. 8vo. New York, 1887.
H 2 T 22, 23

1. Omar Khayyám's Rubáiyát.—Life of Jámí.—Jámí's Salámán and Absál.—Agamemnon, from Æschylus.—Euphranor.—Polonius ; a Collection of Wise Saws.—Essays on Crabbe.
2. Six Dramas of Calderon : The Painter of his own Dishonour.—Keep your own Secret.—Gil Perez, the Gallician.—Three Judgments at a Blow.—The Mayor of Zalamea.—Beware of Smooth Water.—Suffolk Sea Phrases.

FITZGERALD, Mary A. Australian Furs and Feathers. Sm. 4to. Sydney, 1889. MA 2 U 3
King Bungaree's Pyalla, and Stories illustrative of Manners and Customs that prevailed among Australian Aborigines. Sm. 4to. Sydney, 1891. MJ 3 Q 1

FITZGERALD, P. History of Pickwick, with a Bibliography. 8vo. Lond., 1891. J 3 S 22
Chronicles of Bow-street Police Office. 2 vols. 8vo. Lond., 1888. B 4 T 23, 24
Life and Times of John Wilkes, Lord Mayor of London. 2 vols. 8vo. Lond., 1888. C 15 Q 1, 2
Life of Mrs. Catherine Clive ; with an Account of her Adventures on and off the Stage ; a Round of her Characters. 8vo. Lond., 1888. C 3 R 18
Lives of the Sheridans. 2 vols. 8vo. Lond., 1886.
C 13 T 9, 10

FITZGIBBON, E. G. By-Laws, Regulations, &c., of the Corporation of the City of Melbourne, 1870. Roy. 8vo. Melb., 1870. MF 2 T 59

FITZHERBERT, Judge A. La Graunde Abridgement. 2 vols. (in 1.) Fol. Lond., 1565. F 38 Q 20 ‡

FITZPATRICK, Wm. J. Curious Family History ; or, Ireland before the Union. Fifth edition. 12mo. Dublin, 1869. B 29 P 13
Secret Service under Pitt. 8vo. Lond., 1892. B 24 T 10
[See O'Connell, D.]

FLANAGAN, R. J. Aborigines of Australia. 8vo. Sydney, 1888.* MA 1 P 49

FLAUBERT, G. Par les Champs et par les Grèves. 12mo. Paris, 1886. D 18 P 14
Correspondance. 3 vols. 12mo. Paris, 1891.
C 14 P 23-25
Madame Bovary. 12mo. Paris, 1891. J 18 P 36
Salambô. 12mo. Paris, 1892. J 18 P 37
La Tentation de Saint Antoine. 12mo. Paris, 1891.
J 18 P 38
L'Education Sentimentale 12mo. Paris, 1891. J 18 P 39
Bouvard et Pécuchet. 12mo. Paris, 1891. J 18 P 40
Trois Contes : Un cœur simple ; La Légende de St. Julien l'Hospitalier ; Hérodias. 12mo. Paris, 1890. J 18 P 41

FLAXMAN, J. Drawings of. [See Colvin, S.]

FLEAY, F. G. Biographical Chronicle of the English Drama, 1559-1642. 2 vols. 8vo. Lond., 1891.
C 18 Q 13, 14
Chronicle History of the London Stage, 1559-1642. 8vo. Lond., 1890. B 6 S 6
Shakespeare Manual. 12mo. Lond., 1876. H 7 U 30

FLECKEISON, A. [See Plautus M. A., and Terentius, P.]

FLEMING, G. Roaring in Horses (Laryngismus paralyticus) : its History, Nature, Causes, Prevention, and Treatment. 8vo. Lond., 1889. A 1 T 37
Practical Horse Keeper. 8vo. Lond. (n.d.) A 18 R 10

FLEMMIGIUS, C. F. De Commodis Vitæ Sobriæ. Sm. 4to. Vitembergæ, 1705. F 11 Q 28

FLETCHER, A. E. [*See* Sonnenschein, S., & Co.]

FLETCHER, C. W. Handbell Ringing. 12mo. Lond. (n.d.) A 23 Q 18

FLETCHER, J. Best Plays. [*See* Beaumont, F.]

Bonduca. [*See* Beaumont, F.]

The Chances : a Comedy. [*See* British Drama, Modern, 3.]

The False One. [*See* Beaumont, F.]

A King and no King. [*See* Beaumont, F.]

The Maid's Tragedy. [*See* Beaumont, F.]

Philaster. [*See* Beaumont, F.]

Rule a Wife and Have a Wife : a Comedy. [*See* British Drama, Modern, 3.]

Thierry and Theodoret. [*See* Beaumont, F.]

Two Noble Kinsmen. [*See* Shakespeare, W.]

The Widow : a Comedy. [*See* Jonson, B.]

FLETCHER, J. J. Catalogue of Papers and Works relating to the Mammalian Orders, Marsupialia and Monotremata. 8vo. Sydney (n.d.) MK 1 T 31

FLETCHER, J. S. Short Life of Cardinal Newman. 8vo. Lond., 1890. C 16 Q 19

FLETCHER, P. [*See* Indian and Colonial Exhibition, 1886.]

FLETCHER, W. I. [*See* Co-operative Index, &c., *and* Poole, W. F.]

FLETCHER, W. Roby. Egyptian Sketches. 8vo. Adelaide, 1892. MB 2 P 51

FLEURIEU, C. Découvertes des François en 1768-69, dans le sud-est de la Nouvelle Guinée. 4to. Paris, 1790. MD 7 P 11 †

FLEURY de CHABOULON, Le Baron de, Mémoires pour servir à l'histoire de. La Vie Privée, du Retour, et du Règne de Napoléon en 1815. 2 vols. (in 1). 8vo. Lond., 1819. C 18 Q 3

FLIGHT, W. A Chapter in the History of Meteorites. 8vo. Lond., 1887. A 3 T 44

FLINDERS, M. Ontdekkings-Reis naar het Groote Zuidland anders Nieuw Holland, 1801-3. 4 vols. 8vo. Haarlem, 1815-16. MD 6 8 16-19

FLINN, D. E. Ireland ; its Health Resorts and Watering Places. 8vo. Lond., 1888. D 18 U 4

FLORUS, L. A. Epitome Rerum Romanarum ; adnotationes addidit C. A. Dukerus. 2 vols. (in 1). 8vo. Lugd. Bat., 1744. B 30 R 2

FLOWER, W. H. The Horse : a Study in Natural History. 8vo. Lond., 1891. A 18 Q 21

FLOWER, Dr. W. H., and LYDEKKER, R. Introduction to the Study of Mammals, living and extinct. 8vo. Lond., 1891. A 14 S 54

FLOYER, A. M. The Evolution of Ancient Hinduism. 8vo. Lond., 1888. G 13 T 43

FLUGEL, Dr. J. G. Practical Dictionary of the English and German Languages. 2 vols. 8vo. Leipsic, 1847. K 12 U 18, 19

FLUKE, The. What it is, Why it is, How to get rid of it. 8vo. Hobart (n.d.) MA 3 Q 31

FLYNN, P. J. Irrigation Canals and other Irrigation Works. Roy. 8vo. San Francisco, 1892. A 22 V 24

FOIGNY, G. de. Nieuwe Reize na het Zuid-Land, Behelzende de Gewoontens en Zeden der Zuidlanders, der zelver Godtsdienst, Oeffeningen, Studien, Oorlogen, Gediertens, en alle de voornaamste Zeldsaamheden welke aldaar gevonden worden, door Jacques Sadeur. Sm. 4to. Amsterdam, 1701. MJ 2 T 43

Voyage de la Terre Australe par Mr. Sadeur. 18mo. Lyon, 1695. MJ 3 P 3

FOL, Dr. H. Lehrbuch der vergleichenden mikroskopischen Anatomie, mit einschluss der vergleichenden Histologie und Histogenie. Roy. 8vo. Leip., 1884. A 29 V 5

FOLK-LORE (*incorporating the Archæological Review and The Folk-Lore Journal*). Vols. 1, 2. 8vo. Lond., 1890-91.

FOLK-LORE JOURNAL, The (*from 1890 continued as Folk-Lore*). Vols. 3-7. 8vo. Lond., 1885-89 E

FOLK-LORE SOCIETY. Publications. 8vo. Lond., 1888-90. E

Studies on the Legend of the Holy Grail.
Folk-Tales of the Magyars.
Folk and Hero Tales.
Exempla of J. de Vitry.
Hand-Book of Folk-lore.

FONSECA, Dr. J. S. da. Viagem ao Redor do Brasil, 1875-78. 2 vols. Imp. 8vo. Rio de Janeiro, 1880-81. D 15 V 1, 2

FONTAINE, La. [*See* La Fontaine.]

FONTAINE, N., "Sieur de Royaumont." History of the Old and New Testaments. Illustrated, with Appendices. 2 vols. fol. Lond., 1688-90. G 12 Q 14, 15‡

FONTANE, M. Histoire Universelle. Les Iraniens : Zoroastre. 8vo. Paris, 1890. B 35 T 3

FOOTE, S. The Author : a Comedy. [*See* British Drama, Modern.]

The Commissary : a Comedy. [*See* British Drama, Modern, 5.]

The Devil upon two Sticks : a Comedy. [*See* British Drama, Modern, 5.]

Dr. Last in his Chariot : a Comedy. [*See* Bickerstaff, I.]

Englishman in Paris : a Comedy. [*See* British Drama, Modern, 5.]

Englishman returned from Paris : a Comedy. [*See* British Drama, Modern, 5.]

The Knights : a Comedy. [*See* British Drama, Modern, 5.]

The Lame Lover : a Comedy. [*See* British Drama, Modern, 5.]

FOOTE, S.—*contd.*
The Liar: a Comedy. [*See* British Drama, Modern, 5.]
The Maid of Bath: a Comedy. [*See* British Drama, Modern, 5.]
The Mayor of Garratt: a Comedy. [*See* British Drama, Modern, 5.]
The Minor: a Comedy. [*See* British Drama, Modern, 5.]
The Orators: a Comedy. [*See* British Drama, Modern, 5.]
The Patron: a Comedy. [*See* British Drama, Modern, 5.]
Taste: a Comedy. [*See* British Drama, Modern, 5.]

FOOTT, M. H. Morna Lee, and other Poems. 2nd edition. 8vo. Lond., 1890. M H 1 U 13

FORBES, Anna. Insulinde: Experiences of a Naturalist's Wife in the Eastern Archipelago. 8vo. Edinb., 1887. D 17 R 3

FORBES, Archibald: The Afghan Wars, 1839–42 and 1878–80; with Portraits and Plans. 8vo. New York, 1892. B 17 Q 7
Havelock. (English Men of Action.) 12mo. Lond., 1890. C 12 P 34
William of Germany: a Succinct Biography of William I., German Emperor and King of Prussia. 8vo. Lond., 1888. C 14 Q 22

FORBES, Bishop A. P.: a Memoir; by the Rev. D. J. Mackey. 8vo. Lond., 1888. C 13 R 19

FORBES, D. Hindūstānī Manual. New edition, revised by J. T. Platts. 18mo. Lond., 1874. K 16 P 19

FORBES, G. A Course of Lectures on Electricity. 8vo. Lond., 1888. A 21 Q 5

FORBES, Dr. J. Physiological Effects of Alcoholic Drinks; with Documents and Records of the Massachusetts Temperance Society. 12mo. Boston, 1848. F 11 P 37

FORBES-MACKENZIE ACT, Evidence on the. 12mo. Manchester, 1878. F 11 P 56

FORBIN, Count de. Recollections of Sicily. [*Bound with Cramp's "Voyage to India."*] 8vo. Lond., 1823. M D 7 R 38

FORCELLINI, A. Totius Latinitatis Lexicon. Tomes 1–11. Prati, 1858–87. K 14 R 1–11 †
[*See also* Facciolati, J.]

FORD, H. Theory and Practice of Archery; revised by W. Butt. 8vo. Lond., 1887. A 17 W 39

FORD, J. Best Plays; edited, with an Introduction and Notes, by H. Ellis. (Mermaid Series.) 8vo. Lond., 1888. H 4 Q 29
The Lover's Melancholy.—'Tis Pity she's a Whore.—The Broken Heart.—Love's Sacrifice.—Perkin Warbeck.
The Broken Heart: a Tragedy. [*See* British Drama, Modern, 1.]

FORD, R. Handbook for Travellers in Spain. (Murray's Handbooks.) 7th edition. 2 vols. 12mo. Lond., 1890. D 12 S 4, 5

FOREIGN ARMIES: their Formation, Organization, and Strength. 8vo. Lond., 1886. A 29 Q 17

FOREIGN FIELD SPORTS, FISHERIES, SPORTING ANECDOTES, &c., from Drawings by Messrs. Howitt, Atkinson, Clark, &c.; with a Supplement of New South Wales. 4to. Lond., 1819. M A 12 Q 42 †

FOREIGN OFFICE LIST. 6 vols. 8vo. Lond., 1887–92. E

FOREMAN, John. The Philippine Islands. 8vo. Lond., 1890. D 16 U 20

FORESTER, H. [*See* Sophia, Electress of Hanover.]

FORLONG, Maj.-Gen. J. G. R. Rivers of Life; or, Sources and Streams of the Faiths of Man in All Lands. 2 vols. 4to., and chart. Lond., 1883. G 13 S 9–11 †

FORNERON, H. Louise de Kerouaille, Duchess of Portsmouth, 1649–1734; or, how the Duke of Richmond gained his Pension. 8vo. Lond., 1887. C 13 T 1

FORREST, A. Journal of Expedition from De Grey to Port Darwin. Fol. Perth, 1880. M D 2 P 3 ‡

FORREST, J. [*See* Denison, Sir W.]

FÖRSTEMANN, E. Geschichte des deutschen Sprachstammes. 2 vols. roy. 8vo. Nordhausen, 1874. K 16 Q 24, 25

FORSTER, Dr. G. Florulæ Insularum Australium Prodromus. 8vo. Gottingæ, 1786. M A 3 S 17
De Plantis Esculentis Insularum Oceani Australis Commentario Botanica. 12mo. Berolini, 1786. M A 3 P 13

FORSTER, H. O. Arnold-. Laws of Every-day Life : for the use of schools. 12mo. Lond., 1881. F 14 Q 5

FORSTER, J. R. Observations made during a Voyage round the World, on Physical Geography, &c. 4to. Lond., 1778. M A 2 P 2 †

FORSTER, Jos. Four Great Teachers: John Ruskin, Thomas Carlyle, Ralph Waldo Emerson, and Robert Browning. 8vo. Orpington, 1890. C 12 Q 11
Some French and Spanish Men of Genius. 8vo. Lond., 1891. C 16 P 11

FORSTER, W. Midas. 8vo. Lond., 1884. MH 1 R 29

FORSTER, Rt. Hon. W. E. Life of; by T. W. Reid. 2 vols. Roy. 8vo. Lond., 1888. C 12 T 7, 8

FORSTER, W. T. The Wreck of the Maria; or Adventures of the New Guinea Prospecting Association. 8vo. Sydney, 1872. M D 3 S 51

FORSYTH, A. Australian National Federation on Democratic Lines. 12mo. Sydney, 1891. M F 2 P 67

FORSYTH, Sir D. Autobiography and Reminiscences of; edited by Ethel Forsyth. 8vo. Lond., 1887. C 13 U 20

FORSYTH, W. Cases and Opinions on Constitutional Law, and Various Points of English Jurisprudence. Roy. 8vo. Lond., 1869. F 12 R 25

FORTNIGHTLY REVIEW. New Series, Vols. 39–51.
Roy. 8vo. Lond., 1886–92. E

FORTUNATIANUS, C., and DIONYSIUS HALICAR-
NASSENSIS.
OPUSCULA. Sm. 4to. [n.p. n.d.] G 16 S 48
Chirii Consultii Fortunatiani Rhetoricorum libri tres.
Dialectica [ejusdem].
Computus [ejusdem].
Francisci Puteolani Epistola ad Jacobum Antiquarium.
Dionysii Halycarnasei præcepta de oratione nuptiali per Theo-
dorum Gazen e Græco in Latinum traducta.
Dionysii Halycarnasei præcepta de oratione natalitia per Theo-
dorum Gazen e Græco in Latinum traducta.
Dionysii Halycarnasei præcepta de compouendis epithalamiis
per Theodorum Gazen e Græco traducta.
Oratio nuptialis.

FORTUNES MADE IN BUSINESS; a Series of
Sketches, from the recent History of Industry and
Commerce; by Various Writers. 3 vols. 8vo. Lond.,
1884–87. C 13 T 11–13

FORUM, The. Vols. 1–13. 8vo. New York, 1886–91. E

FOSCOLO, U. Poesie. 8vo. Firenze, 1888. H 8 Q 41

FOSS, H. E. [*See* Theophrastus.]

FOSTER, C. W., and GREEN, J. J. History of the
Wilmer Family, together with some account of their
Descendants. 4to. Leeds, 1888. C 12 V 8

FOSTER, F. [*See* Puseley, D.]

FOSTER, J. Alumni Oxonienses : the Members of the
University of Oxford, 1500-1886. 8 vols. Imp. 8vo.
Oxford, 1887–92. C 17 U 5–12
Pedigrees recorded at the Visitations of the County Pala-
tine of Durham, 1575, 1615, and 1666; edited by J.
Foster. 8vo. Lond., 1887. K 12 V 5
Register of Admissions to Gray's Inn, 1521–1889, together
with the Register of Marriages in Gray's Inn Chapel,
.1695–1754. Roy. 8vo. Lond., 1889. K 8 U 3
Visitation of Middlesex,, began in 1663; by W. Ryley
and H. Dethick; edited by J. Foster. Roy. 8vo. Lond.,
1887. K 8 U 4
[*See* Chester, Col. J. C.]

FOSTER, J. J. The Jenolan Caves. 8vo. Sydney, 1890.
MD 2 W 32

FOSTER, W. J. District Courts' Act of 1858 and District Courts' Amendment Act of 1859, with Practical
Notes. 8vo. Sydney, 1859. MF 1 T 68

FOTHERGILL, J. M. Food for the Invalid, the Con-
valescent, the Dyspeptic, and the Gouty. 8vo. Lond.,
1884. A 22 Q 3
Manual of Dietetics. Roy. 8vo. Lond., 1887. A 26 U 2

FOTHERINGHAM, J. Studies in the Poetry of Robert
Browning. 8vo. Lond., 1887. J 5 Q 36

FOTHERINGHAM, L. M. Adventures in Nyassaland :
a Two Years' Struggle with Arab Slave-dealers in Central Africa. 8vo. London, 1891. D 14 Q 8

L

FOURNIER, M. Les Statuts et Privilèges des Univer-
sités Françaises depuis leur fondation jusqu'en 1789.
Tome 1. 4to. Paris, 1890. F 29 Q 11 ‡

FOWLER, F. Last Gleanings. 8vo. Lond., 1864.
MJ 1 T 39

FOWLER, T. [*See* Wilson J. M.]

FOWLER, W. Appreciation of Gold : an Essay. 8vo.
Lond., 1886. F 5 Q 42

FOWLER, W. W. Tales of the Birds. 8vo. Lond.,
1888. J 12 Q 27

FOX, C. J. Life of ; by H. O. Wakeman. (Statesmen
Series.) 8vo. Lond., 1890. C 12 R 33
Early History of ; by G. O. Trevelyan. 8vo. Lond., 1880.
O 11 P 36

FOX, G. Journal ; or, Historical Account of the Life, &c.,
of. 3rd edition. Fol. Lond., 1765. C 42 S 17 ‡

FOX-BOURNE. [*See* Bourne, H. R. Fox-.]

FOY-VAILLANT, J. Seleucidarum Imperium, sive Historia Regum Syriæ. 2nd edition. Sm. fol. Hagæ-
Comitum, 1732. B 42 P 20 ‡

FRAGMENTA GENEALOGICA. Vol. I. Imp. 8vo.
Lond., 1889. K 12 S 23 †

FRANC, M. J. Vermont Vale; or, Home Pictures in
Australia. 3rd edition. 8vo. London, 1876. MJ 1 U 12

FRANCE. Travaux des Tribunaux en Matière Commer-
ciale, &c. 4to. Paris, 1888. E
Statistique des Perches Maritimes et de l'Ostréiculture,
1886–87. 2 vols. 8vo. Paris, 1888–89. E
Compte de l'Exploitation du Monopole des Tabacs,
1886–87. 2 vols. 4to. Paris, 1888–89. E
Annuaire des Syndicats Professionels, &c., 1890. 8vo.
Paris, 1890. E

FRANCESCHI, E. L. Dialoghi di Lingua Parlata. 8vo.
Torino, 1888. J 11 W 16

FRANCIS I. [*See* Coignet, Clarisse.]

FRANCIS, John, Publisher of the *Athenæum* ; A Literary
Chronicle of Half-a-century : Compiled by J. C. Francis.
2 vols. 8vo. Lond., 1888. C 14 Q 15, 16

FRANCIS, John C. John Francis, Publisher of the
Athenæum ; A Literary Chronicle of Half-a-century.
2 vols. 8vo. Lond., 1888. C 14 Q 15, 16

FRANCIS, Sir Phillip. [*See* Bustecd, H. E.]

FRANCK, S. "The Totalisator. The Instrument Can't
Lie." 12mo. Sydney, 1879. MA 2 P 71

FRANCKLIN, T. [*See* Sophocles.]

FRANKENSTEIN, E. N. [*See* Chess Problem.]

FRANKLIN, B., as a Man of Letters; by J. B. Macmaster. (American Men of Letters.) 12mo. Boston, 1887.   C 1 R 42

Complete Works of ; including his Autobiography. Compiled and edited by J. Bigelow. 10 vols. 8vo. New York, 1887-88.   J 3 V 7-16

[Life of]; by J. T. Morse, jr. (American Statesmen). 12mo. Boston, 1889.   C 13 Q 4

Vie de Franklin ; par. F. A. M. Mignet. 3rd edition. 12mo. Paris, 1887.   C 14 P 20

[*See* Hale, E. E.]

FRANKLIN, Sir J. Sir John Franklin's Expedition. [*See* Osborn, Lieut. S.]

Life of, and The North West Passage, by Captain A. H. Markham. 8vo. Lond., 1891.   C 15 Q 16

Acts of Lieutenant-Governors of Tasmania. [*See* Tasmania.]

Discovery of the Fate of Sir John Franklin. [*See* Maclintock, Sir F. L.]

The Last of the Arctic Voyages. [*See* Belcher, Sir E.]

FRANKLIN, Dr. T. Earl of Warwick : A Tragedy. [*See* British Drama, Modern, 2.]

Matilda : A Tragedy. [*See* British Drama, Modern, 2.]

FRANKLYN, Dr. H. B. Great Battles of 1870 and Blockade of Metz. Roy. 8vo. Lond., 1887.   B 26 U 9

FRANKLYN, H. Mortimer. Unit of Imperial Federation: a Solution of the Problem. 8vo. Lond., 1887. MF 1 R 50

FRANQUEVILLE, Comte de. [*See* Cobden Club.]

FRANZ, D. Alcohol: quid in respiratione cordisque actione efficiat. 8vo. Gryphiswaldiae, 1862.   F 11 Q 5

FRASER, A. A. Daddy Crips' Waifs : A Tale of Australasian Life and Adventure. 8vo. Lond., 1887.   MJ 1 Q 46

FRASER, Prof. A. C. [Life of] Locke. 12mo. Edinb., 1890.   C 12 P 20

FRASER, Right Rev. J., second Bishop of Manchester : a Memoir, 1818-85 ; by T. Hughes. 8vo. Lond., 1887.   C 13 U 12

FRASER, Major James. Major Fraser's Manuscript : his Adventures in Scotland and England ; his Mission to, and Travels in, France in Search of his Chief; his Services in the Rebellion (and his Quarrels) with Simon Fraser, Lord Lovat ; 1696-1737. Edited by Lieut.-Colonel A. Ferguson. 2 vols. 12mo. Edinb., 1889.   C 2 P 7, 8

FRASER, Dr. John. Aborigines of Australia. Stories about the Kamilaroi Tribe. Imp. 8vo. Maitland, 1882.   MA 1 U 47

Aborigines of New South Wales. 8vo. Sydney, 1883.   MA 3 S 16

Another Copy. 8vo. West Maitland (n.d.)   MA 1 R 39

The Latin Verb *Jubere*: A Linguistic Study. 8vo. Sydney, 1888.   MK 1 T 33

The Numerals in the Etruscan Language. 8vo. Sydney, 1888.   MK 1 T 32

FRASER, J. B. Views in the Himala Mountains. Fol. Lond., 1820.   D 43 P 16‡

FRASER, M. A. C. Western Australian Year Book for 1890-91. 8vo. Perth, 1891-1892   ME 6 S

FRASER, Simon. [*See* Lovat, Lord.]

FRASER, Sir Wm. The Lennox Family : Memoirs and Muniments. 2 vols. 4to. Edinb., 1874.   B 13 S 15, 16

Words on Wellington : the Duke—Waterloo—the Ball. 8vo. Lond., 1889.   C 13 R 12

Disraeli and his Day. 8vo. Lond., 1891.   C 13 S 6

FRATER, W. J. Tour in New Zealand and Australia : a Lecture. 18mo. Newcastle-upon-Tyne, 1887. MD 1 S 55

FRAZER, J. G. The Golden Bough : a Study in Comparative Religion. 2 vols. 8vo. Lond., 1890. G 2 S 35, 36

Totemism. 8vo. Edinb., 1887.   G 8 Q 23

FREAM, William. The Rothamsted Experiments on the Growth of Wheat, Barley, and the Mixed Herbage of Grass Land. 8vo. Lond., 1888.   A 18 R 5

FRÉDÉGAIRE. Histoire des Francs. [*See* Grégoire de Tour.]

FREDERICK II, King of Prussia. Youth of Frederick the Great ; by E. Lavisse. Trans. by S. L. Simeon. 8vo. Lond., 1891.   C 18 Q 6

FREDERICK WILLIAM III. Frederick, Crown Prince and Emperor : a biographical sketch dedicated to his memory ; by Rennell Rodd. 8vo. Lond., 1888.   C 12 Q 6

Two Royal Lives : the Crown Prince and Princess of Germany ; by Dorothea Roberts. 12mo. Lond., 1887.   C 12 Q 3

FREDERICKSON, A. D. Ad Orientem. Roy. 8vo. Lond., 1890.   D 17 U 13

FREE CHURCH OF SCOTLAND. Acts of the Synod of the Free Presbyterian Church of Victoria. Part 1. 8vo. Melb., 1851.   MG 1 R 63

Apostasy of the Majority of the Free Synod of Victoria from the protest of the. 8vo. Edinb., 1858. MG 1 R 28

Correspondence between the Free Synod of Victoria and the Dissentient Brethren anent Reconciliation. 8vo. Melb. (n.d.)   MG 1 R 28

Extracts from the records of the Synod of Victoria and the Free Synod of Victoria on the subject of Union between the two Churches. 8vo. Melb., 1857.   MG 1 R 28

The Free Church Narrative. 8vo. Melb., 1857.   MG 1 R 28

Letter from Ministers of the Free Church of Scotland to the Free Presbyterian Synod of Victoria. 8vo. Launceston (n.d.)   MG 1 R 28

Letter to the Moderator and Brethren of the Free Presbyterian Synod of Victoria from the Rev. W. Cunningham and other Ministers. 8vo. Edinb., 1857. MG 1 R 28

FREE CHURCH OF SCOTLAND—*contd.*
Statement of Mr. James Cowan, and Counter Statement by the Committee of Management of Chalmers' Church, Melbourne, relative to Iron Building sent to Melbourne for use of the Free Church. 8vo. Melb., 1860.
MG 1 R 63
Union in Victoria. Extracts from letters recently received from Victoria. 8vo. (n.p.n.d.) MG 1 R 63

FREE TRADE AND LIBERAL ASSOCIATION OF NEW SOUTH WALES. Report of Proceedings of First Annual Conference. Roy. 8vo. Sydney, 1889.
MF 1 S 5

FREEMAN; Prof. E. A. Historical Essays. 4th Series. 8vo. Lond., 1892. B 36 S 2
Four Oxford Lectures, 1887 : Fifty Years of European History.—Teutonic Conquest in Gaul and Britain. 8vo. Lond., 1888. B 25 T 4
History of Sicily from the earliest times. 3 vols. 8vo. Oxford, 1891-92. B 30 U 8-10
Historic Towns : Exeter. 8vo. Lond., 1887. B 22 Q 9
[Life of] William the Conqueror. 8vo. Lond., 1888.
[*See* Britannic Confederation.] C 3 R 17

FREEMAN, H. W. The Thermal Baths of Bath, together with the Aix Massage and Natural Vapour Treatment. 8vo. Lond., 1888. A 13 P 49

FREEMAN, J. Lights and Shadows of Melbourne Life. 8vo. Lond., 1888. MD 4 R 44

FREEMAN, P. Architectural History of Exeter Cathedral. 8vo. Exeter, 1873. B 22 R 14

FREEMAN'S JOURNAL, 1852-53, 1887-91. 11 vols. Fol. Sydney, 1852-91. ME

FREEMASONRY, Etiquette of; by "An Old Past Master." 12mo. Lond., 1890. J 1 S 52
History of the Ancient and Honorable Fraternity of Free and Accepted Masons. Roy. 8vo. Boston, 1891.
B 24 V 12

FREILIGRATH, F. Gedichte. 18mo. Stuttgart, 1855.
H 6 P 51

FREISTMANTEL, Prof. O. Fossil Flora of the Gondwána System. [*See* India—Palæontologia Indica.]

FREMANTLE, Hon. and Rev. W. H. [*See* Grey, A.]

FRESENIUS, Dr. C. R. Quantitative Chemical Analysis. 7th edition. Vol. 1. 8vo. Lond., 1876. A 21 S 1

FRÉVILLE, A. F. J. Histoire des Nouvelles Decouvertes faites dans la Mer du Sud en 1767-70. 2 vols. 8vo. Paris, 1774. MD 7 S 47, 48

FREY, A. R. Sobriquets and Nicknames. 8vo. Lond., 1887. K 19 R 3

FREYCINET, Capt. L. Voyage de Découvertes aux Terres Australes. L'Atlas Historique, Deuxième Partie. 4to Paris, 1811. MD 11 P 15 †

FRIEDEL, H. Deutsche Bucheinbände. [*See* Maul, J.]

FRIENDS. Biographical Catalogue ; being an account of the Lives of Friends and others whose Portraits are in the London Friends' Institute. 8vo. Lond., 1888.
C 14 T 2

FRITH, I. Life of Giordano Bruno, the Nolan ; revised by Prof. M. Carriere. 8vo. Lond., 1887. C 13 S 5

FRITH, W. P. John Leech ; his Life and Work. 2 vols. 8vo. Lond., 1891. C 18 Q 11, 12
My Autobiography and Reminiscences. 2 vols. 8vo. Lond., 1887. C 13 T 5, 6
Further Reminiscences. 3rd edition. (My Autobiography and Reminiscences, vol. 3.) 8vo. Lond., 1888.
C 13 T 7

FROEBEL, F. The Education of Man ; translated and annotated by W. N. Hailmann. 12mo. New York, 1887. G 17 P 41

FROGGATT, W. W. Catalogue of Described Hymenoptera of Australia. 8vo. Sydney, 1890. MA 3 Q 29
Another copy. 8vo. Sydney, 1892. MA 3 S 18

FRONTIN or FRONTINUS, S. J. Opera. 8vo. Biponti, 1788. J 17 Q 3
Les Stratagèmes. [*See* Nisard, D.]

FROST, J. Trial of John Frost for High Treason. 8vo. Lond., 1840. F 9 S 27
Letter on Transportation, &c. 8vo. Lond. (n.d.)
MF 1 R 25

FROST, L. Compendium of Views of Australia. 4to. Sydney (n.d.) MD 1 Q 32 †

FROST, P. Hints for the Solution of Problems in the Third Edition of Solid Geometry. 8vo. Lond., 1887.
A 10 T 28

FROTHINGHAM, O. B. Memoir of William Henry Channing. 8vo. Lond., 1887. C 13 R 13

FROUDE, J. A. Cæsar : a Sketch. 8vo. Lond., 1879.
C 15 U 17
The English in the West Indies ; or, the Bow of Ulysses. 8vo. Lond., 1888. D 15 T 2
The Divorce of Catherine of Aragon: the Story as told by the Imperial Ambassadors at the Court of Henry VIII. 8vo. Lond., 1891. B 24 T 16
[Life of] Lord Beaconsfield. 8vo. Lond., 1890.
C 12 R 37
The Spanish Story of the Armada, and other essays. 8vo. Lond., 1892. B 16 Q 37
Froude's Negrophobia. [*See* Davis, N. D.]
[*See* Firth, J. C.]

FRUIN, Prof. R. Word from Holland on the Transvaal Question. 8vo. Utrecht, 1881. F 8 S 26

FRY, Elizabeth. [*See* Walford, L. B.]

FRY, E. H., "Hawkeye." Coming Events, No. 2. 8vo. Sydney, 1888. ME 5 Q

FRY, Katherine. History of the Parishes of East and West Ham; edited and revised by G. Pagenstecher. 4to. Lond., 1888. B 9 R 8 †

FUCHS, G. F. Die Alkoholismus und seine Bekämpfung. 8vo. Heilbronn, 1883. F 11 S 23

FULLER, Andrew S. Practical Forestry: a treatise on the propagation, planting, and cultivation of all the indigenous trees of the United States. 12mo. New York, 1889. A 18 Q 13

FULLERTON, Lady G. Life of; from the French of Mrs. A. Cravon, by H. J. Coleridge. 8vo. Lond., 1888. C 15 Q 25

FURETIERE, A. Le Roman Bourgeois. (Collection Jannet–Picard.) 2 vols. 12mo. Paris (n.d.) J 15 Q 33, 34

FURLEY, J. The Nunc Dimittis from an Evening Cathedral Service. Fol. Sydney (n.d.) MA 11 Q 15 †

FURNEAUX, H. [*See* Tacitus, C. C.]

FURNESS, H. H. [*See* Shakespeare, W.]

FURNISS, Harry. Royal Academy: an Artistic Joke. 4to. Lond., 1888. A 40 Q 1 ‡

FURNIVAL, F. J. [*See* Early English Text Soc.]

FYFE, H. H. Annals of our Time. Vol. 3, pt. 1. 8vo. Lond., 1889. B 21 T 28

FYFE, J. H. British Enterprise beyond the Seas; or, the Planting of our Colonies. 12mo. Lond., 1863. B 35 P 7

G

G ***, P. Mathias. [*See* Lettres sur les Iles Marquises.]

G. S. Frithiofs Saga. [*See* Tegnér, E.]

GABELENTZ, Prof. G. VON DER. The Languages of Melanesia. 8vo. Lond. (n.d.) MK 1 T 17

GABELENTZ, G. von der, and MEYER, A. B. Beiträge zur Kenntniss der Melanesischen, Mikronesischen und Papuanischen Sprachen. Imp. 8vo. Leipzig, 1892. MK 1 U 23

GÆDEKEN, Prof. C. G. Om Brændevinsdrik. 8vo. Kjöbenhavn, 1880. F 11 Q 54

GAINFORD, T. Memoir of Incidents in the Life and Labours of. Compiled by J. and W. R. Gainford. 8vo. Sunnyside, 1886. MC 1 Q 42

GAINSBOROUGH, T. Collection of Prints, Illustrative of English Scenery. Fol. Lond., 1802–05. A 40 P 10‡

Studies of Figures, by T. Gainsborough. Executed in exact imitation of the originals, by R. Lane. 4to. Lond., 1825. A 8 U 30

GAIRDNER, James. Henry the Seventh. 8vo. Lond., 1889. C 16 Q 8

GAIRDNER, Prof. W. T. The Physician as Naturalist. Addresses and Memoirs on the History and Progress of Medicine. 8vo. Glasgow, 1889. A 13 P 42

GAIUS. Institutionum Commentarii Quattuor. 8vo. Berolini, 1842. F 1 Q 31

GALE, F. The Game of Cricket. 8vo. Lond., 1887. A 16 Q 27

GALE, Dr. James. Story of a Blind Inventor, being some account of the Life and Labours of; by John Plummer. 8vo. Lond., 1868. C 14 Q 19

GALILEO GALILEI LINCEO. Galileo and his Judges: by F. R. Wegg-Prosser. 8vo. Lond., 1889. C 8 P 10

GALL, J., AND ROBERTSON, D. Popular Readings in Science. 8vo. Lond., 1892. A 29 Q 46

GALLENGA, Antonio. "L. Mariotti." Castellamonte; an Autobiographical Sketch illustrative of Italian Life during the Insurrection of 1831. 2 vols. Lond., 1856. C 16 Q 23, 24

Italy : Present and future. 2vols. 8vo. Lond., 1887. B 11 R 24, 25

Country Life in Piedmont. 8vo. Lond., 1858. D 9 Q 46

History of Piedmont. 3vols. 8vo. Lond., 1855. B 30 S 1–3

South America. 2nd edition. Lond., 1881. D 3 U 23

Invasion of Denmark in 1864. 2vols. 8vo. Lond., 1864. B 20 R 13, 14

GALLI, H. L' Allemagne en 1813. 8vo. Paris, 1889. B 26 T 14

L'Armée Française en Allemagne, 1806. 8vo. Paris, 1888. B 26 T 15

GALLIENNE, R. Le. [*See* Le Gallienne, R.]

GALLOWAY, R. Fundamental Principles of Chemistry, practically taught by a new method. 8vo. Lond., 1888. A 21 Q 13

GALLOWAY, W. Battle of Tofrek, fought near Suâkin, March 22, 1885, under Maj.-Gen. Sir J. C. M'Neill, in its relation to the Mahdist Insurrection in the Eastern Sûdan, &c. 4to. Lond., 1887. B 21 V 1

GALTON, A. Character and Times of Thomas Cromwell. 8vo. Birmingham, 1887. C 4 S 35

GALTON, F. Natural Inheritance. 8vo. Lond., 1889. A 1 W 42

GAMBETTA, Léon. Life of; by F. T. Marzials. (Statesmen Series.) 8vo. Lond., 1890. C 12 R 39

GAMBUS, Dr. L. De l'Alcoolisme Chronique. 8vo. Paris. 1873. F 11 R 17

GANDON, P. J. "Ecce Homo," in Political Economy. Letters addressed to Henry George. 8vo. Sydney, 1890. MF 3 P 42

Federation, National and Imperial. 8vo. Sydney, 1890. MF 3 P 41

GANGUILLET, E., AND KUTTER, W. R. General Formula for the uniform Flow of Water in Rivers, and other Channels. 8vo. Lond., 1889   A 22 T 25

GAOLS AND OTHER PLACES OF CONFINEMENT Report from Committees on. Fol. Lond., 1819   MF 1 U 35

GARCKE, E., and FELLS, J. M. Factory Accounts; their Principles and Practice: a Hand-book for Accountants and Manufacturers. 8vo. Lond., 1887.   F 12 Q 35

GARDEN PALACE, SYDNEY. Destruction of the Garden Palace by Fire, Friday 22nd Sept., 1882. Ob. fol. Sydney, 1882.   MB 3 P 13 ‡

GARDENERS' CHRONICLE. 43 vols. 4to. Lond., 1841-71, 1886-92.   E

GARDENER'S MAGAZINE. Vols. 29-34. Lond., 1886-91.   E

GARDINER, C. E. Law of Master and Servant. 12mo. Melb., 1890.   MF 3 P 54

GARDINER, S. R. Constitutional Documents of the Puritan Revolution, 1628-60. Oxford, 1889. B 23 R 5

History of the Great Civil War, 1642-1649. 3 vols. Lond., 1886-91.   B 5 T 39-41

Student's History of England. 8vo. Lond., 1892.   B 22 Q 25

GARDNER, P. New Chapters in Greek History: Results of Recent Excavations in Greece and Asia Minor. 8vo. Lond., 1892.   B 16 Q 36

GARDNER, S. [*See* Melsheimer, R. E.]

GARIBALDI, Giuseppe. Autobiography of. Authorised Translation by A. Werner, with Supplement by Jessie W. Mario. 3 vols. 8vo. Lond., 1889.   C 12 R 1-3

Memoire Autobiografiche. 8vo. Firenze, 1888. C 12 R 4

Garibaldi, di G. Guerzoni. 3rd edizione. 2 vols. 8vo. Firenze, 1889.   C 12 R 5, 6

GARNET, W. [*See* Beaumont. W.]

GARNETT, Lucy M. J. The Women of Turkey and their Folk-lore : with an Ethnographical Map and Introductory Chapters on the Ethnography of Turkey ; and Folk-conceptions of Nature ; and concluding Chapters on the Origins of Matriarchy, by John S. Stuart-Glennie. 2 vols. 8vo. Lond., 1890-91.   A 18 T 22, 23

GARNIER, R. M. History of the English Landed Interest. 8vo. Lond., 1892.   B 24 T 15

GARRAN, Dr. A. Picturesque Atlas of Australasia. 3 vols. fol. Sydney, 1886.   MD 6 P 13-15 ‡

Royal South Australian Almanack and General Directory for 1855. 12mo. Adelaide, 1855.   ME 4 P

GARRETT, E. H. Elizabethan Songs in Honour of Love and Beauty ; Collected and Illustrated by E. H. Garrett. 8vo. Lond., 1891.   H 7 V 31

GARRETT, Dr. J. H. The Action of Water on Lead. 12mo. Lond., 1891.   A 21 P 12

GARRETT, T. W. Ecclesiastical Practice, with Standing Rules and Notes thereon, Forms of Procedure, and Appendix of Acts and Reports of Cases. Roy. 8vo. Sydney, 1889.   MF 3 T 29

GARRICK, D. A Peep Behind the Curtain : a Farce. [*See* British Drama, Modern, 5.]

Bon Ton ; or, High Life Above Stairs : a Farce. [*See* British Drama, Modern, 5.]

The Clandestine Marriage : a Comedy. [*See* Coleman, G.]

The Guardian: a Comedy. [*See* British Drama, Modern, 5.]

High Life Below Stairs : a Farce. [*See* British Drama, Modern, 5.]

The Irish Widow : a Comedy. [*See* British Drama Modern, 5.]

Isabella : a Tragedy. [*See* British Drama, Modern, 1.]

Lethe: a Dramatic Satire. [*See* British Drama, Modern, 5.]

The Lying Valet : a Comedy. [*See* British Drama, Modern, 5.]

The Male Coquette : a Farce. [*See* British Drama, Modern, 5.]

Miss in Her Teens : a Farce. [*See* British Drama, Modern, 5.]

Neck or Nothing: a Farce. [*See* British Drama, Modern, 5.]

GARZIA, Francesco. Istoria della Conversione alla nostra Santa Fede dell' Isole Mariane ; nella Vita, predicatione, e morte del Ven. P. Diego Luigi di Sanvitores. 4to. Napoli, 1686.   C 14 T 23

GASQUET, F. A. Henry VIII., and the English Monasteries. 2 vols. 8vo. Lond., 1888-89. B 23 U 13, 14

GATTY, Mrs. Alfred. Book of Emblems, with Interpretations thereof. 8vo. Lond., 1872.   J 1 U 26

The Book of Sun-dials ; edited by H. K. F. Gatty and Eleanor Lloyd ; with an appendix on the Construction of Dials, by W. Richardson. 8vo. Lond., 1889.   A 29 U 9

GATTY, Rev. Dr. A. Hallamshire : the History of Sheffield. [*See* Hunter, J.]

GATTY, H. K. F. [*See* Gatty, Mrs. A.]

GAUHAROU, L. Géographie de la Nouvelle-Calédonie et Dépendances. 8vo. Nouméa, 1882.   MD 2 W 5

GAUTIER, L. Étude Clinique sur l'Absinthisme Chronique. 8vo. Paris, 1882.   F 11 S 21

GAUTIER, T. Œuvres complètes de. 30 vols. 8vo. Paris, 1880-88.   J 19 U 3-32

1. Caprices et Zigzags.
2. Constantinople.
3. Emaux et Camées.
4. Fusains et Eaux-Fortes.
5. Guide de l'Amateur au Musée du Louvre ; suivi de la Vie et les Œuvres de quelques Peintres.
6. Histoire du Romantisme ; suivie de Notices Romantiques et d'une Etude sur la Poésie Française, 1830-68.
7, 8. Le Capitaine Fracasse.
9. Le Roman de la Momie.
10. Les Grotesques.

GAUTIER, T.—*contd.*

11. Les Jeunes-France, Romans Goguenards; suivis de Contes Humoristiques.
12. Les Vacances du Lundi.—Tableaux de Montagnes.
13. Loin de Paris.
14, 15. L'Orient.
16. Mademoiselle de Maupin.
17. Nouvelles : Fortunio.—La Toison d'or.—Omphale.—Le petit chien de la Marquise.—Le Nid de Rossignols.—La Morte amoureuse.—La Chaîne d'or, ou l'Amant partagé.—Une Nuit de Cléopâtre.—Le roi Candaule.
18, 19. Poésies complètes.
20. Portraits contemporains ; Littérateurs, Peintres, Sculpteurs, Artistes dramatiques ; avec un Portrait de Théophile Gautier.
21. Portraits et Souvenirs littéraires :—Gérard de Nerval.—Madame Émile de Girardin.—Henri Heine.—Charles Baudelaire.—Achim d'Arnim
22. Romans et Contes.
23. Souvenirs de Théâtre, d'Art, et de Critique.
24. Spirite : Nouvelle Fantastique.
25. Tableaux à la Plume.
26. Tableaux de Siège, Paris, 1870-71.
27. Théâtre ; Mystère, Comédies, et Ballets :—Un Larme du Diable.—La Fausse Conversion, ou Bou Sang ne peut Mentir.—L'Amour Souffle ; ou, il veut.—Le Tricorne Enchanté.—Perrot Posthume.—Prologue de Falstaff.—Prologue d'Ouverture de l'Odéon.—Pierre Corneille.—La Femme de Diomède.—Prologue de Henriette Maréchal.—Prologue de Strucusée.—Le Sélam.—Giselle ; ou, les Wilis.—La Péri.—Paquerette.—Gemma.—Yanko, le Bandit.—Saccuntalâ.
28. Voyage en Espagne. (Tra los Montes.)
29. Voyage en Italie.
30. Voyage en Russie.

[*See* Villon, F.]

GAY, J. The Beggar's Opera. [*See* British Drama, Modern, 5.]

GAYLL, A. [*See* Donohue, F. J.]

GAZETTE DES BEAUX-ARTS. 65 vols. roy. 8vo. Paris, 1859-92. E

GEDDIE, Rev. J. Missionary Life among the Cannibals; being the Life of the Rev. J. Geddie ; by the Rev. G. Patterson. 8vo. Toronto, 1882. MC 1 Q 46

GEE, W. W. H. [*See* Stewart, Prof. B.]

GEFFCKEN, Dr. F. H. The British Empire ; with Essays on Prince Albert, Lord Palmerston, Lord Beaconsfield, Mr. Gladstone, and Reform of the House of Lords ; translated by S. J. Macmullan. 8vo. Lond., 1889. B 21 S 20

GEGENBAUR, Dr. C. Amphibien. 4to. Halle, 1861. A 42 R 13‡
Elements of Comparative Anatomy ; translated by J. Jeffrey Bell ; translation revised and preface written by E. R. Lankester. Roy. 8vo. Lond., 1878. A 27 U 2

GEIKIE, Prof. Archibald. Scenery of Scotland, viewed in connection with its Physical Geology. 2nd ed. 8vo. Lond., 1887. A 24 Q 1
The Teaching of Geography. 12mo. Lond., 1887. G 17 P 51

GEIKIE, Rev. Dr. A. C. Christian Missions to Wrong Places, Among Wrong Races, and in Wrong Hands. 8vo. Sydney, 1871. MD 5 P 31

GEIKIE, Rev. C. Holy Land and the Bible: a Book of Scripture Illustrations gathered in Palestine. 2 vols. 8vo. Lond., 1887. D 17 U 5, 6

GELDART, E. M. Simplified Grammar of Modern Greek. 8vo. Lond., 1883. K 20 Q 9

GELLIUS, A. Noctium Atticarum Libri XX. 2 vols. 8vo. Biponti, 1784. J 17 Q 1, 2
Noctium Atticarum Libri XX. ; ex recensione M. Hertz. 2 vols. (in 1). 12mo. Lipsiæ, 1853. J 15 R 44

GENEALOGIST, The. New Series. Vols. 3-7. 8vo. Lond., 1886-91. E

GENLIS, Comtesse de. Les Parvenus ; ou, les aventures de Julien Delmours. 2 vols. 8vo. Paris, 1819. J 5 Q 1, 2

GENTLEMAN'S MAGAZINE. Vols. 255-72. 8vo. Lond., 1887-92. E

GENTLEMAN'S MAGAZINE LIBRARY. Publications. 8vols. 4to. Lond., 1887-92. E
Architectural Antiquities. Parts 1, 2.
Bibliographical Notes.
English Topography. Parts 1, 2.
Literary Curiosities and Notes.
Romano-British Remains. Parts 1, 2.

GEOFFREY, Gaimar. Lestorie des Engles. [*See* Chronicles and Memorials of Great Britain, &c.]

GEOGHEGAN, H. C. Divorce Extension Justified ; by "An Irish Anglican." 8vo. Melb., 1888. MF 1 Q 24

GEOGRAPHICAL SOCIETY of Australasia. [*See* Royal Geographical Society.]

GEOGRAPHICAL SOCIETY of London. [*See* Royal Geographical Society.]

GEOLOGICAL MAGAZINE. 5 vols. 8vo. Lond., 1887-91. E

GEOLOGICAL SOCIETY of London. Quarterly Journal. Vols. 43-47. 8vo. Lond., 1887-91. E
Charter and Bye-laws. 8vo. Lond., 1877. F 9 R 29
List, 1883 and 1889. 2 vols. 8vo. Lond., 1883-89. E

GEOLOGISCHEN Reichs-Museums in Leiden, Sammlungen des, Herausgegeben von K. Martin und A. Wichmann. 1to. serie. Beiträge zur Geologie Ost-Asiens und Australiens. Bände 1-4. 8vo. Leiden, 1881-89. ME 9 4

GEOMETRY IN RELIGION, and the Exact Dates in Biblical History after the Monuments. Lond., 1890. G 12 S 36

GEORGE III. [*See* Preston, T.]

GEORGE, Henry. The Condition of Labour ; an Open Letter to Pope Leo XIII. 12mo. Lond., 1891. F 8 U 29
[*See* Cotton, F.]

GEPP, H. M. [*See* Nansen, F.]

GERARD, E. Land beyond the Forest : Facts, Figures, and Fancies from Transylvania. 2 vols. 8vo. Edinb., 1888. D 18 S 1, 2

GERMAIN, A. La Nouvelle-Calédonie au point de vue de l'Acclimatation. Roy. 8vo. Paris, 1875. MA 3 R 22

GERMAN LADY, A. [*See* New Zealand, Notes of a Tour through.]

GERMANN, Dr. H. Die Branntweinbesteuerung. 8vo. Berlin, 1886. F 11 S 22

GERMANY. Respublica et Status Imperii Roman-Germanici. 32mo. 2 vols. (in 1.) Lugd. Bat., 1634-40. B 27 P 1

GERMOND DE LAVIGNE, L. A. G. La Célestine. (Collection Jannet-Picard.) 12mo. Paris (n.d.) H 1 R 42
Histoire de Don Pablo Sécovie. [*See* Quercdo-Villegas, F. de.]

GERNING, Baron J. J. Von. Picturesque Tour along the Rhine, from Mentz to Cologne; translated from the German by J. Black. 2 vols. 4to. Lond., 1820. D 40 Q 13, 14 ‡

GERRALD, J. Trial of Joseph Gerrald, delegate from the London Corresponding Society to the British Convention, at Edinburgh, 1794, for Sedition. 8vo. Edinb., 1794. F 12 P 27

GERSTAËCKER, F. Two Convicts. 8vo. Lond., 1887. MJ 1 U 21

GESCHICHTE DER WISSENSCHAFTEN IN DEUTS-CHLAND. Geschichte der Kriegswissenschaften Vornehmlich in Deutschland; und Geschichte der Medicinischen Wissenschaften. Bande 21, 22. 2 vols. (in 4). 8vo. Munchen, 1889-93. A 17 V 36-39

GESELLSCHAFT ZUR BEKÄMPFUNG DER TRUNKSUCHT, Eingabe. 8vo. Basel, 1882. F 11 R 18

GESNER, J. M. Scriptores Rei Rusticæ Veteres Latini. [*See* Scriptores, and Lucian.]

GESSI, R. Séven Years in the Soudan. Illustrated. 8vo. Lond., 1892. D 14 U 12

GIBB, W., SKELTON, Dr. J., and HOPE, W. H. St. J. The Royal House of Stuart. Illustrated. 4to. Lond., 1890. B 40 P 2 ‡

GIBBINS, H. de B. English Social Reformers. 12mo. Lond., 1892. F 9 U 6
History of Commerce in Europe. 12mo. Lond., 1891. F 14 P 49

GIBBS, SHALLARD & CO. Illustrated Guide to Sydney and its suburbs, &c. 12mo. Sydney, 1882. MD 2 W 18

Illustrated Sydney News New South Wales Annual for 1873. 8vo. Sydney, 1873. ME 3 T

GIBSON, A. [*See* Bennett, G.]

GIBSON, G. R. The Stock Exchanges of London, Paris, and New York : a Comparison. 8vo. New York, 1889. F G R 37

GIBSON, J. Westby-. Bibliography of Shorthand. 8vo. Lond., 1887. K 19 R 2

GIBSON, Rev. M. Has Humanity gained from Unbelief ? Two nights' Debate between the Rev. M. Gibson and C. Bradlaugh. 12mo. Lond., 1889. G 2 V 27

GIDUMAL, Dayaram. Behramji M. Malabari : a Biographical Sketch. 12mo. Lond., 1892. C 16 P 18

GIELGUD, A. [*See* Czartoryski, Prince A.]

GIFFORD, J. Life of Wm. Pitt. [*See* Green, J. R.]

GILBERT, Elizabeth, and her Work for the Blind ; by Frances Martin. 8vo. Lond., 1887. C 16 Q 7

GILBERT, John T. History of the Irish Confederation and the War in Ireland, 1643-49. Vols. 1-5, and 7. 6 vols. 4to. Dublin, 1882-91. B 29 V 12-18
Jacobite Narrative of the War in Ireland, 1688-91. Sm. 4to. Dublin, 1892. B 24 V 15

GILBERT, P. H. [*See* New South Wales Sporting Annual.]

GILBERT, W. S. Songs of a Savoyard. 8vo. Lond., 1890. H 6 U 30

GILCHRIST, Anne ; her Life and Writings ; edited by H. H. Gilchrist, with Prefatory Notice by W. M. Rossetti. 8vo. Lond., 1887. C 15 U 2

GILCHRIST, H. H. [*See* Gilchrist, Anne.]

GILDER, W. H. Ice-pack and Tundra ; account of the Search for the "Jeannette," with Maps and Illustrations. Roy. 8vo. Lond., 1883. D 16 V 4

GILES, E. Australia Twice Traversed : the Romance of Exploration, being a Narrative compiled from Journals of Five Exploring Expeditions into and through South and Western Australia, 1872-76. 2 vols. 8vo. Lond., 1889. MD 3 S 52, 53

GILES, Dr. J. A. [*See* Bede, Ven., *and* Terentius Afer, P.]

GILL, G. Oxford and Cambridge Arithmetic. 12mo. Lond., 1886. A 25 P 30
The Student's Geography, Physical and Descriptive, Industrial and Commercial, Political and Social, Etymological and Historical. 8vo. Lond., 1890. D 11 R 21

GILL, Rev. S. T. Sketches in Victoria ; drawn on stone. 2 vols. ob. 12mo. Melb., 1854-55. MD 1 P 64, 65

GILL, T. Bibliography of South Australia. 8vo. Adelaide, 1886. MK 1 R 31

GILL, Rev. W. Selections from the Autobiography of. 8vo. Lond., 1888. MC 1 T 3

GILL, Rev. Wm. Wyatt. The South Pacific and New Guinea, Past and Present ; with Notes on the Hervey Group, an Illustrative Song, and various Myths. Roy. 8vo. Sydney, 1892. MD 7 U 8

GILLES, Pierre. De Bosporo Thracio, libri III. 24mo. Lugd. Bat., 1632. B 34 P 12

GILLESPIE, A. Bills of Sale and Interpleader in the Small Debts' Court of New South Wales. 12mo. Sydney, 1888. MF 3 P 55

GILLMORE, Parker. Through Gasa Land, and the Scene of the Portuguese Aggression. 8vo. Lond., 1890.
D 14 U 20

"Ubique." Days and Nights by the Desert. 8vo. Lond., 1881.
D 14 U 15

GILLRAY, J. Works of; edited by T. Wright. 4to. Lond. {(n.d.)
J 39 Q 26 ‡

GILMAN, A. The Saracens, from the Earliest Times to the fall of Bagdad. 8vo. Lond., 1887.
B 14 P 52

GILMAN, N. P. Profit Sharing between Employer and Employee. 8vo. Lond., 1890.
F 14 P 25

GIPPS, F. B. Comparison between the Prospect and Kenny Hill Schemes for Sydney Water Supply. 8vo. Sydney, 1880.
MA 3 Q 34

GIPPS, F. B., and CAMPBELL, W. Description of Wattle Flat Gold Field. 8vo. Sydney, 1873.
MD 3 S 40

GIPPS, Sir G. Speech of His Excellency on Immigration. 8vo. Sydney, 1842.
MF 2 Q 8
[*See* New South Wales—Crown Lands.]

GIRALDUS CAMBRENSIS. [*See* Barri, G.]

GIRARD, J. La Nouvelle-Guinée, Histoire de la Découverte, Description Géographique, la Race Papoue, Mœurs et Coutumes des Indigénes, Produits du Sol, Colonisation. Roy. 8vo. Paris, 1883.
MD 7 U 7

GIRAUD, Byng. Stable Building and Stable Fitting. 12mo. Lond., 1891.
A 19 Q 1

GISBORNE, W. The Colony of New Zealand: its History, &c. 8vo. Lond., 1888.
MB 1 Q 36
Official Handbook of New Zealand, Part 3. 8vo. Lond., 1884.
MD 7 Q 23

GIUSTI, G. Poesi di. Illustrate da A. Matarelli. Commentate ed annotate dal Prof. G. Cappi. Imp. 4to. Milano, 1887.
H 7 Q 4 †

GLADSTONE, Rt. Hon. W. E. The Impregnable Rock of Holy Scripture. 8vo. Lond., 1890.
G 13 U 49
Landmarks of Homeric Study. 12mo. Lond., 1890.
J 11 S 32
Life of; by G. W. E. Russell. 8vo. Lond., 1891.
C 14 P 28
Mr. Gladstone : a Study; by L. J. Jennings, M.P. 8vo. Edinb., 1887.
C 12 P 26
[*See* Buxton, S., Cobden Club, Geffcken, Dr. F. H., and Lubbock, Sir J.]

GLANCES AT GREAT AND LITTLE MEN; by "Paladin." 8vo. Lond., 1890.
C 15 Q 7

GLASER, L. Album of New Zealand Views. 8vo. Leip., 1887.
MD 3 Q 42

GLASS, H. A. Story of the Psalters : a History of the Metrical Versions of Great Britain and America, 1549–1885. 8vo. Lond., 1888.
G 8 Q 28

GLEICHEN, Count. With the Camel Corps up the Nile. 8vo. Lond., 1888.
D 14 S 1
[*See* Köppen, F. von.]

GLEIG, Rev. G. R. Life of Major-General Sir T. Munro. New edition. 2 vols. 8vo. Lond., 1831.
C 18 Q 20, 21.

GLENELG, Rt. Hon. C. G., Baron. Chaplain's Claims for Compensation. [*See* New South Wales—Crown Lands.]

GLENFIELD, E. On Strike, or where do the Girls Come in ? 12mo. Sydney, 1890.
MJ 1 Q 59

GLENNIE, John S. Stuart. [*See* Garnett, Lucy.]

GLENORCHY MURDERS, The. [*See* Griffiths, W.]

GLOVER, R. Boadicea : a Tragedy. [*See* British Drama, Modern, 2.]

GNEIST, Prof. R. History of the English Constitution. 2nd edition. 2 vols. 8vo. Lond., 1889.
B 5 T 27, 28

GODARD, J. G. George Birkbeck ; the Pioneer of Popular Education. 12mo. Lond., 1888.
C 16 P 26
Poverty : its Genesis and Exodus. 12mo. Lond., 1892.
F 9 U 13

GODDARD, Arthur. Players of the Period : Anecdotal, Biographical, and Critical Monographs of the Leading English Actors of the Day. 1st and 2nd series. 2 vols. 8vo. Lond., 1891.
C 14 R 13, 14

GODEFFROY MUSEUM. Journal des. Vols. 1-4. Imp. 4to. Hamburgh, 1873-74.
MA 3 Q 3-6 †

GODOLPHIN, Mary. Æsop's Fables, in Words of one syllable. Printed in the learners' style of Phonography, by I. Pitman. 12mo. Lond., 1888.
J 7 R 54
Life of ; by J. Evelyn ; edited by E. W. Harcourt. Lond., 1888.
C 14 Q 47

GODOLPHIN, John. Repertorium Canonicum ; or, the Ecclesiastical Laws of this Realm. Sm. 4to. Lond., 1687.
F 3 P 15

GODOLPHIN, Sidney, Earl of. Life of ; by the Hon. Hugh Elliot. 8vo. Lond., 1888.
C 9 U 20

GODWIN, Rt. Rev. F. Rerum Anglicarum Henrico VIII., Edwardo VI., et Maria regnantibus, Annales. Fol. Francfort, 1616.
B 42 S 10 ‡

GOEBEL, Prof. K. Outlines of Classification and Special Morphology of Plants. Roy. 8vo. Oxford, 1887.
A 20 V 4

GOELLER, F. [*See* Thucydides.]

GOETHE, J. W. von. Faust ; with notes by G. G. Zerffi. 8vo. Lond., 1859.
H 4 P 36
Correspondence between Goethe and Carlyle; edited by C. E. Norton. 8vo. Lond., 1887.
C 12 Q 9
Faust. Translated into English verse by Sir T. Martin. 9th edition. 2 vols. 12mo. Edinb., 1887.
H 1 R 24, 25
Goethe's Reineke Fox, West-eastern Divan, and Achilleid. Translated by A. Rogers. 8vo. Lond., 1890.
H 5 R 43

GOLD. Correspondence relative to the Recent Discovery of Gold in Australia. 2 vols. fol. Lond., 1852-57.
MF 8 P 27, 28 †

GOLD AND GOLD DIGGERS. 8vo. (n.p.n.d.)
MA 2 P 72

GOLDEN SHANTY, A. Australian Stories and Sketches in prose and verse. 8vo. Sydney, 1890. MJ 1 T 56

GOLDEN SOUTH, The. Memories of Australian Home Life, 1843–88 ; by "Lyth." 8vo. Lond., 1890.
MD 2 W 4

GOLDING, Charles. The Coinage of Suffolk. 4to. Lond., 1868. A 27 V 3

GOLDMAN, Jhr. W. C. F. Aanteekeningen gehouden op Eene Reis naar Dorei, (Noord-Oostkust van Guinée) 2 vols. (in 1.) 8vo. Amsterdam (n.d.) MD 7 S 45

GOLDSCHMIDT, Madame Jenny Lind. Memoir of, her early art-life and dramatic career, 1820–51 ; by Rev. H. S. Holland and W. S. Rockstro. 2 vols. 8vo. Lond. 1891. C 15 T 13, 14

GOLDSMID, E. [See Ritson, J.]

GOLDSMITH, O. The Good Natured Man : a Comedy. [See British Drama, Modern, 4.]
She Stoops to Conquer : a Comedy. [See British Drama, Modern, 4.]
Essays. [See Universal Library, The.]

GOLDSTEIN, J. R. G. Some New Species of Bryozoa from the Marion Islands, with notes on Bicellaria Grandis. 8vo. Melb., 1881. MA 3 Q 35

GOLLANCZ, Israel. Pearl : an English Poem of the 14th Century. Edited by I. Gollancz. 8vo. Lond., 1891.
H 7 U 26

GOLTGIUS, H. Imperatorum fere omnium vitæ, ac vivæ Imagines, a C. Julio Cæsar ad Carolum V. ex veteribus numismatibus. Fol. Antverp, 1557. A 42 R 23 ‡

GOLTZ, Lieut.-Col. Baron von der. The Nation in Arms ; translated by P. A. Ashworth. 8vo. Lond., 1887.
F 12 Q 37

GOMME, George Laurence. Ethnology in Folklore. 8vo. Lond., 1892. A 18 Q 28
The Village Community, with special reference to the origin and form of its survivals in Britain. 8vo. Lond., 1890. B 23 R 6

GONNER, E. C. K. [See Ricardo, D.]

GONNEVILLE, B. P. de. Première découverte du Monde Austral en 1504. (Prevost, A. F., Suite de l'histoire générale des voyages, tome, 17.) 4to. Amsterdam, 1761.
MD 11 P 16 †

GOOCH, Sir D. Diaries of. 12mo. Lond., 1892.
C 17 Q 25

GOOCH, Fanny C. Face to Face with the Mexicans. Imp. 8vo. Lond., 1887. D 15 V 6

GOOCH, J. Manual of the Act for the Union of Canada, Nova Scotia, and New Brunswick. 8vo. Ottawa, 1867.
F 4 S 27

GOOD WORDS. 5 vols. 8vo. Lond., 1887-91. E

GOODE, G. B. American Fishes : a Popular Treatise upon the Game and Food Fishes of North America. 4to. Lond., 1888. A 13 U 42

GOODE, Rev. Wm. Letter respecting the present state of things in the Church. 8vo. Lond., 1845. G 15 R 27

GOODEVE, T. M. On Gas Engines. 8vo. Lond., 1887.
A 25 Q 1

GOODFELLOW, John. Dietetic Value of Bread. 8vo. Lond., 1892. A 26 P 5

GOODMAN, George. The Church in Victoria during the Episcopate of the Rt. Rev. Chas. Perry, first Bishop of Melbourne. 8vo. Lond., 1892. MG 1 S 44

GOODRICH, H. N. Poetical Works. 12mo. Melb., 1873. MH 1 Q 48

GOODRICH, S. G. Tales about America and Australia, by "Peter Parley." New Edition. 12mo. Lond., 1862.
MB 1 P 27
Another Copy. 12mo. Lond., 1872. MB 1 P 28

GOODRIDGE, C. M. Statistical View of Van Diemen's Land, forming a complete Emigrant's Guide. 12mo. Exeter, 1832. MD 7 T 14

GOODWIN, Rev. H. Parish Sermons. 2nd ed. 8vo. Camb., 1855. G 13 Q 34

GOODWIN, H., and KNIGHT, Prof. Through the Wordsworth Country. Sm. fol. Lond., 1887. H 11 Q 4 †

GOODWIN, J. A. The Pilgrim Republic : an Historical Review of the Colony of New Plymouth. Roy. 8vo. Boston, 1888. B 1 V 17

GOODWIN, Rev. T. A. Seventy-six Years' Tussle with the Traffic. 8vo. Indianapolis, 1883. F 11 Q 49

GOODWIN, T. [See Mason, R.O.]

GOODWIN, Prof. W. W. Syntax of the Moods and Tenses of the Greek Verb. 8vo. Lond., 1889.
K 12 U 22

GORDON, A. The Future of the Empire ; or, a brief Statement of the case against Imperial Federation. 12mo. Lond., 1889. F 1 P 32

GORDON, A. Speech against the Church and School Lands Bill. 8vo. Sydney, 1880. MF 1 T 31

GORDON, Adam Lindsay. Poems. 4th Ed. 8vo. Melb. (n.d.) MH 1 U 8
Ashtaroth : a Dramatic Lyric. 8vo. Melb., 1867.
MH 1 U 7
Sea Spray and Smoke Drift. 8vo. Melb., 1867.
MH 1 S 62
The Laureate of the Centaurs; a Memoir of the Life of By J. Howlett-Ross. 8vo. Lond., 1888. MC 1 Q 30

GORDON, Sir A. H. Letters and Notes written during the Disturbances in the Highlands of Viti Levu, Fiji, 1876. 2 vols., 8vo. Edinb., 1879. MB 1 R 48, 49

M

GORDON, Surgeon-Gen. C. A. Comments on the Report of the Committee on M. Pasteur's Treatment of Rabies and Hydrophobia. 8vo. Lond., 1888.   A 26 S 2

GORDON, Major-Gen. Charles George. [Life of]; by Col. Sir W. F. Butler. (English Men of Action.) 8vo. Lond., 1889.   C 12 Q 34

Fac-simile of his last Journals. Imp. 4to. Lond., 1885.   C 34 P 15‡

Letters of, to his Sister, M. A. Gordon. 8vo. Lond., 1888.   C 4 R 33

[*See* Hake, A. E., and Rutter J.]

GORDON, Lady Duff. Memoirs and Correspondence of. (Three Generations of Englishwomen). By Janet Ross. 2 vols. 8vo. Lond., 1888.   C 14 R 5, 6

GORDON, Rev. G. N. and E. C. The Last Martyrs of Eromanga ; being a Memoir of the Rev. G. N. Gordon and his Wife, E. C. Powell. 8vo. Halifax, 1863.   MC 1 Q 43

GORDON, H. A. A Miner's Guide. 8vo. Wellington, 1889.   MA 2 R 28

GORDON, J. The Emigrant Barque ; with some traits of Australian Life and Character in Prose and Verse. 12mo. Edinb., 1871.   MJ 1 Q 21

GORDON, Mrs. J. E. H. Decorative Electricity ; with a Chapter on Fire Risks. 8vo. Lond., 1891.   A 21 S 5

GORDON, J. F. S. [*See* Shaw, L.]

GORDON, M. A. Letters of Gen. C. G. Gordon to his Sister. 8vo. Lond., 1888.   C 4 R 33

GORDON, P. R. Pastoral Industry. [*See* Indian and Colonial Exhibition, 1886.]

[*See* Agriculture, Department of, Queensland ; and Bailey, F. M.]

GORDON, W. J. The Captain-General, being the Story of the Attempt of the Dutch to colonise New Holland. 8vo. Lond., 1888.   MJ 2 T 12

GORDON AND GOTCH. Australian Handbook. 6 vols. Roy. 8vo. Lond., 1887-92.   ME

GORE, C. Lux Mundi ; a series of Studies in the Religion of the Incarnation. 8th ed. 8vo. Lond., 1890.   G 2 Q 37

GORE, J. E. Planetary and Stellar Studies. 8vo. Lond., 1888.   A 3 S 26

GORE, J. H. Elements of Geodesy. Roy. 8vo. New York, 1886.   A 6 T 26

Geodesy. 12mo. Lond., 1891.   A 22 P 27

GOSS, Sir J. Introduction to Harmony and Thorough Bass. 20th ed. 4to. Lond., 1888.   A 11 P 16 †

GOSSE, E. Gossip in a Library. 12mo. Lond., 1891.   J 11 W 26

History of Eighteenth Century Literature, 1660-1780. 8vo. Lond., 1889.   B 21 S 19

Life of Philip Henry Gosse, F.R.S. 8vo. Lond., 1890.   C 15 U 9

GOSSE, P. H. History of the British Sea-Anemones and Corals. 8vo. Lond.; 1860.   A 27 U 25

Life of ; by his son, Edmund Gosse. 8vo. Lond., 1890.   C 15 U 9

Omphalos : An attempt to Untie the Geological Knot. Illustrated. 8vo. Lond., 1857.   A 24 R 3

[*See* Hudson, C. T.]

GOSSIP, G. H. D. Theory of Chess Openings. Second edition. Roy. 8vo. Lond., 1891.   A 30 T 1

GOTHAISCHER GENEALOGISCHER HOFKA-LENDER. 5 vols. 18mo. Gotha, 1888-92.   E

GOTHAISCHES GENEALOGISCHES TASCHEN-BUCH DER GRÄFLICHEN HÄUSER. 5 vols. 18mo. Gotha, 1888-92.   E

GOTHAISCHES GENEALOGISCHES TASCHEN-BUCH DER FREIHERRLICHEN HÄUSER. 5 vols. 18mo. Gotha, 1888-92.   E

GOTTHELF, J. Ulric, the Farm Servant : a Story of the Bernese Lowland. Edited, &c., by J. Ruskin. 8vo. Orpington, 1888.   J 12 V 18

GOTTLOEBER, F. De Alcoholis Potionumque Alcoholicarum usu et effectu. 8vo. Berolini, 1864.   F 11 Q 6

GOUFFÉ, A. [*See* Gouffé, J.]

GOUFFÉ, J. The Royal Cookery-book ; translated and adapted by A. Gouffé. 3rd edition. Roy. 8vo. Lond., 1880.   A 22 S 1

GOUGH, Hugh, Viscount. Life of. [*See* Yonge, C. D.]

GOULBURN, Very Rev. E. M. John William Burgon, Late Dean of Chichester : a Biography. 2 vols. 8vo. Lond., 1892.   C 14 R 28, 29

GOULD, Chas. Report upon the subject of Gold in Van Dieman's Land. Fol. Lond., 1862.   MA 12 Q 7 †

GOULD, J. Birds of New Guinea and the adjacent Papuan Islands. Vol. 4. Imp. fol. Lond., 1857-88.   A 5 Q 18 ‡

Monograph of the Trochilidæ ; or Family of Humming Birds. (Supplement.) Imp. fol. Lond., 1887. Libr.

Synopsis of Birds of Australia. Parts 1-4. Imp. 8vo. Lond., 1837-38.   MA 2 P 5 †

GOULD, N. "Verax." The Double Event : a Tale of the Melbourne Cup. 8vo. Lond., 1891.   MJ 2 T 11

GOVERNMENT HAND-BOOK. 3rd edition. 8vo. Lond., 1890.   E

GOVERNMENT YEAR-BOOK, The : a Record of the Forms of Government in Great Britain, her Colonies, and Foreign Countries. 2 vols. 8vo. Lond., 1888-89.   E

GOW, J. Companion to School Classics. 8vo. Lond., 1888.   J 6 Q 32

GOWER, Lord R. C. S. L. Rupert of the Rhine: a Biographical Sketch. 8vo. Lond., 1890.   C 12 Q 32

" Bric à brac ;" or, some Photoprints illustrating Art Objects at Gower Lodge, Windsor. Roy. 8vo. Lond., 1888.   A 8 T 28

Stafford House Papers ; edited by Lord R. Gower. 8vo. Lond., 1891.   C 16 T 1

GOWING, Richard. [Life of] Richard Cobden. (The World's Workers.) 12mo. Lond., 1889.   C 14 P 6

GOZZI, Count C. Memoirs of. Translated by J. A. Symonds. 2 vols. roy. 8vo. Lond., 1890. C 12 U 15, 16

GRACE, A. F. Landscape Painting in Oils. 4to. Lond., 1885.   A 40 P 13 ‡

GRACE, Rev. T. S. Te Karere Whakatepe o te Hahi Karaitiana. [Sketches of Church History.] 12mo. Lond. (n.d.)   MG 2 P 28

GRACE, Dr. W. G. Cricket. 8vo. Bristol, 1891.   A 16 T 6

W. G. Grace : a Biography ; by W. M. Brownlee ; with a Treatise on Cricket by W. G. Grace. 8vo. Lond., 1887.   C 3 R 2

GRAETZ, Prof. H. History of the Jews, from the earliest times to the present day. Edited and in part translated by Bella Löwy. 5 vols. 8vo. Lond., 1891–92.   G 2 R 30–34

GRAFF, Dr. K. Der Moselwein als Getränk und Heilmittel. 8vo. Bonn, 1821.   F 11 R 19

GRAGLIA, G. Dictionary of the English and Italian Languages. 18mo. Lond., 1862.   K 16 P 21

GRAHAM, A., and ASHBEE, H. S. Travels in Tunisia. Imp. 8vo. Lond., 1887.   D 2 U 4

GRAHAM, C. H., and LANE, O. F. Excise Laws of New York, including the Rights, Duties, and Liabilities of Hotel Keepers. 8vo. Albany, 1883.   F 11 T 4

GRAHAM, J. [*See* Dundee, Viscount.]

GRAHAM, J. R. Treatise on the Australian Merino. 8vo. Melb., 1870.   MA 3 Q 36

GRAHAM, Dr. T. J. Modern Domestic Medicine. 15th edition. 8vo. Lond., 1882.   A 33 S 7

GRAHAM, Prof. W. Socialism, New and Old. 8vo. Lond., 1890.   F 14 P 8

GRAMMONT, P. Count. Memoirs of the Court of Charles II. Revised edition. 12mo. Lond., 1891.   C 16 P 21

Memoirs of ; by A. Hamilton. Edited, with Notes, by Sir W. Scott. 4to. Lond., 1889.   C 17 U 14

GRAMPIAN CLUB. Publications. 2 vols. Sm. 4to. Edinb., 1889.   E

Book of Wallace ; by Rev. C. Rogers. 2 vols.

GRANT, Sir A. Aristotle. (Ancient Classics for English Readers.) 8vo. Edinb., 1888.   J 14 P 3

Xenophon. (Ancient Classics for English Readers.) 12mo. Edinb., 1889.   J 14 P 28

Ethics of Aristotle. [*See* Aristoteles.]

GRANT, Asahel. The Nestorians ; or, the Lost Tribes, containing Evidence of their Identity, &c. 3rd ed. 12mo. Lond., 1844.   G 4 V 13

GRANT, James. Extrait du Voyage de, à la Nouvelle Calédonie. [*See* Turnbull, J.]

GRAPHIC, The. Vols. 34–45. Fol. Lond., 1886–92.   E

GRAPHIC AUSTRALIAN. Nov. 1889–Jan. 1890. Fol. Sydney, 1889–90.   ME

GRATTAN, Henry. Life of ; by R. Dunlop. (Statesmen Series.) 8vo. Lond., 1889.   C 12 R 31

GRAVES, R. E. [*See* Bryan, M.]

GRAVES, R. P. Life of Sir William Rowan Hamilton, including Selections from his Poems, Correspondence, and Miscellaneous Writings. 3 vols. 8vo. Dublin, 1882–89.   C 14 U 13–15

GRAEVIUS, J. G. [*See* Catullus, C. V.]

GRAY, Prof. Andrew. The Theory and Practice of Absolute Measurements in Electricity and Magnetism. vol. 1 8vo. Lond., 1888.   A 21 Q 16

GRAY, Dr. Asa. Scientific Papers of. Vols. 1 and 2. 8vo. Lond., 1889.   A 20 S 7, 8

Botany : Phanerogamia. (United States Exploring Expedition, 1838–42.) Vol. 1, Text. Roy. 4to. New York, 1854.   A 31 Q 2 ‡

Plates [to the above.] Imp. fol. New York, 1857.   A 31 R 8 ‡

Chloris Boreali-Americana : Illustrations of rare North American Plants cultivated at the Botanic Garden of Harvard University. 4to. Camb., 1846. A 36 P 22 ‡

GRAY, D. J. T. Poultry Ailments and their Treatment, for the use of Amateurs. 2nd edition. 12mo. Dundee, 1889.   A 18 Q 17

GRAY, G. J. Bibliography of the Works of Sir Isaac Newton. 8vo. Camb., 1888.   K 19 R 1

GRAY, G. R. Entomology of Australia, in a Series of Monographs. Part 1. 4to. Lond., 1833.   MA 8 Q 12 †

GRAY, J. E. Catalogue of Seals and Whales in the British Museum. 2nd ed. 8vo. Lond., 1866.   A 14 R 36

GRAY, Thomas. Gray and his Friends : Letters and Relics, in great part hitherto unpublished. Edited by D. C. Tovey. 12mo. Camb., 1890.   C 12 P 44

GREAT BRITAIN AND IRELAND.

BOARD OF HEALTH :

Minutes of Information collected on the Practical Application of Sewer Water and Town Manures to Agricultural Production. Roy. 8vo. Lond., 1852.   A 22 V 25

Minutes of Information collected in respect to the Drainage of the Land forming the Sites of Towns, to Road Drainage and the Facilitation of the Drainage of Suburban Lands. Roy. 8vo. Lond., 1852.   A 22 V 25

Minutes of Information collected with Reference to Works for the Removal of Soil, Water, or Drainage of Dwelling Houses and Public Edifices, and for the Sewerage and Cleansing of the Sites of Towns. Roy. 8vo. Lond., 1852.   A 22 V 25

BOARD OF TRADE :

Agricultural Returns, 1874-76. Roy. 8vo. Lond., 1874-76.   E

Returns. 3 vols. Sm. fol. Lond., 1888-90.   E

Report on Recent Changes in Prices of Exports and Imports. Annual Statement of Trade of United Kingdom with Foreign Countries, 1889.
Progress of Sugar Trade—Report.
Statistical Tables of Corn Prices, 1889.
Seventh Report under Section 131 of the Bankruptcy Act, 1883.
Report upon Working of Boiler Explosions Act, 1882.
Seventh Report of the Comptroller-General of Patents, Designs, &c., 1889.
Statistical Tables relating to Colonial and other Possessions, 1882-84.
Statistical Tables relating to Progress of Foreign Trade.
Returns of Expenditure by Working Men.
Statistical Tables and Report on Trades Unions ; 3rd Report.
Return of Rates of Wages in principal Textile Trades.
Return of Rates of Wages in minor Textile Trades.
Report on Strikes and Lock-outs of 1888.
Railway Returns for England and Wales, Scotland and Ireland, 1889.
Report upon Railway, Canal, Tramway, Gas, Electric Lighting, and Water Bills, 1890.
Return : Maximum Charges of Railway Companies.
General Report : Share and Loan Capital, Traffic in Passengers and Goods, &c., of Railway Companies, 1888.
Statistical Tables relating to Emigration and Immigration.
Navigation and Shipping, Annual Statement, 1889.
Tables showing Progress of British Merchant Shipping.
Abstracts of Shipping Casualities, United Kingdom, 1888-89.
Merchant Shipping : Wages of Seamen.
Sea Fisheries of the United Kingdom.

Statistical Abstract for the Principal and other Foreign Countries, 1860-72, 1878-88. 2 vols. Roy. 8vo. Lond., 1874-89.   E

Statistical Abstract for Colonial and other Possessions, 1858-90. 5 vols. Roy. 8vo. Lond., 1874-91.   E

Statistical Abstract for United Kingdom, 1859-89. 2 vols. Roy. 8vo. Lond., 1874-90.   E

Statistical Tables relating to Colonial and other Possessions, 1868-70. Fol. Lond., 1875.   E

CIVIL SERVICE :

Rules and Regulations for Her Majesty's Colonial Service. 8vo. Lond., 1856.   MF 1 T 23

COLONIAL REPORTS :

Reports on Her Majesty's Colonial Possessions, 1845-69, 1886-90. 14 vols. Sm. fol. Lond., 1846-91.   E

CUSTOMS. Annual Settlement of the Trade of the United Kingdom for 1891. Sm. fol. Lond., 1892.   E

GREAT BRITAIN AND IRELAND—*contd.*

MINERAL STATISTICS for 1886-91. 6vols. Sm. fol. Lond., 1887-92.   E

MINT. Annual Reports, 1870-89. 20 vols. 8vo. Lond., 1871-90.   E

Report of the Deputy-Master of the Mint on European Mints. 8vo. Lond., 1870.   F 4 R 18

PRIVY COUNCIL : Acts of. New Series. Vols. 1-4. 1542-54. Roy. 8vo. Lond., 1890-92.   E

PARLIAMENTARY DEBATES :

First Series. Vols. 1-41. 8vo. Lond., 1802-20.   E
Second Series. Vols. 1-25. 8vo Lond., 1820-30.   E
Third Series. Vols. 310-356. Roy. 8vo. Lond., 1886-92.   E
Fourth Series. Vols. 1-5. Roy. 8vo. Lond., 1892.   E

STATUTES. Statutes at Large. 39 vols. 4to. Lond., 1811-69.   E

Statutes, 1235-1836. Second Revised Edition. Vols. 1-5. Roy. 8vo. Lond., 1888-92.   E

Chronological Tables and Indexes, 1235-1886. 2 vols. Imp. 8vo. Lond., 1879-87.   E

Public General Statutes, 1887-92. 5 vols. 8vo. Lond., 1887-92.   E

Statutes. Revised Edition. Vols. 1-18. 20 Hen. III, 1235; to 72 Vict. 1878. 18 vols. Imp. 8vo. Lond., 1870-85.   E

GREAT BRITAIN (or Harmonia) Galop, The. Fol. Sydney (n.d.)   MB 11 Q 15 †

GREAT STATESMEN, The : A Few Leaves from the History of Antipodea ; by " Can C.", N.S.W., A.D. 3000. 8vo. Sydney, 1885.   MF 1 R 70

GREEN, Dr. F. W. Edridge. Colour Blindness and Colour Perception. 8vo. Lond., 1891   A 12 P 26

GREEN, J. F. Ocean Birds ; with a Treatise on Skinning Birds by F. H. H. Guillemard. Roy. 4to. Lond., 1887.   A 3 P 8 †

GREEN, J. J. [See Foster, C. W.]

GREEN, John Richard. The Conquest of England. 2nd edition. 8vo. Lond., 1884.   B 22 S 28

GREEN, John Richards. History of the Political Life of the Rt. Hon. Wm. Pitt ; by "John Gifford." 3 vols. 4to. Lond., 1809.   C 40 S 12-14 ‡

GREEN, Mrs. J. R. Henry II. (Twelve English Statesmen.) 8vo. Lond., 1888.   C 2 S 1

GREEN, Prof. T. H. Works of ; edited by R. L. Nettleship. 3 vols. 8vo. Lond., 1885-88.   G 9 S 26-28

[See Ritchie, D. G.]

GREEN, Rev. W. S. High Alps of New Zealand. 8vo. Lond., 1883.   MD 5 P 9

Among the Selkirk Glaciers, being the Account of a Rough Survey in the Rocky Mountain Regions of British Columbia. 8vo. Lond., 1890.   D 15 Q 8

GREENE, Prof. Joseph Reay. Manual of the Sub-Kingdom Cœlenterata. 2nd ed. 12mo. Lond., 1863.
A 27 P 26
[*See* Carey, C. T.]

GREENE, Robert. George a Greene: the Pinner of Wakefield: a Comedy. [*See* British Drama, Ancient, I.]

GREENE, W. T. Parrots in Captivity 3 vols. Roy. 8vo. Lond., 1884-87. A 15 R 6-8

GREENER, W. W. Modern Shot Guns. 2nd edition. 8vo. Lond., 1891. A 11 R 26

GREENUP, E. B. [*See* Agriculture, Department of, Queensland.]

GREENUP, R. [*See* Simon, J.]

GREENWICH ROYAL OBSERVATORY: Magnetical and Meteorological Observations, 1840-80. 15 vols. 4to. Lond., 1843-80. A 13 R 1—S 3 †

GREENWOOD, Col. George. The Tree-lifter; or, a New Mode of Transplanting Forest Trees. 8vo. Lond., 1844.
A 18 T 8

GREENWOOD, J. Savage Habits and Customs. 8vo. Lond., 1865. MA 1 R 16

GREENWOOD, T. Public Libraries. 3rd edition. 8vo. Lond., 1890. J 11 S 35

GREG, P. A. Hidden Scenes. 8vo. Newcastle, 1886.
MJ 2 Q 26

GREG, Percy. History of the United States, from the Foundation of Virginia to the Reconstruction of the Union. 2 vols. 8vo. Lond., 1887. B 1 T 40, 41

GRÉGOIRE DE TOURS, et FRÉDÉGAIRE. Histoire des Francs; traduction de M. Guizot. 2 vols. 12mo. Paris, 1874. G 13 U 44, 45

GREGOROVIUS, F. Corsica: Picturesque, Historical, and Social; with a sketch of the Early Life of Napoleon. Translated from the German by E. J. Morris. 8vo. New York (n.d.) B 17 P 20

GREGORY, A. C. and F. T. Journals of Australian Explorations. 8vo. Brisb., 1884. MD 4 U 30

GREGORY, B. The Thorough Business Man: Memoirs of Walter Powell. 8vo. Lond., 1871. MC 1 P 40

GREGORY, W. Journal of a Captured Missionary, designated to the Southern Pacific Ocean, in the Second Voyage of the ship "Duff." 8vo. Lond., 1800.
MD 5 S 32

GRESWELL, Richard. [Life of;] by the Very Rev. J. W. Burgon. (Lives of Twelve Good Men.) 2 vols. 8vo. Lond., 1888. C 13 R 10-11

GRESWELL, Rev. W. P. Geography of Africa, South of the Zambesi; with 3 maps. 8vo. Oxford, 1892.
D 14 Q 15
Geography of the Dominion of Canada and Newfoundland. 12mo. Oxford, 1891. D 15 Q 7
History of the Dominion of Canada. 8vo. Oxford, 1890.
B 18 Q 4

GREVILLE, C. C. F. The Greville Memoirs: a Journal of the Reigns of King George :v and King William iv, and a Journal of the Reign of Queen Victoria, from 1852-60. 8 vols. 8vo. Lond., 1875-87. B 5 U 36-43

GREVILLE, E. Year Book of Australia. 5 vols. 8vo. Sydney, 1888-92. ME

GREVILLE, Dr. R. K. Icones Filicum. [*See* Hooker, Dr. W. J.]

GREVILLEA: A Monthly Record of Cryptogamic Botany, &c. Vols. 1-20. 8vo. Lond., 1872-92. E

GREY A., and FREMANTLE, Hon. and Rev. W. H. Church Reform. 8vo. Lond., 1888. G 8 Q 29

GREY, Charles, Second Earl. Correspondence of Princess Lieven and Earl Grey; edited and translated by G. Le Strange. 3 vols. 8vo. Lond., 1890. C 14 T 7-9

GREY, Henry, Third Earl. Ireland: the Causes of its Present Condition, and the Measures proposed for its Improvement. 8vo. Lond., 1888. F 5 T 40

GREY, D. [*See* Wilson, F. J. F.]

GREY, Sir Geo.: German Colonization: a Review of Recent Anglo-German Negotiations and the Samoan Situation. 8vo. Auckland, 1889. MF 1 S 4
The Irish Land Question. 8vo. Auckland, 1889.
MF 1 T 32
Ko nga mahi a nga Tupuna Maori. 2nd edition. Roy. 8vo. Auckland, 1885. MB 2 R 37
Ko nga Moteatea, me nga Hakirara o nga Maori: Poems, Traditions, and Chaunts of the Maoris. Roy. 8vo. Wellington, 1853. MH 1 S 28
Polynesian Mythology and Ancient Traditional History of the New Zealand Race. Roy. 8vo. Auckland, 1885.
MB 2 R 37
Life and Times of; by William L. and Lily Rees. 2 vols. 8vo. Lond., 1892. MC 1 T 13, 14
Another Copy. 8vo. Auckland, 1892. MC 1 T 15

GREY, Earl. Commercial Policy of the British Colonies and the McKinley Tariff. 8vo. Lond., 1892. F 12 T 1
Another copy. 8vo. Lond., 1892. MF 2 T 60

GRÉZEL, P. Dictionnaire Futunien-Français avec Notes Grammaticales. 8vo. Paris, 1878. MK 1 T 15

GRIBBLE, T. G. Preliminary Survey and Estimates. 12mo. Lond., 1891. A 22 P 28

GRIER, Rev. R. M. The Truth about Sunday-Closing and Local Option. 8vo. Rugeley, 1883. F 11 S 20

GRIFFIN, C. W. New Zealand: her Commerce and Resources. Roy. 8vo. Wellington, 1884. MF 1 S 3
Another copy. Roy. 8vo. Wellington, 1884. MF 3 R 31
New South Wales: her Commerce and Resources. Roy. 8vo. Sydney, 1888.* MF 1 S 32

GRIFFIN, J. Memoirs of Capt. J. Wilson, containing an account of his enterprises, &c. 2nd edition revised. 8vo. Lond. (n.d.) MC 1 R 1

GRIFFIN, Sir L. [Life of] Ranjit Singh. (Rulers of India.) 12mo. Oxford, 1892.   C 16 P 20

GRIFFITH, C. The Present State and Prospects of the Port Phillip District of New South Wales. 8vo. Dublin, 1845.   MD 5 R 30

GRIFFITH, F. L. The Antiquities of Tell el Yahúdiyeh. (Egypt Exploration Fund, 1888–89.) 4to. Lond., 1880.   B 42 R 27 ‡

The Inscriptions of Siût and dèr Rifeh. Roy. 4to. Lond., 1889.   B 4 P 23 †

The Sign Papyrus from Tanis. (Egypt Exploration Fund.) 4to. Lond., 1889.   K 13 P 14 †

GRIFFITHS, Major A. The English Army: its Past History, Present Condition, and Future Prospects. 8vo. Lond. (n.d.)   B 23 S 8

French Revolutionary Generals. 8vo. Lond., 1891.   C 13 R 26

GRIFFITHS, A. B. Treatise on Manures; or, the Philosophy of Manuring. 8vo. Lond., 1889.   A 1 U 24

GRIFFITHS, Rev. Dr. J. [See Oxford University Statutes.]

GRIFFITHS, W. The Glenorchy Murders: a Full Account of the Capture, Trial, and Execution of W. Griffiths for the Murder of George and Sarah Johnson. 8vo. Hobart, 1865.   MF 2 T 26

GRIGOR, John. Arboriculture; or, a practical treatise on Raising and Managing Forest Trees. 2nd edition. 8vo. Edinb., 1881.   A 18 S 5

GRIM, the Collier of Croydon: a Comedy. [See British Drama, Ancient, 3.]

GRIMES, S. [See Agriculture, Dept. of, Queensland.]

GRIMM, Rev. G. Concise History of Australia, being a narrative of the Rise and Progress of New South Wales and her Sister Colonies, with Sketches of New Zealand. 8vo. Sydney, 1891.   MB 2 Q 44

Australian Explorers, their Labours, Perils, and Achievements. 8vo. Melb., 1888.   MD 5 Q 56

Memory, and How to Improve it. 8vo. Sydney, 1891.   MA 3 Q 32

The Unveiling of Africa: A Sketch of Travel and Discovery in the Dark Continent from Clapperton to Stanley. Roy. 8vo. Sydney, 1892.   MD 7 S 46

The Sabbath: Patriarchal, Jewish, and Christian. 8vo. Sydney, 1890.   MG 1 R 43

GRIMM, J. Teutonic Mythology; translated by J. S. Stallybrass. 4 vols. 8vo. Lond., 1880–88. B 27 U 1–4

GRIMM, J. & W. Deutsches Wörterbuch. Imp. 8vo. Leip., 1889.   K 14 R 24

GRIMM, Dr. O. Fishing and Hunting on Russian Waters. (International Fisheries Exhibition, 1883.) Imp. 8vo. St. Petersburgh, 1883.   A 14 U 9

GRIMWOOD, Mrs. E. St. C. My Three Years in Manipur and Escape from the recent Mutiny. 8vo. Lond., 1891.   D 17 V 12

GRINDON, L. H. British and Garden Botany, preceded by an Introduction to Structure and Physiological Botany. 8vo. Lond., 1864.   A 20 S 9

GROCERS' AND SHOPKEEPERS' LICENSES, Evils of. 8vo. Lond., 1883.   F 11 R 20

GROCERS' LICENSES (SCOTLAND COMMISSION), Report on. Edinb., 1878.   F 42 P 10 ‡

GROMATICI VETERES, ex recensione C. Lachmanni. Die Schriften der Römischen Feldmesser. 2 vols. 8vo. Berolini, 1848–52.   B 30 S 8, 9

GRONLUND, L. The Co-operative Commonwealth; an exposition of modern socialism. 8vo. Lond., 1886.   F 14 P 42

GRONOV, A. [See Mela, P.]

GRONOV, J. [See Cicero, M. T.]

GRONOW, Capt. R. H. Reminiscences and Recollections of Captain Gronow; being Anecdotes of the Camp, Court, Clubs, and Society, 1810–60. 2 vols. Imp. 8vo. Lond., 1889.   C 12 V 10, 11

GROSVENOR NOTES. [See Blackburn, H.]

GROTE, G. History of Greece. 4th edition. 12 vols. 8vo. Lond., 1852–56.   B 27 T 11–22

[See Plato.]

GROTIUS, H. De Jure Belli ac Pacis, libri tres. 12 mo. Amst., 1632.   F 14 Q 11

De Jure Belli et Pacis, libri tres; accompanied by an abridged translation by Prof. W. Whewell. 3 vols. 8vo. Camb., 1853.   F 4 S 24–26

De Veritate Religionis Christianæ. 12mo. Lond., 1823.   G 16 P 36

GROVE, F. C. [See Fencing.]

GROVE, Sir G. Dictionary of Music and Musicians, 1450–1889; with Index. 5 vols. 8vo. Lond., 1879–90.   K 18 Q 7–11

GRUNDTVIG, N. F. S. Phenix-Fuglen et Angelsachsisk Koad. Roy. 8vo. Kjöbenhavn, 1840.   H 6 V 33

GRUNOW, A. Die Diatomeen von Franz Josefs-land. 4to. Wien, 1884.   A 42 R 14 ‡

[See Cleve, P. T.]

GUARDIAN OF THE POOR, A. [See Irish Peasant.]

GUBERNATIS, A. de. Dictionnaire International des Ecrivains du Jour. 3 vols. Imp. 8vo. Florence, 1891.   C 12 V 13–15

GUDGEON, T. W. History and Doings of the Maoris. 1820–40. 8vo. Auckland, 1885.   MB 2 T 6

GUERS, Rev. E. How French Soldiers fared in German Prisons. 8vo. Lond., 1890.   B 20 S 2

GUERZONI, Giuseppe. Garibaldi. 3rd ed. 2 vols. 8vo. Firenze, 1889.   C 12 R 5, 6

GUIGARD, J. Bibliothèque Héraldique de la France. 8vo. Paris, 1861.   K 7 S 18

GUILFORD, Baron. [*See* North, Rt. Hon. F.]

GUILLAUME, H. The Amazon Provinces of Peru, as a Field for European Emigration. 8vo. Lond., 1888.
D 15 Q 5

GUILLEMARD, F. H. H. Life of Ferdinand Magellan, and the First Circumnavigation of the Globe, 1480–1521. 8vo. Lond., 1890. C 14 Q 7
Cruise of the *Marchesa* to Kamschatka and New Guinea. 2 vols. roy. 8vo. Lond., 1886. MD 4 U 47, 48
[*See* Green, J. F.]

GUILLEMIN, A. Electricity and Magnetism ; revised and edited by Prof. S. P. Thompson. Roy. 8vo. Lond., 1891. A 21 V 4

GUIMPS, Roger de. Pestalozzi : his Life and Work. 12mo. New York, 1890. C 12 P 5

GUIZOT, F. P. G. Corneille et son Temps. 8vo. Paris, 1889. C 17 Q 30
Dictionnaire Universel des Synonymes de la Langue Française. Roy. 8vo. Paris, 1885. K 14 Q 4
Discours. 8vo. Paris, 1866. J 15 S 29
Discours Académiques. 12mo. Paris, 1862. J 16 R 31
Discours sur la Révolution d'Angleterre. 8vo. Paris, 1850. B 24 S 25
Essais sur l'Histoire de France. 14e éd. 12mo. Paris, 1878. B 26 Q 10

Étude Historique sur Washington. [*See* Witt, C. de.]

Études sur les Beaux Arts. Nouvelle éd. 12mo. Paris, 1851. A 23 Q 31
General History of Civilisation in Europe. 2nd ed. 8vo. Oxford, 1838. B 7 T 33
Histoire de Charles I. 12e éd. 2 vols. 12mo. Paris, 1882. B 23 Q 8, 9
Histoire de la Civilisation en Europe. 22e éd. 12mo. Paris, 1889. B 25 P 1
Histoire de la Civilisation en France. 15e éd. 4 vols. 12mo. Paris, 1884. B 26 Q 11–14
Histoire de la République d'Angleterre et de Cromwell. 7e éd. 2 vols. 12mo. Paris, 1888. B 23 Q 10, 11
Histoire de France ; [par] Grégoire de Tours et Frédegaire. Traduction de M. Guizot. 2 vols. 12mo. Paris, 1874. G 13 U 44, 45
Histoire des Origines du Gouvernement Représentatif. 2 vols. 12mo. Paris, 1880. F 9 U 25, 26
Histoire du Protectorat de Richard Cromwell. 2e éd. 2 vols. 12mo. Paris, 1881. B 23 Q 12, 13
Méditations et Etudes Morales. 12mo. Paris, 1889. G 13 U 38
Ménandre : Etude historique et littéraire sur la Comédie et la Société Grecque. 8vo. Paris, 1886. B 27 Q 18
Monk. 12mo. Paris, 1874. C 17 Q 27
Portraits Politiques. 7e éd. 12mo. Paris, 1874. C 16 P 29
Sir R. Peel : Etude d'Histoire Contemporaine. 8vo. Paris, 1858. C 17 T 19

GUIZOT, F. P. G., and E. C. P. Le Temps Passé. 2 vols. 12mo. Paris, 1887. J 16 R 32, 33

GUIZOT, F. P. G., and Mme. Abailard et Héloïse. 12mo. Paris, 1876. C 17 Q 29

GUMLEY, R. Brief History of Tasmania. 12mo. Lond., 1889. MB 1 P 26

GUNJL, J. "Dreams on the Ocean " Waltzes. Fol. Sydney, (n.d.) MA 11 Q 15 †

GÜNTHER, A. Guide to the Gallery of Reptilia in the Department of Zoology of the British Museum (Natural History.) 2nd ed. 8vo. Lond., 1886. A 27 T 17

GÜNTHER, Dr. Ueber die Biere. 8vo. Berlin, 1826. F 11 Q 48

GURNEY, Baron. Charge of, to the Grand Jury of the County of Gloucester, 1832. 8vo. Gloucester, 1832. G 15 R 27
Charge of, to the Grand Jury of the County of Essex, 1832. 8vo. Chelmsford, 1832. G 15 R 27

GUNTHER, Rev. Canon W. J. The Church of England in Australia from 1788–1829 : a Lecture. 8vo. Parramatta, 1888. MG 1 R 38

GUNTON, G. Wealth and Progress : a Critical Examination of the Wages Question, &c. 8vo. Lond., 1888. F 5 T 41

GUPPY, H. B. Homes of Family Names in Great Britain. 8vo. Lond., 1890. K 18 P 3
The Solomon Islands and their Natives. Roy. 8vo. Lond., 1887. MA 1 S 23
The Solomon Islands : their Geology, General Features, and Suitability for Colonization. Roy. 8vo. Lond., 1887. MA 1 S 24

GURNER, H. F. Practice of the Criminal Law of Colony of Victoria. 8vo. Melb., 1871. MF 3 T 13

GURNEY, E. Tertium Quid : Chapters on Various Disputed Questions. 2 vols. 8vo. Lond., 1887. J 5 P 36, 37

GURNEY, Jos. J. Thoughts on Habit and Discipline. 3rd edition. 8vo. Lond., 1845. G 15 R 27

GUSTAFSON, A. Some Thoughts on Moderation. 12mo. Lond., 1885. F 11 P 26

GUTHRIE, C. J. [*See* Guthrie, Rev. D. K.]

GUTHRIE, Rev. D. K., and GUTHRIE, C. J. Autobiography of T. Guthrie, D.D., and Memoir ; by his Sons. 8vo. Lond., 1877. C 13 R 22

GUTHRIE, Rev. Dr. T. Autobiography of ; and Memoir, by his Sons, Rev. D. K. Guthrie and C. J. Guthrie. 8vo. Lond., 1877. C 13 R 22
Christ and the Inheritance of the Saints. 8vo. Edinb., 1858. G 13 Q 37

GUTHRIE, W. Geographical, Historical, and Commercial Grammar. 24th ed. 8vo. Lond., 1827. D 12 T 10

GWATKIN, H. M. The Arian Controversy. 12mo. Lond., 1889. G 19 P 11

GWILT, J. Grecian Architecture. [*See* Chambers Sir W.]

H

H.A.S. [*See* Darwin, C.]

H.E.S.L. [*See* Ferns which grow in New Zealand.]

H.H. [*See* Scientific Education of Dogs.]

HAAST, J. von. Humanism and Realism in their relations to Higher Education. Roy. 8vo. Dunedin (n.d.)
MG 1 T 29

HABITUAL DRUNKARDS, Report on. Fol. Lond., 1872.   F 42 P 11 ‡

HACKE, Capt. W. Collection of Original Voyages. 12mo. Lond., 1699.   D 20 Q 9

HADDEN, J. C. [Life of] George Frederick Handel. 12mo. Lond., 1888.   C 2 R 21

HADDEN, Rev. R. H. Reminiscences of William Rogers, Rector of St. Botolph, Bishopsgate. 8vo. Lond., 1888.
C 15 Q 24

HADDON, Prof. A. C. Introduction to the Study of Embryology. Roy. 8vo. Lond., 1887.   A 26 U 1

HAECKEL, E. The Evolution of Man. 2 vols. 8vo. Lond., 1883.   A 27 Q 33, 34

Metagenesis und Hypogenesis von *Aurelia Aurita* 4to. Jena, 1881.   A 40 Q 23 ‡

Die Familie der Rüsselquallen (Geryonida). 8vo. Leip., 1865.   A 14 T 9

HAGGERSTON, W. J. Catalogue of the Juvenile Lending Department, Newcastle-upon-Tyne Public Libraries. Roy. 8vo. Lond., 1887.   K 8 R 18

HAGUE, A. and J. D. [*See* United States Geol. Exploration of 40th Parallel.]

HAIGH, A. E. The Attick Theatre, a description of the Stage and Theatre of the Athenians, and of the Dramatic Performances at Athens. 8vo. Oxford, 1889. B 27 U 11

[*See* Virgilius Maro, P.]

HAILMANN, W. N. [*See* Froebel, F.]

HAINES, C. R. Islam, as a Missionary Religion. (Non-Christian Religious System.) 12mo. Lond., 1889.
G 4 V 1

HAKE, A. E. Events in the Taeping Rebellion : being reprints of MSS. copied by General Gordon. 8vo. Lond., 1891.   B 20 S 3

HAKE, O. Toboggaming. [*See* Heathcote, J. M.]

HAKLUYT SOCIETY. Publications. 10 vols. 8vo. Lond., 1887-91.   L

Diary of Wm. Hedges, 1681-87.
Voyage of François Pyrard to the East Indies.
Tractatus de Globis : by R. Hues.
Conquest of River Plate, 1535-55. 1. Voyage of U. Schmidt to the Rivers La Plata and Paraguai. 2. The Commentaries of Alvar Nuñez Cabeza de Vaca.
Voyage of F. Laguat.

HALDANE, J. W. C. Civil and Mechanical Engineering, popularly and socially considered. 8vo. Lond., 1887.
A 6 S 33

HALDANE, R. Workshop Receipts. [*See* Spon, E.]

HALE, E. E. Life of George Washington studied anew. 8vo. New York, 1888.   C 4 V 37

HALE, E. E. and E. E., junr. Franklin in France ; from original Documents. Roy. 8vo. Boston, 1887. B 26 U 12

HALE, Rt. Rev. M. B. Aborigines of Australia ; being an account of the institution for their education at Poonindie, in South Australia. 8vo. Lond., 1889.
MA 2 P 73

HALE, Susan. Mexico (Story of the Nations Series). 8vo. Lond., 1891.   B 1 Q 58

HALES, A. G. The Wanderings of a Simple Child ; or, Sketches of Life in the Back Country, by "Smiler." 8vo. Sydney, 1890.   MJ 2 T 13

HALKETT, S., and LAING, Rev. J. Dictionary of Anonymous and Pseudonymous Literature. 4 vols. roy. 8vo. Edinb., 1882-88.   K 17 R 1-4

HALL, G. S., and MANSFIELD, J. M. Hints toward a Select and Descriptive Bibliography of Education. 8vo. Boston, 1886.   K 19 P 2

HALL, H. The Antiquities and Curiosities of the Exchequer. (Camden Lib.) 8vo. Lond., 1891.   B 23 S 7

HALL, J. Mundus alter et idem sive Terra Australis antehac semper incognita. 32mo. Ultrajecti, 1643.
MJ 3 P 4

HALL, J. [*See* United States Geol. Expl. of 40th Parallel.]

HALL, Dr. J. Drink Thirst : its medical treatment. 8vo. Lond. (n.d.)   F 11 R 14

HALL, T. Trial of. [*See* Wheeler, J. C.]

HALL, T. D. Grammar of the Latin Language. [*See* Smith, W.]

HALL, W. E. Treatise on International Law. 3rd ed. 8vo. Oxford, 1890.   F 9 S 14

HALL, Wm. Ham. Irrigation Development. 8vo. Sacramento, 1886.   A 22 T 27

Irrigation in California (Southern). 8vo. Sacramento, 1888.   A 22 T 28

HALLACK, E. H. Western Australia and the Gilgarn Goldfields. Roy. 8vo. Adelaide, 1891.   MD·7 R 45

HALLETT, Holt S. A Thousand Miles on an Elephant in the Shan States. Roy. 8vo. Edinb., 1890. D 17 U 12

[*See* Colquhoun, A. R.]

HALLIDAY, Rev. S. D. [*See* Abbott, Rev. L.]

HALLIWELL-PHILLIPS, J. O. Voiage and Travaile. [*See* Maundevile, Sir J.]

HALLORAN, H. Discovery of Eastern Australia: a Prize Poem. 12mo. Sydney, 1879. MH 1 Q 66

In Memoriam. Elizabeth Henrietta Halloran, of Mowbray, Ashfield Park. Sq. 8vo. Sydney, 1890. MH 1 S 49

A Few Love Rhymes of a Married Life. Sq. 8vo. Sydney, 1890. MH 1 S 48

Poems, Odes, Songs. Sm. 4to. Sydney, 1887. MH 1 T 15

A Centennial Ode (an impromptu) in commemoration of the Completion of the First Hundred Years of Settlement in New South Wales. Roy. 8vo. Sydney, 1888. MH 1 T 16

HALMA, F. Woordenboek der Nederduitsche en Fransche Taalen. 4to. Leiden, 1758. K 18 S 8

Le Grand Dictionnaire François et Flamand. 4to. Leiden, 1761. K 18 S 7

HALYBURTON, A. Ledger of, 1492-1503. Roy. 8vo. Edinb., 1867. B 13 S 19

HAM, T. Squatters' Directory, and Key to Ham's Squatting Map, 1859. 12mo. Melb., 1859. ME 8 P

Squatting Map of Victoria. [Folded.] 12mo. Melb. (n.d.) M E 8 P

HAMANN, Dr. O. Der Organismus der Hydroidpolypen. Roy. 8vo. Jena, 1882. A 15 Q 16

HAMERTON, P. G. Human Intercourse. 12mo. Lond., 1891. G 13 U 37

The Saône: a Summer Voyage. Illustrated by J. Pennell and the Author. Roy. 8vo. Lond., 1887. D 16 U 1

French and English : a Comparison. 8vo. Lond., 1889. J 9 S 39

HAMILTON, A. Memoirs of Count Grammont ; edited by Sir W. Scott. 4to. Lond., 1889. C 17 U 14

HAMILTON, Prof. D. J. Text-book of Pathology, systematic and practical. Vol. 1. Roy. 8vo. Lond., 1889. A 26 U 10

HAMILTON, Edward B. The Judicature Act, 1883, and the rules of the Supreme Court, 1884. 8vo. Melb., 1884. MF 2 T 62

HAMILTON, Emma, Lady. Memoirs of, with Illustrative Anecdotes of many of her most particular Friends and distinguished Contemporaries. 2nd edition. 8vo. Lond., 1815. C 21 Q 21

Another Copy. [Reprint of 2nd edition.] Edited by W. H. Long. 8vo. Lond., 1891. C 15 Q 28

Lady Hamilton and Lord Nelson : a Historical Biography; by J. C. Jeaffreson. 2 vols. 8vo. Lond., 1888. C 15 Q 26, 27

HAMILTON, G. Voyage round the World in the *Pandora*. 8vo. Berwick, 1793. MD 1 U 31

HAMILTON, J. A. Life of Daniel O'Connell. (Statesmen Series.) 8vo. Lond., 1888. C 12 R 32

HAMILTON, Walter. Parodies of the Works of English and American Authors. 6 vols. 4to. Lond., 1884-89. H 7 V 10-15

N

HAMILTON, Sir Wm. Discussions on Philosophy and Literature, Education, and University Reform. 8vo. Lond., 1853. G 16 T 26

Lectures on Metaphysics and Logic. 4 vols. 8vo. Edinb., 1859-60. G 16 T 9-12

HAMILTON, Rev. W. Practical Discourses, intended for circulation in the interior of New South Wales. Roy. 8vo. Sydney, 1843. MG 1 T 25

HAMILTON, Wm. D. [*See* Calendar of State Papers.]

HAMILTON, Sir William Rowan. Life of, including selections from his poems, correspondence, and miscellaneous writings ; by R. P. Graves. 3 vols. 8vo. Dublin, 1882-89. C 14 U 13-15

HAMLET, W. M. Anthrax in Australia, with some Account of Pasteur's Method of Vaccination. 8vo. Melb., 1889. MA 2 T 57

On the Action of the Nepean Water on Tubes and Boiler Plates, with some remarks on Corrosion generally. 8vo. Melb., 1889. MA 2 T 57

On the Action of Metallic Salts in the Development of Aspergillus Nigrescens. 8vo. Melb., 1889. MA 2 T 57

On the Presence of Fusil Oil in Beer. 8vo. Sydney, 1887. MA 2 T 58

HAMLEY, Gen. Sir E. B. The War in the Crimea. 8vo. Lond., 1891. B 31 R 2

The Operations of War explained and illustrated. 5th edition. Sm. 4to. Edinb., 1889. A 29 V 9

HAMMILL, Mrs. H. Life and Adventures of the Dog "Oscar." Sq. 8vo. Melb., 1889. MJ 2 Q 29

HAMMOND, A. Art of Practical Brickcutting and Setting, with Remarks on Building Materials. (Weale.) 12mo. Lond., 1889. A 17 R 21

HAMY, Dr. E. T. Centenaire de la Mort de Cook : Cook et Dalrymple. 8vo. Paris, 1879. MC 1 T 4

HANCE, J. L. End of the World ; or, Prophecy, a Lost Science, Revealed. 8vo. Sydney, 1881. MG 1 Q 45

First and Second Numbers of the Atlas Series of Australian Pamphlets, entitled the End of the World or Prophecy, a Lost Science,, recovered. 3rd ed. Sydney, 1891. . . MG 1 Q 65

The Third and Fourth Numbers of the Atlas Series of Australian Pamphlets, entitled a New Era and a New Element, being a Scientific Demonstration of the Materiality of Spirit. 2nd ed. 8vo. Sydney, 1892. M G 1 Q 65

Fifth and Sixth Numbers of the Atlas Series of Australian Pamphlets, entitled our Social Privileges ; or, an Address to the World's Workers. 2nd ed. 8vo. Sydney, 1892. MG 1 Q 65

..New Era and a New Element, being a Scientific Demonstration of the Materiality of Spirit. 8vo. Sydney, 1882. MA 3 V 46

HAND-BOOK OF INFORMATION for the Colonies and India. Roy. 8vo. Brisbane, 1888.* MD 5 V 41

HAND-BOOK to the Desk, Office, and Platform. New edition. 12mo. Lond. (n.d.) K 14 P 29

HANDEL, G. F. [Life of]; by J. C. Hadden. 12mo. Lond., 1888. C 2 R 21

HANKINS, G. T. On the Diet of Infants in Health and Sickness. 12mo. Sydney, 1882. MA 3 P 24

HANNAFORD, S. The Wild Flowers of Tasmania. 12mo. Melb., 1866. MA 1 V 33

HANNAY, David. Rodney. (English Men of Action.) 8vo. Lond., 1891. C 16 P 7

HANNINGTON, Rt. Rev. J. The Last Journals of Bishop Hannington ; being Narratives of a Journey in Palestine, Masai-Land, and U-Soga in 1884-85 ; edited by E. C. Dawson. 8vo. Lond., 1888. D 17 Q 2

HANSARD'S PARLIAMENTARY DEBATES. [*See* Great Britain and Ireland.]

HANSON, J. F. Alkohol afmasket. 18mo. Kjöbenhavn, 1882. F 11 P 7

HANSON, W. The Pastoral Possessions of New South Wales. 8vo. Sydney, 1859. MF 2 R 57

HARCOURT, E. W. [*See* Godolphin, Mrs. M.]

HARCOURT, L. F. Vernon. Achievements in Engineering during the last Half Century. 8vo. Lond., 1891. A 22 R 27

HARCUS, W. South Australia : its History, Resources, and Productions. 8vo. Adelaide, 1876. MB 2 R 43

HARDINGE, Charles, Viscount. [Life of Henry] Viscount Hardinge. (Rulers of India.) 8vo. Oxford, 1891. C 17 Q 10

HARDINGE, Henry, Viscount. [Life of;] by his son Charles Viscount Hardinge. (Rulers of India.) 8vo. Oxford, 1891. C 17 Q 10

HARDOIN, N. "Dick de Lonlay." A travers la Bulgarie. Illustré de 20 dessins par l'auteur. 8vo. Paris, 1888. D 18 T 17

L'Armée Russe en Campagne. 8vo. Paris, 1888. B 16 Q35

Les Marins Français. 8vo. Paris, 1888. B 26 T 12

HARDWICKE'S SCIENCE GOSSIP. Vols. 24-27 roy. 8vo. Lond., 1888-91. E

HARDY, A. S. Reports on the working of the Tavern and Shop Licenses, 1884-85. 8vo. Toronto, 1885-86. F 11 S 24, 25

HARDY, E. G. [*See* Plinius Cæcilius Secundus, C.]

HARDY, J. R. Squatters and Gold Diggers : their claims and rights. 8vo. Sydney, 1855. MF 2 R 56

HARDY, T. D. Modus Tenendi Parliamentum : an ancient treatise on the mode of holding the Parliament in England. 8vo. Lond., 1846. F 14 T 23

Rotuli de Liberate ac de Misis et Præstitis, regnante Johanne. (Record Com. Pubs.) Roy. 8vo. Lond., 1844 B 15 T 30

HARE, A. J. C. Days near Paris. 8vo. Lond., 1887. D 19 Q 22

Paris. 8vo. Lond., 1887. D 19 Q 21

Cities of Southern Italy and Sicily. 8vo. Lond., 1883. D 19 Q 16

Cities of Northern Italy. 2 vols. 8vo. Lond., 1884. D 19 Q 17, 18

Days Near Rome. 3rd edition. 2 vols. Lond., 1884. D 19 Q 19, 20

Florence. 2nd ed. 8vo, Lond., 1887. D 19 Q 23

North-Eastern France. 8vo. Lond., 1890. D 19 Q 27

South-Eastern France. 8vo. Lond., 1890. D 19 Q 28

South-Western France. 8vo. Lond., 1890. D 19 Q 20

Venice. 2nd ed. 8vo. Lond., 1888. D 19 Q 24

Walks in Rome. 12th edition (revised). 2 vols. 8vo. Lond., 1883-89. D 19 Q 25, 26

HARE, Francis A. The Last of the Bushrangers ; an account of the Kelly Gang. 8vo. Lond., 1892. MB 1 B 42

HARE, J. C. and A. W. Guesses at Truth. 5th edition. 8vo. Lond., 1859. G 16 R 33

HARFORD, J. S. Life of Michael Angelo Buonarotti ; with translations of his Poems and Letters. 2vols. 8vo. Lond., 1858. C 14 V 9, 10

HARGRAVE, J. F. Introductory Lecture on General Jurisprudence. 8vo. Sydney, 1860. MF 1 T 33

HARGRAVES, Dr. W. Alcohol and Science ; or, Alcohol, what it is, and what it does. 12mo. Lond. (n.d.) F 11 P 32

HARGREAVES, J. G. Literary Workers ; or, Pilgrims to the Temple of Honour. Sm. 4to. Lond., 1889. J 8 S 33

HARLAND, J. [*See* Baines, E.]

HARLEIAN SOCIETY. Publications. 14 vols. imp. 8vo. Lond., 1887-91. E
  Registers of Stourton, Co. Wilts, 1570-1800.
  Registers of St. James, Clerkenwell. Vol. 3.
  Visitation of Yorkshire in 1564.
  Visitation of Shropshire, 1623. Pts. 1, 2.
  Register of Baptisms and Marriages at St. George's Chapel, May Fair.
  Allegations for Marriage Licences issued by the Vicar-General of the Archbishop of Canterbury, 1679-94.
  Parish Register of Kensington, 1539-1675.
  Register of Marriages, Parish of St. George, Hanover Square, Vol. 2, 1788-1809.
  Visitacion of Norfolk, 1563.
  Marriages Licences, Bishop of London, 1520-1628. 2 vols.
  Visitation of Worcestershire in 1569.

HARLIN, T. Selections from Milton, Dryden, Gray, Keats, Addison, and De Quincey, as prescribed for Melbourne University Matriculation Exams. 8vo. Melb., 1886. MH 1 P 38

HARPER, C. G. English Pen Artists of to-day. 4to. Lond., 1892. A 40 S 3 ‡

HARPER, H. A. The Bible and Modern Discoveries 3rd ed. 8vo. Lond., 1890. G 2 Q 36

HARPER'S MONTHLY MAGAZINE. 10 vols. roy. 8vo. New York, 1886–92. E

HARPUR, C. A Poet's Home. 8vo. Sydney, 1862. MH 1 S 15

HARRIS, E. [*See* Wiclif, J.]

HARRIS, E. Socialism and the Church : a Lecture. 8vo. Sydney, 1890. MG 1 S 56

HARRIS, E. C. New Zealand Ferns, 4to. Nelson (n.d.) MA 11 P 10 †
New Zealand Flowers. 4to. Nelson (n.d.) MA 11 P 11 †
New Zealand Berries. 4to. Nelson (n.d.) MA 11 P 12 †

HARRIS, G. F. Granites and our Granite Industries. 8vo. Lond., 1888. A 24 Q 7

HARRIS, J. R. Origin of the Leicester Codex of the New Testament. 4to. Lond., 1887. G 13 P 9 †

HARRIS, Dr. S. Craving for Drink ; its causes, nature, treatment, and curability. 3rd ed. 12mo. Lond., 1883. F 11 P 13

HARRIS, W. B. The Land of an African Sultan ; Travels in Morocco, 1887–89. 4to. Lond., 1889 D 15 V 13

HARRISON, Rev. A. J. What Does Christian Theism Teach ? Verbatim Report of Two Nights' Discussion between the Rev. A. J. Harrison and C. Bradlaugh. 2nd ed. 12mo. Lond., 1884. G 2 V 27

HARRISON, C. Stray Records. 2 vols. 8vo. Lond., 1892. C 13 Q 19, 20

HARRISON, F. The Transvaal : a Citizen to a Minister. 8vo. Lond. (n.d.) F 8 S 26
Oliver Cromwell. (Twelve English Statesmen.) 8vo. Lond., 1888. C 15 Q 2

HARRISON, F. B. The Contemporary History of the French Revolution, compiled from the " Annual Register." 8vo. Lond., 1889. B 26 Q 1

HARRISON, I. H. Complete Course of Volapük ; with Grammar and Exercises adapted from the French of Prof. A. Kerckhoffs. 8vo. Lond., 1888. K 12 Q 46

HARRISON, Jane E. [*See* Verrall, M. de G.]

HARRISON, W. J. History of Photography ; with Appendix by Dr. Maddox. 8vo. Bradford, 1888. A 23 T 1

HART, Francis. Western Australia in 1891. 8vo. Perth, 1891. MD 7 S 49

HART, G. E. The Fall of New France, 1755–60. 8vo. Montreal, 1888. B 1 S 5

HART, H. C. Some Account of the Fauna and Flora of Sinai, Petra, and Wâdy 'Arabah. 4to. Lond., 1891. A 36 P 26 ‡

HART, Lieut. Gen. H. G. The new Annual Army List, 1859–92. 34 vols. roy. 8vo. Lond., 1859–92. E

HART, T. . Poems. Select Works by. 12mo. (u.p. n.d.) MH 1 U 9

HART, W. F. Trade Marks : their object, use, and protection in Great Britain and Ireland. 8vo. Lond., 1889. F 6 P 47

HART, W. H. H. District Irrigation Laws of California. 8vo. Sacramento, 1891. F 9 S 3

HARTLAND, E. S. The Science of Fairy Tales : an Inquiry into Fairy Mythology. 8vo. Lond., 1891. J 1 U 45

HARTLEY, L. L. [*See* Hartley Library.]

HARTLEY, Prof. W. N. Course of Quantitative Analysis for Students. 12mo. Lond., 1887. A 21 P 4

HARTLEY LIBRARY. Sale Catalogue of the Library of the late L. L. Hartley ; compiled by J. C. Anderson. 3 vols. roy. 8vo. Lond., 1885–87. K 8 Q 13–15

HARTMAN, H. G. Kleinhandel in Sterken Drank. 8vo. Haarlem, 1881. F 11 Q 61

HARTMANN, F. Magic, White and Black ; containing Practical Hints for Students of Occultism. 3rd ed. 8vo. Lond., 1888. A 24 Q 25

HARTMANN, Dr. F. [*See* Boehme, J.]

HARTOG, M. M. [*See* Baillon, H.]

HARTSHORNE, A. Hanging in Chains. 12mo. Lond., 1891. F 9 U 30

HARTSON, H. Countess of Salisbury : a Tragedy. [*See* British Drama, Modern.]

HARTTUNG, Prof. J. V. Pflugk-. [*See* Pflugk-Harttung.]

HARVARD COLLEGE. Museum of Comparative Zoology. Bulletin. Vols. 11–22. 8vo. Camb., Mass., 1882–91. E
Record of the Commemoration (Nov. 5 to Nov. 8, 1886) on the 250th Anniversary of the Founding of Harvard College. Roy. 8vo. Camb., 1887. B 1 V 13

HARVEN, Emile de. La Nouvelle Zélande au Point de Vue Economique de la Belgique. Roy. 8vo. Anvers, 1884. MD 7 R 44

HARVEY, W. H. Nereis Australis ; or, Algæ of the Southern Ocean. Imp. 8vo. Lond., 1847. MA 1 P 25 †

HARVEY, W. F. Simplified Grammar of the Spanish Language. 8vo. Lond., 1890. K 20 Q 23

HARVIE-BROWN. [*See* Brown, J. A. Harvie-.]

HASE, C. B. [*See* Estienne, H.]

HASELFOOT, F. K. H. [*See* Dante, A.]

HASKINS, C. E. [*See* Lucanus, M. A.]

HASKINS, D. G. Ralph Waldo Emerson : his Maternal Ancestors, with some Reminiscences of him. 12mo. Lond., 1886. C 2 R 19

HASLAM, J. A Glimpse of Australian Life. 12mo. Sydney, 1890. MD 3 P 51

HASLUCK, P. N.   Mechanic's Workshop Handy-book.
8vo. Lond., 1888.   A 25 Q 8

Pattern-maker's Handy-book.   8vo. Lond., 1887.
                                            A 25 Q 7

Watch-jobber's Handy-book.   8vo. Lond., 1887. A 25 Q 6

Wood-turner's Handy-book.   8vo. Lond., 1887. A 25 Q 5

HASSALL, A.   Life of Viscount Bolingbroke. (Statesmen
Series.)   8vo. Lond., 1889.   C 12 R 30

HASSALL, A. H.   Adulterations Detected ; or, Instructions for the Discovery of Frauds in Food and Medicine.
8vo. Lond., 1857.   A 26 Q 17

HASSENCAMP, Dr. R.   History of Ireland from the
Reformation to the Union ; translated by E. A. Robinson.
8vo. Lond., 1888.   B 29 U 11

HASTIE, W.   [*See* Kant, I., and Levy, Prof. D.]

HASTINGS, Warren.   Life of ; by Sir A. Lyall. (English
Men of Action.)   12mo. Lond., 1889.   C 12 P 35

Life of ; by Capt. L. J. Trotter. (Rulers of India). 12mo.
Oxford, 1890.   C 12 P 36

[*See* Busteed, H. E.]

HATCH, Rev. E.   Essays in Biblical Greek.   8vo.
Oxford, 1889.   G 6 Q 32

Influence of Greek Ideas and Usages upon the Christian
Church.   8vo. Lond., 1890.   G 13 P 43

HATCH, Dr. F. H.   [*See* Posewitz, Dr. T.]

HAUGHTON, Rev. S.   Manual of Geology.   4th ed.
12mo. Lond., 1876.   A 24 P 3

HAUPTMANN, M.   Letters of a Leipzig Cantor ; translated by A. D. Coleridge.   2 vols. 8vo. Lond., 1892.
                                            C 18 Q 17, 18

HAUSER, M.   Hungarian Airs arranged for the Pianoforte.   Fol. Sydney (n.d.)   MA 11 Q 15 †

HAUSRATH, Dr. A.   History of the New Testament
times ; translated from the German ; by C. T. Poynting
and P. Quenzer.   2 vols. 8vo. Lond., 1878–80.
                                            G 4 U 12, 13

HAVARD, W.   King Charles I.: a Tragedy.   [*See*
British Drama, Modern, 2.]

HAVELOCK, Gen. Sir Henry.   [Life of] ; by Archibald
Forbes. (English Men of Action.)   12mo. Lond., 1890.
                                            C 12 P 34

HAVERCAMP, S.   Medailles de Grand et Moyen Bronze
du Cabinet de la Reine ;Christine.   Fol.   La Haye,
1742.   A 40 R 4 ‡

HAVILAND, E. C.   The Jenolan Caves.   Sm. 4to.
Sydney, 1890.   MH 1 S 50

Spirits and their Friends ; being an Appeal to Reason and
Justice, in answer to Mediums and their Dupes.   8vo.
Sydney, 1879.   MG 1 S 54

HAVILAND, E. C., and Mrs. E. C.   Voices from
Australia ; by "Philip Dale" and Cyril Haviland. 12mo.
Lond., 1892   MH 1 U 26

HAWAIIAN ALMANAC AND ANNUAL for
1887–92.   5 vols. 8vo. Honolulu, 1886–91.   ME 3 S

HAWAIIAN CLUB PAPERS, October 1866.   8vo.
Boston, 1868.   MJ 3 R 2

HAWEIS, Rev. H. R.   The Broad Church ; or, What is
coming.   12mo. Lond., 1891.   G 13 U 46

My Musical Life.   3rd ed.   12mo. Lond., 1891.
                                            C 18 P 6

HAWKESWORTH, A.   Raw Wools and Specimens to
Illustrate the Woollen Manufacture. (Technological
Museum, Sydney. Descriptive Catalogue No. 1.)   Roy.
8vo. Sydney, 1890.   MA 1 S 46

HAWKESWORTH, J.   Account of Voyages undertaken
for making Discoveries in the Southern Hemisphere.
3rd ed. 4 vols. 8vo. Lond., 1785.   MD 6 S 20–23

Relation des Voyages pour faire des Découvertes dans
l'Hemisphere Méridional, et successivement exécutés par
le Commodore Byron, le Capt. Carteret, le Capt. Wallis,
et le Capt. Cook.   4 vols. sm. 4to. Paris, 1774.
                                            MD 12 P 10–13 †

Cartes et Figures [to the above].   Sm. 4to.   Paris, 1774.
                                            MD 12 P 14 †

HAWKEYE.   [*See* Fry, E. H.]

HAWKINS, B. W.   [*See* Huxley, Prof. T. H.]

HAWKINS, Rev. C. H.   [*See* Winchester College
Shakspere Society.]

HAWKINS, Rev. Edward.   Life of. [*See* Burgon, Very
Rev. J. W.]

HAWKINS, E.   The Silver Coins of England.   8vo.
Lond., 1841.   A 27 T 3

Another Copy.   3rd ed.   Roy. 8vo. Lond., 1887.
                                            A 13 S 48

HAWKINS, F.   French Stage in the 18th Century,
1699–1799.   2 vols. 8vo. Lond., 1888.   B 26 U 6, 7

HAWKINS, H. S.   Practical Astronomy as applied to
Land Surveying.   8vo. Sydney, 1890.   MA 3 Q 37

HAWKINS, Sir J.   [*See* Candish, T.]

HAWKINS, Mary W. S.   Plymouth Armada Heroes:
the Hawkins Family.   Sm. 4to. Plymouth, 1888.
                                            C 9 V 7

HAWKINS, S.   Wagga Express Riverine Directory
for 1892.   12mo. Wagga, 1892.   ME 6 T

HAWTREY, Rev. M.   An Earnest Address to New
Zealand Colonists, with reference to their intercourse
with the Native Inhabitants.   12mo. Lond., 1840.
                                            MF 3 P 56

HAY, Sir A. L.   Narrative of the Peninsular War.   3rd
ed. Views and Map.   8vo. Lond., 1839.   B 19 S 18

HAY, James.   Swift : the mystery of his life and love.
8vo. Lond., 1891.   C 15 Q 8

HAY, John.   [*See* Nicolay, J. G.]

HAY, W. D. Elementary Text-book of British Fungi. Roy. 8vo. Lond., 1887. A 20 T 1

HAYDEN, F. V., and SELWYN, A. R. C. North America. 8vo. Lond., 1883. D 15 S 6

HAYDEN, Very Rev. T. Catechism on the Gospels of St. Matthew and St. John ; edited by the Rev. T. Hayden. 4th ed. 12mo. Sydney, 1858. MG 2 P 16

HAYDN, J. Vie de ; par M. H. Beyle. 12mo. Paris, 1887. C 14 P 18

HAYDON, T. Australasian Coursing Calendar for the Season, 1877. 8vo. Melb., 1878. ME 3 S

HAYES, Capt. M. H. Illustrated Horse Breaking. 8vo. Lond., 1889. A 1 U 25

Veterinary Notes for Horse Owners : a manual of horse medicine, written in popular language. 4th edition. 12mo. Lond., 1891. A 18 Q 14

Soundness and Age of Horses : a Veterinary and Legal Guide. 8vo. Lond., 1887. A 1 U 21

HAYNES, H V. Federation : or a Machiavelian Solution of the Australian Labour Problem. 8vo. Sydney, 1891. MF 2 T 27

HAYNES, J. F. Student's Guide to the Jurisdiction and Practice of the Admiralty Sub-Division of the High Court of Justice. 8vo. Lond., 1880. F 9 S 4

HAYR, J. H. The Latest Guide to the Hot Lakes, Terraces, and Geysers. 12mo. Auckland (n.d.) MD 2 W 34

HAYTER, H. H. My Christmas Adventure.—Carboona, and other Poems. 8vo. Melb., 1887. MII 1 Q 6

Victorian Year-Book, 1875-82, 1884-91. 16 vols. 8vo. Melb., 1876-90. ME 3 T

HAYTI. The Treatment of British Subjects in Hayti. 8vo. Lond., 1887. B 19 S 2

HAYWARD, H. [*See* Bismark, Prince von.]

HAZELL'S ANNUAL. 6 vols. 8vo. Lond., 1887-92. E

HAZLITT, W. C. Collections and Notes, 1867-1876. 1st series. 8vo. Lond., 1876. K 17 Q 16

Bibliographical Collections, and Notes on Early English Literature. 3rd series, 1474-1700. 8vo. Lond., 1887. K 17 Q 18

A Hundred Merry Tales. Imp. 8vo. Lond., 1887. J 7 V 11

Gleanings in Old Garden Literature. 12mo. Lond., 1887. A 18 P 1

The Livery Companies of the City of London. Roy. 8vo. Lond., 1892. B 24 V 10

Jests, New and Old. 8vo. Lond., 1886. J 3 V 18

Manual for the Collector and Amateur of Old English Plays. Sm. 4to. Lond., 1892. K 17 Q 14

Schools, School-books, and Schoolmasters. 12mo. Lond., 1888. G 17 P 34

Studies in Jocular Literature. 12mo. Lond., 1890. J 7 R 46

HEAD, B. V. Historia Numorum : a Manual of Greek Numismatics. Roy. 8vo. Oxford, 1887. A 27 V 1

HEAD, R. Congleton, Past and Present. Imp. 8vo. Congleton, 1887. B 24 V 1

HEADLAM, J. W. Election by Lot at Athens. 8vo. Camb., 1891. F 6 P 42

HEALES, Major Alfred. Architecture of the Churches of Denmark. Roy. 8vo. Lond., 1892. A 3 P 35

HEALEY, D. The Seven Christians of Championdom. 4to. Sydney, 1885. MJ 1 V 11

HEALTH LECTURES FOR THE PEOPLE. 2nd series. 8vo. Melb., 1889. MA 3 P 14

HEANLEY, Rev. R. M. Memoir of Edward Steere, third Missionary Bishop in Central Africa. 8vo. Lond., 1888. C 12 R 11

HEARD, A. F. The Russian Church and Russian Dissent. 8vo. Lond., 1887. G 16 S 32

HEARN, W. E. The Aryan Household, its Structure and Development. Roy. 8vo. Melb., 1878. MF 3 T 50

Theory of Legal Duties and Rights : an Introduction to Analytical Jurisprudence. Roy. 8vo. Melb., 1883. MF 3 T 14

HEATH, Prof. R. S. Treatise on Geometrical Optics. 8vo. Camb., 1887. A 21 T 13

HEATHCOTE, C. G. Lawn Tennis. [*See* Tennis, &c.]

HEATHCOTE, J. M. Tennis. [*See* Tennis, &c.]

HEATHCOTE, J. M., and TEBBUTT, C. G. Skating : Figure-Skating, by T. M. Witham ; with Contributions on Curling, by Rev. J. Kerr ; Tobogganing, by O. Hake ; Ice-Sailing, by H. A. Buck ; Bandy, by C. G. Tebbutt. (Badminton Lib.) 8vo. Lond., 1892. A 29 R 13

HEATON, Mrs. C. Concise History of Painting. New edition ; revised by C. Monkhouse. 12vo. Lond., 1888. A 23 Q 5

HEATON, J. H. Australian Dictionary of Dates. Roy. 8vo. Sydney, 1879. MK 1 S 46

HEBENSTREIT, E. B. G. De Potulentorum Cura in Republica bene ordinata ad sanitatis leges componenda. 12mo. Lipsiæ, 1778. F 11 P 49

HECTOR, Sir J. Geology of New Zealand. Reports of Geological Explorations, 1882-87, 1890-91. 4 vols. 8vo. Wellington, 1886-92. ME 2 S

Meteorological Reports, 1880. 8vo. Wellington, 1881. ME 2 S

Outlines of New Zealand Geology. (Geol Surv. of N.Z.) Roy. 8vo. Wellington, 1886. MA 2 R 33

Phormium Tenax as a fibrous plant. 2nd ed. Roy. 8vo. Wellington, 1889. MA 1 T 44

HEDDERWICK, T. C. H. The Old German Puppet Play of Dr. Faust, turned into English. 8vo. Lond., 1887. H 4 R 34

HERD BOOK OF HEREFORD CATTLE. (*Formerly* Eyton's Herd Book.) 12 vols. (in 11.) 8vo. Hereford, 1858-81. A 18 Q 1-11

HERDER, J. G. von. Der Cid. 18mo. Leipzig (n.d.) H 6 P 52

HEREMITE, Jaques L'. [*See* L'Hermite, J.]

HERETIC, The ; Feb.-July, 1886. 4to. Lond., 1886. E

HERFORD, R. B. [*See* Baines, E.]

HERKLESS, Rev. John. Cardinal Beaton : Priest and Politician. 12mo. Edinb., 1891. C 12 P 45

HERMANN, G. Epitome Doctrinæ Metricæ. 8vo. Lipsiæ, 1818. J 17 P 38

HERMAS. [*See* Lambros, Prof. S. P.]

HERNANDEZ, P., and LE ROY, A. Morceaux choisis en prose et en vers des Classiques Espagnols. 3rd ed. 18mo. Paris, 1876. J 15 Q 12

HERODAS. Facsimile of Papyrus cxxxv in the British Museum. Sm. 4to. Lond., 1892. H 7 V 28

HERODIAN. Ab excessu Divi Marci libri octo ; ab I. Bekkero recogniti. 12mo. Lipsiæ, 1855. B 30 Q 8

HERODOTUS. History of. Translated by G. C. Macauley. 2 vols. 8vo. Lond., 1890. B 35 Q 2, 3

Historiarum libri ix ; Annotationes Variorum adjecit T. Gaisford. 4 vols. 8vo. Oxford, 1824. B 35 T 10-13

History of ; translated by G. Rawlinson. 4 vols. 8vo. Lond., 1858-60. B 35 T 18-21

Euterpe: being the Second Book of the famous History of Herodotus ; edited by A. Lang. 8vo. Lond., 1888. B 21 Q 1

Herodotus : by G. C. Swayne. (Ancient Classics for English Readers.) 12mo. Edinb., 1885. J 14 P 10

HERON, Mrs. E. A. The Balance of Pain, and other poems ; "Australie" (Miss Manning). 8vo. Lond., 1877. MH 1 U 10

HERRENSCHMIDT, H. On the Treatment of Mangani. ferous Cobalt and Nickel Ores. 8vo. Sydney, 1884. MA 2 P 15

HERRERA, A. de. Novus Orbis sive Descriptio Indiæ occidentalis. 4to. Amst., 1622. D 40 Q 16†

HERSCHEL, Sir J. F. W. Physical Geography of the Globe. 8vo. Edinb., 1872. A 29 S 4

[*See* Proctor, R. A.]

HERTWIG, Prof. O. Das Problem der Befruchtung und der Isotropie des Eies, eine Theorie der Vererbung. Roy. 8vo. Jena, 1884. A 15 Q 15

HERTWIG, Dr. R. Die Actinien der Challengerexpedition. 4to. Jena, 1887. A 40 Q 7†

Organismus der Radiolarien. 4to. Jena, 1879. A40 S 2†

HERTZ, M. [*See* Gellius, A.]

HERVEY, Gen. C. Some Records of Crime ; being the Diary of an Officer of the Dacoit Police. 2 vols. 8vo. Lond., 1892. F 14 T 10, 11

HERVEY, M. H. Dark Days in Chile ; an account of the Revolution of 1891 ; illustrated. 8vo. Lond., 1891-92. D 15 S 19

The Trade Policy of Imperial Federation. 12mo. Lond., 1892. F 9 U 2

[*See* Britannic Confederation.]

HERVEY, T. K. The Poetical Sketch-Book, including a third edition of Australia. 12mo. Lond., 1829. MH 1 Q 53

HESIOD. Carmina : (Gr. et Lat.) Edidit F. S. Lehrs. Imp. 8vo. Parisiis, 1841. H 7 V 24

Carmina ; curante, C. H. Weiser, (Gr. text.) 18mo. Lipsiæ, 1844. H 11 P 6

Epics of ; with an English Commentary, by F. A. Paley. 8vo. Lond., 1861. H 10 R 14

Hesiod and Theognis ; by Rev J. Davies. (Ancient Classics for English Readers.) 12mo. Edinb., 1881. J 14 P 11

HESSEL, Rev. W. Letter to the Editor of the *Sydney Morning Herald*, on the Subject of State Aid. 8vo. Sydney, 1859. MG 1 S 55

HESSELS, J. H. Haarlem the Birthplace of Printing, not Mentz. Roy. 8vo. Lond., 1887. B 36 V 4

HESSEY, Rev. J. A. Sunday ; in Origin, History, and Present Obligation. 4th ed. 8vo. Lond., 1880. G 13 Q 41

HETHERINGTON, F. W. Immigrants Prospects in South Australia, Hand-book of Information, Resources, Advantages, and Attractions, Soil, Climate, &c. Roy 8vo. Lond., 1892. MD 7 U 13

HETLEY, Mrs C. The Native Flowers of New Zealand, illustrated in colours. Fol. Lond., 1888. MA 1 R 19 ‡

HETTINGER, Prof. F. Dante's Divina Commedia : its Scope and Value ; edited by H. S. Bowden. 8vo. Lond., 1887. H 8 S 44

HEUSINGER, O. Ueber die Getränke. 8vo. (n.p.n.d.) F 11 R 29

HEWITSON, Rev. W. H. Memoir of ; by John Baillie. 8th ed. 12mo. Lond., 1858. C 14 Q 28

HEYLIGERS, J. C. T. De Dronkenschap. 8vo. Zalt-Bommel, 1874. F 11 R 23

HEYWOOD, Capt. P. Memoirs of the late Capt. P. Heywood ; with extracts from his Diaries, &c., by E. Tagart. 8vo. Lond., 1832. MC 1 R 29

HEYWOOD, T. Best Plays ; edited by A. W. Verity. (Mermaid Series ; edited by H. Ellis.) 8vo. Lond., 1888. H 4 Q 28

A Woman killed with Kindness.—The Fair Maid of the West.—The English Traveller.—The Wise Woman of Hogsdon.—The Rape of Lucrece.

The Four P's. : a Merry Interlude. [*See* British Drama, Ancient, 1.]

HEYWOOD, T.—*contd.*
A Woman killed with Kindness : a Tragedy. [*See* British Drama, Ancient, 2.]
Foure Prentises of London : an Historical Play. [*See* British Drama, Ancient, 3.]

HICKES, G. Grammaticæ Anglo-Saxonicæ, et Moeso-Gothicæ. Sm. 4to. Oxoniæ, 1689. K 14 T 35

HICKS, C. Stansfeld-. Yachts, Boats, and Canoes. 8vo. Lond., 1887. A 2 S 41

HICKS, Dr. G. B. Alcohol in Health and Disease. 12mo. Lond., 1885. F 11 P 15

HICKSON, Sydney J. A Naturalist in North Celebes. 8vo. Lond., 1889. D 16 U 21

HIEROCLES. De Providentia et Fato, L. Gyraldi interpretatione. 18mo. Lond., 1673. G 8 P 31

HIGGINS, Charles L. Life of. [*See* Burgon, Very Rev. J. W.]

HIGINBOTHAM, A. J., and ROBINSON, H. E. C. Yachting and Excursion Map of Port ¡Phillip and the Surrounding Country. (Folded.) 8vo. Melb. (n.d.) MD 1 U 38

HIGINBOTHAM, A. J., ROBINSON, H. E. C., and HARRISON. Atlas of the Suburbs of Sydney. Fol. Sydney, 1889. MD 8 P 9†

HILDYARD, H. J. T. [*See* Verdy du Vernois, Col. I. von.]

HILDEBRAND. [*See* Stephens, W. R. W.]

HILL, Aaron. Zara : a Tragedy. [*See* British Drama, Modern, 2.]

HILL, A. Essays upon Educational Subjects. 8vo. Lond., 1857. G 17 P 48

HILL, A. S. The Australian Grand Waltzes. Fol. Sydney (n.d.) MA 11 Q 15†

HILL, F. Crime : its Amount, Causes, and Remedies. 8vo. Lond., 1853. F 11 R 12

HILL, F. H. George Canning. (English Worthies.) 12mo. Lond., 1887. C 12 P 27

HILL, F. S. T. Poems and Recollections of the Past. 12mo. Sydney, 1840. MH 1 U 25

HILL, Miss G. Pleasures and Profits of Our Little Poultry Farm. 12mo. Lond., 1879. A 18 Q 16

HILL, Rev. George. Historical Account of the Plantation in Ulster, 1608–1620. Sm. 4to. Belfast, 1877. B 11 R 2
[*See* Montgomery, W.]

HILL, G. B. Boswell's Correspondence with the Hon. Andrew Erskine and his Journal of a Tour to Corsica. 12mo. Lond., 1879. C 18 P 5
Footsteps of Dr. [S.] Johnson. 4to. Lond., 1890. C 42 R 26‡
Letters of S. Johnson. [*See* Johnson, S.]
Writers and Readers. 8vo. Lond., 1892. J 11 W 22
[*See* Boswell, J.]

HILL, G. W. New Theory of Jupiter and Saturn. [*See* Newcomb, Prof. S. Astronomical Papers, vol. 4.]

HILL, Gray. With the Beduins : a Narrative of Journeys and Adventures in Syria. 8vo. Lond., 1891. D 16 U 22

HILL, J. W. Management and Diseases of the Dog. 8vo. Lond., 1888. A 1 T 32

HILL, S. S. Travels in the Sandwich and Society Islands. 8vo. Lond., 1856. MD 6 S 5

HILL, W. [*See* Agriculture, Dept. of, Queensland.]

HILLARD, Katharine. [*See* Dante Alighieri.]

HILLEBRAND, W. Flora of the Hawaiian Islands : a Description of the Phanerogams and Vascular Cryptogams. 8vo. Lond., 1888. MA 1 T 41

HILLER, Dr. F. Comsumption and its Prevention, with remarks on Koumiss, as a Hygenic Remedy for Debilitating, Nervous, and Wasting Diseases. 8vo. Sydney, 1878. MA 3 S 21

HILLIER, G. L. [*See* Bury, Viscount.]

HILTON, John. Defence of Legislation on the Lines of Local Option. 8vo. Manchester, 1885. F 11 R 21

HIME, M. C. Home Education ; or, Irish *v.* English Grammar Schools for Irish Boys. 8vo. Lond., 1887. G 17 P 39

HIND, R. D. Archer-. [*See* Plato.]

HINTON, C. H. New Era of Thought. 8vo. Lond., 1888. G 8 Q 24

HIORNS, Arthur H. Mixed Metals or Metallic Alloys. 12mo. Lond., 1890. A 24 P 2

HIPPOCAMPUS. [*See* David, the Shepherd King.]

HIPPOCRATES. Hippocratis Aphorismi, Hippocratis et Celsi parallelis illustrati, studio et curâ Janssonii ab Almeloveen ; editionem curavit A. C. Lorry, M.D. 32mo. Parisiis, 1759. Libr.

HIRTIUS, A. [*See* Cæsar, C. J.]

HISLOP, Stephen. Pioneer Missionary and Naturalist in Central India, 1844–63 ; by Dr. G. Smith. 8vo. Lond., 1888. C 15 T 17

HISSEY, J. J. Across England in a Dog-cart ; from London to St. David's and back. 8vo. Lond., 1891. D 18 T 16
A Holiday on the Road : an Artist's Wanderings in Kent, Sussex, and Surrey. 8vo. Lond., 1887. D 8 U 25

HISTOIRE DES DIABLES DE LOUDUN. 18mo. Amsterdam, 1693. B 26 P 2

HISTOIRE LITTÉRAIRE DE LA FRANCE. Tomes 1–30. 4to. Paris, 1733–1888. B 11 R 1–S 10 †

HISTORIÆ AUGUSTÆ SCRIPTORES VI., accurante C. Schrevelio. 12mo. Lugd. Batav., 1661. B 30 Q 5

HISTORIÆ ROMANÆ SCRIPTORES MINORES. 8vo. Biponti, 1789. B 30 R 7

HISTORICAL MANUSCRIPTS COMMISSION. Reports and Appendices. 23 vols. roy. 8vo. Lond., 1885-92. E

HISTORICAL REVIEW of the Question of the Immortality of the Soul, by "Esegar." Australian Edition. 12mo. Brisbane, 1890. MG 2 P 30

HITCHCOCK, H. R. English-Hawaiian Dictionary. 8vo. San Francisco, 1887. MK 1 P 62

HITCHMAN, F. Richard F. Burton : his Early, Private, and Public Life ; with an Account of his Travels and Explorations. 2 vols. 8vo. Lond., 1887. C 13 U 24, 25

HIUEN-TSIANG. Life of ; by the Shamans Hwui Li and Yen-Tsung ; with a preface by Prof. S. Beal. 8vo. Lond., 1888. C 14 S 3

HOADLY, John. The Suspicious Husband : a Comedy. [*See* British Drama, Modern, 4.]

HOBART, Lord. The "Mission of Richard Cobden. 12mo. Lond., 1867. F 12 S 4

HOBART EXHIBITION of Fine Arts, 1887. Catalogue. 8vo. Hobart, 1887. MK 1 T 11

HOBART TOWN ALMANACK and Van Diemen's Land Annual. [*See* Ross, J.]

HOBBS, T. Grecian War. [*See* Thucydides.]

HOBDAY, E. Villa Gardening : a Hand-book for Amateur and Practical Gardeners. 8vo. Lond., 1887. A 1 U 11

HOBLYN, R. D. Dictionary of Terms used in Medicine and the Collateral Sciences. 11th edition, revised by J. A. P. Price. 8vo. Lond., 1887. K 19 P 8

HOBSON, J. A. Problems of Poverty. 8vo. Lond., 1891. F 14 P 9

HOCHE, Gén. L. Généraux de Vingt Ans ; par F. Tulou. 8vo. Paris, 1891. C 18 S 14

HOCKINGS, A. J. Queensland Garden Manual. 2nd thousand. 12mo. Brisb., 1875. MA 3 P 34

HODDER, E. Life of Samuel Morley. 8vo. Lond., 1887. C 13 U 15

George Fife Angas, Father and Founder of South Australia. 8vo. Lond., 1891. MC 1 T 6

HODDER, G. Memories of my Time ; including Personal Reminiscences of Eminent Men. 8vo. Lond., 1870. C 13 U 14

HODGINS, T. Canadian Franchise Act. 12mo. Toronto, 1886. F 6 P 38

Supplement to [the above.] 12mo. Toronto, 1886. F 6 P 38

Manual on the Law Affecting Voters' Lists for Elections in Ontario. 2nd edition. Toronto, 1886. F 6 P 39

HODGKINSON, S. Hand-book to the Colony of Queensland. 8vo. Lond., 1861. MD 1 W 31

O

HOE, R. A Lecture on Bookbinding as a Fine Art. Illustrated. 4to. New York, 1886. A 11 V 16

HÖEGH GULDBERG, O. C. Dissertatio de Delirio Tremente. 2 vols. 8vo. Hauniæ, 1836. F 11 Q 9, 10

HOFF, Prof. J. H. van't. [*See* VAN'T HOFF, Prof. J. H.]

HÖFFDING, H. Outlines of Psychology ; translated by Mary E. Lowndes. 12mo. Lond., 1891. G 13 U 47

HOFFMANN, E. T. W. The Serapion Brethren ; translated by Lt.-Col. A. Ewing. Vol. 2. 8vo. Lond., 1892. J 12 P 28

Weird Tales ; with a Biographical Memoir, by J. T. Bealby. 2 vols. Roy. 8vo. Lond., 1885. J 6 U 12, 13

HOFFMANN-MERIAM, T. Zur Alkoholfrage. 8vo. Bern, 1883. F 11 R 27

HOGAN, J. F. The Australian in London and America. 8vo. Lond., 1889. MD 2 Q 22

The Convict King ; being the Life and Adventures of Jorgen Jorgenson. 12mo. Lond., 1891. MC 1 S 8

Irish in Australia. 8vo. Lond., 1887. MB 2 T 15

HOGARTH, William. Genuine Works of. 2 vols. 4to. Lond., 1808-10. A 39 Q 24, 25‡

HOHENLOHE-INGELFINGEN, Kraft, Prinz zu. Letters on Cavalry translated by Lieut-Col. N. L. Walford. 8vo. Lond., 1889. A 29 Q 12

Letters on Artillery ; translated by Lieut.-Col. N. L. Walford. 2nd edition. 8vo. Lond., 1890. A 29 Q 11

Letters on Infantry ; translated by Lieut.-Col. N. L. Walford. 8vo. Lond., 1889. A 29 Q 10

HOLBERG, L. Samtlige Comœdier. 8vo. Kiobenhavn, 1843. H 2 T 24

HOLBROOK, M. L. Dr. Holbrook's American Cookery, with an Australian Appendix of over 100 refreshing drinks for all Seasons. 12mo. Melb., 1888. MA 3 P 15

HOLCOMBE, W. H. Lazarus of Bethany ; the Story of his Life in both Worlds. 12mo. Melb., 1872. MJ 1 U 10

HOLDEN, F. G. Her Father's Darling, and other Child Pictures. 12mo. Sydney, 1887. MH 1 P 51

The Travels of Red-Jacket and White-Cap ; or, a History of the Circulation of the Blood. 12mo. Sydney, 1884. MA 3 P 35

HOLDEN, J. W. A Wizard's Wanderings from China to Peru. 8vo. Lond., 1886. D 20 Q 1

HOLDER, C. F. Living Lights : a Popular Account of Phosphorescent Animals and Vegetables. 8vo. Lond., 1887. A 27 R 25

HOLDSWORTH, P. J. [*See* Smith, W. H., and Sons.]

HOLDSWORTH, W. A. Law of Wills, Executors, and Administrators. 22nd ed. 12mo. Lond., 1886. F 1 P 31

HOLLAND, Rev. H. S., and ROCKSTRO, W. S. Memoir of Madame Jenny Lind-Goldschmidt, 1820–51. 2 vols. 8vo. Lond., 1891.   C 15 T 13, 14

HOLLAND, T. E. Elements of Jurisprudence. 5th edition. 8vo. Oxford, 1890.   F 9 S 15

HOLMAN, H. Handy Book for Shipowners and Masters. 3rd edition. Roy. 8vo. Lond., 1892.   F 12 R 28

HOLMES, G. C. V. The Steam-engine. 12mo. Lond., 1887.   A 22 P 26

HOLMES, O. W. Over the Teacups. 8vo. Lond., 1890.   J 5 P 46
Our Hundred Days in Europe. 12mo. Lond., 1887.
                                    D 18 P 4

HOLROYD, Dr. A. T. Bowls and Bowling, with the laws and rules of the game. 12mo. Sydney, 1874. MA 2 V 39

HOLST, Dr. H. von. Constitutional Law of the United States of America. Roy. 8vo. Chicago, 1887.   F 10 S 22

HOLT, T. Christianity, the Poor Man's Friend. 8vo. Bexley, 1888.   MG 2 P 5

HOLTZAPFFEL, John J. [*See* Leland, Charles G.]

HOLTZENDORFF, F. von. Psychologie des Mordes. 8vo. Berlin, 1875.   G 12 S 40

HOLYOAKE, G. J. The Co-operative Movement to-day. 8vo. Lond., 1891.   F 14 P 43
Self-help a hundred years ago. 8vo. Lond., 1888.
                                    F 14 Q 34

HOME, J. Douglas : a Tragedy. [*See* British Drama, Modern, 2.]

HOME, D. D. : his Life and Mission ; by Mme. D. Home. 8vo. Lond., 1888.   C 13 U 1

HOMER. Eustathii in Homeri Iliadis et Odysseæ libros Parecbolæ. [Gr. text.] 2 vols. Fol. Basileæ, 1560.
                                    H 42 Q 2, 3 ‡
Copiæ Cornu, sive Oceanus Enarrationum Homericarum, Hadriano Junio autore. Fol. Basileæ, 1558.
                                    H 42 Q 5 ‡
Familiar Studies in. [*See* Clarke, Agnes M.]
Companion to the Iliad. [*See* Leaf, Dr. W.]
Hymni Homerici, ex recensione A. Baumeister. (Gr. text.) 8vo. Lipsiæ, 1858.   H 10 Q 18
Index Vocabulorum. [*See* Seberus, W.]
Iliad ; by Rev. W. L. Collins. (Ancient Classics for English Readers.) 12mo. Edinb., 1886.   J 14 P 12
Iliad ; edited by W. Leaf. (Gr. text.) 2 vols. 8vo. Lond., 1886–88.   H 10 S 1, 2
Iliad, done into English Verse ; by A. S. Way. Vols. 1 and 2. Sm. 4to. Lond., 1886–88.   H 10 S 3, 4
Iliad of Homer ; translated by J. Purves, and edited by Dr. E. Abbott. 8vo. Lond., 1891.   J 3 T 16
Odyssey ; by Rev. W. L. Collins. (Ancient Classics for English Readers.) 12mo. Edinb., 1882.   J 14 P 13

HOMER—*contd.*
Odyssey, done into English Verse ; by W. Morris. 8vo. Lond., 1887.   H 8 Q 26
Odyssey, done into English Verse ; by A. S. Way. 2nd edition. Sm. 4to. Lond., 1886.   H 9 S 22
Odyssea. (Greek text and notes.) 2 vols. 8vo. Oxon., 1782.   H 2 T 28, 29
Ilias [ed Didynii]. (Greek text and notes.) 2 vols. 8vo. Oxon., 1792.   H 6 T 26, 27
Opera Omnia ; cura J. A. Ernesti. (Gr. et Lat.) 5 vols. (in 2). 8vo. Lipsiæ, 1824.   H 4 U 25, 26
The Odyssey of, done into English Verse by W. Morris. 2 vols. 4to. Lond., 1887.   H 6 S 35, 36
[*See* Jebb, R. C.]

HONE, W. Every-day Book. 2 vols. 8vo. Lond. (n.d.)
                                    J 10 V 7, 8
Table Book of Daily Recreation and Information. 8vo. Lond. (n.d.)   J 10 V 9
The Three Trials of William Hone for Publishing three Parodies. 8vo. Lond., 1818.   F 1 Q 28
Year Book of Daily Recreation and Information. 8vo. Lond. (n.d.)   J 10 V 10
Trial by Jury and Liberty of the Press ; Proceedings at the public meeting, Dec. 29, 1817. 6th ed. Lond., 1818.   F 1 Q 28

HOOD, T. H. Cockburn-. Was New Zealand a Post-glacial Centre of Creation ? Roy. 8vo. Wellington, 1876.   MA 2 R 38
The Pacific Region in the Past and Present. Roy. 8vo. Wellington, 1880.   MA 2 R 41
Remarks upon the Footprints of Moas at Poverty Bay, and upon their recent Extinction. 8vo. Waikato, 1872.   MA 2 T 56

HOOK, Rev. Dr. W. F. Letter to. [*See* Burgess, Rev. R.]

HOOKER, Sir J. D. Botany. (Science Primers.) 18mo. Lond., 1881.   A 20 P 8
Botany of the Antarctic Voyage of H.M. Ships Erebus and Terror, 1839–43. 4to. Lond., 1844.   A 36 P 22 ‡
Handbook of the New Zealand Flora. 8vo. Lond., 1867.   MA 1 T 29
Introductory Essay to the Flora of New Zealand. 4to. Lond., 1853.   MA 1 Q 12 †
Another copy. Roy. 4to. Lond., 1853.   A 36 P 22 ‡
On the Flora of Australia ; its Origin, &c. Roy. 4to. Lond., 1859.   MA 1 Q 14 †

HOOKER, Sir W. J. Notes on the Botany of the Antarctic Voyage conducted by Capt. J. C. Ross in Her Majesty's Discovery Ships, Erebus and Terror ; with Observations on the Tussac Grass of the Falkland Islands. 8vo. Lond., 1843.   MA 1 U 48

HOOKER, Sir W. J., and GREVILLE, Dr. R. K. Icones Filicum : Figures and Descriptions of Ferns. 2 vols. Fol. Lond., 1831.   A 37 P 24 25 ‡

HOOLE, Elijah. Year Book of Missions: containing a Comprehensive Account of Missionary Societies, British, Continental, and American, &c. 8vo. Lond., 1847.
MG 1 S 62

HOOPER, G. Abraham Fabert, Governor of Sedan, Marshal of France, the First who rose from the Ranks. 8vo. Lond., 1892. C 14 V 11

Campaign of Sedan: Downfall of the Second Empire, August-September, 1870. 8vo. Lond., 1887. B 26 U 8

[Life of] Wellington. 8vo. Lond., 1889. C 12 Q 19

Waterloo: the downfall of the First Napoleon. New edition. 8vo. Lond., 1890. B 26 Q 5

HOPE, A. Chronicles of an Old Inn; or, a Few Words about Gray's Inn. 8vo. Lond., 1887. C 12 R 22

HOPE, W. H. St. J. Royal House of Stuart. [See Gibb, W.]

HOPEFUL. [See "Taken In."]

HOPKINS, A. A. The Scientific American Cyclopedia of Receipts. 8vo. New York, 1892. K 4 S 21

HOPKINS, I. The Illustrated Australasian Bee Manual, and complete guide to modern Bee-culture in the Southern Hemisphere. 3rd ed. 8vo. Auckland, 1886.
MA 1 Q 16

HOPPE, C. E. L. De Spirituosis. 8vo. Berolini, 1862.
F 11 Q 29

HOPPNER, R. B. [See Kruseustern, Capt. A. J. von.]

HOPPUS, Rev. Dr. Account of Lord Bacon's Novum Organum Scientiarum. 8vo. Lond. (n.d.) G 12 Q 37

HORAPOLLO. Hieroglyphica, Grœce & Latine, curante J. Cornelio. Sm. 4to. Traj. ad Rhenum, 1727. J 17 U 1

HORATIUS FLACCUS, Q. Horace: by Sir T. Martin. (Ancient Classics for English Readers.) 12mo. Edinb., 1887. J 14 P 14

Lyra Romana; or, Extracts from Horace (Lyric only.) 18mo. Sydney, 1870. MH 1 P 48

Opera: illustravit L. Desprey. 8vo. Lond., 1815.
H 10 R 17

Q. Horatius Flaccus: cum Commentariis, &c., J. C. Messeni. Sm. 4to. Raphelengii, 1611. H 10 Q 14

Opera: plurimis in locis emendavit notisque illustravit, C. Fea. 8vo. Romœ, 1811. H 4 S 33

Q. Horatius Flaccus ad editionem R. Bentleii expressus. 12mo. Cantab., 1713. H 10 P 18

Odes, and Carmen Sœculare of Horace; translated into English Verse by Prof. J. Conington. 9th edition. 12mo. Lond., 1882. H 6 Q 6

Satires and Epistles. (Lat. text.) Notes and Excursus, by T. Keightley. 8vo. Lond., 1848. H 10 Q 14

Satires, Epistles, and Art of Poetry of Horace; translated into English Verse by Prof. J. Conington. 6th edition. 12mo. Lond., 1883. H 6 Q 37

[See Janin, J.]

HORE, E. C. Tanganyika: eleven years in Central Africa. 8vo. Lond., 1892. D 14 R 12

HORNBROOK, A. [See Cooper, T.]

HORNE, H. P. [See Nero, and other Plays.]

HORNE, R. H. H. Orion: an Epic Poem. 12mo. Lond., 1843. H 8 P 40

HORNE, Mrs. S. G. The Next World: Communications from eminent Historians, Authors, &c., now in Spirit-life. 8vo. Lond., 1890. G 8 R 28

HORNE, Rev. T. H. Illustrated Record of Important Events in Europe, 1812-15. Fol. Lond., 1815.
D 41 P 14 ‡

HORNEMANN, Dr. E. Hygieiniske Meddelelser. 8vo. Kjöbenhavn, 1874. F 11 Q 63

HORNUNG, E. W. A Bride from the Bush. New edition. Lond., 1891. MJ 2 T 31

HORSEY, J. G. Voyage from Australia to England: an interesting account of all incidents occurring on board the Blackwall Liner " Dover Castle," on her voyage from Melbourne to London, 1867, published on board that ship as a weekly newspaper under the title of the " Dover Castle News." Roy. 8vo. Lond., 1867.
MD 7 R 46

HORSTMAN, Dr. C. Early South-English Legendary. [See Early Eng. Text Soc.]

HORT, Mrs. A. Hena: or, Life in Tahiti. 2 vols. 8vo. Lond., 1866. MJ 1 U 43, 44

HORT, D. Tahiti, the Garden of the Pacific. 8vo. Lond., 1891. MD 7 S 25

HORTON, Rt. Hon. Sir R. W. Letter addressed to the Anonymous Author of "England and America," [Edward G. Wakefield.] 8vo. Colombo, 1834. MF 2 T 64

HORTON, S. D. The Silver Pound, and England's Monetary Policy since the Restoration. Roy. 8vo. Lond., 1887. F 10 T 20

HOSACK, J. Mary Stewart: Statement of the Charges brought against her, with Answers to same. 8vo. Lond., 1888. G 16 P 5

HOSIE, Alexander. Three Years in Western China. Roy. 8vo. Lond., 1890. D 17 U 14

HOSMER, Prof. J. K. Life of young Sir Henry Vane, with a consideration of the English Commonwealth as a forecast of America. 8vo. Lond., 1888. C 12 S 29

Short History of German Literature. 8vo. Lond., 1892. B 16 S 6

HOSTE, Sir W. Service Afloat; or, the Naval Career of. 8vo. Lond., 1887. C 12 Q 24

HOUGH, Franklin B. Elements of Forestry, designed to afford information concerning the planting and care of forest trees for ornament or profit. 8vo. Cincinnati, 1882. A 18 R 7

HOUGH, W. S. History of Philosophy. [See Erdmann, J. E.]

HOUGHTON, Richard Monckton Milnes, First Lord. Life, Letters, and Friendships of; by T. W. Reid. 2 vols. 8vo. Lond., 1890.   C 13 U 10, 11

HOUISON, Dr. A. History of the Post-office, together with an Historical Account of the Issue of Postage Stamps in New South Wales. 4to. Sydney, 1890.   MB 7 P 12 †

HOULDING, J. R. Australian Capers. 8vo. Lond., 1867.   MJ 1 Q 3

Investing Uncle Ben's Legacy: A Tale of Mining and Matrimonial Speculation; by "Old Boomerang." 8vo. Melb., 1876.   MJ 1 S 41

HOUSTON, M. G. Trial of. [*See* Wheeler, J. C.]

HOVELACQUE, A. Science of Language; translated by A. H. Keane. 8vo. Lond., 1877.   K 12 U 16

HOW TO SETTLE ON THE LAND IN QUEENSLAND. [*See* Indian and Colonial Exhibition, 1886.]

HOWARD, A. Beauties of Byron. [*See* Byron, Lord.]

HOWARD, Prof. G. E. [*See* Johns Hopkins University Studies.]

HOWARD, J. J. Miscellanea Genealogica et Heraldica. Series 2, vols. 1-3. Imp. 8vo. Lond., 1886-90.   K 8 U 5-7

HOWARD, J. J., and BURKE, H. F. Genealogical Collections, illustrating the History of Roman Catholic Families of England. 2 vols. Fol. Lond, 1887.   K 44 Q 1, 2‡

HOWARD, L. Barometrographia: 20 years' variation of the Barometer in the Climates of Britain. Fol. Lond., 1847.   A 8 R 14‡

HOWARD, Sir R. The Committee: a Comedy. [*See* British Drama, Modern.]

HOWE, R. Australasian Almanack for 1827. 8vo. Sydney, 1827.   ME 4 Q

Australian Almanac, 1829. 12mo. Sydney, 1829.   ME 4 Q

HOWELL, G. Trade Unionism, New and Old. 8vo. Lond., 1891.   F 14 P 26

Conflicts of Capital and Labour, Historically and Economically considered. 2nd ed. Lond., 1890.   F 14 P 27

HOWELL, James. The Familiar Letters of; edited by Joseph Jacobs. 2 vols. roy. 8vo. Lond., 1892.   C 13 V 7, 8

HOWELL, J. Rose Leaves from an Australian Garden. 8vo. Adelaide, 1884.   MH 1 S 51

HOWELLS, W. D. Modern Italian Poets: Essays and Versions. 8vo. Edinb., 1887.   H 8 S 42 [*See* Alfieri, V.]

HOWES, G. R. [*See* Huxley, Prof. T. H.]

HOWITT, A. W. Australian Group Relations. Roy. 8vo Washington, 1885.   MA 1 T 9

HOWITT, Margaret. [*See* Howitt, Mary.]

HOWITT, Mary. An Autobiography; edited by her Daughter, Margaret Howitt. 2 vols. Lond., 1889.   C 12 U 25, 26

HOWITT, William. Land, Labour, and Gold; or, Two Years in Victoria, with Visits to Sydney and Van Diemen's Land. 2 vols. 8vo. Lond., 1858.   MD 7 T 16, 17

Boy's Adventures in the Wilds of Australia. 12mo. Lond., 1854.   MD 1 P 2

HOWLAND, G. Practical Hints for the Teachers of the Public Schools. 12mo. New York, 1889.   G 18 Q 12

HOWLETT, Ross J. [*See* Gordon, A. L.]

HOWORTH, D. F. Coins and Tokens of the English Colonies. 12mo. Lond., 1890.   A 27 Q 1

HOWORTH, H. H. History of the Mongols from the 9th to 19th Century. Parts I-III (in 4 vols.) roy. 8vo. Lond., 1876-88.   B 20 V 1-4

HOWSON, Rev. J. S. Lectures on the Character of St. Paul. 8vo. Lond., 1864.   G 12 Q 32

HOYLE, Wm. Our National Drink Bill, as it Affects the Nation's well-being. 8vo. Glasgow, 1884.   F 11 Q 8

The Drinking System and its Evils. 8vo. Manchester, 1879.   F 11 R 25

Remedies for the Poverty, Degradation, and Misery which exist. 8vo. Lond., 1882.   F 11 R 26

Our National Resources, and how they are Wasted. 12mo. Manchester, 1882.   F 11 P 34

[*See* Caine, W. S.]

HOZIER, Charles d'. [*See* Hozier, L. P. et A. M. d'.]

HOZIER, Louis Pierre, et Antoine Marie d'. Armorial Général, ou Régistres de la Noblesse de France. 10 vols. fol. Paris, 1738-68.   K 6 Q 1-10‡

Indicateur du grand Armorial Général de France par Charles d' Hozier. 2 vols. (in 1). 8vo. Paris, 1866.   K 8 R 19

HUBBARD, Bela. Memorials of a Half-Century. 8vo. New York, 1887.   D 15 R 4

HUC, l' Abbé E. R. Travels in Tartary, Thibet, and China during the Years 1844-6. 2nd ed. 2 vols. 12mo. Lond. (n.d.)   D 5 P 37, 38

HUCHER, E. F. F. Calques des Vitraux Peints de la Cathédrale du Mans. Fol. Paris, 1864.   A 43 P 4‡

HUDSON, C. T., and GOSSE, P. H. The Rotifera; or, Wheel-Animalcules, both British and Foreign. Text, Plates, and Supplement. 3 vols. imp. 8vo. Lond., 1886-89.   A 14 V 4 6

HUDSON, G. V. Elementary Manual of New Zealand Entomology, being an introduction to the study of our Native Insects. 8vo. Lond., 1892.   MA 3 S 20

HUDSON, H. Descriptio ac delineatio Geographica Detectionis Freti sive Transitus ad Occasum suprà terras Americanas, in Chinam atque Japonem ducturi; item exegesis Regi Hispaniæ facta, super tractu recens detecto, in quintâ Orbis parte, cui nomen, Australis Incognita. Sm. 8vo. Amsterodami, 1613. MD 1 R 46

HUDSON, J. [*See* Josephus, F.]

HUDSON, W. H. The Naturalist in La Plata. 8vo. Lond., 1892. A 14 T 51
[*See* Sclater, P. L.]

HUDSPETH, B. M. Santa Claus and the Shadow. Roy. 8vo. Sydney (n.d.) MJ 3 R 1

HUEFFER, F. [*See* Wagner, R.]

HUES, R. Tractatus de Globis. [*See* Hakluyt Society.]

HUET, C. B. Land of Rubens : a Companion for Visitors to Belgium; translated by A. D. Vandam. 8vo. Lond., 1888. D 8 S 14

HUG, Mrs. Lina, and STEAD, R. Switzerland. (Story of the Nations Series.) 8vo. Lond., 1890. B 25 R 1

HUGGARD, J. J. The Christian Armed; a popular summary of Christian doctrine in verse, with other Poems. 12mo. Sydney, 1871. MH 1 Q 54

HUGHES, E. Outlines of Physical Geography. 7th ed. 12mo. Lond., 1856. A 29 P 20

HUGHES, Mrs. F. My Childhood in Australia, a story for my children. 8vo. Lond., 1892. MD 7 T 15

HUGHES, G. M. History of Windsor Forest, Sunninghill, and the Great Park. 4to. Lond., 1890. B 2 T 19

HUGHES, H. S. The Registers of Llantrithyd, Glamorganshire : Christenings, 1597–1810; Burials, 1571–1810 ; Marriages, 1571–1752. Roy. 8vo. Lond., 1888. B 3 V 19

HUGHES, J. Siege of Damascus : a Tragedy. [*See* British Drama, Modern.]

HUGHES, Prof. The Plain Speaker. 12mo. Sydney, 1882. MJ 2 P 42

HUGHES, Prof. T. M. [*See* Clark, J. W.]

HUGHES, T. James Fraser, second Bishop of Manchester ; a Memoir, 1818–85. 8vo. Lond., 1887. C 13 U 12
Tom Brown's School Days. 8vo. Lond., 1877. J 9 Q 38
Tom Brown at Oxford. 8vo. Lond., 1886. J 9 Q 39
[Life of] David Livingstone. (English Men of Action.) 8vo. Lond., 1889. C 15 Q 11

HUGHES, W. The Australian Colonies; their Origin and Present Condition. New edition. Lond., 1853. MD 6 P 4

HUGHES, W. Manual of Geography, Physical, Industrial, Political. 12mo. Lond., 1887. D 11 Q 7
Training-School Atlas. Fol. Lond., 1861. D 37 Q 12 ‡

HUGHES, W. R. A Week's Tramp in Dickens-Land. Illustrated. 8vo. Lond., 1891. D 18 T 18

HUGO, T. The Bewick Collector : a descriptive Catalogue of the Works of Thomas and John Bewick ; with Supplement. 2 vols. 8vo. Lond., 1866–68. K 8 Q 33, 34

HUGO, Victor Marie, Vicomte. Dramatic Works of : Hernani.—The King's Diversion.—Ruy Blas ; translated by F. L. Slous and Mrs. N. Crosland. 8vo. Lond., 1887. H 4 P 34

Œuvres Complètes de. 46 vols. roy. 8vo. Paris, 1880–85. J 17 S 1-T 11

Actes et Paroles, 1841–76. 3 vols.

Drame. Vols. 1–4.
1. Cromwell.
2. Hernani.—Marion de Lorme.—Le Roi s'amuse.
3. Lucrèce Borgia.—Marie Tudor.—Angelo, Tyran de Padoue.
4. La Esmeralda.—Ruy Blas.—Les Burgraves.

Histoire. Vols. 1–3.
1. Napoléon le Petit.
2, 3. Histoire d'un Crime.

Le Rhin. Vols. 1, 2.

Philosophie. 2 vols.
1. Littérature et Philosophie Mêlées, 1819–34.
2. William Shakespeare.

Poésie. Vols. 1–16.
1. Odes et Ballades.
2. Les Orientales.—Les Feuilles d'Automne.
3. Les Chants du Crépuscule.—Les voix intérieures.—Les Rayons et les Ombres.
4. Les Châtiments.
5. Les Contemplations.—Autrefois 1630–43.
6. Les Contemplations.—Aujourd 'hui 1843–55.
7–10. La Légende des Siècles.
11. Les Chansons des Rues et des Bois.
12. L'Année Terrible.
13. L'Art d'être Grand-Père.
14. Le Pape.—La Pitié Suprême.—Religions et Religion.—L'Ane.
15, 16. Les quatre vents de l'esprit : 1. Le Livre Satirique. 2. Le Livre Dramatique. 3. Le Livre Lyrique. 4. Le Livre Épique.

Roman. Vols. 1–14.
1. Han d'Islande.
2. Bug-Jargal.—Le dernier jour d'un Condamné.—Claude Gueux.
3, 4. Notre Dame de Paris.
5. Les Misérables.—Fantine.
6. Les Misérables.—Cosette.
7. Les Misérables.—Marius.
8. Les Misérables.—L'Idylle Rue Plumet et l'Epopée Rue Saint-Denis.
9. Les Misérables.—Jean Valjean.
10, 11. Les Travailleurs de la Mer.
12, 13. L'Homme qui rit.
14. Quatrevingt-treize.

Victor Hugo raconté; par " Un Témoin de sa vie." Vols. 1, 2.

Things seen (Choses vues). 2 vols. 8vo. Lond., 1887. B 26 U 4, 5

Notre Dame de Paris; translated by A. L. Alger. (Edition de Luxe.) 2 vols. roy. 8vo. Lond. (n.d.) J 7 U 29, 30

HUIDEKOPER, Dr. R. S. Age of the Domestic Animals. 8vo. Philad., 1891. A 27 T 21

HUIE, J. A. History of Christian Missions, from the Reformation to the Present Time. 2nd edition. 12mo. Edinb., 1842. G 8 P 24

HUISH, M. B. The Year's Art. 4 vols. 8vo. Lond., 1889-92.   E

HÜLPHERS, H. W. Om Bruket af Destillerade Spritdrycker frän militärhygienisk synpunkt. 8vo. Stockholm, 1881.   F 11 R 22

HULL, A. F. B. The Stamps of Tasmania : a History of the Postage Stamps, Envelopes, Post Cards, adhesive and impressed Revenue, and Excise Stamps of Tasmania. Imp. 8vo. Lond., 1890.   MB 2 V 16

HULL, E. Sketch of Geological History : being the Natural History of the Earth and of its Pre-Human Inhabitants. 12mo. Lond., 1887.   A 9 P 52

HULTON, S. F. Rixæ Oxonienses. 8vo. Oxford, 1892.   B 22 Q 24

HUME, D. History of England from the Invasion of Julius Cæsar to 1688. 8 vols. 8vo. Lond., 1789.   B 22 T 11–18

Philosophical Works. 4 vols. 8vo. Boston, 1854.   G 4 T 11–14

Treatise on Human Nature ; edited by L. A. Selby-Bigge. 8vo. Oxford, 1888.   G 13 T 48

HUME, M. A. S. Chronicle of King Henry VIII. of England ; translated, with Notes and Introduction by M. A. S. Hume. 8vo. Lond., 1886.   B 22 S 1

HUMFREY, J. Horse-breeding and Rearing in India. 8vo. Calcutta, 1887.   A 1 U 20

HUMOURIST, The : a Collection of Entertaining Tales, with Illustrations ; by G. Cruikshank. 4 vols. 8vo. Lond., 1892.   J 12 Q 35–38

HUMPHREYS, G. [*See* Bazalgette, C. N.]

HUMPHREYS, Capt. H. M. Men of the Time in Australia. Victorian Series, 2nd ed. 8vo. Melb., 1882.   MC 1 T 11

HUNGERFORD, F. R. British Difficulties under Solution. 12mo. Lond. (n.d.)   MF 3 P 43

HUNT, J. Life of ; by G. S. Rowe. 8vo. Lond., 1859.   MC 1 Q 33

Another Copy. 6th thousand. 8vo. Lond., 1886.   MC 1 Q 34

HUNT, James Henry Leigh. Poems of ; edited by R. B. Johnson. 18mo. Lond., 1881.   H 6 P 45

Essays of ; edited by R. B. Johnson. 18mo. Lond., 1891.   J 7 P 31

Autobiography of. New edition. 12mo. Lond., 1860.   C 13 Q 10

HUNT, J. L. Hunt's Book of Bonanzas. 8vo. Sydney, 1889.   MJ 2 P 41

HUNT, T. S. Mineral Physiology and Physiography. 8vo. Boston, 1886.   A 24 U 3

Another copy. 2nd ed. 8vo. New York, 1891.   A 24 U 9

HUNT, T. S.—*contd.*
New Basis for Chemistry ; a Chemical Philosophy. 8vo. Boston, 1887.   A 21 Q 14

Another copy. 3rd. ed. 8vo. New York, 1891.   A 21 Q 26

Chemical and Geological Essays. 3rd ed. 8vo. New York, 1891.   A 21 R 3

Systematic Mineralogy based on a Natural Classification. 2nd ed. Roy. 8 vo. New York, 1892.   A 24 V 10

HUNT, W. Historic Towns : Bristol. 8vo. Lond., 1887.   B 22 Q 5

The English Church in the Middle Ages. 12mo. Lond., 1888.   G 19 P 7

HUNTER, C. Mechanical Dentistry : a Treatise on the Construction of Artificial Dentures. (Weale.) 3rd ed. 12mo. Lond., 1887.   A 17 R 17

HUNTER, Rev. Jos. The Great Roll of the Pipe, 1189–90. [Record Com. Pubs.] Roy. 8vo. Lond., 1844.   B 15 T 31

Hallamshire : the History and Topography of the Parish of Sheffield. New edition. by Rev. Dr. A. Gatty. Fol. Lond. (n.d.)   B 40 Q 19‡

HUNTER, R. Encyclopædic Dictionary. 7 vols. 4to. Lond., 1879–88.   K 16 U 13–19

HUNTER, W. Biggar, and the House of Fleming. Roy. 8vo. Edinb., 1867.   B 31 T 24

HUNTER, W. A. Systematic and Historical Exposition of Roman Law in the Order of a Code. 2nd edition. 8vo. Lond., 1885.   F 8 S 25

[*See* Muluk Chand.]

HUNTER, Sir W. W. Bombay, 1885–90 : a Study of Indian Administration. 8vo. Lond., 1892.   F 9 S 2

The Earl of Mayo. (Rulers of India.) 8vo. Oxford, 1891.   C 17 Q 8

The Marquess of Dalhousie. (Rulers of India.) 8vo. Oxford, 1890.   C 12 Q 36

HUNTER-DUVAR, John. [*See* Duvar, John Hunter-.]

HUNTERIAN CLUB. Publications. 3 vols. 4to. Lond., 1876–88.   E
No. 35. Scillaes Metamorphosie ; by T. Lodge. 1589.
No. 36. A Margarite of America ; by T. Lodge. 1596.
No. 63. Index and Glossary to Works of T. Lodge.

HUNTING, J. D. The French Revolution. [*See* Rocquain, F.]

HURBERT, W. H. France and the Republic : a Record of Things seen and learned in the French provinces during the "Centennial" year 1889. 8vo. Lond., 1890.   B 8 R 37

HURST, C. H. [*See* Marshall, A. M.]

HUSMANN, G. Grape-culture and Wine-making in California. 8vo. San Francisco, 1888.   A 1 U 8

HUSS, Dr. Magnus. Jubelfest. 8vo. Stockholm, 1886.   F 11 R 39

HUTCHINSON, Ellen M. American Literature. [*See* Stedman, E. C.]

HUTCHINSON, F., and MYERS, F. The Australian Contingent : a History of the Patriotic Movement in New South Wales. 8vo. Sydney, 1885.   MB 2 R 4

HUTCHINSON, H. G. Golf. (Badminton Library.) 12mo. Lond., 1890.   A 17 U 43

HUTCHINSON, M. L. Commercial Exchange Map of the City of Melbourne. [Folded.] 8vo. Melb., 1877.   MD 3 P 17

HUTCHINSON'S AUSTRALASIAN ENCYCLOPÆ-DIA. [*See* Levey, G. C.]

HUTH, A. H. Marriage of Near Kin considered with respect to the Law of Nations, the Results of Experience, and the Teachings of Biology. 2nd ed. Roy. 8vo. Lond., 1887.   A 26 V 5

HUTH, F. H. Works on Horses and Equitation : a Bibliographical Record of Hippology. 4to. Lond., 1887.   K 19 S 1

HUTTEN, Ulrich von. His Life and Times; by D. F. Strauss. 8vo. Lond., 1874.   C 21 Q 20

HUTTON, A. W. [Life of] Cardinal Manning. 12mo. Lond., 1892.   C 16 P 27

HUTTON, Prof. F. W. Biology in our Arts Curriculum. 8vo. Dunedin, 1882.   MA 3 R 46

Catalogue of New Zealand Diptera, Orthoptera, and Hymenoptera. 8vo. Wellington, 1881.   MA 2 U 7

Report on the Tarawera Volcanic District. Roy. 8vo. Wellington, 1887.   MA 2 R 32

HUTTON, I. [*See* Actors and Actresses.]

HUTTON, Richard H. [Life of] Cardinal Newman. 12mo. Lond., 1891.   C 12 Q 3

Essays on some of the Modern Guides of English Thought in Matters of Faith. 12mo. Lond., 1887.   G 19 P 1

HUTTON, Rev. W. H. S. Thomas of Canterbury : an Account of his Life and Fame. 16mo. Lond., 1889.   C 13 P 6

Misrule of Henry III. (English History by Contemporary Writers.) 18mo. Lond., 1887.   B 22 P 1

Simon de Montfort and his Cause, 1251–66. (English History by Contemporary Writers.) 18mo. Lond., 1888.   B 22 P 2

HUTTON, W. S. Practical Engineer's Hand-book, comprising a Treatise on Modern Engines and Boilers. Roy. 8vo. Lond., 1887.   A 16 U 16

Steam-Boiler Construction : a Practical Hand-book of Engineers, Boilermakers, and Steam Users. 8vo. Lond., 1891.   A 25 U 1

HUXLEY, Prof. T. H. Critiques and Addresses. 8vo. Lond., 1873.   J 10 V 29

Essays upon some Controverted Questions. 8vo. Lond., 1892.   G 12 S 39

HUXLEY, Prof. T. H., and HAWKINS, B. W. Elementary Atlas of Comparative Osteology. 4to. Lond., 1864.   A 40 S 6 ‡

HUXLEY, Prof. T. H., and MARTIN, H. N. A Course of Elementary Instruction in Practical Biology ; revised edition, extended and edited by G. B. Howes and D. H. Scott. 8vo. Lond., 1888.   A 14 Q 58

HWUI LI and YEN-TSUNG. Life of Hiuan-Tsiang ; with a preface by Prof. S. Beal. 8vo. Lond., 1888.   C 14 S 3

HYATT, A. Observations on Polyzoa, sub-order Phylactolæmata. 8vo. Salem, 1866–68.   A 14 T 50

HYDE, Dr. D. Beside the Fire : a collection of Irish Gaelic Folk Stories. 8vo. Lond., 1890.   J 3 S 25

HYDE, J. W. A Hundred Years by Post : a Jubilee Retrospect. 12mo. Lond., 1891.   B 23 R 10

HYGIEINISKE CONGRES I KJOBENHAVN, 1858. Imp. 8vo. Kjöbenhavn, 1858.   F 11 V 1

HYGIEJNISKE MEDDELELSER, Tredie Række. Förste Bind. 8vo. Kjöbenhavn, 1882.   F 11 Q 64

[*See* Hornemann, Dr. E.]

HYNDMAN, H. M. Commercial Crisis of the Nineteenth Century. 12mo. Lond., 1892.   F 9 U 1

Historical Basis of Socialism in England. 8vo. Lond., 1883.   F 14 R 1

Eight Hours' Movement : Verbatim Report of a Debate between H. M. Hyndman and C. Bradlaugh. 12mo. Lond., 1890.   F 5 Q 11

Will Socialism benefit the English People ? Verbatim Report of a Debate between H. M. Hyndman and C. Bradlaugh. 12mo. Lond., 1884.   F 5 Q 11

I

IBANEZ Y GARCÍA, L. de. Historia de las Islas Marianas con su derrotero, y de las Carolinas y Palaos, desde el Descubrimiento por Magallanes. 8vo. Granada, 1886.   MB 2 R 44

IBBETSON, W. J. Elementary Treatise on the Mathematical Theory of perfectly Elastic Solids. Roy. 8vo. Lond., 1887.   A 6 T 29

IBIS, The : a Quarterly Journal of Ornithology. Series 5, vols. 5 and 6 ; series 6, vols. 1–3. 8vo. Lond., 1887–91. E

IBRAHIM-HILMY, Prince. The Literature of Egypt and the Soudan : a Bibliography. 2 vols. 4to. Lond., 1886–88.   K 17 S 11, 12

IBSEN, H. A Doll's House : a Play in 3 Acts. Sm. 4to. Lond., 1889.   H 4 S 31

Hedda Gabler : a Drama in 4 Acts. 8vo. Lond., 1891.   H 4 Q 34

IBSEN, H.—_contd._

Prose Dramas. 5 vols. 8vo. Lond., 1890–91.　H 4 Q 35–39
1. The League of Youth : The Pillars of Society : A Doll's House.
2. Ghosts : An Enemy of the People : The Wild Duck.
3. Lady Inger of Ostråt : The Vikings of Helgeland : The Pretenders.
4. Emperor and Galilean : a World-historic Drama.
5. Rosmerholm : The Lady from the Sea : Hedda Gabler.
Life of ; by H. Jæger ; translated by Clara Bell. 8vo. Lond., 1890.　　　　　　　　　C 16 P 12

IDDESLEIGH, Sir Stafford Northcote, First Earl of. Life, Letters, and Diaries of ; by A. Lang. 2 vols. 8vo. Edinb., 1890.　　　　　　　　C 13 R 23, 24
Lectures and Essays. 8 vo. Edinb., 1887.　　J 3 V 6

ILLAWARRA STEAM NAVIGATION COMPANY. Deed of Settlement. 8vo. Wollongong, 1862.
　　　　　　　　　　　　　　　　　MF 1 T 35

ILLINGWORTH, T. Distribution Reform, the Remedy for Industrial Depression &c. 8vo. Lond., 1885.
　　　　　　　　　　　　　　　　　F 5 Q 44

ILLICIT DISTILLATION. Report on the consequences of extending the Functions of the Constabulary in Ireland to the Suppression or Prevention of Illicit Distillation. Fol. Lond., 1854.　　F 42 P 14 ‡

ILLUSTRATED LONDON NEWS. Vols. 89–100. Fol. Lond., 1886–92.　　　　　　　　　　　　E

ILLUSTRATED SYDNEY NEWS, 1853–55, 1887–92. Fol. 7 vols. Sydney, 1853–92.　　　　ME

ILLUSTRATED SYDNEY NEWS NEW SOUTH WALES WEATHER ALMANAC for 1873. 8vo. Sydney, 1873.　　　　　　　　　　　　ME

ILLUSTRATED WORDS OF GRACE. Vol. 5. 4to. Sydney, 1880–81.　　　　　　　　　ME 2 U

ILLUSTRATIONS OF ARMORIAL CHINA. Fol. Privately printed, 1887.　　　　　　K 34 P 14 ‡

IMBERT, DE SAINT AMAND, Arthur Léon, Baron.
Citizeness Bonaparte ; trans. by T. S. Perry. 8vo. Lond., 1891.　　　　　　　　　　C 14 Q 9
Court of the Empress Josephine ; trans. by T. S. Perry. 8vo. Lond., 1891.　　　　C 14 Q 11
The Duchess of Argoulome and the Two Restorations ; trans. by J. Davis. 8vo. Lond., 1892.　C 16 P 19
Happy Days of the Empress Marie Louise ; trans. by T. S. Perry. 8vo. Lond., 1891.　　C 14 Q 12
Marie Antoinette and the End of the Old Régime ; trans. by T. S. Perry. 8vo. Lond., 1891.　C 14 Q 8
Marie Louise and the Decadence of the Empire ; trans. by T. S. Perry. 8vo. Lond., 1891.　C 14 Q 13
Marie Louise : the Island of Elba, and the Hundred Days ; trans. by T. S. Perry. Lond., 1891.　C 14 Q 14
The Wife of the First Consul ; trans. by T. S. Perry. 8vo. Lond., 1891.　　　　　C 14 Q 10

IMHAUS, E. N. Les Nouvelles-Hébrides. Roy. 8vo. Paris, 1890.　　　　　　　　　MD 7 R 34

IMPEY, Sir Elijah. [See Busteed, H. E.]

IMMIGRATION, Debate in the Legislative Council of New South Wales on. 8vo. Sydney, 1840. MF 1 R 57

IMPERIAL INSTITUTE, Year Book of. 8vo. Lond., 1872.　　　　　　　　　　　　　　E

INAGAKI, M. Japan and the Pacific, and a Japanese View of the Eastern Question. 8vo. Lond., 1890.
　　　　　　　　　　　　　　　　B 35 R 2

INCORPORATED SOCIETY OF AUTHORS. The Grievances between Authors and Publishers : being the Report of the Conferences in March, 1887. 8vo. Lond., 1887.　　　　　　　　　　　　F 6 T 36

INDERWICK, F. A. The Interregnum, 1648–1660 ; Studies of the Commonwealth, legislative, social, and legal. 8vo. Lond., 1891.　　　　B 24 R 2
Side-lights on the Stuarts. 8vo. Lond., 1888. B 22 U 11

INDEX MEDICUS : a Monthly Classified Record of the Current Medical Literature of the World. Vols. 1–13. 4to. Boston, 1879–91.　　　　　　　　　E

INDEX SOCIETY. Publications. 2 vols. sm. 4to. Lond., 1887–89.　　　　　　　　　　　　E
Bibliography and Chronology of Hales Owen ; by H. Ling Roth. Index to Engravings in the Proceedings of the Society of Antiquaries ; by E. Peacock.
[_See_ British Record Society.]

INDIA. Civil Service Examination of Candidates for Writerships. July, 1855. 8vo. Cheltenham, 1855.
　　　　　　　　　　　　　　　　G 17 R 21
Memoirs of the Geological Survey of India. Vols. 23–24. 2 vols. roy. 8vo. Calcutta, 1891–92.　　E
Memoirs of the Geological Survey of India. Palaeontologia Indica. 5 vols. fol. Calcutta, 1871–87.　E
Records of the Geological Survey of India. Vols. 19–24. roy. 8vo. Calcutta, 1886–91.　　　　E
Contents and Index of the First Twenty Vols. of the Records, 1868–87. Roy 8vo. Calcutta, 1890.　　E
MADRAS.
Annual Returns of the Civil Hospitals and Dispensaries, 1888, 1890. Sm. fol. Madras, 1889–90.　E
Report on the Administration of the Presidency, 1888, 1890–91. 2 vols. sm. fol. Madras, 1889–91.　E
Reports on Public Instruction, 1888–91. 3 vols. sm. fol. Madras, 1888–91.　　　　　　　E
Report on Administration, 1887–90. 2 vols. sm. fol. Madras, 1888–90.　　　　　　　E
Report on Public Instruction, 1887–88. Sm. fol. Madras, 1888.　　　　　　　　　　E
Returns of the Civil Hospitals and Dispensaries, 1887, 1890. 2 vols. sm. fol. Madras, 1888–91.　E

INDIA LIST, Civil and Military. 12 vols. 8vo. Lond., 1887–92.　　　　　　　　　　　　E

INDIA OFFICE LIST. 5 vols. 8vo. Lond., 1887–92. E

INDIAN AND COLONIAL EXHIBITION, 1886. Queensland; its Resources and Institutions. Essays. 8vo. Lond., 1886. M A 2 V 45

Boyd, A. J. Queensland; an Introductory Essay.
Poole, Rev. W. Education in Queensland.
Earle, II. Commerce and Industries of Queensland.
Staiger, K. T. Mineral Industries of Queensland.
Fletcher, P. Agriculture in Queensland.
,, Sugar Industry of Queensland.
,, Hints to Immigrants.
,, Natural History of Queensland.
Gordon, P. R. Pastoral Industry.
Wright, T. Horticulture.
Bailey, F. M. Flora of Queensland.
Jack, R. L. Geology of Queensland.
Bancroft, J. Contribution to Pharmacy from Queensland.
Emigration to Queensland.
How to settle on the Land in the Colony of Queensland.

Reports on the Colonial Sections of the Exhibition; edited by H. T. Wood. 8vo. Lond., 1887. MK 2 P 43

Report of the Royal Commission. 8vo. Lond., 1887. MF 2 P 42

INDIAN ANTIQUARY, The. Vols. 15–20. 4to. Bombay, 1886–91. E

INDO-CHINA. Miscellaneous Papers relating to Indo-China. [1st series.] 2 vols. 8vo. Lond., 1886. A 29 T 8, 9

Miscellaneous Papers relating to Indo-China and the Indian Archipelago. 2nd series. 2 vols. 8vo. Lond., 1887. A 29 T 10, 11

INDUSTRIAL REMUNERATION CONFERENCE, Report of the Proceedings and Papers, 1885. 8vo. Lond., 1885. F 14 S 6

INGE, W. R. Society in Rome under the Cæsars. 8vo. Lond., 1888. B 12 Q 13

INGEGNARIA CIVILE L'E LE ARTI INDUSTRIALI. 5 vols. Roy. 4to. Torino, 1886–91. E

INGERSOLL, Col. R. G. Complete Lectures. 8vo. (n.p.n.d.) G 6 Q 36

INGLEBY, C. M. Essays; edited by his Son. 8vo. Lond., 1888. J 5 Q 38

INGLIS, Rev. J. In the New Hebrides: Reminiscences of Missionary Life and Work, 1850–77. 8vo. Lond., 1887. MD 4 S 49

Bible Illustrations from the New Hebrides. 8vo. Lond., 1890. MG 1 Q 59

INGLIS, J., "Maori." Our Australian Cousins. 8vo. Lond., 1880. MD 5 T 38

Our New Zealand Cousins. 8vo. Lond., 1887. MD 1 Q 9

Tent Life in Tigerland, with which is incorporated Sport and Work on the Nepaul Frontier. Roy. 8vo. Sydney, 1888. MD 6 U 25

INGRAM, Rear-Adm. H. F. Winnington. Hearts of Oak. Sm. 4to. Lond., 1889. D 20 U 1

INGRAM, J. H. Elizabeth Barrett Browning. (Eminent Women Series.) 8vo. Lond., 1888. C 12 Q 27

P

INGRAM, T. D. History of the Legislative Union of Great Britain and Ireland. 8vo. Lond., 1887. B 29 U 12

England and Rome: a History of the Relations between the Papacy and the English State and Church, from the Conquest to 1688. 8vo. Lond., 1892. B 24 T 19

INNOCENT III., Pope. [See Deaumont, W.]

IN SOUTHERN SEAS: a Trip to the Antipodes; by "Petrel." Sm. 4to. Edinb., 1888. *MD 5 V 21

INSTÄDTEN, C. S. E. von. Die Zillerthaler Alpen. 4to. Gotha, 1872. A 36 P 17 ‡

INSTITUTE OF ACTUARIES, Journal of. April-July, 1890. 8vo. Lond., 1890. E

INSTITUTE OF BRITISH ARCHITECTS. [See Royal Institute of British Architects.]

INSTITUTE OF ARCHITECTS OF NEW SOUTH WALES. Professional Practice and Charges. Fol. Sydney, 1891. MF 11 P 8 †

Rules and Regulations. 8vo. Sydney, 1877. MF 2 P 6 8

INSTITUTION OF CIVIL ENGINEERS. Minutes of Proceedings. Vols. 87–108. Roy. 8vo. Lond., 1886–92. E

Charter; Supplemental Charter; By-laws and List of Members. 8vo. Lond., 1889. E

INSTITUTION OF MECHANICAL ENGINEERS. Proceedings 1847–90 and Catalogue. 41 vols. 8vo. Birm. and Lond., 1849–91. E

INSTITUTO NACIONAL DE GEOGRAFÍCA Y ESTADÍSTICA DE LA REPÚBLICA MEXICANA. [See Sociedad de Geografica.]

INSURANCE AND SAVING. A Report on the existing opportunities for Working-class Thrift. 12mo. Lond., 1892. F 9 U 4

INTEMPERANCE. [First to fourth Reports on.] 4 vols. Fol. Lond., 1877–78. F 42 P 4–7 ‡

Report of Committee on. 8vo. Lond., 1869. F 11 R 31

Intemperance: its Bearing upon Agriculture. 8vo. (n.p.n.d.) F 11 R 32

INTERCOLONIAL MEDICAL CONGRESS of Australasia. Transactions, 1887. Roy. 8vo. Adelaide, 1888. ME

Transactions of the Second Session, held in Melbourne, 1889. Roy. 8vo. Melb., 1889. ME 1 T

INTERCOLONIAL TARIFF ARRANGEMENTS [Correspondence with the Australian Colonies with reference to Proposals for]. 2 vols. (in 1.) fol. Lond., 1887. MF 4 S 22

INTERCOLONIAL TRADES UNION CONGRESS.
Second Official Report. 8vo. Melb., 1884. ME 8 S
Third Official Report. 8vo. Sydney, 1885. ME 8 S
Fifth Official Report. 8vo. Brisbane, 1888. ME 8 S
Sixth Official Report. 8vo. Hobart, 1889. ME 8 S

INTERNATIONAL ATLAS AND GEOGRAPHY.
Fol. Lond., 1881.   D 41 P 13 ‡

INTERNATIONAL CODE OF SIGNALS, for the use
of all nations. Imp. 8vo. Washington, 1879.
                                      K 12 S 25 †

INTERNATIONAL SCIENTISTS' DIRECTORY. 8vo.
Boston, 1888.   E

INTERNATIONAL TEMPERANCE AND PROHIBI-
TION CONVENTION, 1862. Proceedings. 8vo.
Lond., 1862.   F 11 R 30

IONA CLUB. Collectanea de Rebus Albanicis; edited by
the Iona Club. 8vo. Edinb., 1847.   E

IRELAND. Calendar of the State Papers relating to
Ireland, 1603-1625; edited by Rev. C. W. Russell and
J. P. Prendergast. 5 vols. imp. 8vo. Lond., 1872-80.
                                      B 28 V 2-6

Calendar of the Patent and Close Rolls of Chancery in
Ireland in the Reign of Charles I. ; by J. Morrin. Roy.
8vo. Dublin, 1863.   B 11 R 3

Liber Munerum Publicorum Hiberniæ, 1152-1827; or, the
Establishments of Ireland. 2 vols. fol. Lond., 1827.
                                      B 38 Q 16, 17 ‡

IRELAND, Mrs. A. . Life of Jane Welsh Carlyle. 8vo.
Lond., 1891.   C 13 R 3

IRELAND, S. Picturesque Views on the River Medway.
4to. Lond., 1793.   D 18 V 1

Picturesque Views on the River Wye. Roy. 8vo. Lond.,
1797.   D 18 V 2

IRELAND, W. H. [*See* Voltaire, F. M. A. de.]

IRISH PEASANT, THE : a Sociological Study ; by "A
Guardian of the Poor." 12mo. Lond., 1892. F 9 U 3

IRON. Vols. 28-39. Fol. Lond., 1886-92.   E

IRON, Ralph. [*See* Schreiner, Olive.]

IRVINE, J. C. Our Dishonest Voting System Exposed,
and its remedy. 8vo. Sydney, 1877.   MF 1 T 34

IRVINE, W. H. Justices of the Peace, their authority
and Functions out of Sessions, and in Courts of Petty
Sessions, to which is appended the Justices of the Peace
Act 1887, and the rules with notes. 8vo. Melb., 1888.
                                      MF 2 T 65

IRVING, J. Supplement to the Annals of Our Time,
July, 1878, to June, 1887. 8vo. Lond., 1889.
                                      B 21 T 27

IRVING, J. T. Indian Sketches taken during a U.S.
Expedition to make Treaties with the Indians in 1833.
8vo. Lond., 1888.   D 15 Q 13

IRVING, W. Tales and Sketches. (In the corresponding
style of phonography.) 12mo. Lond., 1884. J 7 R 51

IRWIN, Capt. F. C. State and Position of Western
Australia. 8vo. Lond., 1835.   MD 4 U 24

ISAEUS. Orationes ; edidit C. Scheibe. 12mo. Lipsiæ,
1860.   F 14 Q 9

ISOCRATES. Opera Omnia ; notas adjunxit G. Battie.
2 vols. 8vo. Lond., 1749.   F 2 U 28, 29

ITALY. Gli Albori della Vita Italiana. 3 vols. 8vo.
Milano, 1890-91.   B 17 P 21-23

IVIMEY, Aleck J. All about Queensland. 8vo. Maryborough, 1889.   M D 7 S 56

The Gympie Mining Handbook, 1887. 8vo. Brisb.,
1887.   MA 3 Q 39

Mining and Descriptive Queensland ; or, Travels through
the Queensland Goldfields. 8vo. Brisb., 1889.
                                      MD 7 S 26

J

JACK, R. L. The Mineral Wealth of Queensland. 8vo.
Brisb., 1888.   MA 2 P 59

Geology of Queensland. [*See* Indian and Colonial
Exhib., 1886.]

JACKSON, Catherine Charlotte, Lady. The First of the
Bourbons, 1589-95. 2 vols. 8vo. Lond., 1890.
                                      B 26 R 4, 5

The Last of the Valois, and Accession of Henry of
Navarre, 1559-89. 2 vols. 8vo. Lond., 1888.
                                      B 26 R 3, 2

JACKSON, F. G. Lessons on Decorative Design. 8vo.
Lond., 1888.   A 23 S 2

JACKSON, Dr. H. W. Addresses delivered at the New
Temperance Hall before Sydney New Church Society.
8vo. Sydney, 1891.   MG 2 P 42

JACKSON, James. James Cook : Cartographie et Bibliographie. 8vo. Paris (n.d.)   MK 1 T 19

JACKSON, Lewis d'A. Aid to Survey Practice. 2nd
edition. 8vo. Lond., 1889.   A 22 R 26

JACKSON, T. G. Dalmatia :—the Quarnero and Istria.
3 vols. 8vo. Oxford, 1887.   B 25 T 6-8

JACKSON, W. H. [*See* Rolleston, Prof. G.]

JACKY JACKY, Statement of. [*See* Carron, W.]

JACOB, Col. S. S. Jeypore Portfolio of Architectural
Details. 6 parts, fol. Lond., 1890. A 31 R 9-14 ‡

JACOBI, C. T. Printing : a practical treatise on the art
of Typography as applied more particularly to the printing
of books. 12mo. Lond., 1890.   A 25 P 1

JACOBI, H. [*See* Müller, F. Max, Sacred Books, 22.]

JACOBS, G. S. The Masonic Guide of New South Wales.
18mo. Sydney, 1890.   ME 8 P

JACOBS, Very Rev. H. Colonial Church Histories :
New Zealand, containing the Dioceses of Auckland,
Christchurch, Dunedin, Nelson, Waiapu, Wellington,
and Melanesia. 12mo. Lond., 1887.   MG 2 P 29

JACOBS, Dr. H. E. The Lutheran movement in England
during the reigns of Henry VIII. and Edward VI., and its
literary monuments. 8vo. Lond., 1892.   G 2 P 38

JACOBS, Jos. The Familiar Letters of James Howell. [*See* HOWELL, James.] [*See* Æsop.]

JACOBS, J. [*See* Anglo-Jewish Historical Exhibition.]

JACOBS, T. J. Scenes, Incidents, and Adventures in the Pacific Ocean. 8vo. New York, 1844. MD 1 R 21

JACOBSON, H. C. Tales of Banks Peninsula. 12mo. Akaroa, 1884. MB 1 P 32

JACOBSON, William. Life of. [*See* BURGON, Very Rev. J. W.]

JACQUEMART, A. History of Furniture; edited by Mrs. Bury Palliser. Roy. 8vo. Lond., 1878. A 11 V 9

JÆGER, Henrik. Life of Henrik Ibsen; translated by Clara Bell. 8vo. Lond., 1890. C 16 P 12

JAGO, F. W. P. An English-Cornish Dictionary. 4to. London, 1887. K 13 T 13

JAHRESBERICHTE ÜBER DIE FORSTSCHRITTE DER ANATOMIE UND PHYSIOLOGIE. Bande 14-18, 1885-89. Roy. 8vo. Leip., 1886-90. E

JALÁLU-D-DIN, M. M. I. Rúmí. Masnavi I Ma' Navi: the Spiritual Couplets of; translated and abridged by E. H. Whinfield. 8vo. Lond., 1887. H 2 R 34

JAMAICA. Hand-book of. 6 vols. 8vo. Lond., 1887-92. E

JAMES, Capt. C. Universal Military Dictionary in English and French. 4th ed. 8vo. Lond., 1816. A 29 T 14

JAMES, Croake. Curiosities of Law and Lawyers. New edition. 8vo. Lond., 1891. F 9 S 16

Curiosities of Christian Literature prior to the Reformation. 8vo. Lond., 1892. G 8 R 31

JAMES, E. Expedition from Pittsburgh to the Rocky Mountains, 1819-20; compiled from the notes of Major S. H. Long. 3 vols. 8vo. Lond., 1823. D 15 S 24-26

JAMES, F. L. The Unknown Horn of Africa: an exploration from Berbera to the Leopard River; with additions by J. G. Thrupp. 8vo. Lond., 1888. D 14 U 13

JAMES, George L. Shall I try Australia? or, Health, Business, and Pleasure in New South Wales. 8vo. Liverpool, 1892. MD 7 T 25

JAMES, Col. Sir H. Facsimiles of National Manuscripts from William the Conqueror to Queen Anne. Parts 1-4. 4 vols. 4to. Southampton, 1865. B 6 R 11-14 ‡

JAMES, Henry. Partial Portraits. 12mo. Lond., 1888. C 2 R 22

JAMES, H. E. M. The Long White Mountain; or, a Journey in Manchuria. 8vo. Lond., 1888. D 17 U 7

JAMES, J. Temperance Legislation and Licensing Reform. 2nd edition. 8vo. Lond., 1885. F 11 R 33

JAMESON, Dr. J. F. Essays in the Constitutional History of the United States, 1775-89. Edited by J. F. Jameson. 8vo. Boston, 1889. B 1 Q 57

JAMESON, J. S. Story of the Rear Column of the Emin Pasha Relief Expedition. 8vo. Lond., 1890. D 14 U 5

JAN, Prof. G. Iconographie Générale des Ophidiens. 3 vols. fol. Milan, 1861-68. A 40 S 8-10 ‡

JANIN, J. G. Œuvres Diverses de. 20 vols. 8vo. Paris, 1876-83. J 19 U 33-V 5
1, 2. Barnave.
3, 4. Contes et Nouvelles.
5. Correspondance.
6-9. Critique Dramatique : 1. La Comédie. 2. La Tragédie. 3. Le Drame. 4. Théâtre de Genre.
10. Deburau : Histoire du Théâtre à quatre sous pour faire suite à l'Histoire du Théâtre-Français.
11. L'Ane Mort et la Femme Guillotinée.
12, 13. Les Œuvres d'Horace : Poëte Latin du Siècle d'Auguste ; Odes—Satires—Epîtres. Traduction de Jules Janin.
14, 15. Mélanges et Variétés.
16. Petite Critique.
17. Petits Contes.
18. Petits Mélanges.
19. Petits Romans.
20. Petits Souvenirs.

La Poésie et l'Eloquence à Rome au temps des Césars. 12mo. Paris, 1864. B 17 P 31

JANSEN, Dr. A. De l'Usage et de l'Abus des Boissons et des Liqueurs Alcooliques. 12mo. Namur, 1880. F 11 P 21

JANSEN, H. J. Voyage à Batavia. [*See* Stavorinus, J. S.]

JANSEN, Reinier. Biographical Notice of. [*See* Smith, Jos.]

JAPHET IBN ALI. Commentary on the Book of Daniel. [*See* Anecdota Oxoniensia.]

JAPP, Dr. A. H. De Quincey Memorials; edited by A. H. Japp. 2 vols. 8vo. Lond., 1891. C 16 T 6, 7

JARRETT, F. C. Jottings from the Log of a New South Welshman; or, Six Years in the Opium Trade. 8vo. Sydney, 1867. MD 7 S 57

JARVES, J. J. Kiana: a Tradition of Hawaii. 8vo. Boston, 1857. MB 2 P 46

JARVIE, Rev. A. J. Memorials of a Ministry in Dunfermline and Sydney; Biographical Sketch of Rev. A. M. Jarvie; with selected sermons. 8vo. Edinb., 1888. MG 1 Q 53

JASCHKE, H. A. Tibetan Grammar. 2nd edition. 8vo. Lond., 1883. K 20 Q 11

JASMIN, J. Barber, Poet, Philanthropist; by S. Smiles. 12mo. Lond., 1891. C 17 Q 12

JAUBERT, J. B. Dictionnaire raisonné universel des Arts et Métiers. 5 vols. 8vo. Lyon, 1801. K 18 P 17-21

JAY, John. Life of; by George Pellew (American Statesmen.) 12mo. Boston, 1890. C 13 Q 7

JEAFFRESON, J. C. Lady Hamilton and Lord Nelson: an Historical Biography, based on Letters and other Documents. 2 vols. 8vo. Lond., 1888. C 15 Q 26, 26

The Queen of Naples and Lord Nelson. 2 vols. 8vo. Lond., 1889. C 14 Q 23, 24

JEANS, J. S. Railway Problems: an Inquiry into the Economic Conditions of Railway Working in different countries. 8vo. Lond., 1887. F 5 U 38

Waterways and Water Transport in Different Countries. 8vo. Lond., 1890. A 22 S 28

JEBB, Prof. R. C. Homer: an Introduction to the Iliad and the Odyssey. 8vo. Glasgow, 1887. H 7 S 16

[*See* Sophocles.]

JEEP, J. [*See* Justinus.]

JEFFERIES, R. Field and Hedgerow, being the last Essays of Richard Jefferies; collected by his widow. 8vo. Lond., 1889. A 29 R 4

JEFFERIS, Rev. J. The Chinese and the Seamen's Strike; a Lecture. 8vo. Sydney, 1878. MF 1 T 36

Other Bibles and other Beliefs: a Series of Eight Lectures delivered as a help to Young Men of Free Thought. 8vo. Sydney, 1882. MG 1 R 46

JENAISCHE ZEITSCHRIFT FÜR NATURWISSEN-SCHAFT. Bande 20–26. Jena, 1887–91. E

JENKIN, Prof. F. Papers, Literary, Scientific, &c.; edited by S. Colvin and J. A. Ewing; with Memoir by R. L. Stevenson. 2 vols. 8vo. Lond., 1887. J 3 V 22, 23

JENKINS, E. [*See* Mennell, P.]

JENKINS, H. M. On some Tertiary Mollusca from Mount Sela, in the Island of Java. 8vo. Lond., 1864. A 27 T 16

JENKINS, J. H. Davenport Brothers and Prof. W. M. Fay: a Short Sketch of the Lives, Travels, and Performances of the Brothers Davenport and Prof. Fay. 8vo. Tamworth, 1877. MC 1 Q 44

JENKINS, R. L. Considerations that should Guide the Breeders and Graziers of Cattle in New South Wales. 8vo. Sydney, 1874. MA 3 T 39

JENKINS, William H. The Family Medical Index; or, What to do in Cases of Emergency. 8vo. Melb., 1874. MA 3 Q 38

JENKS, E. The Constitutional Experiments of the Commonwealth, 1649–60. 8vo. Camb., 1890. B 23 R 8

Government of Victoria (Australia). Roy. 8vo. Lond., 1891. MF 3 T 15

JENKYNS, C. C. Hard Life in the Colonies, and other Experiences by Sea and Land. 8vo. Lond., 1892. MJ 3 Q 2

JENNER, E. Enquiry into the Causes and Effects of the Variolæ Vaccinæ, known by the name of the Cow Pox. 2nd ed. (*Fac-simile.*) 4to. Sydney, 1884. MA 1 P 28 †

JENNINGS, Rev. A. C. Chronological Tables: a Synchronistic Arrangements of the Events of Ancient History. 8vo. Lond., 1888. B 14 R 35

JENNINGS, H. The Rosicrucians: their Rites and Mysteries. 2 vols. 8vo. Lond., 1887. G 12 T 42, 43

JENNINGS, H. J. Cardinal Newman: the Story of his Life. 12mo. Birmingham, 1888. C 12 P 29

JENNINGS, L. J. Mr. Gladstone: a Study. 8vo. Edinb., 1887. C 12 P 26

[*See* Churchill, Lord R.]

JEPHSON, A. J. Mounteney-. Emin Pasha and the Rebellion at the Equator. 8vo. Lond., 1890. D 14 U 8

Emin Pascià; Capitano Casati e la Ribellione all' Equatoria. Traduzione di A. Massoni. 8 vo. Milano, 1890. D 14 U 9

JEPHSON, H. The Platform: its Rise and Progress. 2 vols. 8vo. Lond., 1892. B 24 S 21, 22

JERDON, T. C. The Birds of India; being a Natural History of all Birds known to inhabit Continental India. (With Memoir of Dr. T. C. Jerdon, by Sir W. Elliot.) 2 vols. (in 3.) Roy. 8vo. Calcutta, 1862–64. A 13 T 31–33

Illustrations of Indian Ornithology. Imp. 4to. Madras, 1847. A 11 Q 5 †

JERVOIS, Lieut.-Gen. Sir W. F. D. Defence of New Zealand: an Address. Illustrated with Charts, &c. Fol. Wellington, 1884.* MA 6 P 1 †

JESSEN, C. F. G. Prasiolæ Generis Algarum Monographia. 4to. Kiliæ, 1848. A 36 P 22 ‡

JESSOPP, Rev. Dr. A. The Coming of the Friars, and other Historic Essays. 8vo. Lond., 1889. B 21 S 22

Arcady: for Better for Worse. 8vo. Lond., 1887. J 5 Q 37

[*See* North, Hon. R.]

JEVONS, W. S. Letters and Journal of. Edited by his wife, Harriet A. Jevons. 8vo. Lond., 1886. MC 1 T 5

Pure Logic, and other Minor Works. 8vo. Lond., 1890. G 12 S 34

The State in Relation to Labour. 8vo. Lond., 1887. F 14 P 14

JEWELD, J. Apologia Ecclesiæ Anglicanæ. 12mo. Lond., 1837. G 16 R 34

JEWS in Russia, Persecution of. 8vo. Lond., 1891. B 31 S 1

JOHN BULL'S LETTERS to his Family on the Subject of the New Standard Weights and Measures. 8vo. Lond., 1826. F 5 T 42

JOHNS, Rev. C. A. Home Walks and Holiday Rambles. 12mo. Lond., 1863. A 28 P 2

JOHNS HOPKINS UNIVERSITY. Studies in Historical and Political Science. Herbert B. Adams, Editor. 14 vols. Roy. 8vo. Baltimore, 1883-91. B 18 S 1-14

Vol. 1. Local Institutions.
Vol. 2. Institutions and Economics.
Vol. 3. Maryland, Virginia, and Washington.
Vol. 4. Municipal Government and Land Tenure.
Vol. 5. Municipal Government, History and Politics.
Vol. 6. History of Co öperation in the United States.
Vol. 7. Social Science, Municipal and Federal Government.
Vol. 8. Beginnings of American Nationality ; by A. W. Small.
Vol. 9. Education, History, and Politics.
Extra vol. 1. The Republic of New Haven ; by C. H. Levermore.
Extra vol. 2. Philadelphia, 1681-1887 ; by E. P. Allinson and B. Penrose.
Extra vol. 3. Baltimore and the 19th April, 1861 ; by G. W. Brown.
Extra vol. 4. Introduction to the Local Constitutional History of the United States ; by Prof. G. E. Howard.
Extra vol. 5. The Negro in Maryland ; by J. R. Brackett.

JOHNSON, C. The Rifle, and how to use it. 12mo. Sydney, 1888. MA 2 V 40

JOHNSON, C. P. Early Writings of William Makepeace Thackeray. 8vo. Lond., 1888. J 2 P 28

Hints to Collectors of Original Editions of the Works of W. M. Thackeray. 8vo. Lond., 1885. K 19 P 4

JOHNSON, E. The Rise of Christendom. 8vo. Lond., 1890. G 6 S 36

JOHNSON, Rev. E. The Psalms. [*See* Ewald, Dr. G. H. A. v.]

JOHNSON, G. W. The Agricultural and Horticultural Uses of Gas Lime, Ammoniacal Liquor, and Tar. 8vo. (Lond., n.d. *reprinted*.) Parramatta (n.d.) MA 1 R 57

JOHNSON, J. The First Hymn for Christmas Day. "High let us Swell our Tuneful Notes." Fol. Sydney (n.d.) MA 11 Q 15 †

JOHNSON, R. B. [*See* Hunt, J. H. L.]

JOHNSON, Dr. S. Footsteps of ; by G. B. Hill. 4to. Lond., 1890. C 42 R 26 ‡

Letters of ; collected by G. B. Hill. 2 vols. 8vo. Oxford, 1892. C 18 R 16, 17

Lives of the Poets ; edited by Mrs. A. Napier. 3 vols. 12mo. Lond., 1890. C 12 P 17-19

Irene : a Tragedy. [*See* British Drama, Modern, 2.]

Boswell's Life of, including Boswell's Journal of a Tour to the Hebrides, and Johnson's Diary of a Journey into North Wales; edited by G. B. Hill. 6 vols. Roy. 8vo. Oxford, 1887. C 12 U 7-12

JOHNSTON, A. Connecticut : a Study of a Commonwealth Democracy. 12mo. Boston, 1887. B 17 P 5

JOHNSTON, A. R. Campbell. South Africa ; its difficulties and present state. 8vo. Lond., 1877. F 8 S 26

JOHNSTON, A. W. The New Utopia ; or, Progress and Prosperity. 8vo. Sydney, 1890. MF 2 P 55

JOHNSTON, H. H. Livingstone and the Exploration of Central Africa. 8vo. Lond., 1891. D 14 Q 5

JOHNSTON, R. M. Handbook of Tasmania for 1892. 8vo. Hobart, 1892. ME 8 S

Systematic Account of the Geology of Tasmania. 4to. Hobart, 1888. MA 12 P 22 †

Tasmanian Official Record, 1890-92. 3 vols. Roy. 8vo. Hobart, 1890-92. ME 7 R

JOHNSTONE, C. L. Historical Families of Dumfriesshire and the Border Wars. Sm. 4to. Edinb., 1888. B 31 T 22

JOHNSTONE, W. Australian Agriculture and Live Stock Farming, their Practical Defects, &c. 8vo. Sydney, 1886. MA 1 R 56

JOLLY, Prof. J. Mânava Dharma-Sàstra : the Code of Manu : Original Sanskrit Text; with critical Notes. 8vo. Lond., 1887. F 4 Q 28

[*See* Müller, F. Max.]

JOMINI, Baron de. The Art of War. 8vo. Philad., 1879. A 29 Q 9

JONES, —. Life and Adventure in the South Pacific by "Roving Printer." 8vo. Lond., 1861. MD 1 R 42

JONES v. JENKYNS ; or, the Bushranger's Revenge; by "Walker." 8vo. Sydney (n.d.) MJ 2 S 27

JONES, B. [*See* Acland, A. H. D.]

JONES, C. Introduction to the Science and Practice of Photography. 8vo. Lond., 1888. A 23 Q 3

JONES, F. H. New Testament. [*See* Schmidt, Prof. P. W.]

JONES, Rev. Harry. Holiday Papers. 8vo. Lond., 1884. J 9 S 39

JONES, Henry. The Earl of Essex : a Tragedy. [*See* British Drama, Modern, 2.]

JONES, Prof. Henry. Browning as a Philosophical and Religious Teacher. 12mo. Glasgow, 1891. G 13 U 36

JONES, J. Atlas of the Australian Colonies. 4to. Sydney, 1864. MD 8 Q 11 †

Australian Geography for the use of Schools. 18mo. Sydney, 1857. MD 1 P 67

JONES, Rev. J. Correspondence respecting the Expulsion of the Rev. J. Jones from Maré, one of the Loyalty Islands, by the French Authorities. Fol. Lond., 1888. MF 12 Q 10 †

JONES, Rev. Jesse H. [Life of] Henry Kemble Oliver. Roy. 8vo. Boston, 1886. C 9 V 6

JONES, Robert H. Asbestos ; its properties, occurrence, and uses. 8vo. Lond., 1890. A 24 Q 10

Asbestos: its Production and Use; with some Account of the Asbestos Mines of Canada. 8vo. Lond., 1888. A 24 T 2

JONES, T. R. Mammalia. 8vo. Lond. (n.d.) A 27 R 28

Organization of the Animal Kingdom, and Manual of Comparative Anatomy. 4th ed. 8vo. Lond., 1871. A 27 T 34

The Animal Creation. 8vo. Lond. (u.d.) A 27 Q 38

Natural History of Birds. 8vo. Lond. (u.d.) A 27 Q 37

JONQUET, A. Sketches for Art Furniture, in the Jacobean, Queen Anne, and other Styles. 2nd ed. Imp. 4to. Lond., 1880. A 23 S 17 ‡

JONSON, B. The Alchemist: a Comedy. [*See* British Drama, Modern, 3.]

Eastward Hoe. [*See* Chapman, G.]

Every Man in His Humour : a Comedy. [*See* British Drama, Modern, 3.]

Volpone, or the Fox : a Comedy. [*See* British Drama, Modern, 3.]

JONSON, B., FLETCHER, J., and MIDDLETON, T. The Widow [*See* British Drama, Ancient, 3.]

JORDAN, Dr. W. Die Geographischen Resultate der Expedition in die libysche Wüste. 8vo. Berlin, 1875. D 17 T 14

JORGENSEN, I. En kostbar Vane. 18mo. Kjöbenhavn, 1882. F 11 P 5

Bidrag til Belysning af Drinkspörgsmaalet. 18mo. Kjöbenhavn, 1882. F 11 P 8

JORGENSON, J. The Convict King: being the Life and Adventures of J. Jorgenson ; retold by J. F. Hogan. 12mo. Lond., 1891. MC 1 S 8

JORNANDES. Œuvres de. [*See* Nisard, D.]

JOSA, Rev. F. P. L. "The Apostle of the Indians of Guiana": a Memoir of the Life and Labours of the Rev. W. H. Brett. 8vo. Lond., 1887. C 3 R 4

JOSE, A. W. Sun and Cloud on River and Sea : Verses ; by "Ishmael Dare." 12mo. Sydney, 1888. MH 1 Q 50

JOSEPH, R. E. Electric Fire Alarms. 8vo. Melb., 1881. MA 3 Q 46

Electric Lighting. 8vo. Melb., 1882. MA 3 Q 45

Electric Lighting for Mines. 8vo. Melb., 1883. MA 3 Q 44

On Recent Improvements in Electric Lighting. 8vo. Melb., 1886. MA 3 Q 43

Incandescent Lamps for Surgical and Microscopical Purposes. 8vo. Melb., 1883 MA 3 Q 42

JOSEPHINE, Empress of France. Citizeness Bonaparte ; by [Baron A. L.] Imbert de Saint-Amand. Translated by T. S. Perry. 8vo. Lond., 1891. C 14 Q 9

The Wife of the First Consul ; by [Baron A. L.] Imbert de Saint-Amand. Translated by T. S. Perry. 8vo. Lond., 1891. C 14 Q 10

The Court of the Empress Josephine ; by [Baron A. L.] Imbert de Saint-Amand. Translated by T. S. Perry. 8vo. Lond., 1891. C 14 Q 11

JOSEPHUS, F. Opera Omnia ; notis illustravit J. Hudsonus. 2 vols. Fol. Oxonii, 1720. G 29 Q 15, 16 ‡

Opera Omnia, ab A. Bekkero recognita. (Greek text.) 6 vols. (in 3.) 12 mo. Lipsiæ, 1855-56. G 2 U 15-17

Works of. Whiston's translation, revised by Rev. A. R. Shilleto. 5 vols. 12 mo. Lond., 1889-90. G 2 V 2-6

Works of. Translated by W. Whiston. 12 mo. Lond., 1873. G 2 V 1

JOUAN, Lieut. H. Archipel des Marquises. 8vo. (n.p. n.d.) MD 7 S 55

Les Iles Loyalty. 8vo. Paris (n.d.) MD 8 Q 33

Remarques Météorologiques et Nautiques faites pendant un Voyage de France à la Nouvelle-Calédonie et dans la partie Sud-Ouest de l'Ocean-Pacifique. 8vo. (n.p. n.d.) MA 3 S 23

Note sur les Iles Basses et les Récifs de Corail du Grand Océan. 8vo. Cherbourg, 1859. MA 3 S 22

JOUBERT, Gén. B. C. Généraux de Vingt Ans ; par F. Tulou. 8vo. Paris, 1891. C 18 S 14

JOUBERT, Prof. J. [*See* Mascart, Prof. E.]

JOUFFROY, T. Mélanges Philosophiques. 4e édition. 12mo. Paris, 1866. G 7 U 29

Nouveaux Mélanges Philosophiques. 4e édition. 12mo. Paris, 1882. G 7 U 28

Cours d'Esthétique. 4e édition. 12mo. Paris, 1883. G 7 U 27

JOULE, J. P. Joint Scientific Papers of J. P. Joule ; published by the Physical Society of London. 2 vols. 8vo. Lond., 1887. A 17 W 51, 52

JOURNAL ASIATIQUE. 8e serie. Tomes 7-18. 8vo. Paris, 1886-91. E

JOURNAL DES ECONOMISTES. 4th series. Tomes 36-48. 5th series. Tomes 1-10. 8vo. Paris, 1886-92. E

JOURNAL OF CLASSICAL AND SACRED PHILOLOGY. Vol. 1, vol. 2, Nos. 4-6; vol. 3, Nos. 8, 9. 3 vols. 8vo. Lond, 1854-56. E

JOURNAL OF COMMERCE OF VICTORIA, THE. A Weekly Record of Trade and Shipping Intelligence. Fol. Melb., 1858. ME

JOURNAL OF INDIAN ART. Vols. 2-4. Roy. 4to. Lond., 1888-92. E

JOURNAL OF PRIMARY EDUCATION, Vol. 1. 1871-72. ME 8 Q

JOUSSELIN, H. Nos Petits Rois: Fables et poésies enfantines. Roy. 8vo. Paris, 1877. H 7 V 30

JOYCE, P. W. Origin and History of Irish Names of Places. 1st series. 4th edition. 12mo. Dublin, 1875. K 16 P 30

Another Copy. 2nd series. 12mo. Dublin, 1875. K 16 P 31

Irish Local Names Explained. New edition. 12mo. Dublin (n.d.) K 16 P 29

JUBILEE OF CONGREGATIONALISM in Australia, 1883. 8vo. Sydney, 1883. MG 1 S 51

JUDSON, Rev. Dr. A. Grammar of the Burmese Language. 8vo. Rangoon, 1888. K 12 U 35

JUKES, J. B. The Students' Manual of Geology. 8vo. Lond., 1857. A 24 R 7

JUKES-BROWNE. [*See* Browne, A. J. Jukes-.]

JULIAN, Emperor; containing Gregory Nazianzen's two Invectives and Libanius' Monody; with Julian's extant Theosophical Works; translated by C. W. King. 8vo. Lond., 1888. G 16 Q 26

JULIAN, Rev. J. Dictionary of Hymnology. Roy. 8vo. Lond., 1892. K 18 R 34

JULIEN, A. Richard Wagner, sa vie et ses œuvres. 4to. Paris, 1886. C 13 P 8 †

JUNKER, Dr. W. Travels in Africa, 1875-88. Translated by A. H. Keane. 3 vols. 8vo. Lond., 1890-92. D 14 S 14-16

JUSSERAND, J. J. English Warfaring Life in the Middle Ages. (XIV. Century.) Translated by Lucy T. Smith. 8vo. Lond., 1889. B 23 U 4

JUSTI, Prof. Carl. Diego Velazquez and his Times. Translated by Prof. A H. Keane. Imp. 8vo. Lond., 1889. C 18 U 4

JUSTINIAN. Corpus Juris Civilis. 3 vols. Imp. 8vo. Lipsiæ, 1856. F 11 V 10-12

Institutes of; with English Notes by T. G. Sanders. 8vo. Lond., 1853. F 3 P 14

JUSTINUS. Justinus cum notis. 12mo. Amst., 1669. B 35 P 17

Historiarum Philippicarum epitoma; reconsuit J. Jeep. 12mo. Lipsiæ, 1859. B 35 P 13

JUVENALIS, D. J. Thirteen Satires of; with Commentary by J. E. B. Mayor. 2 vols 12mo. Lond., 1889. J 11 W 30, 31

Thirteen Satires of Juvenal; edited, with Notes, by C. H. Pearson and H. A. Strong. (Clarendon Press.) 8vo. Oxford, 1887. J 5 P 10

Juvenal; by E. Walford. (Ancient Classics for English Readers.) 12mo. Edinb., 1880. J 14 P 15

D. Junii Juvenalis et A. Persii Flacci Satiræ. 18mo. Oxonii, 1845. , H 11 P 3

K

KAISERLICH - KÖNIGLICHE GEOLOGISCHEN REICHSANSTALT. Verhandlungen. 5 vols. Roy. 8vo. Wien, 1887-91. E

Jahrbuch. 5 vols. Roy. 8vo. Wien, 1886-91. E

General Register. Roy. 8vo. Wien, 1872. E

KAMPEN, N. G. van. Geschiedenis der Nederlanders Buiten Europa, of Verhaal van de Togten, ontdekkingen, oorlogen, veroveringen en inrigtingen der Nederlanders in Aziën, Afrika, Amerika, en Australië. 3 vols. (in 4). 8vo. Haarlem, 1831-33. MD 7 S 51-54

KANT, I. Philosophy of Law; translated by W. Hastie. 8vo. Edinb., 1887. F 6 Q 38
[*See* Fischer, Prof. K.]

KARPINSKI, Capt. On the Gold Washings in Russia. [In Russian.] 8vo. St. Petersburg, 1840. A 24 T 5

KARR, H. W. S. Shores and Alps of Alaska. 8vo. Lond., 1887. D 3 U 40

KATHOLIKOS. [*See* King's Brotherhood, The.]

KAUFMANN, Rev. M. Socialism; its nature, its dangers, and its remedies considered. 8vo. London, 1874. F 14 P 10

Utopias; or, Schemes of Social Improvement. 8vo. Lond., 1879. F 14 P 11

Socialism and Communism in their practical application. 12mo. Lond., 1883. F 14 P 12

Christian Socialism. 8vo. Lond., 1888. F 14 P 13

KAVANAGH, Rt. Hon. A. M.: a Biography; compiled by Sarah L. Steele. 8vo. Lond., 1891. C 15 T 16

KAVANAGH, Julia. Women of Christianity, exemplary for acts of Piety and Charity. 8vo. Lond., 1852. G 11 P 18

KAY, D. Memory: what it is, and how to improve it. 8vo. Lond., 1888. G 13 R 47

KAY, J. Free Trade in Land. 9th ed. 8vo. Lond., 1885. F 5 Q 43

KAYE, Sir John, and MALLESON, Col. G. B. History of the Indian Mutiny of 1857-8; with an Analytical Index. Cabinet edition. 6 vols. 8vo. Lond., 1888-89. B 29 Q 1-6

KAYSER, C. G. Vollständiges Bücher-Lexicon, 1750-1890. 26 vols. Imp. 8vo. Leip., 1834-91. Libr.

Sachregister zum Kayser'schen Bücher-Lexicon. Imp. 8vo. Leip., 1838. Libr.

KEAN, Edmund. Life and Adventures of, 1787-1833; by J. F. Molloy. 2 vols. 8vo. Lond., 1888. C 14 Q 20, 21

KEAN, Rev. James, M.A. Among the Holy Places; a Pilgrimage through Palestine. 8vo. Lond., 1891. D 16 U 14

KEANE, Prof. A. H. Asia; edited by Sir R. Temple. (Standford's Compend. of Mod. Geog.) 8vo. Lond., 1882. D 16 T 4

Eastern Geography: a Geography of the Malay Peninsula, Indo-China, the Eastern Archipelago, the Philippines, and New Guinea. 8vo. Lond., 1887. D 11 S 11

Science of Language. [*See* Hovelacque, A.]
[*See* Junker, Dr. W., *and* Justi, Prof. C.]

KEANE, John F. T. "Hajj Mohammed Amin:" Six Months in the Hejaz. 8vo. Lond., 1887. D 17 Q 10

Three Years of a Wanderer's Life. 2 vols. 8vo. Lond., 1887. D 10 Q 30, 31

KEARY, C. F. Norway and the Norwegians. 8vo. Lond., 1892. B 17 P 30

The Vikings in Western Christendom, 789-888. 8vo. Lond., 1891. B 20 T 13

KEATING, J. General History of Ireland; translated by D. O'Connor. 2 vols. (in 1). 8vo. Dublin 1841. B 29 R 12

KEATS, John. Letters of, to his family and friends; edited by S. Colvin. 12mo. Lond., 1891. C 14 P 1

[Life of]; by S. Colvin. (English Men of Letters.) 8vo. Lond., 1887. C 1 U 39

KEBBEL, T. E. Life of the Earl of Derby. (Statesmen Series.) 8vo. Lond., 1890. C 12 R 36

Life of Lord Beaconsfield. (Statesmen Series.) 8vo. Lond., 1888. C 3 R 19

KEENE, C. S. Life and Letters of; by G. S. Layard. 8vo. Lond., 1892. C 18 R 8

KEENE, H. G. [Life of] Mádhava Ráo Sindhia, otherwise called Madhoji (Rulers of India). 12mo. Oxford, 1891. · C 17 Q 19

The Turks in India. 8vo. Lond., 1879. B 29 T 3

KEENE, J. B. Handbook of Hydrometry. 8vo. Lond., 1875. F 11 Q 31

KEESE, Oline. [*See* Leakey, Miss C.]

KEIGHTLEY, T. [*See* Horatius Flaccus, Q.]

KEIM, Dr. Theodore. The History of Jesus of Nazareth. 6 vols. 8vo. Lond., 1873. G 4 U 3-8

KEIMER, Samuel. Biographical Notice of. [*See* Smith, Jos.]

KEITH-FALCONER. [*See* Falconer, Hon. I. Keith-.]

KELLETT, F. W. Pope Gregory the Great, and his relations with Gaul. 8vo. Camb., 1889. G 7 R 35

KELLNER, Dr. L. Caxton's Blanchardyn and Eglantine. [*See* Early Eng. Text Soc.]

KELLY, A. C. Wine-growing in Australia. 8vo. Adelaide, 1867. MA 1 Q 77

KELLY, C. Selections of Voyages and Travels, from the Days of Columbus to the late Voyages of Captains Parry, Ross &c. 8vo. Lond. (n.d.) MD 7 P 14

KELLY, J. L. The South Sea Islands; possibilities of trade with New Zealand. 8vo. Auckland, 1885. MD 4 U 51

KEMBLE, Frances Anne. Further Records, 1848-83: a Series of Letters; forming a Sequel to Records of a Girlhood, and Records of Later Life. 2 vols. 8vo. Lond., 1890. C 17 Q 2, 3

KEMMIS, Rev. T. Five Lectures on the Antiquity and Independence of the British Church. 8vo. Sydney, 1876. MG 1 R 45

KEMP, E. How to lay out a Garden: a Guide in Choosing, Forming, or Improving an Estate. 8vo. Lond., 1864. A 1 T 34

KEMP, H. T. First Step to Maori Conversation. 8vo. Auckland (n.d.) MK 1 P 34

KEMP, Rev. J. The Difficult Arrest, Fair Trial, Just Sentence, and Unfortunate Liberation of Sir John Barleycorn; a Speech. 12mo. Hobart (n.d.) MF 2 P 71

KEMPFIUS, C. [*See* Valerius Maximus.]

KEMPIS, T. à. The Imitation of Christ. 4th ed. 18mo. Glasgow, 1825. G 9 U 5

De Christo Imitando. 12mo. Lond., 1709. F 14 S 1

Notes of a Visit to the Scenes in which his Life was spent, &c. [*See* Cruise, F. R.]

KEMPNER, N. Commonsense Socialism. 8vo. Lond., 1887. F 14 S 1

KEN, Rt Rev. Thos. Life of; by E. H. Plumptree. 2 vols. 8vo. Lond., 1889. C 12 U 4, 5

KENDALL, H. Kinship of Men: an Argument from Pedigrees; or, Genealogy viewed as a Science. 8vo. Lond., 1888. K 19 Q 2

KENDALL, May. Dreams to Sell. 12mo. Lond., 1887. H 5 Q 28

KENNAN, G. Siberia and the Exile System. [Illustrated.] 2 vols. 8vo. Lond., 1891. D 17 V 10, 11

KENNARD, Mrs. A. Mrs. Siddons. (Eminent Women.) 8vo. Lond., 1887. C 3 R 49

KENNEDY, E. B. Blacks and Bushrangers: Adventures in Queensland. 8vo. Lond., 1889. MJ 1 S 52

KENNEDY, Prof. A. B. W. Mechanics of Machinery. 8vo. Lond., 1886. A 11 Q 29

KENNEDY, D., the Scottish Singer: Reminiscences of his Life and Work; by Marjory Kennedy. 8vo. Paisley, 1887. C 14 S 4

KENNEDY, Marjory. David Kennedy, the Scottish Singer: Reminiscences of his Life and Works. 8vo. Paisley, 1887. C 4 S 4

KENNEL CLUB Calendar and Stud-book. Vols. 14-18. 8vo. Lond., 1887-91. E

KENNET, Rt. Rev. Bishop. Complete History of England. 3 vols. fol. Lond., 1706. ¦ B 44 Q 6-8 ‡

KENRICK, W. Falstaff's Wedding: a Comedy. [*See* British Drama, Modern, 4.]

KENT, C. B. R. Essays in Politics. 8vo. Lond., 1891. F 14 P 48

KENT, J. Racing Life of Lord George Cavendish Bentinck. 8vo. Edinb., 1892. C 18 Q 16

KENT ARCHÆOLOGICAL SOCIETY. Archæologia Cantiana. Vols. 17-19. 8vo. Lond., 1887-92. E

KENTISH, N. L. Valedictory ("P.P.C.") Letter to his acquaintances on leaving for a few months his adopted Country, Melbourne and Victoria. 8vo. Melb., 1858. MF 1 T 1

Treatise on Penal Discipline; depicting various modes of treatment of Criminals under penal sentences of Courts of Law. 8vo. Melb., 1858. MF 1 T 1

KENYON, F. G. [*See* Aristoteles.]

KEPPEL, Capt. H. Visit to the Indian Archipelago, in H.M. Ship Mæander. 2 vols. roy. 8vo. Lond., 1853.
MD 5 V 23, 24

KER, Mrs. A. M. Australian Poems by A. M. K. 8vo. Melb. (n.d.)
MH 1 U 15

KERCHOFFS Prof. A. Complete Course of Volapük. [*See* Harrison, I. H.]

KERFORD, G. B. Digest of Cases in the Supreme Court of Victoria. [*See* Victoria.]

KERGUELEN-TRÉMAREC, J. J. Y. J. de. Relation de Deux Voyages dans les Mers Australes et des Indes, faits en 1771-74. 8vo. Paris, 1782.
MD 3 T 39

KERN, H. De Fidjitaal vergeleken met hare verwanten in Indonesië en Polynesië. 4to. Amsterdam, 1886.
MK 1 U 24
[*See* Müller, F. Max; Sacred Books, 21.]

KEROUALLE, Louise de. [*See* Portsmouth, Duchess of.]

KERR, James. Carlyle as seen in his Works: his Characteristics as a Writer and as a Man. 8vo. Lond., 1887.
C 12 Q 10

KERR, Rev. John. History of Curling, Scotland's Ain Game. 8vo. Edinb., 1890.
A 30 T 3
Curling. [*See* Heathcote, J. M.]

KERR, Dr. N. Mortality from Intemperance. 12mo. Lond., 1879.
F 11 P 28

Truth about Alcohol: a Lecture. 12mo. Lond., 1885.
F 11 P 48

Unfermented Wine, a Fact. 5th ed. 12mo. Lond., 1882.
F 11 P 57

Treatment of Inebriates. 2nd. ed. 8vo. Lond, 1885.
F 11 R 34

KEW ROYAL GARDENS. Bulletin. 5 vols. 8vo. Lond., 1887-91.
E

KEY, T. H. Latin Grammar. 8vo. Lond., 1846.
K 12 V 15

KEYNES, J. N. Scope and Method of Political Economy. 8vo. Lond., 1891.
F 6 P 50

KEYSER, A. An Exile's Romance or Realities of Australian Life. 8vo. Lond., 1888.
MJ 1 S 53

KEYTS, JEAN. Voyage à la Nouvelle Guinée en 1678 (Prévost, A. F., Suite de l'histoire générale des Voyages, tome 17). 4to. Amsterdam, 1761.
MD 11 P 16†

KHUSH-HAL KHAN KHATAK. Afghan Poetry of the Seventeenth Century: being Selections from the Poems of Khush-hal Khan Khatak, with translations, &c. Edited by C. E. Biddulph. 4to. Lond., 1890.
H 5 V 30

KIASH, K. D. Ancient Persian Sculptures; or, the Monuments, Buildings, Bas-reliefs, Rock Inscriptions, &c., belonging to the Kings of the Achæmenian and Sassanian Dynasties of Persia. (In English, Gujarati, and Persian). Roy. 8vo. Bombay, 1889.
A 8 R 3S

KICK, Prof. F. Flour Manufacture: a Treatise on Milling Science and Practice: translated by H. H. P. Powles. Imp. 8vo. Lond., 1888.
A 11 V 19

KIDD, J. Adaption of external nature to the Physical Condition of Man. 8vo. Lond., 1838.
A 26 U 17

KIDDER, J. H. Contributions of the Natural History of Kerguelen Island. Roy. 8vo. Wash., 1876.
A 30 U 1

KIDSON Joseph R. and Frank. Historical Notices of the Leeds Old Pottery. 4to. Leeds, 1892.
A 11 V 21

KIESSLING, T. [*See* Tacitus.]

KILLEBREW, J. B. Tennesee: its Agricultural and Mineral Wealth. 8vo. Nashville, 1876.
A 24 U 16

KILLEGREW, T. The Parson's Wedding: a Comedy. [*See* British Drama, Ancient, 3.]

KINDERMANN, C. G. De usu vini therapeutico. 8vo. Lipsiæ (n.d.)
F 11 Q 65

KING, Lieut.-Col. C. History of Berkshire. (Popular County Histories.) 8vo. Lond., 1887.
B 23 U 3

KING, C. [*See* U.S. Geol. Expl. of 40th Parallel.]

KING, C. W. The Gnostics and their Remains, Ancient and Mediæval. Roy. 8vo. Lond., 1887.
G 3 V 1
[*See* Julian the Emperor.]

KING, E. M. Truth, Love, Joy, &c. 8vo. Melb. 1864.
MG 1 Q 10

KING, H. Savage London: Lights and Shadows of Riverside Character, and Queer Life in London Dens 8vo. Lond., 1888.
J 9 Q 43

KING, J. E., and COOKSON, C. Principles of Sound and Inflexion, as illustrated in the Greek and Latin Languages. 8vo. Oxford, 1888.
K 12 U 12

KING, J. W. [*See* United States.]

KING, Hon. P. G. Comments on Cook's Log (H.M.S. "Endeavour," 1770), with Extracts, Charts, and Sketches. 4to. Sydney, 1892.
MD 12 P 16†

KING, R. Ohio: First Fruits of the Ordinance of 1787. 12mo. Boston, 1888.
B 17 P 7

KING, Ven. Archdeacon R. I. Atoning Sacrifice of Messiah: Three Sermons preached in St. Andrew's Cathedral, Sydney. 12mo. Sydney, 1875.
MG 1 Q 7

KING, W. F. H. Classical and Foreign Quotations, Law Terms and Maxims, Proverbs, Mottoes, Phrases, and Expressions. 8vo. Lond., 1887.
K 19 P 7

KINGLAKE, A. W. The Invasion of the Crimea; its Origin, and an Account of its Progress down to the death of Lord Raglan. 8 vols. 8vo. Lond., 1863-87.
B 12 U 23-30

KINGLAKE, E. The Australian at Home; Notes and Anecdotes of Life at the Antipodes, including useful hints to those intending to settle in Australia. 8vo. London, 1892.
MD 7 T 24

KING'S BROTHERHOOD, The. An Appeal for Christian Unity in Australia, and a suggestion towards its attainment; by "Katholikos." 12mo. Melb., 1891.   MG 2 P 41

KING'S COLLEGE, LONDON. Calendar, 1887-93. 6 vols. 12mo. Lond., 1887-92.   E

KING'S HIGHWAY, The. [Song] written by "Australie." Music composed by "E. M. W." Fol. Sydney, 1892.   MA 11 Q 15†

KING'S MESSENGERS; or what shall I do with my Money? 12mo. Sydney, 1870.   MJ 1 R 48

KINGSCOTE, H. Letter to the Archbishop of Canterbury on the Present Wants of the Church. 8vo. Lond., 1846.   G 15 R 27

KINGSFORD, Wm. The History of Canada. Vols. 1-5. 1608-1775. 8vo. Lond., 1888-92. B 17 R 1-5

KINGSLAND, W. G. Robert Browning, chief Poet of the Age: an Essay. 12mo. Lond., 1887.   C 13 P 3

KINGSLEY, Rev. C. Alexandria and her Schools. 8vo. Camb., 1854.   G 13 Q 39

Works of. 26 vols. 8vo. Lond., 1888-90. J 14 Q 1-26
  Alton Locke, Poet and Tailor.
  At Last; a Christmas in the West Indies.
  Discipline, and other Sermons.
  Glaucus: or, the Wonders of the Shore.
  Good News of God: Sermons.
  Hereward the Wake; 'Last of the English.'
  The Hermits.
  The Heroes: or, Greek Fairy Tales.
  Historical Lectures and Essays.
  Hypatia: or, New Foes with an Old Face.
  Literary and General Lectures and Essays.
  Madam How and Lady Why; or First Lessons in Earth Lore.
  Plays and Puritans, and other Historical Essays.
  Poems.
  Prose Idylls, New and Old.
  Roman and the Teuton.
  Sanitary and Social Lectures and Essays.
  Scientific Lectures and Essays.
  Sermons on National Subjects.
  Two Years Ago.
  Village Sermons, and Town and Country Sermons.
  The Water Babies.
  Water of Life, and other Sermons.
  Westminster Sermons.
  Westward Ho.
  Yeast: a Problem.

KINGSLEY, H. The Recollections of Geoffry Hamlyn. 12mo. Lond. (n.d.)   MJ 2 T 15

KINGSTON, A. Phonography in the Office: a complete Shorthand Clerk's Guide. 12mo. Lond., 1888.   K 20 P 17

KINGSTON, W. Beatty-. A Wanderer's Notes. 2 vols. 8vo. Lond., 1888.   D 8 U 23, 24

Monarchs I have met. 2 vols. 8vo. Lond., 1887.   C 13 U 5, 6

KINLOCH, M. G. J. History of Scotland, chiefly in its Ecclesiastical Aspect. 2 vols. 12mo. Edinb., 1888.   B 31 P 12, 13

KINNEAR, J. B. Principles of Civil Government. 8vo. Lond., 1887.   F 6 Q 39

KINNS, REV. S. Graven in the Rock: or, the Historical Accuracy of the Bible. 8vo. Lond., 1891. G 12 S 30

KINTORE, Earl of. Despatch from the Earl of Kintore, Governor of South Australia, reporting upon his visit to Port Darwin, and upon the Affairs of the Northern Territory of South Australia. Fol. Lond., 1891.   MD 12 Q 11 †

KIPLING, R. Barrack-room Ballads. 12mo. Lond., 1892.   H 9 P 8

KIPPIS, Dr. A. Vie du Capitaine Cook, traduite de l'Anglois. 4to. Paris, 1789.   MC 11 P 18 †

Narrative of Voyages of Captain J. Cook. [See Cook, Capt. J.]

KIRBY, Rev. J. C. The Liquor Laws of New South Wales. 8vo. Sydney, 1877.   MF 1 T 37

KIRBY, J. [See Brumfitt, G.]

KIRBY, T. F. Winchester Scholars: List of the Wardens, Fellows, and Scholars of St. Mary College, of Winchester. 8vo. Lond., 1888.   C 13 T 23

KIRBY, Rev. W. Monographia Apum Angliæ. 2 vols. (in 1). 8vo. Ipswich, 1802.   A 27 U 10

Power, Wisdom, and Goodness of God as manifested in the Creation of Animals. 8vo. Lond., 1838. A 27 U 7

KIRBY, Rev. W., and SPENCE, William. Introduction to Entomology. 2 vols. 8vo. Lond., 1816. A 27 U 5, 6

KIRCHHOFF, A. Das Stadrecht van Bantia. 8vo. Berlin, 1853.   K 15 R 6

KIRCHHOFF, A. [See Plotinus.]

KIRCHOFF, Prof. A. [See Leutemann, H.]

KIRK, John Foster. Supplement to Allibone's Critical Dictionary of English Literature and British and American Authors. [See Allibone, S. A.]

KIRK, Prof. T. Forest Flora of New Zealand. Fol. Wellington, 1889.   MA 11 P 9 †

Fruit-Blights and Diseases of Fruit Trees. Interim Report. 8vo. Brisb., 1886.   MA 3 Q 41

Fruit-Blights and Diseases of Fruit Trees. 8vo. Sydney, 1889.   MA 1 T 66

KIRKBRIDE, T. S. On the Construction, Organization, and General Arrangements of Hospitals for the Insane. 2nd ed. Roy. 8vo. Philad., 1880.   A 26 U 8

KIRKPATRICK, A. F. The Divine Library of the Old Testament; its origin, preservation, inspiration, and permanent value. 8vo. Lond., 1891.   G 13 U 40

KIRKPATRICK, J. Streets and Lanes of the City of Norwich. Fol. Norwich, 1889.   B 40 Q 8 ‡

KIRKPATRICK, Prof. J. Octocentenary Festival of the University of Bologna, June, 1888. 12mo. Edinb., 1888.   B 12 P 42

KIRKUP, T. An Inquiry into Socialism. 8vo. Lond., 1887.   F 6 Q 40

KITCHIN, Very Rev. G. W. Historic Towns: Winchester.
8vo. Lond., 1890. B 22 Q 11

KITTON, F. G. Charles Dickens by Pen and Pencil.
Illustrated. 2 vols. 4to. Lond., 1890. C 6 R 1, 2‡

KITTS, E. J. Compendium of the Castes and Tribes
found in India. Fol. Bombay, 1885. F 42 R 8 ‡

KLEINENBERG, Dr. N. Hydra. 4to. Leipzig, 1872.
A 36 P 30 ‡

KLEINHANDEL IN STERKEN DRANK en tot beten-
geling van openbare dronkenschap. 18mo. (n.p. n.d)
F 11 P 3
Ontwerp van wet tot regeling van den Kleinhandel in
sterken drank. 18mo. 'sGravenhage, 1881.
F 11 P 4
Handleiding voor Tappers. 12mo. Amsterdam, 1881.
F 11 P 11
Wet van den 28 Junij, 1881. 8vo. (n.p.) 1881.
F 11 R 35

KLENCKE, Prof. H. K. Untersuchungen über die
Wirkung des Branntwein-Genusses auf den lebenden
Organismus. 8vo. Braunschweig, 1848. F 11 Q 32

KLOTZ, R. [See Cicero, M. T.]

KLUSSMANN, E. C. Naevii poetæ Romani vitam
descripsit, carminum reliquias collegit, poesis rationem
exposuit. 8vo. Jenæ, 1843. J. 15 S 23

KNAGGS, R. C., and CO. Newcastle Nautical Almanac,
Directory and Guide to the Port of Newcastle, 1889-93.
5 vols. 8vo. Newcastle, 1888-92. ME 3 8

KNAGGS, Dr. S. T. Recreations of an Australian
Surgeon. 8vo. Sydney, 1888. MA 2 Q 68

KNIBBS, G. H. Prize Essay on the Nature and Public
Utility of Trigonometrical, General and Cadastral
Survey. Roy. 8vo. Sydney, 1891. MA 3 R 8

KNIGHT, C. [See Shakespeare, W.]

KNIGHT, E. F. Cruise of the "Alerte"; the Narrative of a Search for Treasure on the Island of Trinidad.
12mo. Lond., 1890. D 20 Q 10

KNIGHT, J. G. The Northern Teritory of South Australia. 8vo. Adelaide, 1880. MD 4 U 40

KNIGHT, R. P. The Symbolical Language of Ancient
Art and Mythology. A new edition by A. Wilder. 8vo.
New York, 1892. A 23 V 8

KNIGHT, Prof. Wm. A. Principal Shairp and his Friends.
8vo. Lond., 1888. C 9 T 48
Life of William Wordsworth. 3 vols. roy. 8vo. Edinb.,
1889. C 17 T 9-11
Memorials of Coleorton : being Letters from Coleridge,
Wordsworth, and his Sister, Southey, and Sir W. Scott,
to Sir George and Lady Beaumont, 1803-34; edited by
W. Knight. 2 vols. 8vo. Edinb., 1887.
C 16 P 13, 14
[See Goodwin, H.]
[See Wordsworth, W.]

KNIGHTON, H. Chronicon. [See Chronicles and
Memorials of Great Britain, &c.]

KNIGHTS TEMPLAR OF MICHIGAN. 36th Annual
Conclave, Proceedings. 2 vols. 8vo. Michigan,
1891-92. . E

KNIGHTS TEMPLAR OF KENTUCKY. 44th and
45th Annual Conclave, Proceedings. 2 vols. 8vo.
Kentucky, 1891-92. E

KNIGHTS TEMPLAR OF NEW HAMPSHIRE. 32nd
Annual Conclave, Proceedings. 8vo. Concord, 1891. E

KNIGHTS TEMPLAR OF NORTH DAKOTA. 2nd
Annual Conclave, Proceedings. 8vo. 1891. E

KNIGHTS TEMPLAR OF PENSYLVANIA. 28th
Annual Conclave, Proceedings, 8vo. Philad., 1891.
E

KNOLLYS, Major H. Sketches of Life in Japan. 8vo.
Lond., 1887. D 17 R 4

KNORR, G. W. Die Naturgeschichte Versteinerungen.
5 vols. fol. Nurenberg, 1773. A 40 P 5-9 ‡
Verlustiging der oogen en van den Geest, of Verzameling
van allerley bekende Hoorens en Schulpen. 6 vols. (in 2).
4to. Amsterdam, 1770-75. A 30 V 2, 3

KNOS, T. Bilder ur Lifvet i Australien. Reseskildringar.
8vo. Stockholm, 1875. MD 4 U 50

KNOWLEDGE: an Illustrated Magazine of Science,
Literature, and Art. Vols. 10-13, n.s. 4to. Lond.,
1886-90. E

KNOWLES, Rev. J. H. Folk-tales of Kashmir. 8vo.
Lond., 1888. J 7 S 29

KNOX, G. Vitality or Endowments? the present needs
of the University of Sydney. 8vo. Sydney, 1880.
MG 1 R 44

KNOX, R. Manual of Zoology. [See Edwards, H. Milne.]

KNOX, T. W. The Boy Travellers in Australasia. 8vo.
New York, 1889. MD 4 V 34
Decisive Battles since Waterloo, 1815-87. 8vo. New
York, 1887. B 25 T 3

KNOX, Rev. W. Liberal Education. 6th ed. 12mo.
Lond., 1783. G 17 P 47

KOCH, A. Prince Alexander of Battenberg: Reminiscences
of his Reign in Bulgaria. 8vo. Lond., 1887. C 12 T 11

KOEBLE, A. Report of a trip to Australia to investigate
the Natural Enemies of the Fluted Scale. 8vo. Washington, 1890. MA 3 T 48

KOECHLY, A. [See Manetho ; Nonnus Panopoletanus ;
Onosander ; and Quintus Smyrnaeus.]

KOELLE, S. W. Mohammed and Mohammedanism Critically Considered. 8vo. Lond., 1889. G 12 T 34

KOLBE, Rev. F. W. Language Study based on Bantu;
or, an Inquiry into the Laws of Root-formation. 8vo.
Lond., 1888. K 12 U 11

KOLFF, T. H. Reize door den Weinig Bekenden Zuidelijken Molukschen Archipel en langs de Geheel Onbekende Zuidwest kust van Nieuw-Guinea. 8vo. Amsterdam, 1828.   MD 7 S 50

KÖLLIKER, A. Icones Histiological. 4to. · Leip., 1864.
                                                      A 40 S 1 ‡

KOLOKOTRONÊS, T. Kolokotronês, the Kleptit and the Warrior : an Autobiography ; translated by Mrs. Edmonds. 8vo. Lond., 1892.   C 13 S 20

KÖPPEN, F. von. The Armies of Europe (illustrated), translated by Count Gleichen. 4to. Lond., 1890.
                                                      A 30 V 4

KORALEVSKY, M. Modern Customs and Ancient Laws of Russia. 8vo. Lond., 1891.   F 14 T 25

KORAN, The ; or, Alcoran of Mohammed ; with explanatory Notes by G. Sale. 8vo. Lond., 1876. G 16 T 34
The Koran ; translated by G. Sale. 2 vols. . 8vo. Lond., 1825.   G G P 37, 38

KORT EN NAUWKEURIG VERHAAL van de Reize, door drie Schepen in 't Jaar 1721. Sq. 8vo. Amsterdam, 1727.   M D 7 T 23

KOREN, J., og DANIELSSEN, D. C. Nye Alcyonider, Gorgonider, og Pennatulider tilhørende Norges Faurna. (Bergens Museum.) 4to. Bergen, 1883. A 40 S 4 ‡

KÖRNER, T. Rosamunde. 18mo. Leip. (n.d.)
                                                      H 2 P 48

KOTZEBUE, Otto von. A New Voyage Round the World, 1823-26. 2 vols. 8vo. Lond., 1830.
                                                      M D 7 T 20, 21

KRAUS, Emil. Adventures of Count George Albert of Erbach ; translated by H.R.H. Princess Beatrice. 8vo. Lond., 1890.   C 16 Q 26

KREFFT, J. L. G. Descriptions of New Australian Snakes. 8vo. Lond., 1869.   M A 3 S 20
On Australian Entozoa. 8vo. Sydney, 1871.
                                                      M A 2 U 50

KRIEGER, J. A. De Alcoholismo Chronico. 8vo. Berolini, 1864.   F 11 Q 33

KRILOF, or Kruilov, I. A. Krilof and his Fables ; by W. R. S. Ralston. 4th ed. 8vo. Lond., 1883. J 5 P 41

KROEGER, A. E. [*See* Fichte, J, G.]

KROUPA, B. An Artist's Tour : Gleanings and Impressions of Travels in North and Central America and the Sandwich Islands. Imp. 8vo. Lond., 1890. ·
                                                      D 15 V 7

KROPOTKINE, P. In Russian and French Prisons. 8vo. Lond., 1887.   F 6 T 33

KRUILOV, I. A. [*See* Krilof, I. A.]

KRUSENSTERN, Capt. A. J. von. Voyage round the World, in the years 1803-6 ; translated from the German by R. B. Hoppner. 2 vols. 4to. Lond., 1813.
                                                      D 12 Q 15, 16 †

KRÜGELSTEIN, Dr. F. C. C. Getränke Verfälschung. 8vo. Erlangen, 1846.   F 11 Q 30

KUGLER, F. T. Hand-book of Painting : the Italian Schools ; based on the Hand-book of Kugler. 5th ed., revised, &c., by A. H. Layard. 2 vols. 8vo. Lond., · 1887.   A 23 S 4, 5

KÜHN, J. [*See* Pausanias.]

KUMAR, Maharaja Nanda. Trial of. [*See* Beveridge, H.]

KUNZ, G. F. Gems and Precious Stones of North America. Imp. 8vo. New York, 1890. A 9 V 26

KUSTER, L. [*See* Aristophanes.]

KUTTER, W. R. [*See* Ganguillet, E.]

KUZ. [*See* Duun, F.]

KYD, Thomas. Jeronimo [Part the First] ; a Tragedy [*See* British Drama, Ancient, 1.]
The Spanish Tragedy : a Comedy [*See* British Drama, Ancient, 1.]

KYNSEY, Dr. W. R. Report on Anæmia ; or, Beri-Beri of Ceylon. Sm. fol. Colombo, 1887.   A 7 Q 20 †

L

L., H. E. S. [*See* Ferns which grow in New Zealand.]

LABBERTON, R. H. New Historical Atlas and General History. 4to. Lond., 1887.   B 9 P 27 †

LABILLIERE, F. P. de. History of a Covenol Family. 8vo. Lond., 1888.   B 26 T 1

LACE-MAKING. Renascence of the Irish Art of Lace-making : Notes and Descriptions ; by A. S. Cole. 8vo. Lond., 1888.   A 11 S 25

LACHMANN, C. [*See* Gromatic Veteres ; *and* Lucretius Carus, T.]

LACOUPERIE, Prof. T. de. [*See* Terrein de Lacouperie, A. E. J. B.]

LACY, G. Liberty and Law. 8vo. Lond., 1888.
                                                      F 8 R 8

LADD, Prof. G. T. Elements of Physiological Psychology. Roy. 8vo. Lond., 1887.   A 26 U 5

LADIES OF SYDNEY WALTZES, The. Fol. Sydney (n.d.)   MA 11 Q 15 †

LA FONTAINE, J. de. Contes Nouvelles. (Collection Jannet-Picard.) 2 vols. 12mo. Paris (n.d.)
                                                      H 1 P 43, 44
Fables. (Collection Jannet-Picard.) 2 vols. 12mo. Paris (n.d.)   H 1 P 53, 54
Fables Choisies de. 2 vols. (in 1.) 8vo. Bruxelles, 1838.
                                                      H 6 U 31

LAFARGUE, P. Evolution of Property from Savagery to Civilization. 8vo. Lond., 1890.   F 14 P 28

LA FAYETTE, Marie Madeline. La Princesse de Clèves. (Collection Jannet-Picard.) 12mo. Paris (n.d.) J 15 Q 28

LAGRANGE, Dr. F. Physiology of Bodily Exercise. 12mo. Lond., 1889. A 26 Q 12

LAGRANGE, J. L. Œuvres. 14 vols. 4to. Paris, 1867-92. A 32 U 1–14

LAING, Edward. Letter from New South Wales on Scurvy, &c. [*See* Trotter, Thomas.]

LAING, Rev. J. [*See* Halkett, S.]

LAING, S. Human Origins. 8vo. Lond., 1892. A 1 W 45

Modern Science and Modern Thought. 8vo. Lond., 1890. G 6 P 38

Problems of the Future, and Essays. 8vo. Lond., 1890. G 12 S 31

LAISHLEY, R. Report upon State Education in Great Britain, France, United States, &c. Sm. fol. Wellington, 1886. MG 10 Q 6 †

LAKE, H. Personal Reminiscences of the Rt. Hon. Benjamin Disraeli, Earl of Beaconsfield. 8vo. Lond., 1891. C 12 R 38

LAKE, J. Official Guide to the Picture Galleries and Catalogue of Fine Arts, Melbourne Centennial International Exhibition, 1888. 3rd ed. 8vo. Melb., 1888. MA 3 Q 53

LALANDE, J. Bibliographie Astronomique avec l' Histoire de l'Astronomie, 1781-1802. 4to. Paris, 1803. K S T 4

LAMARTINE, A. de. Graziella. 8vo. Paris, 1891. J 5 P 43

Harmonies : Poétiques et Religieuses. 8vo. Paris, 1879. H 3 Q 31

Jocelyn : épisode, journal trouvé chez un curé de village. 8vo. Paris, 1888. H 5 R 44

Jocelyn. 8vo. Paris, 1882. H 3 Q 30

La Chute d'un Ange. 8vo. · Paris, 1879. H 6 T 31

Méditations Poétiques suivies de la Mort de Socrate, de Pèlerinage de Childe-Harold, et du Chant du sacre. 8vo. Paris, 1881. H 6 T 32

Memoirs of Celebrated Characters. 2 vols. 8vo. Lond. 1854. C 2 T 16, 17

1. Nelson, Heloise, Columbus, Palissy, Roostam, Cicero.
2. Milton, Socrates, Jacquard, Joan of Arc, Cromwell, Homer, Gutenberg, Fénelon.

Voyage en Orient. 2 vols. 8vo. Paris, 1875. D 17 V 15, 16

Life of : by Lady M. Domvile. 8vo. Lond., 1888. C 5 Q 3

LAMAZE, Rt. Rev. (—). Les Missions Catholiques en Océanie. Roy. 8vo. Lyon, 1889. M D 7 U 11

LAMB, Charles. In the Footprints of; by B. E. Martin. Roy. 8vo. Lond., 1891. C 16 U 1

[Life of]; by Rev. A. Ainger. 12mo. Lond., 1888. C 2 R 5

Letters of; edited by A. Ainger. 2 vols. 12mo. Lond., 1888. C 12 P 12, 13

LAMB, S. [*See* Agriculture, Dept. of, Queensland.]

LAMB, S. E. [*See* Cockshott, H. M.]

LAMB, William [*See* Melbourne, Lord.]

LAMBROS, Prof. S. P. Collation of the Athos Codex of the Shepherd of Hermas; translated and edited by J. A. Robinson. 8vo. Camb., 1888. J 16 S 1

LAMENNAIS, F. Œuvres Posthumes : Correspondance. 2 vols. 8vo. Paris, 1859. C 16 S 23, 24

Discussions, Critiques et Pensées diverses sur la Religion et la Philosophie 8vo. Paris, 1841. G 11 U 3

Esquisse d'une Philosophie. 4 vols. 8vo. Paris, 1840-46. G 11 U 4–7

Essai sur l'Indifférence en matière de Religion. 4 vols. 8vo. · Paris, 1859. G 11 U 8–11

LA MOTTE, Jeanne de Luz, Comtesse de Valoise de. Authentic Adventures of the celebrated Countess de la Motte. 12mo. Lond., 1787. C 13 P 4

[*See* Macmahon, P.]

LAMPLOUGH, E. Yorkshire Battles. 8vo. Hull, 1891. B 5 T 33

LAMPSON, F. Locker-. [*See* Locker-Lampson, F.]

LANCELOTT, F. Australia as it is ; its Settlements, &c. 2 vols. 8vo. Lond., 1852. MD 15, 16

LANCEREAUX, Dr. E. De l'Alcoolisme et de ses conséquences. 8vo. Paris, 1878. F 11 S 29

LANCET, The. 28 vols. 8vo. Lond., 1868-75, 1888-92. E

LANCIANI, Prof. R. Ancient Rome, in the light of recent discoveries. Roy. 8vo. Boston, 1890. B 11 R 26

LANDOR, I. W. S. [*See* Casati, Capt. G.]

LANDSTAD, M. B. Norske Folkeviser. 8vo. Christiania, 1853. H 10 R 13

LANE, O. F. [*See* Graham, C. H.]

LANE, R. [*See* Gainsborough, T.]

LANE, William. The Workingman's Paradise : An Australian Labour Novel, by "John Miller." 8vo. Sydney, 1892. MJ 2 T 34

LANEHAM, Robert. [*See* Shakespeare Society, New.]

LANE-POOLE, S. [*See* Poole, S. Lane-.]

LANG, Andrew. Life, Letters, and Diaries of Sir Stafford Northcote, First Earl of Iddesleigh. 2 vols. 8vo. Edinb., 1890 C 13 R 23, 24

Old Friends : Essays in Epistolary Parody. 12mo. Lond., 1890. J 5 P 42

Aucassin and Nicolette ; done into English. 12mo. Lond., 1887. H 5 Q 29

Ballads of Books. 12mo. Lond., 1888. H 5 Q 30

Books and Bookmen. 8vo. Lond., 1887. J 5 R 37

Myth, Ritual, and Religion. 2 vols., 8vo. Lond., 1887. G 8 Q 25

[*See* Herodotus.]

LANG, J. Assigned to his Wife ; or the Adventures of George Flower, the Celebrated Detective Officer. 8vo. Lond. (n.d.)   MJ 2 Q 31

LANG, Rev. Dr. J. D. Discourse delivered in the Scots Church, on the occasion of the death of the Hon. R. Campbell. 12mo. Sydney, 1859.   MG 2 P 31

Historical and Statistical Account of New South Wales. 3rd ed. 2 vols. 8vo Lond., 1840.   MB 1 S 30, 31.

LANGE, L. [*See* Leipziger Studien.]

LANGER, Dr. Das Aquarium und seine Bewohner. S.4to. Berlin, 1877.   A 27 Q 27

LANGFORD, J. A. On Sea and Shore. 12mo. Lond., 1887.   MH 1 R 38

LANGLEY, B. and T. The Builders Jewel, &c. ; with a Dictionary of Terms used in Architecture. 18mo. Haddington, 1805.   A 2 R 43

LANGMEAD, T. P. T. English Constitutional History from the Teutonic Conquest to the Present Time. 4th ed. Revised by C. H. E. Carmichael. 8vo. Lond., 1890.   .   B 24 S 19

LANGSTROTH, L. L. On the Hive and Honey Bee ; Revised enlarged and completed by Chas. Dadant and Son. 8vo. Hamilton, 1890.   A 18 R 3

LANGTON, R. Childhood and Youth of Charles Dickens. 8vo. Lond., 1891.   C 15 Q 17

LANGTON, William. Mark Anderson : a tale of Station Life in New Zealand. 8vo. Dunedin (n.d.) MJ 2 T 33

LANIN, E. B. Russian Characteristics. 8vo. Lond., 1892.   F 14 T 13

LANKESTER, E. [*See* Schleiden, Dr. J. M.]

LANKESTER, E. Ray. The Advancement of Science ; occasional Essays and Addresses. 8vo. Lond., 1890.   A 30 T 2

Comparative Anatomy. [*See* Gegenbaur, C.]

LANSDELL, H. Through Central Asia. 8vo. Lond., 1887.   D 16 U 13

LA PEROUSE, J. F. de Galaup, Comte de. Découvertes dans la Mer du Sud, 1794. Paris (n.d.)   MD 7 S 59

La Pérouse : Récit de son Voyage Expédition envoyée à sa recherche le Capitaine Dillon, &c. ; édition du Centennaire. Publiée par G. Marcel. 8vo. Paris (n.d.) MC 1 Q 45

Voyage round the World in the Years 1785-88. Translated from the French. 3 vols. 8vo. Lond., 1798.   MD 5 U 41-43

Voyage de la Pérouse autour du Monde ; rédigé par L. A. Milet-Mureau. 4 vols. 4to. Paris, 1797.   MD 8 Q 17-20 †

Atlas [to the above]. Fol. Paris (n.d.)   MD 3 Q 1 ‡

Voyages et Aventures de : par F. Valentin. 12mo. Tours, 1839.   MD 2 W 24

LAPLACE, P. S., Le Marquis. Exposition du Système du Monde. 6e. éd. 4to. Paris, 1835.   A 19 V 9

LAPPENBURG, J. M. History of England under the Norman Kings ; translated from the German by B. Thorpe. 8vo. Oxford, 1857.   B 22 U 18

LARDEN, W. Electricity for Public Schools and Colleges, 8vo. Lond., 1887.   A 22 Q 15

LARKIN, M. Catalogue of a Collection of Books illustrative of Discovery and Colonisation in Australasia. Roy. 8vo. Lond., 1890.   MK 1 S 31

LARKWORTHY, F. New Zealand Revisited. 2nd ed. 8vo. Lond., 1881.   MD 3 T 38

Another copy. 2nd ed. 8vo. Lond., 1882.   MD 3 S 38

LARNACH, W. J. M. Hand-book of New Zealand Mines ; with Maps and Illustrations. 8vo. Wellington, 1887.   MA 2 Q 45

LARWOOD, Jacob. [*See* Sadler, L. R.]

LAS CASES, M. J. E. A. D., Comte de. Private Life of the Emperor Napoleon at Saint Helena. 8 vols. 8vo. Lond., 1823.   C 15 R 1-8

LASCELLES, R. Liber Munerum Publicorum Hiberniæ; or, the Establishments of Ireland, 1152-1827. 2 vols. fol. Lond., 1852.   B 38 Q 16, 17 ‡

LATHAM, R. G. The English Language. 3rd ed. 8vo. Lond., 1850.   K 16 T 18

The Germania of Tacitus, with Ethnological Dissertations and Notes. Roy. 8vo. Lond., 1851.   B 27 V 5

Handbook of the English Language. 2nd. ed. 8vo. Lond., 1855.   K 16 P 37

LATIMER, J. Annals of Bristol in the 19th Century. 8vo. Bristol, 1887.   B 22 U 4

LATIN ACCIDENCE, The; arranged in progressive lessons for the use of Junior Pupils in the Sydney Grammar School. 12mo. Sydney, 1865.   MK 2 P 4

LATROBE, C. J. The Rambler in Mexico, 1834. 8vo. Lond., 1836.   D 15 R 16

LAUD, W., Archbishop of Canterbury : a Study ; by A. C. Benson. 8vo. Lond., 1887.   C 17 Q 5

[*See* Oxford Univerity Statutes.]

LAUGHING JACKASS, The: a weekly journal of Satire. Vol. 1. 4to. Sydney, 1867-68.   ME 8 T

LAUGHTON, Prof. J. K. Studies in Naval History Biographies. 8vo. Lond., 1887.   C 13 R 25

LAUNCESTON EXAMINER, The. Fol. Launceston, 1848.   ME

LAURIE, Dr. S. S. Teachers' Guild, Addresses, and the Registration of Teachers. 12mo. Lond., 1892. G 18 Q 11

LAURIE, Col. W. P. B, Sketches of Distinguished Anglo-Indians. 1st, 2nd series. 2 vols. 8vo. Lond., 1887-88.   C 16 Q 3, 4

LAVELEYE, Prof. É de. Socialism of To-day ; translated by G. H. Orpen, with an account of Socialism in England. 8vo. Lond., 1884.   F 14 P 15

LAVELEYE, Prof. E. de—*contd.*
Luxury. 8vo. Lond., 1891.　　　　F 14 P 29

The Balkan Peninsula ; translated by Mrs. Mary Thorpe.
8vo. Lond., 1887.　　　　D 18 U 1

LAVIGNE, L. A. G.　Germond de.　[*See* Germond de
Lavigne, L. A. G.]

LAVISSE, E.　The Youth of Frederick the Great.　8vo.
Lond., 1891.　　　　C 18 Q 6

LAW, E.　The History of Hampton Court Palace.　3 vols.
sm. 4to.　Lond., 1885-91.　　　　B 22 S 2-4

LAW, J.　The Farmer's Veterinary Adviser : a Guide to
the Prevention and Treatment of Disease in Domestic
Animals.　8vo.　Edinb., 1887.　　　　A 1 U 12

LAW, SOMNER and CO.　Hand-book to the Garden for
New South Wales.　8vo.　Sydney, (n.d.)　　　MA 3 S 24

LAW LIST OF AUSTRALASIA.　The, 1891-92.　8vo.
Melb., 1891.　　　　ME 6 R

LAW MAGAZINE AND REVIEW.　4th Series.　Vols.
12-16.　8vo.　Lond., 1887-91.　　　　E

LAW REPORTS OF THE COUNCIL OF LAW RE-
PORTING FOR ENGLAND AND WALES.　Edited
A. P. Stone.　3 vols. roy. 8vo.　Lond., 1892.
F 11 T 13-15

LAWES, Rev. W. G.　Grammar and Vocabulary of Language spoken by Motu Tribes, New Guinea.　2nd ed.
8vo.　Sydney, 1888.*　　　　MK 1 P 51

LAWLESS, Hon. Emily.　Ireland ; with some Additions
by Mrs. A. Bronson.　8vo.　Lond., 1887.　　　B 29 S 11

LAWRANCE, Chas.　Ready Reckoner of Agents' Commissions on Land Sales and Money Loans.　12mo.
Adelaide, 1884.　　　　MA 3 P 37

LAWRENCE, John Laird Mair, Lord.　[Life of] by Sir
Richard Temple.　(Englishmen of Action.)　8vo.　Lond.,
1889.　　　　C 12 R 28

LAWRENCE, W. B.　International Law.　[*See* Wheaton,
Dr. H.]

LAWRENCE-ARCHER.　[*See* Archer, Maj. J. H. L.]

LAWS, B. G.　[*See* Chess Problem, The.]

LAWSON, H.　[*See* Quatrefages, A. de.]

LAYARD, A. H.　Hand-book of Painting.　[*See* Kugler,
F. T.]

LAYARD, G. S.　Life and Letters of Charles Samuel
Keane.　8vo.　Lond., 1892.　　　　C 18 R 8

LAYARD, Sir H.　Early Adventures in Persia, Susiana,
and Babylonia.　2 vols. 8vo.　Lond., 1887.　E 17 R 1, 2

LAYARD, Thomas L.　[*See* Du Noyer, Mme.]

LAYMAN, A.　[*See* Virtue, P.]

LEA, H. C.　History of the Inquisition of the Middle Ages.
3 vols. 8vo.　Lond., 1888.　　　　G 12 T 38-40

LEADER, W.　Manual of the Law of Evidence.　8vo.
Melb., 1889.　　　　MF 3 T 5

LEAF, Dr. W.　Companion to the Iliad for English
Readers.　8vo.　Lond., 1892.　　　　J 11 W 23
[*See* Homer.]

LEAKEY, Miss C.　The Broad Arrow ; being passages
from the History of Maida Gwynnham, a Lifer ; by
"Oline Keese."　2 vols. (in 1.)　8vo.　Hobart, 1860.
MJ 1 T 52

Another copy (Australian Edition).　8vo.　Lond., 1887.
MJ 1 T 53

LEAVITT, T. W. H., and LIBURN, W. D.　Jubilee
History of Victoria and Melbourne.　Illustrated.　2 vols.
4to.　Melb., 1888.　　　　MB 1 U 21, 22

LEBIGRE, E.　Catalogue de la Bibliothèque de feu E.
Lebigre.　Roy. 8vo.　Paris, 1889.　　　　K 8 R 10

LEBON, L.　De l'Alcoolisme en Belgique.　8vo.　Bruxelles,
1883.　　　　F 11 S 28

LECKY, W. E. H.　History of Rationalism in Europe.
2nd ed.　2 vols. 8vo.　Lond., 1865-68.　G 4 W 42, 43

Poems.　12mo.　Lond., 1891.　　　　H 8 P 50

History of England in the 18th Century.　Vols. 1-6.　8vo.
Lond., 1878-87.　　　　B 5 P 13-18

LE CONTE, J.　Evolution and its Relation to Religious
Thought.　8vo.　Lond., 1888.　　　　G 13 R 40

LEDLIE, J. C.　Roman Law.　[*See* Sohm, R.]

LE DUC, W. G.　[*See* United States, Sorghum Sugar.]

LEE, A.　Marble and Marble-workers : a Hand-book for
Architects, Artists, Masons, and Students.　12mo.　Lond.,
1888.　　　　A 2 4 44

LEE, Rev. F. G.　The Directorium Anglicanum.　2nd ed.
Sm. 4to.　Lond., 1865.　　　　G 3 V 19

Reginald Pole, Cardinal Archbishop of Canterbury : an
Historical Sketch.　8vo.　Lond., 1888.　　　C 13 S 9

LEE, H.　The Vegetable Lamb of Tartary : a Curious Fable
of the Cotton Plant ; with a History of Cotton and the
Cotton Trade.　8vo.　Lond., 1887.　　　A 1 T 30

LEE, N.　The Rival Queens ; a Tragedy.　[*See* British
Drama, Modern, 1.]

Theodosius ; a Tragedy.　[*See* British Drama, Modern, 1.]

LEE, Mrs. R.　Adventures in Australia.　3rd ed.　12mo.
Lond., 1869.　　　　MJ 2 P 35

LEE and ROSS'S Handbook to the City of Sydney ;
compiled by G. R. Addison.　8vo.　Sydney, 1880.
MD 3 T 40

LEECH, H. J.　[*See* Bright, Rt. Hon. J.]

LEECH, J., his life and work ; by W. P. Frith.　2 vols.
8vo.　Lond., 1891.　　　　C 18 Q 11-12

Pictures of Life and Character.　Vols. 2, 3.　Roy. 4to.
Lond., 1887.　　　　A 2 R 26, 27†

LEES, Dr. F. R. One hundred objections to a Maine Law. 12mo. Manchester, 1857. F 11 P 51

Argument for the Legislative Prohibition of the Liquor Traffic. 12mo. Lond., 1857. F 11 P 71

The Strong Drink Question; Total Abstinence from all intoxicating beverages, and the language of the Holy Scriptures harmonised. 12mo. Leeds, 1842. F 11 P 39

Illustrated History of Alcohol. 8vo. Lond., 1846. F 11 S 27

LEFÉBURE, E. Embroidery and Lace: their Manufacture and History. 8vo. Lond., 1888. A 11 Q 30

LEFEVRE, T. Guide pratique du Compositeur d'imprimerie. 2 vols. roy. 8vo. Paris, 1880. A 25 U 2, 3

LEFEVRE, Rt. Hon. G S. Peel and O'Connell : a Review of the Irish Policy of Parliament, from the Act of Union to the Death of Sir Robert Peel. 8vo. Lond., 1887. F 5 P 13

LEFFINGWELL, Dr. Albert. Illegitimacy and the influence of Seasons upon conduct. 12mo. Lond., 1892. F 9 U 21

LEFFINGWELL, Dr. Albert Tracy. Rambles through Japan without a Guide; by "Albert Tracy." 12mo. Lond., 1892. D 17 P 3

LEGAL YEAR-BOOK OF AUSTRALASIA, 1892. 8vo. Sydney, 1892. ME 6 R

LE GALLIENNE, R. Volumes in folio. 12mo. Lond., 1889. H 5 Q 31

LEGG, J. W. [*See* Quignon, Card. F.)

LEGGE, Prof. J. The Nestorian Monument of Hsi an Fú ; relating to the diffusion of Christianity in China. Text and Translation. 8vo. Lond., 1888. G 6 Q 31
[*See* Müller, F. Max, Sacred Books.]

LEGGO, Wm. History of the Administration of Rt. Hon. Frederick Temple, Earl of Dufferin, late Governor-General of Canada. 8vo. Montreal, 1878. B 19 T 1

LEHMANN, C. [*See* Preiss, L.]

LEHRS, F. S. [*See* Hesiod.]

LEIBIUS, A. President's Address delivered to the Royal Society of New South Wales. 8vo. Sydney, 1891. MA 2 T 67

LEICHHARDT, Dr. L. Notes on the Geology of parts of New South Wales and Queensland in 1842–43 ; edited by the Rev. W. B. Clarke. 12mo. Sydney, 1866. MA 2 P 66

LEIGH, S. T., and Co. Masonic Year-Book and Directory of New South Wales, 1892. 12mo. Sydney, 1892. ME 8 P

Hand-book to Sydney and Suburbs ; with a Plan of the City and Map of the Roads of the Colony. 8vo. Sydney, 1867. MD 7 Q 39

LEIPZIGER STUDIEN ZUR CLASSISCHEN PHILOLOGIE. Herausgegeben von G. Curtius, L. Lange, O. Ribbeck, H. Lipsius, C. Wachsmuth. 13 vols. 8vo. Leipzig, 1878-91. 19 S 5–17

LEITE, T. Compendio para o ensino dos surdos-mudos. 8vo. Rio de Janeiro, 1891. K 11 T 46

LELAND, C. G. Gipsey Sorcery and Fortune-telling. 4to. Lond., 1891. A 24 V 26

Manual of Wood-carving.; revised by John J. Holtzapffel. Sm. 4to. Lond., 1890. A 23 T 7

Leather-work : a practical Manual for Learners. Sm. 4to. Lond., 1892. A 23 T 10

Practical Education. Treating of the Development of Memory, &c. 8vo. Lond., 1888. G 17 P 36
[*See* Barrière, A.]

LELEWEL, J. Géographie du moyen age ; accompagnée d'atlas et de Cartes dans chaque volume. 4 vols. 8vo. Brusselles, 1852. D 12 T 11–14

Atlas [to above.] Ob. 8vo. Brusselles, 1850. D 37 Q 7 ‡

LELY, J. M. [*See* Chitty, J., and Wharton, J. S.]

LE MAIRE, J. Ephemides sive Descriptio Navigationis Australia, 1615. Imp. 4to. Amsterd, 1621. MD 7 Q 3†
[*See* Spilbergen, G. de.]

LE MESSURIER, Col. A. From London to Bokhara and a ride through Persia. 8vo. Lond., 1889. D 16 U 17

Game, Shore, and Water Birds of India. Roy. 8vo. Calcutta, 1888. A 15 R 12

LEMIRE, Rev. A. D'Irlande en Australie : Souvenirs et Impressions de Voyage. Roy. 8vo. Lille, 1890. MD 7 R 48

LEMOS, B. A. Dissertatio Inauguralis Medica de cerevisia Interdicendis. Sm. 4to. Halæ Magdeburgicæ, 1735. F 11 Q 34

LENDENFELD, Dr. R. von. Descriptive Catalogue of Sponges in the Australian Museum, Sydney. Roy. 8vo. Lond., 1888. MA 2 U 51

Monograph of the Horny Sponges. 4to. Lond., 1889. MA 1 P 36 †

LENEY, Rev. A. Compendium of Geography. 2nd ed. 12mo. Dublin, 1807. D 11 Q 8

LENO, J. B. Art of Boot and Shoe making. 2nd ed. (Weale.) 12mo. Lond., 1887. A 17 R 22

LENORMANT, Comte de F. Lettres Assyriologiques ; 2ᵉ série. Etudes Accadiennes. 3 vols. 4to. Paris, 1872–79. K 17 S 17–19

LENTZ, Dr. F. De l'Alcoolisme et de ses diverses manifestations. 8vo. Bruxelles, 1884. F 11 S 26

LENTZNER, K. Colonial English : a Glossary of Australian, Anglo-Indian, Pidgin-English, West Indian, and South African Words. Roy. 8vo. Lond., 1891. MK 1 R 16

LEO XIII, Pope. Encyclical Letter of Our Holy Father, by Divine Providence, on the Condition of Labour. (Official Translation.) 8vo. Sydney, 1891. MF 2 T 30

Life of, from an authentic Memoir furnished by his order ; by B. O'Reilly. Roy. 8vo. Lond., 1887. C 12 U 1

LEONHARD, K. C. von. Fremdenbuch für Heidelberg und die umgegend. 8vo. Heidelberg, 1834. D 18 T 7

LEOPARDI, G. Opere di. 4 vols. 12mo. Firenze, 1889.
J 11 T 34–37

LEPAGE, J. B., and his Art : a Memoir, by A. Theuriet. Roy. 8vo. Lond., 1892. C 19 M 12

LE PETIT, J. Bibliographie des Principales Editions originales d'Ecrivains Français du 15e au 18e siècle. Imp. 8vo. Paris, 1888. K 8 R 15

LE ROY, A. [*See* Hernandez, P.]

LE ROY, G. Australia's Welfare. 8vo. Adelaide, 1892.
MJ 2 T 32

LE SAGE, A. R. Le Diable Boiteux. (Collection Jannet-Picard.) 2 vols. 12mo. Paris (n.d.) J 15 Q 38, 39
Œuvres de. Imp. 8vo. Paris, 1876. J 2 U 21
1. Gil Blas.
2. Guzman d'Alforache.
3. Théâtre.

LESLIE, J. Historie of Scotland. [*See* Scottish Text Soc.]

LESLIE, Robert C. Old Sea Wings, Ways, and Words, in the days of oak and hemp. 8vo. Lond., 1890.
A 19 T 2

LESSEPS, F. de. Recollections of Forty years ; translated by C. B. Pitman. 2 vols. 8vo. Lond., 1887.
C 12 T 22, 23

LESSING, G. E. Dramatische Meisterwerke. 18mo. Leip., 1847. H 2 P 47

LESSING, J. Ancient Oriental Carpet Patterns, after pictures and originals of the 15th and 16th centuries. Fol. Lond., 1879. A 32 P 22 ‡

LESSON, R. P. Voyage autour du Monde sur la Corvette *La Coquille*. 2 vols. 8vo. Paris, 1838–39.
MD 7 R 29, 30
Voyage Médical autour du Monde, exécuté sur la Corvette du Roi *La Coquille* commandée par L. I. Duperrey, 1822-25. 8vo. Paris, 1829. MD 7 S 58

L'ESTRANGE, Rev. A. G. Lady Belcher and her Friends. 8vo. Lond., 1891. C 14 T 12

LE STRANGE, Guy. Palestine under the Moslems : a description of Syria and the Holy Land, 650–1500. 8vo. Lond., 1890. B 20 R 3
Correspondence of Princess Lieven and Earl Grey. [*See* Lieven, Princess D.]

L'ESTRANGE, Capt. W. D. Under Fourteen Flags ; being the Life and Adventures of Brigadier-Gen. MacIver. 2 vols. 8vo. Lond., 1884. C 14 P 3, 4
Another copy. 8vo. Melb., 1884. MC 1 P 38

LETOURNEAU, C. Biology ; translated by W. Maccall. 8vo. Lond., 1878. A 27 Q 32

LETTERS FROM SETTLERS and Labouring Emigrants in the New Zealand Company's Settlement of Wellington, &c. 8vo. Lond., 1843. MD 3 Q 30

R

LETTRES SUR LES ILES MARQUISES ; par le P. Mathias G. * * * 8vo. Paris, 1843. MD 7 S 24

LEUSDEN, J. Grammaticæ Hebræe. [*See* Buxtorf, J.]

LEUTEMANN, H. Graphic Pictures of Native Life in Distant Lands ; explanatory text by Prof. A. Kirchoff ; translated by G. Philip, Junr. 4to. Lond., 1888.
A 36 P 24 ‡

LEVERMORE, C. H. Republic of New Haven. [*See* Johns Hopkins University Studies.]

LEVEY, G. C. Handy Guide to Australasia, including [New Zealand, Fiji, and New Guinea.] 8vo. Lond., 1891. MD 2 W 1 9
Hutchinson's Australasian Encyclopædia, comprising a description of all places in the Australasian Colonies, an account of the events which have taken place in Australasia from its Discovery to the present date, and Biographies of distinguished Early Colonists. 8vo. Lond., 1892. MK 2 P 3

LEVEY, M. The Venus Polka. Fol. Sydney (n.d.)
MA 11 Q 15 †
The I Don't Know Polka. Fol. Sydney (n.d.)
MA 11 Q 15 †

LEVEY, W. The Victorian Stud Book, containing pedigrees of Race Horses, &c. 2 vols. 8vo. Melb., 1859-65.
MA 3 Q 24, 25

LEVI, L. International Law. 8vo. Lond., 1887.
F 6 Q 41

LEVISON, J. L. Lecture on the Hereditary Tendency of Drunkenness. 18mo. Lond., 1839. F 11 P 6

LEVY, Amy. A Minor Poet, and other verse. 2nd ed. 12mo. Lond., 1891. H 8 T 50

LEWES, G. H. Biographical History of Philosophy. 4 vols. (in 2) 18mo. Lond., 1845-51. G 9 U 1, 2
Another copy. 8vo. Lond., 1857. G 16 S 39
Studies in Animal Life. 8vo. Lond., 1862. A 27 Q 40

LEWIN, F. S. Songs of the South. 12mo. Adelaide, 1884. MH 1 Q 67

LEWIN, J. W. Natural History of the Lepidopterous Insects of New South Wales. 4to. Lond., 1822.
MA 1 P 37 †

LEWIS, Bailie. The Gothenburg Licensing System. 8vo. Edinb., 1873. F 11 R 38

LEWIS, D. Britain's Social State. 18mo. Glasgow, 1878. F 11 P 1
Drink Traffic in the 19th Century. 12mo. Lond., 1885. F 11 P 43
Drink Problem and its Solution. 2nd ed. 8vo. Lond., 1883. F 11 Q 11

LEWIS, Mrs. L. L. Fatal Shadows. 12mo. Bristol, 1887. MJ 1 P 37

LEWIS, N. E. The Law relating to Parliamentary Elections in Tasmania. 12mo. Hobart, 1886. MF 2 P 69

LEWIS, T. Hope. Medical Guide to the Mineral Waters of Rotorua. 12mo. Auckland, 1885.　　MA 3 P 36

LEXICON GRÆCO-LATINUM. Fol. Basileœ, 1541.　　K 42 Q 8 ‡

LEYDEN, John. Historical Account of Discoveries and Travels in Africa; enlarged and completed by H. Murray. 2 vols. 8vo. Edinb., 1817.　　D 14 T 2, 3

LEYLAND, John. The Peak of Derbyshire. 8vo. Lond., 1891.　　D 18 R 6

The Yorkshire Coast and the Cleveland Hills and Dales. Illustrated. 8vo. Lond., 1892.　　D 18 R 16

LEYS, Thompson W. A Weird Region: New Zealand Lakes, Terraces, Geysers, and Volcanoes. Roy. 8vo. Auckland, 1887.　　MD 7 R 47

The Doctrine of Evolution. 8vo. Auckland, 1882.　　MA 3 S 25

[*See* Sherrin, R. A. A.] .

L'HERMITE, J. Journael van de Nassausche Vloot, 1623–1626. 8vo. Amstalredam, 1648.　　MD 1 R 47

[*See* Candish, T.]

L'HOPITAL, Chancelier M. Vie du; par A. F. Villemain. 12mo. Paris, 1874.　　B 35 R 26

LIBANIUS. [*See* Julian, Emperor.]

LIBRARY, The: a magazine of Bibliography, &c. Vols. 1–3. 8vo. Lond., 1889–91.　　E 1. 25

LIBRARY ASSOCIATION OF THE UNITED KINGDOM, Transactions and Proceedings of. 3 vols., 1880–81. Imp. 8vo. Lond., 1890.　　E 1. 74

LIBRARY CHRONICLE, The. Vols. 3–5. Roy. 8vo. Lond., 1886–88.　　E 1. 59

LIBRARY JOURNAL. Vols. 11–16. 4to. New York, 1886–91.　　E 2. 75

LIBURN, W. D. [*See* Leavitt, T. W.]

LICENSING SYSTEM. Report by Her Majesty's Commissioners for enquiring into the Licensing System and Sale and Consumption of Excisable Liquors in Scotland. 2 vols. roy. 8vo. Edinb., 1860.　　F 11 T 5, 6

LICTOR, The: an Illustrated Political, Facetious, and Satirical Journal. 4to. Sydney, 1869–70.　　MF 17 S

LIDDELL, Col. R. S. Memoirs of the Tenth Royal Hussars. Roy. 8vo. Lond., 1891.　　D 5 V 4

LIEBE, Julic. [*See* Burnouf, E.]

LIEBERMANN, F. Ungedruckte Anglo-Normannische Geschichtsquellen. 8vo. Strassburg, 1879.　　B 6 S 12

LIEBETRUT, Dr. F. Brœndevinsdrikkens Nytte og Skade. 12mo. Bergen, 1841.　　F 11 P 22

LIEBIG, J. von, Baron. Familiar Letters on Chemistry in its relations to Physiology, Dietetics, Agriculture, Commerce, and Political Economy. 4th ed. edited by J. Blyth. 8vo. Lond., 1859.　　A 21 R 4

LIEVEN, Princess D. Correspondence of Princess Lieven and Earl Grey; edited and translated by Guy Le Strange. 3 vols. 8vo. Lond., 1890.　　C 14 T 7–9

LIFE AND DEATH OF THOMAS LORD CROMWELL: a Tragedy. [*See* British Drama, Ancient.]

LIFE, ADVENTURES, AND CONFESSIONS OF A SYDNEY BARMAID. 12mo. Sydney, 1891.　　MC 1 Q 54

LIGHTFOOT, Rev. John. Eternal Torment: a written debate between the Rev. J. Lightfoot and C. Bradlaugh. 12mo. Lond., 1884.　　G 2 V 27

LIGHTFOOT, Rt. Rev. Dr. Jos. B. Essays on the work entitled Supernatural Religion. 8vo. Lond., 1889.　　G 6 R 36

St. Paul's Epistles to the Colossians and to Philemon. 8th ed. 8vo. Lond., 1886.　　G 6 R 37

St. Paul's Epistle to the Galatians. 9th ed. 8vo. Lond., 1887.　　G 6 R 38

St. Paul's Epistle to the Philippians. 8th ed. 8vo. Lond., 1888.　　G 6 R 39

LIGHTHOUSES. Report on the Necessity of a Lighthouse on Cape Pine, Newfoundland. Statement of Progress in the Construction of a Lighthouse on Barbadoes. Statement of Measures taken with reference to Management of Lighthouses in the British Colonies. Fol. Lond., 1849.　　MF 12 Q 15 †

Statement of what Measures have been adopted respecting the Erection, Management, and Superintendence of Lighthouses in the British Colonies and Possessions; and, Abstract of any Returns received from the Colonies upon the Subject since 1849. Fol. Lond., 1850. MF 12 Q 15†

LIGNE, Princesse Hélène de. Memoirs of; edited by L. Percy, translated by L. Ensor. 2 vols. 8vo. Lond., 1887.　　C. 13 R 5, 6

LIGUE PATRIOTIQUE. Journal de la Ligue Patriotique contre l'Alcoolisme. 4to. Bruxelles, 1884–86.　　F 42 R 25 ‡

LILLIE, A. Buddhism in Christendom; or, Jesus, the Essene. 8vo. Lond., 1887.　　G 12 T 37

LILLO, George. Arden of Feversham: a Tragedy. [*See* British Drama, Modern, 2.]

Fatal Curiosity: a Tragedy. [*See* British Drama, Modern, 2.]

George Barnwell: a Tragedy. [*See* British Drama, Modern, 2.]

LILLY, W. S. Century of Revolution. 8vo. Lond., 1889.　　B 26 U 1

On Shibboleths. 8vo. Lond., 1892.　　G 12 S 37

On Right and Wrong. 8vo. Lond,, 1890.　　G 12 S 35

LILLYWHITE, W. Lillywhite's Hand-book of Cricket. [*See* Cricket, Chronicles of.]

LINCOLN, Abraham: a History; by J. G. Nicolay and J. Hay. 10 vols. 8vo. New York, 1890.　　C 15 T 1–10

LINCOLNE, A. The Farm and Selection, containing useful information to the Farmer and Selector. 12mo. Sydney, 1878. MA 1 P 76

LINCOLN'S INN. Catalogue of printed books in the Library of the Hon. Society of Lincoln's Inn; by W. H. Spilsbury. 8vo. Lond., 1859. K 8 R 13 †
Supplementary Volume [to Catalogue] containing additions, 1859-1890; by J. Nicholson. 8vo. Lond., 1890. K 8 R 14 †

LINCOLNSHIRE NOTES AND QUERIES. Vols. 1, 2. 8vo. Horncastle, 1889-91. E 1. 40

LIND, Jenny. [*See* Goldschmidt, Mdme. Jenny Lind.]

LIND, Dr. J. G. De Delirio Tremente sic dicto. 8vo. Hauniæ, 1822. F 11 Q 12

LINDLEY, J. Elements of Botany, with a Glossary of Technical Terms. New ed. 8vo. Lond., 1849. A 20 T 4
Introduction to Botany. 4th ed. 2 vols. 8vo. Lond., 1848. A 20 T 2, 3
Medical and Œconomical Botany. 2nd ed. Illustrated. 8vo. Lond., 1856 A 20 T 5
Note upon a handsome and hardy plant called *Clianthus Puniceus.* 4to. Lond., 1834. A 36 P 22 ‡

LINDLEY, W., and WIDNEY, J. P. California of the South; its Climate, Resources, Routes of Travel, Physical Geography, and Health Resorts. 8vo. New York, 1888. D 15 Q 1

LINDSAY, J. A. Climatic Treatment of Consumption. 8vo. Lond., 1887. A 13 P 50

LINDSAY, J. L. [*See* Crawford and Balcarros, Earl of.]

LINDSAY, W. L. Contributions to New Zealand Botany. 4to. Lond., 1868. MA 12 P 15 †

LINDSEY, Rev. Theophilus. Memoirs of; by the Rev. T. Belsham. 8vo. Lond., 1812. C 15 U 6

LINDT, J. W. Picturesque New Guinea. Roy. 8vo. Lond., 1887. MD 3 V 35

LINES WRITTEN ON FIRST SEEING THE COMET (of September, 1882); by H. J. C. 8vo. Sydney, 1882. MH 1 Q 70

LINGARD, J. History of England, from the First Invasion by the Romans to 1688. 6th ed. 10 vols. 8vo. Lond., 1854-55. B 22 Q 12-22

LINGHAM, H. C. J. Juvenal in Melbourne; a Satire, Social and Political. 8vo. Melb., 1892. MH 1 U 27

LINNÆUS, Carl von. Through the Fields with Linnæus. 2 vols. 8vo. Lond., 1887. C 12 Q 14, 15
[*See* Clarson, W.]

LINNEAN SOCIETY, LONDON. Transactions. 2nd Series—Botany. Vol. 2. 4to. Lond., 1881-87. E 2. 67
Transactions. 2nd Series—Zoology. Vols. 2-4. 4to. Lond., 1879-88. E 2. 67
Journal. Zoology. Vols. 22-23. 8vo. Lond., 1888-91. E 1. 68

LINNEAN SOCIETY, LONDON—*contd.*
Journal. Botany. Vols. 22-28. 8vo. Lond., 1886-91. E 1. 68
General Index to the First Twenty Volumes of the Journal (Botany). 8vo. Lond., 1888. E 1. 68

LINNEAN SOCIETY OF NEW SOUTH WALES. Proceedings. Vols. 2-6, 2nd Series. 5 vols. 8vo. Sydney, 1887-92. ME 2 P & Q
Rules, with List of Members and Catalogue of the Library. 8vo. Sydney, 1882. MK 1 T 30
Account of Proceedings connected with the Dedication of a New Hall, Laboratory and Chambers. 8vo. Sydney, 1885. MB 1 Q 46
List of the Names of Contributors to the First Series of the Proceedings. 8vo. Sydney, 1887. ME 2 Q
Act of Incorporation, Rules, Lists of Members, &c., March, 1889. 8vo. Sydney, 1889. MF 4 R 22
Rules and List of Members, &c., July, 1883. 8vo. Sydney, 1883. MF 4 R 22
Rules and List of Members, &c., February, 1885. 8vo. Sydney, 1885. MF 4 R 22

LINTERN, W. The Mineral Surveyor and Valuer's Guide; with new Traverse Tables. (Weale.) 2nd ed. 12mo. Lond., 1887. A 17 R 19

LINTON, Mrs. Eliza Lynn. An Octave of Friends, with other Silhouettes and Stories. 8vo. Lond., 1891. J 1 U 12

LINTON, W. J. The English Republic; with notes by K. Parkes. 12mo. Lond., 1891. F 9 U 12
The Masters of Wood-engraving. Fol. New Haven, Conn., 1889. A 32 P 21 ‡

LINWOOD, Rev. W. Lexicon to Æschylus (Greek and Eng.) 8vo. Lond., 1843. K 19 S 30
Treatise on Greek Tragic Metres. 8vo. Lond., 1855. J 10 V 30

LIOY, Prof. D. The Philosophy of Right; translated by W. Hastie. 2 vols. 8vo. Lond., 1891. G 13 S 41, 42

LIPPINCOTT, J. R. & CO. Lippincott's Gazetteer of the World. Complete Pronouncing Gazetteer of the World. Imp. 8vo. Philad., 1880. D 11 V 10

LIPPMANN, F. Art of Wood-engraving in Italy in the 15th Century. Imp. 8vo. Lond., 1888. A 8 T 29

LIPSIUS, H. [*See* Leipziger Studien.]

LIQUOR LAWS. Papers regarding the Present Working of the Liquor Laws in Canada, the Australian Colonies, and New Zealand. Fol. Lond., 1891. MF 12 Q 14†

LISIANSKY, Capt. U. Voyage round the World, 1803-6. 4to. Lond., 1814. D 36 P 18†

LISZT, F. Correspondence of Wagner and Liszt, 1841-61; translated by F. Hueffer. 2 vols. 8vo. Lond., 1888. C 14 R 2, 3
Recollections of a Compatriot; by J. Wohl. 8vo. Lond., 1887. C 15 Q 22

LITERARISCHES CENTRALBLATT FÜR DEUTSCHLAND. 4to. Berlin, 1886-91. E 2. 78

LITHGOW, William. Statement of value of Compensations for Land. [*See* New South Wales—Crown Lands.]

LITTLE, A. J. Through the Yang-tze Gorges ; or, Trade and Travel in Western China. 8vo. Lond., 1888.
D 16 U 6

LITTLE, Rev. H. W. Henry M. Stanley, his Life, Travels, and Explorations. 8vo. Lond., 1890.　　C 12 S 7

LITTLE, J. W. Treatise on the Orchards and Gardens of the Western Districts. 8vo. Bathurst, 1877.
MA 2 T 62

LITTLETON, Dr. Adam. Linguæ Romanæ Dictionarium Luculentum Novum. Sm. 4to. Camb., 1693.　K 14 Q 37

LITURGIA, cu Liber Precum Communium in Ecclesia Anglicana Receptus. 12mo. Lond., 1706.　G 8 P 28

LIVERSIDGE, Prof. A. Analyses of Queensland Soils. 8vo. Lond., 1881.　　MA 3 R 23

Anniversary Address [delivered to the Royal Society of New South Wales, 1890.] 8vo. Sydney, 1890.
MA 2 T 61

Australian Meteorites. 8vo. Melb., 1890. MA 3 R 23

Chalk and Flints from the Solomon Islands. 8vo. Melb., 1890.　　MA 3 R 23

Deniliquin or Barratta Meteorite. 8vo. Sydney, 1883.
MA 3 R 23

Examples of Pseudo-Crystallization. 8vo. Sydney, 1876.
MA 3 R 23

List of Mineral Localities of New South Wales. Roy. 8vo. Lond. (n.d.)　　MA 3 R 23

List of Scientific Papers and Reports by. 8vo. Sydney, 1892.　　MA 3 R 23

Metallic Meteorite, Queensland. 8vo. Sydney, 1887.
MA 3 R 23

Minerals of New South Wales, &c. Roy. 8vo. Lond., 1888.　　MA 2 R 27

Note on some Bismuth Minerals, Molybdenite and Enhydros. Roy. 8vo. Sydney, 1892.　MA 3 R 23

Notes on the Bingera Diamond Field, with Notes on the Mudgee Diamond Field. 8vo. Sydney (n.d.)
MA 3 R 23

Notes on some New South Wales Minerals. (Notes 3–6.) 8vo. Sydney, 1885–91.　　MA 3 R 23

Notes on some Rocks and Minerals from New Guinea. 8vo. Sydney, 1887.　　MA 3 R 23

On Iron Rust possessing Magnetic Properties. 8vo. Hobart, 1892.　　MA 3 R 23

On the Bingera Meteorite, New South Wales. 8vo. Sydney, 1883.　　MA 3 R 23

On the Chemical Composition of Certain Rocks, New South Wales. 8vo. Sydney, 1883.　MA 3 R 23

On the Composition of Some Pumice and Lava from the Pacific. 8vo. Sydney, 1887.　MA 3 R 23

On the Presence of Magnetite in Certain Minerals and Rocks. 8vo. Hobart, 1892.　MA 3 R 23

On the removal of Gold from Suspension and Solution by Fungoid Growths. 8vo. Melb., 1890.　MA 3 R 23

LIVERSIDGE, Prof. A.—*contd.*
A Peculiar Copper Ore from Coombing Copper Mine, New South Wales. 8vo. Sydney, 1881.　MA 3 R 23

President's address [delivered to the Royal Society of N.S.W., 1886.] 8vo. Sydney, 1886.　MA 2 T 60

The Proposed Chemical Laboratory at the University of Sydney. Fol. Sydney, 1888.　MA 3 P 15 ‡

Rocks from New Britain and New Ireland. 8vo. Sydney, 1883.　　MA 3 R 23

Stilbite from Kerguelen's Island. 8vo. Hobart, 1892.
MA 3 R 23

LIVING LEADERS OF THE WORLD. 4to. Lond., 1889.　　C 12 V 9

LIVINSTONE, David. [Life of ;] by Thomas Hughes. 8vo. Lond., 1889.　　C 15 Q 11

Livingstone and the Exploration of Africa. [*See* Johnston, H. H.]

LIVIUS, T. Historiarum libri qui supersunt ; accurante T. Ruddimanno. 4 vols. 12mo. Edinb., 1772.
B 30 P 3–6

Historiarum libri qui supersunt omnes, ex recensione A. Drakenborchii. 3 vols. 8vo. Lond., 1842.
B 30 V 8–10

Livy ; by Rev. Canon Collins. (Ancient Classics for English Readers.) 12mo. Edinb., 1880.　J 14 P 16

LLOYD, Eleanor. [*See* Gatty, Mrs. Alfred.]

LLOYD, Mrs. G. A. The Wheel of Life : a Domestic Tale of Australian Life. 8vo. Sydney, 1880.　MJ 1 R 18

LOBLEY, Prof. J. L. Mount Vesuvius : a descriptive, historical, and geological account of the Volcano and its surroundings. 8vo. Lond., 1889.　A 24 U 5

LOBOS, Prof. R. Villa- [*See* Villa-Lobos, Prof. R.]

LOCAL LETTER CARRIER, A. [*See* After Twenty Years.]

LOCAL OPTION at Bessbrook, the Temperance Colony in Ireland. 12mo. Lond., 1884.　F 11 P 30

LOCH, Sir Henry B. Extracts from a Report of the Reception of Sir Henry Loch on his assuming the Governorship of South Africa, &c. 8vo. Auckland, 1890.
MB 2 Q 47

Personal Narrative of Occurrences during Lord Elgin's Second Embassy to China, 1860. 2nd ed. 8vo. Lond., 1870.　　D 17 Q 3

LOCHER, C. An Explanation of the Organ Stops ; with Hints for Effective Combinations ; translated by Agnes Schauenburg. 8vo. Lond., 1888.　A 23 T 3

LOCK, C. G. W. Workshop Receipts. [*See* Spon, E.]

LOCK, Rev. J. B. Treatise on Elementary Trigonometry and Higher Trigonometry. 12mo. Lond., 1889.
A 25 P 31

LOCKE, John. [Life of] ; by Prof. A. C. Fraser. 12mo. Edinb., 1890.　　C 12 P 20

Essays. [*See* Universal Library, The.]

Works. New ed. 10 vols. 8vo. Lond., 1823.
J 17 P 25–34

LOCKER, A. [*See* Caldecott, R.]

LOCKER-LAMPSON, F. Lyra Elegantiarum, social and occasional verse, by deceased English authors. 12mo. Lond., 1891. H 6 R 45

LOCKETT, G. F. Mining Manual and Handy Compendium of "The Mining Companies' Act, 1871." 8vo. Melb., 1871. MF 2 T 29

LOCKHART, W. Life of A. Rosmini-Serbati, Founder of the Institute of Charity. 2nd ed. 2 vols. 8vo. Lond., 1886. C 16 Q 9, 10

LOCKYER, Prof. J. N. The Meteoritic Hypothesis : a statement of the Results of a Spectroscopic Inquiry into the Origin of Cosmical Systems. 8vo. Lond., 1890. A 19 T 20

Studies in Spectrum Analysis. 8vo. Lond., 1878. A 21 Q 36

Chemistry of the Sun. Roy. 8vo. Lond., 1887. A 3 U 29

Outlines of Physiography : the Movements of the Earth. 12mo. Lond., 1887. A 19 P 25

LOCKWOOD, C. & SON. Lockwood's Dictionary of Terms used in the Practice of Mechanical Engineering. 8vo. Lond., 1888 K 18 P 30

LODGE, E. Peerage and Baronetage of the British Empire, 1888–92. 5 vols. roy. 8vo. Lond., 1888–92. E

LODGE, H. C. [Life of] George Washington. (American Statesmen.) 2 vols. 12mo. Boston, 1889. C 13 Q 5, 6

Boston. (Historic Towns.) 8vo. Lond., 1891. B 3 Q 6

LODGE, Prof. Oliver J. Lightning Conductors and Lightning Guards. 8vo. Lond., 1892. A 21 Q 35

Modern Views of Electricity. 12mo. Lond., 1889. A 21 P 1

LODGE, T. [*See* Hunterian Club.]

LOEWE, J. K. G. [Life of ;] by A. B. Bach. Sm. 4to. Edinb., 1890. C 14 R 32

LOEWE, Dr. L. [*See* Montefiore, Sir M.]

LOFTIE, W. J. Kensington, picturesque and historical. Roy. 8vo. Lond., 1888. B 3 V 6

London City. 4to. Lond., 1891. D 19 V 15

Orient Line Guide : chapters for Travellers by Sea and by Land. 3rd ed. Sm. 4to. Lond., 1889. D 10 S 31

Another copy. Sm. 4to. Lond., 1885. MD 5 R 50

Westminster Abbey. 8vo. Lond., 1891. B 5 T 32

LOFTUS, Rt. Hon. A. W. F. S., Lord. Diplomatic Reminiscences of; 1837–62. 2 vols. 8vo. Lond., 1892. C 18 Q 4, 5

LOGEMAN, Dr. H. The Rule of St. Benet. [*See* Early Eng. Text Soc.]

LOGEMAN, W. S. [*See* Strong, Prof. H. A.]

LOGGAN, D. Oxonia Illustrata. Fol. Oxoniæ, 1675. B 29 Q 14 ‡

LOGIN, Sir John, and Duleep Singh; by Lady Login. 8vo. Lond., 1890. C 15 U 10

LOGIN, Lina, Lady. Sir John Login and Duleep Singh. 8vo. Lond., 1890. C 15 U 10

LOIR, A. La Microbiologie en Australie ; études d'Hygiène et de Pathologie comparée poursuivies à l'Institut Pasteur de Sydney. Roy. 8vo. Paris, 1892. MA 3 R 24

[*See* Bruce, A.]

LOMAX, B. Bells and Bellringers. 12mo. Lond., 1879. A 23 Q 16

LOMBROSO, Prof. C. Alcoolismo acuto e chronico, e delle Leggi per prevenirlo. 8vo. Torino (n.d.) F 11 S 30

The Man of Genius. 8vo. Lond., 1891. A 26 Q 15

LONDON, Edinburgh, and Dublin Philosophical Magazine. [*See* Philosophical Magazine.]

LONDON DIALECTICAL SOCIETY. Report on Spiritualism. 8vo. Lond., 1871. G 12 S 38

LONDON POST OFFICE DIRECTORY. Roy. 8vo. Lond., 1890. E 1. 78

LONDON SCHOOL BOARD. Code of Regulations for the Guidance of Managers and Teachers. Sm. fol. Lond., 1879. G 39 P 18 †

LONDON PRODIGAL, The : a comedy. [*See* British Drama, Ancient, 1.]

LONDON TO MELBOURNE; by "Marchamp Longway." (J. C. P. W.) 8vo. Lond., 1889. MD 3 P 52

LONDON UNIVERSITY CALENDAR. 6 vols. 12mo. Lond., 1887–92. E 2. 80

LONDON, The. Wreck of. 8vo. Lond., 1866. MD 2 R 39

LONDONDERRY, Marquess of. Story of the Peninsular War. New ed. 8vo. Lond., 1849. B 17 P 24

LONG, Major S. H. Expedition to the Rocky Mountains. [*See* James, E.]

LONG, W. H. [*See* Hamilton, Emma, Lady, *and* Oglander, Sir J.]

LONG TIME AGO. [Song.] Fol. Sydney (n.d.) MA 11 Q 15 †

LONGFELLOW, H. W. Final Memorials of ; edited by Samuel Longfellow. 8vo. Lond., 1887. C 5 U 28

LONGFELLOW, S. [*See* Longfellow, H. W.]

LONGINUS, D. C. Libellus [De Sublimitate], cum notis, &c., T. Fabri. 18mo. Salmurii, 1663. G 9 U 10

De Sublimitate ; J. Tollius emendavit. [With French translation by Mons. Despreaux.] (Gr., Lat., and French.) Sm. 4to. Traj. ad Rhen., 1694. J 18 V 20

LONGMAN'S MAGAZINE. Vols. 4–12. 8vo. Lond., 1885–88. E 2. 44

LONGMAN'S NEW ATLAS, Political and Physical; edited by G. G. Chisholm. 4to. Lond., 1889. D 33 Q 18 ‡

LONGMAN'S SCHOOL GEOGRAPHY. [*See* Chisholm, G. G.]

LONGMORE, Sir T. Richard Wiseman, Surgeon to Charles II; a Biographical Study. 8vo. Lond., 1891.
C 17 T 20

LONGSTAFF, G. B. Studies in Statistics, social, political, and medical. Roy. 8vo. Lond., 1891. F 1 V 1

LONGUS. Pastorales de Longus ou Daphnis et Chloé. (Collection Jannet-Picard.) 12 mo. Paris (n.d.) J 15 Q 23

LONGWAY, Marchamp. [*See* London to Melbourne.]

LONLAY, Dick de. [*See* Hardoin, N.]

LOOMIS, Prof. Elias. Treatise on Astronomy. 8vo. New York, 1880. A 19 U 28

Treatise on Meteorology. 8vo. New York, 1890.
A 19 U 29

LORD'S DAY OBSERVANCE. First and Second Annual Reports of the New South Wales Society for Promoting the Observance of the Lord's Day. 8vo. Sydney, 1857-58. ME 6 Q

Progress Report of the Committee of the N. S. W. Society for Promoting the Observance of the Lord's Day. 8vo. Sydney, 1883. ME 6 Q

LORD'S SUPPER, Observations on the Nature of the Sacrament of the. 2nd ed. 8vo. Oxford, 1852.
G 16 R 35

LORENZ, Otto. Catalogue Général de la Librairie Française depuis 1840. Tomes IX-XI. Roy. 8vo. Paris, 1886-88. Libr.

LORNE, Marquis of. [*Life of*] Viscount Palmerston. 2nd ed. 12mo. Lond., 1892. C 13 Q 21

LORRY, Dr. A. C. Hippocratis Aphorismi. [*See* Hippocrates.]

LOSERTH, Dr. J. [*See* Wiclif, J.]

LOTT, Emmeline. The Governess in Egypt : Harem Life in Egypt and Constantinople. 2 vols. 8vo. Lond., 1865.
D 1 T 25, 26

LOVAT, Simon Fraser, Lord. Major Fraser's Manuscript : his Adventures in Scotland and England ; his Mission to and Travels in France in search of his Chief ; his Services in the Rebellion (with his quarrels) with Simon Fraser, Lord Lovat, 1696-1737 ; edited by Lieut.-Col. A. Fergusson. 2 vols. 12mo. Edinb., 1889. C 2 P 7, 8

LOVE, Jas. Scottish Church Music, its composers and sources. 8vo. Edinb., 1891. A 23 R 5

LOVELESS, G. Victims of Whiggery, &c.; with Reflections upon the present system of Transportation, and an Account of Van Dieman's Land. 8vo. Lond., 1837.
MF 3 R 20

LOVELL, J. The Great Trial : Fair Trade v. Free Trade. 8vo. Lond., 1886. F 5 U 35

LOVETT, Rev. Richard. Irish Pictures drawn with Pen and Pencil. Imp. 8vo. Lond., 1888. D 19 V 3

London Pictures drawn with Pen and Pencil. Imp. 8vo. Lond., 1890. D 19 V 4

Pictures from Holland, drawn with pen and Pencil. Imp. 8vo. Lond., 1887. D 19 V 2

LOW, C. R. Memoir of Lieut.-Gen. Sir Garnet J. Wolseley. 2 vols. 8vo. Lond., 1878. C 12 Q 22, 23

LOW, D. Domesticated Animals of the British Islands. 8vo. Lond. (n.d.) A 27 U 11

LOW, D. A. Introduction to Machine Drawing and Design. 8vo. Lond., 1887. A 22 Q 28

LOW, S., & CO. English Catalogue of Books, 1872-80. 8vo. Lond., 1882. Libr.

English Catalogue of Books, 1887-91. 8vo. Lond., 1888-91. Libr.

LOWE, R. Letter to the Hon. J. T. Bigge, in reply to four questions on Convict discipline and Agriculture. 5th July, 1820. 8vo. Sydney, 1890. MF 2 P 56

LOWE, Rt. Hon. Robert, Viscount Sherbrooke. [*See* Sherbrooke, Viscount.]

LOWE, Robert W. Thomas Betterton. (Eminent Actors.) 12mo. Lond., 1891. C 12 P 42

Bibliographical Account of English Theatrical Literature, from the Earliest Times to the Present Day. Imp. 8vo. Lond., 1888. K 19 V 3

[*See* Cibber, C.]

[*See* Doran, J.]

LOWE, S., MARSTON, and CO. English Catalogue of Books. Vol. 4. 1881-89. 8vo. Lond., 1891. Libr.

LOWELL, J. R. Latest Literary Essays and Addresses. 8vo. Lond., 1891. J 11 W 19

Political Essays. 8vo. Lond., 1888. F 6 T 34

Writings of. 10 vols. 8vo. Lond., 1890. J 11 R 32-41
1—4. Literary Essays.
5. Political Essays.
6. Literary and Political Addresses.
7—10. Poems.

LÖWENTHAL, J. The Chess Congress of 1862 : a Collection of Games played, and a Selection of the Problems sent in for Competition ; with an Account of the Proceedings and a Memoir of the British Chess Association ; by G. W. Medley. 8vo. Lond., 1889. A 29 P 6

LOWNDES, Mary E. Psychology. [*See* Höffding, H.]

LOWTH, Rt. Rev. R. De Sacra Poesi Hebræorum. 8vo. Oxonii, 1821. H 10 R 16

Isaiah : a new Translation ; with Notes. 8vo. Lond., 1833. G 16 S 49

LÖWY, Bella. [*See* Graetz, Prof. H.]

LUARD, H. R. Flores Historiarum. [*See* Chronicles and Memorials of Great Britain, &c.]

LUBBOCK, Sir J. On the Senses, Instincts, and Intelligence of Animals, with special reference to Insects. 3rd ed. (Inter. Scient. Series.) 8vo. Lond., 1889.
A 14 Q 55
Origin of Civilisation and the Primitive Condition of Man ; Mental and Social Condition of Savages. 5th ed. 8vo. Lond., 1890.
A 18 T 25
Pre-historic Times, as Illustrated by Ancient Remains, Manners and Customs of Modern Savages. 5th ed. 8vo. Lond., 1890.
A 18 T 26
The Pleasures of Life. 2 vols. 12mo. Lond., 1890.
G 16 Q 47, 48
The Races of the British Isles—Mr. Gladstone and the Nationalities of the United Kingdom: a Series of Letters to the *Times.* Sm. 4to. Lond., 1887.
A 1 W 41

LUCANUS, M. A. De Bello Civili ; accurante C. Schrevelio. 12mo. Amstel., 1658.
H 10 P 19
Pharsalia Studiis Societatis Bipontinæ. 8vo. Biponti, 1783.
H 10 R 4
Pharsalia; edited, with English Notes by C. E. Haskins. 8vo. Lond., 1887.
H 6 S 34

LUCAS, C. P. Historical Geography of the British Colonies. Vols. 1 & 2. 8vo. Oxford, 1888-90.
D 11 S 13, 14
Introduction to a Historical Geography of the British Colonies. 8vo. Oxford, 1887.
D 11 S 12

LUCAS, Rev. D. V. Australia and Homeward. 8vo. Toronto, 1888.
MD 7 P 13

LUCAS, F. W. Appendiculæ Historicæ ; or, Shreds of History hung on a Horn. 4to. Lond., 1891. D 18 V 8

LUCAS, J. Letter on the Land Question written to the Hon. James Martin, M.P. 8vo. Sydney, 1867.
MF 1 T 2

LUCAS, R. B. Review of Existing Legislation on Weights and Measures in the Australian Colonies, together with a Scheme for Unification System, in view of Federation. 8vo. Adelaide, 1891.
MF 2 T 28

LUCAS, Dr. T. P. True Action and Physiological Results of Alcohol. 12mo. Lond. (n.d.)
F 11 P 33
Laws of Life and Alcohol. 12mo. Lond., 1877.
F 11 P 50

LUCIAN. Opera, cum nova versione T. Hemsterhusii et J. M. Gesneri. (Great Lat.) 3 vols. 4to. Amstelodami, 1743.
J 18 V 14-16
Index verborum ac, phrasium Luciani, à C. C. Reitzio. 4to. Rhenum, 1746.
J 18 V 17
Lucian ; by the Rev. Canon Collins. (Ancient Classics for English readers.) 12mo. Edinb., 1880. J 14 P 17
Lucian's Dialogues of the Gods, and of the Dead, &c.; translated by H. Williams. 8vo. Lond., 1688. J 11 Q 35

LUCK, H. C. Queensland ; a Sketch. 8vo. Melb., 1888.
MD 3 T 41

LUCRETIUS CARUS, T. Lucretius ; by W. H. Mallock. (Ancient Classics for English Readers.) 12mo. Edinb., 1887.
J 14 P 18
De Rerum Natura et Commentarius ; recensuit C. Lachmannus. 8vo. Berolini, 1850-53. H 10 R 16

LUDWIG SALVATOR, Archduke. Hobarttown oder Sommerfrische in den Antipoden. 4to. Prag, 1886.
MD 1 Q 31 †

LUMHOLTZ, C. Among Cannibals, an account of four years' Travels in Australia. 8vo. Lond., 1889.
MD 7 S 5
Blandt Menneskeædere ; fire aars Reise i Australien. 8vo. Kjobenhavn, 1888. MD 5 T 4

LUND, T. W. M. Como and Italian Lake-land. 8vo. Lond., 1887.
D 19 Q 11

LUNDIE, G. A. Missionary Life in Samoa, as exhibited in the Journals of the late George A. Lundie. 12mo. Edinb., 1846.
MD 2 Q 23

LUNGE, Dr. G. Coal Tar and Ammonia. 8vo. Lond., 1887
A 5 T 19

LUNGE, Dr. G., MEYER, Dr. V., and SCHULZE, Dr. E. Zur Alkoholfrage ; Fuselöls im Sprit. 8vo. Bern, 1884.
F 11 R 40

LUNIER, Dr. L. De la Production et de la Consommation des Boissons Alcooliques en France. roy. 8vo. Paris, 1877.
F 11 T 7

LUNN, H. C. Musings of a Musician. 12mo. Lond., 1854.
A 23 Q 43

LUPTON, J. H. Life of John Colet, D.D. 8vo. Lond., 1887.
C 12 T 21

LUTHER, M.: his Life and Work; by P. Bayne. 2 vols. 8vo. Lond., 1887.
C 13 T 17, 18
Hauspostill. Fol. Jhena, 1568. G 39 P 7 ‡

LUTTEROTH, H. O—Taïti Histoire et Enquête. Roy. 8vo. Paris, 1843.
MB 2 R 45

LYALL, Sir Alfred. Warren Hastings. (English Men of Action.) 12mo. Lond., 1889. C 12 P 35

LYDEKKER, R. [*See* Flower, Dr. W. H.]

LYDGATE, John. Temple of Glas. [*See* Early English Text Soc.]

LYELL, A., and GOWAN, J. D. The Victorian Insolvent list, comprising Insolvencies and Assignments from June 1862 to December, 1866. 4to. Melb., 1867. MF 1 U 39

LYELL, Sir C. Manual of Elementary Geology. 5th ed. 8vo. London, 1855.
A 24 T 7
The Student's Elements of Geology. 3rd ed., illustrated. 8vo. Lond., 1878.
A 24 P 8

LYLY, J. Alexander and Campaspe. [*See* British Drama, Ancient, 1.]

LYNCH, J. Egyptian Sketches. 8vo. Lond., 1890.
D 14 U 18

LYNE, C. Industries of New South Wales. Roy. 8vo. Sydney, 1882.   MF 2 S 8

LYONS, J. C. The Chemistry of Soils and Manures. 2nd ed. 8vo. Sydney, 1873.   MA 2 T 63

LYRA ROMANA ; or, Extracts from Horace. [*See* Horatius Flaccus, Q.*]

LYSIAS. Quæ exstant omnia, illustravit G. S. Dobson. 8vo. Lond., 1828.   F 1 Q 32

LYTH. [*See* Golden South.]

LYTTELTON, R. H. [*See* Steel, A. G.]

LYTTON, E. G. E. L. Bulwer-Lytton, Baron. Speeches of. 2 vols. 8vo. Edinb., 1874.   F 13 Q 29, 30
The Coming Race. 8vo. Lond., 1871.   J 8 U 25

LYTTON, E. R. L. Bulwer-Lytton, Earl of. " Owen Meredith." Marah. 12mo. Lond., 1892.   H 8 T 51

LYTTON, Rosina, Lady Life of; with numerous Extracts from her MS. Autobiography, by Louisa Devey. 8vo. Lond., 1887.   C 12 8 19

M

MABINOGION, The Text of the, and other Welsh Tales, from the Red Book of Hergest; edited by Prof. J. Rhys and J. G. Evans. Roy. 8vo. Oxford, 1887.   J 4 U 7

MACALPINE, Prof. A. N. [*See* Stebler, Dr. F. G.]

M'ARTHUR, A. Transportation to Western Australia. Three Letters. 8vo. Lond., 1864.   MF 1 T 41

McARTHUR, Dr. J. [*See* Clarke, Rev. J. S.]

M'ARTHUR, Sir Wm. A Biography, religious, parliamentary, municipal, commercial ; by T. McCullagh. 8vo. Lond., 1891.   C 14 R 8

MACARTNEY, Rev. H. B. Conference Addresses delivered at St. Mary's, Caulfield, August, 1875. 12mo. Melb., 1875.   MG 2 P 32

MACASSEY, L. I. Private Bill Legislation and Provisional Orders: Hand-book for the use of Solicitors and Engineers. 8vo. Lond., 1887.   F 10 S 26

MACAULAY, G. C. [*See* Herodotus.]

MACAULAY, Dr. Jas. Victoria: her Life and Reign. Roy. 8vo. Lond., 1887.   C 12 V 7
[*See* Albert Edward, H.R.H., Prince of Wales.]

MacCALL, W. Biology. [*See* Letourneau, C.]

MacCALLUM, Prof. M. W. George Meredith : Poet and Novelist. A Public Lecture. 12mo. Sydney, 1892.   MC 1 P 66
Specimens of old French. Printed privately for class use in Sydney University. 8vo. Sydney, 1887.   MJ 3 Q 25

McCANN, Rev. Dr. Secularism, unphilosophical, immoral, and anti-social : verbatim report of a three-nights' debate between the Rev. Dr. McCann and C. Bradlaugh. 12mo. Lond., 1881.   G 2 V 27

MacCARTHY, J. Choix de Voyages ou Précis des Voyages les plus intéressans, par Terre et par Mer, entrepris depuis l'année 1806. 2 vols. 8vo. Paris, 1822.   MD 1 R 43, 44

McCARTHY, Justin H. History of the Four Georges. Vol. 2. 8vo. Lond., 1890.   B 23 U 17
The French Revolution. Vols. 1, 2. 8vo. Lond., 1890.   B 26 U 13, 14
Case for Home Rule. 8vo. Lond., 1887.   F 6 Q 42
Ireland since the Union: Sketches of Irish History 1798-1886. 8vo. Lond., 1887.   B 29 Q 12
Sir Robert Peel. 8vo. Lond., 1891.   C 16 Q 22
[*See* Omar Khayyam.]

McCARTHY, Justin, PRAED, Mrs. Campbell, and MEMPES, M. The Grey River. 4to. London, 1889.   D 6 R 3‡

MacCARTY, L. P. Annual Statistician. 5 vols. 8vo. San Francisco, 1887-92.   E

McCAUSLAND, D. Sermons in Stones ; or, Scripture confirmed by Geology. New ed. 12mo. Lond., 1857.   A 24 P 6

McCLELLAN, G. B. Macclellan's Own Story: the War for the Union. Roy. 8vo. Lond., 1887.   B 1 V 12

M'CLINTOCK Capt. Sir Francis Leopold. Voyage of the Fox in the Artic Seas : Narrative of the discovery of the Fate of Sir John Franklin and his Companions. 8vo. Lond., 1859.   D 4 R 20

McCONNOCHIE, A. J. [Description of] Bennachie. 12mo. Aberdeen, 1890.   B 13 P 6

McCOSH, Dr. T. The Prevailing Types of Philosophy, can they logically reach Reality? 8vo. Lond., 1891.   G 8 R 32

McCOSH, J. Psychology: the Motive Powers, Emotions, Conscience, Will. 8vo. Lond., 1887.   G 11 P 41
Realistic Philosophy defended in a Philosophic Series. 2 vols. 8vo. Lond., 1887.   G 11 P 36, 37

MacCOLI, N. [*See* Calderon de la Barca, Don P.]

McCOY, Prof. F. Natural History of Victoria ; Prodromus of the Zoology of Victoria ; or, Figures and Descriptions of the Living Species of all Classes of Victorian Indigenous Animals. Vol. 2, decades XI-XX., imp. 8vo. Melb., 1890.   MA 2 P 30†

McCRAE, G. G. The Story of Balladeádro. 8vo. Melb., 1867.   MH 1 S 53

M'CULLAGH, T. Sir William McArthur, K.C.M.G., a Biography. 8vo. Lond., 1891.   C 14 R 8

McCULLOCH, H. Men and Measures of Half a Century ; Sketches and Comments. Roy. 8vo. Lond., 1888.   B 1 V 18

McCULLOCH, J. R. Treatise on the Principles and Practical Influence of Taxation and the Funding System, 3rd ed. Roy. 8vo. Edinb., 1863. F 10 S 23

McCURE, J. B. My Log-book; or, the History of my Voyage from London to Sydney. 8vo. Lond., 1868-69. MD 3 Q 29

McCUTCHEON, Capt. J. W. Catechism on Squad and Company Drill, Skirmishing and Attack. 12mo. Sydney, 1889. MA 2 V 42

McDERMOTT, F. Life and Work of Joseph Firbank, Railway Contractor. 8vo. Lond., 1887. C 7 T 10

MACDONALD, A. Too Late for Gordon and Khartoum, 8vo. Lond., 1887. D 14 S 2

MACDONALD, Donald. Gum Boughs and Wattle Bloom gathered on Australian Hills and Plains. 8vo. Lond., 1888. MD 1 Q 21

MACDONALD, Rev. D. Oceania: Linguistic and Anthropological. 8vo. Melb., 1889. MK 1 P 58
South Sea Languages: a Series of Studies on the Languages of the New Hebrides and other South Sea Islands. 2 vols. 12mo. Melb., 1889-91. MK 2 P 8, 9
Vol. 1—Three New Hebrides Languages (Efatese, Eromangan, Santo).
Vol. 2—Tangoan-Santo, Malo-Malekula, Epi (Baki and Bierian), Tauna and Futuna.

MACDONALD, D. C. [*See* Ogilvie, W.]

MACDONALD, G. A Threefold Cord : Poems by Three Friends; edited by G. Macdonald. 18mo. Lond., 1883. H 6 P 54

MACDONALD, James. [*See* Stephens, H.]

MACDONALD, Sir John. Anecdotal Life of ; by E. B. Biggar. 8vo. Montreal, 1891. C 18 R 20
Life and Career of; by G. M. Adam. 8vo. Lond., 1892. C 18 S 6

MACDONALD, J. D. Herald Waltzes. Fol. Sydney, (n.d.) MA 11 Q 15 †

McDONALD, J. D. Proceedings of the Expedition for the Exploration of the Rewa River and its Tributaries in Na Viti Levu, Fiji Islands. 8vo. Lond., 1857. MD 7 S 60

MACDONALD, J. M. The Great Volcano of Kilauea, Hawaiian Islands. 8vo. Honolulu, 1889. MD 7 S 27

MACDONALD, Marshal J.E.J.A., Duke of Tarentum, Recollections of ; edited by Camille Rousset; trans. by S. L. Simeon. 2 vols. 8vo. Lond., 1892. C 14 V 12, 13

MACDONALD, W. The Fair Apostate : a Tragedy. [*See* British Drama, Modern 2.]

MACDONALD, W. R. [*See* Napier, J.]

MACDONELL, Arthur A. Camping Voyages on German Rivers. 12mo. Lond., 1890. D 18 Q 15

MACDOUGALL, Rev. J. Folk and Hero Tales. (Waifs and Strays of Celtic Tradition). 8vo. Lond., 1891. B 32 T 13

M'DOUGALL, R. The Victorian Herd Book of 1870-75. 8vo. Melb., 1875. MA 3 Q 52

MACDOUGALL, W. J. The Lucy Escott Polka. Fol. Sydney (n.d.) MA 11 Q 15 †
Lurline Quadrilles. Fol. Sydney (n.d.) MA 11 Q 15 †

M'DOWALL, W. Among the Old Scotch Minstrels. 12mo. Edinb., 1888. H 5 S 43

McFARLANE, Rev. S. Among the Cannibals of New Guinea. 8vo. Lond., 1888. MD 1 Q 22
[*See* Murray, Rev. A. W.]

MACFARREN, Sir G. A. Addresses and Lectures. 8vo. Lond., 1888. A 8 P 49
[*See* Day, A.]

MACGIBBON, D. The Architecture of Provence and the Riviera. 8vo. Edinb., 1888. A 3 P 25

MACGIBBON, David, and ROSS, Thomas. The Castellated and Domestic Architecture of Scotland, 12th to the 18th Century. Vols. 1-5. roy. 8vo. Edinb., 1887-92. A 3 Q 21-25

McGILCHRIST, John. The Mutineers; a Poem. 12mo. Edinb., 1859. MH 1 U 30

M'GILL, P. The Victorian Almanac for 1862. 12mo. Melb., 1862. ME 4 P

MACGILLIVRAY, P. H. A Catalogue of the Marine Polyzoa of Victoria. 8vo. Melb., 1886. MA 3 Q 51
Descriptions of new or little known Polyzoa, Parts 1-12. 8vo. Melb., 1881-87. MA 3 Q 48

MACGREGOR, Major-Gen. Sir Charles M. Life and Opinions of ; edited by Lady C. MacGregor. 2 vols. 8vo. Edinb., 1888. C 13 U 21, 22

MACGREGOR, Charlotte, Lady. [*See* MacGregor, Sir C.M.]

MACHIAVELLI, N. Le Démon Marié. [*See* Contes Fantastiques.]
Il Principe ; edited by L. A. Burd. 8vo. Oxford, 1891. F 6 U 34

MACHIN, L. The Dumb Knight. [*See* Markham, J.]

M'HUTCHESON, W. The New Zealander Abroad. 8vo. Glasgow, 1888. MD 1 Q 50

MACINTYRE, Major-Gen. Donald, V. C., &c. Hindu-Koh ; Wanderings and Wild Sport on and beyond the Himalayas. Roy. 8vo. Edinb., 1889. D 17 U 3

McINTYRE, W. D. Manual of the Law of Real Property in force in New South Wales. 8vo. Sydney, 1892. MF 2 T 67

MACIVER, Brig.-Gen. R. Under Fourteen Flags: being the Life and Adventures of; by Capt. W. D. L'Estrange. 2 vols. 8vo. Lond., 1884. C 14 P 3, 4
Another copy. 8vo. Melb., 1884. MC 1 P 38

MACKAY, Æ. J. C. Sketch of the History of Fife and Kinross. 8vo. Edinb., 1890. B 32 Q 1

MACKAY, A. M. Pioneer Missionary of the Church Missionary Society to Uganda. [Life of] by his Sister. 8vo. Lond., 1890. C 5 Q 29

9

MACKAY Angus. Australian Agriculturist and Colonists' Guide. 2nd ed. 8vo. Sydney, 1890. MA 3 P 2
Grazing, Farm, and Garden Soils of New South Wales. 12mo. Sydney, 1888. MA 2 P 16
Introduction to Australian Agricultural Practice, arranged for Teachers and Pupils of the Public Schools. 8vo. Sydney, 1890. MA 3 P 1
Semi-Tropical Agriculturist and Colonists' Guide. 8vo. Brisb., 1875. MA 3 Q 47

MACKAY, Chas. Lost Beauties of the English Langauge. 8vo. Lond. (n.d.) K 16 P 36
Poetical Works of. 8vo. Lond., 1876. H 8 Q 34
Selected Poems and Songs of. 12mo. Lond., 1888. H 6 Q 42
Dictionary of Lowland Scotch. Sm. 4to. Edinb., 1888. K 12 U 7
Glossary of Obscure Words and Phrases in the Writings of Shakspeare and his Contemporaries. 8vo. Lond., 1887. K 12 U 6
Through the Long Day; or, Memorials of a Literary Life during Half-a-century. 2 vols. 8vo. Lond., 1887. C 12 R 23, 24

MACKAY, G. The History of Bendigo. 8vo. Melb., 1891. MB 2 Q 45

MACKAY, James. Our Dealings with Maori Lands. Roy. 8vo. Auckland, 1887. MF 3 T 7

McKAY, James. Pendle Hill in History and Literature. Roy. 8vo. Lond., 1888. B 21 U 20

MACKAY, Jessie. The Spirit of the Rangatira, and other Ballads. 8vo. Melb., 1889. MH 1 U 31
The Sitter on the Rail, and other poems. 12mo. Christchurch, 1891. MH 1 U 29

MACKAY, K. Stirrup Jingles from the Bush, Turf, &c. 2nd ed. 8vo. Sydney, 1887. MH 1 P 28

MACKAY, M. Substance of a Speech relative to the Erection of a Presbyterian College in connection with the University of Sydney. 8vo. Sydney, 1857. MG 1 R 63

MACKAY, R. W. A Sketch of the Rise and Progress of Christianity. 8vo. Lond., 1854. G 13 S 39

MACKAY, T. The English Poor: a Sketch of their Social and Economic History. 8vo. Lond., 1889. F 14 P 30
A Plea for Liberty ; an Argument against Socialism and Socialistic Legislation. 8vo. Lond., 1891. F 9 S 22

M'KEAN, J. A Treatise on the Law of Divorce and Matrimonial Causes in Victoria. 8vo. Melb., 1861. MF 3 T 16

McKELLAR, Campbell. The Premier's Secret, and other Tales. 12mo. Melb., 1887. MJ 3 P 15

MACKELLAR, Dr. C. K. Federal Quarantine. 8vo. Sydney, 1883. MA 2 T 13

McKENDRIK, Prof. J. G. Text-book of Physiology ; including Histology by P. Stöhr. 2 vols. 8vo. Glasgow, 1888-89. A 26 T 2, 3

McKENNEY, T. L. History of the Indian Tribes of North America, with Sketches of the Principal Chiefs. 3 vols. 4to. Philad., 1870. A 36 P 19-21‡

MACKENZIE, John. Austral Africa: Losing it, or Ruling it; being Incidents and Experiences in Bechuana-land, Cape Colony, and England. 2 vols. 8vo. Lond., 1887. B 16 T 25, 26

MACKENZIE, John, F.G.S. Description of Seams of Coal worked in New South Wales. 4to. Sydney, 1888.* MA 1 Q 36 †

MACKENZIE, Capt. T. A., EWART, Lieut. J. S., and FINDLAY, Lieut. C. Historical Records of the 79th Queen's Own Cameron Highlanders. 8vo. Lond., 1887. B 31 T 20

MACKEY, A. G. Lexicon of Freemasonry. 6th ed.; revised by D. Campbell. 8vo. Lond., 1873. K 11 P 22

MACKEY, Rev. D. J. Bishop Forbes: a Memoir. 8vo. Lond., 1838. C 13 R 19

MACKINNON, Rev. J. South African Traits. 8vo. Edinb., 1887. D 14 U 21

MACKINNON, L. B. Some Account of the Falkland Islands. 8vo. Lond., 1840. D 15 S 2

MACKINTOSH, Dr. J. Scotland, from the earliest times to the present century. (Story of the Nations Series.) 8vo. Lond., 1890. B 32 R 3
History of Civilization in Scotland. Vols. 1-4. 8vo. Lond., 1878-88. B 32 T 1-4

MACKLIN, Charles. [Life of ;] by E. A. Parry. (Eminent Actors.) 8vo. Lond., 1891. C 16 P 10
Love a la Mode : a Farce. [See British Drama, Modern, 5.]

MACKLIN, Rev. H. W. Monumental Brasses. 8vo. Lond., 1890. A 23 Q 43

MACKONOCHIE, Rev. A. H. A Memoir [by Mrs E. A. Towle] ; edited by F. F. Russell. 8vo. Lond., 1890. C 12 R 12

McLACHLAN, C. Copies of Two Letters to the Secretary of State for the Colonies, 24th and 27th February, 1846, on Transportation to Van Diemen's Land. Fol. London, 1846. MF 11 Q 33 †

MACLAINE, Rev. A. Ecclesiastical History. [See Mosheim, J. L.].

MACLAREN, C. Sketch of the Geology of Fife and the Lothians. 2nd ed. 8vo. Edinb., 1866. A 24 Q 2

McLAUGHLIN, Prof. A. C. [Life of] Lewis Cass. (American Statesmen.) 12mo. Boston, 1891. C 13 Q 8

McLEAN, H. R. Twenty Standard Songs arranged for voices of Medium Register. 8vo. Sydney (n.d.) MA 2 P 60

MACLEAY, Sir Alexander. Presentation of a piece of plate to, by a numerous body of his fellow Colonists, Inhabitants of New South Wales. 8vo. Sydney, 1843.
MC 1 T 16

MACLEAY, Sir W. On the Clupeidæ of Australia. 8vo. Sydney, 1879. MA 3 Q 2

On the Mugilidæ of Australia. 8vo. Sydney, 1879.
MA 3 Q 1

MACLEOD, H. D. Theory of Credit. Vol. 2. pt. 2. 8vo. Lond., 1891. F 8 S 32

Theory and Practice of Banking. 4th ed. 2 vols. 8vo. Lond., 1883–86. F 7 S 10, 11

MACMAHON, P. Memorial, or Brief for the Comte de Cagliostro in the Cause of the Cardinal de Rohan, Comtesse de La Motte, and others. 8vo. Lond., 1786. B 26 T 2

MACMASTER, J. B. Benjamin Franklin as a Man of Letters. (American Men of Letters.) 12mo. Boston, 1887. C 1 R 42

MACMILLAN, Rev. Hugh. Roman Mosaics; or, Studies in Rome and its Neighbourhood. 12mo. Lond., 1888.
D 18 P 3

McMILLAN, Hon. W. Financial Statement of. 8vo. Sydney, 1889. MF 1 T 3

Supplementary Financial Statement, made 8th Oct., 1889. 8vo. Sydney, 1889. MF 1 T 4

MACMILLAN, W. G. Treatise on Electro-Metallurgy. 8vo. Lond., 1890. A 24 R 2

MACMILLAN'S MAGAZINE. Vols. 54–65. Lond., 1886–92. E 1. 27

MACMULLAN, S. J. [*See* Geffcken, Dr. F. H.]

MACMULLEN, J. History of Canada. 8vo. Brockville, 1868. B 1 T 43

McMURDO, Edward. History of Portugal. Vols. 1 and 2. 8vo. Lond., 1888–89. B 34 S 1, 2

[Note.—A Translation of Herculano's Historia de Portugal.]

McMURTRIE, Wm. Report of the Culture of the Sugar Beet, and the Manufacture of Sugar therefrom, in France and the United States. 8vo. Washington, 1880.
A 18 U 14

MACNEILL, Maj.-Gen. Sir J. C. [*See* Galloway, W.]

MACNISH, R. Anatomy of Drunkenness. 5th ed. 8vo. Glasgow, 1834. F 11 P 31

MACONOCHIE, Capt. A. [*See* Convicts.]

MACOUN, J. Catalogue of Canadian Plants. Part 3. Apetalæ. (Geol. and Nat. Hist. Survey of Canada.) 8vo. Montreal, 1886. A 20 V 24

MACPHAIL, M. The Australian Squatting Directory, 1871. Roy. 8vo. Sydney, 1871. ME 10 P

MACPHERSON, A. Mount Abundance; or Experiences of a Pioneer Squatter in Australia thirty years ago. 8vo. Lond. (n.d.) MD 1 R 22

MACPHERSON, H. A. [*See* Pidsley, W. E. H.]

MACPHERSON, Rev. P. Astronomy of the Australian Aborigines. 8vo. Sydney, 1881. MA 3 Q 49

Astronomy of the Australian Aborigines. 8vo. Sydney, 1883. MA 3 S 28

McPHUN, W. R. McPhun's Australian News and Record of Commercial Progress in Australia. Fol. Glasgow, 1853. ME 17 S

MACRAY, W. D. Annals of the Bodleian Library, Oxford. 2nd ed. 8vo. Lond., 1890. B 6 S 44

MACREADY, William Charles. [Life of]; by William Archer. (Eminent Actors). 12mo. Lond., 1890.
C 12 P 43

MACROBIUS, A. S. Opera quae supersunt; emendavit, L. Janus. 2 vols. 8vo. Quedlinburgi et Lipsiæ, 1848–52. J 15 S 18, 19

MADAN, A. C. Kiungani; or, Story and History from Central Africa; written by Boys in the Schools of the Universities' Mission to Central Africa. 8vo. Lond., 1887. D 14 Q 4

MADAN, F. Rough List of Manuscript Materials relating to the History of Oxford. 8vo. Oxford, 1887. K 12 V 4

MADDEN, F. W. [*See* Stevenson, S. W.]

MADDEN, Mrs. H. Memoir of Rt. Rev. R. Daly. 8vo. Lond., 1875. C 22 P 2

MADDEN, R. L. [*See* Harrison, W. J.]

MADDEN, Dr. R. R. The Memoirs of. (Chiefly Autobiographical), from 1798 to 1886. 8vo. Lond., 1891.
C 17 T 18

[*See* Daly, J. B.]

MADDOCK, W. Guide to Sydney, with which is incorporated the Tourists' Handbook and Description of New South Wales. 7th ed. 12mo. Sydney, 1889.
MD 7 T 30

Another Copy. 8th ed. Sydney (n.d.) MD 7 T 31

MADHOJI. [*See* Sindhia Mádhava Rao.]

MADRAS PRESIDENCY. Annual Returns of the Civil Hospitals and Dispensaries for 1886. Sm. fol. Madras, 1887. E 2. 16

Manual of the Administration of the. Vol. 1. Sm. fol. Madras, 1885. E 2. 16

Report on the Administration of the, 1886–87. Sm. fol. Madras, 1887. E 2. 16

MAGAZINE OF AMERICAN HISTORY. Vols. 17–27. Sm. 4to. New York, 1887–92. E 1. 16

MAGELLAN, Ferdinand. Life of, and the first Circumnavigation of the Globe, 1480–1521; by F. H. H. Guillemard. 8vo. Lond., 1890. C 14 Q 7

MAGNAN, Dr. V. De l'Alcoolisme des diverses formes du Délire Alcoolique et de leur traitement. 8vo. Paris, 1874. F 11 S 31

MAGNÚSSON, E. [*See* Morris, W.]

MAGNY, Ludovic Marquis de. Le Nobiliaire Universel. 20 vols. 4to. Paris, 1854–90. K 13 Q 1–20 †

MAGUIRE, J. F. Father Mathew : a Biography. Abridged and re-edited by Miss Rosa Mulholland. 8vo. Dublin, 1891 C 16 P 6

MAGUIRE, Rev. T. [*See* Pope, Rev. R.P.T.]

MAHAFFY, J. P. Greek World under Roman Sway, from Polybius to Plutarch. 8vo. Lond., 1890.
B 27 Q 16

Greek Pictures drawn with Pen and Pencil. Imp. 8vo. Lond., 1890. D 19 V 5

Problems in Greek History. 8vo. Lond., 1892.
B 17 P 18

Greek Life and Thought, from the age of Alexander to the Roman Conquest. 8vo. Lond., 1887. B 27 Q 11

Rambles and Studies in Greece. 3rd ed. 8vo. Lond., 1887. D 18 R 2

MAHAN, Capt. A. T. Influence of Sea Power upon History ; 1660–1783. 8vo. Lond., 1889. B 36 T 6

MAHÁVANSA. The Mahávansa ; translated from the original Páli ; by L. C. Wijesinha. Roy. 8vo. Colombo, 1889. G 6 T 26

MAIDEN, J. H. Bibliography of Australian Economic Botany. Roy. 8vo. Sydney, 1892. MR 3 R 25

Hints for the Collection and Preservation of Raw Products suitable for Technological Museums. Roy. 8vo. Sydney, 1890. MA 3 R 1

Useful Native Plants of Australia (including Tasmania). 8vo. Sydney, 1889. MA 1 R 54

Wattles and Wattle-Barks, being Hints on the Conservation and Cultivation of Wattles. Roy. 8vo. Sydney, 1890.
MA 3 R 9

Another Copy. 2nd ed. Roy. 8vo. Sydney, 1891.
MA 3 R 10

MAIER, J. [*See* Preece, W. H.]

MAIL, The. 13 vols. Fol. Lond., 1886–92. E

MAIMON, Solomon: an Autobiography ; translated by J. C. Murray. 8vo. Lond., 1888. C 12 Q 5

MAIMONIDES. The Writings of. [Hebrew Text.] 8 vols. (in 4). Fol. Berlin, 1862–64. G 33 Q 20–23 †

MAINE, H. S. International Law : a Series of Lectures. 8vo. Sydney, 1888. F 8 S 22

MAINTENON, Françoise d'Aubigné, Marquise de. [Life of] Madame de Maintenon ; by Emily Bowles. 8vo. Lond., 1888. C 13 R 9

MAINZER, M. Ueber die Wirkung des Alkohols auf die Temperatur des gesunden Menschen. 8vo. Bonn, 1871.
F 11 R 41

MAISTRE, X. de, Le Comte. Œuvres complètes. Roy. 8vo. Paris, 1862. J 18 V 27

MAITLAND, F. W. [*See* Bracton's Note-book.]

MAITLAND, William. [*See* Skelton, J.]

MAJOR, Jno. History of Greater Britain. [*See* Scottish History Soc., 10.]

MAJORANA, A. Codice Scolastico. [*See* Cogliolo, P.]

MALABARI, B. M. A Biographical Sketch ; by Dayaram Gidumal. 12mo. Lond., 1892. C 16 P 18

MALAY LANGUAGE. The Travellers' Malay Pronouncing Hand-book. 2nd ed. 18mo. Singapore, 1889.
K 16 P 12

MALDEN, Mrs. Charles. Jane Austen. (Eminent Women Series.) 8vo. Lond., 1889. C 12 Q 26

MALET, W. E. The Australian Wine-growers' Manual. 12mo. Lond., 1880.* MA 1 P 37

MALFATTI, Prof. G. Dall' Uomo all' Infusorio. Imp. 8vo. Milano, 1888. A 28 V 12

MALHERBE, F. Poésies Complètes. (Collection Jannet-Picard.) 12mo. Paris (n.d.) H 1 P 48

MALLESON, Col. G. B. Akbar. (Rulers of India.) 12mo. Oxford, 1890. C 12 P 37

Dupleix. (Rulers of India.) 12mo. Oxford, 1890.
C 12 P 38

Life of the Marquess Wellesley. 8vo. Lond., 1889.
C 12 Q 21

Life of Prince Metternich. (Statesmen Series.) 8vo. Lond., 1888. C 15 Q 6

Prince Eugene of Savoy. 8vo. Lond., 1888. C 13 R 9
[*See* Kaye, Sir J.]

MALLET, F. R. Manual of the Geology of India. Part 4. Mineralogy. Roy. 8vo. Calcutta, 1887. A 9 U 5

MALLET, Rt. Hon. Sir L. Free Exchange : including chapters on Law of Value and Unearned Increment. 8vo. Lond., 1891. F 6 U 29

National Income and Taxation. 8vo. Lond. (n.d.)
F 5 Q 45

MALLOCK, W. H. In an Enchanted Island : or, a Winter in Cyprus. 8vo. Lond., 1889. D 6 Q 1

Lucretius. (Ancient Classics for English Readers.) 12mo. Edinb., 1887. J 14 P 18

MALONE, R. E. Three Years' Cruise in the Australian Colonies. 8vo. Lond., 1854. MD 1 W 12

MALORY, Sir T. Le Mort D'Arthur. The Original Edition of William Caxton now reprinted and edited by H. O. Sommer. Vols. 1–3. Imp. 8vo. Lond., 1889–91.
J 6 V 1–3

MALTHUS, T. R. [*See* Ricardo, D.]

MALTON, Capt. W. D. The Duties of Markers in Company Battalion, and Brigade. 18mo. Sydney, 1873.
MA 2 P 74

MAN AT THE WHEEL, The. A New Ballad to an old tune. 8vo. (n.p. n. d.) H 9 P 12

MANCHESTER. The Court Leet Records of the Manor of Manchester, 1552-1687, and 1731-1846. Vols. 1-12. Imp. 8vo. Manchester, 1884-90. B 22 V 1-12

MANCHESTER GEOLOGICAL SOCIETY. Transactions. Vols. 18-21. 8vo. Manch., 1886-92. E 1. 42

MANCHESTER GUIDE, THE. Historical Description of Manchester and Salford. 8vo. Manch., 1804. B 23 T 9

MANCHESTER QUARTERLY. Vols. 6-10. 8vo. Manch., 1887-91. E 1. 58

MANDAT-GRANCEY, Baron E. de. Cowboys and Colonels: Narrative of a Journey across the Prairie and over the Black Hills of Dakota; with additional Notes by W. Conn. 8vo. Lond., 1887. D 15 T 3

MANDEVILLE, Sir J. de. Voiage and Travaile of; with an introduction by J. O. Halliwell. 8vo. Lond., 1839. D 16 T 8

Voiage and Travayle of Sir John Maundeville; edited, in Facsimile, by J. Ashton. 8vo. Lond., 1887. D 16 U 8

MANETHO. Apotelesmaticorum libri VI, relegit A. Koechly. 12mo. Lipsiæ, 1858. H 10 P 24

MANING, F. E. History of the War in the North of New Zealand against the Chief Heke, in 1845; by "A Pakeha Maori." 8vo. Auckland (n.d.) MB 2 Q 41

Another Copy. 2nd ed. 8vo. Auckland, 1864. MB 2 Q 42

MANN, J. F. Eight Months with Dr. Leichhardt in the years 1846-47. Roy. 8vo. Sydney, 1888. MD 7 R 14

MANN, Dr. R. J. Domestic Economy and Household Science. 5th ed. 12mo. Lond., 1887. A 22 P 2

MANNERING, George E. With Axe and Rope in the New Zealand Alps. Roy. 8vo. Lond., 1891. MD 7 R 51

MANNERS, J. Lord. The Church of England in the Colonies: a Lecture. 8vo. Lond., 1851. MG 1 R 48

MANNING, F. E. Old New Zealand : a Tale of the Good Old Times. 8vo. Auckland, 1863. MD 5 R 33

MANNING, H. E. Cardinal. [Life of]; by A. W. Hutton. 12mo. Lond., 1892. C 16 P 27

A Cardinal's Broken Oath. [See Bradlaugh, C.]

MANNING, J. Notes on Aborigines of New Holland. 8vo. Sydney, 1883. MA 3 S 29

MANNING, J. E. Correspondence relative to default of, late Registrar of the Supreme Court of New South Wales; also copy of any Orders of the Government for Security taken from. Fol. Lond., 1845. MF 12 Q 25 †

MANSEL, Rev. H. L. The Gnostic Heresies of the First and Second Centuries. 8vo. Lond., 1875. G 16 T 27

Life of. [See Burgon, Very Rev. J. W.]

[See Aldrich, Rev. H.]

MANSEL-PLEYDELL. [See Pleydell, J. C. Mansel-.]

MANSERGH, James. Report on the Sewerage and Sewage Disposal of the Proposed Melbourne Metropolitan District. Fol. Melb., 1890. MA 12 Q 16 †

MANSFIELD, J. M. [See Hall, G. S.]

MANTELL, G. A. Medals of Creation; or First Lessons in Geology. 2nd ed. 2 vols. 8vo. Lond., 1854. A 24 R 8, 9

MANTON, T. One hundred and ninety Sermons on the 119th Psalm. Fol. Lond., 1681. G 40 T 12 ‡

MANZONI, A. The Betrothed. 12mo. Lond., 1889. J 7 Q 49

MAORI. [See Inglis, J.]

MAORI CONVERSATION. [See Aubert, Sister.]

MAPOTHER, Prof. E. D. The Body and its Health, with Teachers' Aid and Questions. 18mo. Dublin (n.d.) A 12 P 47

MAR, Earldom of. Nuda Veritas. Shall Wrong Prevail? 12mo. Lond., 1888. C 12 P 22

MARBOT, J. B. A. M., Baron de. Memoirs of; translated by A. J. Butler. 2 vols. 8vo. Lond., 1892. C 18 S 15, 16

MARCEAU, Gén. F. S. Généraux de Vingt Ans; par F. Tulou. 8vo. Paris, 1891. C 18 S 14

MARCEL, G. La Pérouse, Récit de son Voyage Expédition envoyée a sa recherche le Capitaine Dillon, &c. Edition du Centenaire. 8vo. Paris (n.d.) MC 1 Q 45

MARCELLINUS, A. Rerum Gestarum qui de 31 supersunt, libri 18. Fol. Parisiis, 1681. B 42 Q 4 ‡

MARCET, Dr. W. On chronic Alcoholic Intoxication. 2nd ed. 12mo. Lond., 1862. F 11 P 20

MARCHANT, W. T. In Praise of Ale; or, Songs, Ballads, Epigrams, and Anecdotes relating to Beer, Malt, and Hops. 8vo. Lond., 1888. H 7 Q 39

MARCKWALD, A. Movements of Respiration, and their Innervation in the Rabbit. Roy. 8vo. Lond., 1888. A 26 V 1

MARCUS and ANDREW, Messrs. Sydney Trades Directory of City and Suburbs. 2 vols. 8vo. Sydney 1890-91. ME 10 S

MARENZELLER, Dr. E. von. Die Coelenteraten der K.K. österreichisch-ungarischen Nordpol'-Expedition. 4to. Wien, 1877. A 42 R 18‡

MARGAROT, M. The Trial of Maurice Margarot, at Edinburgh, 1794, on an Indictment for Seditious Practices. 8vo. Lond., 1794. F 12 P 26

MARGERISON, S. Registers of the Parish Church of Calverley, in the County of York. 3 vols 8vo. Bradford, 1880-87. B 24 Q 1-3

MARGOLIOUTH, Prof. D. S. [*See* Anecdota Oxoniensia.]

MARGOLLÉ, Lieut. E. Volcanoes and Earthquakes. [*See* Zurcher, F.]

MARGUERITÉ DE VALOIS, Queen of Navarre. Memoirs of ; translated with notes by Violet Fane. 8vo. Lond., 1892. C 18 S 8

L'Heptameron des nouvelles de Marguerité D'Angoulême. (Collection Jannet-Picard.) 2 vols. 12mo. Paris (n.d.) J 15 Q 23, 24

MARIE ANTOINETTE, Queen of France, and the End of the Old Régime ; by [A. T., Baron] Imbert de Saint-Amand ; translated by T. S. Perry. 8vo. Lond., 1891. C 14 Q 8

MARIE CAROLINE, Queen of Naples. The Queen of Naples and Lord Nelson ; by J. C. Jeaffreson. 2 vols. 8vo. Lond., 1889. C 14 Q 23, 24

MARIE DE MEDICIS, Queen of France. Life of ; by Julia S. H. Pardoe. 3 vols. 8vo. Lond., 1890. C 17 T 6-8

MARIE LOUISE, Empress of France. Happy days of ; by [Baron A. L.] Imbert de Saint-Amand. Trans. by T. S. Perry. 8vo. Lond., 1891. C 14 Q 12

Marie Louise and the Decadence of the Empire ; by [Baron A. L.] Imbert de Saint-Amand. Trans. by T. S. Perry. 8vo. Lond., 1891. C 14 Q 13

Marie Louise, the Island of Elba, and the Hundred Days ; by [Baron A. L.] Imbert de Saint-Amand. Trans. by T. S. Perry. 8vo. Lond., 1891. C 14 Q 14

[*See* Durand, Mme. la Gén.]

MARIETTE, A., Pacha. Monuments divers recueillis en Égypte et en Nubie. Texte par G. Maspero. Fol. Paris, 1889. B 6 S 7 ‡

MARIN LA MESLÉE, E. Past Exploration in New Guinea, and a Project for the Scientific Exploration of the Great Island. 8vo. Sydney, 1883. MD 7 S 7

MARINDIN, G. E. [*See* Smith, Dr. W.]

MARINER, W. An Account of the Natives of the Tonga Islands, compiled by J. Martin. 2 vols. 8vo. Lond., 1817. MD 7 R 12, 13

Histoire des Naturels des Iles Tonga ou des Amis, depuis leur découverte par le Capt. Cook. Rédigée par John Martin. 2 vols. 8vo. Paris, 1817. MD 3 S 31, 32

Voyage aux Iles des Amis, 1805-10 ; avec l'Histoire des Habitans depuis leur découverte ; par le Capt. Cook. Traduit de l'Anglais. 2ᵉ éd. 2 vols. 8vo. Paris, 1819. MD 7 T 26, 27

MARIO, Jessie W. [*See* Garibaldi, G.]

MARIOTTI, L. [*See* Gallenga, A.]

MARITIME NOTES AND QUERIES. Vol. 7. 8vo. Lond., 1888. E 1. 58

MARK LANE EXPRESS. Fol. Lond., 1881, 1886-91. E 1. 83

MARK TWAIN. [*See* Clemens, S. L.]

MARKHAM, C. R. "The Fighting Veres." Lives of Sir F. and Sir H. Vere. Roy. 8vo. Lond., 1888. C 11 P 42

MARKHAM, J., and MACHIN, L. The Dumb Knight ; a Historical Comedy. [*See* British Drama, Ancient, 2.]

MARKHAM, Capt. A. H. Life of Sir John Franklin, and the north-west passage. 8vo. Lond., 1891. C 15 Q 16

MARLBOROUGH, (John Churchill) Duke of. Life of ; [*See* Yonge, C. D.]

John Churchill, Duke of Marlborough : The "Mob,' the 'Scum,' and the 'Dregs," by C. Bradlaugh. 3rd ed. 12mo. Lond., 1884. F 7 V 21

MARLOWE, C. Edward II. ; a Tragedy. [*See* British Drama, Ancient, 1.]

The Jew of Malta ; a Tragedy. [*See* British Drama, Ancient, 1.]

Best Plays; edited by H. Ellis. (Mermaid Series.) 8vo. Lond., 1887. H 4 Q 17

Tamburlane the Great.—The Tragical History of Dr. Faustus —The Jew of Malta.—Edward II.

MARMION, S. The Antiquary. [*See* British Drama, Ancient, 3.]

MARMONTEL, J. F. Contes Moraux. 3 vols. 18mo. Lond., 1798. J 15 Q 16-18

MAROT, C. Œuvres Complètes. (Collection Jannet—Picard.) 4 vols. 12mo. Paris (n.d.) H 1 P 49-52

MARRIOTT, Charles. Life of. [*See* Burgon, Very Rev. J. W. T.] C 12 R 10, 11

MARRIOTT, Rev. W. B. Vestiarium Christianum ; the origin and development of the Dress of Holy Ministry in the Church. Roy. 8vo. Lond., 1868. G 3 V 18

MARSDEN, R. Cotton-spinning ; its Development, Principles, and Practice. 12mo. Lond., 1884. A 11 P 29

MARSH, H. The Chusan Waltz. Fol. Sydney, (n.d.) MA 11 Q 15 †

The Crœsus Polka. Fol. Sydney (n.d.). MA 11 Q 15 †

MARSH, J. E. [*See* Van 'T Hoff, Prof. J. H.]

MARSH, S. H. The All England Eleven Polka. Fol. Sydney (n.d.) MA 11 Q 15 †

MARSHALL, A. Specimens of Antique Carved Furniture and Woodwork. 4to. Lond., 1888. A 37 P 3 ‡

MARSHALL, A. M., and HURST, C. H. Junior Course of Practical Zoology. 8vo. Lond., 1887. A 27 Q 25

MARSHALL, Prof. A. Principles of Economics. Vol. 1. 8vo. Lond., 1890. F 10 Q 23

MARSHALL, Major G. F. L., and NICEVILLE, L. de. The Butterflies of India, Burmah, and Ceylon. Vols. 1-3. (2nd and 3rd vols. by L. de Nicéville only.) 3 vols. roy. 8vo. Calcutta, 1882-90. A 15 Q 19-21

MARSHALL, Mrs. Julian. Life and Letters of Mary Wollstonecraft Shelley. 2 vols. 8vo. Lond., 1889. C 14 U 4, 5

MARSTON, E. Copyright, National and International, with some Remarks on the Position of Authors and Publishers, by "A Publisher." 8vo. Lond., 1887. F 7 Q 30

MARSTON, J. The Malcontent: a Tragi-Comic [*See* British Drama, Ancient, 2.] Eastward Hoe; a Comedy. [*See* Chapman, G.]

MARTEN, F. [*See* Voyages and Discoveries.]

MARTIALIS, M. V. Epigrammata. 18mo. Lond., 1816. H 11 P 4
Epigrammata cum notis, accurante C. Schrevell. 8vo. Lugd. Bat., 1670. H 10 Q 20.

MARTIN, Annie. Home Life on an Ostrich Farm. 8vo. Lond., 1890. D 14 Q 9

MARTIN, A. P. Australia and the Empire. 8vo. Edinb., 1889. MF 1 P 6
Lays of To-day; Verses in jest and earnest. Sm. 4to. Melb., 1878. MH 1 S 85

MARTIN, B. E. In the Footprints of Charles Lamb. Roy. 8vo. Lond., 1891. C 16 U 1

MARTIN, Frances. Elizabeth Gilbert and her Work for the Blind. 8vo. Lond., 1887. C 16 Q 7

MARTIN, H. N. [*See* Huxley, Prof. T. H.]

MARTIN, J. Origin and History of the New Testament. 12mo. Melb. 1871. MG 2 P 20

MARTIN, J. [*See* Mariner, W.]

MARTIN, J., and PANTER, F. K. Report for the Information of His Excellency the Governor of Western Australia and the Promoters of the North Western Expedition of 1864 on the Voyage and the Resources of the Districts Explored. 8vo. (u.p. n.d.) MD 7 S 28

MARTIN, K., and WICHMAN, A. Beiträge zur Geologic Ost-Asiens und Australasiens. 3 vols. roy. 8vo. Leiden, 1881-87. ME 18 R

MARTIN, L. C., and TRUBNER, C. Current Gold and Silver Coins of all Countries. Roy. 8vo. Lond., 1863. Libr.

MARTIN, Mrs. Patchett. Coo—ee. Tales of Australian Life; by Australian Ladies. 8vo. Lond., 1891. MJ 2 T 16

MARTIN, Sir T. Faust, by Goethe; translated into English verse. 9th ed. 2 vols. 12mo. Edinb., 1887. H1 R 24-25
Horace. (Ancient Classics for English Readers.) 12mo. Edinb., 1887. J 14 P 14
Shakespeare or Bacon? 8vo. Edinb., 1888. J 5 R 35

MARTIN, W. R. Treatise on Navigation and Nautical Astronomy. Roy. 8vo. Lond., 1888. A 3 U 30

MARTINEAU, J. Study of Religion: its Sources and Contents. 2 vols. 8vo. Oxford, 1888. G 8 T 22, 23

MARTINIÈRE, H. M. P. de la. Morocco: Journeys in the Kingdom of Fez and to the Court of Mulai Hassan. 8vo. Lond., 1889. D 14 R 6

MARTINUCI. De Quibusdam Officiis Episcopi. [*See* Offices of the Bishop.]

MARTIUS, C. F. P. de Historia Naturalis Palmarum. 3 vols. Fol. Lipsiæ, 1850. A 43 Q 16-18 ‡
Nova Genera et Species Plantarum quas in itinere per Brasiliam, 1817-20. 3 vols. 4to. Monachii, 1824-29. A 40 Q 9-11 ‡

MARTIUS, Dr. W. Der Kampf gegen den Alkoholmissbranch. Roy. 8vo. Halle, 1884. F 12 R 26

MARTYN, T. The Universal Conchologist. 4to. Lond., 1789. A 40 Q 12 ‡

MARVELL, A. Satires of; edited by G. A. Aitken. 12mo. Lond., 1892. H 8 P 49
Poems of; edited by G. A. Aitken. 12mo. Lond., 1892. H 8 P 48

MARWICK, J. G. Spare Moments in Australia. 8vo. Sydney. 1877. MJ 1 U 45

MARWOOD, J. Treatise on the Forest Laws. 4th ed. Corrected and enlarged by W. Nelson. 8vo. Lond., 1717. F 2 U 27

MARX, Karl. The Students' Marx. [*See* Aveling, Dr. E. B.]
Capital: a Critical Analysis of Capitalist Production; edited by F. Engels. 2 vols. 8vo. Lond., 1887. F 10 S 24, 25

MARY CALLINACK POLKA, The. Fol. Sydney (n.d.) MA 11 Q 15 †

MARY OF CASTLE CARY. [Song.] Fol. Sydney (n.d.) MA 11 Q 15 †

MARY STUART, Queen of Scots. Histoire de Marie Stuart. 6e. éd. 2 vols. 12mo. Paris, 1885. C 14 P 21, 22
Brief Statement of the Principal Charges brought against her, with Answers to the Same; by J. Hosack. 8vo. Lond., 1888. C 16 P 5
[*See* Sharman, J. *and* Skelton, J.]

MARZIALS, F. T. Life of Léon Gambetta. (Statesmen Series.) 8vo. Lond., 1890. C 12 R 39

MASING, R. De Mutationibus Spiritus Vini in Corpus ingesti. 8vo. Dorpati Livonorum, 1854. F 11 S 32

MASCART, Prof. E., and JOUBERT, Prof. J. Treatise on Electricity and Magnetism. 2 vols. 8vo. Lond., 1883-88. A 5 U 32, 33

MASKELL, W. M. Account of Insects noxious to Agriculture and Plants in New Zealand. (Scale Insects.) Roy. 8vo. Wellington, 1887.* MA 2 U 18

MASNAVI I MA'NAVI. [*See* Jálálu-d-Din.]

MASON, Amelia G. The Women of the French Salons. Roy. 8vo. Lond., 1891. C 17 U 3

MASON, R. H. History of Norfolk. Vol. 1 and vol. 2, pt. I. 2 vols. fol. Lond., 1884-85. B 6 S 1, 2 ‡
[*See* Woodgate, W. B.]

MASON, R. O. Sketches and Impressions, Musical, Theatrical, and Social (1799-1885). From the After-dinner Talk of T. Goodwin. 12mo. New York, 1887. J 7 Q 48

MASON, W. Caractacus : a Tragedy. [*See* British Drama, Modern, 2.]

Elfrida : a Tragedy. [*See* British Drama, Modern, 2.]

MASON, W. B. Handbook for Travellers in Japan. [*See* Murray, J.]

MASON, W. S. Statistical Account, or Parochial Survey of Ireland. 3 vols. 8vo. Dublin, 1814-19.   F 10 P 25-27

MASON, FIRTH, & M'CUTCHEON Victorian Almanac for 1890. 12mo. Melb., 1890.   ME 4 U

MASPERO, Prof. G. Egyptian Archæology ; translated by A. B. Edwards. 8vo. Lond., 1887.   B 2 S 19
[*See* Mariette, A.]

MASSEE, George. Monograph of the Myxogastres. Roy. 8vo. Lond., 1892.   A 20 V 20

MASSEY, C. C. [*See* Du Prel, Dr. C.]

MASSEY, G. The Secret Drama of Shakespeare's Sonnets. 8vo. Lond., 1888.   H 10 S 5

MASSEY, W. N. History of England during the Reign of George III (1745-1802). 4 vols. 8vo. Lond., 1855-63.   B 21 T 17-20

MASSINA, A. H. Massina's Guide to Melbourne. 12mo. Melb., 1882-3.   MD 1 P 54

MASSINGER, P. Best Plays of the Old Dramatists. Philip Massinger ; edited by A. Symons. (Mermaid Series.) 2 vols. 8vo. Lond., 1887-89.   H 4 Q 18, 19,
     I. The Duke of Milan.—A New Way to pay Old Debts.—The Great Duke of Florence.—The Maid of Honour.—The City Madam.
     II. The Roman Actor.—The Fatal Dowry.—The Guardian.— The Virgin-Martyr.—Believe as you list.

The Bondman: a Tragedy. [*See* British Drama, Modern, 1.]

The Fatal Dowry , a Tragedy. [*See* British Drama, Modern, 1.]

New Way to pay Old Debts : a Comedy. [*See* British Drama, Modern, 3.]

MASSON, Prof. D. Chronological and Historical Atlas of the Middle Ages. Fol. Lond., 1849.   B 41 P 2 ‡

MASSON, G. Mediæval France from the reign of Hugues Caput to the beginning of the 16th Century. 8vo. Lond., 1888.   B 26 R 1
[*See* Dudevant, Madame.]

MASSONI, A. [*See* Stanley, H. M., *and* Jephson, A. J. M-.]

MATARELLI, A. [*See* Giusti, G.]

MATHER, Rev. G., and BLAGG, C. J. Bishop Rawle : a Memoir. 8vo. Lond., 1890.   C 12 R 13

MATHERS, Helen. [*See* Reeves, Mrs. H.]

MATHERS, S. L. M. The Key of Solomon the King. 4to. Lond., 1889.   A 24 V 25
The Kabbalah Unveiled. 8vo. Lond., 1887.   A 24 T 25

MATHEW, Father T. A Biography ; by J. F. Maguire. Abridged and re-edited by Miss Rosa Mulholland. 8vo. Dublin, 1891.   C 16 P 6

MATHEWS, P. J. Rough Jottings on Tasmanian Legislation. 12mo. Launceston, 1884.   MF 2 P 70

MATHEWS, R. H. Handbook to Magisterial Inquiries and Coroners' Inquests in New South Wales. 2nd ed. 8vo. Sydney. 1890.   MF 3 T 6
Hand-book to Magisterial Inquiries in New South Wales. 8vo. Sydney, 1888.   MF 3 R 32

MATTHEW, J. E. Popular History of Music, &c., from St. Ambrose to Mozart. Roy. 8vo. Lond., 1888.   A 8 R 35
[*See* Pougin, A.]

MATTHEWS, B. [*See* Actors and Actresses.]

MATTHEWS, James E. Manual of Musical History. 8vo. Lond., 1892.   A 23 R 6

MATTHEWS, J. W. Incwadi Yami ; or, Twenty Years' Personal Experience in South Africa. Roy. 8vo. Lond., 1887.   D 14 V 1

MAUDSLAY, A. Highways and Horses. 8vo. Lond., 1888.   A 17 W 37

MAUGNY, Comte de. Souvenirs of the Second Empire ; or, the Last Days of the Court of Napoleon. 8vo. Lond., 1891.   B 26 S 1

MAUL, J., und FRIEDEL, H. Deutsche Buchoinbände der Neuzeit. 4to. Leipzig, 1888.   A 40 Q 24 ‡

MAUNDEVILE, Sir John. [*See* Mandeville, Sir J. de.]

MAUNSELL, Rt. Rev. R. Grammar of the New Zealand Language. 2nd ed. 12mo. Auckland, 1862.   MK 2 P 5
Another Copy. 3rd ed. 12mo. Melb., 1882.   MK 1 P 64

MAURICE, C. E. Revolutionary Movement of 1848-49 in Italy, Austria-Hungary, and Germany. 8vo. Lond., 1887.   B 25 T 2

MAURICE, Col. J. F. Balance of Military Power in Europe. 8vo. Lond., 1888.   F 6 Q 43

MAURY, M. F., LL.D. The Physical Geography of the Sea. 2nd ed. Roy. 8vo. Lond., 1855.   A 29 V 10
Life of ; by Diana F. M. Corbin. 8vo. Lond., 1888.   C 12 S 18

MAWR, Mrs. E. B. Analogous Proverbs in Ten Languages. 8vo. Lond., 1885.   K 19 P 9

MAXTED, Edward. Sketches of the Poor. Sm. 4to. Sydney, 1892.   MF 1 U 41.

MAXWELL, Sir H. E. Studies in the Topography of Galloway. 8vo. Edinb., 1887.   D 18 U 5

MAXWELL, J. C. Scientific Papers of ; edited by W. D. Niven. 2 vols. 4to. Camb., 1890.   A 42 R 21, 22 ‡
Substanz und Bewegung. 12mo. Braunschweig, 1879.   A 29 P 16

MAXWELL, W. E. Manual of the Malay Language. 2nd ed. 12mo. Lond., 1888.   K 14 P 26

MAXWELL, Sir W. S. Works of. 6 vols. 8vo. Lond., 1891. J 6 U 18-23

MAY, T. The Heir: a Comedy. [*See* British Drama, Ancient, 1.]
The Old Couple: A Comedy. [*See* British Drama, Ancient, 3.]

MAYER, Brantz. Captain Canot; or, Twenty Years of an African Slaver. 8vo. New York, 1854. D 1 R 13

MAYER, Dr. S. French Code of Commerce as revised to the end of 1886. 8vo. Lond., 1887. F 10 Q 25

MAYES, C. Victorian Contractors' and Builders' Price-book. 12mo. Melb., 1859. MA 3 P 16
Australian Builders' Price-book. 12mo. Melb., 1886. MA 1 T 7

MAYHALL, John. Annals of Yorkshire. 8vo. Leeds, 1862. B 23 R 9

MAYHEW, Rev. A. L., and SKEAT, Rev. W. W. Concise Dictionary of Middle English, 1150–1580. 8vo. Oxford, 1888. K 11 V 54

MAYHEW, H. London Labour and the London Poor. [Vol. 4.] Those that will not work; comprising Prostitutes, Thieves, Swindlers, Beggars. Roy. 8vo. Lond., 1861. F 14 S 14

MAYNE, J. The City Match: A Comedy. [*See* British Drama, Ancient, 2.]

MAYNE, J. D. Commentaries on the Indian Penal Code. 6th ed. 8vo. Madras, 1869. F 9 S 21

MAYO (Richard Southwell Bourke), sixth Earl of. [Life of;] by Sir W. W. Hunter. (Rulers of India.) 8vo. Oxford, 1891. C 17 Q 8

MAYOR, J. E. B. Satires of Juvenal. [*See* Juvenalis, D. J.]

MAZZINI, G. Doveri dell' Nomo. 8vo. Firenze, 1891. G 16 Q 45
Life and Writings of. 6 vols. 8vo. Lond., 1890-91. J 10 R 34-39
[*See* Bradlaugh, C. — Five Dead Men.]

MAZZINGHI, T. J. de'. Sanctuaries. Roy.8vo. Stafford, 1887. B 24 V 2

MEAD, T. H. Horsemanship for Women. 8vo. New York, 1887. A 29 Q 3

MEARS, Mrs. Amelia Garland. Idylls, Legends, and Lyrics. 8vo. Lond., 1890. H 5 R 42

MECHANICAL ENGINEERS, Institution of. [*See* Institution of Mechanical Engineers.]

MEDICAL BILL. Report of a Meeting of the Medical Profession held at Sydney on Tuesday, 2nd June, 1875, to take into consideration the speech by the Dean of the Faculty of Medicine, in the Sydney University, on the proposed Medical Bill for New South Wales. 8vo. Sydney, 1875. MF 4 R 23

MEDICAL REGISTER. 6 vols. roy. 8vo. Lond., 1887-92. E

MEDICAL TEMPERANCE JOURNAL. Vols. 1–6 (in 3 vols.) 8vo. Lond., 1870-75. F 11 Q 55-57

MEDLEY, G. W. [*See* Löwenthal, J.]

MEEK, F. B. [*See* U.S. Geol. Expl. of 40th Parallel, 4.]

MEGSON, J. Excelsior Polka. Fol. Sydney (n.d.) MA 11 Q 15 †

MEIDINGER, H. First Lessons in German. 12mo. Frankfort, 1848. K 16 P 24

MEIKLE, J. [*See* Shields, H.]

MEINEKE, A. Fragmenta Comicorum Graecorum. 8vo. Berolini, 1847. H 10 R 12
[*See* Athenæus; Strabo; *and* Stobæus, J.]

MEISSAS, l'Abbe de. Journal d'un Aumonier Militaire. 8vo. Paris, 1890. B 26 T 26

MÉJAN, M. [*See* Causes Célèbres.]

MELA, P. De Situ Orbis Libri III; cum notis, &c.; curante A. Gronovio. 8vo. Lug. Bat., 1722. D 11 R 24

MELBOURNE (William Lamb), Lord. [Life of]; by H. Dunckley. 8vo. Lond., 1890. C 16 Q 17

MELBOURNE CENTENNIAL INTERNATIONAL EXHIBITION, 1888. Catalogue of Exhibits in the New South Wales Court. Roy. 8vo. Sydney, 1888 MK 1 R 51
Catalogue of Exhibits in the Queensland Court. 8vo. Brisbane, 1888. MK 1 T 5
Catalogue of Minerals exhibited in the Queensland Court. 8vo. Brisbane, 1888. MK 1 T 4
New South Wales Mineral Court: Descriptive Catalogue of Exhibits of Metals, Minerals, Fossils, and Timbers. Roy. 8vo. Sydney, 1888.* MK 1 R 1
New South Wales Mineral Court. Descriptive Catalogue of Exhibits. Roy. 8vo. Sydney, 1889. MK 1 R 52
Official Guide to the Picture Galleries and Catalogue of Fine Arts; by J. Lake. 3rd ed. 8vo. Melb., 1888. MA 3 Q 53
Photographic Views of the New South Wales Court. Ob. fol. Melb., 1889. MA 2 P 27 ‡
Report by the Hon. R. B. Smith, Executive Commissioner. Roy. 8vo. Sydney, 1890. MK 1 S 32
Report of the Royal Commission to the Queen's most Excellent Majesty. 8vo. Lond., 1889. MK 1 T 6

MELBOURNE HOSPITAL. Report, 1883. 8vo. Melb., 1884. ME 6 Q

T

MELBOURNE PUBLIC LIBRARY, MUSEUMS, AND NATIONAL GALLERY. Catalogue of Newspapers, Magazines, Reviews, Publications of Societies, and Government Periodical Publications currently received. 8vo. Melb., 1891.   MK 1 T 20

Catalogue of Oil Paintings, Water-Colour Drawings and Portraits in the National Gallery. 8vo. Melb., 1889.   MK 1 T 26

Another Copy. 2nd ed. 8vo. Melb., 1891.   MK 1 T 28

MELBOURNE PUNCH, The. 4 vols. 4to. Melb., 1882-85.   ME 9 P 24-27 †

MELBOURNE UNIVERSITY. Calendars for the Years 1883-1887, and 1888-91. 7 vols. 12mo. Melb., 1884-90.   ME 5 S

Examination Papers., 1876, 1878, 1885-87. 5 vols. (in 3). 12mo. Melb., 1876-87.   ME 5 P

MELCOMBE, Lord. [*See* Dodington, G. B.]

MELDOLA, Prof. R. The Chemistry of Photography. 12mo. Lond., 1889.   A 21 P 3

MELSHEIMER, R. E., and GARDNER, S. Law and Customs of the Stock Exchange. 3rd ed. 8vo. Lond., 1891.   F 12 P 33

MELVILLE, H. Present State of Australasia, including New South Wales, &c. 8vo. Lond., 1851. MB 1 Q 13

MELVILLE, H. Narrative of a Four Months' Residence in the Marquesas Islands. 12mo. Lond., 1846. MD 4 P 21

Omoo: a Narrative of Adventures in the South Seas; being a Sequel to the "Residence in the Marquesas Islands." 12mo. Lond., 1847.   MD 4 P 23

MEMBER OF THE NEW ZEALAND BAR, A. [*See* Smythies, H.]

MEMNON. Excerpta historiæ, Græce et Latine H. Stephani et L. Rhodomanni interpretatione. 12mo. Amst., 1594.   B 35 P 14

MEMORIAL CATALOGUE of the French and Dutch Loan Collection. [*See* Edinburgh Intern. Exhibition.]

MEMORIES OF THE PAST. Auckland, from 1847; by "An Old Hand." 8vo. Auckland (n.d.) MB 1 P 29

MEMPES, M. The Grey River. [*See* McCarthy, J.]

MEN AND WOMEN OF THE TIME: a Dictionary of Contemporaries. 13th ed.; by G. W. Moon. Roy. 8vo. Lond., 1891.   C 12 U 18

MEN OF THE TIME: a Dictionary of Contemporaries. 12th ed., edited by T. H. Ward. 8vo. Lond., 1857. Libr.

MÉNARD, L. and R. De la Sculpture antique et moderne. 2ᵉ ed. 12mo. Paris, 1868.   A 23 Q 9

MENDANA, Dom A. [*See* Mendoce, Dom A.]

MENDENHALL, T. C. A Century of Electricity. (Nature Series.) 12mo. Lond., 1887.   A 21 Q 2

MENDOCE, Dom Alvare de, et MENDANA Dom Alvare, Voyage de, en 1567 (Prévost, A. F., Suite de l'histoire générale, tome 17). 4to. Amsterdam, 1761.   MD 11 P 16 †

MENNELL, P. The Coming Colony; Practical Notes on Western Australia. 8vo. Lond., 1892. MD 1 R 45

In Australian Wilds, and other Colonial Tales and Sketches. 2nd ed. 8vo. London, 1889. MJ 2 T 1

MENZIES, Rev. A. Church History. [*See* Baur, Dr. F. C.]

[*See* Pfleiderer, Dr. O.]

MENZIES, Rev. P. S. Sermons. 8vo. Melb., 1875.   MG 2 P 17

MENZIES, W. Forest Trees and Woodland Scenery, as described in ancient and modern Poets. 4to. Lond., 1875.   A 40 Q 6 ‡

MERCANTILE NAVY LIST and Maritime Directory. 6 vols. Roy. 8vo. Lond., 1887-92.   E

MERCIER, C. Sanity and Insanity. 12mo. Lond., 1890.   A 26 Q 4

The Nervous System and the Mind: a Treatise on the Dynamics of the Human Organism. 8vo. Lond., 1888.   A 12 U 34

MEREDITH, George. Poet and Novelist: a Public Lecture; by Prof. M. W. Maccallum. 12mo. Sydney, 1892.   MC 1 P 66

MEREDITH, Mrs. L. A. Bush Friends in Tasmania. Native Flowers, Fruits, and Insects, drawn from Nature. Last Series. Fol. Lond., 1891.   MA 7 Q 34 †

Travels and Stories in our Gold Colonies. 8vo. Lond. (n.d.)   MD 7 P 29

MEREDITH, Owen. [*See* Lytton, E. R. L. Bulwer-Lytton, Earl.]

MÉRIMÉE, Prosper. An Author's Love; being the unpublished Letters of P. Mérimée's "Inconnue." 2 vols. 8vo. Lond., 1889.   C 14 S 6, 7

Lettres à M. Panizzi, 1850-70. 5th ed. 2 vols. 8vo. Paris, 1881.   C 16 T 2, 3

Ouvrages de. 17 vols. 8vo. Paris, 1874-91. J 19 R 11-27

Carmen, Arsène Guillot, L' Abbé Aubain, La Dame de Pique, Les Bohémiens, Le Hussard, Nicolas Gogol.
Chronique du Règne de Charles IX.
Colomba, La Vénus d' Ille, Les Ames du Purgatoire.
Les Cosaques d'autrefois.
Dernières Nouvelles-Lokis, Il Viccolo di Madama Lucrezia, La Chambre Bleue, Djoumane, Le Coup de Pistolet, Federigo, Les Sorcières espagnoles.
Les Deux Héritages, suivis de L' Inspecteur Général, et des Débuts d'un Aventurier.
La Double Méprise, La Guzla.
Épisode de l' Histoire de Russie, Les Faux Démétrius.
Études sur les Arts au moyen Âge.
Études sur l' Histoire Romaine, Guerre Sociale, Conjuration de Catilina.
Lettres à une Autre Inconnue.
Lettres à une Inconnue.
Mélanges historiques et littéraires.
Mosaïque—Mateo Falcone, Vision de Charles XI, L' Enlèvement de la Redoute, Tamango, La Perle de Tolède, La Partie de Trictrac, La Vase Étrusque, Les Mécontents, Lettres d' Espagne.
Portraits historiques et Littéraires.
Théâtre de Clara Gazul, suivi de La Jaquerie, et de La Famille Carvajal.

MERIVALE, C. The Fall of the Roman Republic. 2nd
ed. 8vo. Lond., 1853. B 30 Q 9

MERIVALE, Prof. J. H. Notes and Formulæ for Mining
Students. 12mo. Lond., 1887. A 24 P 1

MERKEL, R. [*See* Apollonius Rhodius.]

MERLÉ D'AUBIGNE, J. H. History of the Reformation of the 16th Century : translated by H. White. 5
vols. 8vo. Edinb., 1846. G 8 S 28-32

MÉRODE, F. F. X. de, Archbishop of Melitinensis; his
Life and Works; by M. Besson. 8vo. Lond., 1887.
C 15 Q 20

MERRY ENGLAND. Vols. 8-18. 8vo. Lond., 1886-92
E.

MERRYWEATHER, James Compton. The Fire Brigade
Handbook. 8vo. Manchester, 1888. A 25 T 1

Fire Brigade Hand-book. 8vo. Lond., 1888. F 7 Q 32

MESSENIUS, J. G. [*See* Horatius Flaccus, Q.]

MESSURIER, Col. A. Le. [*See* Le Messurier, Col. A.]

MESTON, A. Report on Government Scientific Expedition to Bellenden-Ker Range (Wooroonooran), North
Queensland. Fol. Brisbane, 1889. MD 11 Q 13 †

METASTASIO, P. A. D. B. Vie de Métastase ; par M. H.
Boyle. 12mo. Paris, 1887. C 14 P 18

METEOROLOGICAL OBSERVATIONS at the Foreign
and Colonial Stations of the Royal Engineers and the
Army Medical Department 1852-86. 4to. Lond, 1890.
A 42 R 10 ‡

METTERNICH, Prince C. W. N. L. Life of; by Col.
G. B. Malleson. (Statesmen Series.) 8vo. Lond., 1888.
C 15 Q 6

MEURSIUS, J. [*See* Constantinus, VII.]

MEW, James, and ASHTON, John. Drinks of the World.
8vo. Lond., 1892. A 22 S 2

MEYER, A. B. [*See* Gabelentz, G. von der.]

MEYER, Prof. E. von. History of Chemistry, from
earliest times to the present day. 8vo. Lond., 1891.
A 21 S 8

MEYER, Prof. G. H. Why the Shoe Pinches: a contribution to applied anatomy, translated from the German by
John Stirling Craig. 12mo. Edinb. 1860. A 26 P 16

MEYER, Dr. Hans. Across East African Glaciers : an
account of the first ascent of Kilimanjaro ; translated by
E. H. S. Calder. Imp. 8vo. Lond., 1891. D 2 U 14
Gutenbergs' Album. 4to. Braunschweig, 1840.
H 13 P 1 †

MEYER, Prof. Lothar. Outlines of Theoretical Chemistry ;
translated by Prof. P. Phillips Bedson and Prof. W. C.
Williams. 8vo. Lond., 1892. A 21 S 9

Modern Theories of Chemistry. 8vo. Lond., 1888.
A 5 T 22

MEYER, O. [*See* New Zealand and South Seas Exhibition.]

MEYER, Dr. V. [*See* Lunge, Dr. G.]

MEYMOTT, C. New Truths and their reception : a
Lecture. 12mo. Sydney, 1858. MA 2 P 62

MICHAEL, J. L. John Cumberland. 8vo. Sydney (n.d.)
MH 1 P 19

MICHAEL, W. H., and WILL, J. S. The Law relating
to Gas and Water. 3rd ed. 8vo. Lond., 1884.
F 9 S 20

MICHEL, Ernest. A Travers l'Hémisphère Sud ou Mon
Second Voyage autour du Monde. 3 vols. 8vo. Paris,
1887-90. MD 8 R 9-11

MICHEL, F. Les Écossais en France : les Français en
Écosse. 2 vols. 8vo. Lond., 1862. B 26 T 6, 7

MICHELL, E. B. Boxing. [*See* Fencing.]

MICHELET, C. L. Aristotelis Ethicorum Nicomacheorum
libri decem ; commentarium. 8vo. Berolini, 1848.
G 13 P 21

MICHELET, J. Life of Luther. [*See* Universal Library,
The.]

Histoire du 19ᵉ Siècle. 3 vols. 12mo. Paris, 1880.
B 34 P 27-29

Un Hiver en Italie. 2ᵉ ed. 12mo. Paris (n.d.) D 18 P 15

La Montagne. 12mo. Paris, 1887. A 20 Q 12

Ma Jeunesse. 7ᵉ ed. 12mo. Paris, 1884. C 14 P 16

Mon Journal, 1820-23. 12mo. Paris, 1888. C 14 P 15

Nos Fils. 12mo. Paris (n.d.) G 18 P 9

Précis de l' Histoire de France jusqu' à la Révolution
Française. 2nd ed. 8vo. Paris, 1834. B 26 T 5

Rome. 12mo. Paris, 1891. D 18 P 16

La Sorcière. 12mo. Paris, 1867. G 2 V 31

MICHIE, Sir A. Retrospects and Prospects of the Colony :
a Lecture. 8vo. Melb., 1866. MF 1 T 69

MICHIE, C. Y. The Practice of Forestry. 8vo. Edinb.
1887. A 1 U 25

MICHIELS, A. La Case de l'Oncle Tom. [*See* Stowe,
Mrs. Harriet B.]

MIDDLEMASS, Miss Hume. "Mignonette." [*See* Browne,
Lady H. G.]

MIDDLETON, Prof. J. H. The Engraved Gems of Classical Times, with a Catalogue of the Gems in the Fitz-
william Museum. Roy. 8vo. Camb., 1891. A 8 R 41

MIDDLETON, T. [Plays of ;] edited by H. Ellis. (Mer-
maid Series). 2 vols. 8vo. Lond., 1887-90. Unex-
purgated edition. H 4 Q 30, 31
[Life of] Thomas Middleton.
A Trick to Catch the Old One.
The Changeling.
A Chaste Maid in Cheapside.
Women beware Women.
The Spanish Gipsy.
The Roaring Girl.
A Fair Quarrel.
The Witch.
Mayor of Queenborough.
The Widow.

MIDDLETON, T.—*contd.*

A Mad World, my Masters: a Comedy. [*See* British Drama, Ancient, 2.]

The Mayor of Quinborough : a Comedy. [*See* British Drama, Ancient, 3.]

The Widow : a Comedy. [*See* Jonson, B.]

The Witch : a Tragi-comedy. [*See* British Drama, Ancient, 3.]

MIDDLETON, T., and DEKKER, T. The Roaring Girl, or Moll Cut-purse : a Comedy. [*See* British Drama, Ancient, 2.]

MIDSHIPMAN ON BOARD THE SAID SHIP, A. [*See* Byron, Commodore J.]

MIGNE, J. P. [*See* Aquinas, St. T.]

MIGNET, F. A. M. Antonio Perez et Philippe II. 12mo. Paris, 1881.   B 16 Q 35

Charles-Quint ; son abdication, son sejour et sa mort au monastère de Yuste. 2ᵉ éd. Paris, 1891.   B 26 Q 34

Etudes Historiques ; la Germanie aux 8ᵉ et 9ᵉ Siècles ; Formation de la France ; Etablissement de la Réforme a Genéve, introduction a l' Histoise de la Succession d' Espagne. 5ᵉ éd. 12mo. Paris, 1884.   B 34 P 30

Histoire de la Marie Stuart. 6ᵉ éd. 2 vols. 12mo. Paris, 1885.   C 14 P 21, 22

Histoire de la Révolution Française, 1789–1814. 2 vols. 8vo. Paris, 1880.   B 26 Q 7, 8

Histoire de la Révolution Française, depuis 1789 jusqu'en 1814. 5ᵉ éd. 2 vols. 12mo. Paris, 1884.   B 26 Q 32, 33

Notice historique sur la Vie et les Travaux de Victor Cousin. 8vo. Paris, 1869.   C 21 R 8

Nouveau Eloges Historiques ; De Savigny, Alexis de Tocqueville, Victor Cousin, Lord Brougham, Charles Dunoyer, Victor de Broglie, Amédée Thiery. 2ᵉ éd. 12mo. Paris, 1878.   B 26 Q 29

Rivalité de François I et de Charles V. 2 vols. 12mo. Paris, 1886.   B 26 Q 30–31

Vie de Franklin. 3e éd. 12mo. Paris, 1887.   C 14 P 20

MIGNONETTE. [*See* Middlemas, Miss H.]

MIJATOVICH, C. Constantine : the conquest of Constantinople by the Turks. 8vo. Lond., 1892.   B 17 P 16

MILBOURN, S. Love's Memories, Song. 2nd ed. Fol. Adelaide, 1890.   MA 7 Q 31†

MILBOURN, S., Junr. Eden-Love Valse. Fol. Melb., 1892.   MA 7 Q 31†

The Yacht Club Mazurka. Fol. Melb. (n.d.)   MA 7 Q 31†

MILES, J. Vindication of Admiral Lord Nelson's Proceedings in the Bay of Naples. 12mo. Lond., 1843.   C 17 P 23

MILES, W. A. Description of the Deverel Barrow, opened A.D. 1825 ; also a minute account of the Kimmeridge Coal Money. Imp. 8vo. Lond., 1826.   B 23 V 3

MILES, W. A.—*contd.*

[A letter on the above from Lord Colchester.] 4to. Lond., 1826.   B 23 V 3

The Correspondence of William Augustus Miles on the French Revolution, 1789–1817. 2 vols. 8vo. Lond., 1890.   B 26 U 15–16

MILET-MUREAU, M.L.A. [*See* La Perouse, J. F. G. de.]

MILITARY TEXT-BOOKS. Provisional Infantry Drill. 16mo. Lond., 1892.   A 29 R 23

Queen's Regulations and Orders for the Army. Parts 1, 2. 8vo. Lond., 1889.   F 6 R 44, 45

MILL, Rev. John. Diary of. [*See* Scottish History Society, 5.]

MILL, J. S. [*See* Bradlaugh, C., Ritchie, D. G., and Robertson, J. M.]

MILLAR, W J. The Clyde, from its Source to the Sea. 8vo. Lond., 1888.   D 18 R 1

MILLER, Annie Jenness. Physical Beauty ; how to obtain and how to Preserve it. 8vo. Lond., 1892.   A 26 S 7

MILLER, Ellen E. Alone through Syria. 8vo. Lond., 1891.   D 17 Q 9

MILLER, H. The Old Red Sandstone ; or, New Walks in an Old Field. 20th ed. 8vo. Lond., 1875.   A 24 R 6

MILLER, Prof. J. Alcohol : its place and power. 12mo. Glasgow, 1880.   F 11 P 25

MILLER, John. [*See* Lane, W.]

MILLER, J. Mahomet : a Tragedy. [*See* British Drama, Modern, 2.]

MILLER, J. J. Sporting Pamphlet and Official Trotting Record, 1883–84. 12mo. Melb., 1884.   MA 2 V 41

MILLER, R. C. Books ; their History and Influence. 8vo. Melb., 1883.   MB 1 Q 39

MILLIGAN, Joseph. Reports on the Coal Basins of Van Diemen's Land. 8vo. Hobart, 1849.   MA 3 S 59

MILLINGEN, Dr. J. G. Curiosities of Medical Experience. 2nd ed. 8vo. Lond., 1839.   A 13 R 16

MILLS, Evelynne. The Modern Lyric from a Musical Standpoint. 8vo. Hobart, 1892.   MA 3 S 26

MILLS, Rev. J. G. Sunday Closing of Public Houses. 12mo. Lond. (n.d.)   F 11 P 54

MILLS, L. H. [*See* Müller, F. Max, Sacred Books, 31.]

MILLSPAUGH, C. F. American Medicinal Plants: an illustrated and descriptive Guide to the American Plants used as Homœopathic Remedies. 3 vols. roy. 4to. New York, 1887.   A 9 R 1–3 †

MILMAN, Rev. Dr. H. H. History of Latin Christianity. 2nd ed. 6 vols. 8vo. Lond., 1857.   G 16 T 28–33

MILNE, D. A Readable English Dictionary, etymologically arranged. 8vo. Lond., 1888.   K 11 V 55

MILNE, Rev. J. Frazer Prize Essay on Secularism in Relation to Christianity. 8vo. Sydney, 1889.
MG 1 T 26
Frazer Prize Essay on Agnosticism. [*See* Burgess, Rev. H. T.]

MILNE, Rev. J. J. Weekly Problem Papers, with notes. 12mo. Lond., 1886. A 25 P 28
Companion to the Weekly Problem Papers. 8vo. Lond., 1888. A 25 Q 26

MILNE-EDWARDS, M. [*See* Edwards, M. Milne —.]

MILNER, H. E. Art and Practice of Landscape Gardening; with Plans and Illustrations. 4to. Lond., 1890. A42 R 4 ‡

MILNER, Rev. J. Collectanea Latina Minora, designed for the use of Schools, with critical and explanatory notes. 12mo. Sydney, 1853. MK 1 P 59
A Few Plain Words about Baptismal Regeneration. 8vo. Sydney, 1851. MG 1 R 62
[*See* Euripides.]

MILNE, Rev. T. Gallery of Geography. Imp. 8vo. Lond., 1864. D 11 W 1

MILNES, Richard Monckton. [*See* Houghton, Lord.]

MILTON, John. Poetical Works of; edited by Prof. D. Masson. 3 vols. 8vo. Lond., 1890. H 5 T 38–40
Poetical Works of; edited by Sir E. Bridges; with Imaginative Illustrations by J. M. W. Turner. 6 vols. 12mo. Lond., 1835. H 5 S 13–18
1. Life of Milton.
2, 3. Paradise Lost.
4. Paradise Regained.
5. Remarks on Milton's Versification.— Samson Agonistes.— Comus. —Arcades.
6. L'Allegro and Il Penseroso.— Sonnets.—On the Morning of Christ's Nativity.—The Passion.—Odes. Miscellanies.—Translations.—Joannis Miltoni Londinensis Poemata.— Elegiarum Liber.—Epigrammatum Liber.—Silvarum Liber.
Comus : a Mask. [*See* British Drama, Modern.]
[*See* Powning, W.]

MIND : a Quarterly Review of Psychology and Philosophy. Vols. 1–6, 12–16. 8vo. Lond., 1876–91. E

MINGHETTI, Marco. The Masters of Raffaello. 8vo. Lond., 1882. A 2 T 83

MINING MANUAL, The. 2 vols. 8vo. Lond., 1890–91 E

MINNESOTA. [*See* United States of America.]

MIRABEAU, Honoré Gabriel Riquetti, Comte de. Mirabeau : a Life-History. 2 vols. 8vo. Lond., 1848. C 12 R 18, 19

MIRAMS, J. The Land Question in Victoria : a Speech. 8vo. Melb. (n.d.) MF 2 T 66

MISCELLANEA GENEALOGICA ET HERALDICA. Vol. 1-4. Imp. 8vo. Lond., 1886-92. K 8 U 5–8

MISOPSEUDES : a Vision, and Extracts from Letters. 2nd. ed. 8vo. Melb., 1873. MG 1 S 64

MITCHEL, J. Jail Journal; or, Five Years in British Prisons. 8vo. New York, 1854. MC 1 P 42
Life of; by W. Dillon. 2 vols. 8vo. Lond., 1888. C 12 T 1, 2

MITCHELL, A. [*See* Coombe, A.]

MITCHELL, Sir C. Report in connection with the Recent Disturbances in, and the affairs of Tonga. Fol. Lond., 1887. MF 12 Q 17 †

MITCHELL, H. Diamonds and Gold of South Africa, with the Transvaal Gold Law. 8vo. Lond., 1888. A 24 T 3

MITCHELL, Lieut.-Col. Sir T. L. The Australian Geography; with the Shores of the Pacific and those of the Indian Ocean. 12mo. Sydney, 1851. MD 3 P 19
Three Expeditions into the Interior of Eastern Australia ; with Descriptions of Australia Felix and New South Wales. 2 vols. 8vo. Lond., 1839. MD 2 T 33, 34

MITCHELL, Rev. W. A. Geology. [*See* Ansted, Prof. D. T.]

MITCHELL & CO. The Newspaper Press Directory. Imp. 8vo. Lond., 1890. E

MITFORD, Mary R. Christina, the Maid of the South Seas ; a Poem. 8vo. Lond., 1811. MH 1 S 64

MITFORD, Maj.-Gen. R. C. W. R. Orient and Occident : a Journey East from Lahore to Liverpool. 8vo. Lond., 1888. D 10 R 23

MITTEN, W. Australian Mosses. 8vo. Melb., 1882. MA 1 U 49

MIVART, St. G. Essays and Criticisms. 2 vols. 8vo. Lond., 1892. J 3 T 5, 6
On Truth : a Systematic Enquiry. 8vo. Lond., 1889. G 12 P 38

MOBERLEY, Rev. C. E. The Early Tudors, Henry vii and Henry viii. 18mo. Lond., 1887. B 21 P 26

MODERATE DRINKING. Opinions of Sir Henry Thompson ; Dr. B. W. Richardson ; Rev. Canon Farrar ; Admir. Sir B. J. Sulivan ; Rev. H. S. Paterson ; E. Baines, &c. 12mo. Lond., 1885. F 11 P 52
Speeches by the Lord Bishop of Exeter ; Dr. A. Carpenter ; Mr. J. J. Ritchie ; Dr. B. W. Richardson ; Rev. C. B. Symes ; and His Eminence Cardinal-Archbishop Manning. 12mo. Lond., 1884. F 11 P 65

MODESTUS. Œuvres de. [*See* Nisard, D.]

MOELLMANN, W. De Alcoholica Intoxicatione Chronica. 8vo. Berolini, 1862. F 11 Q 36

MOFFAT, Rev. Adam. Sermons. 8vo. Melb., 1878. MG 2 R 13

MOHAMMED, D. E. [*See* Djémal-eddin-Mohammed.]

MOHL, Julius and Mary. Letters and Recollections of by M. C. M. Simpson. 8vo. Lond., 1887. C 13 T 14

MOISTER, Rev. W. Evil and the Remedy ; or, the Sin and Folly of Intemperance and the Wisdom and Excellence of Total Abstinence. 8vo. Lond. 1884. F 11 Q 13

MOLESCHOTT, J. Die Einheit der Wissenschaft. 12mo.
Gietzen (n.d.)   H 1 R 34–41

MOLESWORTH, Sir W.   [*See* Danson, J. T.*]

MOLIERE, J. B. P. Œuvres complètes. (Collection
Jannet-Picard.) 8 vols. 12mo. Paris (n.d.)
                                                  H 1 R 34–41

MOLI, A. Hypnotism. 12mo. Lond., 1890.   A 26 Q 8

MÖLLENDORFF, P. G. and O. F. Manual of Chinese
Bibliography. 8vo. Shanghai, 1876.   K 7 R 49

MOLLOY, J. F. The Faiths of the People. 2 vols.
roy. 8vo. Lond., 1892.   G 6 T 23, 24

Life and Adventures of Edmund Kean, Tragedian, 1787–
1833. 2 vols. 8vo. Lond., 1888.   C 14 Q 21, 21

MOLONEY, Alfred. Sketch of the Forestry of West
Africa. 8vo. Lond., 1887.   A 1 U 13

MOLTKE, H. Count von. The Franco-German War of
1870–71. 2 vols. 8vo. Lond., 1891.   B 26 T 3, 4

MOMBERT, J. I. Charles the Great. [*See* Charlemagne.]

MOMMSEN, T. History of Rome; translated by the
Rev. W. P. Dickson. Vols. 1–3. 8vo. Lond., 1862-63.
                                                 B 30 Q 11–13

History of Rome; translated by W. P. Dickson. Vols. 1–6.
8vo. Lond., 1868–86.   B 11 T 25–30

MONCELON, Leon. Les Canaques de la Nouvelle-Calédonie et des Nouvelles-Hébrides. Roy. 8vo. Paris, 1886.
                                                  MF 3 T 31

Le Bagne et la Colonisation Pénale à la Nouvelle-Calédonie.
Roy. 8vo. Paris, 1886.   MF 3 T 32

MONCK, Frances E. O. My Canadian Leaves ; Account
of a Visit to Canada, 1864-65. 8vo. Lond., 1891.
                                                   D 15 S 17

MONEY, W. History of Newbury, in the County of Berks.
Roy. 8vo. Oxford., 1887.   B 21 U 18

MONGREDIEN, A. Free Trade and English Commerce.
8vo. Lond., 1881.   F 5 Q 46

On the Displacement of Labour and Capital. 8vo. Lond.,
1886.   F 5 Q 47

The Western Farmer of America. . 8vo. Lond., 1886.
                                              F 5 S 47

MONIER-WILLIAMS, Sir M. [*See* Williams, Sir M.
Monier-.]

MONK, Very Rev. Dean James Henry. Life of Richard
Bentley, D.D. 4to. Lond., 1830.   C 42 S 11 ‡

MONK, Gen. George, Duke of Albemarle. [Life of];
by Julian Corbett. 12mo. Lond., 1889.   C 12 P 32

Monk: Chute de la République et Rétablissement de la
Monarchie en Angleterre, en 1660 ; Etude Historique par
M. Guizot. 12mo. Paris, 1874.   C 17 Q 27

MONKHOUSE, William Cosmo. The Earlier English
Water-Colour Painters. Imp. 8vo. Lond., 1890.
                                                  A 8 T 32

[*See* Heaton, Mrs. C.]

MONMOUTH, Robert Cary, Earl of. Memoirs of the
Life of ; written by himself. 2nd ed. 8vo. Lond.,
1759.   C 18 S 11

MONNIER, Rev. J. Memoir of; translated by W. A.
Duncan. 8vo. Sydney, 1876.   MC 1 P 39

MONNIER, M. Un Printemps sur le Pacifique : Iles
Hawaï. 8vo. Paris 1885.   MD 1 Q 20

MONTAGU, Basil. Some Enquiries into the Effects of
Fermented Liquors ; by "A Water Drinker." 2nd ed.
8vo. Lond., 1818.   F 11 R 42

MONTAGU, Irving. Camp and Studio. 8vo. Lond.,
1890.   C 12 T 34

Wanderings of a War Artist. 8vo. Lond., 1889.
                                                  D 18 U 2

MONTAGU, Lady M. W. Letters and Works of; edited
by Lord Wharncliffe; with a Memoir, &c., by W. M.
Thomas. 2 vols. 8vo. Lond., 1887.   C 12 P 14, 15

MONTAGUE, Francis C. Life of Sir Robert Peel. (Statesmen Series.) 8vo. Lond., 1888.   C 12 R 35

The Old Poor-Law and the New Socialism ; or, Pauperism
and Taxation. 8vo. Lond., 1886.   F 5 S 38

Technical Education. 12mo. Lond., 1887.   G 18 P 11

MONTAIGNE, M. de. Essais de. 3 vols. 4to. Paris,
1725.   J 39 Q 21–23 ‡

[Life of]; by A. Sorel. (Great French Writers.) 8vo.
Lond., 1887.   C 11 P 19

Persian Letters ; translated by J. Davidson. 2 vols. 8vo.
Lond., 1892.   J 12 Q 41, 42

MONTFORT, Simon de. [*See* Hutton, Rev. W. H.]

MONTGOMERIE, A. Poems of. (Scottish Text Soc.)
8vo. Edinb., 1887.   E

MONTGOMERY, W. The Montgomery Manuscripts ;
(1603–1706) ; edited, with Notes, by Rev. G. Hill. Sm.
4to. Belfast, 1869.   C 18 T 17

MONTH, The : a Catholic Review. Vols. 1–13, 44, 59–75.
8vo. Lond., 1864–92.   E

MONTHLY REVIEW, The. Vols. 7, 8, 1752–53. 8vo.
Lond., 1753.   E

MONTH IN THE BUSH OF AUSTRALIA. Journal
of one of a Party of Gentlemen who recently travelled
from Sydney to Port Phillip. 8vo. Lond., 1838.
                                                  MD 7 S 18

MONTROSE, James Graham, Marquis of. [Life of] by M.
Morris. (English Men of Action.) 12mo. Lond., 1892.
                                                  C 17 Q 20

MONTT, Pedro. Exposition of the Illegal Acts of Ex-President Balmaceda which caused the Civil War in Chile. 8vo. Washington, 1891. B 18 R 12

MONUMENTOS ARQUITECTONICOS DE ESPAÑA. 7 vols. Fol. Madrid, 1876–81. A 43 P 8-14 ‡

MOODIE, D. C. F. The History of the Battles and Adventures of the British, the Boers, and the Zulus, &c., in South Africa, from the time of Pharoah Necho to 1880. 2 vols. 8vo. Cape Town, 1888. B 16 P 25, 26

MOODIE, G. P. Annexation of the Transvaal. 8vo. Lond., 1881. F 8 S 26

MOODY, J. J. The Borough Elector's Manual, and Municipal Councillor's Vade Mecum. 8vo. Melb., 1863. MF 3 Q 23

MOON, G. W. The Dean's English : a Criticism on the Dean of Canterbury's Essays on the Queen's English. 9th ed. 12mo. Lond., 1874. K 16 P 14
Men and Women of the Time. [*See* Men and Women of the Time.]

MOORE, Charles. Notes on the Genus Doryanthes, with a Notice and Description of a new Species. 8vo. Sydney, 1884. MA 3 T 52

MOORE, C. H. Development and Character of Gothic Architecture. 8vo. Lond., 1890. A 19 T 5

MOORE, Rev. E. Contributions to the Textual Criticism of the Divina Commedia. 8vo. Camb., 1889. H 10 S 6
Dante and his early Biographers. 8vo. Lond., 1890. C 12 R 8
The Time-References in the Divina Commedia. 8vo. Lond., 1887. J 9 Q 40

MOORE, E. The Gamester : a Tragedy. [*See* British Drama, Modern, 2.]

MOORE, F. F. Coral and Cocoa-nut : the Cruise of the Yacht "Fire-Fly" to Samoa. 8vo. Lond., 1890. MJ 2 T 36

MOORE, J. Brief Grammar of Modern Geography, for the Use of Schools. 2nd ed. 12mo. Sydney, 1853. MD 2 W 35

MOORE, Sir John. Life of ; by J. C. Moore. 2 vols. (in 1.) 8vo. Lond., 1834. C 14 S 12

MOORE, J. C. Life of Sir John Moore. 2 vols. (in 1.) 8vo. Lond., 1834. C 14 S 12

MOORE, J. J. Australian Almanac. 11 vols. 8vo. Sydney, 1874–85. ME

MOORE, J. M. New Zealand for the Emigrant, Invalid, and Tourist. 8vo. Lond., 1890. MD 7 P 39

MOORE, J. Sheridan. The Bronze Trumpet : a Satirical Poem. 12mo. Sydney, 1866. MH 1 U 28

MOORE, Thomas. Irish Melodies. 12th ed. 12mo. Lond., 1834. H 3 P 46

MOOREHEAD, W. K. Wanneta : the Sioux. 8vo. Lond., 1891. J 11 V 12

MOORHOUSE, Rt. Rev. James. The Bishop of Melbourne in reply to Judge Williams on Religion without Superstition. 8vo. Melb., 1855. MG 1 S 65

MOORS, H. On the Sea-cell as a possible source of danger in Torpedo Experiments. 8vo. Melb., 1881. MA 3 Q 50

MORA, F. [*See* Becker, S. C.]

MORDAUNT, Charles. [*See* Peterborough, Earl of.]

MORE, Hannah [Life of]; by Charlotte M. Yonge. (Eminent Women.) 8vo. Lond., 1888. C 12 Q 28
[*See* Walford, L. B.]

MORE, Sir Thomas. Life and Writings of ; by the Rev. T. E. Bridgett. 8vo. Lond., 1891. C 16 Q 16

MOREHEAD, R. A. A. Letter to the Miners at Lambton Colliery. 8vo. Sydney, 1879. MF 1 T 42
Primary Education, as Administered in New South Wales. 8vo. Sydney, 1876. M 1 R 47
Notes, and Further Notes on the Coal Trade of New South Wales. 8vo. Sydney, 1872. MF 1 T 43

MORELI, Sir C. Tales of the Genii; or, the Delightful Lessons of Horam, the Son of Asmar. 2 vols. 8vo. Lond., 1805. J 3 V 19, 20

MORELL, G. A. On the Defences of Port Jackson. 8vo. Sydney, 1865. MA 3 Q 4

MORELLUS, Frédéric. [*See* Philostratus.]

MORERY, L. Le Grand Dictionaire Historique ou le melange curieux de l' Histoire Sacrée et Profane. 2 vols. fol. Amst., 1692. K 33 P 11, 12

MOREWOOD, S. Essay on Inventions and Customs of Ancients and Moderns in the use of Inebriating Liquors. 8vo. Lond., 1824. F 11 R 43

MORFILL, W. R. Russia. (Story of the Nations Series.) 8vo. Lond., 1890. B 31 R 1
Simplified Grammar of the Polish Language 8vo. Lond., 1884. K 20 Q 15
Simplified Grammar of the Serbian Language. 8vo. Lond., 1887 K 20 Q 20

MORGAN, A. Digest Shakespeareanæ. [*See* New York Shakespeare Society.]
Shakespeare in Fact and in Criticism. 8vo. New York, 1888. J 5 R 34
[*See* Shakespeare, W.]

MORGAN, Prof. C. L. Animal Life and Intelligence. 8vo. Lond., 1890–91. A 14 T 43
Animal Sketches. 8vo. Lond., 1891. A 28 S 26

MORGAN, Delmar. Early Discovery of Australia. [*See* Royal Geographical Society of Australasia.]

MORGAN, J. The Municipal Act, with observations on the Several Clauses, and on the most Equitable mode of Assessment, &c. 8vo. Hobart, 1852. MF 2 T 31

MORHANGE, S. Etude sur l' Australie, 1862-69. 12mo. Bruxelles, 1869. MD 7 T 22

MORICE, Rev. F. D. Pindar. (Ancient Classics for English Readers.) 12mo. Edinb., 1879. J 14 P 20

MORISON, J. C. Service of Man: an Essay towards the Religion of the Future. 8vo. Lond., 1887. G 12 P 36

MORLEY, Prof. H. A Bundle of Ballads; edited by H. Morley. 18mo. Lond., 1891. H 6 P 44

English Writers: an Attempt towards a History of English Literature. Vols. 1-8. 8vo. Lond., 1887-92. B 21 R 25-32
1. Introduction.--Origins.—Old Celtic Literature.—Beowulf.
2. From Cædmon to the Conquest.
3. From the Conquest to Chaucer.
4-5. The Fourteenth Century.
6. From Chaucer to Caxton.
7. From Caxton to Coverdale.
8. Surry to Spenser.

MORLEY, H. F. [*See* Watts, H.]

MORLEY, J. Aphorisms: an Address delivered before the Edinburgh Philosophical Institution, November 11th, 1887. 12mo. Lond., 1887. G 8 P 26

Studies in Literature. 8vo. Lond., 1891. J 1 W 47

Walpole. 8vo. Lond., 1889. C 12 R 34

Life of Richard Cobden. 4to. Lond., 1882. C 17 U 20

MORLEY, S. Life of; by E. Hodder. 2nd ed. 8vo. Lond., 1887. C 13 U 15

MORPHOLOGISCHES JAHRBUCH. Bande 13-18. 8vo. Leip., 1887-92. E

MORRIN, Jas. Calendar of the Patent and Close Rolls of Chancery of Ireland. [*See* Ireland.]

MORRIS, Anne C. [*See* Morris, G.]

MORRIS, E. E. [*See* Cassell's Picturesque Australasia.]

MORRIS, E. J. Corsica. [*See* Gregorovius, F.]

MORRIS, E. R. The Official Newspaper Atlas of Australasia. 4to. Sydney, 1891. MD 11 P 4 †

MORRIS, Gouverneur. Diary and Letters of. Edited by Anne C. Morris. 2 vols. 8vo. Lond., 1889. C 13 T 15, 16

[Life of]; by T. Roosevelt. (American Statesmen.) 12mo. Boston, 1888. C 2 R 24

MORRIS, H. Simplified Grammar of the Telugu Language. 8vo. Lond., 1890. K 20 Q 24

MORRIS, Isabel. A Summer in Kieff; or, Sunny Days in Southern Russia. 8vo. Lond., 1891 D 18 T 4

MORRIS, M. Montrose. (English Men of Action.) 12mo. Lond., 1892. C 17 Q 20

Claverhouse. (English Worthies.) 8vo. Lond., 1887. C 12 P 28

MORRIS, Rev. M. G. F. Yorkshire Folk-Talk. 12mo. Lond., 1892. K 14 P 28

MORRIS, Wm. Æneids of Virgil done into English Verse. 2nd ed. 8vo. Lond., 1889. W 8 Q 23

Defence of Guenevere, and other Poems. 8vo. Lond., 1889. H 8 Q 24

Dream of John Bull, and a King's Lesson. 12mo. Lond., 1888. J 1 U 40

Signs of Change: Seven Lectures delivered on various occasions. 8vo. Lond., 1888. F 6 Q 44

[*See* Homer.]

Life and Death of Jason: a Poem. 9th ed. 8vo. Lond., 1889. H 8 Q 25

Love is Enough; or, the Freeing of Pharamond. 3rd. ed. 8vo. Lond., 1889. H 8 Q 21

News from Nowhere; or, an Epoch of Rest, being some Chapters from a Utopian Romance. 12mo. Lond., 1891. J 1 W 48

The Roots of the Mountains. Sm. 4to. Lond., 1890. J 5 P 45

The Odyssey of Homer, done into English Verse. 8vo. Lond., 1887. H 8 Q 26

Poems by the Way. Sm. 4to. Lond., 1891. H 8 T 55

Story of Sigurd the Volsung, and the Fall of the Niblungs, 4th ed. 8vo. Lond., 1887. H 8 Q 27

Story of the Glittering Plain. 12mo. Lond., 1891. J 11 W 9

Tale of the House of the Wolfings, and all the Kindreds of the Mark. 8vo. Lond., 1889. H 8 Q 22

A Vision of Saints. 12mo. Lond., 1890. H 6 K 44

MORRIS, W., and MAGNÚSSON, E. The Saga Library. [*See* Saga Library, The.]

MORRIS, W. O'C. Great Commanders of Modern Times, and the Campaign of 1815. Roy. 8vo. Lond., 1891. C 13 V 4

MORRISON, A. J. W. Ancient Philosophy. [*See* Ritter, Dr. H.]

MORRISON, G. B. Ventilation and Warning of School Buildings. 8vo. New York, 1887. A 2 R 42

MORRISON, Rev. W. D. Crime and its Causes. 8vo. Lond., 1891. F 6 R 41

The Jews under Roman Rule. (Story of the Nations Series.) 8vo. Lond., 1890. B 28 R 6

MORRISON, W. F. The Aldine Centennial History of New South Wales, Illustrated. 2 vols. 4to. Sydney, 1888 MB 2 V 14, 15

The Aldine History of Queensland, Illustrated. 2 vols. 4to. Sydney, 1888. MB 2 V 12, 13

MORSE, J. T., jun. [Life of] Benjamin Franklin. (American Statesmen.) 12mo. Boston, 1889. C 13 Q 4

MORTIMER, H. W. Refutation of the Personal Reign of our Lord Jesus Christ, and a Vindication of the Restoration of the Jews. 2nd ed. 12mo. Melb., 1868. MG 2 P 21

MORTIMER, Mrs. M. The Night of Toil. 3rd ed. 12mo. Lond., 1849. MD 3 P 23

MORTIMER-FRANKLYN, H. [*See* Franklyn, H. M.-]

MORTON, Alexander. [*See* Royal Society of Tasmania.]

MORTON, Mrs. A. Heroes of Notasia ; a Record of Australian Exploration ; by "Dio." 8vo. Hobart, 1888. MD 1 R 24
Maria Island ; its Past, Present, and Probable Future ; by "Dio." 8vo. Hobart, 1888. MD 4 P 50

MORTON, J. Vaccination and its Evil Consequences ; Cowpox and its Origin, Small Pox, &c. 8vo. Parramatta, 1875. MA 3 Q 3

MORTON, P. Geometry, Plain, Solid, and Sperical. 8vo. Lond., 1830. A 25 S 25

MOSBLECH, L'Abbé B. Vocabulaire Océanien-Français et Français-Océanien. 8vo. Paris, 1843. MK 1 P 65

MOSER, T. Mahoo Leaves ; being a selection of sketches of New Zealand and its Inhabitants. 12mo. Wellington, 1863. MD 1 P 52
Another copy. 2nd ed. 12mo. Wanganui, 1888. MD 1 P 53

MOSHEIM, J. L. De Rebus Christianorum ante Constantinum Magnum. Sm. 4to. Helmstadii, 1753. G 16 S 46
Ecclesiastical History ; translated from the Latin by A. Maclaine, D.D. New ed. 6 vols. 8vo. Lond., 1782. G 4 S 24-29

MOSS, Dr. E. L. Shores of the Polar Sea. Fol. Lond., 1878. D 41 P 15 ‡

MOSS, F. J. Through Atolls and Islands in the Great South Sea. 8vo. Lond., 1889. MD 7 P 40

MOSSMAN, S. A Voice from Australia, giving Practical Advice and True Information. 8vo. Lond., 1852. MD 4 U 41

MOTLEY, J. L. Correspondence of. Edited by G. W. Curtis. 2 vols. 8vo. Lond., 1889. C 12 T 9, 10
History of the United Netherlands. 2 vols. 8vo. Lond., 1860. B 30 U 15
The Rise of the Dutch Republic. 3 vols. 8vo. Lond., 1858. B 30 R 16-18

MOTTE, Countess de la. [*See* La Motte Countess de.]

MOUAT, Dr. F. J., and SNELL, H. S. Hospital Construction and Management. 4to. Lond., 1889. A 36 S 6 ‡

MOUAT, James. The Rise of the Australian Wool Kings : a Romance of Port Phillip. 8vo. Lond., 1892. MJ 2 T 35

MOULE, Ven. Arthur E. New China and Old ; Personal Recollections and Observations of Thirty Years. 8vo. Lond., 1891. D 17 R 9

MOULE, H. G. C. [Life of] Charles Simeon. 12mo. Lond., 1892. C 14 Q 31

MOULTON, R. G. The Ancient Classical Drama ; a Study in Literary Evolution. 8vo. Oxford, 1890. H 4 Q 40

U

MOUNTENEY-JEPHSON, A. J. [*See* Jephson, A. J. M.]

MOWAT, J. L. G. Alphita : a Medico-Botanical Glossary. [*See* Anecdota Oxoniensia.]

MOWLE, A. [*See* New South Wales Bankruptcy Act.]

MOWLE, S. M. Aboriginal Songs. (A Few words of their Language and mis-spelt names of places.) 8vo. Sydney, 1891. MK 1 T 25

MOZART, W. A. Vie de ; par M. H. Beyle. 12mo. Paris, 1887. C 14 P 18

MOZLEY, Anne. Letters and Correspondence of John Henry Newman during his Life in the English Church, with a brief autobiography. 2 vols. 8vo. Lond., 1891. C 15 U 11, 12

MOZLEY, Rev. T. Letters from Rome on the occasion of the Œcumenical Council, 1869-70. 2 vols. 12mo. Lond., 1891. G 13 U 42, 43

MUELLER, C. O. [*See* Festus, S. P.]

MUELLER, Sir F. von, Baron. Catalogue of Plants collected during Mr. Alexander Forrest's geographical exploration of North-west Australia in 1879. 8vo. Sydney, 1880. MA 1 V 61
Iconography of Australian Salsolaceous Plants. 1st-4th Decades. 4to. Melb., 1889-90. MA 8 Q 24 †
Iconography of Australian Species of Acacia and Cognate Genera. Vol. 1. [1st to 13th Decades.] 4to. Melb., 1877-88. MA 11 P 7 †
Introduction to Botanic Teachings at the Schools in Victoria. 8vo. Melb., 1877. MA 1 V 4
Key to the System of Victorian Plants. 2 vols. 8vo. Melb., 1885-88. MA 3 P 4, 5
Plants indigenous to the Colony of Victoria. 2 vols. roy. 4to. Melb., 1860-65. MA 2 Q 19, 20 †
1. Thalamiflorae.
2. Lithogramns.
Report on the Forest Resources of Western Australia. Roy. 4to. Melb., 1879. MA 1 Q 7 ‡
Vegetation of the Chatham Islands. Roy. 8vo. Melb., 1864. MA 3 R 26

MUIR, M. M. P. [*See* Watts, H.]

MUIR, T. Trial of Thomas Muir ; at Edinburgh, 1793, for Sedition. 8vo. Lond., 1793. F 13 P 23
[*See* Adam, Wm.]

MULCASTER, R. Positions wherin those primitive circumstances be examined, which are necessarie for the Training up of Children. (Reprint, 1581.) With Appendix by R. H. Quick. 8vo. Lond., 1887. G 17 Q 33

MULHALL, M. G. Dictionary of Statistics. Imp. 8vo. Lond., 1892. F 14 V 16
Balance-sheet of the World, 1870-80. 8vo. Lond., 1881. F 6 P 21
Dictionary of Statistics. 8vo. Lond., 1886. F 6 R 26
Progress of the World, since the beginning of the 19th Century. 8vo. Lond., 1880.* F 6 R 25

MULHALL, M. G. and E. T.   Manual de las Repúblicas
del Plata.   8vo.   Buenos Aires, 1876.   D 15 Q 9

MULHOLLAND, Miss Rosa.   [*See* Maguire, J. F.]

MULL, M.   Macbeth.   [*See* Shakespeare, W.]

MÜLLENHOFF, Karl.   Ueber den Ernährungs, und
Athmungsprocess der Pflanzen im Vergleich mit dem
der Thiere.   8vo.   Berlin, 1874.   A 20 Q 5

MULLENS, J.   Some Elucidations of Old Testament
History from the Records of Assyria and Egypt.   8vo.
Sydney, 1884.   MG 1 S 63

MÜLLER, Dr. E.   Simplified Grammar of the Pali Language.   8vo.   Lond., 1884.   K 20 Q 16

MÜLLER, Dr. F.   Symptomatologie und Therapie der
Tabes Dorsalis im Initialstadium.   8vo.   Graz, 1880.
A 26 U 14

MÜLLER, Prof. F. Max.   Natural Religion.   (The Gifford
Lectures, 1888.)   12mo.   Lond., 1889.   G 7 R 36

The Origin and Growth of Religion.   8vo.   Lond., 1878.
G 16 T 18

Physical Religion.   8vo.   Lond., 1891.   G 13 U 50

Anthropological Religion.   8vo.   Lond., 1892.   G 13 T 47

Rig-Veda-Samhita ; the Sacred Hymns of the Brahmans.
2nd ed.   4 vols.   4to.   Lond., 1890-92.   G 10 V 7-10

Biographies of Words, and the Home of the Aryas.   8vo.
Lond., 1888.   K 12 P 43

Sacred Books of the East.   Vols. 1-35, 37, 39, 40.   8vo.
Oxford, 1879-92.   G 20 R 1-8 G

1. The Khándogya-upanishad.--The Talavakára-upanishad.—
    The Aitareya-áranyaka.—The Kaushítaki-bráhmana-upani-
    shad.—and the Vágasaneyi-samhítá-upanishad.
2. The Sacred Laws of the Aryas; translated by G. Bühler.
    Part 1. Apastamba and Gautama.
3. The Sacred Books of China. The texts of Confucianism
    translated by J. Legge. Part 1. The Shû King; the Religious
    Portions of the Shih King; the Hsiâo King.
4. The Zend-Avesta. Part 1. The Vendidâd; translated by
    J. Darmesteter.
5. Pahlavi Texts; translated by E. W. West. Part 1. The
    Bundahis, Bahman Yast, and Shâyast lâ-shâyast.
6. The Qur'ân; translated by E. H. Palmer. Part 1, Chapters
    1-16.
7. The Institutes of Vishnu; translated by J. Jolly.
8. The Bhagavadgîtâ with the Sanatsugâtîya and the Anugîtâ;
9. The Qur'ân; translated by E. H. Palmer. Part 2, Chapters
    17-114.
10. The Dhammapada; translated by F. Max Müller.
11. Buddhist Suttas; translated by T. W. Rhys Davids. The
    Mahâ-parinibbâna Suttanta.—The Dhamma-kakka-ppavattana
    Sutta.—The Tevigga Suttanta.—The Akankheyya Sutta.—
    The Ketokhila Sutta.—The Mahâ-sudassana Suttanta.—The
    Sabbâsava Sutta.
12. The Satapatha-bráhmana; translated by J. Eggeling. Books
    1, 2.
13. Vinaya Texts; translated by T. W. Rhys Davids and H.
    Oldenberg. Part 1. The Pâtimokkha.—The Mahâvagga, 1-4.
14. The Sacred Laws of the Aryas; translated by G. Bühler.
    Part 2. Vasishta and Baudhâyana.
15. The Upanishads; translated by F. Max Müller. Part 2. The
    Katha-upanishad.—The Mundaka-upanishad.—The Taittirî-
    yaka-upanishad.—The Brihadâranyaka-upanishad.—The Svetâs-
    vatara-upanishad.—The Prasña-upanishad.—The Maitrâyana-
    bráhmana-upanishad.
16. The Sacred Books of China. The texts of Confucianism;
    translated by J. Legge. Part 2. The Yî King.

MÜLLER, Prof. F. Max—*contd.*
17. Vinaya Texts; translated by T. W. Rhys Davids, and H.
    Oldenberg. Part 2. The Mahâvagga, 5-10. The Kullavagga,
    1-3.
18. Pahlavi Texts; translated by E. W. West. Part 2. The
    Dâdistân-i-Dînîk and the Epistles of Mânûskihar.
19. The Fo-sho-hing-tsan-king. A Life of Buddha; translated
    by S. Beal.
20. Vinaya Texts; translated by T. W. Rhys Davids and H.
    Oldenberg. Part 3. The Kullavagga, 4-12.
21. The Saddharma-pundarîka; or, the Lotus of the true law;
    translated by H. Kern.
22. Gaina Sûtras; translated by H. Jacobi. Part 1. The Akâ-
    rânga Sûtra. The Kalpa Sûtra.
23. The Zend-Avesta. Part 2. The Sîrôzahs, Yasts, and Nyâyis;
    translated by J. Darmesteter.
24. Pahlavi Texts; translated by E. W. West. Part 3. Dînâ-î
    Maînôg-î Khirad.--Sikand-gûmânik Vigar.— Sad Dar.
25. The Law of Manu; translated by G. Bühler.
26. The Satapatha-bráhmana; translated by J. Eggeling. Part
    2, Books 3, 4.
27, 28. The Sacred Books of China. The texts of Confucianism;
    translated by J. Legge. Parts 3, 4. The Lî Kî, 1-46.
29, 30. The Grihya-Sûtras. Parts 1 and 2; trans. by H.
    Oldenburg.
31. The Zend-Avesta. Part 3; trans. by L. H. Mills.
32. Vedic Hymns. Part 1; trans. by F. Max Müller.
33. Minor Law Books. Part 1; trans. by J. Jolly.
34. The Vedanta-Sutras. Part 1; trans. by G. Thibaut.
35. The Questions of King Melinda. Part 1; trans. by T. W.
    Rhys Davids.
37. Pahlavi Texts. Part 4; trans. by E. W. West.
39, 40. Sacred Books of China : The Texts of Taoism. Parts
    1, 2 ; trans. by J. Legge.

Science of Language.   8vo.   Lond., 1861.   K 16 T 20

Suggestions for Learning the Languages of the Seat of
War in the East.   8vo.   Lond., 1854.   K 16 T 23

The Science of Thought.   8vo.   Lond., 1887.   G 12 P 39

Three Introductory Lectures on the Science of Thought,
delivered at the Royal Institution, London, March, 1887.
8vo.   Chicago, 1888.   G 15 R 24

MÜLLER, Dr. J.   Die Wissenschaftlichen Vereine und
Gesellschaften Deutschlands im neunzehnten Jahrhundert
Bibliographie ihrer Veröffenlichungen seit ihrer Begrün
dung bis auf die Gegenwart.   8vo.   Berlin, 1883-87.
K 17 R 14

MÜLLER, K. O., and DONALDSON, J. W.   A History
of the Literature of Ancient Greece.   3 vols.   8vo.   Lond.,
1858.   B 27 V 13-15

MULLINGER, J. B.   History of the University of Cambridge.   8vo.   Lond., 1888.   B 21 Q 24

MULLINS, George L.   Register of Administrations of
Anæsthetics for use in Hospitals, Public Institutions and
Private Practice.   4to.   Sydney, 1892.   MA 11 P 32†

MULLINS, J. D.   Catalogue of Birmingham Free Libraries.
8vo.   Birm., 1890.   Libr.

MULUK CHAND, Trial of, for the Murder of his own
Child; with an Introduction by W. A. Hunter.   8vo.
Lond., 1888.   F 7 Q 31

MULVANY, T. J.   New Zealand Products and Manufacture   8vo.   Tauranga, 1880.   MF 1 R 6

MUNCH, Prof. P. A.   Den Ældre Edda ; samling af
Norrøne oldkvad indeholdende Nordens Ældste Gude-
og Helte-Sagn.   Sm. 4to.   Christiania, 1847.   J 15 S 20

MUNICIPAL ASSOCIATION OF NEW SOUTH
WALES. Proceedings at the 10th Session, 1892. 8vo.
Sydney, 1892. ME 6 R

MUNK, Dr. E. De Fabulis Atellanis. 8vo. Lipsiæ,
1840. J 15 8 23

MUNRO, J. E. C. The Constitution of Canada. 8vo.
Camb., 1889. F 9 S 19

MUNRO, Dr. R. Lake Dwellings of Europe. Imp. 8vo.
Lond., 1890. B 25 U 1

MUNRO, R. D. Steam Boilers: their Defects, Management, and Construction. 8vo. Lond.,1887. A 22 Q 30

MUNRO, Major-Gen. Sir T. Life of ; by the Rev. G. R.
Gleig. New ed. 2 vols. 8vo. Lond., 1831.
C 18 Q 20, 21

MUNRO, Surg.-Gen. W. Records of Service and Cam-
paigning in Many Lands. 2 vols. 8vo. Lond., 1887.
C 12 R 20, 21

MUNROE, Dr. H. Physiological Action of Alcohol : a
Lecture. 12mo. Lond., 1865. F 11 P 69

MUNTER, Prof. J. Ueber Muscheln, Schnecken, und
verwandte Weichthiere. 8vo. Berlin, 1876. A 27 S 25

MUNTHE, A. Letters from a Mourning City (Naples,
Autumn, 1884); translated by Maude V. White. 8vo.
Lond., 1887. D 19 Q 3

MÜRATORI, L. A. Novus Thesaurus Veterum Inscrip-
tionum. 4 vols. fol. Mediolani, 1739–42. B 34 Q 3–6 ‡

MURGER, H. Œuvres complètes de. 14 vols. 8vo.
Paris, 1875–88. J 19 P 26–39

1. Dona Sirène.
2, Le Dernier Rendez-vous.—La Résurrection de Lazare.
3. Le Pays Latin.
4. Le Roman de toutes les Femmes.
5. Le Sabot Rouge.
6. Les Buveurs d'Eau.
7. Les Nuits d'Hiver : Poésies complètes.
8. Les Roueries de l'Ingenue.—La Scène du Gouverneur.—La
Nostalgic.—Les Sirènes.
9. Les Vacances de Camille : Scenes de la Vie Réelle.
10. Madame Olympe.
11. Propos de Ville et Propos de Théâtre.
12. Scènes de Campagne.—Adeline Protat.
13. Scènes de la Vie de Bohème.
14. Scènes de la Vie de Jeunesse.

MURCHISON, Sir R. I. Siluria. 3rd. ed. 8vo. Lond.,
1859. A 24 U 15

MURPHY, A. The Apprentice : a Farce. [*See* British
Drama, Modern, 5.]

The Citizen : a Comedy. [*See* British Drama, Modern, 5.]

The Grecian Daughter : a Tragedy. [*See* British Drama,
Modern, 2.]

The Old Maid : a Comedy. [*See* British Drama,
Modern, 5.]

The Orphan of China : a Tragedy. [*See* British Drama,
Modern, 2.]

Three Weeks after Marriage : a Comedy. [*See* British
Drama, Modern, 2.]

The Upholsterer : a Farce. [*See* British Drama,
Modern, 5.]

MURPHY, A.—*contd.*
The Way to Keep him ; a Comedy. [*See* British Drama,
Modern, 4.]

Zenobia : a Tragedy. [*See* British Drama, Modern, 2.]

MURPHY, G. M. Life of ; by Annie Taylor. 8vo.
Lond., 1888. C 12 P 16

MURPHY, M. Handbook of Gardening for New Zealand,
with Chapters on Poultry and Bee-Keeping. 2nd ed.
8vo. Christchurch, 1888. MA 3 P 3

MURRAY, Miss Alma. Portrait as Beatrice Cenci ; with
Critical Notes containing four Letters from Robert
Browning. 8vo. Lond., 1891. C 14 S 8

MURRAY, A. S. Handbook of Greek Archæology. 8vo.
Lond., 1892. A 23 S 8

MURRAY, A. Victoria Nautical and Commercial Almanac. 8vo. Melb., 1855. ME 4 Q

MURRAY, Rev. A. W. The Bible in the Pacific. 8vo.
Lond., 1888. MG 2 P 18

Forty Years' Mission Work in Polynesia and New
Guinea, 1835–75. 8vo. Lond., 1876. MD 6 S 11

MURRAY, Rev. A. W., and MACFARLANE, Rev. S.
Journal of a Missionary Voyage to New Guinea. Roy.
8vo. Lond., 1872. MD 7 R 31

MURRAY, E. C. G. Side Lights on English Society ; or,
Sketches from Life, Social and Satirical. 2 vols. 8vo.
Lond., 1881. J 12 Q 29, 30

MURRAY, G. [*See* Bennett, A. W.]

MURRAY, G. A. [*See* Aytoun, W. E.]

MURRAY, H. Historical Account of Discoveries and
Travels in North America. 2 vols. 8vo. Lond., 1829.
D 15 S 4, 5

Historical Account of Discoveries and Travels in Asia.
3 vols. 8vo. Edinb., 1820. D 16 T 5–7

MURRAY, J. [*See* Thomson, Sir C. W.]

MURRAY, John. Handbook of the Bengal Presidency ;
by E. B. Eastwick. 12mo. Lond., 1882. D 12 S 7

Handbook for Lincolnshire. 12mo. Lond., 1890.
D 12 R 28

Handbook for Travellers in Berks, Bucks, and Oxfordshire.
3rd ed. 12mo. Lond., 1882. D 12 R 26

Handbook for Travellers in Denmark, Schleswig and
Holstein, and Iceland. 5th ed. 12mo. Lond., 1883.
D 12 S 12

Handbook for Travellers in France, containing Provence,
Dauphiné, and the Riviera, from Marseilles to Mentone.
12mo. Lond., 1890. D 12 S 6

Handbook for Travellers in Gloucestershire, Worcestershire, and Herefordshire. 3rd ed. 12mo. Lond., 1884.
D 12 R 25

MURRAY, John—*contd.*

Handbook for Travellers in Greece. 5th ed. 2 vols. 12mo. Lond., 1884.   D 12 S 2, 3

Handbook for Travellers in India and Ceylon. 12mo. Lond., 1891.   D 12 S 9

Handbook for Travellers in Japan. 3rd ed. ; revised by B. H. Chamberlain and W. B. Mason. 12mo. Lond., 1891.   D 12 S 11

Handbook for Travellers in Lower and Upper Egypt; Part 1. 8th ed., 12mo. Lond., 1891.   D 12 S 13

Handbook for Travellers in North Wales. 5th ed. 12mo. Lond., 1885.   D 12 S 1

Handbook for Travellers in Spain. 7th ed. 2 vols. 12mo. Lond., 1890.   D 12 S 4, 5

Handbook for Travellers in Wiltshire, Dorsetshire, and Somersetshire. 4th ed. 12mo. Lond., 1882. D 12 R 24

Handbook for Travellers in Yorkshire. 3rd ed. 12mo. Lond., 1882.   D 12 R 27

Handbook to the Cathedrals of Wales. Llandaff, St. Davids, St. Asaph, Bangor. 2nd ed. 12mo. Lond., 1887.   D 12 R 23

Handbook to the English Lakes included in the Counties of Cumberland, Westmorland, and Lancashire. 12mo. Lond., 1889.   D 12 R 29

Handbook to the Cathedrals of England. 5 vols. 12mo. Lond., 1869-81.   D 12 R 18-22

Eastern Division : Oxford, Peterborough, Norwich, Ely, Lincoln. Northern Division : Part 1—York, Ripon, Carlisle ; Part 2—Durham, Chester, Manchester. Western Division : Gloucester, Hereford, Worcester, Bristol, Lichfield, St. Paul's.

A Publisher and his Friends ; Memoirs and Correspondence of John Murray. 2 vols. 8vo. Lond., 1891.   C 10 S 18, 19

MURRAY, J. A. H. New English Dictionary on historical principles. Vol. 1, Pts. 1-6, and vol. 3, Pt. 1. AAC–CON, E–EVE. 7 vols. imp. 4to. Oxford, 1883-91.   K 20 V

MURRAY, Dr. J. C. Introduction to Ethics. 12mo. Paisley, 1891.   G 13 U 51

MURRAY, Hon. R. D. Summer at Port Phillip. 12mo. Edinb., 1843.   MD 2 Q 41
[*See* Maimon, S.]

MURRAY, R. L. The Austral-Asiatic Review. 8vo. Hobart, 1828.   ME 3 R

MURRAY, R. W. South Africa from Arab Domination to British Rule. 8vo. Lond., 1891.   B 16 T 27

MURRAY'S MAGAZINE. Vols. 1-6. 8vo. Lond., 1887-89.   E

MURRAY RIVER, Australia. Despatches on the subject of the Navigation of. Fol. Lond., 1854.   MF 4 S 16

MUSEE FRANCAISE Le. 5 vols. Fol. Paris, 1803-9.   A 43 Q 12-16 ‡

MUSKETT, P. E. The Feeding and Management of Australian Infants. Sm. 4to. Sydney, 1889. MA 2 T 41

Health and Diet of Children in Australia. Sm. 4to. Sydney, 1889.   MA 2 T 40

Prescribing and Treatment in the Diseases of Children. 18mo. Edinb., 1891.   MA 3 P 17

MUSQUETIER, H. A. Tekst der Wet van den, 28 Junij, 1881, regeling van den Kleinhandel in Sterkin Drank. 8vo. 's Gravenhage, 1886.   F 11 Q 35

Wet van den, 28 Juni, 1881, tot regeling van den Kleinhandel in Sterken Drank. 8vo. 'sGravenhage, 1885.   F 11 Q 37

MUSSCHENBROEK, S. C. J. W. van. Dagboek van Dr. H. A. Bernstein's Laatste Reis van Ternate naar Nieuw-Guinea, Salawati en Batanta, 1864-65 ; 8vo. 's Gravenhage, 1883.   MD 7 R 5

MUSSET, Louis Charles Alfred de. [Life of] ; by C. F. Oliphant. 12mo. Edinb., 1890.   C 14 P 2

Œuvres Complètes de. 9 vols. 8vo. Paris, 1887-88.   J 19 V 6-14

1. La Confession d'un Enfant du Siècle.
2. Mélanges de Littérature et de Critique.
3. Nouvelles.—Les Deux Maitresses.—Emmeline.—Le Fils du Titien.—Frédéric et Bernerette.--Margot.
4. Œuvres Posthumes.
5. Poésies Nouvelles, 1836-52.
6. Premières Poésies, 1829-35.
7-9. Comedies et Proverbs : -1. La Nuit Vénitienne.—André del Sarto.—Les Caprices de Marianne.—Fantasio · On ne badine pas avec l'Amour.—Barberine. 2. Lorenzaccio.--Le Chandelier.—Il ne faut jurer de rien. 3. Un Caprice.—Il faut qu'une porte soit ouverte ou fermée.—Louison.—On ne saurait penser a tout.--Carmosine.—Bettine.

MYERS, F. Beautiful Manly ; its Approaches, Surroundings, Charms, and History ; with Visitors' Guide. Sm. 4to. Sydney, 1885.   MD 3 V 31
[*See* Hutchinson, F.]

MYERS, F. W. H. [Life of] Wordsworth. (English Men of Letters.) 12mo. Lond., 1888.   C 1 U 40

MYERS, Capt. John. Life, Voyages, and Travels of, detailing his adventures during four voyages round the World. 8vo. Lond., 1817.   MD 8 R 20

N

NABBES, T. Microcosmus : a Moral Masque. [*See* British Drama, Ancient, 2.]

Works of ; edited by A. H. Bullen. (Old English Plays.) Vols. 1, 2. 8vo. Lond., 1887.   H 4 T 1, 2

1. Covent Garden.—Totenham Court.—Hannibal and Scipio.
2. The Bride.--The Unfortunate Mother.—Microcosmus—The Spring's Glory. · Miscellaneous Verses.

NAEGELI, Prof. C., and SCHWENDENER, Prof. S. The Microscope in Theory and Practice. 8vo. Lond., 1887.   A 29 U 4

NAGLER, Dr. G. K. Neuesallgemeines Künstler-Lexicon. 22 vols. 8vo. München, 1835-52.   C 15 S 2-23

NANSEN, Fridtjof. The First Crossing of Greenland; translated by H. M. Gepp. 2 vols. 8vo. Lond., 1890.
D 4 S, 39, 40

NANSON, W. [*See* Ferguson, R. S.]

NAPHEYS, G. H. The Body and its Ailments. 8vo. Lond., 1876.
A 12 R 13

NAPIER, Mrs. A. [*See* Johnson, Dr. S.]

NAPIER, Sir Charles. [Life of]; by Col. Sir W. F. Butler. (English Men of Action.) 8vo. Lond., 1890.
C 12 Q 35

Life of. [*See* Yonge, C. D.]

Life and Correspondence of; by Maj.-Gen. E. Napier. 2 vols. 8vo. Lond., 1862.
C 18 R 11, 12

NAPIER, Maj.-Gen. E. Life and Correspondence of Adm. Sir C. Napier. 2 vols. 8vo. Lond., 1862.
C 18 R 11; 12

NAPIER, John. The Construction of the Wonderful Canon of Logarithms. Translated by W. R. Macdonald. Sm. 4to. Edinb., 1889.
A 10 T 30

NAPIER, Sir Joseph. Lectures, Essays, and Letters of; with an Introduction by his Daughter. 8vo. Dublin, 1888.
C 13 T 4

Life of; from his Private Correspondence, by A. C. Ewald. 8vo. Lond., 1887.
C 13 T 3

NAPOLEON BONAPARTE. Bonaparte and the French People under his Consulate. 2nd ed. 8vo. Lond., 1804.
C 18 S 9

Confidential Correspondence of Napoleon Bonaparte with his Brother Joseph. 2nd ed. 2 vols. 8vo. Lond., 1856.
C 18 R 9, 10

Copies of Letters from the Army of Bonaparte in Egypt, intercepted by the Fleet under Lord Nelson. 8vo. Lond., 1798.
C 14 S 9

Histoire de Napoléon et de la Grand Armée pendant l' année 1812; par le Gén. Comte de Ségur. 2 vols. (in 1.) 8vo. Paris, 1852.
C 18 Q 2

Eighteen Original Journals of the Campaigns of the Emperor Napoleon. Trans. from the French. 8vo. Lond., 1817.
C 18 R 18

Journal of the Private Life and Conversations of the Emperor Napoleon at St. Helena; by the Count de Las Cases. 8 vols. 8vo. Lond., 1823.
C 15 R 1-8

Letters written on board H.M.S. "Northumberland," and [at] St. Helena; by Wm. Warden. 4th ed. 8vo. Lond., 1816.
C 18 S 10

Mémoires Historiques de Napoléon. 8vo. Lond., 1820.
B 26 T 25

Mémoires pour servir à l'Histoire de France sous Napoléon. 4 vols. 8vo. Lond., 1823-24.
B 26 T 16-19

Mémoires pour servir à l'Histoire de France sous Napoléon: Mélanges Historiques. 3 vols. 8vo. Lond., 1823.
B 26 T 20-22

Mémoires pour servir á l'Histoire de la Vie Privée, du Retour, et du Règne de Napoléon en 1815. 2 vols. 8vo. Lond., 1819-20.
B 26 T 23, 24

NAPOLEON BONAPARTE—*contd.*
Napoleon and his Detractors; by H.I.H. Prince Napoleon. Trans. by R. L. de Beaufort. 8vo. Lond., 1888.
C 10 R 4

Vie de Napoléon; par M. H. Boyle. 12mo. Paris, 1882.
C 14 P 19

La Vie Privée, du Retour, et du Règne de Napoléon en 1815; par Fleury de Chaboulon. 2 vols. (in 1.) 8vo. Lond., 1819.
C 18 Q 3

[*See* Browning, O., and Durard, Mme. la Gén.]

NAPOLEON III. Last Days of the Court of Napoleon. [*See* Maugny, Comte de.]
Life and Times of; by S. M. Schmucker. 8vo. Philad., 1890.
C 14 R 27

NAPOLEON, Louis. [*See* Baxter, Rev. M.]

NAPOLEON, Prince Jérôme. Napoleon and his Detractors. Trans. by R. L. de Beaufort. 8vo. Lond., 1888.
C 10 R 4

NAQUET, Prof. A. Collectivism and the Socialism of the Liberal School. 8vo. Lond., 1891.
F 14 P 31

NARBOROUGH, Sir J. [*See* Voyages and Discoveries.]

NARRIEN, John. Historical account of the Origin and Progress of Astronomy. 8vo. Lond., 1833. A 19 T 28

NASH, A. [*See* Watkins, J. L.]

NASH, R. L. The Investor's Sinking-fund and Redemption Tables. 2nd ed. 4to. Lond., 1883.
K 33 P 13

[*See* Fenn, C.]

NASH, T. A. Life of Richard Lord Westbury, with selections from his correspondence. 2 vols. 8vo. Lond., 1888.
C 12 T 26, 27

NATION, The, with which is incorporated the Express. 3 vols. fol. Sydney, 1887-89.
ME

NATIONAL Life and Thought of the various Nations throughout the World. 8vo. Lond., 1891.
J 6 U 17

NATIONAL REVIEW. Vols. 1-11, 13, 14, 13 vols., 8vo. Lond., 1883-91.
E

NATIONAL RIFLE ASSOCIATION. Proceedings, 1888-91. 4 vols. 8vo. Lond., 1889-91.
E

NATIONAL SOCIETY FOR WOMEN'S SUFFRAGE. Occasional Paper, May, 1892: Debate in the House of Commons. 8vo. Lond., 1892.
F 2 V 2

NATIONAL TEMPERANCE CONGRESS, Liverpool, 1884. 8vo. Lond., 1884.
F 11 R 60

NATURE. Vols. 35-45. 4to. Lond., 1887-92.
E

NAUCK, A. [*See* Porphyrius.]

NAUMANN, E. and M. Zur Geologie und Paläontologie von Japan. 4to. Wien, 1890.
A 42 R 3‡

NAUTICAL ALMANAC, 1767-1879, 1890-95. 100 vols. 8vo. Lond., 1766-91.
E

NAUTICAL MAGAZINE. Vols. 57–60. 8vo. Lond., . 1889–91. ·   E

NAVAL ANNUAL, The, 1887. Roy. 8vo. Portsmouth, 1888.   E

NAVILLE, F. Bubastis. (Egypt Exploration Fund.) Fol. Lond., 1891   B 42 S 8 ‡
The Mound of the Jew and the City of Onias. (Egypt Exploration Fund, 1888–89.) 4to. Lond., 1890.
                                              B 42 R 27 ‡
The Shrine of Saft el Henneh, und the Land of Goshen, 1885. Fifth Memoir of the Egypt Exploration Fund. Roy. 4to. Lond., 1887.   B 2 R 31†

NAVY LIST. 26 vols. 12mo. Lond., 1882–88.   E

NAYSMITH, D. Makers of Modern Thought. 2 vols. 12mo. Lond., 1892.   C 17 Q 17, 18

NAZIANZEN, G. [*See* Julian, Emperor.]

NEAL, D. History of the Puritans. 2 vols. 4to. Lond., 1754.   G 3 V 20, 21

NEAVES, Lord. Greek Anthology. (Ancient Classics for English Readers.) 12mo. Edinb., 1877. J 14 P 9

NECKER, Anne Louise Germaine. [*See* Staël–Holstein, Baronne de.]

NEGUS, R. P. Essay on Leeches: a Practical Handbook. 12mo. Melb., 1861.   MA 3 P 19

NELSON, Vice-Adm. Horatio, Viscount. Horatio Nelson and the Naval Supremacy of England; by W. Clark Russell. 8vo. New York, 1890.   C 12 R 44
Lady Hamilton and Lord Nelson : an Historical Biography; by J. C. Jeaffreson. 2 vols. 8vo. Lond., 1888.
                                              C 15 Q 26, 27
Life of; by Rev. J. S. Clarke, and Dr. J. McArthur. 2 vols. 4to. Lond., 1889.   C 33 P 18, 19 ‡
Life and Naval Memoirs of; by Col. J. M. Tucker. 8vo. Lond. (n.d.)   C 18 R 15
Life and Services of; by the Rev. J. S. Clarke, and J. McArthur. 3 vols. 8vo. Lond. (n.d.) C 16 R 3–5
Memoirs of the Professional Life of; by J. White. 3rd ed. 12mo. Lond., 1806.   C 14 P 10
Nelson's Words and Deeds; by W. C. Russell. 12mo. Lond., 1890.   C 16 P 22
The Queen of Naples and Lord Nelson ; by J. C. Jeaffreson. 2 vols. 8vo. Lond., 1889. C 14 Q 23, 24
Nelson : the public and private life of, as told by himself, his comrades and his friends ; by G. L. Browne. 8vo. Lond., 1891.   C 15 U 13
Vindication of Admiral Lord Nelson's Proceedings in the Bay of Naples ; by J. Miles. 12mo. Lond., 1843.
                                              C 17 P 23

NELSON, J. H. Indian Usage and Judge-made Law in Madras. 8vo. Lond., 1887.   F 6 V 24

NELSON, R. Companion for the Festivals of the Church of England. 22nd ed. 8vo. Dublin, 1763. G 13 Q 38
Festivals and Fasts of the Church of England. 36th ed. 8vo. Lond., 1826.   G 13 R 43

NELSON, Dr. W. Five years at Panama—the Trans-Isthmian Canal. 12mo. Lond., 1891.   D 15 Q 11

NELSON, W. Forest Laws. [*See* Marwood, J.]

NEMESIS TIMES, The : a weekly journal of Literature and Art, 1876–77. 8vo. Melb., 1877.   ME 6 R

NEPOS, Cornelius. Selectæ Vitæ excellentium Imperatorum. [*See* Brain, T. H.]
Vitæ excellentium Imperatorum. 8vo. Biponti, 1789.
                                              C 14 U 19

NERO, and other Plays ; edited by H. P. Horne, H. Ellis, A. Symons, and A. W. Verity. 8vo. Lond., 1888.   H 4 Q 25
Nero.—The Two Angry Women of Abington.—The Parliament of Bees.—Humour out of Breath.—Woman is a Weathercock.—Amends for Ladies.

NESFIELD, H. W. A Chequered Career; or, Fifteen Years' Experience in Australia and New Zealand. 8vo. Lond., 1887.   MD 3 R 41

NESFIELD, W. E. Specimens of Mediæval Architecture of the 12th and 13th Centuries in France and Italy. Fol. Lond., 1862.   A 37 P 4 ‡

NETHERCOTE, H. O. The Pytchley Hunt, Past and Present. 8vo. Lond., 1888.   B 21 R 22

NETTLEROTH, H. Kentucky Fossil Shells : a Mono-graph of the Fossil Shells of the Silurian and Devonian Rocks of Kentucky. Fol. Frankfort, Kentucky, 1889.
                                              A 30 R 4 ‡

NETTLESHIP, Prof. H. [*See* Pattison, M., *and* Seyffert, Dr. O.]

NETTLESHIP, R. L. [*See* Green, Prof. T. H.]

NEUMAN, H., and BARETTI, G. Dictionary of the Spanish and English Languages. 4th ed. 2 vols. 8vo. Lond., 1823.   K 12 T 33, 34

NEUMANN, J. C. The Masonic Guide of Victoria 1889-90. 18mo. Melb., 1889.   MJ 3 P 5

NEUMAYER, Dr., and BÖRGEN, Dr. C. Die Interna-tionale Polarforschung, 1882–83. Die Beobachtungs-Ergebnisse der Deutschen Stationen. 2 vols. roy. 4to. Berlin, 1886.   A 4 P 24, 25 †

NEVE, J. Concordance to the Poetical Works of W. Cowper. Roy. 8vo. Lond., 1887.   K 17 R 22

NEVILLE, Henry. Nouvelle Découverte de l' Isle Pinés. Sm. 4to. Paris, 1668.   MJ 3 R 3

NEVILLE, Ralph. Old Cottage and Domestic Archi-tecture in South-west Surrey. 2nd ed. 4to. Guilford, 1891.   A 19 V 1

NEW GUINEA. Annual Reports on ; 1887–90. 2 vols. 8vo. Lond., 1888–91.   ME 8 R
Arrangement between Great Britain and Germany relative to their respective spheres of Action in Portions of. Fol. Lond., 1885,   MF 12 Q 28 †
Correspondence respecting New Guinea, the New Hebrides, and other Islands in the Pacific. Fol. Lond., 1883.
                                              MF 12 Q 27 †

NEW GUINEA—*contd.*

Correspondence respecting New Guinea and other Islands, and the Convention at Sydney of Representatives of the Australasian Colonies. Fol. Lond., 1884.

MF 12 Q 27 †

Declarations between the Governments of Great Britain and the German Empire relating to the demarcation of the British and German Spheres of Influence in the Western Pacific, and to reciprocal Freedom of Trade and Commerce in the British and German possessions and protectorates in those regions. Fol. Lond., 1886.

MF 12 Q 28 †

Description Geographique d'une Côte de la Nouvelle Guinée, en 1705. (Prévost, A. F., Suite de l'histoire générale des voyages, tome 17.) 4to. Amsterdam, 1761.

MD 11 P 16 †

Instruments and Instructions for erecting certain British Territory in New Guinea and the adjacent Islands into a Separate Possession and Government by the name of British New Guinea, and for the Government thereof. Fol. Lond., 1888.

MF 12 Q 26 †

Memoranda of Conversations at Berlin on Colonial Matters. Fol. Lond., 1885.

MF 12 Q 28 †

Narrative of Expedition of Australian Squadron to. 4to. Sydney, 1885.

MD 3 P 12 ‡

NEW REVIEW, The. Vols. 1-6. 8vo. 1889-92. E

NEW SHAKESPEARE SOCIETY.

[*See* Shakespeare Society, New.]

NEW SOUTH WALES.

BLUE BOOK. 1882-90. Sm. fol. Sydney, 1883-91. ME

BULLI COLLIERY ACCIDENT.

Report of Royal Commission. Fol. Sydney, 1887.

MA 3 Q 28 †

CAPITAL PUNISHMENT.

Correspondence relating to the Exercise of the Prerogative of Pardon. Fol. Lond., 1875. MF 12 Q 22 †

Report of the Capital Punishment Commission. Roy. 8vo. Sydney, 1868. MF 3 R 42

CENSUS, 1881. Fol. Sydney, 1884. ME

CHARITIES.

Report of the Department of Charitable Institutions, 1891. Roy. 8vo. Sydney, 1892. ME 8 R

Government Asylums Inquiry Board, Report. Fol. Sydney, 1887. MF 2 U 52

State Children's Relief Dept. Reports. Sm. fol. Sydney, 1885-88. ME

State Children's Relief Department, Report for 1892. Roy. 8vo. Sydney, 1892. ME 8 R

CHINESE QUESTION.

Proceedings of the Conference, held in Sydney, June, 1888. Fol. Sydney, 1888. MF 2 U 53

CIVIL SERVICE.

Civil Service Board, Report, 1889. Fol. Sydney, 1890. ME

NEW SOUTH WALES—*contd.*

CONSTITUTION.

An Act to confer a Constitution on New South Wales, and to Grant a Civil List to Her Majesty. Fol. Lond., 1855. MF 12 Q 20 †

An Act to explain and amend the Act for the Government of New South Wales and Van Diemen's Land. Fol. Lond., 1844. MF 12 Q 19 †

An Act for the Government of New South Wales and Van Diemen's Land. Fol. Lond., 1842.

MF 12 Q 19 †

Copies or Extracts of Despatches between the Colonial Department and the Governor of New South Wales, relating to the Proposed Changes in the Constitution of Australia. Fol. Lond., 1849. MF 11 Q 21 †

Despatch from Earl Grey to the Governor of New South Wales and other Despatches and Correspondence relating thereto. [Separation of Victoria and Responsible Government in New South Wales.] Fol. Lond., 1848. MF 12 Q 21 †

Papers relative to the Separation of Moreton Bay District from New South Wales. Fol. Lond., 1858.

MF 12 Q 23 †

Papers respecting New South Wales. Fol. Lond., 1841. MF 8 Q 30 †

Report of Proceedings of the General Meeting of the supporters of the Petition [to extend the Legislature], to His Majesty and the House of Commons. 8vo. Sydney, 1836. MF 1 R 58

CROWN LANDS.

Copies of any Correspondence relative to Crown Lands and Emigration in New South Wales. Parts 3-6. Fol. Lond., 1845-46. MF 12 Q 8 †

Copies or Extracts of a Despatch, dated 24th Feb., 1841, with Enclosures, between Sir George Gipps and Lord John Russell, relative to Condition of Licensed Occupiers of Crown Lands in Port Phillip and New South Wales, and Subsequent Correspondence. Fol. Lond., 1844. MF 12 Q 8 †

Copies of the Royal Instructions to Governors of New South Wales, Van Diemen's Land, and Western Australia, as to the mode to be adopted in disposing of Crown Lands; or to the means by which Emigration may be facilitated. Fol. Lond., 1831.

MF 11 Q 5 †

Correspondence between the Secretary of State for the Colonies and the Governor of New South Wales, 1834-5 on the Appropriation of the Revenue arising from Crown Lands. Correspondence dated 28th June 1840, relative to Finances of the Colony, and Application of Land Sales to Police and Gaols. Fol. Lond., 1840.

MF 12 Q 9 †

Crown Lands Act of 1884. Analytical Index to Reports of Cases heard before the Court of Appeal, 1885-88 (inclusive). 8vo. Sydney, 1889. ME 6 U

Crown Lands Acts and Regulations of 1861. 8vo. Sydney, 1861. MF 1 T 71

Crown Lands Act of 1884, and the Regulations thereto 3rd. ed. Roy. 8vo. Sydney, 1889. MF 3 R 17

NEW SOUTH WALES—*contd.*

CROWN LANDS—*contd.*

Crown Lands Act of 1884. Report of Cases heard before the Court of Appeal. Vol. 1 and Vol. 2. Part 1. 8vo. Sydney, 1887-90.   ME 6 U

Crown Lands Act of 1889. Regulations under. Fol. Sydney, 1889.   MF 2 U 57

Department of Lands. Reports, 1882-91. Sm. fol. Sydney, 1883-92.   ME

Despatch from the Rt. Hon. Lord Glenelg to His Excellency Sir Richard Bourke, on the subject of claims of certain Chaplains of Church of England, to Compensation in lieu of Grants of Land. Fol. Sydney, 1836.   MF 11 Q 46 †

Laws and Regulations of Waste Land. 8vo. Sydney, 1858.   MF 1 R 8

Letter signed by Sir E. Deas Thompson to accompany the above. (MS.) Fol. Sydney, 1837.   MF 11 Q 46 †

List of Pastoral Leases. Roy. 8vo. Sydney, 1818. MF

Handbook to the Crown Lands Acts. 8vo. Sydney, 1889.   MF 3 T 8

List of Crown Lands that may be selected at the upset price, 1882. Fol. Sydney, 1882.   ME

List of Pastoral Leases showing the dates upon which the Rents are Payable, 1892-93. Sydney, 1892.   ME 3 R

Papers relative to the Occupation of, 1848-50. 2 vols. (in 1). Fol. Lond., 1848.   MF 11 Q 32 †

Real Property Acts Inquiry Commission. Report. Fol. Sydney, 1879.   MF 2 U 51

Statement of the Present Value, on 30th July, 1837, of Compensations for land promised to the families of certain Chaplains of the Church of England, New South Wales, by William Lithgow. Fol. Sydney, 1837.   MF 11 G 46 †

CUSTOMS.

Customs Hand-book, revised and corrected to 1858. Roy. 8vo. Sydney, 1888.   MF

Particulars of Customs Receipts. Collections for the Year 1888. Roy. 8vo. Sydney, 1889. ME 8 R

DRINK COMMISSION.

Intoxicating Drink Inquiry Commission Report. Part 1. Sm. fol. Sydney, 1887.   MF 3 R 19

EDUCATION.

Calendar of the Technical College. 8vo. Sydney, 1881.   ME

Public Schools Act of 1866, with Regulations of 8th March, 1869, thereunder. 8vo. Sydney, 1871.   MF 1 T 46

Reports of the Department of Public Instruction, 1881-88. 2 vols. fol. Sydney, 1882-89.   ME

Report of the Technical College, 1881. Fol. Sydney, 1881.   ME

ELECTORAL ACT.

Electoral Act. [12 July, 1880.] 8vo. Sydney, 1887.   MF 3 R 25

NEW SOUTH WALES—*contd.*

ELECTORAL ROLLS.

Electoral Rolls, 1888-93. 10 vols. fol. Sydney, 1888-92.   ME

EMIGRATION AND IMMIGRATION.

Copy of a Despatch from the Governor, transmitting the Report of a Committee of the Legislative Council on the subject of Emigration. Fol. Lond., 1841.   MF 12 Q 13 †

Copy of a Despatch from the Governor, to the Secretary of State for the Colonies, containing Resolutions of the Legislative Council on the subject of Emigration. Fol. Lond., 1841.   MF 12 Q 13 †

Copy of a Despatch from Governor, Sir George Gipps, relative to the Introduction of Emigrants upon Bounty into New South Wales. Fol. Lond., 1841.   MF 12 Q 13 †

Copy of a Report of the Committee of the Legislative Council on the subject of Immigration. Fol. Lond., 1846.   MF 12 Q 13 †

Copy of a Despatch from the Governor of New South Wales, bearing date 4th Dec., 1839 ; with copy of Report made by Committee of Legislative Council of that Colony, appointed to consider the subject of Immigration. Fol. Lond., 1840.   MF 12 Q 13 †

FINANCES.

Public Accounts for the Year 1887, accompanied by the Seventeenth Annual Report of the Auditor-General. Fol. Sydney, 1888.   ME

Estimates of Ways and Means, 1889. Sm. fol. Sydney, 1888.   ME

Schedule to Estimates-in-Chief, 1889. Sm. fol. Sydney, 1888.   ME

Supplementary Estimates of Expenditure. Sm. fol. Sydney, 1888.   ME

FISHERIES.

Report of Royal Commission appointed to inquire into and report upon the actual state and prospect of the Fisheries. 8vo. Sydney, 1880.   MA 2 U 56

Report from Select Committee on Working of Fisheries Act. Fol. Sydney, 1889.   MF 2 U 56

Report on Fisheries of the Colony. Fol. Sydney, 1887.   ME

GEOLOGICAL SURVEY.

Geological Reports and Articles on the Basaltic Country lying between the Forest Reefs, Lucknow, and Benerre Goldfields. 8vo. Sydney, 1883.   MA 3 Q 33

Memoirs of Geological Survey. Palæontology, No. 2. Contributions to the Tertiary Flora of Australia, by Dr. C. B. von Ettingshausen. 4to. Sydney, 1888.   ME

Memoirs of Geological Survey. Palæontology, No. 8. Contributions to a Catalogue of Works, &c., on the Anthropology, Ethnology, and Geological History of Australian and Tasmanian Aborigines. Part I. 4to. Sydney, 1890.   ME

NEW SOUTH WALES—*contd.*

GEOLOGICAL SURVEY—*contd.*

Memoirs of Geological Survey. Monograph of Carboniferous and Permo-Carboniferous Invertebrata of New South Wales. Part 1. Cœlentercœta, by R. Etheridge, Jun. 4to. Sydney, 1891.　　ME

Records of Geological Survey. Vols. 1 and 2. Roy. 8vo. Sydney, 1889-92.　　ME 15 T

[*See* Etheridge, R.]

GOVERNMENT GAZETTE.

N.S.W. Government Gazette, 1886-91. 22 vols. fol. Sydney, 1886-91.　　ME

INSANE.

Report of Inspector-General of Insane, 1888. Fol. Sydney, 1889.　　ME

LEGISLATIVE ASSEMBLY.

Alleged Attempted Bribery of Members of Parliament. Report of Royal Commission. Fol. Sydney, 1889.　　MF 2 U 12

Votes and Proceedings, 1885-91. 35 vols. Sm. fol. Sydney, 1886-91.　　ME

Report upon the Proposed Standing Orders. Sm. fol. Sydney, 1888.　　ME

LEGISLATIVE COUNCIL.

Journal of, 1885-90. 24 vols. sm. fol. Sydney, 1886-90.　　ME

LICENSING DISTRICTS.

Boundaries of the Licensing Districts. 8vo. Sydney, 1890.　　MF 1 T 47

LUNACY.

Lunacy Rules. Roy. 8vo. Sydney, 1887.　　MF 3 R 28

MINES.

Annual Reports, 1885-88, 1890-91. Sydney, 1886-92.　　ME

Stock and Brands Branch, Reports, 1881-84. Sm. fol. Sydney, 1881-85.　　ME

[*See* N.S.W.—Geological Survey.]

OYSTER CULTURE.

Report of Royal Commission. Fol. Sydney, 1877.　　MA 3 Q 13 †

PARLIAMENTARY DEBATES.

Parliamentary Debates. Vols. 28-50, and 52-58. roy. 8vo. Sydney, 1887-92.　　ME

PARLIAMENTARY HANDBOOK.

2nd ed. 8vo. Sydney, 1881. 1881.　　MF 3 Q 66

Another copy. 3rd ed. 8vo. Sydney, 1891. MF 2 T 33

PARLIAMENTARY LIBRARY.

Supplementary Catalogue of Books added since 1886. Roy. 8vo. Sydney, 1887.　　MK 1 R 10

PATENTS.

Letters of Registration. Name Index of Grantees, 1854-1887. Roy. 8vo. Sydney, 1889-92. ME 6 U

NEW SOUTH WALES—*contd.*

PATENTS—*contd.*

Name Index of Applicants for Certificates of Provisional Protection and Letters Patent, August, 1887-July, 1888. Roy. 8vo. Sydney, 1889.　　ME 6 U

Letters of Registration of Inventions for 1883. Sm. fol. Sydney, 1887.　　ME

POLICE.

Rules and Regulations for the Government and Guidance of the Constabulary Force. 8vo. Sydney, 1852.　　MF 3 P 57

Boundaries of the Police Districts. 8vo. Sydney, 1888.　　MF 3 Q 20

POSTMASTER-GENERAL.

Annual Reports of Postmaster-General, 1881-86 and 1888. Fol. Sydney, 1882-89.　　ME

Postal Conference. Sm. fol. Sydney, 1888.　　ME

PUBLIC WORKS.

Plans, Public Works Committee, 1890. Fol. Sydney, 1890.　　ME

Report and Evidence, Board of Inquiry. Fol. Sydney, 1887.　　MF 2 U 54

Parliamentary Standing Committee on Public Works. General Report. Fol. Sydney, 1888.　　ME

Report on Storage Reservoir at Potts' Hill, and Second line of Pipes to Crown Street. Fol. Sydney, 1888.　　MA 3 Q 19 †

Royal Commission of inquiry into construction of Public Tanks and Wells of New South Wales. Report. Fol. Sydney, 1888.　　MA 3 Q 14 †

Tanks and Wells, a Statement in Reply, tendered in Evidence, but refused by the Royal Commission of Inquiry into Public Tanks and Wells. Fol. Sydney, 1889.　　MA 3 Q 15 †

Report on Drainage Works, North Shore. Fol. Sydney, 1888.　　MA 3 Q 21 †

Report on Drainage Works, Manly. Fol. Sydney, 1888.　　MA 3 Q 20 †

Parliamentary Standing Committee on Public Works, Report on Improvements to Circular Quay. Fol. Sydney, 1888.　　MA 3 Q 25 †

Parliamentary Standing Committee on Public Works, Report relating to the Proposed Bridge at the Spit, Middle Harbour. Fol. Sydney, 1889.　　MA 3 Q 24 †

Parliamentary Standing Committee on Public Works, Report on Proposed Improvements and Additions to the Wharfage accommodation, Woolloomooloo Bay. Sydney, 1889.　　MA 3 Q 23 †

Parliamentary Standing Committee on Public Works, Report on New Central Police Court. Fol. Sydney, 1888.　　MA 3 Q 22 †

RAILWAYS.

Hawkesbury Railway Bridge, Opening of: Celebration at the Hawkesbury, 1st May, 1889. 8vo. Sydney, 1889.　　MF 1 T 6

Peat's Ferry Railway Accident. Sm. fol. Sydney, 1888.　　ME

x

NEW SOUTH WALES—*contd.*

RAILWAYS—*contd.*

Railways and Tramways. Reports, 1872–77, 1882–87. 1890, 4 vols. sm. fol. Sydney, 1872–90. ME

Railway Tourists' Guide. Division I., Southern and Illawarra Lines. Division II., Western and Northern Lines. 8vo. Sydney, 1889. MD 7 S 29

REGISTRATION OF BIRTHS, DEATHS, AND MARRIAGES.

Report from the Select Committee on Registration of Births, Deaths, and Marriages. Fol. Sydney, 1886. ME

SANITARY CONFERENCE.

Australasian Sanitary Conference of Sydney, 1884. Report, &c. Fol. Sydney, 1884. MA 3 Q 16 †

STATISTICS.

Vital Statistics, 1887. Sm. fol. Sydney, 1889. ME

Statistical Registers, 1867–68, 1881–86. Sm. fol. Sydney, 1868–87. ME

[*See* Coghlan, T. A.]

STATUTES.

Acts of Council, 1824–30. Sm. fol. Sydney, 1824–30. ME

Acts and Ordinances of the Governor and Council of New South Wales. Sydney, 1821.

The Common Law Procedure Acts and the Law of Evidence Amendment Act, indexed by H. Cary. 8vo. Sydney, 1868. MF 2 T 69

Private Acts, 1832–62, 1879–85. 2 vols. fol. Sydney, 1863–85. ME

Licensing Act. Roy. 8vo. Sydney, 1882. MF 1 S 13

Mining Act. Roy. 8vo. Sydney, 1887. MF 1 S 18

Navigation Act. 8vo. Sydney, 1872. MF 3 Q 22

Stamp Duties Act and Regulations; Stamp Duties Act Amendment Act of 1886; and Transfer of Mining Stock Stamp Duty Exemption Act. Roy. 8vo. Sydney, 1891. MF 3 T 19

Statutes, 1875–89, 1891–92. Sm. fol. Sydney. 1876–92. ME

STOCKOWNERS.

List of Stockowners and Licensees in the Colony having not less than 1000 Sheep or 100 Head of Cattle. Sm. 4to. Sydney, 1891. ME 7 Q

STRIKES.

Report of the Royal Commission on Strikes. Fol. Sydney, 1891. MF 4 S 30

Another Copy. Fol. Sydney, 1891. MF 11 Q 6 †

SUPREME COURT.

Bankruptcy Cases, together with Reports of Cases under the Companies Acts. Vols. 1 and 2, July, 1890–July, 1892. 2 vols. roy. 8vo. Sydney, 1891–92. ME 7 R

Law Reports. Vols. 1–12, 1880–91. 8vo. Sydney, 1881–92. ME 21

Supreme Court, Regulæ Generales. Roy. 8vo. Sydney, 1891. MF 3 T 18

General Rules under the Bankruptcy Act, 1887. Roy. 8vo. Sydney, 1888. MF 1 S 33

NEW SOUTH WALES—*contd.*

SUPREME COURT—*contd.*

General Rules made pursuant to Section 119 of the Bankruptcy Act, 1887. Index compiled by Aubrey Mowle. Roy. 8vo. Sydney, 1891. MF 3 T 17

Reports of Cases Argued and Determined in the Supreme Court. Vols. 1–13, and vols. 1 and 2, new series, 1863–79. 15 vols. 8vo. Sydney, 1863–1880. ME

Reserved and Equity Judgments. Roy. 8vo. Sydney, 1846. ME

In Equity. Consolidated Standing Rules, 1883. 8vo. Sydney, 1883. MF 3 R 16

Weekly Notes. Vols. 1–8. Roy. 8vo. Sydney, 1884–92. ME 7 R

SURVEYS.

Public Surveys. 8vo. Sydney, 1866. MA 3 Q 9

Trigonometrical Survey, 1890. Roy. 8vo. Sydney, 1891. MA 3 R 12

TANKS AND WELLS.

Public Tanks and Wells. Information respecting their Construction and Maintenance. Sm. fol. Sydney, 1888. ME

TRANSPORTATION.

New South Wales: an Article from the *Quarterly Review*, Oct., 1838, on Transportation, &c. 8vo. Lond., 1838. MF 3 T 1

UNEMPLOYED.

Casual Labour Board Inquiry Commission, Report. Fol. Sydney, 1889. MF 2 U 55

Progress Report from Select Committee on Work of Unemployed on Roads at Hornsby and Holt-Sutherland Estate. Fol. Sydney, 1888. MF 2 U 49

WATER SUPPLY AND SEWERAGE.

Board of Water Supply and Sewerage. Metropolitan Water By-laws. 2 vols. (in 1). 4to. Sydney, 1889. MF 2 S 48

NEW SOUTH WALES AUXILIARY BIBLE SOC. Reports, 1849, 1869, 1870, 1873. 8vo. Sydney, 1850–74. ME 6 R

NEW SOUTH WALES BENEVOLENT SOCIETY. Help for the Poor and Afflicted. 4to. Sydney, 1891. MF 1 U 38

A Merry Christmas to the Poor, and a Christmas Page from Dickens: An Appeal to the Charitable. 4to. Sydney, 1891. MF 1 U 37

NEW SOUTH WALES DEAF, DUMB, AND BLIND INSTITUTION. Report for 1872. 8vo. Sydney, 1872. ME 6 S

NEW SOUTH WALES GOOD TEMPLAR AND RECHABITE JOURNAL. Fol. Sydney, 1887. ME

NEW SOUTH WALES INDEPENDENT. Vol. 1. Fol. Sydney, 1875. ME 8 T

NEW SOUTH WALES LAW ALMANAC, 1889–1891. 3 vols. 12 mo. Sydney, 1889–91. ME 4 Q

NEW SOUTH WALES MEDICAL GAZETTE. Vol. 5. Oct., 1874–March, 1875. 8vo. Sydney, 1874–75. ME 8 Q

NEW SOUTH WALES MUNICIPAL ASSOCIATION. Proceedings at Eighth Session. 8vo. Sydney, 1890. ME 8 Q

NEW SOUTH WALES MUNICIPAL DIRECTORY, 1890, 1892-93. 3 vols. 8vo. Sydney, 1890–92. ME 6 T

NEW SOUTH WALES POST OFFICE DIRECTORY. [*See* Wise, H., and Co.]

NEW SOUTH WALES PROTECTIVE INSTITUTE. Trade Report. Vols. 17–18. 4to. Sydney, 1888. ME

NEW SOUTH WALES RIFLE ASSOCIATION. Reports, 1888–90. 8vo. Sydney, 1889-91. ME 2 Q

NEW SOUTH WALES SAVINGS BANK, Rules and Regulations. 12mo. Sydney, 1840. MF 2 P 53

NEW SOUTH WALES SOCIETY FOR THE PREVENTION OF CRUELTY TO ANIMALS. First Annual Report. 8vo. Sydney, 1874. ME 6 Q

NEW SOUTH WALES SPORTING ANNUAL, 1884; edited by P. H. Gilbert. 8vo. Sydney, 1884. ME 4 S

NEW SOUTH WALES WEALTH AND INDUSTRIAL EXHIBITION, 1884. Official Catalogue. 8vo. Sydney, 1884. ME 7 R

NEW SOUTH WALES ZOOLOGICAL SOCIETY. Annual Report, 1884. 8vo. Sydney, 1884. ME 6 S

Rules and By-laws. 8vo. Sydney (n.d.) MF 2 P 51

NEW WORLD, The, in 1859. Roy. 8vo. Lond., 1859. D 15 T 7

NEW WORLD BOOK LIST. 8vo. Bristol, 1890. K 7 R 48

NEW YORK STATE. [*See* United States.]

NEW YORK SHAKESPEARE SOCIETY. Digesta Shakespeareana. Parts 1 and 2. Compiled by A. Morgan. 8vo. New York, 1886-87. K 19 P 6

NEW YORK STATE AGRICULTURAL SOCIETY. Transactions. Vol. 34. Roy. 8vo. New York, 1889. E

NEW ZEALAND.

All about New Zealand; being a Complete Record of Colonial Life. 8vo. Glasgow, 1875. MD 2 S 19

New Zealand : a Poem. 8vo. Lond., 1842. MH 1 W 32

Correspondence relating to the Policy of Confiscation adopted by the New Zealand Legislature. Fol. Lond., 1864. MF 11 Q 48†

Correspondence with the Secretary of State relative to New Zealand. Fol. Lond., 1840. MF 3 U 25

Despatches from the Governor of New South Wales containing the Reports of Captain Hobson of his proceedings on his arrival at New Zealand. Fol. Lond., 1840. MF 3 U 25

History of the Carved House " Matatua " (exhibited by the New Zealand Government at the Sydney Exhibition). Fol. Wellington, 1879. MA 12 P 24†

NEW ZEALAND—*contd.*

Notes of a Tour through various parts of New Zealand, including a visit to the Hot Springs; by " A German Lady." 8vo. Sydney, 1877. MD 5 U 44

Papers relative to the Affairs of New Zealand, 1845. Fol. Lond., 1845. MF 1 U 45

Papers and Further Papers relative to New Zealand. Fol. Lond., 1847–48. MF 1 U 48

Further Papers relative to Affairs of New Zealand. 3 vols. Fol. Lond., 1849–51. MF 1 U 49–51

New Zealand, the Wonderland of the World. 8vo. Dunedin (n.d.) MD 7 T 32

Report from Select Committee on [with map]. Fol. Lond., 1844. MF 12 Q 41†

History, Institutions, and Industries. 8vo. Lond., 1888. MB 1 R 37

Maps of the North and Middle Islands. Fol. M

Sounds, Lakes, and Rivers. 4to. Wellington, 1885.* MA 7 P 19 †

Thermal Springs of the North Island. 4to. Wellington, 1881. MD 7 P 21 †

CENSUS.

Census, 1887. Sm. fol. Wellington, 1888. ME

CONSTITUTION.

Act to Grant a Representative Constitution to New Zealand. Fol. Lond., 1852. MF 12 Q 30†

Correspondence relative to [Colonization of New Zealand]. Fol. Lond., 1841. MF 3 U 25

Correspondence relative to the Establishment of a Proprietary Government in the Islands of New Zealand. 2 vols. (in 1). Fol. Lond., 1845. MF 12 Q 33†

Papers and Further Papers relative to the Proposed Constitution. 2 vols. (in 1). Fol. Lond., 1852. MF 12 Q 31†

Correspondence on the Subject of Responsible Government. Fol. Lond., 1855. MF 12 Q 32 †

CROWN LANDS.

Certain Acts passed by the Legislatures of South Australia and New Zealand relating to the Registration and Transfer of Land, together with reports and regulations relating to those Acts. Fol. Lond., 1862. MF 11 Q 17 †

Crown Lands Department, Annual Report, 1890. Fol. Wellington, 1891. ME

Crown Lands Guide, Nos. 9–12. 4 vols. 8vo. Wellington, 1888-92. ME 8 S

Handy-book on the Land Transfer Act, 1885. 8vo. Wellington, 1886. MF 2 P 50

History and Policy of the Native Land Laws, 1840–86. 12mo. Napier, 1886. MF 3 P 58

Important Judgments delivered in the Compensation Court and Native Land Court, 1866–79. 8vo. Auckland, 1879. MF 1 T 11

List of Original Land Purchases and Holders of Pasturage Runs to accompany Map of the Canterbury Province. 8vo. Lond., 1856. MD 7 R 16

NEW ZEALAND—*contd.*

CROWN LANDS—*contd.*

Papers relative to Land Claims, 1845–46. Fol. Lond.,
1845–46.	MF 1 U 46

Papers relative to Waste Lands Acts 1856–58, and to
the Grants made under the authority of those Acts.
Fol. Lond., 1859.	MF 12 Q 40 †

CUSTOMS.

Customs Tariff. 8vo. Wellington, 1891.	MF 2 T 68

EMIGRATION.

Correspondence on Emigration. Fol. Lond., 1860.
	MF 1 U 53

Emigrant's Guide to New Zealand, comprising every
requisite information for intending emigrants relative
to the Southern Settlements of New Zealand ; by "A
late resident in the colony." 6th edition. 12mo.
Lond., 1850.	MD 2 W 38

Information respecting the Settlement of New Plymouth,
together with Terms of Purchase for Lands, Regulations for labouring emigrants, &c., &c. 8vo. Lond.,
1841.	MD 5 U 45

Letters from Emigrants, published by the New Zealand
Company for the Information of the Labouring Classes.
8vo. Lond., 1841.	MD 7 S 8

FINANCE.

Correspondence on Proposed Guaranteed Loan. Fol.
Lond., 1869.	MF 12 Q 36 †

Correspondence having Reference to the Proposed
Guaranteed Loan of £1,000,000. Fol. Lond., 1870.
	MF 12 Q 36 †

Letter calling attention of Secretary of State to certain
Evidence given before a Committee of the House of
Commons in favour of a Guarantee by the Imperial
Legislature of a Loan of £500,000. Fol. Lond.,
1859.	MF 12 Q 35 †

Papers relating to a proposal that Parliament should
guarantee a loan to be received by the Government to
meet the expenses arising out of the Native War. Fol.
Lond., 1864.	MF 12 Q 35 †

Resolution adopted with reference to a loan of £500,000
which was to be solicited from the British Legislature.
Fol. Lond., 1858.	MF 12 Q 35 †

GAZETTE.

Gazette. Vols. 1, 2. Sm. fol. Wellington, 1887. ME

LEGISLATIVE COUNCIL.

Standing Orders, 1889. 12mo. Wellington, 1889.
	MF 2 P 57

MINES AND MINING.

Report on Goldfields, Roads, Water-races, and other
works in connection with Mining, 1886, 1889–91. 5
vols. Fol. Wellington, 1886–91.	ME

Mining Industry. Report. 8vo. Wellington, 1887. ME

Geological Survey. Reports of Geological Explorations
for 1885–87. Nos. 17, 18. Roy. 8vo. Wellington,
1886–87.	ME

Geological Survey. Index to Reports, 1866–85. Roy.
8vo. Wellington, 1887.	ME

NEW ZEALAND—*contd.*

NATIVE AFFAIRS.

Correspondence relative to an Attack on the British
Settlement at the Bay of Islands by the Natives. Fol.
Lond., 1845.	MF 3 Q 26

Correspondence relating to the Abandonment of Imperial
Control over Native Affairs in that Colony. Fol.
Lond., 1863.	MF 1 U 53

Correspondence relating to the War in New Zealand.
Fol. Lond., 1869.	MB 8 Q 29 †

Correspondence respecting a Memorial brought to this
Country by certain Maori Chiefs, 1884. 2 vols. (in 1).
Fol. Lond., 1885.	MF 12 Q 38 †

Correspondence relative to Native Affairs. Fol. Lond.,
1863.	MF 1 U 53

Correspondence relative to New Zealand, 1845–46. Fol.
Lond., 1845–46.	MF 1 U 46

Correspondence and Further Correspondence respecting
Native Affairs, and the Imprisonment of Certain
Maoris. 2 vols. (in 1). Fol. Lond., 1882–83.
	MF 1 U 59

Despatch from the Governor of New Zealand together
with a translation of a letter from the Chief Tawhiao
to the Governor. Fol. Lond., 1886. MF 12 Q 38 †

Despatch relative to Native Affairs. Fol. Lond., 1860.
	MF 1 U 53

Despatches relating to Management of Native Affairs and
the Purchase of Native Land, and the Proposed Establishment of a Native Council ; with Map. Fol. Lond.,
1860.	MF 1 U 53

Further Papers relating to the War in New Zealand.
Fol. Lond., 1864.	MF 1 U 54

Further Papers relative to the Affairs of New Zealand.
Fol. Lond., 1864–70.	MF 1 U 54–58

Memorial to his Grace the Secretary of State for the
Colonies, together with a Memorandum on New Zea-
land Affairs. 8vo. Lond., 1861.	MF 2 T 70

Papers relative to the Affairs of New Zealand. 3 vols.
Fol. Lond., 1845–54.	MF 1 U 42–44

Papers relative to Affairs of New Zealand. Fol. Lond.
1847.	MF 1 U 47

Papers and Further Papers relating to the recent disturbances. 2 vols. (in 1). Fol. Lond., 1861–62.
	MF 12 Q 34 †

Papers relative to Native Affairs. Fol. Lond., 1862.
	MF 1 U 52

Papers relating to certain allegations respecting the Treatment of Native Prisoners and others. Fol. Lond.,
1868.	MF 11 Q 47 †

Papers relating to Affairs of New Zealand. Part 1. War.
2 vols. (in 1). Fol. Lond., 1869.	MF 1 U 57

Vindication of the Character of the Missionaries and
Native Churches. 8vo. Lond., 1861.	MG 1 S 66

PARLIAMENTARY DEBATES.

Parliamentary Debates. 6 vols. 8vo. Wellington, 1887–88.
	ME

NEW ZEALAND—*contd.*

STATUTES.

Debtors and Creditors Act, 1876. Fol. Wellington, 1876.   MF 11 Q 4 †

Laws and Ordinances passed by the Governor and Council. 2 vols. (in 1.) Fol. Lond., 1842–44. MF 12 Q 39 †

Ordinances passed in the first ten Sessions of the General Legislative Council, 1841–49. 8vo. Wellington, 1850.
                                                MF 2 T 32

STATISTICS.

Statistics, 1887. Sm. fol. Wellington, 1888.   ME

NEW ZEALAND AND SOUTH SEAS EXHIBITION, Dunedin, 1889–90. Report of Oscar Meyer, Commissioner for New South Wales. Sm. 4to. Sydney, 1890. MA 2 V 47

Catalogue of Exhibits in the New South Wales Court. 8vo. Sydney, 1890.   MK 1 T 8

Papers read at the Mining Conference held at Dunedin, March, 1890. 8vo. Wellington, 1890.   MA 3 Q 54

NEW ZEALAND COMPANY. Correspondence between the Commissioners for the affairs of the New Zealand Company, the Directors, and the Colonial Office. Fol. Lond., 1852.   MF 12 Q 37 †

Correspondence relating to Manakau, New Zealand Company. Fol. Lond., 1845.   MF 1 U 46

Petition of the New Zealand Company. Fol. Lond. (n.d.)   MF 11 Q 22 †

Papers and Further Papers relating to the Surrender of their Charters, by the New Zealand Company. Fol. Lond., 1851–52.   MF 11 Q 22 †

NEW ZEALAND COUNTRY JOURNAL. Vol. 1, No. 4. Oct. 1877. 8vo. Christchurch, 1877.   ME 6 R

NEW ZEALAND INSTITUTE. Transactions and Proceedings, 1888–91. 4 vols. Roy. 8vo. Wellington, 1889–92.   ME 2 R

NEW ZEALAND JURIST, THE. Vols. 1 and 2, 1873–75, and vols. 1–3 (New Series), 1875–78. 5 vols. 4to. Dunedin, 1873–78.   ME 7 Q

NEWALL, Major-Gen. D. J. F. Highlands of India. 2 vols. 8vo. Lond., 1882–87.   D 16 U 11, 12

NEWBERRY, P. [*See* Carlyle, T.]

NEWCASTLE NAUTICAL ALMANAC. [*See* Knaggs & Co.]

NEWCASTLE-UPON-TYNE PUBLIC LIBRARIES. Catalogue of the books in the Juvenile Lending Department. Compiled by W. J. Haggerston. Roy. 8vo. Lond., 1887.   K 8 R 18

NEWCOMB, Prof. S. Astronomical Papers for the American Ephemeris, &c. Vol. 4, New Theory of Jupiter and Saturn, by G. W. Hill. 4to. Washington, 1890.   E

NEWFOUNDLAND. Acts to amend Licensing Acts. 3 vols. (in 1.) 8vo. St. Johns, 1873–84.   F 11 T 2

NEWMAN, Prof. F. W. History of the Hebrew Monarchy. 2nd edition. 8vo. Lond., 1853.   G 13 S 36

Miscellanies. 5 vols. 8vo. Lond., 1869–91.   J 3 T 8–12

Political Economy ; or the Science of the Market, especially as affected by Local Law. 8vo. Lond., 1890.
                                                F 8 Q 18

Regal Rome. 8vo. Lond., 1852.   B 30 Q 10

NEWMAN, Cardinal J. H. Anglican Career of ; by E. A. Abbott. 2 vols. 8vo. Lond., 1892.   C 18 S 17, 18

Callista ; a Tale of the Third Century. 8vo. Lond., 1891.
                                                J 11 W 29

Letters and Correspondence of, during his life in the English Church. Edited by Anne Mozley. 2 vols. 8vo. Lond., 1891.   C 15 U 11, 12

[Life of] ; by R. H. Hutton. 12mo. Lond., 1891.
                                                C 12 Q 2

Short Life of Cardinal Newman ; by J. S. Fletcher. 8vo. Lond., 1890.   C 16 Q 19

The Story of his Life ; by H. J. Jennings. New edition. 12mo. Birmingham, 1888.   C 12 P 29

NEWMAN, W. L. Politics of Aristotle. [*See* Aristoteles.]

NEWMARCH, Rosa. [*See* Brahms, J.]

NEWTON, G. W. Treatise on the Growth and Future Management of Timber Trees, and on other rural subjects. 8vo. Lond., 1859.   A 18 T 3

NEWTON, Sir I. Principia. [Philosophiæ naturalis principia mathematica.] Reprinted for Sir W. Thomson and H. Blackburn. Roy. 8vo. Glasgow, 1871. A 25 V 26

Bibliography of the Works of. [*See* Gray, G. J.]

NEY, N. En Asie Centrale. 3e édition. 8vo. Paris (n.d.)   D 17 U 20

NIBELUNGEN LIED, Der. 8vo. Berlin, 1810.
                                                H 10 R 10

Lay of the Nibelung; translated by A. G. Foster-Barham. 8vo. Lond., 1887.   H 7 Q 42

NICATI, Dr. W. [*See* Ranvier, L.]

NICÉVILLE, L. de. Butterflies of India. [*See* Marshall, Major G. F. L.]

NICHOL, Prof. J. Francis Bacon, his Life and Philosophy. 2 vols. 12mo. Edinb., 1888–89.   C 12 P 50, 51

[Life of] Thomas Carlyle. (Eng. Men of Letters.) 12mo. Lond., 1892.   C 1 U 41

Tables of European History, Literature, Science, and Art, A.D. 200–1888; and of American History, &c. 4th ed. 4to. Glasgow, 1888.   B 35 T 2

NICHOL, J. P. Cyclopædia of the Physical Sciences. 8vo. Lond., 1857.   K 16 Q 30

NICHOLAS, Sir E. Correspondence of. [*See* Camden Society.]

NICHOLS, F. M. Mirabilia Urbis Romæ : The Marvels of Rome, or a Picture of the Golden City. 8vo. Lond., 1889.   B 12 Q 43

NICHOLS, G. R. The Administration of Justice Acts, and the Protection of Justices Act, together with the Local Statute, the Duties of Justices Act. 8vo. Sydney, 1851.   MF 1 T 70

NICHOLS, T. N. What's in a Name; being a popular explanation of ordinary Christian names of men and women. 12mo. Lond., 1859.   K 19 P 15

NICHOLSON, Sir Chas. Ægyptinca, comprising a Catalogue of Egyptian Antiquities in the Museum of the University of Sydney, together with an account of some remains of the Disk Worshippers. Roy. 8vo. Lond., 1891.   MB 2 U 23

NICHOLSON, G. Illustrated Dictionary of Gardening: a practical and scientific Encyclopædia of Horticulture for Gardeners and Botanists. With supplement. 4 vols. 4to. Lond., 1885–89.   K 4 Q 15–18

NICOLSON, H. A. Manual of Palæontology for the Use of Students. 2nd ed. Roy. 8vo. Edinb., 1879.
                    A 24 T 8, 9

Manual of Zoology. 5th ed. 8vo. Lond., 1878.
                    A 27 Q 35

[*See* White, C. A.]

NICHOLSON, J. Beacons of East Yorkshire. 8vo. Hull, 1887.   B 22 Q 3

[*See* Lincoln's Inn.]

NICHOLSON, J. H. Moike ; or Melbourne in a Muddle : a Farcical Comedy in Two Acts. 12mo. Brisbane, 1886.   MH 1 Q 54

NICHOLSON, Prof. J. S. Effects of Machinery on Wages. 12mo. Lond., 1892.   F 9 U 40

Treatise on Money, and Essays on present Monetary Problems. 8vo. Edinb., 1888.   F 6 Q 45

NICHOLSON, P. W. Dante Gabriel Rossetti, Poet and Painter. (Round Table Series.) 8vo. Edinb., 1886.
                    C 7 T 9

NICKSON, C. History of Runcorn; with an Account of the Ancient Village of Weston. 4to. Lond., 1887.
                    B 9 R 6 †

NICOL, D. Political Life of Our Time. 2 vols. 8vo. Lond., 1889.   F 8 S 23, 24

[*See* Britannic Confederation.]

NICOL, Walter. The Practical Planter ; or, a Treatise on Forest Planting. 2nd ed. 8vo. Lond., 1803.
                    A 18 T 9

NICOLAS, Sir H. Chronology of History. 2nd ed. 12mo. Lond., 1838.   B 35 P 15

NICOLAY, J. G., and HAY, J. Abraham Lincoln : a History. 10 vols. 8vo. New York, 1890.
                    C 15 T 1–10

NICOLS, A. Wild Life and Adventure in the Australian Bush. 2 vols. 8vo. Lond., 1887.   MJ 2 P 1, 2

NICOLSON, Right Rev. W. English, Scotch, and Irish Historical Libraries. 3 vols. (in 1). Fol. Lond., 1736.
                    B 42 Q 7 ‡

NICOLSON, Wm. Letter to the Rev. J. Bonar on the Free Church of Scotland. 8vo. Hobart, 1852.
                    MG 1 R 28

NIECKS, Frederick. Frederick Chopin as a Man and Musician. 2 vols. 8vo. Lond., 1888.   C 13 U 7, 8

NIGHTINGALE, T. Oceanic Sketches. 8vo. Lond., 1835.   MD 6 S 3

NIMMO, Jas. Narrative of. [*See* Scottish History Society, 6.]

NINETEENTH CENTURY, The. Vols. 21–31. Roy. 8vo. Lond., 1887–1892.   E

NIPHER, F. E. Theory of Magnetic Measurements. 12mo. New York, 1886.   A 21 Q 3

NISARD, D. Histoire de la Littérature Française. 6e édition. 4 vols. 12mo. Paris, 1889.   B 26 Q 19–22

Collection des Auteurs Latins avec la Traduction en Français. 3 vols. Imp. 8vo. Paris, 1850–51.
                    J 18 V 24–26

Sénèque Œuvres complètes de.
Théâtre Complet des Latins comprenant Plaute, Térence, et Sénèque le Tragique.
Ammien Marcellin, Jornandès, Frontin (les Stratagèmes), Végèce, Modestus.

NISBET, Hume. "Bail Up" : a Romance of Bushrangers and Blacks. 8vo. Lond., 1891.   MJ 2 T 38

A Colonial Tramp : Travels and Adventures in Australia and New Guinea. 2 vols. 8vo. Lond., 1891.
                    MD 7 S 30, 31

The Land of the Hibiscus Blossom : a Yarn of the Papuan Gulf. 8vo. Lond., 1888.   MJ 2 Q 28

NISBET, J. F. The Sanity of Genius, and the General Inequality of Human Faculty, physiologically considered. 8vo. Lond., 1891.   A 12 T 29

NIVEN, R. The British Angler's Lexicon. Illustrated. 12mo. Lond., 1892.   A 29 Q 45

NIVEN, W. D. Scientific Papers of J. C. Maxwell. 2 vols. 4to. Camb., 1890.   A 42 R 21, 22 ‡

NOBLE, Rev. L. L. After Icebergs with a Painter : a Summer Voyage to Labrador and around Newfoundland. 8vo. Lond., 1862.   D 15 R 3

NODAL, Garcie de. Voyage de, en 1618. (Prévost, A. F., Suite de l'Histoire Générale des Voyages, tome 17). 4to. Amsterdam, 1781.   MD 11 P 16 †

NODIER, C. Le Génie Bonhomme. Roy. 8vo. Paris, 1873.   J 18 V 28

NOEL, Hon. R. [*See* Otway, T.]

NOEL, T. Rymes and Roundelayes. 12mo. Lond., 1841.   H 8 P 28

NONIUS MARCELLUS. De Compendiosa Doctrina. Roy. 8vo. Basiliæ, 1842.   J 13 U 27

NONNUS PANOPOLITANUS. Dionysiacorum libri xlviii., recensuit A. Koechly. (Gr. text.) 2 vols. (in 1.) 12mo. Lipsiæ, 1857–58.   H 10 P 25

NOORT, O. van, and NECK, J. van. Wonderlijcke Voyagie, by de Hollanders gedaen door de Strate Magalanes, ende voorts den gantschen kloot des Aertbodems om, met vier Schepen ; onder den Admirael O. van Noort, uytghevaren, 1598. Hier achter is by·gevoeght de Tweede Voyagie van Jacob van Neck naer Oost Indien. 8vo. Amstelrodam, 1648. MD 1 R 48

NORDENSKIÖLD, A. E. Facsimile-Atlas. Translated from the Swedish by J. A. Ekelöf and C. R. Markham. Fol. Stockholm, 1889. D 8 Q 1 ‡

NORFOLK ARCHÆOLOGICAL SOCIETY. Publications. Norfolk Archæology. Vols. 10, 11. 8vo. Norwich, 1888–92. E

NORFOLK RECORDS, edited by Walford D. Selby. Vol. 1. 8vo. Norwich, 1886. E

NORFOLK ISLAND. Correspondence on Removal of Inhabitants of Pitcairn's Island to Norfolk Island. Fol. Lond., 1857. MF 12 Q 24†
Further Papers on Removal of Inhabitants of Pitcairn's Island. Vols. 1 & 2. Fol. Lond., 1857. MF 12 Q 24†
Correspondence in reference to Pitcairn Islanders settled in Norfolk Island. Fol. Lond., 1863. MF 12 Q 24†

NORGATE, Miss Kate. England under the Angevin Kings. 2 vols. 8vo. Lond., 1887. B 22 U 8, 9

NORMAN, Capt. C. B. The Corsairs of France. 8vo. Lond., 1887. B 26 U 3

NORMAN, H. The Real Japan. Illustrated. 8vo. Lond., 1892. D 17 S 7

NORTH, A. J. Descriptive Catalogue of the Nests and Eggs of Birds found breeding in Australia and Tasmania. Roy. 8vo. Sydney, 1889. MA 2 U 55

NORTH, Rt. Hon. F., Baron Guilford ; the Hon. Sir Dudley, and the Hon. and Rev. Dr. John, Lives of ; by the Hon. Roger North. Edited by Rev. A. Jessopp, D.D. 3 vols., 8vo. Lond., 1890. C 12 P 2–4

NORTH, Marianne. Recollections of a Happy Life. 2 vols., 8vo. Lond., 1892. C 14 R 25, 26

NORTH, Hon. Roger. Lives of the Rt. Hon. Francis North, Baron Guilford ; the Hon. Sir Dudley North ; and the Hon. and Rev. Dr. John North. Edited by Rev. A. Jessopp, D.D. 3 vols., 8vo. Lond., 1890. C 12 P 2–4
Autobiography of; edited by Rev. A. Jessopp. 4to. Lond., 1887. C 12 V 12

NORTH, Sir T. [*See* Pilpay.]

NORTH, W. Cooley's Cyclopædia. [*See* Cooley, A. J.]

NORTH AMERICAN REVIEW. Vols. 144–154. 8vo. New York, 1887–92. E

NORTH BRITISH AGRICULTURIST. 6 vols., fol. Edinb., 1886–91. E

NORTHBROOK, Earl of. Descriptive Catalogue of the Collection of Pictures belonging to. 4to. Lond., 1889. A 42 R 5‡

NORTHCOTE, Sir Stafford. [*See* Iddesleigh, Earl of.]

NORTON, C. E. [*See* Carlyle, Thomas ; and Goethe, J. W.]

NORTON, C. L. Political Americanisms : a Glossary of Terms and Phrases current in American politics. 12mo. Lond., 1890. K 16 P 15.

NORTON, J. History of Capital and Labour in all Lands and Ages ; their past condition, present relations, and outlook for the future. Roy. 8vo. Sydney, 1888. MF 3 R 39

NOTES AND QUERIES. 7th Series, Vols. 2–12, 8th Series, Vol. 1. Sm. 4to. Lond., 1886–92. E

NOTES GRAMMATICALES SUR LA LANGUE DE LIFU (LOYALTYS.) D'après les manuscrits du P. F. P. Par le P. A. C. 8vo. Paris, 1882. MK 1 T 21

NOTTINGHAM. Records of the Borough of Nottingham, being a series of extracts from the Archives of the Corporation of Nottingham. Vols. 1–4. 1155–1625. Roy. 8vo. Lond., 1882–89. B 21 V 11–14

NOURSE, Prof. J. E. American Explorations in the Ice Zones. 4to. Boston, 1884. D 16 S 1

NOWELL, E. C. History of the Relations between the Two Houses of Parliament in Tasmania and South Australia in regard to Amendments to Bills containing provisions relating to the Public Revenue or Expenditure. 8vo. Hobart, 1890. MF 1 T 44

NUNEZ CABEZA DE VACA, Alvar. Commentaries of. [*See* Hakluyt Soc.]

NUNN, John. [*See* Clarke, Dr. W. B.]

NYLANDER, W. Lichenes Novæ Zelandiæ. 8vo. Paris, 1888. MA 1 T 67

NYREN, J. Nyren's "Cricketer's Guide." [*See* Cricket, Chronicles of.]

O

OAKESHOTT, G. J. Detail and Ornament of the Italian Renaissance. 4to. Lond., 1888.

OBERMULLER, J. Samoa : Zur Geschichte der deutschen Colonien in du Süd-See mit befonderer Rücksicht auf die Kämpfe um diefelben und die Ereignissi von 1888–89. 12mo. Leip., 1889. MD 2 W 6

O'BRIEN, Capt. Captivity in France. [*See* Choyce, J.]

O'BRIEN, R. B. Thomas Drummond, Under-Secretary in Ireland, 1835–40, Life and Letters. 8vo. Lond., 1889. C 13 U 4
Irish Wrongs and English Remedies, with other Essays. 8vo. Lond., 1887. F 6 Q 46

OBSERVATIONS upon a Petition recently addressed to the Lieut. Governor and Legislative Council of Van Diemen's Land, by Free Roman Catholic Inhabitants. 8vo. Sydney, 1840. MG 1 R 36

O'BYRNE, J. [*See* Sullivan, S.]

OCEAN STEAMSHIPS. A Popular Account of their Construction, &c. Roy. 8vo. Lond., 1892.   A 3 P 36

O'CLERY, P. K. "The O'Clery." The Making of Italy. 8vo. Lond., 1892.   B 16 R 5

O'CONNELL, Daniel. Correspondence of. Edited by W. J. Fitzpatrick. 2 vols. 8vo. Lond., 1888.   C 12 T 13, 14
Life of; by J. A. Hamilton. (Statesmen Series.) 8vo. Lond., 1888.   C 12 R 32
[*See* Lefevre, Rt. Hon. G. S.]

O'CONNOR, Evangeline M. An Index to the Works of Shakspere. 8vo. Lond., 1887.   K 19 P 1

O'CONNOR, Dr. M. [*See* St. Augustine's Literary Institute.]

O'CONNOR, R. New South Wales Parliamentary Handbook. 8vo. Sydney, 1872.   MF 1 T 7

O'CONNOR, R. E. [*See* Watkins, J. L.]

O'CONOR, W. A. History of the Irish People. 2nd edition. 2 vols. 8vo. Manchester, 1886–87.   B 29 T 12, 13

O'DONOVAN, J. Grammar of the Irish Language. 8vo. Dublin, 1845.   K 12 V 17

OEHLER, F. [*See* Tertullianus, Q. S. F., *and* Varro, M. T.]

OESTLUND, O. W. Synopsis of the Aphididæ of Minnesota. (Geol. Survey of Minnesota, &c.) Roy. 8vo. St. Paul, 1887.   E

OFFICER IN THE VICTORIAN POLICE, An. [*See* Borlase, J.S.]

OFFICES OF THE BISHOP. Martinuci de Quibusdam Officiis Episcopi. 8vo. Sydney (n.d.)   MG 1 R 14
Ordo Divini Officii Recitandi, &c. 12mo. Sydney, 1869.   MG 1 Q 5

OGILBY, J. D. Description of a little-known Australian Fish, of the Genus Girella. 8vo. Lond., 1887.   MA 3 T 36
On an undescribed fish of the Genus Prionurus, from Australia. 8mo. Lond., 1887.   MA 3 T 36

OGILVIE, W. Birthright in Land, with Biographical Notes, by D. C. Macdonald. 12mo. Lond., 1891.   F 9 U 41

OGLANDER, Sir J. The Oglander Memoirs; edited by W. H. Long. Sm. 4to. Lond., 1888.   B 23 U 10

O'HARA, John B. Songs of the South. 12mo. Lond., 1891.   MH 1 U 34

O'HARA, Kane. Midas: an English Burletta. [*See* British Drama, Modern, 5.]
The Two Misers, a Musical Farce. [*See* British Drama, Modern, 5.]

O'HART, J. Irish Pedigrees. 3rd edition. 8vo. Dublin, 1881.   K 12 V 10
Irish and Anglo-Irish Landed Gentry when Cromwell came to Ireland. 8vo. Dublin, 1884.   K 12 V 11
Irish Landed Gentry when Cromwell came to Ireland. 8vo. Dublin, 1887.   K 12 V 13

OKES, R. Musæ Etonenses. Series nova. 8vo. Etonæ, 1869.   H 9 S 24

OLCOTT, H. S. [*See* D'Assier, A.]

OLD BOHEMIAN, An. [*See* Strauss, G. L. M.]

OLD BOOMERANG. [*See* Houlding, J. R.]

OLD EXPLORER, An. [*See* Queenslanders' New Colonial Camp Fire Song Book.]

OLD HAND, An. [*See* Memories of the Past.]

OLD HAND, An. [*See* Reminiscences of Early Days.]

OLD IDENTITY, An. [*See* Walker, T.]

OLD PAST MASTER, An. [*See* Freemasonry.]

OLDEN, Rev. C. Protection of Girls and Young Women, and the Legislative Repression of Vice generally : a Lecture. 8vo. Sydney, 1886.   MF 1 T 79

OLDENBURG, H. [*See* Müller, F. Max, Sacred Books.]

OLDFIELD, A. Practical Manual of Typography, and Reference Book for Printers. 12mo. Lond., 1890.   A 25 Q 11

OLIPHANT, Alice. Memoir of the Life of Laurence Oliphant and of Alice Oliphant, his wife. 2 vols. 8vo. Edinb., 1891.   C 13 R 27, 28

OLIPHANT, C. F. Alfred de Musset. 12mo. Edinb., 1890.   C 14 P 2

OLIPHANT, Laurence. Memoir of, and of Alice Oliphant, his wife ; by Margaret Oliphant W. Oliphant. 2 vols. 8vo. Edinb., 1891.   C 13 R 27, 28
Episodes in a Life of Adventure. 8vo. Lond., 1887.   C 12 R 42
Haifa; or, Life in Modern Palestine. 8vo. Edinb., 1887.   D 16 T 1
Scientific Religion; or, Higher Possibilities of Life and Practice. 8vo. Lond., 1888.   G 12 P 25

OLIPHANT, Mrs. Margaret O. W. Jerusalem : its History and Hope. 8vo. Lond., 1891.   B 16 S 34
Makers of Venice: Doges, Conquerors, Painters, and Men of Letters. 8vo. Lond., 1887.   B 11 T 38
Memoir of the Life of Laurence Oliphant and of Alice Oliphant, his wife. 2 vols. 8vo. Edinb., 1891.   C 13 R 27, 28
Memoir of the Life of John Tulloch, D.D., &c. 8vo. Edinb., 1888.   C 13 T 22
Royal Edinburgh, her saints, kings, prophets, and poets. 8vo. Lond., 1890.   B 32 T 12

OLIVER, D. Lessons in Elementary Botany. New edition. 12mo. Lond., 1888.   A 20 P 10

OLIVER, Edward E. Across the Border ; or Pathán and Biloch. 8vo. Lond., 1890.   D 16 U 19

OLIVER, Henry K. [Life of]; by Rev. Jesse H. Jones. Roy. 8vo. Boston, 1886.   C 9 V 6

OLIVER, Prof. T. Lead Poisoning in its acute and chronic forms. 8vo. Edinb., 1891.   A 26 T 5

OLIVER AND BOYD. Edinburgh Almanac. 6 vols. 12 mo. Edinb., 1887-92.   E

OLLIFF, A. S. Australian Butterflies; a brief account of the native Families, with a chapter on collecting and Preserving Insects. 8vo. Sydney, 1889.   MA 2 T 43
A Chapter on Collecting and Preserving Insects. 8vo. Sydney, 1889.   MA 2 T 42

OLLIVANT, J. E. Hine Moa, the Maori Maiden. 12mo. Lond (n.d.)   MH 1 Q 79

OMAI. Narrations d'Omai Insulaire de la Mer du Sud, ami et compagnon de voyage du Captaine Cook [composée par l'abbé G. A. R. Baston]. 4 vols. 8vo. Rouen, 1790.   MD 6 S 24-27

OMAN, C. W. C. The Byzantine Empire. 8vo. Lond., 1892.   B 17 Q 6
Warwick, the King-maker. (English Men of Action.) 8vo. Lond., 1891.   C 15 Q 12

OMAN, Prof. John Campbell. Indian Life: Religious and Social. 8vo. Lond., 1889.   D 17 R 5

OMAR KHAYYAM. Rubaiyat of; translated by Justin Huntly M'Carthy. 12mo. Lond., 1889.   H 6 Q 41

O'MEAGHER, J. C. Some Historical Notices of the O'Meaghers of Ikerrin. Roy.8vo. Lond.,1887. B 29 V 11

OMOND, G. W. T. Arniston Memoirs, 1571-1838. Roy. 8vo. Edinb., 1887.   B 31 U 12

O'NEIL, C. A. American Electoral System. 8vo. New York, 1887.   F 6 Q 47

O'NEILL, H. Sculptured Crosses of Ancient Ireland. Fol. Lond., 1857.   B 41 P 21 ‡

ONLY WILLIAM, The. [See Schmidt, William.]

ONOSANDER. De Imperatoris Officio liber; recensuit A. Koechly. 8vo. Lipsiæ, 1860.   A 29 R 7

OPPEN, E. A. Description of the Northern Territory of South Australia. 8vo. Hertford, 1864.   MD 8 R 1

OPPENHEIM, J. Wet tot Regeling van dem Kleinhandel in Sterken Drank, &c. 8vo. Groningen, 1885.   F 11 S 33

ORANGE, Rev. J. Life of George Vason; with a preliminary essay on the South Sea Islands. 12mo. Lond., 1840.   MC 1 Q 55

ORDINAIRE, F. La Nouvelle-Calédonie. Roy. 8vo. Lyon, 1889.   MD 7 U 12

ORDEN, Wappen, und Flaggen aller Regenten und Staaten, mit Specielle Beschreibung. 2 vols. roy. 8vo. Leipsic, 1883-88.   K 8 S 1, 2

O'REILLY, Rev. Bernard. Life of Leo XIII, from an authentic Memoir furnished by his order. Roy. 8vo. Lond., 1887.   C 12 U 1

O'REILLY, D. "A Pedlar's Pack." 12mo. Sydney, 1888.   MH 1 P 34

O'REILLY, J. B. Life of; by J. J. Roche; with his complete poems and speeches; edited by Mrs. J. B. O'Reilly. Roy. 8vo. Lond., 1891.   C 12 U 19
Another Copy. Roy. 8vo. Lond., 1891.   MC 1 R 38

O'REILLY, Mrs. J. B. Complete Poems and Speeches of John B. O'Reilly. [See O'Reilly, J. B.]

O'RELL, Max. [See Blouet, P.]

ORIENT LINE GUIDE. [See Loftie, W. J.]

ORLEBAR, Lieut. J. Midshipman's Journal, on board H.M.S. *Seringapatam* during the year 1830, containing observations on Pitcairn's Island, &c. 8vo. Lond., 1833.   MD 7 S 9

ORME, W. Defence of Missions in the South Sea and Sandwich Islands. Roy.8vo. Lond.,1827. MG 1 R 13

ORMEROD, Eleanor A. Notes of Observations of Injurious Insects. Reports, 1879-80. Roy. 8vo. Lond., 1880-81.   E
Reports of Observations of Injurious Insects and Common Farm Pests. 10 vols. (in 8.) Roy. 8vo. Lond., 1882-92.   E
Notes on the Australian Bug in South Africa. 8vo. Lond., 1887.   MA 2 T 16

ORMONDE, B. W. Few Words about Life Assurance, in reply to a pamphlet by Henry Francis. 8vo. Sydney, 1882.   MF 1 T 51

ORPEN, G. H. Song of Dermot and the Earl; an old French poem from the Carew MSS. No. 596; edited, with translation, notes, and map, by G. H. Orpen. 12mo. Oxford, 1892.   R 3 P 44
[See Laveleye, E. de.]

ORR, Mrs. Andrew. Sunny Australia for Australia's Children. Sm. 4to. Sydney, 1892.   MH 1 T 20

ORR, Mrs. S. Life and Letters of Robert Browning. 8vo. Lond., 1891.   C 14 R 30

ORR, W. S. and Co. Circle of the Sciences. 2 vols. 8vo. Lond., 1854.   A 29 S 5, 6
1. Principles of Physiology—Structure of the Skeleton and Teeth—Varieties of the Human Race.
2. Botany, Structural and Systematic—Zoology, Invertebrated Animals.

OSBORN, Emily F. D. [See Osborn, Hon. Mrs. S.]

OSBORN, Prof. H. S. Practical Manual of Minerals, Mines, and Mining. 8vo. Philad., 1888.   A 24 U 4

OSBORN, Hon. Mrs. Sarah. Political and Social Letters of a Lady of the 18th Century, 1721-71. Edited by Emily F. D. Osborn. 8vo. Lond., 1890   C 15 U 14

Y

OSBORN, Rear-Adm. Sherard. Stray Leaves from an Arctic Journal ; or, Eighteen Months in the Polar Regions in search of Sir J. Franklin's Expedition in 1850–51. 8vo. Lond., 1852.   D 16 R 1

OSBORNE, Dorothy. [*See* Temple, Lady.]

OSBORNE, Rev. Lord S. G. Letters of S.G.O. Edited by A. White. 2 vols. 8vo. Lond., 1891.   F 8 S 27, 28

OSBOURNE, Lloyd. [*See* Stevenson, R. L.]

OSBURNE, R. History of Warrnambool, 1847–86. 8vo. Prahran, 1887.   MB 2 P 43

O'SHEA, J. A. Roundabout Recollections. 2 vols. 8vo. Lond., 1892.   C 18 S 3, 4
Military Mosaics : Tales and Sketches on Soldierly Themes. 8vo. Lond., 1888.   J 5 Q 42

O'SULLIVAN, D. A. Government in Canada. 2nd edition. 8vo. Toronto, 1887.   F 4 S 29
Manual of Government in Canada. 12mo. Toronto, 1879.   F 6 P 40

OTAGO UNIVERSITY. Calendar for 1892. 8vo. Dunedin, 1892.   ME 5 S

OTAHEITE. [*See* Tahiti.]

O'TOOLE, Rev. P. L. History of the Clan O'Toole and other Leinster Septs. 4to. Dublin, 1890.   B 28 V 1

OTTÉ, E. C. How to Learn Danish (Dano-Norwegian). 3rd edition. 8vo. Lond., 1887.   K 20 Q 4
Simplified Grammar of the Danish Language. 8vo. Lond., 1884.   K 20 Q 12

OTWAY, T. The Best Plays of the Old Dramatists. Thomas Otway, with Notes by the Hon. Roden Noel. (Mermaid series.) 8vo. Lond., 1888.   H 4 Q 32
Don Carlos.—The Orphan.—The Soldier's Fortune.—Venice Preserved.
The Cheats of Scapin : a Farce. [*See* British Drama, Modern, 5.]
Venice Preserved : a Tragedy. [*See* British Drama, Modern, 1.]
The Orphan : a Tragedy. [*See* British Drama, Modern, 1.]

OUR AMERICAN COUSINS and their Political Life ; by "One of Themselves" [E. A.] 8vo. Lond., 1887.   F 5 U 40

OUR HOMES AND HOW TO MAKE THEM HAPPY ; by "An Australian." 12mo. Sydney, 1887.   MJ 2 T 17

OUR NATIONAL CATHEDRALS, their History and Architecture from their Foundation to Modern Times. Vol. 1. Roy. 8vo. Lond., 1887.   A 19 V 4

OUR PRESENT PARLIAMENT [opened 17th November, 1885, dissolved 26th January, 1887]. What it is Worth. By an "Ex-M.L.A." 8vo. Sydney, 1887.   MF 3 P 61

OUR PUBLIC SCHOOLS. 12mo. Lond., 1881.   G 18 Q 24

OUR RIVER : A Practical Suggestion to British Patriots, by "A Colonial Briton." 12mo. Lond., 1871.   MF 2 P 76

OVERLAND MONTHLY. 2nd series. vols. 8–18. Roy. 8vo. San Francisco, 1886–92   E

OVERLANDER. [*See* Australian Sketches.]

OVERTON, J. H. [Life of] John Wesley. 8vo. Lond., 1891.   C 15 Q 10

OVERTON, J. H., and WORDSWORTH, Elizabeth. Christopher Wordsworth, Bishop of Lincoln, 1807–85. 8vo. Lond., 1888.   C 12 S 28

OVIDIUS NASO, P. Carmina. Edidit A. Riese. 3 vols. (in 1.) 8vo. Lipsiæ, 1871–74.   H 10 R 5
Epistolarum Heroidum Liber. 8vo. Lond., 1702.   H 10 Q 19
Le Metamorposi di Ovidio, ridotti da G. Andrea. Roy. 8vo. Venetia, 1584.   H 6 V 30
Ovid ; by Rev. A. Church. (Ancient Classics for English Readers.) 12mo. Edinb., 1880.   J 14 P 19
Quaedam Fabellæ ex Ovidio. [*See* Brain, T. II.]

OWEN, D. Declaration of War ; a Survey of the Position of Belligerents and Neutrals with relative considerations of Shipping during War. 8vo. Lond., 1889.   F 9 T 1

OWEN, Dr. Dialogue on Baptism. 8vo. Sydney, 1886.   MG 1 Q 11

OWEN, Col. John. Memoirs of above Half-a-century ; by "Owen Square." 8vo. Lond., 1889.   C 13 T 24

OWEN, J. W. The Common Salvation of Our Lord and Saviour Jesus Christ. 8vo. Melb., 1891.   MG 1 R 29

OWEN, R. Palæontology. 8vo. Edinb., 1860.   A 24 T 10

OWEN, Robert, the Founder of Socialism in England [Life of ;] by A. J. Booth. 8vo. Lond., 1869. C 16 Q 20
[*See* Bradlaugh, C.—Five Dead Men.]

OWEN SQUARE. [*See* Owen, Col. John.]

OWEN, T. C. The Tea Planter's Manual. 8vo. Colombo, 1886.   A 18 S 3

OWENS, E. M. Ovariotomy : with notes on two Successful Cases. 8vo. Brisb., 1888.   MA 3 S 37

OXFORD ARCHITECTURAL SOCIETY. Reports, 1851–53. 8vo. Oxford, 1853.   E
Rules and List of Members. 8vo. Oxford, 1851.   E

OXFORD UNIVERSITY. Calendars. 6 vols. 12mo. Oxford, 1878–92.   E
Statutes of. 3 vols. 8vo. Oxford, 1853.   F 1 Q 20–22
Statutes. Codified in 1636, under authority of Archbishop Laud ; edited by Rev. Dr. J. Griffiths. 4to. Oxford, 1888.   F 9 R 25 †
Statuta Universitatis Oxoniensis. 8vo. Oxonii, 1883.   F 1 Q 27

OXLEY, John. Reizen in de Binnenlanden van Australie, 1817–18. 8vo. Dordrecht, 1821.   MD 8 Q 1

P

P. W. [*See* Albanian Language.]

PACIFIC ISLANDS. Sailing Directions for Western, Central, and Eastern Groups. Second edition. 2 vols. Roy. 8vo. Lond., 1890-91. MD 5 V 46, 47

PACKARD, A. S., Jun. Zoology. Fourth edition. 8vo. New York, 1883. A 27 Q 39

PACKER, C. S. The Royal Charlie Polka. Fol. Sydney (n.d.) MA 11 Q 15 †

PAGE, D. Hand-book of Geological Terms and Geology. 8vo. Lond., 1859. . K 18 P 31

PAGE, H. W. Railway Injuries ; with special reference to those of the back and nervous system. Roy. 8vo. Lond., 1891. A 12 U 1

PAGE, John Lloyd Warden. Exploration of Exmoor and the Hill Country of West Somerset. 8vo. Lond., 1890. D 18 R 7

PAGE, T. Land Settlement and Congested Population. [Sheet Folded.] Roy. 8vo. Grafton, 1892. MF3 T 43

PAGENSTECHER, G. [*See* Fry, Katherine.]

PAGET, Sir J. [*See* Alcohol Question.]

PAINTER, Prof. F. V. N. History of Education. 8vo. New York, 1886. G

PALADIN. [*See* Glances at Great and Little Men.]

PALÆOGRAPHICAL SOCIETY, The. Fac-similes of Ancient Manuscripts, &c. Series 2, part 4-6. Imp. fol. Lond., 1886-89. E

PALÆONTOGRAPHICA. Bande 1-38. Roy. 4to. Stuttgart, &c., 1851-92. E
Supplements. 10 vols. roy. 4to. (Plates 4to.) Cassel, 1866-80. E

PALÆONTOLOGISCHE ABHANDLUNGEN. Bande 3, 4. Roy. 4to. Berlin, 1886-89. E

PALATINE NOTE-BOOK, The. Vol. 4. Sm. 4to. Manchester, 1884. E

PALESTINE, Map of. Fol. Lond., 1890. D 41 P 19

PALESTINE EXPLORATION FUND. Quarterly Statements, 1869-91. 22 vols. 8vo. Lond., 1869-91. E
Survey of Eastern Palestine. Memoirs, Vol. 1. The 'Adwân Country. By Major C. R. Conder. 4to. Lond., 1889. D 3 R 16 †
The Survey of Western Palestine : a General Index to the Memoirs, the Special Papers, the Jerusalem Volume, the Flora and Fauna of Palestine, the Geological Survey and to the Arabic and English Name Lists. Compiled H. C. Stewardson. 4to. Lond., 1888. D 4 V 12
Northern 'Ajlân. [*See* Schumacher, G.]

PALEY, F. A. Epics of Hesiod. [*See* Hesiod.]

PALEY, W. Horæ Paulinæ. 8vo. Lond., 1852. G 16 P 42

PALGRAVE, Prof. F. T. Treasury of Sacred Song. Sm. 4to. Oxford, 1889. H 5 T 41

PALGRAVE, R. F. D. Oliver Cromwell, the Protector ; an appreciation based on contemporary evidence. 8vo. Lond., 1890. C 12 R 45
House of Commons: Illustrations of its History and Practice. 8vo. Lond., 1878. D 10 S 28

PALGRAVE, W. G. Ulysses ; or, Scenes and Studies in Many Lands. 8vo. Lond., 1887. D 10 S 28

PALING, W. H. Sydney Railway Waltz. Fol. Sydney, 1855. MA 11 Q 15 †

PALLADIUS, Rutilius Taurus Æmilianus. [*See* Agronomes Latins, Les.]

PALLISER, Mrs. B. Historic Devices, Badges, and War-Cries. 8vo. Lond., 1870 K 12 V 12
[*See* Jacquemart, A.]

PALMÉN, Dr. J. A. Zur Morphologie des Tracheen-systems. 8vo. Helsingfors, 1877. A 14 T 48

PALMER, Prof. E. H. Simplified Grammar of Hindûstânî, Persian, and Arabic. 3rd ed. 8vo. Lond., 1890. K 20 Q 5
[*See* Besant, W., *and* Müller, F. Max—Sacred Books.]

PALMER, Rev. H. A. Necromancy ; or Intercourse with the Spirits of the Dead. Two Sermons. 8vo. Sydney, 1874. MG 1 S 58

PALMER, S. Index to the *Times* Newspaper, 1840-52, 1866, and 1886-91. Sm. 4to. Lond., 1876-92. E

PALMER, Rev. T. F. Account of the Trial of Thomas Fyshe Palmer, at Perth, 1793, for Sedition. 8vo. Perth, 1793. F 12 P 28
Narrative of the Sufferings of T. F. Palmer and W. Skirving. 8vo. Cambridge, 1797. ˙ MC 1 Q 24
Trial of the Rev. Thomas Fyshe Palmer, at Perth, 1793, on an Indictment for Seditious Practices, with an appendix. 8vo. Edinb., 1793. F 12 P 25
[*See* Adam, Wm.]

PALMERSTON, Henry John Temple, Viscount. [Life of] ; by the Marquis of Lorne. 12mo. Lond., 1892. C 13 Q 21
Life of ; by L. C. Sanders. (Statesmen Series.) 8vo. Lond., 1888. C 12 Q 38
[*See* Geffcken, Dr. F. H.]

PAMELY, C. The Colliery Manager's Handbook. 8vo. Lond., 1891. A 24 V 7

PANIZZI, A. Lettres à ; par Prosper Mérimée. 5th ed. 2 vols. 8vo. Paris, 1881. C 16 T 2, 3

PANTER, F. K. [*See* Martin, J.]

PAOLI, P. [*See* Boswell, J.]

PAPENDIEK, Mrs. C. L. H. Court and Private Life in the Time of Queen Charlotte : edited by Mrs. V. D. Broughton. 2 vols. 8vo. Lond., 1887.   C 13 S 21, 22

PAPILLON, A. F. W. Memoirs of Thomas Papillon, of London, Merchant, 1623-1702. 8vo. Reading, 1887.
                                                    C 13 S 7

PAPILLON, T. Memoirs of, 1623-1702; by A. F. W. Papillon. 8vo. Reading, 1887.   C 13 S 7

PAPILLON, Rev. T. L. [_See_ Virgilius Maro, P.]

PARDOE, Julia S. H. Life of Marie de Medicis, Queen of France. 3 vols. 8vo. Lond., 1890.   C 17 T 6-8

PÂRIS, Vice-Adm. E. Collection de Plans ou Dessins de Navires et de Bateaux Anciens ou Modernes. 2 vols. L. 4to. Paris, 1882-84.   A 8 R 5, 6 ‡

PARIS as it is ; an Illustrated Souvenir of the French Metropolis. Ob. 8vo. Paris, 1892.   D 18 R 13

PARIS SALON. Catalogue illustré. 6 vols. 8vo. Paris, 1887-92.   E

PARK, Mungo. [_See_ Thomson, Jos.]

PARKE, T. H. My Personal Experiences in Equatorial Africa, with Map and Illustrations. 8vo. Lond., 1891.
                                                    D 14 U 24

PARKER, C. S. [_See_ Peel, Sir R.]

PARKER, F. W. How to Study Geography. (Intern. Educ. Series.) 8vo. New York, 1889.   D 11 R 18

PARKER, Roan. Round the Compass in Australia. Roy. 8vo. Lond., 1892.   MD 8 R 3

PARKER, G. W. Concise Grammar of the Malagasy Language. 8vo. Lond., 1883.   . K 20 Q 8

PARKER, J. Introduction to the History of the Successive Revisions of the Book of Common Prayer. 8vo. Oxford, 1877.   G 7 R 34

PARKER, T. Theism, Atheism, and the Popular Theology. 8vo. Lond., 1853.   G 13 S 40

PARKER, Prof. T. J. Lessons in Elementary Biology. 8vo. Lond., 1891.   A 14 Q 60

Studies in Biology for New Zealand Students, No. 4. The Skeleton of the New Zealand Crayfishes (Palinurus and Paranephrops). Roy. 8vo. Wellington, 1889.
                                                    MA 3 R 4

PARKER, W. R. Science of Life ; or, Self-preservation. 18mo. Sydney (n.d.)   MA 2 S 42

PARKES, Prof. E. A. Manual of Practical Hygiene. 7th ed. 8vo. Lond., 1887.   A 12 U 32

PARKES, Sir H. The Case of the Prisoner Gardiner, the Prerogative of Pardon : a Chapter of History. 8vo. Melb., 1876.   MF 1 R 65

The Chinese in Australia : a Speech. Roy. 8vo. Sydney, 1888.   MF 3 T 9

Correspondence respecting Orangemen in Public Schools. [_See_ Reynolds, M.]

Federal Government in Australasia : Speeches. 8vo. Sydney, 1890.   MF 2 T 7

PARKES, Sir H.—_contd._

Freehold Homes in a Gold Country : Two Public Addresses. 12mo. Birmingham, 1861.   MF 3 P 62

Manuscript Letter to Joseph Mayer, with full length photograph. 8vo. Sydney, 1880.   MC 1 T 23

Present Condition and Future Prospects of Australia : a Speech. 8vo. Melb., 1880.   MF 1 R 66

Mr. Gladstone and English Liberalism from an Australian Point of View : Speech. 8vo. Sydney, 1878.
                                                    MF 1 T 49

Murmurs of the Stream. 12mo. Sydney, 1857.
                                                    MH 1 Q 68

Public Schools Act : Speech. 8vo. Sydney, 1870.
                                                    MF 1 T 50

[_See_ Reid, G. H.]

PARKES, K. [_See_ Linton, W. J.]

PARKES, L. C. [_See_ Corfield, Prof. W. H.]

PARKES, S. Chemical Catechism. 13th ed., revised by E. W. Brayley. 8vo. Lond., 1834.   A 5 T 20

PARKES, S. H. Unfinished Worlds : a Study in Astronomy. 8vo. Lond., 1887.   A 19 R 25

PARKIN, G. R. Imperial Federation. 12mo. Lond., 1892.   F 9 U 19

PARKIN, J. Are Epidemics Contagious? 8vo. Lond., 1887.   A 13 P 46

Volcanic Origin of Epidemics. 8vo. Lond., 1887. A 13 P 47

PARKINSON, J. Theatrum Botanicum. The Theater of Plants, or, an Herball of a large extent. Fol. Lond., 1641.   A 39 S 3 ‡

PARKINSON, S. Voyage autour du Monde sur le Vaisseau de sa Majesté Britannique l'Endeavour. 2 vols. 8vo. Paris, 1797.   MD 8 Q 4, 5

PARKINSON, S. Scenes from the "George Eliot" Country. 8vo. Leeds, 1888.   D 19 Q 2

PARKINSON, Rev. T. Yorkshire Legends and Traditions. 8vo. Lond., 1888.   B 23 U 9

PARKMAN, F. A Half-Century of Conflict. 2 vols. 8vo. Lond., 1892.   B 19 S 6, 7

Conspiracy of Pontiac, and the Indian War. Vol. 1. 8vo. Lond., 1885.   B

PARLEY, Peter. [_See_ Goodrich, S. G.]

PARNELL, Hon. Col. A. War of the Succession in Spain, 1702-11. 8vo. Lond., 1888.   B 13 T 15

PARNELL, E. B. [_See_ Watson, R. H. L.]

PARNELLITE SPLIT, THE ; or, the Description of the Irish Parliamentary Party. 8vo. Lond., 1891. F 7 P 9

PARRY, Rev. D. Signals Hoisted ; being a series of short Lectures. 12mo. Hobart, 1874.   MG 2 P 44

PARRY, E. A. [Life of] Charles Macklin. (Eminent Actors.) 8vo. Lond., 1891. C 16 P 10

Letters from Dorothy Osborne to Sir W. Temple, 1652–54. 8vo. Lond., 1888. C 15 U 4

PARRY, E. G. Reynell Taylor: a Biography. 8vo. Lond., 1888. C 13 S 1

PARSONS, Rev. B. The Wine Question settled, in accordance with the inductions of Science and the facts of History. 12mo. Lond., 1841. F 11 P 39

PARSONS, J. L. The Sugar Industry in the Mackay District : Notes of a Trip among the Mackay Sugar Plantations : the Coloured Labour Question in Queensland : and the Northern Territory as a country for the Growth of Sugar, &c. : and the advantages of Coolie Labour for the Northern Territory. 8vo. Adelaide, 1883. MA 3 Q 11

PASCAL, B. Thoughts of; translated by C. K. Paul. 8vo. Lond., 1885. G 8 R 30

PASK, Arthur T. The Eyes of the Thames. 8vo. Lond., 1889. D 19 Q 10

PASTEUR, L. Report on Experiments demonstrating the efficacy of Pasteur's Vaccine of Anthrax. 8vo. Sydney, 1889. MA 1 S 44

[*See* Suzor, R.; Gordon, Surgeon-Gen. C. A.]

PASTORALIST, THE. May, 1889–August, 1891. 3 vols. Fol. Sydney, 1889–91. ME

PASTORALISTS' FEDERAL COUNCIL OF AUS-TRALIA. Official Statement of Facts and History of the Shearing Difficulty in Australia. Fol. Sydney, 1891. MF 11 Q 51 †

PATER, W. Imaginary Portraits. 8vo. Lond., 1887. J 5 R 38

The Renaissance : Studies in Art and Poetry. 8vo. Lond., 1886. A 23 R 2

PATERSON, A. Physical Health of Woman : Useful Knowledge for Maiden, Wife, and Mother. 8vo. Sydney, 1890. MA 3 Q 12

PATERSON, A. B. Australia for the Australians : a Political Pamphlet showing the Necessity for Land Reform combined with Protection. 8vo. Sydney, 1889. MF 2 T 34

PATMORE, Coventry K. D. Poems. 4th edition. 2 vols. 12mo. Lond., 1890. H 8 P 46, 47

PATON, Jas. Scotish National Memorials. 4to. Glasgow, 1890. B 39 P 19 ‡

PATON, J. G. Missionary to the New Hebrides. An Autobiography. 2 vols. 8vo. Lond., 1889. MC 1 Q 31, 32

PATON, W. A. Down the Islands: a Voyage to the Caribbees. Roy. 8vo. Lond., 1888. D 15 U 1

PATOUILLET, J. Trois Ans en Nouvelle Caledonie. 12mo. Paris, 1873. MD 7 T 33

PATRICK, R. W. Cochran-. Early Records relating to Mining in Scotland. Roy. 4to. Edinb., 1878. A 4 R 4 †

Mediæval Scotland. 8vo. Glasgow, 1892. B 24 S 14

PATRIOT'S LETTERS on Free Trade v. Protection and Encouragement to Native Industries. 8vo. Sydney, 1877. MF 1 R 68

PATRONATO DI TEMPERANZA in Milano, Statistica, 1885. 8vo. Milano, 1885. F 11 S 34

PATTERSON, Rev. G. Missionary Life among the Cannibals ; being the Life of the Rev. J. Geddie. 8vo. Toronto, 1882. MC 1 Q 46

PATTERSON, R. Introduction to Zoology. 12mo. Lond., 1857. A 27 Q 30

PATTISON, M. Essays by the late Mark Pattison, sometime Rector of Lincoln College. Collected and arranged by H. Nettleship. 2 vols. 8vo. Oxford, 1889. J 3 V 24, 25

[Life of] Isaac Casaubon. 2nd ed. 8vo. Oxford, 1892. C 18 Q 8

PATTISON, S. R. Gospel Ethnology. 8vo. Lond., 1888. A 1 V 20

PATTON, Prof. A. St. G. Modern History. [*See* Rawlinson, Prof. G.]

PATTON, J. H. Concise History of the American People. 2 vols. 8vo. Lond., 1887. B 1 S 48, 49

Natural Resources of the United States. 8vo. New York, 1888. A 29 T 1

PAUL, C. Kegan. Faith and Unfaith, and other essays. 12mo. Lond., 1891. J 5 P 8

[*See* Pascal, B.]

PAUL, Prof. H. Principles of the History of Language, translated by H. A. Strong. 8vo. Lond., 1888. K 12 U 9

PAUSANIAS. Graeciæ Descriptio accurata. Annotationes G. Xylandri et F. Sylburgii, notæ J. Kuhnii. [Gr. et Lat.] Fol. Leip., 1696. D 42 Q 7 ‡

PAUW, J. C. de. Horapollinis Hieroglyphica. [*See* Horapollo.]

PAVY, F. W. Treatise on Food and Dietetics, physiologically and therapeutically considered. 2nd ed. 8vo. Lond., 1875. A 12 U 33

PAWLOFF, Mons. Interprète Française, Russe, Allemand. 12mo. Leipzig, 1856. K 16 P 24

PAYNE, A. G. Choice Dishes at Small Cost. 12mo. Lond., 1888. A 22 P 1

PAYNE, E. J. History of the New World called America. Vol. 1. 8vo. Oxford, 1892. B 19 S 10

PAYNE, J. [*See* Boccacci, G.]

PAYNE, W. H. [*See* Compayré, G.]

PAYTON, E. W. Round about New Zealand. 8vo. Lond., 1888. MD 1 R 23

PEABOBY, C. H. Thermodynamics of the Steam Engine and other Heat Engines. Roy. 8vo. Lond., 1889.
A 6 U 17

PEABODY, Elizabeth P. Education in the Home, the Kindergarten, and the Primary School. 8vo. Lond., 1887.
G 17 P 38

PEACH, R. E. M. Bath, Old and New : a Handy Guide and History. 8vo. Lond., 1888.
B 21 R 19

PEACOCK, E. Glossary of words used in Manley and Corringham. [*See* English Dialect Soc.]
Index to Engravings in Proceedings of Society of Antiquaries. [*See* Index Soc.]

PEACOCK, G. Life of Dr. T. Young. [*See* Young, Dr. T.]

PEACOCKE, G. Rays from the Southern Cross. 8vo. Lond., 1876.
MH 1 U 14

PEARL. [*See* Gollancz, I.]

PEARSON, A. N. A Search for Knowledge, and other papers. 8vo. Melb., 1889.
MG 1 S 57

PEARSON, C. H. The Early and Middle Ages of England. 8vo. Lond., 1861.
B 22 S 10
[*See* Juvenalis D. J.]

PEARSON, Rt. Rev. John. An Exposition of the Creed. 5th edition. Fol. Lond., 1683.
G 39 S 8‡

PEARSON, K. Socialism in theory and Practice. 2nd edition. 12mo. Lond., 1887.
F 14 P 20

PEARSON, L. The Emigrants' Guide to Port Curtis and the Canoona Gold Regions, New South Wales. 12mo. Melb., 1858.
MD 2 W 22

PEARSON, Miss M. J. Cookery Recipes for the People. 8vo. Melb., 1888.
MA 3 Q 56

PECHEY, W. C. Fijian Cotton Culture and Planter's Guide to the Islands. 12mo. Lond., 1890. MA 2 P 64

PECK, B. C. Recollections of Sydney. 12mo. Lond., 1850.
MD 1 P 17

PECK, G. Australian Masonic Waltz. Fol. Sydney (n.d.)
MA 11 Q 15 †
Peck's Australian Bouquet, a collection of choice popular Songs, Operatic Airs, &c. Fol. Sydney (n.d.)
MA 11 Q 15†

PECK, W. Handbook and Atlas of Astronomy. 4to. Lond., 1888.
A 36 S 21‡

PEEL, Sir R. Étude d' Histoire Contémporaire ; par M. Guizot. 8vo. Paris, 1858.
C 17 T 19
Life of : by F. C. Montague. (Statesmen Series.) 8vo. Lond., 1888.
C 12 R 35
Peel ; by J. R. Thursfield. (English Statesmen.) 8vo. Lond., 1891.
C 16 Q 21
Sir Robert Peel ; by Justin McCarthy. 8vo. Lond., 1891.
C 16 Q 22
Sir Robert Peel, in Early life, as Irish Secretary, and as Secretary of State : from his Private Correspondence. Edited by C. S. Parker. Lond., 1891.
C 13 T 2
[*See* Lefevre, Hon. G. S.]

PEELE, G. Works of ; edited by A. H. Bullen. 2 vols. 8vo. Lond., 1888.
H 2 R 32, 33
1. The Arraignment of Paris.—Edward I.—The Battle of Alcazar.—The Old Wives' Tales.—The Device of the Pageant, &c.—Descensus Astræe.
2. David and Bathsabe.—Sir Clyomon and Sir Clamydes.—A Farewell to Sir John Norris and Sir Francis Drake, &c., and a Tale of Troy.—An Eclogue Gratulatory.—Polyhymnia.—Speeches to Queen Elizabeth at Theobald's.—The Honour of the Garter.—Anglorum Feriæ, England's Holidays.—Miscellaneous Poems.—Merry conceited Jests of George Peele.

PREETERS, Dr. J. A. L'Alcool : Physiologie, Pathologie, Médecine légale. 8vo. Paris, 1885.
F 11 R 44

PELHAM, C. The World: a Collection of Voyages and Travels. 2 vols. (in 3) roy. 4to. Lond., 1806-8.
D 9 S 11-13 †

PELHAM, Rt. Hon. H. Memoirs of the Administration of ; by Rev. W. Coxe. 2 vols. Lond., 1829. C 13 P 2, 3†

PELL, M. B. On the Constitution of Matter. 8vo. Sydney, 1871.
MA 3 Q 10

PELLEW, George. [Life of] John Jay. (American Statesmen.) 12mo. Boston, 1890.
C 13 Q 7

PELLICO, Silvio. Cantiche e Poesie varie di. 8vo. Firenze, 1860.
H 7 P 45
Epistolario di, raccolto e pubblicato per cura di G. Stefani. 12mo. Firenze, 1880.
C 12 P 7
Lettere di, a Giorgio Briano. 12mo. Firenze, 1861.
C 12 P 6
My Confessions to Silvio Pellico ; the Autobiography of Guido Sorelli. 8vo. Lond., 1836.
C 13 S 4
My Imprisonments; Memoirs of; translated by T. Roscoe. 12mo. Lond., 1833.
C 13 P 2
Prose di. 8vo. Firenze, 1856.
J 7 Q 44
Le mie Prigioni. Addizone alle mie Prigioni. Dei Doveri degli Uomini. Critica Dramatica. Letteratura e Morale. Racconti.
Tragedie di. 8vo. Firenze, 1883.
H 7 P 44

PELLOW, Thomas. Adventures of Thomas Pellow, of Penryn, Mariner. Three and twenty Years in Captivity among the Moors. Edited by Dr. R. Brown. 8vo. Lond., 1890.
C 13 S 14

PEMBERTON, T. E. Charles Dickens and the Stage. 8vo. Lond., 1888.
C 12 R 41

PEMBROKE, Gilbert de Clare, Earl of, "Strongbow." [*See* Barnard, F. P.]

PEMBROKE, G. R. C., Earl of. Roots: a Plea for Tolerance. 8vo. Lond., 1873.
MG 1 T 33

PENDLETON, J. Newspaper Reporting in the Olden Time and To-day. 12mo. Lond., 1890. J 7 R 45

PENDRED, H. W. Iron Bridges of Moderate Span ; their Construction and Erection. (Weale.) 12mo. Lond., 1887.
A 17 R 18

PENINSULA AND ORIENTAL STEAM NAVIGATION CO. Traveller's P. and O. Pocket-book. 18mo. Lond., 1888.
D 20 P 1

PENITENTIARY HOUSES, Report from the Committee on the Laws relating to. Fol. Lond., 1811. MF 11 Q 49†

PENNEFATHER, F. W., and BROWN, E. B. The Code of Civil Procedure in the Supreme Court of New Zealand; with notes and index. 8vo. Wellington, 1885.
MF 3 R 40

PENNELL, J. Pen Drawing and Pen Draughtsmen. 4to. Lond., 1889. A 33 P 14 ‡
[*See* Hamerton, P. G.]

PENNELL, Joseph and Elizabeth Robins. The Stream of Pleasure : a Narrative of a Journey on the Thames from Oxford to London. 4to. Lond., 1891. D 18 T 5
Our Sentimental Journey through France and Italy. 8vo. Lond., 1888. D 18 Q 2

PENNY, Rev. A. Ten Years in Melanesia. 12mo. Lond., 1887. MD 2 W 8
Another Copy. 2nd ed. 8vo. Lond., 1888. MD 2 W 9

PENNY POSTAGE. Account of the Celebration of the Jubilee of Uniform Inland Penny Postage. 2nd edition. 8vo. Lond., 1891. B 24 T 10

PENROSE, B. [*See* Johns Hopkins University Studies.]

PÉPIN, A. [*See* Bonvalot, G.]

PEPYS, W. C. Genealogy of the Pepys Family, 1273–1887. Sm. 4to. Lond., 1887. C 13 R 7

PEPYS FAMILY. Genealogy of, 1273–1887; by W. C. Pepys. Sm. 4to. Lond., 1887. C 13 R 7

PERCIVAL, William Spencer. The Land of the Dragon : My Boating and Shooting Excursions to the Gorges of the Upper Tangtze. 8vo. Lond., 1889. D 16 U 9

PERCY, C. M. Mine Rents and Mineral Royalties. 8vo. Liverpool, 1888. F 14 T 29

PERCY, Dr. J. Metallurgy. 8vo. Lond., 1875.
A 24 T 13

PEREY, L. [*See* Ligne, Princess de.]

PERIODICALS, Annual Index to, 1886–87. 2 vols. roy. 8vo. Bangor, U.S., 1887–88. E

PERKINS, E. T. Na Motu : or, Reef-Rovings in the South Seas : a Narrative of Adventures at the Hawaiian, Georgian, and Society Islands. Roy. 8vo. New York, 1854. MD 5 V 48

PERKINS, G. J. Mackay : an Essay upon the Rise, Progress, Industries, Resources, and Prospects of Mackay. 8vo. Mackay, 1888. MD 7 S 11

PERKINS, J. B. France under the Regency. 8vo. Lond., 1892. B 26 Q 16

PÉRON, Captain F. A. Mémoirs du, sur ses Voyages aux côtes d'Afrique, en Arabie, a l'Ile d'Amsterdam, aux Iles d'Anjouan et de Mayotte, aux Côtes Nord Ouest de l'Amerique, aux Iles Sandwich, &c. 2 vols. 8vo. Paris, 1824. MD 8 Q 2, 3

PERONNE, Dr. C. De l'Alcoolisme dans ses rapports avec le Traumatisme. 8vo. Paris, 1870. F 11 S 36

PERRAULT, C. Les Contes. (Collections Jannet-Picard.) 12mo. Paris (n.d.) J 15 Q 27

PERRET, L. Catacombes de Rome. 3 vols. Fol. Paris, 1855. B 8 R 1–3 ‡

PERROT, Prof. Georges, and CHIPIEZ, Charles. History of Art in Persia. Roy. 8vo. Lond., 1892. A 23 V 6
History of Art in Phrygia, Lydia, Caria, and Lycia. Roy. 8vo. Lond., 1895. A 23 V 7
History of Art in Sardinia, Judæa, Syria, and Asia Minor. 2 vols. Imp. 8vo. Lond., 1890. A 8 S 29, 30

PERRY, G. G. History of the English Church : 3rd period, from the accession of the House of Hanover to the Present Time. 8vo. Lond., 1887. G 16 R 29

PERRY, T. S. [*See* Imbert de Saint-Amand, A. L., Baron.]

PERSIUS, C. Rouge et Noir : the Academicians of 1823; or, the Crooks of the Palais Royal, and the Clubs of St. James's. 8vo. Lond., 1823. A 17 U 5

PERSIUS FLACCUS, A., and JUVENAL, D. J. Satiræ. 8vo. Lipardi, 1785. H 10 R 6
Satires. (Lat. text.) English Notes ; by C. W. Stocker. 8vo. Lond., 1845. H 10 R 11
[*See* Juvenal, D. J.]

PESTALOZZI, Henry, his Life and Work ; by R. de Guimps. 12mo. New York, 1890. C 12 P 5

PETERBOROUGH AND MONMOUTH, Earl of (Charles Mordaunt) : a Memoir ; by Col. F. S. Russell. 2 vols. 8vo. Lond., 1887. C 12 T 29, 30
[Life of] ; by W. Stebbing. (English Men of Action.) 12mo. Lond., 1890. C 12 P 3

PETER, E. [*See* Pfleiderer, O.]

PETERS, Edward D., Jun. Modern American Methods of Copper Smelting. Roy. 8vo. New York, 1887.
A 24 V 3

PETERS, F. H. [*See* Verestchagin, V.]

PETERSON, P. O. Practical Treatise on the Hive and Honey Bee. 8vo. Melb., 1878. MA 3 Q 55

PETHERICK, E. A., and Co. Monthly Catalogue, Literary, Artistic, Scientific. Vol. 1. 4to. Melb., 1890. MK 1 U 1
Catalogue of the York Gate Library. [*See* York Gate Library.]

PETIT, J. Le. [See Le Petit, J.]

PETREL. [*See* In Southern Seas.]

PETRIE, W. M. F. The Geographical Papyrus, Tanis. (Egypt Exploration Fund.) 4to. Lond., 1889.
K 13 P 14 †
A Season in Egypt, 1887. Roy. 4to. Lond., 1888. B 3 S 19 †
Kahun, Gurob, and Hawara. 4to. Lond., 1890. B 42 R 16 ‡

PETRIE, W. M. F.—*contd.*
Historical Scarabs ; arranged chronologically. 12mo.
Lond., 1889. B 21 Q 23
Medum. [Illustrated.] 4to. Lond., 1892. B 13 P 5†
Tanis. Parts 1 and 2. (Egypt Exploration Fund.)
2 vols. 4to. Lond., 1885–88. B 39 P 20, 21 ‡

PETRONIUS ARBITER, T. Satiricon. [*Bound with
Nepos.*] 8vo. Biponti, 1790. C 14 U 19
Satyricon. 12mo. Lipsiæ, 1731. J 19 R 36

PETTIGREW, F. J. Bibliotheca Sussexiana : a Catalogue
of the MSS. and printed Books in the Library of the Duke
of Sussex. Vol. 2. Imp.8vo. Lond.,1839. K 8 R 23 †

PFEIFFER, Emily. Women and Work : an Essay on the
relation to health and physical development, of the higher
education of girls, &c. 8vo. Lond., 1888. A 26 Q 2

PFLEIDERER, Dr. O. Paulinism ; translated by E.
Peters. 2 vols. 8vo. Lond., 1877. G 4 U 1, 2
Philosophy of Religion ; translated by A. Stewart and A.
Menzies. 4 vols. 8vo. Lond., 1886. G 4 U 32–35

PFLUGK–HARTTUNG, Prof. J. v. Acta Pontificum
Romanorum inedita. 3 vols. Imp. 8vo. Tübingen and
Stuttgart, 1881–88. G 6 T 21–23

PHÆDRUS. Fabulæ Æsopiæ. 8vo. Biponti, 1784.
H 10 R 4

PHARMACEUTICAL SOCIETY, The. Journal. Series
3, vols. 17–21 Roy. 8vo. Lond., 1887–91. E

PHILADELPHIA ACADEMY OF NATURAL
SCIENCES. [*See* Academy of Natural Sciences.]

PHILADELPHIA CENTENNIAL EXHIBITION.
Collection of the Netherlands Treasury Department.
(Pam. Co.) [Analytical Chemistry.] 8vo. Amst.
1876. A 16 U 23

PHILALETHES, E. [See Vaughan, T.]

PHILIP, G. Philip's Handy General Atlas of America ;
with Index and Statistical Notes, by J. Bartholomew.
Imp. 4to. Lond., 1879. D 33 P 0 ‡

PHILIP, G., Jun. [See Leutemann, H.]

PHILIP, J. The Grumoid. [*See* Scottish History Soc., 3.]

PHILIPPSON, F. C. [*See* Cobden Club.]

PHILIPS, A. The Distrest Mother : a Tragedy. [*See*
British Drama, Modern, 1.]

PHILLIMORE, Catherine M. Studies in Italian Literature, Classical and Modern. 8vo. Lond.,1887. B 30 Q 2

PHILLIMORE, Sir R. Commentaries upon International
Law. 3rd ed. 4 vols. 8vo. Lond., 1879–89.
F 9 T 2–5
Principal Ecclesiastical Judgments delivered in the Court
of Arches, 1867–75. 8vo. Lond., 1876. F 10 S 28

PHILLIMORE, W. P. W. How to Write the History of
a Family : a Guide for the Genealogist. 8vo. Lond.,
1887. K 19 Q 1

PHILLIP, Capt. A. Voyage du Gouverneur à Botany-Bay.
8vo. Paris, 1791. MD 1 R 18

PHILLIPS, J. A. Elements of Metallurgy ; revised by
H. Bauerman. Roy. 8vo. Lond., 1887. A 24 V 0

PHILLIPS, W. Manual of the British Discomycetes.
8vo. Lond., 1887. A 20 P 3

PHILLIPS, J. Manual of Geology. Edited by R.
Etheridge and H. G. Seeley. In two parts. Pt. 1 :
Physical Geology and Palæontology, by H. G. Seeley.
Pt. 2 : Stratigraphical Geology and Palæontology, by R.
Etheridge. Maps, &c. 2 vols. 8vo. Lond., 1885.
A 24 U 13, 14
Rivers, Mountains, and Sea Coast of Yorkshire, 2nd
edition. 8vo. Lond., 1855. D 18 S 3
Treatise on Geology. 12mo. Lond., 1852. A 24 P 4, 5

PHILLIPS, J. T. Compendious Way of Teaching
Languages. 8vo. Lond., 1750. G 17 Q 34

PHILO JUDÆUS. Operum Omnium. (Gr. text.) 8
vols. (in 4). 12mo. Lipsiæ, 1828–30. G 16 Q 29–32

PHILOLOGICAL SOCIETY. Transactions. 4 vols·
8vo. Lond., 1880–81, 1885–87, 1891. E

PHILOSOPHICAL MAGAZINE, London, Edinburgh,
and Dublin. 5th series. vols. 23–33. 8vo. Lond.,
1887–92. E

PHILOSOPHICAL SOCIETY OF NEW SOUTH
WALES. [*See* Royal Society of N.S.W.]

PHILOSTRATUS. Opera. (Gr. et Lat.) Edidit F.
Morellus. Fol. Parisiis, 1608. J 39 S 6 ‡

PHILP, John A. The Frozen Meat Industry : a Compendium of Facts and Figures relating to the Frozen
Meat Industry. 8vo. Sydney, 1892. MA 3 S 19

PHILP, R. K. Enquire Within upon Everything. 86th
edition. 8vo. Lond., 1892. K 9 T 2

PHIPSON, C. B. Redemption of Labour ; or, Free Labour
upon Freed Land. 2 vols. 8vo. Lond., 1888–92.
F 10 S 29, 30

PHONETIC JOURNAL. Vols. 38, 45–50. 4to. Lond.,
1879–91. E

PHOTOGRAPHS. [*See* Sydney.]

PHYFE, W. H. P. Seven Thousand Words often Mis-
pronounced. 10th edition. 12mo. New York, 1891.
K 16 P 13

PHYSICAL SOCIETY of London. [*See* Joule, J. P.]

PICTURESQUE TASMANIA : a Guide for Visitors.
8vo. Launceston, 1886. MD 5 P 41

PICKARD, J. L. School Supervision. 12mo. New
York, 1890. G 18 Q 8

PICKERING, Dr. C. The Races of Man, and their
Geographical Distribution. New edition. 8vo. Lond.,
1876. A 18 Q 32

PICTORIAL WORLD. Vols. 10–19. New series, vols.
1–2. Fol. Lond., 1887–92. E

PIDDINGTON, A. B. [*See* Addison, J.]

PIDDINGTON, H. The Sailor's Horn-book for the Law of Storms. 7th edition. 8vo. Lond., 1889. A 19 S 24

PIDSLEY, W. E. H. The Birds of Devonshire; edited by H. A. Macpherson. 8vo. Lond., 1891. A 14 T 46

PIERCE, G. A., and WHEELER, W. A. The Dickens Dictionary. 8vo. Lond., 1891. K 17 R 27

PIERROT, J. [*See* Seneca, L.A.]

PIESSE, Dr. G. W. S. The Art of Perfumery, and the methods of obtaining the odours of plants, &c. 4th edition. 8vo. Lond., 1879. A 11 R 25

PIETZCKER, C. F. De Cerevisia. 8vo. Berolini, 1835. F 11 Q 39

PIGGOTT, F. T. Exterritoriality: the Law relating to Consular Jurisdiction and to Residence in Oriental Countries. Roy. 8vo. Lond., 1892. F 11 T 23

PIKE, W. The Barren Ground of Northern Canada. 8vo. Lond., 1892. D 15 S 15

PIKE & OWEN. Atlas of the Suburbs of Sydney. Fol. Sydney, 1887. MD 2 P 35 ‡

PILCHER, C. E. Common Law Procedure Acts, New South Wales, 1853-57. 8vo. Sydney, 1881. MF 2 R 9

PILLANS, James. Elements of Physical and Classical Geography. 12mo. Edinb., 1854. D 11 Q 9

PILPAY (or Bidpai). The earliest version of the Fables of Bidpai, "The Morall Philosophie of Doni"; by Sir T. North. 8vo. Lond., 1888. J 5 Q 34

PILSBRY, H. A. [*See* Tryon, G. W., Jun.]

PINDARUS. Carmina; recensuit A. Boeckhius. (Gr. text.) 12mo. Lipsiæ (n.d.) H 8 T 49

Pindar; by Rev. F. D. Morice. (Ancient Classics for English Readers.) Edinb., 1879. J 14 P 20

PINETUM BRITANNICUM, The. A Descriptive Account of Hardy Coniferous Trees cultivated in Great Britain. 3 vols. fol. Edinb., 1884. A 8 R 7-9 ‡

PINNOCK, Rev. W. H. The Bible and Contemporary History. 2 vols. 8vo. Lond., 1887. G 10 T 26, 27

PIONEER MODEL SABBATH-SCHOOL INSTITUTE, BUNINYONG. Annual Report, 1875. 8vo. Buninyong, 1876. ME 6 Q

PITCAIRN, W. D. Two Years among the Savages of New Guinea, with Introductory Notes on North Queensland. 8vo. Lond., 1891. MD 2 W 20

PITMAN, C. B. [*See* Lesseps, Baron F. de.]

PITMAN, Isaac. Biography of; by T. A. Reed. 8vo. Lond., 1890. C 16 Q 18

Extracts Nos. 1-3 in the Corresponding Style of Phonography. 12mo. Lond., 1882-89. J 7 R 54

Hints on Lecturing. 12mo. Lond., 1879. J 7 R 55

History of Shorthand. 3rd edition. 12mo. Lond., 1891. K 20 P 10

z

PITMAN, Isaac—*contd.*

Manual of Phonography; or, Writing by Sound. 12mo. Lond., 1887. K 20 P 5

Another copy. New edition. 12mo. Lond., 1889. K 20 P 6

New Testament in Phonography. [*See* Bible.]

Phonographic and Pronouncing Dictionary of the English Language. 6th edition. 12mo. Lond., 1889. K 20 Q 2

The Phonographic Phrase Book. 12mo. Lond., 1889. K 20 P 3

Phonographic Legal Phrase Book. 12mo. Lond. (n.d.) K 20 P 11

Phonographic Reader: a Course of Reading in Phonetic Shorthand. 12mo. Lond., 1887. K 20 P 7

The Phonographic Reporter; or, Reporter's Companion. 12mo. Lond., 1889. K 20 P 4

Phonographic Teacher. 12mo. Lond., 1887. K 20 P 8

Phonography adapted to French. [*See* Bruce, J. R.]

Progressive Studies in Phonography. 2nd edition. 12mo. Lond., 1888. K 20 P 9

Selections, Nos. 1-3; in the Reporting Style of Phonography. 12mo. Lond., 1881-85. J 7 R 53

[*See* Æsop.]

PITT, Rt. Hon. Wm. Political Life of; by "John Gilford." 3 vols. 4to. Lond., 1809. C 40 S 12-14 ‡

[Life of;] by Lord Rosebery. 12mo. Lond., 1891. C 18 P 8

PIXLEY, F. W. The Shareholder's Handbook. 2nd edition. 8vo. Lond., 1886. F 5 U 41

The Director's Handbook. 2nd edition. 8vo. Lond., 1890. F 5 U 42

PIZZAMIGLIO, Dr. L. Distributing Co-operative Societies: an Essay on Social Economy. 8vo. Lond., 1891. F 14 P 44

PLANCK, C. [*See* Chess Problem, The.]

PLANIA, L. H. National Drunkenness and the English Sabbath. 8vo. Sydney (n d.) MG 1 R 50

PLANTÉ, G. Storage of Electrical Energy. 8vo. Lond., 1887. A 5 U 21

PLATO. Convivium, cum epistola ad Thompsonum, edidit C. Badham. (Gr. text.) 8vo. Lond., 1866. G 14 T 19

Euthydemus et Laches. (Gr. text) Praefixa est epistola ad Senatum Lugdunensem Batavorum auctore C. Badham. 8vo. Jena, 1865. G 16 S 42

Lexicon Platonicum. [*See* Astius, F.]

Opera omnia, edidit G. Stallbaumius. (Gr. text.) Imp. 8vo. Lipsiæ, 1850. J 39 P 22 ‡

The Philebus of. (Gr. text.) English notes by E. Poste. 8vo. Oxford, 1860. G 12 Q 38

Philebus (Gr. text), with Introduction and Notes by Prof. C. Badham. 8vo. Lond., 1855. G 16 S 41

Philebus (Gr. text), with Introduction and Notes by Prof. C. Badham. 2nd edition with Australian postscript. 8vo. Lond., 1878. G 16 S 40

PLATO—*contd.*

Plato and the other Companions of Sokrates; by George Grote. 3 vols. 8vo. Lond., 1865. G 16 T 13–15

Plato: by C. W. Collins. (Ancient Classics for Eng. Readers.) 12mo. Edin., 1886. J 14 P 21

The Theætetus of. (Gr. text.) English Notes by Rev. L. Cameron. 8vo. Oxford, 1861. G 12 Q 33

Timæus of; edited, with Introduction and Notes, by R. D. Archer-Hind. 8vo. Lond., 1888. G 14 T 2

PLATTNER, C. F. Manual of Qualitative and Quantitative Analysis with the Blowpipe. Revised and enlarged by Prof. T. Richter. 8vo. Lond., 1875. A 21 S 7

PLATTS, J. S. Hindustani Manual. [*See* Forbes, D.]

PLAUTUS, M. A. Comœdiæ : ex recognitione A. Fleckeiseni. 12mo. Lipsiæ, 1881. H 2 Q 43

Comœdiæ : recensuit C. H. Weise. 2 vols. 8vo. Quedlinb., 1847–48. H 9 S 7, 8

Œuvres de. [*See* Nisard, D.]

Plautus and Terence ; by Rev. W. L. Collins. (Ancient Classics for English Readers.) 12mo. Edin., 1880. J 14 P 22

PLAYFAIR, Rt. Hon. Sir L. Effect of Protection on Wages. 8vo. Lond., 1888. F 14 T 28

Industrial Competition and Commercial Freedom. 8vo. Lond., 1888. F 14 T 27

Subjects of Social Welfare. 2nd edition. Lond., 1889. F 6 R 12

Tariffs of the United States in relation to Free Trade. 8vo. Lond., 1890. F 7 V 29

Wages and Hours of Labour. 12mo. Lond., 1891. F 12 S 5

[*See* Cobden Club.]

PLEYDELL, J. C. Mansel. The Birds of Dorsetshire. 8vo. Lond., 1888. A 14 T 37

PLINIUS CAECILIUS SECUNDUS, Caius. Epistolarum libri X ; cum commentariis J. M. Catanaei. 8vo. Paris, 1625. C 17 T 15

Epistolæ et Panegyricus. 8vo. Biponti, 1789. C 14 U 18

Epistolæ ad Traianum Imperatorem cum ejusdem responsis ; edited by E. G. Hardy. 8vo. Lond., 1889. C 13 U 19

Pliny's Letters ; by Rev. A. Church and Rev. W. J. Brodribb. (Ancient Classics for English Readers.) 12mo. Edinb., 1888. J 14 P 23

PLINIUS SECUNDUS, Caius. Naturalis Historiæ Libri 37; recognovit L. Janus. 4 vols. 8vo. Lipsiæ, 1854–59. A 28 P 18–21

PLOTINUS. Opera quæ extant omnia. (Gr. et Lat.) Fol. Basileæ, 1615. G 39 S 9 †

Opera ; recognovit A. Kirchhoff. (Gr. Text.) 2 vols. (in 1.) 12mo. Lipsiæ, 1856. G 13 T 45

PLOWRIGHT, C. B. Monograph of the British Uredineæ and Ustilagineæ, with an account of their biology, germination of their spores, and of their experimental culture. 8vo. Lond., 1889. A 4 S 23

PLUMMER, A. The Church of the Early Fathers. 8vo. Lond., 1887. G 19 P 15

PLUMMER, John. New South Wales Railway Tourists' Guide. 12mo. Sydney, 1892. MD 7 T 34

The Story of a Blind Inventor ; being some account of the Life and Labours of Dr. James Gale. 8vo. Lond., 1868. C 14 Q 19

PLUMPTRE, C. E. Natural Causation: an Essay in four Parts. 8vo. Lond., 1888. G 4 R 38

PLUMPTRE, E. H. [*See* Dante Alighieri.]

PLUMPTREE, Very Rev. Dr. E. H. Life of Thomas Ken, D.D., Bishop of Bath and Wells. 2 vols. Roy. 8vo. Lond., 1889. C 12 U 4, 5

Tragedies of Sophocles. [*See* Sophocles.]

Tragedies of Æschylus. [*See* Æschylus.]

PLUTARCH. Plutarch's Morals, Ethical Essays ; translated with Notes and Index by A. R. Shilleto. 12mo. Lond., 1888. G 16 R 26

Plutarchi quæ supersunt Omnia. Græce et Latine. 12 vols. 8vo. Lipsiæ, 1774–82. J 17 Q 9–20

Les Romains Illustres ; édition à l'usage de la jeunesse. 8vo. Paris, 1890. C 18 S 22

POCKET DICTIONARY of 1,000 Christian Names, with their meaning explained. 3rd edition. 8mo. Lond. (n.d.) K 19 R 13

POCKET DICTIONARY of the English and Dutch Languages. 18mo. Leip., 1870. K 16 P 20

POCOCKE, Dr. R. Travels. [*See* Camden Soc.]

POETARUM Scenicorum Græcorum, Æschyli, Sophoclis, Euripidis, et Aristophanis, Fabulæ quæ extant omnes, ex recensione Guil. Dindorfii. Roy. 8vo. Oxonii, 1846. H 7 V 23

POETICAL REGISTER and Repository of Fugitive Poetry, 1801–11. 8 vols. 8vo. Lond., 1803–15. H 10 Q 1–8

POLE, R., Archbishop of Canterbury : an Historical Sketch ; by the Rev. F. G. Lee. 8vo. Lond., 1888. C 13 S 9

POLE, Wm. Life of Sir Wm. Siemens. 8vo. Lond., 1888. C 6 S 15

POLLARD, A. [*See* Sidney, Sir P.]

POLLARD, A. W. English Miracle Plays, Moralities, and Interludes ; edited by A. W. Pollard. 8vo. Oxford, 1890. H 4 R 35

Odes from the Greek Dramatists ; edited by A. W. Pollard. 12mo. Lond., 1890. H 6 R 43

Last Words on the History of the Title Page, with notes on some Colophons and fac-similes of Title Pages. 4to. Lond., 1891. B 42 R 14 ‡

[*See* Wiclif, J.]

POLLEN, J. H. Supplement to Universal Catalogue of Books on Art. 8vo. Lond., 1877. Libr.

Ancient and Modern Furniture and Woodwork. (South Kens. Mus.) 8vo. Lond., 1875. A 23 R 25

POLLOCK, Sir F. Personal Remembrances of. 2 vols. 8vo. Lond., 1887. C 12 Q 12, 13

POLLOCK, W. H. [*See* Fencing.]

POLYÆNUS. Strategicon Libri Octo; recensuit E. Woelfflin. 8vo. Lipsiæ, 1860. A 29 R 7

POLYBIUS. Historiarum Libri qui supersunt: interprete I. Casaubono, J. Gronovius recensuit. (Gr. et Lat.) 3 vols. (in 2.) 8vo. Amst., 1670. B 30 Q 6, 7

POMPALLIER, Rt. Rev. J. B. F. Early History of the Catholic Church in Oceania. Roy. 8vo. Auckland, 1888. MG 1 T 27

PONTEY, Wm. The Forest Pruner; or, Timber Owner's Assistant. 8vo. Huddersfield, 1805. A 18 T 4

The Profitable Planter : a treatise on the theory and practice of planting forest trees. 4th edition. 8vo. Lond., 1828. A 18 T 5

POOL, J. J. Woman's Influence in the East; as shown in the noble Lives of Past Queens and Princesses of India. 8vo. Lond., 1892. C 14 R 31

POOLE, Rev. M. Annotations upon the Holy Bible. 2 vols. fol. Lond., 1696. G 40 R 1, 2 ‡

POOLE, R. Lane. Wycliffe and Movements for Reform. 12mo. Lond., 1889. G 19 P 9

POOLE, S. Lane. The Barbary Corsairs. (Story of the Nations.) 8vo. Lond., 1890. B 1 P 50

Catalogue of the Mohammadan Coins preserved in the Bodleian Library at Oxford. 4to. Oxford, 1888. A 10 S 18 †

History of the Mogul Emperors of Hindustan, illustrated by their Coins. 8vo. Westminster, 1892. B 16 R 3

Life of the Rt. Hon. Stratford Canning, Viscount Stratford de Redcliffe. 2 vols. 8vo. Lond., 1888. C 12 T 3, 4

Moors in Spain. 8vo. Lond., 1887. B 34 Q 1

Turkey. 8vo. Lond., 1888. B 34 Q 12

[*See* Bowen, Sir G. F.]

POOLE, Rev. W. Education in Queensland. [*See* Indian and Colonial Exhibition, 1886.]

POOLE, W. F., and FLETCHER W. I. Index to Periodical Literature. 4to. Boston, 1885. E

Poole's Index to Periodical Literature. The First Supplement. Imp. 8vo. Lond., 1888. Libr.

POPE, A. Works of. 10 vols. 8vo. Lond., 1871-89. J 2 8 18-27

POPE, J. H. The State: Rudiments of New Zealand Sociology. 8vo. Wellington, 1887.* MF 3 Q 9

Health for the Maori. 12mo. Wellington, 1884.* MA 2 8 39

Te Ora mo te Maori : He Pukapuka mo nga Kura Maori, 12mo. Poneke, 1884. MA 2 8 41

POPE, Rev. R. T. P., and MAGUIRE, Rev. T. Discussion between, in Dublin, 1827. 12mo. Dublin, 1827. G 16 P 50

POPULAR SCIENCE MONTHLY. Vols. 30-40. Roy. 8vo. New York, 1887-92. E 1. 21

PORPHYRIUS. Philosophi Platonici Opuscula Tria ; recognovit A. Nauck. 12mo. Lipsiæ, 1860. G 13 T 44

PORSON, R. Works of. 6 vols. 8vo. Lond, 1790-1822. J 8 S 35-40

1. Letters to Travis.
2. Tracts and Criticisms.
3. Aristophanica.
4. Adversaria.
5, 6. Photi Lexicon.
[*See* Euripides.]

PORT AUGUSTA, the Natural Shipping Port of Inlet and Outlet for the Barrier Traffic. 12mo. Port Augusta, 1889. MD 2 W 21

PORT ESSINGTON, Copies or Extracts of any Correspondence relative to the Establishment of a Settlement at. Fol. Lond., 1843. MF 8 P 29 †

PORT JACKSON, Laws and Regulations to be observed in the Harbour of. Roy. 8vo. Sydney, 1892. MF 3 T 35

PORTAL, G. H. My Mission to Abyssinia ; with map and illustrations. 8vo. Lond., 1892. D 14 V 9

PORTER, D. D. Naval History of the Civil War. 4to. Lond., 1887. B 18 V 7

PORTER, Major-Gen. W. History of the Corps of Royal Engineers. 8vo. Lond., 1889. B 6 S 29, 30

PORTFOLIO, The: an artistic periodical. 3 vols. 4to. Lond., 1870, 1890-91. E 2. 71

PORTSMOUTH, Louise de Kerouallo, Duchess of. [Life of], 1649-1734 ; or, How the Duke of Richmond gained his Pension. Compiled by H. Forneron. 8vo. Lond., 1887. C 13 T 1

POSEWITZ, Dr. T. Borneo : its Geology and Mineral Resources ; maps and illustrations. 8vo. Lond., 1892. A 24 S 9

POSSELT, E. A. Structure of Fibres, Yarns, and Fabrics. 2 vols. (in 1.) 4to. Philad., 1891. A 42 R 9 ‡

POSTE, E. [*See* Plato.]

POTTER, Beatrice. The Co-operative Movement in Great Britain. 8vo. Lond., 1891. F 14 P 45

POTTER, Rev. Canon. [*See* Church History.]

POTTER, Thomas Bayley. [*See* Cobden Club.]

POTTIE, J. Every Man his Own Farrier : How to know Disease in Horses at a glance, and how to cure Disease quickly. 8vo. Sydney, 1891. MA 3 Q 57

POTTS, J. H. Three Tables of Interested Products, or Factors, for Four, Eight, and Ten per cent. Fol. Sydney, 1841. MA 3 P 16 ‡

POUGEOIS, l'Abbé A. Vansleb, savant orientaliste et voyageur : sa vie, sa disgrace, ses œuvres. Roy. 8vo. Paris, 1869 C 13 V 3

POUGIN, A. Verdi: an Anecdotic History of his Life and Works; translated by J. E. Matthew. 8vo. Lond., 1887.   C 13 R 2

POULTON, E. B. Colours of Animals, their Meaning and use, especially considered in the case of insects. 8vo. Lond., 1890.   A 14 Q 13

POULTRY for Exhibition, Home, and Market; with a Chapter on Pheasants and Pheasantries, by "A Poultry Farmer." Sm. 4to. Lond., 1888.   A 18 S 4

POULTRY FARMER, A. [*See* Poultry.]

POWELL, J. The Customs Laws, and Regulations of New South Wales: An Address. 8vo. Sydney, 1875.   MF 1 T 48

POWELL, Captain R. S. S. Baden. Pigsticking or Hog-hunting: a complete Account for Sportsmen and others. 8vo. Lond., 1889.   A 29 T 12

POWELL, W. Unter den kannibalen von New-Britannien. Roy. 8vo. Leipzig, 1884.   MD 8 R 2

POWELL, W., the thorough Business Man, Memoirs of; by B. Gregory. 8vo. Lond., 1871.   MC 1 P 40

POWELL, Wilfred. Wanderings in a Wild Country. 8vo. Lond., 1884.   MD 5 U 27

POWER, T. P. The Footballer: an Annual Record of Football in Victoria, &c. 12mo. Melb., 1877.   ME 5 Q

POWLES, H. H. P. [*See* Kick, Prof. F.]

POWLES, L. D. Land of the Pink Pearl; or, Life in the Bahamas. 8vo. Lond., 1888.   D 15 S 1

POWNALL, R. W. Illustrated Guide to the West Coast of the North Island, New Zealand. 8vo. Wanganui, 1885.   MD 1 U 39

POWNING, W. Milton's L'Allegro and Tennyson's (Enone (analysed according to Morell.) 8vo. Melb., 1893   MH 1 Q 71

POYNTING, C. T. New Testament Times. [*See* Hawsrath, Dr. A.]

PRAED, Mrs. Campbell. The Grey River. [*See* McCarthy, J.]

PRAED, W. M. Political and Occasional Poems; edited, with Notes, by Sir G. Young. 8vo. Lond., 1888.   H 7 Q 40

PRÆGER, F. Wagner as I knew Him. 12mo. Lond., 1892.   C 13 Q 18

PRAIRIE FARMER. 6 vols. Fol. Chicago, 1886–91 E

PRATT, A. E. To the Snows of Tibet through China. 8vo. Lond., 1892.   D 16 V 6

PRATT, E. H. L. On the Treatment and Permanent Cure of Stricture of the Urethra. 12mo. Sydney, 1875.   MA 2 P 54

PRATT, W. T. Colonial Experiences; or, Incidents and Reminiscences of thirty-four years in New Zealand; by "An Old Colonist." 8vo. Lond., 1877.   MD 4 R 29

PRATTEN, Mary A. My Hundred Swiss Flowers; with a Short Account of Swiss Ferns. 8vo. Lond., 1887.   A 4 Q 26

PRAYER-BOOK, the First, of Edward VI compared with the successive Revisions of the Book of Common Prayer. 8vo. Lond., 1883.   G 16 R 30

PREECE, W. H. The Progress of Electricity (a reprint). Sm. 4to. Lond., 1892.   MA 2 R 26

PREECE, W. H., and MAIER, J. The Telephone. 8vo. Lond., 1889.   A 21 Q 7

PREECE, W. H., and SIVEWRIGHT, J. Telegraphy. 9th edition. 12mo. Lond., 1891.   A 21 P 13

PREISS, L. Plantæ Preissianæ sive enumeratio Plantarum quas in Australasia Collegit, annis 1838–41. 2 vols. 8vo. Hamburg, 1844–47.   MA 1 V 30, 31

PRELLER, L. [*See* Ritter, H.]

PRENDERGAST, J. P. Ireland from the Restoration to the Revolution, 1660–90. 8vo. Lond., 1887.   B 29 T 11

[*See* Ireland State Papers.]

PRENDERGAST, T. The Mystery of Languages; or, the Art of Speaking Foreign Tongues Idiomatically. 8vo. Lond., 1864.   K 16 T 19

PRESBYTERIAN CALENDAR OF AUSTRALASIA for 1892. 8vo. Melb., 1892.   ME 4 R

PRESBYTERIAN CHURCH of Eastern Australia. Minutes of the Synod of, for 1882 and 1884–87. 8vo. Sydney, 1888.*   MG 2 Q 5

PRESBYTERIAN CHURCH OF NEW SOUTH WALES: Code of Rules, Forms of Procedure and Styles for the Use of the. 8vo. Sydney, 1882.   MG 2 R 14

PRESBYTERIAN CHURCH OF VICTORIA. Proceedings of the General Assembly. 8vo. Melb., 1877.   MG 1 R 28

Rules and Forms of Procedure in the Courts and Congregations. 12mo. Melb., 1877.   MG 2 P 45

PRESBYTERIAN CHURCHES OF AUSTRALIA AND TASMANIA, Directory for the Public Worship of God in. 12mo. Sydney, 1892.   MG 2 R 15

PRESCOTT, H. P. Strong Drink and Tobacco Smoke. 8vo. Lond., 1869.   F 11 S 35

PRESCOTT, W. H. Charles V. [*See* Robertson, W.]

PRESHAW, G. O. Banking under Difficulties; or, Life on the Goldfields of Victoria, New South Wales, and New Zealand; by "A Bank Official." 8vo. Melb., 1888.   MD 7 S 10

PRESS, T. Hertfordshire Men of Mark. 8vo. St. Albans, 1887.   C 16 P 1

PRESTON, E. Index to Next of Kin, &c. [*See* Chambers, R.]

PRESTON, H. W. Documents illustrative of American History, 1606–1863. 8vo. New York, 1886. B 1 S 36

PRESTON, S. H. [*See* Chambers, R.]

PRESTON, S. P. Pasture Grasses and Forage Plants. 8vo. Lond., 1887. A 1 U 10

PRESTON, T. The Jubilee of George III, 25th October, 1809. Sm. 4to. Lond., 1887. B 6 R 31

PRESTON, W. Reprint of the 1772 Edition of Preston's Illustrations of Masonry. 8vo. Lond., 1887. J 9 Q 12

PRESTWICH, Prof. J. Geology, Chemical, Physical, and Stratigraphical. 2 vols. roy. 8vo. Oxford, 1886-88. A 9 S 39, 40

PRETORIUS, H. P. N. Letter to Col. O. Lanyon, on Probable Hostilities. 8vo. Lond., 1880. F 8 S 26

PRÉVOST, l'Abbé A. F. Histoire de Manon Lescaut et du Chevalier des Grieux. (Collection Jannet-Picard.) 12mo. Paris (n.d.) J 15 Q 26

PREVOST, C. [*See* Fencing.]

PREVOST, Ven. Sir G. [*See* Williams, I.]

PREVOST, Dr. J. L. Étude clinique sur le Délire Alcoolique. 8vo. Genève, 1875. F 11 R 45

PREYER, W. The Mind of the Child. Part 1. The Senses and the Will. 8vo. New York, 1888. G 19 P 5

PRICE, Annie N. True to the Best. 12mo. Lond. (n.d.) MJ 1 U 23

PRICE, Rev. C. Life and Work of; by James Fenton. 12mo. Melb., 1886. MC 1 P 60

PRICE, J. A. P. [*See* Hoblyn, R. D.]

PRICE, J. E. Descriptive Account of the Guildhall of the City of London : its History and Associations. Imp. 4to. Lond., 1886. B 37 P 5

PRICE, J. M. From the Arctic Ocean to the Yellow Sea : Narrative of a Journey in 1890-91 across Siberia, Mongolia, Gobi Desert, and North China. Illustrated. 8vo. Lond., 1892. D 17 V 13

PRICHARD, Dr. J. C. The Natural History of Man. 8vo. Lond., 1848. A 18 U 21

PRICKARD, A. O. Aristotle on the Art of Poetry : a Lecture. 8vo. Lond., 1891. J 11 W 10

PRINCE, Br. The Counsel of God in Judgment : or, Br. Prince's Testimony to the Closing of the Gospel Dispensation, &c. 12mo. Halle, 1887. G 10 P 31

PRINCE ALFRED HOSPITAL, Sydney. Reports, 1883-87, 1890. 8vo. Sydney, 1883-88, 1891. ME 6 S
Statistics of, for 1883. 8vo. Sydney, 1883. ME 6 S
Bylaws of. 8vo. Sydney, 1883. MF 1 T 10

PRINSEP, H. T. Code of Criminal Procedure, British India. 3rd ed. Roy. 8vo. Calcutta, 1869. F 12 R 24

PRIOR, S. H. Handbook of Australian Mines. Imp. 8vo. Sydney, 1890. MA 2 R 42

PRISON MATRON, A. [*See* Robinson, F. W.]

PRITCHARD, G. The Missionary's Reward ; or, the Success of the Gospel in the Pacific. 12mo. Lond., 1844. MG 2 R 16

PRITCHARD, Rev. W. C. [*See* Church History.]

PRITCHETT, R. Smokiana : Historical and Ethnographical. Roy. 8vo. Lond., 1890. J 6 U 16

PRITT, T. E. Book of the Grayling : being a Description of the Fish, and the Art of Angling for him. Roy. 8vo. Leeds, 1888. A 13 U 41

PROBYN, J. W. Italy : from 1815 to 1890. 8vo. Lond., 1891. B 17 P 28
Local Government and Taxation in the United Kingdom. 8vo. Lond., 1882. F 5 R 7
[*See* Cobden Club.]

PROCTER, F. Elementary History of the Book of Common Prayer. 12mo. Camb., 1862. G 9 U 15

PROCTER, W. C. Round the Globe, through Greater Britain. 8vo. Lond., 1887. D 20 Q 2

PROCTOR, R. The New Evangel, according to R. Proctor. 12mo. Maitland, 1891. MG 2 P 49

PROCTOR, R. A. Chance and Luck : a Discussion on the Laws of Luck, Coincidences, Wagers, Lotteries, and the Fallacies of Gambling. 8vo. Lond., 1887. A 29 V 2
Cycloid and all Forms of Cycloidal Curves. 8vo. Lond., 1878. A 10 S 30
Other Suns than Ours ; with Two Essays on Whist, and Correspondence with Sir John Herschel. 8vo. Lond., 1887. A 19 Q 26
Watched by the Dead : a Loving Study of Dickens' half-told Tale. 8vo. Lond., 1887. J 9 Q 41

PROPERT, J. L. History of Miniature Art ; with Notes on Collectors and Collections. Imp. 4to. Lond., 1887. A 7 Q 7 †

PROPERTIUS, S. A. [*See* Catullus, C. V., *and* Davies, Rev. J.]

PROPHETS, The, and Holy Writings, with Commentaries and Annotations by ancient Rabbins (Hebrew text). 6 vols. 4to. Velino, 1860. G 39 T 21-26‡

PROSSER, F. R. Wegg-. Galileo and his Judges. 8vo. Lond., 1889. C 8 P 10

PROTESTANT STANDARD. 7 vols. Folio. Sydney, 1886-92. ME

PROTHERO, G. W. Memoir of Henry Bradshaw. 8vo. Lond., 1888. C 15 U 3

PROTHERO, R. E. Pioneers and Progress of English Farming. 8vo. Lond., 1888. A 1 U 15

PROUT, Dr. W. Chemistry, Meteorology, and Function of Digestion. (Bridgewater Treatises.) 8vo. Lond., 1838. C 16 S 44

PRUEN, S. T. The Arab and the African : experiences in Eastern Equatorial Africa during a residence of three years. 8vo. Lond., 1891. D 14 R 7

PSYCHICAL RESEARCH, Society for. Proceedings. Vols. 5–7. 8vo. Lond., 1889–91.   E 1. 56

PTOLEMÆUS, C. Geographicæ enarrationes libri octo. Fol. Lugduni, 1535.   D 40 Q 27‡

PUBLIC HOUSES, Reports from Committee on. 2 vols. Sm. fol. Lond., 1853–54.   F 42 P 8, 9‡

PUBLIC OPINION. Vols. 50–61. Sm. fol. Lond., 1886–92.   E 2. 78

PUBLISHER, A. [*See* Marston, E.]

PUFFENDORF, S. Introduction to the History of Europe. 9th edition. 8vo. Lond., 1728.   B 25 R 2

PUGH, T. P. Queensland Almanac and Gazetoor, 1875, 1883–84. 12mo. Brisbane, 1875–84.   ME 4 P

PUGIN, A. W. Details of Ancient Timber Houses of 15th and 16th Centuries. 4to. Lond., 1836. A 36 P 23‡
Gothic Furniture of the 15th Century. 4to. Lond., 1835.   A 36 P 23‡
Designs for Gold and Silversmiths. 4to. Lond., 1830.   A 36 P 23‡
Designs for Iron and Brass-work. 4to. Lond., 1836.   A 36 P 23‡

PUIBUSQUE, L. V. de. Lettres sur la Guerre de Russie en 1812. 8vo. Paris, 1817.   B 19 S 16

PULLAN, R. P. [*See* Burges, W.]

PULLING, F. S. Life and Speeches of the Marquis of Salisbury. 2 vols. 8vo. Lond., 1885.   C 16 P 3, 4

PULSFORD, E. Notes on Customs Duties, with special Reference to the Proposals lately made by Mr. Copeland. 8vo. Sydney, 1886.   MF 1 T 52
Notes on Capital and Finance in Australasia. 8vo. Sydney, 1892.   MF 3 P 63
Thoughts and Suggestions concerning the Commerce and Progress of New South Wales. 2nd edition. 8vo. Melb., 1884.   MF 1 R 67
Freedom in New South Wales *versus* Oppression in Victoria. Sm. 4to. Sydney, 1887.   MF 3 Q 16

PULSIFER, W. H. Notes for a History of Lead, and an Inquiry into the Development of the Manufacture of White Lead and Lead Oxides. Roy. 8vo. New York, 1888.   A 24 V 5

PULSZKY, Prof. A. Theory of Law and Civil Society. 8vo. Lond., 1888.   F 10 S 27

PUNCH. Vols. 91–102. 4to. Lond., 1886–92.   E 2. 73

PUNCH STAFF PAPERS: a Collection of Tales, &c. 8vo. Sydney, 1872.   MJ 2 S 19

PURDIE, A. Studies in Biology for New Zealand Students. No. 3. Anatomy of the Common Mussels. Roy. 8vo. Wellington, 1887.   MA 2 U 32

PURDY, J. The Oriental Navigator; or directions for Sailing to, from, and upon the Coasts of the East Indies, China, Australia, &c. 4to. Lond., 1816. MD 8 Q 16†

PURSER, C. L. [*See* Tyrrell, Prof. R. Y.]

PURVES, J. Iliad of Homer [*See* Homer.]

PUSELEY, Daniel. Number One; or, The Way of the World; by "Frank Foster" [with a Colonial Directory, 1862, including Sydney, Melbourne, and New Zealand]. Roy. 8vo. Lond., 1862.   MJ 1 V 12
Number One; or, The Way of the World; by "Frank Foster." 2nd ed. 2 vols. 8vo. Lond.,1863. MJ 1 R 46,47

PUTSCHINS, H. Grammaticæ Latinæ Auctores Antiqui. Sm. 4to. Hanoviæ, 1605.   K 16 Q 28

PYKE, V. The Adventures of George Washington Pratt. 8vo. Melb., 1874.   MJ 2 S 53
Handy Book of Local Government Law, for the use of County Councils and Road Boards. 8vo. Dunedin, 1882.   MF 1 T 8
The Story of Wild Will Enderby. 2nd ed. 8vo. Melb., 1873.   MJ 2 S 53
Another Copy. 3rd. ed. 8vo. Melb., 1873.   MJ 2 S 54

PYLE, H. [*See* Buccaneers.]

PYNE, Geo. Practical Rules on Drawing, for the Operative Builder and Young Student in Architecture. 2nd edition. 4to. Lond., 1864.   A 8 S 31

PYRARD, F. Voyage of. [*See* Hakluyt Society.]

PYRMONT BRIDGE COMPANY. Deed of Settlement and Supplemental Deed with Act of Incorporation. 8vo. Sydney, 1858.   MF 1 R 69

Q

Q.P. ANNUAL INDEX to Periodicals, 1886–87. 2 vols. 8vo. Bangor, 1887–88.   E 2. 21

QUAIFE, Dr. B. The Intellectual Sciences. Outline Lectures. 2 vols. 8vo. Sydney, 1872.   MG 2 P 2, 3

QUARITCH, B. Catalogue of 1500 Books, remarkable for the Beauty, or the Age of their Bindings. 2 vols. (in 1.) 4to. Lond., 1889.   K 36 S 7 ‡

QUARLES, F. Emblems, Divine and Moral. New edition, with a Sketch of the Life and Times of the Author. 8vo. Lond., 1866.   G 16 P 46

QUARLL, P. The Hermit; or, the Sufferings and Adventures of Mr. P. Quarll. 12mo. Lond., 1768.   J 11 W 5

QUARTERLY JOURNAL OF MICROSCOPICAL SCIENCE. Vols. 27–32. Roy. 8vo. Lond., 1886–91.   E 2. 54

QUARTERLY REVIEW, The. Vols. 163–173. 8vo. Lond., 1886–91.   E 1. 6

QUATREFAGES, A. de. The Human Species. 2nd edition. 8vo. Lond., 1879.   A 18 Q 29
Metamorphoses of Man and the Lower Animals. Trans. by H. Lawson. 8vo. Lond., 1864.   A 27 R 29

QUEBEC. Journals of Legislative Assembly of Province of. Vol. 21. Roy. 8vo. Quebec, 1887.   E

QUEEN'S REGULATIONS and Orders for the Army. [*See* Military Text-books.]

QUEENSLAND. Papers relative to the Affairs of, 1861. Fol. Lond., 1861. MF 4 S 42

Almanac and Gazetteer. [*See* Pugh, T. P.]

Hand-book to Colony of. [*See* Hodgkinson, S.]

AGRICULTURE, DEPARTMENT OF.
Annual Report, 1889-90. Fol. Brisb., 1890. ME 2. 58
[*See also* Agriculture.]

CONSTITUTION.
Correspondence respecting the powers of the two houses of the Legislature of Queensland, in respect to Money Bills. Fol. Lond., 1886. MF 4 S 19

CROWN LANDS.
Acts and Regulations relating to the Waste Lands of the Colony of Queensland, together with an explanatory digest of the Land Act of 1876. 8vo. Brisbane, 1879. MF 2 T 3

Correspondence between the Secretary of State for the Colonies, and the Governors of the Australian Colonies, respecting the Annexation of the Crown Lands around the Gulf of Carpentaria. Fol. Lond., 1863 MF 12 Q 29 †

Department of Public Lands, Annual Report, 1889. Fol. Brisb., 1890. ME 2. 58

EDUCATION.
Report of Secretary for Public Instruction, 1889. Fol. Brisb.,'1890. ME 2. 58

GAOLS.
Sheriff's Report upon the Gaols of the Colony, 1889. Fol. Brisb., 1890. ME 2. 58

GOVERNMENT GAZETTE.
Government Gazette, Jan.-Dec., 1889. 3 vols. Fol. Brisbane, 1889. ME 2. 58

GYMPIE GOLD-FIELD.
Report by Wm. H. Rands. Sm. fol. Brisb., 1889. MA 12 Q 43 †

METEOROLOGY.
Meteorological Report for 1887. Fol. Brisb., 1889. ME 2. 58

MINES.
Annual Report of the Department of Mines, 1889. Fol. Brisb., 1890. ME 2. 58

PATENTS.
Fourth Report of the Registrar of Patents, Designs, and Trade Marks. Fol. Brisb., 1890. ME 2. 58

POLYNESIAN LABOUR.
Correspondence relative to Introduction of Polynesian Labourers. Fol. Lond., 1873. MF 11 Q 53 †

Correspondence relating to Polynesian Labour. Fol. Lond., 1892. MF 11 Q 54 †

QUEENSLAND—*contd.*
POST AND TELEGRAPHS.
Report of Post and Telegraph Department, 1889. Fol. Brisb., 1890. ME 2. 58

RAILWAYS.
Report of the Railway Commissioners, for Eighteen Months, ending 30th June, 1890. Fol. Brisb., 1890. ME 2. 58

STATISTICS.
Statistics for 1889. Fol. Brisb., 1890. ME 2. 58
Vital Statistics, 1889. 13th Annual Report by Registrar-General. Fol. Brisb., 1890. ME 2. 58

STATUTES.
Acts of Parliament, 1887-91. 6 vols. Roy. 8vo. Brisb., 1887-92. ME 2. 58

Gold-field Acts, together with Regulations for the Management of Gold-fields of the Colony. 8vo. Brisb., 1881. MF 2 P 52

STOCK AND BRANDS.
Report of the Chief Inspector of Stock and Brands for 1889. Fol. Brisb., 1890. ME 2. 58

WATER SUPPLY.
Report of Hydraulic Engineer. Fol. Brisb., 1890. MA 11 Q 12 †

QUEENSLAND MUSEUM. Annual Report. Fol. Brisb., 1890. ME 2. 58

QUEENSLAND NATIONAL BANK, Limited: Half-yearly Reports, 1872-85. 8vo. Brisbane, 1885. MF 3 Q 21

QUEENSLAND OFFICIAL DIRECTORY. [*See* Wise, H. & Co.]

QUEENSLANDERS' NEW COLONIAL CAMP FIRE SONG BOOK, containing Popular Songs of the Day never before printed ; by "An Old Explorer" (or any other man) 1st. No. 12 mo. Sydney, 1865. MH 1 Q 69

QUEKETT, Rev. W. "My Sayings and Doings"; with Reminiscences of my Life. 8vo. Lond., 1888. C 7 P 27

QUENZER, P. New Testament Times. [*See* Hausrath, Dr. A.]

QUEVEDO-VILLEGAS, F. de. Histoire de Don Pablo de Ségovie ; traduit par L. A. G. Germond de Lavigne. (Collection Jannet-Picard.) 12mo. Paris, 1868. J 15 Q 25

QUIDELL BROS. The Sheep-breeder's Guide. 8vo. Newark, 1888. A 18 S 1

QUICK, R. H. Essays on Educational Reformers. 8vo. Lond., 1868. G 17 P 52
[*See* Mulcaster, R.]

QUIGNON, Cardinal F. Breviarum Romanum. Editum et recognitum juxta editionem Venetiis, A.D. 1535, impressam curante J. W. Legg. 8vo. Cantab., 1888. G 12 T 33

QUIN, J., Comedian. Life of; with the History of the Stage, and his Trial for the Murder of W. Bowen. 8vo. Lond., 1887. C 12 Q 39

QUINET, E. Œuvres Complètes. 29 vols. 12mo. Paris,
1857-76. J 18 P 1-29

1. Le Génie des Religions, De l'origine des Dieux.
2. Le Jésuites, L'Ultramontanisme.
3. Le Christianisme et la Révolution Française.
4, 5. Les Révolutions d'Italie.
6. Marnix de Sainte-Aldegonde, Philosophie de l'Histoire de
France.
7. Les Roumains, Allemagne et Italie.
8. Ahasvérus, Les tablettes do Juif Errant.
9. Prométhée, Les Esclaves.
10. Mes Vacances en Espagne.
11. Histoire de mes Idées, Documents inédits.
12. L'Enseignement du l'euple, Œuvres Politiques avant l'exil.
13-15. La Révolution.
16. Histoire de la Campagne de 1815.
17, 18. Merlin l'Enchanteur.
19, 20. La Création.
21. Le Siège de Paris. Œuvres Politiques après l'exil.
22. La République.
23. L'Esprit Nouveau.
24. La Livre de l'exilé.
25. Vie et Mort du Génie Grec.
26. La Grèce Moderne, Histoire de la Poésie.
27. Premiers Travaux, Vie de Jésua.
28, 29. Correspondance.

QUINTILIANUS, M. F. Opera. 4 vols. 8vo. Biponti,
1784. F 2 U 33-36

QUINTUS SMYRNÆUS. Posthomericorum libri XIV,
relegit A. Koechly. 12mo. Lipsiæ, 1853. H 10 P 23

QUINZE JOYES DE MARIAGE, Les. (Collection
Jannet-Picard.) 12mo. Paris (n.d.) J 15 Q 19

QUIROS, P. F. de. Historia del Descubrimiento de las
Regiones Austrialcs Hecho por El General P. F. de
Quiros. Publicada por Don J. Zaragoza. Tom. 1 and 2.
2 vols. 8vo. Madrid, 1876-80. MB 2 R 47, 48

Voyage de, en 1606. (Prévost, A. F. Suite de l'Histoire
Générale des Voyages, tome 17.) 4to. Amsterdam, 1761.
MD 11 P 16 †

R

RABBE, F. Shelley: the Man and the Poet. 2 vols. 8vo.
Lond., 1888. C 12 Q 16, 17

RABELAIS, F. Œuvres. (Collection Jannet-Picard.) 7
vols. 12mo. Paris (n.d.) J 15 Q 40-46

RABONE, Rev. S. Vocabulary of the Tonga Language,
to which is annexed a list of Idiomatical Phrases. 8vo.
Vavau, 1845. MK 1 T 12

RACINE, J. Phèdre : Tragédie en Cinq Actes, with
Grammatical and Explanatory Notes by H. Bué. 2nd
edition. 8mo. Lond., 1880. H 3 U 16

RADCLIFFE, A. G. Schools and Masters of Painting ;
with an Appendix on the Principal Galleries of Europe.
8vo. New York, 1888. A 23 S 1

RADCLIFFE, C. B. Behind the Tides. 8vo. Lond.,
1888. A 3 T 43

RADIGUET, Maximilien René. Les Derniers Sauvages.
Souvenirs de l'Occupation Française aux Iles Marquises,
1842-59. 12mo. Paris, 1861. MD 7 T 40

RAE, G. M. The Syrian Church in India. 8vo. Edinb.,
1892. G 8 R 29

RAE, John. Contemporary Socialism. 2nd edition. 8vo.
Lond., 1891. F 14 S 2

RAE, John. Stanley Gordon : a Historical Tale of the
Peninsular War and Waterloo. 8vo. Melb., 1869.
MJ 2 T 18

RAE, W. F. Austrian Health Resorts, and the Bitter
Waters of Hungary. 8vo. Lond., 1888. D 8 S 15

RAFFALOVICH, A. L'Impot sur les Alcools et le
Monopole en Allemagne. 8vo. Paris, 1886. F 11 R 48

RAGGED SCHOOLS, SYDNEY. Thirteenth Annual
Report of Kent Street, Globe Street, and the Glebe
Ragged Schools, Sydney. 12mo. Sydney, 1873.
ME 8 P

RAGOZIN, Z. A. Assyria : from the Rise of the Empire
to the Fall of Nineveh (continued from "Chaldea"). 8vo.
Lond., 1888. B 28 R 2

Chaldea, from the Earliest Times to the Rise of Assyria.
8vo. Lond., 1887. B 28 R 1

Media, Babylon, and Persia, including a Study of the
Zend-Avesta. (The Story of the Nations.) 8vo. Lond.,
1889. B 16 Q 2

RAHILLY, J. F. The Liquor Licensing Law of the
Colony of Victoria. 8vo. Melb., 1890. MF 2 T 8

RAIKES, Harriet. Private Correspondence of T. Raikes
with the Duke of Wellington, and other Distinguished
Contemporaries. 8vo. Lond., 1861. C 18 R 19

RAIKES, Thomas. [_See_ Raikes, Harriet.]

RAILWAYS IN AUSTRALIA. Despatches to and from
Australian Governors relative to the Gauge of. Fol.
Lond., 1863. MF 4 S 4

RAILWAYS OF AMERICA, their construction, &c.
Roy. 8vo. Lond., 1890. A 6 U 23

RAINES, Rev. F. R. Fellows of the Collegiate Church
of Manchester. [_See_ Chetham Soc., n.s. 21, 23.]

RALEIGH, Sir W. A Biography ; by W. Stebbing. 8vo.
Oxford, 1891. C 18 Q 9

RALSTON, W. R. [_See_ Krilof, I. A.]

RAMBLINGS ; by "A Tramp." 1st series. 12mo. Auckland, 1888. MD 7 T 42

RAMSAY, C. J. The Tasmanian House of Boys ; or,
Mimic Parliament. 8vo. Hobart, 1875. MJ 2 S 37

RAMSAY, E. P. Catalogue of the Australian Birds in
the Australian Museum. Parts 1-3 and supplement. 4
vols. (in 3). 8vo. Sydney, 1876-91. MA 3 V 1-3

1. Accipitres ; or, Diurnal Birds of Prey, and Supplement.
2. Striges ; or, Nocturnal Birds of Prey.
3. Psittaci ; or, Parrot Tribe.

Catalogue of the Exhibits in the New South Wales Court.
(Great International Fisheries Exhibition, London, 1883.)
8vo. Lond., 1883. MK 1 S 48

RAMSAY, E. P.—*contd.*
Contributions to the Zoology of New Guinea. Pts. 1-3. 8vo. Sydney (n.d.) MA 2 T 48
Hints for the Preservation of Specimens of Natural History. 4th ed. 8vo. Sydney, 1890. MA 3 Q 58
Papers read before the Linnean Society of New South Wales. 8vo. Sydney, 1877. MA 2 T 49
1. Zoology of the "Chevert."
2. Description of two supposed new species of Mus and of a Pteropine Bat.
3. On a new species of Platycercus, New South Wales.
4. Description of a new species of Pelodryas.
5. Description of a species of Echidna (Tachyglossus).
6. Description of a new species of Gerygone.
7. Some further remarks on Poëphila Gouldiæ and Poëphila Mirabilis (Homb. et Jacq.)
8. Description of a supposed new species of Acanthophis.
9. Description of some new species of Birds from New Britain, New Ireland, Duke of York Island, &c.
10. Description of some Rare Eggs of Australian Birds, and a note on Eggs of certain species of Megapondius.
11. Note on Macgillivray's Snake.
Tabular List of all the Australian Birds at present known to the Author. Sm. 4to. Sydney, 1888. MA 2 U 52

RAMSAY, J. Scotland and Scotsmen in the 18th Century; edited by A. Allardyce. 2 vols. 8vo. Edinb., 1888. B 13 R 22, 23

RAMSAY, Sir J. H. Lancaster and York : a Century of English History. (A.D. 1399-1485.) 2 vols. 8vo. Oxford, 1892. B 24 T 11, 12

RAMSAY, Prof. Wm. System of Inorganic Chemistry. 8vo. Lond., 1891. A 21 S 6

RAND, E. A. Up North in a Whaler. 8vo. Lond., 1890. J 11 W 15

RAND, Rev. S. T. Dictionary of the Language of the Micmac Indians. 4to. Halifax, N.S., 1888. K 15 S 12

RAND, McNALLY, & CO. Business Atlas and Shippers Guide, together with a complete Reference Map of the World. Imp. 4to. Chicago, 1887. D 33 P 10 †
Quarterly Postal and Shipping Bulletin, Jan. and July, 1888. Imp. 4to. Chicago, 1888. E 2. 15

RANDOLPH, Edmund. Omitted Chapters of History disclosed in the Life and Papers of ; by M. D. Conway. Roy. 8vo. New York, 1888. C 12 U 3

RANDOLPH, Edmund, Jun. The New Eve ; a Study in Recent Evolution. 2 vols. 8vo. Lond., 1889. J 1 U 41, 42

RANDOLPH, Rev. H. Life of General Sir R. Wilson. 2 vols. 8vo. Lond., 1862. C 18 R 1, 2

RANDOLPH, T. The Muse's Looking-glass : a Comedy. [British Drama, Ancient, 2.]

RANDOM RECOLLECTIONS of Courts and Society ; by " A Cosmopolitan." 8vo. Lond., 1888. B 25 T 5

RANDS, W. H. Gympie Gold Field, Report. Sm. Fol. Brisb., 1889. MA 12 Q 43†

RANFT, J. A. H. T. Origin and Formation of Auriferous Rocks and Gold. 12mo. Sydney, 1889. MA 2 P 65

2 A

RANGERS, The, Mossman's Bay [with description and illustrations]. Ob. 8vo. Sydney, 1886. MD 12 P 18†

RANJIT SINGH, Mahárájá. [Life of], by Sir L. Griffin. (Rulers of India.) 12mo. Oxford, 1892. C 16 P 20

RANKE, L. von. History of the Latin and Teutonic Nations, 1494-1514. 8vo. Lond., 1887. B 25 Q 1
Sämmtliche Werke. 52 vols. (in 41) 8vo. Leipsic, 1867-88. B 14 W 1-41
1-6. Deutsche Geschichte im Zeitalter der Reformation. 6 vols.
7. Zur deutschen Geschichte ; vom Religionsfrieden bis zum dreissigjährigen Krieg. 1 vol.
8-13. Französische Geschichte, vornehmlich in sechzehnten und siebzehnten Jahrhundert. 6 vols.
14-22. Englische Geschichte, vornehmlich in siebzehnten Jahrhundert, 9 vols.
23. Geschichte Wallensteins. 1 vol.
24. Abhandlungen und Versuche. 1 vol.
25-29. Zwölf Bücher preussischer Geschichte. 5 vols. (in 3)
30. Zur Geschichte von Oesterreich und Preussen, zwischen den Friedensschlüssen zu Aachen und Hubertusburg. 1 vol.
31, 32. Die deutschen Mächte und der Fürstenbund. Deutsche Geschichte von 1780 bis 1790. 2 vols. (in 1).
33, 34. Geschichte der romanischen und germanischen Völker, von 1494 bis 1514. 2 vols. (in 1).
35, 36. Die Osmanen und die spanische Mouarchie im 16. und 17. Jahrhundert. 2 vols (in 1)
37-39. Die römischen Päpste in den letzten vier Jahrhunderten. 3 vols.
40, 41. Historisch-biographische Studien. 2 vols.
42. Venezianischen Geschichte.
43, 44. Serbien und die Türkei in neunzehnten Jahrhundert. 2 vols. (in 1).
45. Ursprung und Beginn der Revolutionskriege 1791 und 1792. Zweite Auflage.
46-48. Hardenberg und die Geschichte des preussischen Staates von 1793-1813. Zweite Auflage der in dem Werke "Denkwürdigkeiten des Staatskanzlers Fürsten von Hardenberg" den eigenhändigen Memoiren Hardenberg's beigegebenen historischen Darstellung des Herausgebers. Mit einer Notiz über die Memoiren des Grafen von Haugwitz, und mit einer Denkschrift Hardenberg's über die Reorganisation des preussischen Staates vom Jahre 1807.
49, 50. Zur Geschichte Deutschlands und Frankreichs im neunzehnten Jahrhundert. (2 vols. (in 1).
51, 52. Abhandlungen und Versuche.

RANKEN, George. The Federal Geography of British Australasia. 8vo. Sydney, 1891. MD 1 R 26
Land Law of the Future ; by " Capricornus." 8vo. Sydney, 1877. MF 2 T 9

RANSOME, Prof. C. [*See* Acland, A. H. D.]

RANVIER, L. Technisches Lehrbuch der Histologie ; uebersetzt von Dr. W. Nicati und Dr. H. von Wyss. Roy. 8vo. Leip., 1888. A 26 U 4

RASK, E. Danish Grammar for Englishmen. 2nd edition. 8vo. Lond., 1847. K 12 V 18
Grammar of the Anglo-Saxon Tongue. New edition ; translated by B. Thorpe. 8vo. Copenhagen, 1830. K 12 V 21
Grammar of the Icelandic or Old Norse Tongue ; translated by G. W. Dasent. 8vo. Lond., 1843. K 12 V 16

RATHBONE, Wm. Sketch of the History and Progress of District Nursing. 12mo. Lond., 1890. A 26 Q 5

RATTE, F. Hints for Collectors of Geological and Mineralogical Specimens. (Australian Museum.) 8vo. Sydney, 1887. MA 2 Q 43

RAWLE, Rt. Rev. Richard. · Bishop Rawle : a Memoir ; by Rev. G. Mather and C. J. Blagg. 8vo. Lond., 1890.
     C 12 R 13

RAWLINS, T. The Rebellion : a Tragedy. [*See* British Drama, Ancient, 3.]

RAWLINSON, Prof. G. History of Phœnicia. 8vo. Lond., 1889.   B 28 T 1

Ancient Egypt. 8vo. Lond., 1887.   B 2 S 18

.Phœnicia. (Story of the Nations.) 8vo. Lond., 1889.
     B 28 R 3

History of Herodotus. [*See* Herodotus.]

RAWLINSON, Prof. G., STOKES, Prof. G. T., and PATTON, Prof. A. St. G. Sketch of Universal History. 3 vols. 8vo. Lond., 1887.   B 35 P 3–5

RAWSON, E. S. [*See* Mennell, P.]

RAWSON, Mrs. L. Cookery Book and Household Hints : Enlarged and Revised ; with which is incorporated the Queensland Poultry Book. 3rd ed. 12mo. Rockhampton, 1890.   MA 3 P 6

Mrs. Rawson's Australian Book. 8vo. Sydney, 1893.
     MA 3 P 42

RAWSON, Sir R. W. Synopsis of the Tariffs and Trade of the British Empire. 8vo. Lond., 1888.   F 7 S 25

RAY SOCIETY. Publications. 5 vols. 8vo. Lond., 1887–89.   E

·British Oribatidæ ; by A. D. Michael. Vol. 2.
Larvæ of the British Butterflies and Moths ; by W. Buckler. Vols. 2-4.
Monograph of the British Phytophagous Hymenoptera, Vol. 3 ; by P. Cameron.

RAYNAL, F. E. Wrecked on a Reef ; or, Twenty Months in the Auckland Isles : a True Story of Shipwreck, Adventure, and Suffering. 8vo. Lond., 1889.
     MD 7 T 41

RAYNER, S. History and Antiquities of Pudsey. 8vo. Lond., 1887.   B 6 R 32

READ, Prof. H. Modern Pronunciation of Latin and Greek, as adopted in Universities of Melbourne and Adelaide. 8vo. Adelaide, 1877.   MK 2 P 6

READE, A. A. Study and Stimulants. 8vo. Manchester, 1883.   F 11 Q 14

READE, C.: a Memoir ; compiled chiefly from his Literary Remains, by C. L. Reade and the Rev. C. Reade. 2 vols. 8vo. Lond., 1887.   C 14 R 11, 12

READE, C. L., and READE, Rev. C. Charles Reade, Dramatist, Novelist, Journalist : a Memoir. 2 vols. 8vo. Lond., 1887.   C 14 R 11, 12

READE, Rev. C. [*See* Reade, C. L.] ·

REAY, W. Poems and Lyrics. 8vo. West Maitland. 1886.   MH 1 S 54

RECLUS, E. The British Isles : General Features, Topography, Statistics, Government, and Administration. Imp. 8vo. Lond., 1887.   D 19 V 1

RECLUS, E.—*contd.*
Nouvelle Géographie Universelle. Tomes 12–17. Imp. 8vo. Paris, 1887–91.   D 10 V 12–17

12. l'Afrique Occidentale, Archipels Atlantiques, Sénégambie, et Soudan Occidental.
13. L'Afrique Méridionale, Iles de l'Atlantique Austral, Gabonie, Congo, Angola, Cap, Zambèze, Zanzibar, Côte de Somal.
14. Océan et Terres Océaniques, Iles de l'Ocean Indien, Insulinde, Philippines, Micronésie, Nouvelle-Guinée, Mélanésie, Nouvelle-Calédonie, Australie, Polynésie.
15. Amérique Boréale, Groenland, Archipel Polaire, Alaska, Puissance du Canada, Terre-Neuve.
16. Les Etats-Unis.
17. Indes Occidentales, Mexique, Isthmes Americains, Antilles.

RECORD COMMISSIONERS' PUBLICATIONS :—
The Great Roll of the Pipe, 1189–90 ; by J. Hunter. Roy. 8vo. Lond., 1844.   B 15 T 32

Handbook of the Public Records ; by F. S. Thomas. Roy. 8vo. Lond., 1853.   B 15 T 31

Issue Roll of Thomas de Brantingham, Lord High Treasurer of England, 1370 ; by T. Devon. Roy. 8vo. Lond., 1835.   B 15 T 29

Issues of the Exchequer during the reign of James 1 ; by F. Devon. Roy. 8vo. Lond., 1836.   B 15 T 28

Modus Tenendi Parliamentum : an Ancient Treatise on the Mode of Holding the Parliament in England. 8vo. Lond., 1846.   F 14 T 23

Rotuli de Liberate ac de Misis et Praestitis, regnante Johanne ; cura T. D. Hardy. Roy. 8vo. Lond., 1844.
     B 15 T 30

State Papers : King Henry VIII, 1518–47. 11 vols. 4to. Lond., 1830-52.   F 14 Q 1–11†

RECORDS OF THE PAST : being English Translations of the Ancient Monuments of Egypt and Western Asia. New Series ; edited by Prof. A. H. Sayce. Vols. 1–5. 12mo. Lond., 1888–91.   B 21 Q 14–18

REDFARN, W. B. Ancient Wood and Iron Work in Cambridge ; the letterpress by J. W. Clark. 4to. Camb. (n.d.)   A 40 P 11‡

REDFORD, G. Art Sales : a History of Sales of Pictures and other works of Art, &c. 2 vols. roy. 4to. Lond., 1888.   A 9 S 2, 3†

REDGRAVE, Gilbert R. History of Water-color Painting in England. 8vo. Lond., 1892.   A 23 Q 27

[Lives of] David Cox and Peter de Wint. (Great Artists.) 8vo. Lond., 1891.   C 17 Q 6

REDGRAVE, Richard and Samuel. Century of Painters of the English School. 2nd ed. 8vo. Lond., 1890.
     A 23 R 4

REDGRAVE, Samuel. [*See* Redgrave, R.]

REDHOUSE, J. W. Simplified Grammar of the Ottoman-Turkish Language. 8vo. Lond., 1884.   K 20 Q 13

REED, Sir E. J., and SIMPSON, Rear-Adm. E. Modern Ships of War. Roy. 8vo. Lond., 1888.   A 3 P 24

REED, Lieut. H. A. Photography applied to Surveying. Roy. 4to. New York, 1888.   A 3 P 21†

Topographical Drawing and Sketching, including Applications of Photography. Roy. 4to. New York, 1886.
     A 2 S 12 †

REED, T. A. Biography of Isaac Pitman. 8vo. Lond., 1890.   C 16 Q 18

Leaves from the Note-Book of. (Printed in the reporting style of Phonography.) 2 vols. 12mo. Lond., 1888.   K 20 P 12, 13

The Reporter's Guide. 3rd ed. 12mo. Lond., 1890.   K 20 P 14

French Phonography : an Adaptation of Pitman's Phonetic Shorthand to the French Language. 12mo. Lond., 1882.   K 20 P 15

Technical Reporting : comprising Phonographic Abbreviations. 12mo. Lond., 1886.   K 20 P 16

REED, T. B. History of the Old English Letter Foundries : with Notes on the Rise and Progress of English Typography. 4to. Lond., 1887.   A 25 V 5

REED, W. Recent Wanderings in Fiji : Glimpses of its Villages, Churches, and Schools. 12mo. Lond., 1888.   MD 2 W 39

REES, W. L. The Coming Crisis : a Sketch of the Financial and Political Condition of New Zealand. 8vo. Auckland, 1874.   MF 2 T 10

Sir George Grey and the Constitution : an Answer to Sir W. Fox. 8vo. Auckland, 1890.   MF 2 T 37

REES, William L. and Lily. Life and Times of Sir George Grey, K.C.B. 2 vols. 8vo. Lond., 1892.   MC 1 T 13, 14
Another Copy. 8vo. Auckland, 1892.   MC 1 T 15

REEVE, H. [*See* Vitzthum, Count C. F.]

REEVES, A. M. The Finding of Wineland the Good : the History of the Icelandic Discovery of America ; edited and translated by A. M. Reeves. 4to. Lond., 1890.   B 18 V 6

REEVES, C. E. Heart Diseases in Australia. 8vo. Melb., 1873.   MA 2 S 32

Softening of the Stomach in Children and Adults in Australia. 8vo. Melb., 1867.   MA 2 S 31

REEVES, E. Homeward Bound after Thirty Years ; with illustrations. 8vo. Lond., 1892.   D 20 S 3

REEVES, J. The Rothschilds, the Financial Rulers of Nations. 8vo. Lond., 1887.   C 12 R 25

REEVES, Mrs. H., "Helen Mathers." Sam's Sweetheart. 2nd ed. 3 vols. 8vo. Lond., 1883.   MJ 2 P 21-23

REEVES, W. P. [*See* Williams, G. P.]

REGISTER OF AUSTRALIAN AND NEW ZEALAND SHIPPING, 1880-81, 1884-85. 2 vols. Ob. 8vo. Melb., 1880-84.   ME 6 R

REGISTERS OF THE FRENCH CHURCH at Dover, Kent. [*See* Crisp, F. A.]

REGISTRATION OF TITLE, Return reporting on the Working and Progress of the System of Conveyancing by Registration of Title in operation in the Colonies of South Australia, Queensland, New South Wales, Victoria, Tasmania, Western Australia, New Zealand, British Columbia, and Fiji. Fol. Lond., 1881   MF 4 S 20

REGNIER, M. Œuvres Complètes. (Collection Jannet-Picard.) 12mo. Paris (n. d.)   H 1 P 49

REID, E., and COMPTON, H. The Dramatic Peerage, 1891. 12mo. Lond., 1891.   C 17 P 1

REID, Elizabeth. Mayne Reid : a Memoir of his Life. 12mo. Lond., 1890.   C 12 P 40

REID, Dr. George. Practical Sanitation. 8vo. Lond., 1892.   A 12 Q 48

REID, G. H., and PARKES, Sir H. Free Trade Association of New South Wales.—Speeches on the Second Reading of the Customs Duties Bill. 8vo. Sydney, 1886.   MF 2 T 36

REID, J. A. The Australian Reader : Selections from leading Journals on Memorable Historic Events. Roy. 8vo. Melb., 1882.   MB 2 U 19

REID, J. B. Complete Word and Phrase Concordance to the Poems and Songs of Robert Burns. Imp. 8vo. Glasgow, 1889.   K 19 V 5

REID, Capt. Mayne. A Memoir of his Life ; by Elizabeth Reid, his widow. 12mo. Lond., 1890.   C 12 P 40

REID, T. W. Life, Letters, and Friendship of Richard Monckton Milnes, First Lord Houghton. 2 vols. 8vo. Lond., 1890.   C 13 U 10, 11
Life of the Rt. Hon. W. E. Forster. 2 vols. Roy. 8vo. Lond., 1888.   C 12 T 7, 8

REID, W. M. Culture and Manufacture of Indigo ; with a Description of a Planter's Life and Resources. 8vo. Calcutta, 1887.   A 1 U 7

REIN, Prof. J. J. The Industries of Japan, together with an account of its Agriculture, Forestry, Arts, and Commerce. Roy. 8vo. New York, 1889.   A 29 V 2

REINEKE VOS. Nach der Lübecker Ausgabe vom Jahre, 1498 ; min Einleitung, Glossar, und Anmerkungen von H. von Fallersleben. 8vo. Breslau, 1834   H 10 Q 16

REISKE, J. J. [*See* Demosthenes, and Plutarch.]

REISS, J. Vom Rheinwein eine chemisch-medizinische Abhandlung. 12mo. Mainz, 1791.   F 11 P 55

REISS, W., and STÜBEL, A. Necropolis of Ancon, in Peru : a Contribution to our Knowledge of the Culture and Industries of the Empire of the Incas. 2 vols. 4to. Berlin, 1880-87   B 34 Q 10-12 ‡

REITZIO, C. C. [*See* Lucian.]

RELIGIOUS SYSTEMS OF THE WORLD : a Collection of Addresses delivered at South Place Institute. 2nd edition. 8vo. Lond., 1892.   G 15 R 28

REMARKABLE ADVENTURES from Real Life. 8vo. Lond., 1888.   D 20 Q 4

REMBRANDT-GALERIE. Eine Auswahl von Hundert Gemälden Rembrandts. Herausgegeben von A. von Wurzbach. Roy. 4to. Stuttgart, 1886.   A 34 Q 7 ‡
Plates [to the above]. 4to. Stuttgart, 1884.   A 34 Q 8 ‡

REMINISCENCES OF EARLY DAYS; by "Old Hand." 12mo. Auckland, 1890. MB 1 P 30

REMONDINO, Dr. P. C. The Mediterranean Shores of America : Southern California, its Climate, &c. Illustrated. Roy. 8vo. Philad., 1892. D 15 U 4

REMSEN, Prof. I. Inorganic Chemistry. 8vo. Lond., 1889. A 5 T 23

RÉMUSAT, P. de. Life of A. Theirs. 12mo. Lond., 1892. C 17 Q 22

RENAN, E. The Future of Science : Ideas of 1848. 8vo. Lond., 1891. G 12 U 32

Histoire Générale et Système Comparé des Langues Sémitiques. 5th edition. 8vo. Paris, 1878. K 12 U 34

History of the People of Israel up to the Capture of Samaria. [1st and 2nd divisions.] 2 vols. 8vo. Lond., 1888–89. B 28 U 1, 2

Leaders of Christian and Anti-Christian Thought : translated by W. M. Thomson. 12mo. Lond. (n.d.) G 16 Q 56

The Origins of Christianity. 7 vols. 12mo. Lond. (n.d.) G 16 Q 49–55

   1. Life of Jesus.
   2. The Apostles.
   3. St. Paul.
   4. The Anti-Christ.
   5. The Gospels.
   6. The Christian Church.
   7. Marcus Aurelius.

Studies in Religious History. 8vo. Lond., 1886. G 8 Q 33

RENEY, W. Narrative of the Shipwreck of the Corsair in 1835. 8vo. Lond., 1836. MD 2 Q 53

RENNIE, E. A. The Foundation Strength of Popery ; by "An Old Student of Scripture." 8vo. Sydney, 1888. MG 2 Q 3

RENSSELAER, Mrs. J. K. van. [*See* Van Rensselaer, Mrs. J. K.]

RENTON, E. H. Heraldry in England ; with a Glossary of Terms. Sm. 4to. Lond., 1887. K 12 V 6

REPPLIER, Agnes. Point of View. 12mo. Lond., 1892. J 11 W 6

REPTON, H. and J. A. Fragments on the Theory and Practice of Landscape Gardening, including some remarks on Grecian and Gothic Architecture. L. 4to. Lond., 1816. A 7 S 17 †

RESIDENT, A. [*See* Clayden, A.]

RESPUBLICA, sive Status Regni Scotiæ et Hiberniæ, diversorum autorum. 18mo. Lugd. Bat., 1627. (Elzevier Press.) B 31 P 11

RESTIF, N. E. Les Contemporaines. (Collection Jannet-Picard.) 3 vols. 12mo. Paris (n.d.) J 15 Q 35–37

RETURN FROM PARNASSUS, The; a Comedy. [*See* British Drama, Ancient, 1.]

REVELEY-MITFORD, Major-Gen. R. C. W. [*See* Mitford, Major-Gen. R. C. W. Reveley.]

REVELL, W. F. Browning's Criticism of Life. 12mo. Lond., 1892. J 11 W 1

REVIEW OF REVIEWS. Vols. 1–5. 4to. Lond., 1890–92. E 1. 40

RÉVILLE, Prof. A. Prolegomena of the History of Religions. 8vo. Lond., 1884. G 16 S 38

RÉVOIL, B. H. Le Rêve du Chasseur. Ob. fol. Paris, 1873. A 41 P 4 ‡

REVUE AUSTRALIENNE, Juin, 1874. 8vo. Sydney, 1874. ME 3 R

REVUE COLONIALE INTERNATIONALE Vols. 1, 2, 1886, and vol. 1, 1887. Roy. 8vo. Amsterdam, 1886–87. E 1. 70

REVUE DES ARTS DECORATIFS, 1880–82. 4 vols. Sm. fol. Paris, 1880–82. A 36 S 8, 9 ‡

REVUE DES DEUX MONDES. Tomes 76–111. Paris, 1886–92. E 1. 31–33

REVUE DES QUESTIONS HISTORIQUES. Tomes 41–51. Paris, 1887–92. E 1. 35

REVUE INTERNATIONALE. Tomes 13–27. Rome, 1887–90. E 1. 35

REY, F. G. Les Familles d'outre-mer de du Cange. 4to. Paris, 1869. C 17 U 4

REYNOLDS, M. Orangemen in Public Schools, and Volunteers paraded on the 12th July, 1874 ; being Correspondence between the Bishop of Sydney (Dr. Barker), Lieut.-Col. Richardson, the Hon. H. Parkes, and M. Reynolds. 12mo. Parramatta, 1874. MG 2 P 4

RHATIGAN, John. Lays of Temporal Freedom. 8vo. Sydney, 1890. MH 1 S 55

RHODES, E. W. Defensor's Liber Scintillarum. [*See* Early Eng. Text. Soc.]

RHODOMAN, L. [*See* Mennon.]

RHYS, E. [*See* Dekkar, T.]

RHYS, Prof. J. Studies in the Arthurian Legend. 8vo. Oxford, 1891. B 24 S 12

The Hibbert Lectures, 1886 : Lectures on the Origin and Growth of Religion as illustrated by Celtic Heathendom. 8vo. Lond., 1888. G 4 R 39

[*See* Mabinogion.]

RIBBECK, O. Tragicorum Latinorum Reliquiæ. 8vo. Lipsiæ, 1852. H 2 T 25

[*See* Leipziger Studien.]

RIBERO, D. Carta Universal, &c., 1529, in Fac-simile. Roy. 4to. Lond., 1887. D 2 S 13 †

RIBOT, T. Heredity : a psychological study of its phenomena, laws, causes, and consequences. 2nd edition. 8vo. Lond., 1875. A 18 R 25

RIBTON-TURNER, C. J. [*See* Turner, C. J. Ribton-.]

RICARDO, D. Political Economy and Taxation; edited with notes by E. C. K. Gonner. 12mo. Lond., 1891.
F 9 U 14

Letters to T. R. Malthus, 1810–23; edited by J. Bonar. 8vo. Oxford, 1887.
F 7 Q 33

RICH, G. E. [*See* Rolin, T.]

RICHARD, J. En Campagne. 4to. Paris (n.d.)
A 40 P 1 ‡

RICHARDS, J. W. Aluminium : its History, Occurrence, Properties, Metallurgy, and Applications. 8vo. Philad., 1887.
A 24 S 1

RICHARDSON, Dr. B. W. The Commonhealth : a Series of Essays on Health and Felicity for Every-day Readers. 8vo. Lond., 1887.
A 26 R 12

Moderate Drinking : for and against, from scientific points of view. Lond., 1878.
F 11 R 47

Temperance Lesson Book. 12mo. Lond., 1886.
F 11 P 10

Results of Researches on Alcohol. 12mo. Lond., 1878.
F 11 P 27

On Alcohol : a course of six Cantor lectures. 12mo. Lond., 1880.
F 11 P 38

Action of Alcohol on the Mind. 12mo. Lond., 1877.
F 11 P 42

Total Abstinence. 8vo. Lond., 1878.
F 11 Q 15

RICHARDSON, C. New Dictionary of the English Language. New edition. 2 vols. 4to. Lond., 1856.
K 16 U 20, 21

RICHARDSON, C. F. American Literature, 1607–1885. 2 vols. 8vo. New York, 1887–89.
B 19 T 2, 3

1. The Development of American Thought.
2. American Poetry and Fiction.

RICHARDSON, C. J. [*See* Australian Juvenile Industrial Exhib.]

RICHARDSON, Maj.-Gen. J. S. Correspondence respecting Orangemen in Public Schools. [*See* Reynolds, M.]

RICHARDSON, R. Willow and Wattle. 12mo. Edinb., 1893.
H 8 T 54

Another Copy. 12mo. Edinb., 1893.
MH 1 U 35

RICHARDSON, W. Catalogue of 7,385 Stars, chiefly in the Southern Hemisphere, prepared from Observations made 1822–26, at the Observatory, Parramatta, N.S.W., founded by Sir Thos. M. Brisbane. 4to. Lond., 1835.
MA 1 P 30†

RICHARDSON, W. [*See* Gatty, Mrs. A.]

RICHERIE, E. G. de la. Etablissements Français de l'Océanie. Roy. 8vo. Paris, 1865.
MD 7 R 49

RICHEY, Prof. A. G. Short History of the Irish People, down to the date of the Plantation of Ulster. 8vo. Dublin, 1887.
B 29 T 16

RICHMOND, Duke of. [*See* Portsmouth, Duchess of.]

RICHTER, Prof. V. von. Chemistry of the Carbon Compounds ; or, Organic Chemistry. 8vo. Philad., 1886.
A 21 R 2

Text-book of Inorganic Chemistry. 8vo. Philad., 1885.
A 21 R 1

RICHTER, Prof. T. [*See* Plattner, C. F.]

RIDES Out and About : Rambles of an Australian School Inspector. 12mo. Lond. (n.d.)
MD 1 Q 25

RIDGWAY, R. Manual of North American Birds. 4to. Philad., 1887.
A 13 U 43

Ornithology. [*See* United States of America.]

RIDPATH, J. C. Popular History of the United States of America, from the aboriginal times to the present day. Imp. 8vo. New York, 1887.
B 18 V 1

RIESE, A. [*See* Ovidius Naso, P.]

RIETSTAP, J. B. Armorial Général ; précédé d'un Dictionnaire des termes du Blason. 2 vols. roy. 8vo. Gouda, 1884–87.
K 10 U 1, 2

RIGG, Rev. C. W. Digest of the Laws and Regulations of the Australasian Wesleyan Connexion. 2nd ed. 8vo. Auckland, 1872.
MG 2 P 25

RIGG, E. [*See* Saunier, C.]

RIGUTINI, G. Crestomazia Italiana della Poesia Moderna. 2nd edition. 8vo. Firenze, 1886. H 7 S 41

RIIS, J. A. How the other half lives : studies among the poor. 8vo. Lond., 1891.
F 14 S 7

RILEY, A. Documents substantiating the character and performances of the Entire Irish Race-Horse, Skeleton. 8vo. Lond., 1832.
MA 2 P 67

[Portrait of] Skeleton, the Entire Irish Race-Horse. Ob. fol. Lond., 1832.
MA 3 P 9 ‡

Portraits of a Prize Ram and Ewe, Exhibited at Parramatta from the Electoral Saxon Flocks of Raby. Ob. fol. Lond. (n.d.)
MA 3 P 7 ‡

RILEY, A. Athos ; or, the Mountain of the Monks. 8vo. Lond., 1887.
D 18 U 3

RILEY, W. E. Remarks on Importation of Cashmere and Angora Goats into France ; and the Extraordinary Properties of the new race, Cashmere-Angora, with its capabilities of rendering the common goat of value to the colonies of New South Wales and Van Diemen's Land. 8vo. Lond., 1832.
MA 2 T 47

RIMINI, Griscolli de Vezzani, Baron de. Memoirs of ; Secret Agent of Napoleon III, 1850–58 ; Cavour, 1859–61; Antonelli, 1861–62 ; Francis II, 1862–64 ; Emperor of Austria, 1864–67. 8vo. Lond., 1888.
C 7 P 30

RIMMER, A. Summer Rambles around Manchester. Roy. 8vo. Manchester, 1890.
D 8 U 26

RIMMER, Dr. Wm. Art Anatomy. 4to. Lond., 1884.
A 38 P 22 ‡

RISTORI, Adelaide. Studies and Memoirs. 8vo. Lond., 1888.
C 12 Q 40

RITCHIE, D. G. Principles of State Interference : Essays on the Political Philosophy of Herbert Spencer, J. S. Mill, and T. H. Green. 8vo. Lond., 1891. F 14 P 32

RITCHIE, D. G. [*See* Carlyle, Jane W.]

RITCHIE, J. E. An Australian Ramble, or a Summer in Australia. 8vo. Lond., 1890. MD 3 R 44

Brighter South Africa ; or Life at the Cape and Natal, with map. 12mo. Lond., 1892. D 14 Q 14

Imperialism in South Africa. 8vo. Lond., 1879. F 8 S 26

RITCHIE, L. Wanderings by the Seine. [*See* Turner, J. M. W.]

RITSON, J. Ancient English Metrical Romances ; revised by E. Goldsmid. 3 vols. 8vo. Edinb., 1884–85. H 8 U 10–12

RITTER, Dr. B. Das Bier von Seiten der Medizinalpolizei. 8vo. Erlangen, 1854. F 11 Q 67

RITTER, Prof. C. The Colonization of New Zealand ; translated from the German. 8vo. Lond., 1842. MD 2 P 42

RITTER, Dr. H. The History of Ancient Philosophy ; translated by A. J. W. Morrison. 4 vols. 8vo. Oxford, 1838. G 4 U 38–41

RITTER, H., and PRELLER, L. Historia Philosophiæ Græco-Romanæ. 8vo. Hamburgi, 1838. G 12 Q 35

RIVETT-CARNAC, Col. E. S. [*See* Carnac, Col. E. S. R.]

ROBERT OF TORIGNI. Chronicles. [*See* Chronicles and Memorials of Great Britain, &c.]

ROBERT, Emma. Scenes and Characteristics of Hindostan. 3 vols. 8vo. Lond., 1835. D 5 P 48–50

ROBERT, V. R. L'Architecture Normande aux 11' et 12' siècles en Normandie et en Angleterre. 2 vols. 4to. Paris, 1890. A 40 Q 21, 22 ‡

ROBERTS, Rev. Prof. Alexander. Greek, the Language of Christ and his Apostles. 8vo. Lond., 1888. G 10 T 28

ROBERTS, Alfred. On Pauperism in New South Wales. 8vo. Lond., 1869. MF 4 R 7

ROBERTS, Sir Alfred. Paper on Hospital Accommodation. 8vo. Sydney, 1874. MA 3 T 35

ROBERTS, David. Picturesque Sketches in Spain. Fol. Lond., 1837. D 41 P 1 ‡

ROBERTS, David, and CROLY, Rev. G. The Holy Land. 2 vols. Fol. Lond., 1842–43. D 8 R 17, 18 ‡

ROBERTS, Dorothea. Two Royal Lives : the Crown Prince and Princess of Germany. 8vo Lond., 1887. C 12 Q 3

ROBERTS, Ellis Henry. New York : the Planting and Growth of the Empire State. 2 vols. 12mo. Boston, 1887. B 17 P 2, 3

ROBERTS, G. B. [*See* Sladen, D. W. B.]

ROBERTS, Rev. H. Grammar of the Khassi Language. 8vo. Lond., 1891. K 20 Q 25

ROBERTS, Jane. Two Years at Sea. 2nd edition. 12mo. Lond., 1837. M D 2 W 40

ROBERTS, M. The Western Avernus ; or, Toil and Travel in Further North America. 8vo. Lond., 1887. D 4 P 49

ROBERTS, R. Prophecy and the Eastern Question, &c. 8vo. Melb., 1877. MG 1 Q 44

ROBERTS, R. A. Treatise on the Integral Calculus. Part 1. 8vo. Dublin, 1887. A 25 Q 30

ROBERTS, W. The Earlier History of English Bookselling. 8vo. Lond., 1889. B 21 S 21

ROBERTS-AUSTEN, Prof. W. C. [*See* Austen, Prof. W. C. R.]

ROBERTSON, A. The Kidnapped Squatter, and other Australian Tales. 8vo. Lond., 1891. MJ 2 T 39

ROBERTSON, Rev. A. The Past and Future of the Education Question ; or the late bill, its Merits' and Defects. 12mo. Melb., 1867. MF 2 P 73

ROBERTSON, David. The Naturalist of Cumbrae, a true story ; by the Rev. T. R. R. Stebbing. 8vo. Lond., 1891. C 15 Q 4

ROBERTSON, D. Popular Readings in Science. [*See* Gall, J.]

ROBERTSON, Sir John. Speeches made on the Lands Act Further Amendment Bill. 8vo. Sydney, 1879. MF 1 R 71

[*See* Stephen, Sir A.]

ROBERTSON, J. D. Dialect in Gloucester. [*See* English Dialect Soc.]

ROBERTSON, J. M. Essays towards a Critical Method. 8vo. Lond., 1889. J 9 S 36

Modern Humanists : sociological studies of Carlyle, Mill, Emerson, Arnold, Ruskin, and Spencer, with an epilogue on social reconstruction. 8vo. Lond., 1891. F 14 P 33

The Fallacy of Saving. 12mo. Lond., 1892. F 9 U 20

ROBERTSON, W. Works of ; with an account of the Life of, by D. Stewart. 8 vols. 8vo. Lond., 1827. B 31 T 12–19

History of the reign of Charles V. ; with an account of the Emperor's Life after his abdication, by W. H. Prescott. 8vo. Lond., 1857. B 27 T 2

History of Scotland during the Reigns of Queen Mary and King James VI. New edition. 2 vols. 8vo. Lond., 1781. B 31 T 25–26

ROBINS, E. C. Technical School and College Building, &c. 4to. Lond., 1887. A 9 R 4 †

ROBINSON, Rev. C. J. Register of Scholars admitted into Merchant Taylors' School, 1562–1874. 2 vols. roy. 8vo. Lewes, 1882. C 17 S 1, 2

ROBINSON, Dr. C. S. The Pharaohs of the Bondage and the Exodus. 8vo. New York, 1887. G 8 Q 32

ROBINSON, E. A. [*See* Hassencamp, Dr. R.]

ROBINSON, F. W. Female Life in Prison; by "A Prison Matron." 8vo. Lond., 1864. F 14 Q 4

ROBINSON, G. Treatise on the Use of maize as Human Food. 8vo. Sydney, 1890. MA 3 Q 13

ROBINSON, H. E. C. [*See* Higinbotham, A. J.]

ROBINSON, H. J. Colonial Chronology: Principal events connected with the English Colonies and India; with maps. Imp. 8vo. Lond., 1892. B 36 S 14 ‡
Another copy. Imp. 8vo. Lond., 1892. MB 2 V 17

ROBINSON, J. A. [*See* Lambros, Prof. S. P.]

ROBINSON, M. New Family Herbal; comprising a Description, and the Medical Virtues of British and Foreign Plants. 18mo. Lond., 1888. Libr.

ROBINSON, R. E. Vermont: a Study of Independence. (American Commonwealths.) 12mo. Boston, 1892. B 17 P 32

ROBINSON, W. Cremation and Urn-burial. 8vo. Lond., 1889. A 29 Q 44
Garden Design and Architects' Gardens. 8vo. Lond., 1892. A 18 T 19
The Parks and Gardens of Paris. 2nd edition. 8vo. Lond., 1878. A 18 T 1

ROBINSON, Rev. W. G. Sermon Memorials of; edited by F. T. Whitington. 8vo. Adelaide, 1885. MG 2 Q 11

ROBISON, Capt. Robert. In the King's Bench: Rex v. Robison, Judgment. 8vo. Lond., 1835. MF 1 Q 40

ROBSON, T., Memoir of, a Warrington Artist; by W. Beaumont. 8vo. Warrington, 1886. C 5 U 29

ROBSON, W. James Chalmers, Missionary and Explorer of Rarotonga and New Guinea. 12mo. Lond., 1887. MC 1 P 45

ROCHAS, Dr. Victor de. La Nouvelle Calédonie et ses Habitants. 12mo. Paris, 1862. MD 7 T 39

ROCHE, J. J. Life of J. B. O'Reilly; together with his complete Poems and Speeches; edited by Mrs. J. B. O'Reilly. Roy. 8vo. Lond., 1891. C 12 U 19
Another copy. Roy. 8vo. Lond., 1891. MC 1 R 38
The Story of the Filibusters; to which is added the Life of Col. D. Crockett. 8vo. Lond., 1891. B 19 S 4

ROCHON, Abbé A. Description of Madagascar. [*See* Drury, R.]

ROCKHILL, William Woodville. Land of the Lamas. Roy. 8vo. Lond., 1891. D 16 V 2

ROCKSTRO, W. S. [*See* Holland, Rev. H. S.]

ROCQUAIN, F. The Revolutionary Spirit preceding the French Revolution; translated by J. D. Hunting. 12mo. Lond., 1891. B 26 Q 15

RODD, R. Customs and Lore of Modern Greece; with Illustrations. 8vo. Lond., 1892. D 18 R 14

RODD, Rennell. Frederick, Crown Prince and Emperor: a Biographical Sketch. 8vo. Lond., 1888. C 12 Q 6

RODENBOUGH, T. F. Uncle Sam's Medal of Honor. Some of the noble deeds for which the medal has been awarded; described by those who have won it, 1861-86. 8vo. New York, 1886. B 1 S 47

RODNEY, George Brydges. Life of; by D. Hannay. (English Men of Action.) 8vo. Lond., 1891. C 16 P 7

RODYHOUSE, T. R., and TAPERELL, H. J. The Labour Party in New South Wales: a history of its formation and Legislative Career. 8vo. Sydney, 1892. MF 3 P 64

ROEMER, Prof. J. Origins of the English People and of the English Language. 8vo. Lond., 1888. B 23 U 8

ROGER OF WENDOVER. Chronica. [*See* Chronicles and Memorials of Great Britain, &c.]

ROGERS, A. [*See* Goethe, J. W. von.]

ROGERS, Rev. C. Book of Wallace. [*See* Grampian Club.]

[*See* Stirling, Earl of.]

ROGERS, Prof. J. E. T. The Economic Interpretation of History. 8vo. Lond., 1888. F 14 T 24
Ensilage: and its prospects in English Agriculture. 2nd edition. 12mo. Lond., 1884. A 18 Q 20
First Nine Years of the Bank of England, 1694-1703. 8vo. Oxford, 1887. F 5 P 11
History of Agriculture and Prices in England, 1259-1702. Vols. 1-6. Roy. 8vo. Oxford, 1866-87. F 4 V 1-6
Holland. 8vo. Lond., 1888. D 30 R 15
Local Taxation, especially in English Cities and Towns. 8vo. Lond., 1886. F 5 S 40
Industrial and Commercial History of England. 8vo. Lond., 1892. B 24 S 20

ROGERS, J. W. F. The Australasian Federal Directory of Commerce, Trades, and Professions, 1888-89. Roy. 8vo. Melb., 1888. ME 10 T
Another copy. 2nd edition. Roy. 8vo. Melb. 1891. ME 10 T

ROGERS, Samuel. Rogers and his Contemporaries; by P. W. Clayden. 2 vols. 8vo. Lond., 1889. C 13 R 20, 21
Early Life of; by P. W. Clayden. 8vo. Lond., 1887. C 4 V 38

ROGERS, Rev. W. Reminiscences of; compiled by the Rev. R. H. Hadden. 8vo. Lond., 1888. C 15 Q 24

ROGERS, W. H. H. Memorials of the West, collected on the Borderland of Somerset, Dorset, and Devon. Roy. 8vo. Exeter, 1888. B 24 T 8

ROGERS, W. T. Manual of Bibliography. 8vo. Lond., 1891. K 9 S 14

ROGET, John Lewis. A History of the "Old Water-Colour Society." 2 vols. Roy. 8vo. Lond., 1891. A 23 V 2, 3

ROGET, Dr. P. M. Animal and Vegetable Physiology, considered with reference to Natural Theology. 2 vols. 8vo. Lond., 1838. A 27 U 8, 9

Thesaurus of English Words and Phrases. 8vo. Lond., 1890. K 12 R 42

ROGGEVIEN, J. Histoire de l'Expédition de Trois Vaisseaux aux Terres Australes, 1721 [traduit] par. M. de B***. [C. F. de Behrens.] 12mo. La Hayé, 1739. MD 1 T 14

Voyage aux Terres Australes en 1722. (Prévost, A. F. Suité de l'Histoire Générale des Voyages. Tome 17.) 4to. Amsterdam, 1761. MD 11 P 16 †

ROLAND, A. The Drainage of Land, Irrigation, and Manures. (Farming for Pleasure and Profit. Fifth Section.) 8vo. Lond., 1887. A 18 R S.

Tree-planting for Ornamentation or Profit, suitable to every soil and situation. 8vo. Lond., 1887. A 18 S 6

ROLFE, E. N. Pompeii, Popular and Practical. 8vo. Naples, 1888. B 12 Q 44

ROLIN, F., and RICH, G. E. The Companies Acts of 1874 and 1888. Rules and Forms, together with the No-Liability Mining Companies Act, and other Acts relating to Companies. Roy. 8vo. Sydney, 1890. MF 3 R 43

ROLLESTON, C. Anniversary Address. [Delivered to the Royal Society of New South Wales, 2nd May, 1883.] 8vo. Sydney, 1883. MA 2 T 46

Condition and Resources of New South Wales. 8vo. Lond., 1867. MF 3 Q 25

ROLLESTON, Prof. G. Forms of Animal Life: a Manual of Comparative Anatomy; revised by W. H. Jackson. Roy. 8vo. Oxford, 1888. A 28 V 2

ROLLIAD, The. Probationary Odes for the Laureatship. 8vo. Lond., 1795. H 7 T 34

ROLLIN, Lédru. [See Bradlaugh, C.—Five Dead Men.]

ROMANES, Prof. G. J. Mental Evolution in Man: Origin of Human Faculty. 8vo. Lond., 1888. G 12 P 40

ROME, Dr. T. Notice sur l'Alcool, sa provenance, sa nature, son utilité, son action, et ses éffets. 12mo. Bruxelles, 1885. F 11 P 62

ROMILLY, H. H. From my Verandah in New Guinea: Sketches and Traditions. 8vo. Lond., 1889. MD 2 S 5

ROONEY, J. Ai Vola kei Vuravura. 2nd edition. 12mo. Sydney, 1879. M D 2 Q 52

ROOSEVELT, Blanche. Elizabeth of Roumania: a Study; with two tales from the German of Carmen Sylva. 8vo. Lond., 1891. C 15 U 16

ROOSEVELT, T. New York. (Historic Towns.) 8vo. Lond., 1891. B 19 Q 5

[Life of] Gouverneur Morris. (American Statesmen.) 12mo. Boston, 1888. C 2 R 24

Life of Thos. H. Benton. (American Statesmen.) 12mo. Boston, 1887. C 13 Q 2

ROPER, E. By Track and Trail: a Journey Through Canada. 8vo. Lond., 1891. D 3 U 41

ROQUEFEUIL, C. de. Journal d'un Voyage autour du Monde, 1816–19. 2 vols. 8 vo. Paris, 1823. MD 8 Q 7, 8.

Voyage round the World between the years 1816–19. 8vo. Lond., 1823. MD 8 R 5

ROSA, S. A. The Truth about the Unemployed Agitation of 1890. 8vo. Melb., 1890. MF 2 P 58

RÖSCH, Dr. C. Der Missbrauch geistiger Getränke. 8vo. Tübingen, 1839. F 11 Q 66

ROSCOE, Sir H. E., and SCHORLEMMER, C. A Treatise on Chemistry. 2nd edition. 3 vols. (in 9). Roy. 8vo. Lond., 1878-92. A 21 T 1–9

ROSCOE, T. [See Pellico, S.]

ROSE, Geo. The Great Country: or Impressions of America. 8vo. Lond., 1868. D 15 S 3

ROSE, Sir Hugh. [See Strathnairn, Baron.]

ROSE, Hugh James. Life of. [See Burgon, Very Rev. J. W.]

ROSE, J. Steam-boilers: a Practical Treatise on Boiler Construction and Examination. Roy. 8vo. Philad., Lond., 1888. A 6 U 20

ROSEBERY, Right Hon. Archibald Philip Primrose, Earl of. [Life of Wm.] Pitt. 12mo. Lond., 1891. C 18 P 8

ROSEGGER, P. H. Zither und Hackbrett. 12mo. Graz, 1870. H 5 Q 52

ROSENKRANZ, Prof. J. K. F. Philosophy of Education; translated by Anna C. Brackett. 12mo. New York, 1886. G 17 P 42

ROSENTHAL, Dr. J. Ol og Brændevin og deres Betydning for Sundheden. 8vo. Kjöbenhavn, 1882. F 11 Q 16

ROSINI, G. Storia della Pittura Italiana. 7 vols. 8vo. Pisa, 1848. A 23 U 9–15

ROSMINI-SERBATI, Antonio, Founder of the Institute of Charity. Life of; edited by W. Lockhart. 2nd ed. 2 vols. 8vo. Lond., 1886. C 16 Q 9, 10

Psychology. 3 vols. 8vo. Lond., 1884-88. G 16 T 1–3

ROSNY, L. de. La Patrie des Romains d'Orient. 4to. Paris, 1884. A 37 P 6 ‡

Atlas [to the above]. Fol. Paris, 1884. A 37 P 7 ‡

ROSS, Dr. A. Lecture on Philosophy of Mind and Matter; or, the Immortality of the Soul and Life Beyond the Grave. 8vo. Sydney, 1881. MG 1 S 59

ROSS, A. Steam Communication with Great Britain, by Branch Vessels between Sydney and the Cape of Good Hope. 8vo. Sydney, 1838. MF 1 R 55

ROSS, Rev. C. Stuart. Story of the Otago Church and Settlement. 8vo. Dunedin, 1887. MG 2 Q 10

Education and Educationists in Otago. 8vo. Dunedin, 1890. MG 2 R 18

Colonization and Church Work in Victoria. 8vo. Melb., 1891. MG 2 Q 9

ROSS, F. Legendary Yorkshire. 8vo. Hull, 1892. B 24 S 16

Bygone London. 8vo. Lond., 1892. B 24 S 15

ROSS, J. Van Diemen's Land Annual and Hobart Town Almanack, 1833, 1835. 2 vols. 12mo. Hobart Town, 1833–35. ME 4 P

ROSS, Janet. Early Days Recalled. 8vo. Lond., 1891. C 16 P 9

Three Generations of Englishwomen. Memoirs and Correspondence of Mrs. John Taylor, Mrs. Sarah Austin, and Lady Duff Gordon. 2 vols. 8vo. Lond., 1888. C 14 R 5, 6

ROSS, J. D. Burnsiana: a Collection of Literary Odds and Ends relating to Robert Burns. 4to. Paisley, 1892. J 6 U 29

ROSS, M. Complete Guide to the Lakes of Central Otago; the Switzerland of Australasia. 8vo. Wellington, 1889. MD 7 S 32

ROSS, P. H. W. Federation and the British Colonies: a Paper of Suggestions. 8vo. Lond., 1887. MF 1 R 36

ROSS, Thomas. Castellated and Domestic Architecture of Scotland. [*See* Macgibbon, David.]

ROSSE, J. W. Chronological Tables. [*See* Blair, Rev. J.]

An Index of Dates alphabetically arranged. 2 vols. 8vo. Lond., 1859–68. B 14 P 40, 41

ROSSER, W. H. Wind, Weather, and Currents, &c., together with Sailing Directions, &c., to accompany Charts of the North and South Pacific. 8vo. Lond., 1868. MD 4 S 1

ROSSETTI, D. G., Poet and Painter; by P. W. Nicholson. (Round Table Series.) 8vo. Edinb., 1886. C 7 T 9

ROSSETTI, Lucy Madox. Mrs. Shelley. 12mo. Lond., 1890. C 12 P 46

ROSSETTI, W. M. [*See* Gilchrist, Anne, and Shelley, P. B.]

ROSSINI, L. J. Sette colli di Roma, antica e moderna. Fol. Roma, 1829. A 43 P 15 ‡

Le Antichità di Pompei. Fol. Roma, 1826. B 43 P 7 ‡

ROSSINI, J. Vie de; par M. H. Beyle. 12mo. Paris, 1892. C 14 P 17

ROTH, C. L. [*See* Suetonius Tranquillus, C.]

ROTH, H. L. The Aborigines of Tasmania. 8vo. Lond., 1890. MA 3 Q 15

Guide to the Literature of Sugar. 8vo. Lond., 1890. A 18 T 11

Report of the Sugar Industry in Queensland. 8vo. Brisb., 1880. MA 3 Q 59

2 в

ROTHSCHILDS, The: the Financial Rulers of Nations; by J. Reeves. 8vo. Lond., 1887. C 12 R 25

ROTULI SCACCARII REGUM SCOTORUM. [*See* Scotland.]

ROUAIX, P. Les Styles: 700 Gravures, classées par Epoques. Imp. 4to. Paris, 1888. A 37 P 8 ‡

ROULET AND COMTESSE, MM. L'Alcoolisme on Suisse et les moyens d'en combattre les progrès. 8vo. Neuchâtel, 1881. F 11 R 49

ROUSSEAU, J. J. Œuvres Complètes. 4 vols. Imp. 8vo. Paris, 1861–83. J 2 U 22–25

ROUSSET, C. Recollections of Marshall Macdonald, Duke of Tarentum. Trans. by S. L. Simeon. 2 vols. 8vo. Lond., 1892. C 14 V 12, 13

ROUTH, Dr. E. J. Treatise on Analytical Statics, with numerous examples. Vol. 1. 8vo. Camb., 1891. A 25 T 26

ROUTH, Martin Joseph. Life of. [*See* Burgon, Very Rev. J. W.]

ROUTLEDGE, Rev. C. F. History of St. Martin's Church, Canterbury. 8vo. Lond., 1891. B 23 R 3

ROVING PRINTER, A. [*See* Jones, —.]

ROWBOTHAM, J. F. History of Music. 3 vols. 8vo. Lond., 1885–87. A 23 U 2–4

ROWBOTHAM, T. L. Shower of Diamonds Waltz. Fol. Sydney (n.d.) MA 11 Q 15 †

ROWE, G. S. Life of John Hunt, Missionary to the Cannibals. 8vo. Lond., 1859. MC 1 Q 33

Another Copy. Sixth Thousand. 8vo. Lond., 1866. MC 1 Q 34

ROWE, N. The Fair Penitent : a Tragedy. [*See* British Drama, Modern, 1.]

Lady Jane Gray : a Tragedy. [*See* British Drama, Modern, 1.]

Jane Shore : a Tragedy. [*See* British Drama, Modern, 1.]

Tamerlane : a Tragedy. [*See* British Drama, Modern, 1.]

ROWLAND, T. B. and F. F. The Problem Art: a Treatise on how to compose, and how to solve Chess Problems. 8vo. Dublin, 1887. A 29 P 5

ROWLEY, W. A Match at Midnight : a Comedy. [*See* British Drama, Ancient, 2.]

ROYAL ACADEMY PICTURES. 4to. Lond., 1892. E 1. 79

ROYAL AGRICULTURAL SOCIETY, LONDON. Journal. 2nd Series. Vols. 23–25. 3rd Series, vols, 1, 2. Lond., 1887–91. E 1. 68

General Index to the Second Series of the Journal, Vols. 1–25. 8vo. Lond., 1890. E 1. 68

ROYAL ALBUM of Arts and Industries of Great Britain. Roy. 4to. Lond., 1887. **A 3 P 7 †**

ROYAL ASIATIC SOCIETY. Journal, 1887-91. 5 vols. 8vo. Lond., 1887-91. **E 2. 39**

Straits Branch. Notes and Queries. 8vo. Singapore, 1885. **E 1. 15**

Straits Branch. Journal, 1885-90. 6 vols. 8vo. Singapore, 1886-90. **E 1. 15**

North China Branch. Journal, 1882-90. 8 vols. 8vo. Shanghai, 1882-90. **E 1. 15**

ROYAL BOOK OF CRESTS of Great Britain and Ireland, Dominion of Canada, India, and Australasia. 2 vols. Roy. 8vo. Lond., 1883. **K 8 U 1, 2**

ROYAL CALEDONIAN HORTICULTURAL SOCIETY, Edinburgh. Report of the Apple and Pear Congress, November, 1885. 8vo. Edinb., 1887. **E**

ROYAL COLONIAL INSTITUTE. Proceedings. Vols. 18-23. 8vo. Lond., 1887-92. **E**

ROYAL GEOGRAPHICAL SOCIETY, LONDON. Proceedings. Vol. 22 and New Series, Vols. 9-13. Roy. 8vo. Lond., 1878, 1887-91. **E 1. 48-49**

Supplementary Papers. Vols. 2, 4. Roy. 8vo. Lond., 1889-90. **E 1. 48-49**

ROYAL GEOGRAPHICAL SOCIETY OF AUSTRALASIA. (Queensland Branch.) Proceedings and Transactions, 1889-91. Vol. 5, part 2, and Vol. 6, part 1. 2 vols. 8vo. Brisb., 1889-91. **ME 20 P**

[New South Wales Branch.] Proceedings. Vols. 3, 4 and 5. No. 4. Early Discovery of Australia, with Maps; by Delmar Morgan and G. Collingridge. 8vo. Sydney, 1888-92. **ME 20 P**

New Constitution of. 8vo. Sydney, 1886. **MF 4 R 24**

Proceedings of the Geographical Society of Australasia, New South Wales, and Victorian Branches. 2nd Session. Edited by J. H. Maiden and A. C. Macdonald. Vol. 2. 8vo. Sydney, 1885. **ME 20 P**

(Victorian Branch), Transactions. Part 2, Vol. 7, and Part 2, Vol. 8, 2 vols. 8vo. Melb., 1890-91. **ME 20 P**

ROYAL INSTITUTE OF BRITISH ARCHITECTS. Kalendar, 1887-92. 5 vols. 8vo. Lond., 1887-92. **E 2. 75**

Transactions. New Series. Vols. 3-8. 4to. Lond., 1888-92. **E 2. 75**

Proceedings. Vols. 1-3, n.s., 1884-87. 4to. Lond., 1885-87. **E 2. 75**

ROYAL KALENDAR, The. 4 vols. 12mo. Lond., 1889-92. **E 2. 75**

ROYAL SOCIETY, LONDON. Proceedings. Vols. 42-50. 8vo. Lond., 1887-92. **E 2. 38**

Philosophical Transactions, 1830-34, and Vols. 177-182. 14 vols. 4to. Lond., 1830-34, 1886-92. **E 1. 80**

Catalogue of Scientific Papers, 1874-83. Vol. 9. 4to. Lond., 1891. **K 10 V 14**

ROYAL SOCIETY OF NEW SOUTH WALES *(formerly* Philosophical Society of N.S.W.) Journal and Proceedings, 1878-88 and 1891. 12 vols. 8vo. Sydney, 1878-91. **ME 1 S**

Catalogue of Scientific Books in the Library. Part I. General Catalogue. 8vo. Sydney, 1889. **MK 1 Q 35**

Rules and List of Members, 1876-7. 8vo. Sydney, 1876. **MF 4 R 25**

ROYAL SOCIETY OF SOUTH AUSTRALIA. Transactions and Proceedings and Report, 1886-91. Vols. 10-14. 8vo. Adelaide, 1888-91. **ME 1 S**

ROYAL SOCIETY OF TASMANIA. Papers and Proceedings, 1881, 1884-91. 9 vols. 8vo. Hobart, 1882-92. **ME 1 Q**

Register of Papers published in the Tasmanian Journal, and the Papers and Proceedings, compiled by Alexander Morton. 8vo. Hobart, 1887. **ME 1 Q**

Reports, 1872, 1875, and 1886. 3 vols. 8vo. Hobart, 1873-87. **ME 1 Q**

ROYAL SOCIETY OF VICTORIA. Proceedings. Vols. 1-4. New Series. 8vo. Melb., 1889-92. **ME 1 P**

Transactions. Vol 1. Parts 1 and 2. 4to. Melb., 1888-89. **ME**

Transactions and Proceedings. Vol. 24, part 2. 8vo. Melb., 1888. **ME 1 P**

ROYAUMONT, Sieur de. [*See* Fontaine, N.]

ROYCE, J. California from the Conquest in 1846, to the Second Vigilance Committee in San Francisco. (American Commonwealths.) 12mo. Boston, 1889. **B 17 P 12**

RUDALL, H. A. Beethoven. (Great Musicians.) 12mo. Lond., 1890. **C 12 P 39**

RUDDER, E. W. Incidents connected with the Discovery of Gold in New South Wales in 1851. 8vo. Sydney, 1861. **MA 3 Q 14**

RUDING, Rev. R. Annals of the Coinage of Great Britain and its Dependencies. 3rd ed. (Text and Plates.) 3 vols. 4to. Lond., 1840. **A 4 Q 22-24 †**

RUMBOLD, Sir H. Great Silver River: Notes of a Residence in Buenos Ayres in 1880-81. 8vo. Lond., 1887 **D 15 R 2**

RUPERT, Prince. Rupert of the Rhine : a Biographical Sketch ; by Lord Ronald Gower. 8vo. Lond., 1890. **C 12 Q 32**

RUDDIMAN, T. [*See* Livius, T.]

RUSCHENBERGER, W. S. W. Biographical Notice of George W. Tryon, junior. 8vo. Philad., 1888. **C 16 U 2**

RUSDEN, G. W. Tragedies in New Zealand in 1868 and 1881, discussed in England in 1886 and 1887. 8 vo. Lond., 1888. **MB 1 R 3**

Aureretanga: Groans of the Maoris; edited by G. W. Rusden. 8vo. Lond., 1888.* **MB 1 R 3**

History of Australia. 3 vols. 8vo. Lond., 1883. **MB 2 S 5-7**

RUSKIN, John. The Art Teaching of. [*See* Colling-wood, W. G.]

Examples of the Architecture of Venice. Fol. Orpington, 1887. A 43 P 1 ‡

Fors Clavigera: Letters to the Workmen and Labourers of Great Britain; with Index. 9 vols. (in 6) roy. 8vo. Orpington, 1871–87. A 7 T 27–32

Four Great Teachers: Ruskin, Carlyle, Emerson, and R. Browning; by J. Forster. 8vo. Orpington, 1890. C 12 Q 11

Hortus Inclusus: Messages from the Wood to the Garden. 8vo. Orpington, 1887. C 12 R 27

Modern Painters. 6 vols. Imp. 8vo. Orpington, 1888. A 12 U 11–16 †

"Our Fathers have told us": Sketches of the History of Christendom. Vol. 1. 8vo. Orpington, 1884. G 6 Q 33

Præterita: Outlines of Scenes and Thoughts, perhaps worthy of Memory, in my Past Life. Vol. 2. Roy. 8vo. Orpington, 1887. C 10 V 49

Proserpina: Studies of Wayside Flowers. Vol. 1. 8vo. Orpington, 1882. A 20 S 3

Studies in. [*See* Cook, E. T.]

Modern Humanists. [*See* Robertson, J. M.]

Ulric the Farm Servant: a Story of the Bernese Low-land. [*See* Gotthelf, J.]

[*See* Alexander, F.]

RUSSELL, A. Voices of Doubt; Australian Scenes, and other Poems. 8vo. Adelaide, 1884. MH 1 Q 73

The Seeker, and other Poems; with In Parochiâ. 8vo. Adelaide, 1881. MH 1 Q 72

RUSSELL, Sir C. The Parnell Commission: the Opening Speech for the Defence. 8vo. Lond., 1889. F 10 R 22

RUSSELL, Rev. C. W. [*See* Ireland—State Papers.]

RUSSELL, E. F. [*See* Mackonochie, A. H.]

RUSSELL, Col. F. S. The Earl of Peterborough and Monmouth (Charles Mordaunt): a Memoir. 2 vols. 8vo. Lond., 1887. C 12 T 29, 30

RUSSELL, G. W. E. [Life of] the Rt. Hon. W. E. Gladstone. 8vo. Lond., 1891. C 14 P 28

RUSSELL, H. The Ruin of the Soudan : Cause, Effect, and Remedy : a Resumé of Events, 1883–1891. 8vo. Lond., 1892. B 16 R 1

RUSSELL, H. C. Anniversary Address; delivered to the Royal Society of New South Wales, 3rd May, 1882. 8vo. Sydney, 1882. MA 2 T 44

Astronomical and Meteorological Workers in New South Wales, 1778–1860. 8vo. Sydney, 1888. MA 1 T 72

Causes of Rain. [Part of President's Anniversary Address to Royal Society of New South Wales, 1882.] Sydney, 1882. MA 3 T 46

Cyclonic Storm or Tornado in the Gwydir District. 8vo. Sydney, 1891. MA 3 S 40

Description of the Star Camera at the Sydney Observatory. 4to. Sydney, 1892. MA 12 P 17 †

RUSSELL, H. C.—*contd.*

List of Scientific Papers, Reports, &c., by H. C. Russell, up to 1885. 12mo. Sydney, 1885. MK 1 P 60

Local Variations and Vibrations of the Earth's Surface. 8vo. Sydney, 1885. MA 3 T 46

Notes on the Rate of Growth of some Australian Trees. 8vo. Sydney, 1891. MA 3 S 39

On a New Self-recording Thermometer. 8vo. Sydney, 1889. MA 1 T 75

Photographs of the Milky Way and Nubeculæ, taken at Sydney Observatory, 1890. Fol. Sydney, 1890. MA 11 P 13 †

Physical Geography and Climate of New South Wales. 2nd edition. 8vo. Sydney, 1892. MA 3 R 28

Preparations now being made in Sydney Observatory for the Photographic Chart of the Heavens. 8vo. Sydney, 1891. MA 3 S 38

President's Address, at the first meeting of the Australasian Association for the Advancement of Science. Sydney (n.d.). MA 2 T 45

Proposed Method of Recording Variations in the direction of the Vertical. 8vo. Sydney, 1888. MA 1 T 71

Results of Double Star Measures made at Sydney Observatory. Roy. 8vo. Sydney, 1891. MA 3 R 2

Results of Meteorological Observations made in New South Wales; 1880–84, 1886–87. 4 vols. roy. 8vo. Sydney, 1888–92. ME 16 P

Results of Rain, River, and Evaporation Observations made in New South Wales, in 1879–82, 1887. Roy. 8vo. Sydney, 1880–88. ME 16 T

Source of the Underground Water in the Western Districts. 8vo. Sydney, 1889. MA 1 T 70

Spectrum and Appearance of the Recent Comet. 8vo. Sydney, 1881. MA 3 T 46

Storm of 21st September, 1888. 8vo. Sydney, 1888. MA 1 T 74

Thunderstorm of 26th October, 1888. 8vo. Sydney, 1889. MA 1 T 73

RUSSELL, H. S. Genesis of Queensland: an Account of the first Exploring Journeys to and over the Darling Downs &c. Roy. 8vo. Sydney, 1888.* MB 2 U 9

RUSSELL, J. Schools of Greater Britain: Sketches of the Educational Systems of the Colonies and India. 8vo. Lond., 1888. G 17 Q 32

Another copy. MG 1 R 20

RUSSELL, John, Lord. Life of ; by Spencer Walpole. 2 vols. 8vo. Lond., 1889. C 14 T 5, 6

RUSSELL, P. A Journey to Lake Taupo and Australian and New Zealand Tales and Sketches. 8vo. Lond., 1889. MD 2 W 10

RUSSELL, Hon. R. Epidemics, Plagues, and Fevers. 8vo. Lond., 1892. A 26 T 0

The Spread of Influenza : its supposed relations to Atmospheric Conditions. 8vo. Lond., 1891. A 26 S 6

RUSSELL, Stuart A. Electric Light Cables. 8vo.
Lond., 1892. A 21 Q 33

RUSSELL, T. W. A Social Experiment ; or, Five Years
before and after Sunday Closing in Ireland. 8vo.
Dublin, 1884. F 11 R 46

RUSSELL, W. History of Modern Europe. New edition.
4 vols. 8vo. Lond., 1837. B 25 T 9–12

RUSSELL, W. Clark. [Life of Admiral Lord.] Colling
wood. 8vo. Lond., 1891. C 15 U 8
Horatio Nelson, and the Naval Supremacy of England.
8vo. New York, 1890. C 12 R 44
Nelson's Words and Deeds. 12mo. Lond., 1890.
C 16 P 22
William Dampier. (English Men of Action.) 12mo.
Lond., 1889. C 12 P 30
A Book for the Hammock. 8vo. Lond., 1887.
J 5 P 39

RUSSELL, W. H. Visit to Chili and the Nitrate Fields
of Tarapacá, &c. Imp. 8vo. Lond., 1890. D 15 V 3

RUSTICUS. [See Victoria.]

RUTHERFORD, Dr. W. G. Fourth Book of Thucydides. [See Thucydides.]

RUTLEY, F. Rock-forming Minerals. 8vo. Lond.,
1888. A 24 T 1

RUTTER, J. Gordon Songs and Sonnets; with Notes,
Historical and Biographical, written 1884-85. 8vo.
Lond., 1887. H 8 S 45

RUYSSEN, J. Essays after the Cartoons of Raphael at
Windsor. 2 vols. fol. Lond., 1798–1800. A 43 P 2, 3 ‡

RYAN, Rt. Rev. Vincent W. Two Sermons preached on
the occasion of the Funeral of the Most Rev. Frederic
Barker, Bishop of Sydney; with a brief memoir and
account of his last illness. 8vo. Lond., 1882.
M G 1 S 67

RYDBERG, V. Teutonic Mythology ; translated by R.
B. Anderson. 8vo. Lond., 1889. B 9 R 4
Another Copy. 8vo. Lond., 1891. B 19 S 17

RYE, W. Paper-chasing. [See Shearman, M.]
Records and Record-searching: a Guide to the Genealogist
and Topographer. 8vo. Lond., 1888. K 10 S 30

RYLAND, F. Chronological Outlines of English Literature. 8vo. Lond., 1890. B 23 Q 4

RYLANDS, J. P. Disclaimers at the Heralds' Visitations
of the various Counties of England. 8vo. Guilford,
1888. K 12 V 2
[See Beaumont, W.]

RYLEY, W. [See Foster, J., Visitation of Middlesex.]

RYMER, T. Fœdera, Conventiones, Litteræ &c., inter
Reges Angliæ et alios quosvis Imperatores, &c. Vol 4.
fol. Lond., 1869. B 24 Q 15 ‡

S

S., H. A. [See Darwin, C.]

SAAVEDRA, Don Alvaro de. Voyage de, en 1526. (Prévost, A. F., Suite de l'histoire générale des Voyages,
tome 17). 4to. Amsterdam, 1761. MD 11 P 16 †

SABOUROFF, M. de. La Collection Sabouroff, Monuments de l'Art Grec publiés par adolphe Furtwængler.
2 vols. 4to. Berlin, 1883–87. A 40 Q 25, 26‡

SACCARDO, P. A. Sylloge Fungorum omnium hucusque
cognitorum. 10 vols. roy. 8vo. Patavii, 1882–92.
A 20 V 5–14
Additamenta ad Volumina I–IV, curantibus A. P. Berlese
et P. Voglino. Roy. 8vo. Patavii, 1886. A 20 V 15

SACHAU, Prof. E. C. [See Alberuni.]

SACHS, Prof. Julius von. History of Botany, 1530–1860.
Oxford, 1890. A 20 Q 3
Text-Book of Botany, Morphological and Physiological :
translated and annotated by A. W. Bennett and W. T.
T. Dyer. Roy. 8vo. Oxford, 1875. A 20 V 26
Lectures on the Physiology of Plants ; translated by H.
M. Ward. Roy. 8vo. Oxford, 1887. A 20 V 1

SACKVILLE, T. Ferrex and Porrex : a Tragedy. [See
British Drama, Ancient.]

SACY, Baron Silvestre de. [See Djémal-eddin Mohammed.]

SADEUR, J. [See Foigny, G. de.]

SADLER, L. R. "Jacob Larwood." Story of the London
Parks. 8vo. Lond., 1871 B 23 R 7

SADLER, R. Vox Clamantis. 8vo. Lond., 1891.
G 13 U 38

SAGA LIBRARY, The. Edited by William Morris and
Eirikr Magnússon. Vols. 1, 2. 8vo. Lond., 1891–92.
J 14 Q 27, 28
1. The Story of Howard the Halt.
   The Story of the Banded Men.
   The Story of Hen Thorir.
2. The Story of the Ere-dwellers (Eyrbyggja Saga); with the
   Story of the Heath-slayings.

SAIL, C. R. Farthest East, and South, and West : notes
of a Journey Home through Australasia, Japan, and
America ; by "An Anglo-Indian Globe-Trotter." 8vo.
Lond., 1892. MD 8 R 4

SAINT-AMAND, Arthur Léon Imbert de, Baron. [See
Imbert de Saint-Amand, A. L., Baron.]

SAINT AUGUSTINE'S LITERARY INSTITUTE,
Yass. Two Lectures : The Inaugural Lecture, by the
Rev. P. Bermingham ; "Irish Hearts and Hands," by
M. O'Connor. 8vo. Sydney, 1860. MJ 2 P 8

St. CLAIR, George. Buried Cities and Bible Countries.
8vo. Lond., 1891. D 17 R 8
[See Dawson, G.]

SAINT HELENA. [See Colonial Possessions.]

St. JULIAN, Chas. Notes on the Latent Resources of
Polynesia. 12mo. Sydney, 1851. MD 2 W 44

SAINT LEONARDS, Lord. Handy-book on Property
Law, in a Series of Letters. 8th ed. 12mo. Edinb.,
1869. F 5 S 44

St. LOUIS MERCANTILE LIBRARY. Catalogue of
English Prose Fiction. 8vo. St. Louis, 1862. Libr.

St. MARK. Basilica di San Marco in Venezia. 2 vols.
fol. and 13 vols. 4to. Venezia, 1881-86.
A 43 P 5, 6‡ and A 40 R 5-17‡
The Basilica of S. Mark. [*See* Boito, Prof. C.*]

St. MAUR, Mrs. Algernon. Impressions of a Tenderfoot
during a Journey in Search of Sport in the Far West.
8vo. Lond., 1890. D 4 P 35

SAINT-PIERRE, B. de. Paul et Virginie. (Collection
Jannet-Picard.) 12mo. Paris (n.d.) H 1 R 43

SAINT VINCENT'S HOSPITAL, Sydney. Reports,
1857-1888. 2 vols. 8vo. Sydney, 1857-1889. ME 6 S

SAINTE-BEUVE, C. A. Originaux et Beaux Esprits.
8vo. Paris, 1886. C 18 S 20
Œuvres de. 20 vols. 8vo. Paris, 1850-86.
J 19 V 15-34
1-15. Causeries du Lundi. 15 vols.
16. Portraits de Femmes.
17-19. Portraits Littéraires. 3 vols.
20. Table Générale et Analytique.
[*See* Sévigné, Mme. de.]

SAINTSBURY, G. E. B. Essays on French Novelists. 8vo.
Lond., 1891. J 1 U 44
Essays in English Literature, 1780-1860. 12mo. Lond.,
1890. J 11 W 11
[Life of] the Earl of Derby. 12mo. Lond., 1892.
C 13 Q 22
Miscellaneous Essays. 12mo. Lond., 1892. J 11 W 33
[*See* Dryden, J., *and* Swift, J.]
History of Elizabethan Literature. 8vo. Lond., 1887.
B 21 R 18
Manchester. 8vo. Lond., 1887. B 22 Q 4

SALA, Mrs. G. A. Famous People I have Met. 12mo.
Lond., 1892. C 17 Q 21

SALE, G. The Koran. [*See* Koran, The.]

SALE OF BEER. Report on. Fol. Lond., 1833.
F 42 P 1 ‡
Report on the Operations of the Acts for the Sale of Beer.
Fol. Lond., 1850. F 42 P 3 ‡
Report on the Sale of Beer, &c., Act. Fol. Lond., 1855.
F 42 P 2 ‡
Sale of Intoxicating Liquors in the Colonies, and in Native
Territories under British Protection, Further Papers re-
garding the Laws or Ordinances for regulating. Fol.
Lond., 1888. MF 12 Q 26 †
Sale of Intoxicating Liquors on Sunday (Ireland) Bill.
Fol. Lond., 1877. F 32 P 13 ‡
Sale of Liquors on Sunday Bill. Special Report on. Fol.
Lond., 1868. F 42 P 12 ‡

SALISBURY, Dr. A. The Book of the Nineteenth Century, containing instructions for the safe and certain
cure of every form of Pain and Disease known to Mankind, without the aid of any Medicine whatever. 12mo.
Sydney, 1892. MA 3 P 45

SALISBURY, Robert Cecil, Marquis of. [Life of ;] by H.
D. Traill. 12mo. Lond., 1891. C 16 P 23
Life and Speeches of; by F. S. Pulling. 2 vols. 8vo.
Lond., 1885. C 16 P 3, 4

SALLUSTIUS, C. Opera omnia quæ extant : illustravit
D. Crispinus. 8vo. Lond., 1813. B 30 S 7
Conjuratio Catilinæ, et Bellum Jugurthinum. 12mo.
Antw., 1564. B 30 P 7

SALMON, C. S. Depression in the West Indies. 12mo.
Lond., 1884. F 12 S 6
Crown Colonies of Great Britain : an Inquiry into their
Social Condition, and Methods of Administration. 8vo.
Lond., 1885. F 5 S 41

SALMON, E. Juvenile Literature as it is. 8vo. Lond.,
1888. J 9 S 35

SALMON, N. Lives of the English Bishops, from the
Restauration to the Revolution. (*Bound with the Life
of Dr. S. Clarke.*) 8vo. Lond., 1731. C 4 T 3

SALMON, W. The Reign of Grace. 12mo. Dunedin,
1888. MG 2 P 24

SALOMONS, Sir David. Electric Light Installations and
the Management of Accumulators. New edition. Lond.,
1890. A 21 P 40

SALT, H. S. Life of James Thomson ("B. V.") 8vo.
Lond., 1889. C 14 S 1
Life of Henry David Thoreau. 8vo. Lond., 1890.
C 14 T 16
Percy Bysshe Shelley : a Monograph. 12mo. Lond.,
1888. C 2 R 23

SALUSBURY, F. H. The Bankruptcy Acts, 1887-88,
with the rules and forms thereunder, and the Bills of Sale
Act, with Notes. 8vo. Sydney, 1891. MF 3 T 38

SAMOA. Correspondence respecting the affairs of. Fol.
Lond., 1889. MF 1 P 38 †

SAMUELSON, James Beer, Scientifically and Socially
Considered. 8vo. Lond., 1870. F 11 Q 52
History of Drink. 2nd ed. 8vo. Lond., 1880. F 11 Q 68.
Bulgaria, Past and Present, Historical, Political, and
Descriptive. 8vo. Lond., 1888. B 34 T 13

SANCHEZ or SANCTIUS, Francisco. Minerva seu de
Causis Linguæ Latinæ Commentarius. Ed 4ª. 8vo.
Amstelædami, 1714. K 12 U 21

SAND, G. [*See* Dudevant, Mme.]

SANDARS, T. C. [*See* Justinian.]

SANDERS, William Basevi. Facsimiles of Anglo-Saxon Manuscripts. Photozincographed by Lieut.-Gen. J. Cameron, R.E., Col. A. C. Cooke, C.B., R.E., [and] Col. R. H. Stotherd, R.E., [edited] with translations by W. Basevi Sanders. 3 vols. fol. Southampton, 1878–84.
B 8 Q 6–8 ‡

SANDERS, L. C. Celebrities of the Century : being a Dictionary of Men and Women of the 19th Century ; edited by L. C. Sanders. Roy. 8vo. Lond., 1887.
C 12 U 17

Life of Viscount Palmerston. (Statesmen Series.) 8vo. Lond., 1888. C 12 Q 38

SANDERSON, J. The American in Paris. 2 vols. 8vo. Lond., 1838. D 8 P 22, 23

SANDERSON, Prof. J. Burdon-. Translations of Foreign Biological Memoirs—Memoirs on the Physiology of Nerve, of Muscle, and of the Electrical Organ. Roy. 8vo. Oxford, 1887. A 26 U 3

SANDMANN, Paul. Eine Experimentalstudie über die Wirkung des Alkohol und Aether auf die Circulation. 8vo. Greifswald, 1874. F 11 Q 17

SANDS, J. Sands's Commercial and General Sydney Directory for 1861. 8vo. Sydney, 1864. ME 10 P

Sands's Sydney and Suburban Directory, 1888–92. 5 vols. 8vo. Sydney, 1888–92. ME 10 P–R

Country Directory and Gazetteer of New South Wales, 1889–90. 8vo. Sydney, 1889. ME 10 P

New Atlas of Australia. Roy. fol. Sydney, 1886. MD 5 S 1†

SANDS AND KENNY. Melbourne Directory for 1857 and 1861. 2 vols. 8vo. Melb., 1857–61. ME 11 P–R

SANDS, J., and MACDOUGALL, D. Melbourne and Suburban Directory, 1889. 8vo. Melb., 1889.
ME 11 P–R

Melbourne Directory for 1891. 8vo. Melb., 1891.
ME 11 P–R

Railway Map of Melbourne and Suburbs. [Folded.] Sm. 4to. Melb. (n.d.) MD 7 R 33

South Australian Directory, 1891. 8vo. Adelaide, 1891.
ME 12 T

SANDYS, J. E. An Easter Vacation in Greece ; with Lists of Books on Greek Travel and Topography. 8vo. Lond., 1887. D 19 Q 7

[*See* Seyffert, Dr. O.]

SANDWITH, Dr. Humphrey. Two Lectures on the defective arrangements in large towns to secure the Health and Comfort of their inhabitants. (Pamphlets.) 8vo. Lond., 1843. G 15 R 27

SANITARY ENGINEER, The. [*See* Engineering and Building Record.]

SANSONE, A. Printing of Cotton Fabrics, comprising Calico-Bleaching, Printing, and Dyeing. 8vo. Manchester, 1887. A 11 R 24

SANTAREM, Vicomte de. Essai sur L'Histoire de la Cosmographie et la Cartographie pendant le Moyen-Age. 3 vols. 8vo. Paris, 1849–52. B 35 S 7–9

SANTINI, E. Bêtes et Plantes. 8vo. Paris, 1888.
A 27 T 37

SANVITORES, Ven. Pad. Diego Luigi di. Vita Predicatione, e morte gloriosa per Christo. [*See* Garzia, Francesco.]

SAPPHO. Memoir, Text, Selected Renderings, and a Literal Translation; by H. T. Wharton. 12mo. Lond., 1887. H 6 Q 39

SARGANT, W. L. Inductive Political Economy. Vol. 1. 8vo. Lond., 1887. F 7 Q 34

SARRAZIN, T. Code Pratique des prud 'hommes. 5e éd. 18mo. Paris, 1890. F 14 P 34

SARGANT, E. B., and WHISHAW, B. Guide Book to Books. Roy. 8vo. Lond., 1891. K 8 Q 39

SARGENT, C. S. The Silva of North America. Vols. 1–4. 4to. Boston and New York, 1891–92.
A 40 S 18–21 ‡

SARS, G. O. Additional Notes on Australian Cladocera raised from dried mud. Roy. 8vo. Christiania, 1888.
MA 3 R 29

SATOW, E. M. The Jesuit Mission Press in Japan, 1591–1610. 4to. Lond., 1888. K 12 T 22 †

SATURDAY REVIEW. Vols. 62–73. Fol. Lond., 1886–92. E 2. 76

SAUER, C. M. Italian Conversation-Grammar. 5th edition. 8vo. Lond., 1886. K 12 U 33

SAUNDERS, F. The Story of Some Famous Books. 12mo. Lond., 1887. J 1 S 49

SAUNDERS, W. H. B. Legends and Traditions of Huntingdonshire. 8vo. Lond., 1888. B 6 R 33

SAUNIER, C. The Watchmaker's Hand-book; translated and enlarged by J. Tripplin and E. Rigg. 2nd ed. 12mo. Lond., 1888. A 11 P 16

SAVIGNY, F. C. de. Nouveaux éloges historiques. [*See* Mignet, F. A. M.]

SAVONAROLA, Girolamo. Life and Times of ; by Prof. P. Villari. 2 vols. 8vo. Lond., 1888. C 8 Q 17, 18

SAWYER, Arthur Robert. Mining, Geological, and General Guide to the Murchison Range. 8vo. Manchester, 1892. A 24 U 12

SAY, L. Turgot. (Great French Writers.) 8vo. Lond., 1888. C 14 U 1

SAYCE, Prof. A. H. Assyria, its Princes, Priests, and People. 12mo. Lond., 1891. B 28 Q 2

Fresh Lights from the Ancient Monuments. 5th edition. 12mo. Lond., 1890. B 28 Q 1

The Hibbert Lectures : Lectures on the Origin and Growth of Religion, as illustrated by the Religion of the Ancient Babylonians. 8vo. Lond., 1887. G 4 R 40

Introduction to the Books of Ezra, Nehemiah, and Esther. 3rd edition. 12mo. Lond., 1889. G 16 P 51

SAYCE, Prof. A. H.—*contd.*
Life and Times of Isaiah. (By-paths of Bible Knowledge.)
2nd edition. 12mo. Lond., 1890. G 16 Q 46
The Races of the Old Testament. 12mo. Lond., 1891.
A 8 R 37
[*See* Records of the Past.]

SAYCE, G. C. Twelve Times Round the World. 12mo.
Bristol (n.d.) D 20 Q 8

SAYLE, C. [*See* Wiclif, J.]

SCACCHI, Fortunato. Sacrorum Elæochrismaton My-
rothecia Tria, in quibus exponuntur Olea atque Unguenta
divinos in codices relata. Fol. Amst., 1701. G 44 P 10 ‡

SCARGILL-BIRD, S. R. [*See* Bird, S. R.Scargill.]

SCARLETT, Hon. P. C. South America and the Pacific.
2 vols. 8vo. Lond., 1838. D 15 R 7, 8

SCEPEAUX, François de Sire de Vicilloville. A Gentleman of the Olden Time; by C. Coignet. 2 vols. Lond.,
1887. C 3 S 21, 22

SCEUSA, F. Hail Australia! Morituri te Salutant.
12mo. Sydney, 1888. MF 2 P 72

SCHAEFER, G. H. [*See* Demosthenes.]

SCHÄFER, Prof. E. A. The Essentials of Histology,
Descriptive and Practical. 2nd ed. 8vo. Lond.,
1887. A 26 S 1

SCHAFF, Dr. P. Literature and Poetry: Studies on the
English Language, the Poetry of the Bible, the Dies Iræ,
the Stabat Mater, the Hymns of St. Bernard, the University (ancient and modern), Dante Alighieri, the Divina
Commedia. 8vo. Lond., 1890. G 4 S 38

SCHÄFFLE, Dr. A. Impossiblity of Social Democracy.
12mo. Lond., 1892. F 9 U 24
Quintessence of Socialism. 8vo. Lond., 1889. F 6 R 34
Another copy. 3rd ed. 8vo. Lond., 1891. F 14 P 16

SCHAUENBERG, Agnes. [*See* Locher, C.]

SCHEDEL, J. C. Praktisches Taschenworterbuch der
Waarenkunde. 8vo. Leipzig, 1798. K 16 P 39

SCHEEL, L. V. Brændevinsbrændingen i Danmark. 8vo.
Köbenhavn, 1877. F 11 R 50

SCHELLER, I. J. G. Lexicon Totius Latinitatis: a Dictionary of the Latin Language; translated by J. E.
Riddle. Fol. Oxford, 1835. K 6 R 6 †

SCHERER, E. La Démocratie et la France. 2e édition.
8vo. Paris, 1884. F 14 S 34
Diderot: étude. 12mo. Paris, 1880. G 2 V 22
Essays on English Literature; translated by G. Saintsbury.
12mo. Lond., 1891. J 11 W 18
Études sur la Littérature au 18e Siécle. 12mo. Paris, 1891.
B 34 P 14
Études sur la Littérature contemporaire. 9 vols. 12mo.
Paris, 1885–89. J 18 P 42–50

SCHERER, E.—*contd.*
Mélanges d' Histoire religieuse. 12mo. Paris, 1865.
G 2 V 23
Melchior Grimm. 8vo. Paris, 1887. C 13 S 26
La Révision de la Constitution. 8vo. Paris, 1882.
F 14 S 33

SCHERER, W. Vorträge und Aufsätze. 8vo. Berlin,
1874. B 37 S 1

SCHEWIAKOFF, W. Beitrage zur Kenntnis des Acal-
ephenauges 8vo. (n.p. n.d.) A 27 V 19

SCHILLER, Johann Christoph Frederick von. Sämmtliche
Schriften. 15 vols. roy. 8vo. Stuttgart, 1867–76.
J 13 V 1–15
Sämmtliche Werke. 2 vols. (in 1). imp. 8vo. Paris,
1836–37. J 15 V 7

SCHINCK, J. Lydgate's Temple of Glass. [*See* Early
Eng. Text Soc.]

SCHLEGEL, Caroline, and her Friends; by Mrs. Alfred
Sidgwick. 8vo. Lond., 1889. C 12 R 16

SCHLEGEL, F. Lectures on the History of Literature,
Ancient and Modern. 2 vols. 8vo. Edinb., 1818.
B 36 T 8, 9

SCHLEICHER, A. Compendium of the Comparative
Grammar of the Indo-European, Sanskrit, Greek, and
Latin Languages. 2 vols. 8vo. Lond., 1874–77.
K 16 Q 20, 21

SCHLEIDEN, Dr. J. M. Principles of Scientific Botany,
translated by E. Lankester. 8vo. Lond., 1849. A 20 S 1

SCHLEUSNER, J. F. Novum Lexicon Græco-Latinum
in Novum Testamentum. 2 vols. 8vo. Edinb., 1814.
K 12 U 30, 31

SCHLEYER, J. M. [*See* Scrot, W. A.]

SCHLICH, Prof. William. Manual of Forestry. Vols. 1
and 2. 8vo. Lond., 1889–91. A 18 T 15, 16

SCHLOETEL, J. H. De ratione qua potus spirituosi in
organismum agant. 8vo. Halæ, 1821. F 11 R 53

SCHMIDT, Dr. A. Die Ausscheidung des Weingeistes
durch die Respiration. Roy. 8vo. Berlin, 1875.
F 11 T 8
Ueber die angebliche Ausscheidung des Weingeistes durch
die Lungen. Roy. 8vo. Bonn, 1876. F 11 T 9
De Spirituosorum Usu atque Abusu. 8vo. Berolini, 1863.
F 11 Q 47

SCHMIDT, Julius. De Specificu, quæ abusu potuum spirituosorum exoritur morbosa dispositione ejusque in morbos
febriles effectu. 8vo. Berolini, 1841. F 11 Q 46

SCHMIDT, Prof. O. Die Säugethiere in ihrem Verhältniss
zur Vorwelt. 8vo. Leip., 1884. A 14 Q 27

SCHMIDT, P. Den lille Brændevinshader. 18mo. Viborg,
1879. F 11 P 2

SCHMIDT, P. A. O. De Spirituosorum Abusu. 8vo.
Berolini, 1865. F 11 Q 45

SCHMIDT, Prof. P. W., and HOLZENDORFF, Prof. F. von. Short Protestant Commentary on the New Testament; translated from the German by F. H. Jones. 3 vols. 8vo. Lond., 1882–84.   G 4 U 9-11

SCHMIDT, U. Voyage to La Plata and Paraguai. [*See* Hakulyt Soc.*]

SCHMIDT, WILLIAM. The Flowing Bowl, when and what to drink; by "The only William." 8vo. New York, 1892.   A 22 R 3

SCHMIEDEBERG, Dr. O. Elements of Pharmacology. 8vo. Edinb., 1887.   A 26 T 4

SCHMITZ, A. Beiträge zur diätetischen Beurtheilung des gallisirten Weines. 8vo. Köln, 1878.   F 11 S 37

SCHMITZ, L. Dora. [*See* Shakespeare, W.]

SCHMUCKER, S. M. Life and Times of Louis Napoleon. 8vo. Philad., 1890.   C 14 R 27

SCHNABEL, C. Report on the Treatment of the Sulphides of the Barrier Ranges. Sm. 4to. Melb., 1892.   MA 2 R 43

SCHNEIDER, Dr. Die Medicinisch Polizeiliche. Untersuchung und Prüfung der Biere Deutschlands. 8vo. Erlangen, 1846.   F 11 Q 50

SCHNEIDER, J. G. [*See* Theophrastus.]

SCHNITZER, Dr. E., "Emin Pasha." Emin Pasha in Central Africa; being a Collection of his Letters and Journals. 8vo. Lond., 1888.   D 14 U 7
[*See* Jephson, A.J.M.—]

SCHOCH, G. A. Manual of Instructions for Raising Mulberry Trees and Silkworms. 8vo. Wellington, 1886.*   MA 1 Q 47

SCHOENHOF, J. Industrial Situation and the Question of Wages. 8vo. New York, 1885.   F 14 Q 2

SCHOETENSACK, H. A. Beitrag für etymologische Untersuchungen auf dem Gebiete der französischen Sprache. 8vo. Bonn, 1883.   K 13 S 34

SCHOLEFIELD, J. [*See* Æschylus, and Euripides.]

SCHOLES, S. E. Fiji and the Friendly Isles; Sketches of their Scenery and People. Sq. 18mo. Lond. (n.d.)   MD 2 W 43
Fiji and the Friendly Isles: Sketches of their Scenery and People. 18mo. Lond., 1882   MD 1 P 18

SCHOLL, C. Phraseological Dictionary of Commercial Correspondence in English, German, French, and Spanish Languages. 2nd ed. Roy. 8vo. Liverpool, 1891.   K 9 S 13

SCHOLTZ, F. De Ebriositate. 8vo. Gryphiæ, 1824.   F 11 Q 20

SCHOLZ, Dr. I. M. A. Novum Testamentum Græce. [*See* Bibles, &c.—Greek.]

SCHOMBURGK, Dr. Richard. On the Vegetable Fragments found in the Tombs and other monumental buildings of the Ancient Egyptians. 8vo. Adelaide, 1878.   MA 3 T 37
Catalogue of the Plants under Cultivation in the Government Botanic Garden, Adelaide, South Australia. 8vo. Adelaide, 1878.   MA 1 T 42

SCHÖNER, J. Reproduction of his Globe of 1523; with Translations, and Notes on the Globe, by H. Stevens. 8vo. Lond., 1888.   D 11 R 19

SCHOOLMASTER'S CALENDAR and Handbook of Examinations and Open Scholarships, 1889. 12mo. Lond., 1889.   E 1. 78

SCHOPENHAUER, A. Art of Literature : a series of essays. 8vo. Lond., 1891.   J 1 U 24
Selected Essays of ; with a biographical introduction by E. B. Bax. 12mo. Lond., 1891.   G 16 Q 42
Two Essays. 1. On the fourfold root of the Principle of sufficient Reason. 2. On the Will in Nature. 8vo. Lond., 1889.   G 16 Q 23

SCHORLEMMER, C. Treatise on Chemistry. [*See* Roscoe, Sir H. E.]

SCHOSULAN, J. M. Dissertatio de Vinis. 8vo. Viennæ, 1767.   F 11 Q 43

SCHOUTEN, Gautier. Voiage aux Indes Orientales, 1658–65. 2 vols. 12mo. Amsterdam, 1707.   D 20 P 5, 6

SCHOUTEN, Willem Cornelisz. Diarium vel Descriptio laboriosissimi et molestissimi Itineris, facti à Guilielmo Cornelii Schoutenio, Hornano, 1615–17. 8vo. Amsterdam, 1619.   MD 7 T 46
Journael of te Beschrijvinge van de wonderlijcke Reyse, 1615–17. [*See* Spilbergen, G. de.]
Journael of te Beschrijvinghe van de Wonderlijcke Reyse, 1615-17. 8vo. Hoorn, 1648.   MD 8 Q 9
Journal ou Description du Merveilleux Voyage de. Sm. 4to. Amsterdam, 1619.   MD 1 W 10

SCHRADER, Dr. E. Cuneiform Inscriptions and the Old Testament; translated from the German by Rev. O. E. Whitehouse. 2 vols. 8vo. Lond., 1885–88.   G 4 U 14, 15

SCHRADER, Dr. O. Prehistoric Antiquities of the Aryan Peoples. 8vo. Lond., 1890.   B 36 T 7

SCHREINER, Miss Olive. "Ralph Iron." The Story of an African Farm. 12mo. Lond., 1890.   J 5 P 7

SCHREVEL, C. Lexicon Manuale Græco-Latinum et Latino-Græcum. 8vo. Lond., 1831.   K 12 V 19
[*See* Lucanus, M.A., and Martialis, M. V.]

SCHRÖTER, Dr. C. [*See* Stebler, Dr. F. G.]

SCHUBERT, F. [Life of ;] by A. B. Bach. Sm. 4to. Edinb., 1890.   C 14 R 32

SCHUETZ, W. De Vino. 12mo. Berolini, 1829.   F 11 P 61

SCHULD, J. F. Strafbepalingen tegen Dronkenschap. 8vo. Gorinchem, 1870.   F 11 Q 38

SCHULER, Dr. Zur Alkoholfrage: die Ernährungsweise der arbeitenden Klassen in der Schweiz, &c. 8vo. Bern, 1884.   F 11 R 54

SCHULZE, Dr. E. [*See* Lunge, Dr. G.]

SCHUMACHER, G. Northern 'Ajlûn, "Within the Decapolis." (Palestine Exploration Fund.) 8vo. Lond., 1890.   D 17 R 13

Pella. (Palestine Exploration Fund.) 8vo. Lond., 1888.   D 17 S 5

The Jaulân; surveyed for the German Society for the Exploration of the Holy Land. 8vo. Lond., 1889.   D 17 R 6

SCHUMANN, Robert. Early Letters of, originally published by his wife; translated by May Herbert. 12mo. Lond., 1888.   C 12 P 9

Life of, told in his Letters; translated by May Herbert. 2 vols. 12mo. Lond., 1890.   C 12 P 10, 11

SCHURMAN, J. G. The Ethical Import of Darwinism. 8vo. Lond., 1888.   G 8 Q 34

SCHÜRMANN, C. W. [*See* Teichelmann, C. G.]

SCHURZ, C. Life of Henry Clay. (American Statesmen.) 2 vols. 12mo. Boston, 1887.   C 12 P 48, 49

SCHUSTER, Dr. J. Koe Gaohi Talanoa Meiho Tohi Tapu, Kihe Mama Motua, Moe Tuakava Foou, Ihe Lea Fakatoga. [Biblical History, translated into the language of Tonga, by P. Chevron.] 8vo. Fribourg, 1876.   MG 2 R 11

O Tala Filifilia nui Tusi paia mai le feagaiga tuai ma le feagaiga fou. [Biblical History in the Language of Samoa.] 8vo. Fribourg, 1875.   M G 2 R 17

SCHUURMAN, L. N., and JORDENS, P. H. Wet van den 28 Junij, 1881, houdende Wettelijke Bepalingen tot Regeling van den Kleinhandel in Sterken Drank. 8vo. Zwolle, 1885.   F 11 Q 18

SCHWARZBACH, Dr. B. The Eye and its Care. 8vo. Sydney, 1878.   MA 3 Q 21

SCHWEGLER, A. [*See* Eusebius.]

SCHWEIGÆUSER, J. Lexicon Herodoteum. 8vo. Oxonii, 1840.   K 16 T 23

[*See* Epictetus.]

SCHWENDENER, Prof. S. [*See* Naegeli, Prof. C.]

SCIENCE GOSSIP [*See* Hardwicke's Science Gossip.]

SCIENTIFIC AMERICAN. Vols. 55-66. Fol. New York, 1886-91.   E 1. 100

Scientific American Supplement. Vols. 22-33. Fol. New York, 1886-92.   E 1. 100

Scientific American Architects and Builders Edition. Vols. 1-12. Fol. New York, 1885-91.   E 1. 99

Scientific American Cyclopedia of Receipts. [*See* Hopkins, A. A.]

2 C

SCIENTIFIC EDUCATION OF DOGS FOR THE GUN; by H.H. 8vo. Lond., 1890.   A 29 Q 15

SCIENTIFIC JOURNAL MINING MANUAL. 8vo. Lond., 1888.   E 1. 56

SCLATER, P. L., and HUDSON, W. H. Argentine Ornithology; a Descriptive Catalogue of the Birds of the Argentine Republic. 2 vols. Roy. 8vo. Lond., 1888-89.   A 27 V 20, 21

SCOTCH COLLEGE, Melbourne, Annual Report and Honour List, 1874; Prospectus, 1875. 8vo. Lond., 1874.   ME 6 Q

SCOTLAND, Historians of. Vols. 1-10. 8vo. Edinb., 1871-80.   B 13 P 45-54

Records of the Convention of the Royal Burghs of Scotland, 1295-1738. 5 vols. 4to. Edinb., 1866-85.   B 32 V 1-5

Compota Thesaurariorum Regum Scotorum: Accounts of the Lord High Treasurer of Scotland, edited by T. Dickson. Vol. 1. Roy. 8vo. Edinb., 1877.   B 32 U 1

Records of the Convention of the Royal Burghs, 1295-1738. 5 vols. roy. 8vo. Edinb., 1866-85.   B 32 V 1-5

Rotuli Scaccarii Regum Scotorum: The Exchequer Rolls of Scotland, edited by J. Stuart and G. Burnett. 1264-1513. 13 vols. Roy. 8vo. Edinb., 1878-91.   B 33 T 1-U 1

SCOTT, A. W. Australian Lepidoptera with their Transformations. Vol. 2. Parts 1 and 2. 4to. Sydney, 1890-91.   MA 1 R 8 †

SCOTT, Clement. Blossom-Land and Fallen Leaves. 8vo. Lond., 1890.   D 18 R 5

SCOTT, D. H. [*See* Huxley, Prof. T. H.]

SCOTT, E. G. Development of Constitutional Liberty in the English Colonies of America. 8vo. New York, 1890.   F 4 S 31

SCOTT, H. Fasti Ecclesiæ Scoticanæ: Succession of Ministers in the Parish Churches of Scotland. 3 vols. (in 6) 4to. Edinb., 1866-71.   G 4 R 22-27 †

SCOTT, H. W. Distinguished American Lawyers. 8vo. New York, 1891.   C 17 S 3

SCOTT, John. Berwick-upon-Tweed: the History of the Town and Guild. 4to. Lond., 1888.   B 9 R 7

SCOTT, John and C. Blackfaced Sheep: their History, Distribution, and Management. 8vo. Edinb., 1888.   A 1 U 14

SCOTT, Leader. [*See* Baxter, Mrs. Lucy E.]

SCOTT, T. A. Chowbokiana; or Notes about the Antipodes and the Antipodeans. Roy. 8vo. Bombay, 1875.   MD 7 R 32

SCOTT, Sir Walter. Journal of, from the original manuscript at Abbotsford. 2 vols. 8mo. Lond., 1890.   C 15 U 17, 18

[*See* British Drama, Ancient, Dryden, J., Grammont, Count, an *l* Knight, W.]

SCOTT, Wm. Glance at the Historical Documents relating to the Church of Saint Mark in Venice. 4to. Venice, 1887.   B 30 V 6

[*See* Boito, Prof. C.]

SCOTTISH HISTORY SOCIETY. Publications. Vols. 1–11. 8vo. Edinb., 1887–92.   E 1. 63
1. Tours in Scotland, 1747–60 ; by Rt. Rev. R. Pococke.
2. Diary and General Expenditure Book of Wm. Cunningham of Craigends, 1670–80.
3. The Grameid ; an heroic poem, by J. Philip.
4, 7. Register of Minister Elders, &c., of St. Andrews, 1559–1600. Edited by D. H. Fleming.
5. Diary of Rev. John Mill.
6. Narrative of Jas. Nimmo, 1654–1709.
8. List of Persons concerned in the Rebellion [of 1745]
9. Book of Record ; a Diary, by Patrick, First Earl of Strathmore.
10. History of Greater Britain ; by John Major.
11. Records of the Commissions of the General Assemblies of the Church of Scotland, 1646–47.

SCOTTISH REVIEW. Vols. 8–14. 8vo. Lond., 1886–89.   E 1. 63

SCOTTISH TEXT SOCIETY. Publications. 9 vols. 8vo. Edinb., 1888–92.   E 1. 63
Poems of Alexander Montgomery. The Richt Vay to the Kingdom of Heuine ; by J. Gau.
Actis and Deidis of Schir William Wallace.
Poems of William Dunbar.
Historic of Scotland ; by J. Leslie.
Certain Tractates and Translation of Vincentius Lirinensis, by N. Winzet. Vols. 1 and 2.
Satirical Poems of the Reformation. Vol. 1. Edited by J. Cranstoun.
Vernacular Writings of Geo. Buchanan ; edited by R. H. Brown.

SCOVILLE, Rev. S. [*See* Beecher, Rev. H. W.]

SCRATCHLEY, A. Practical Treatise on Building Societies and Average Investment "Trusts." 7th edition. 8vo. Lond., 1891.   F 9 S 25

SCRATCHLEY, Maj.-Gen. Sir P. H. Australian Defences and New Guinea; compiled by C. H. Cooke. 8vo. Lond., 1887.   MF 1 R 9
Defences of New Zealand : Memorandum on Defence Organization. 8vo. Wellington, 1881.*   MF 3 Q 60

SCRIBE, E. Œuvres Complètes. 10 vols. 12mo. Paris, 1874–82.   J 16 P 43–52

SCRIPTORES REI RUSTICÆ VETERES LATINI, et Lexicon, e recensione J. M. Gesneri. 4 vols. 8vo. Biponti, 1787–88.   A 18 S 7–10

SCRIVENER, F. H. A. [*See* Coadda, St.]

SCRUTTON, T. E. Law of Copyright. 2nd edition. 8vo. Lond., 1890.   F 6 U 32

SEACOLE, Mrs. Wonderful Adventures of, in many Lands, edited by W. J. Seacole. 12mo. Lond., 1857.   C 13 P 7

SEARCY, A. The Custom House Handbook ; being the Merchants' and Importers' Guide to the Business of the Customs Department. 8vo. Adelaide, 1883.   MF 3 T 10

SEBASTIAN, L. B. Law of Trade Marks and their Registration. 8vo. Lond., 1890.   F 9 S 1

SEBERUS, W. Index Vocabulorum in Homeri Iliade atque Odyssea cæterisque quotquot extant Poematis 8vo. Oxonii, 1780.   K 17 R 28

SEDGEFIELD, S. W. Notes on the Practice of the Office of Titles of Victoria. 8vo. Melb., 1879. ·   MF 3 T 37

SEDGWICK, Prof. Adam. Life and Letters of ; by J. W. Clark and Prof. T. M. Hughes. 2 vols.   C 14 U 2, 3

SEEBOHM, F. The Era of the Protestant Revolution. 18mo. Lond., 1887.   G 9 P 50

SEEBOHM, H. The Birds of the Japanese Empire. Imp. 8vo. Lond., 1890.   A 15 R 9
Geographical Distribution of the Family Charadriidæ or the Plovers, Sandpipers, Snipes, and their Allies. 4to. Lond., 1888.   A 42 R 11 ‡

SEELEY, H. G. Geology. [*See* Phillips, J.]

SEELEY, L. B. [*See* Burney, Fanny.]

SEFFERN, W. H. J. Taranaki Almanac and Directory, 1872. New Plymouth, 1872.   ME 4 Q

SÉGUIN, L. G. Walks in Algiers and its Surroundings. 8vo. Lond., 1888.   D 14 Q 1

SEGUR, Gén. Phillipe, Comte de. Histoire de Napoleon et de la Grand Armée, Pendant ·l'année, 1812. 16o éd. 2 vols. (in 1). 8vo. Paris, 1852.   C 18 Q 2

SEISMOLOGICAL SOCIETY OF JAPAN. Transactions. Vols. 6–15.· 8vo. Yokohama, 1883–91.   E 1. 63

SELLAR, W. Y. Roman Poets of the Augustan Age. 8vo. Oxford, 1892.   C 18 Q 10

SELBORNE, Roundell, Earl of. Ancient Facts and Fictions concerning Churches and Tithes. 8vo. Lond., 1888,   G 8 Q 27

SELWAY, G. U. A Mid-Lothian Village : Notes on the Village and Parish of Corstorphine. 4to. Edinb., 1890.   B 13 S 20

SELWYN, A. R. C. North America. [*See* Hayden, F. V.]

SELWYN, Rt. Rev. G. A. Memoir of the Life and Episcopate of ; by the Rev. H. W. Tucker. 2 vols. 8vo. Lond., 1879.   MC 1 R 55, 56
Another copy. 2 vols. 8vo. Lond., 1879. MC 1 R 39, 40
New Zealand : Letters from the Bishop to the Society for the Propagation of the Gospel, together with Extracts from his Visitation Journal. 12mo. Lond., 1847–51.   MD 2 W 25
Sketch of his Life and Work with some further Gleanings from his Letters, Sermons, and Speeches. 8vo. Lond., 1889.   MC 1 Q 52

SEMMES, Adm. R. Service Afloat; or, the Remarkable Career of the Confederate Cruisers *Sumter* and *Alabama* during the War between the States. Roy. 8vo. Lond., 1887.   B 1 V 15

SEMPER, Dr. C. Reisen im Archipel der Philippinen Wissenschaftliche Resultat. Zweiter Band, Heft XV–XVIII; und Supplement, Heft II–IV [und] Fünfte Band, 1o Abtheilung. 2 vols. Roy. 4to. Wiesbaden, 1881–92.   A 9 Q †

SEMPILL, Francis. Australian Etiquette, or the Rules and Usages of the Best Society in the Australasian Colonies. Sydney, 1885.   MJ 2 S 50

Golden Sovereigns for Squatters, Graziers, Free Selectors, Farmers, &c. 8vo. Maitland, 1882.   MF 3 Q 24

SENANCOUR, Etienne Pivert de. Obermann. Nouvelle édition, revue et corrigée. 8vo. Paris, 1882.   J 11 S 2

SENECA, L. A. Opera Philosophica; illustravit N. Bouillet. 5 vols. (in 6). 8vo. Parisiis, 1827–32.   G 3 Q 31–36

Opera Tragica; illustravit J. Pierrot. 3 vols. 8vo. Parisiis, 1829–32.   G 3 Q 37–39

Opera Declamatoria; illustravit N. Bouillet. 8vo. Parisiis, 1831.   G 3 Q 40

Opera. 8vo. Biponti, 1783.   G 16 S 50

Minor Dialogues, together with the Dialogue on Clemency, trans. by A. Stewart. 12vo. Lond., 1889.   G 16 Q 24

Œuvres Complètes. [See Nisard, D.]

Tragœdiæ. 18mo. Lond., 1823.   H 2 P 49

On Benefits; addressed to Æbutins Liberalis; translated by A. Stewart. 12mo. Lond., 1887.   G 16 Q 2

SENIOR, Wm. "Red Spinner." Near and Far: an Angler's Sketches of Home Sport and Colonial Life. 12mo. Lond., 1888.   D 20 Q 5

Another copy. 12 mo. Lond., 1890   MD 2 W 13

The Thames from Oxford to London. Imp. 8vo. Lond., 1891.   D 19 V 6

SERBATI, A. R.- [See Rosmini-Serbati, A.]

SERET, W. A. Grammar, with Vocabularies, of Volapük; translated and published with the consent of the Inventor, J. M. Schleyer. 8vo. Glasgow, 1887.   K 12 Q 45

SERLE, A. Horæ Solitariæ: or, Essays on some Remarkable Names and Titles of Jesus Christ. New edition. 2 vols. 12mo. Dublin, 1836.   G 16 Q 27

SERRANO, Mary J. [See Bashkirtseff, M.]

SERVICE, Dr. J. Thir Notandums, being the Literary Recreations of Laird Canticarl of Mongrynen, to which is appended a Biographical Sketch of James Dunlop. 8vo. Edinb., 1890.   MC 1 Q 48

SETH, Prof. A. Hegelianism and Personality. 12mo. Lond., 1887.   G 19 P 3

SETON-KARR, W. S. The Marquis Cornwallis. (Rulers of India.) 8vo. Oxford, 1890.   C 17 Q 9

SÈVE, Edouard. Le Chili tel qu'il est. Tome I. 8vo. Valparaiso, 1876.   F 12 R 29

SEVERN, J. Life and Letters of; by W. Sharp. 8vo. Lond., 1892.   C 18 R 6

SÉVIGNÉ, Marie de Rabutin Chantal, Marquise de. [Life of]; by G. Boissier. (Great French Writers.) 8vo. Lond., 1887.   C 9 U 19

Lettres Choisies; précédées d'une notice par C. A. Sainte-Beuve. 8vo. Paris, 1886.   C 18 S 23

SEWELL, E. M. Principles of Education. 2 vols. 12mo. Lond., 1865.   G 17 P 45, 46

SEXTUS EMPIRICUS. [Opera] ex recensione I. Bekkeri. 8vo. Berolini, 1842.   G 16 S 43

SEYFFERT, Dr. O. Dictionary of Classical Antiquities, Mythology, Religion, Literature, and Art. Edited by Prof. H. Nettleship and J. E. Sandys. 4to. Lond., 1891.   K 7 Q 14

SEYBERT, H. [See Spiritualism.]

SEYMOUR, Commodore F. B. Report upon Experiments made with Australian Coal at Sydney, July, 1862. Fol. Lond., 1863.   MA 12 P 20 †

SEYMOUR, H. D. Egypt. [See Brugsch, H.]

SEYMOUR, W. D. Home Rule and State Supremacy; or, Nationality reconciled with Empire. 8vo. Lond., 1888.   F 6 S 33

SHAIRP, Principal John Campbell. Principal Shairp, and his Friends; by Prof. W. Knight. 8vo. Lond., 1888.   C 9 T 48

Sketches in History and Poetry. 8vo. Edinb., 1887.   B 31 Q 13

SHAKESPEARE, William. The Bankside Shakespeare. Edited by A. Morgan. Vols. 1–17. 8vo. New York, 1888–92.   H 9 R 1–17

1. The Merry Wives of Windsor.	8. Midsummer Night's Dream.
2. The Taming of the Shrew.	9. Othello.
3. The Merchant of Venice.	10. King Lear.
4. Troilus and Cressida.	11. Hamlet.
5. The Tragedie of Romeo and Juliet.	12, 13. Henry IV.
	14. Pericles, Prince of Tyre.
6. Much ado about Nothing.	15. Richard III.
7. Titus Andronicus.	16. Henry V.
	17. Richard II.

Complete Concordance to. [See Clarke, Mrs. Mary Victoria Cowden.]

Comedies, Histories, Tragedies, and Poems of. Edited by C. Knight. 6 vols. 8vo. Lond., 1851.   H 3 T 14–19

Index to the Works of. [See O'Connor, Evangeline M.]

Julius Cæsar, Latine reddidit H. Denison. 8vo. Oxford, 1856.   H 9 S 1

Macbeth, Lines pronounced corrupt restored, &c.; with notes by M. Mull. 8vo. Lond., 1889.   H 2 R 39

New Variorum Edition of. Vols. 7 and 8. Roy. 8vo. Philad., 1888–90.   H 1 T 7, 8

     7. The Merchant of Venice.
     8. As You Like It.

Noctes Shaksperianæ: a series of Papers edited by Rev. C. H. Hawkins. 8vo. Winchester, 1887.   C 10 T 2

Our English Homes; or, Shakespeare Historically Considered. [See White, T. W.]

Plays of. With Life, &c., by A. Chalmers. 8 vols. 8vo. Lond., 1823.   H 9 S 9–16

SHAKESPEARE, WILLIAM—*contd.*

Secret Drama of Shakespeare's Sonnets. [*See* Massey, G.]

Shakespeare : a critical study of his Mind and Art ; by Prof. E. Dowden. 9th ed. 8vo. Lond., 1889.
     C 16 R 1

Shakespeare Manual ; by F. G. Fleay. 12mo. Lond., 1876.   H 7 U 39

Shakespeare's Sonnets ; edited by T. Tyler. 8vo. Lond., 1890.   H 5 T 37

Shakespeare's Face : a Monologue on the various Portraits of Shakespeare in comparison with the Death Mask in the Grand Ducal Museum at Darmstadt ; by A. H. Wall. Roy. 8vo. Stratford-upon-Avon, 1890.   J 4 U 6

True Life of ; by J. Walter. Imp. 8vo. Lond., 1890.
     C 36 S 14 ‡

William Shakespeare : a Literary Biography ; by Karl Elze ; translated by L. Dora Schmitz. 8vo. Lond., 1888.
     C 12 P 8

Works of. Edited by W. G. Clark and W. A. Wright. 12mo. Lond., 1874.   H 2 Q 44

Youth of Shakspere [by R. F. Williams]. 3 vols. 8vo. Lond., 1839.   C 13 R 16–18

[*See* Beaumont, W. ; Dawson, G. ; Donnelly, I. ; Mackay, C. ; Martin, Sir T. ; Morgan, A. ; Shakespeare Society, New ; New York Shakespeare Society ; *and* Williams, R. F.]

SHAKESPEARE, W., and FLETCHER, J. The Two Noble Kinsmen : a Tragedy. [*See* British Drama, Modern, 1.]

SHAKESPEARE SOCIETY, NEW. Publications. 3 vols. 8vo. Lond., 1886–90.   E

Robert Laneham's Letter, wherein, part of the entertainment untoo the Queen's Maiesty at Killingworth Castl, 1575, is signified, with Forewords describing all the accessible books in Capt. Cox's list, and the complaint of Scotland.
Allusion Books, 3 : Three hundred fresh Allusions to Shakspere in 1594–1693.
Transactions, 1880–86.

SHALER, Nathaniel Southgate. Kentucky, a pioneer commonwealth. (American Commonwealths.) 4th ed. 12mo. Boston, 1888.   B 17 P 9

SHAND, A. I. Half-a-Century ; or, Changes in Men and Manners. 8vo. Edinb., 1887.   J 3 V 21

SHARMAN, H. R. A Cloud of Witnesses against Grocers' Licenses. 8vo. Lond. (n.d.)   F 11 R 57

SHARMAN, J. The Library of Mary Queen of Scots. Sm. 4to. Lond., 1889.   K 7 R 46

SHARP, Abraham. Life and Correspondence of, with Memorials of his Family and Associated Families ; by W. Cudworth. Roy. 8vo. Lond., 1889.   C 12 U 2

SHARP, William. Life and Letters of Joseph Severn. 8vo. Lond., 1892.   C 18 R 5

SHARPE, Charles K. Letters from and to ; edited by A. Allardyce, with a Memoir by the Rev. W. K. R. Bedford. 2 vols. 8vo. Edinb., 1888.   C 12 T 24, 25

SHARPE, Edmund. Architectural Parallels ; or the Progress of Ecclesiastical Architecture in England, through the twelfth and thirteenth centuries. Fol. Lond., 1848.
     A 34 P 20 ‡

SHARPE, Dr. Reginald Robinson. Calendar of Wills in the Court of Husting, London, 1258–1688. Parts 1 & 2. Roy. 8vo. Lond., 1889–90.   F 3 V 1, 2

SHARPE, Samuel. The History of Egypt from the Earliest Times till the Conquest by the Arabs, A.D. 640. 4th edition. 2 vols. 8vo. Lond., 1859.   B 21 T 3, 4

SHAW, L. History of the Province of Moray ; enlarged by J. F. S. Gordon. 3 vols. 8vo. Glasgow, 1882.
     B 31 T 12–14

SHAW, W. A. Minutes of the Manchester Presbyterian Classis. [*See* Chetham Soc., n.s. 20, 22, 24.]

SHEARMAN, M. Athletics and Football ; with a Contribution on Paper-chasing, by W. Rye. 8vo. Lond., 1887.   A 17 U 35

SHEARMAN, Thomas G. [*See* Cobden Club.]

SHEDLOCK, J. S. Wagner's Letters. [*See* Wagner, R.]

SHEEN, J. R. Wines and other fermented liquors, from the earliest ages to the present time. 12mo. Lond., 1864.   F 11 P 17

SHELLEY, Mary Wollstonecraft. Life and letters of ; by Mrs. Julian Marshall. 2 vols. Lond., 1889.
     C 14 U 4, 5

[Life of] ; by Lucy M. Rossetti. 12mo. Lond., 1890.
     C 12 P 46

SHELLEY, Percy Bische : a Monograph ; by H. S. Salt. 12mo. Lond., 1888.   C 2 R 23

Adonais. Edited by W. M. Rossetti. 8vo. Oxford, 1891.
     H 8 Q 20

Concordance to Works of. [*See* Ellis, F. S.]

The Man and the Poet ; from the French of Felix Rabbe. 2 vols. 8vo. Lond., 1888.   C 12 Q 16, 17

Poetical Works of ; edited by R. H. Shepherd. 3 vols. 12mo. Lond., 1888.   H 5 S 44–46

1. Margaret Nicholson.—Correspondence with Stockdale.—The Wandering Jew.—Queen Mab.—Alastor ; or, the Spirit of Solitude. —Mont Blanc.—Lines to a Critic.—Rosalind and Helen.—Eugananea Hills.—Hymn to Intellectual Beauty.—Ozymandias.—Prometheus Unbound.—Miscellaneous Poems.—Adonais : an Elegy on the Death of John Keats.
2. Laon and Cynthia.—The Cenci.—Julian and Maddalo.—Swellfoot, the Tyrant.—To Mary.—The Witch of Atlas.—Epipsychidion.— Hellas.—Lines on hearing of the Death of Napoleon.
3. Posthumous Poems.—Translations.—Fragments.—National Anthem.—To the Lord Chancellor.—To his Son.—The Masque of Anarchy.—The Shelley Papers.—Peter Bell the Third.—England in 1819.—Otho.—To ——.—Song to the Men of England.—Song of Proserpine.—Fragments.—To Constantia.—To Night.—Fragment.—To ——.—To a Lady.—Hymns of Homer.—Epigrams.

Prose Works ; edited by R. H. Shepherd. 2 vols. 12mo. Lond., 1888.   J 1 W 44, 45

SHELTON, F. M. [*See* Agriculture, Dept. of, Queensland.]

SHEPARD, E. M. Martin van Buren. (American Statesmen.) 12mo. Boston, 1888.   C 13 Q 3

SHEPHERD, P. L. C., & Sons. Catalogue and Amateur's Guide for 1889 and 1890. Roy. 8vo. Sydney, 1889.
MA 1 U 44

SHEPHERD, R. H. The Bibliography of Swinburne : a Bibliographical List, arranged in chronological order, of the published writings in Verse and Prose of A. C. Swinburne (1857-87). 8vo. Lond., 1887. K 19 P 5
[*See* Shelley, P. B.]

SHEPPARD, Furman. Constitutional Text Book of the United States. 8vo. Philad., 1856. F 2 U 31

SHERARD, C. A. A Daughter of the South, and other Poems. 8vo. Lond., 1889. MH 1 U 18

SHERBROOKE, Rt. Hon. Robert Lowe, Viscount. Speeches and Letters on Reform. 2nd edition. 12mo. Lond., 1867. F 9 U 5

Poems of a Life. 2nd ed. 8vo. Lond., 1885. MH 1 R 7

SHERER, Major Moyle. Recollections of the Peninsula 8vo. Lond., 1827. B 19 T 13

SHERIDAN, J. B., and BAKEWELL, J. W. The Magistrates' Guide, containing the Ordinary Procedure, Jurisdiction, and Duties of Special Magistrates and Justices of the Peace ; also a Digest of Magisterial Law. 8vo. Adelaide, 1879. MF 1 R 72

SHERIDAN, Gen. Philip Henry. Personal Memoirs. 2 vols. 8vo. Lond., 1888. C 12 S 30, 31

SHERIDAN, Richard Brinsley. The Rivals : a Comedy. [*See* British Drama, Modern, 4.]

The Critic : a Farce. [*See* British Drama, Modern.]

SHERIDANS. Lives of the ; by P. Fitzgerald. 2 vols. 8vo. Lond., 1886. C 13 T 9, 10

SHERRIFF, John L., and DOWNING, Robert. Australasian Almanac for 1864. 8vo. Sydney, 1864. ME 4 R

The Gazetteer of New South Wales. 12mo. Sydney, 1866. MD 2 W 27

SHERRIN, R. A. A. Hand-book of the Fishes of New Zealand. 8vo. Auckland, 1886.* MA 2 U 21

SHERRIN, R. A. A., and WALLACE J. H. Early History of New Zealand ; edited by T. W. Leys. 4to. Auckland, 1890. MB 3 P 15†

SHERWIN, W. [*See* Bennett, G.]

SHIELDS, H., and MEIKLE, T. Famous Clyde Yachts, 1800-87. Fol. Glasgow, 1888. A 32 P 23‡

SHILLETO, Rev. Arthur Richard. [*See* Josephus, F., and Plutarch.]

SHILLIBEER, Lieut. J. Narrative of the Briton's Voyage to Pitcairn's Island. 8vo. Taunton, 1817.
MD 2 V 15

Another Copy. 3rd ed. 8vo. Lond., 1818.
MD 2 V 16

SHIPP, Lieut. John. Memoirs of the Extraordinary Career of ; edited by H. M. Chichester. 8vo. Lond., 1890. C 14 S 6

SHIRLEY, James. The Bird in a Cage : a Comedy. [*See* British Drama, Ancient, 1.]

The Gamester : a Comedy. [*See* British Drama, Ancient, 2.]

Andromana : a Tragedy. [*See* British Drama, Ancient, 3.]

Best Plays. (Mermaid Series ; edited by H. Ellis.) 8vo. Lond., 1888. H 4 Q 24

The Witty Fair One.—The Traitor.—Hyde Park.—The Lady of Pleasure.—The Cardinal.—The Triumph of Peace.

SHIRRIEFF, Miss Emily Anne E. Intellectual Education and its Influence on the Character and Happiness of Women. 8vo. Lond., 1858. G 17 P 49

SHOALBRED, J. N. [*See* Couche, C.]

SHOALHAVEN ESTATES. First Subdivision Sales of ; [with Plans and Illustrations.] 4to. Sydney, 1892. MD 12 P 19†

SHOLL, Martin, and ALLOM. Supplement to the Handy Book of Tasmanian Mines and Mining. 8vo. Launceston, 1890. MA 3 S 44

SHONE, J. Critique upon Mr. Mansergh's Report on the Drainage of Melbourne. 2nd ed. Roy. 8vo. Lond., 1891. MA 3 R 14

SHOOTING, Practical Hints on ; being a Treatise on the Shot-gun and its Management, Game, Wild-fowl, and Trap-shooting ; by "20-Bore." 8vo. Lond., 1887. A 16 T 22

SHORE, Margaret Emily. Journal of. 8vo. Lond., 1891. C 16 Q 25

SHORE, T. W. History of Hampshire, including the Isle of Wight. (Popular County Histories.) 8vo. Lond., 1892. B 24 S 17

SHORT, Rt. Rev. A. The Poonindie Mission described in a letter from the Lord Bishop of Adelaide. 12mo. Lond., 1853. MD 1 P 66

Story of a Thirty-four Years Episcopate ; by F. T. Whitington. 8vo. Lond., 1888. MC 1 Q 35

SHORTLAND, Vice-Adm. P. F. Nautical Surveying. 8vo. Lond., 1890. A 22 S 29

SHORTT, Rev. J. [*See* Smith, T. C.]

SHOWERS, Lieut.-Gen. C. L. A Missing Chapter of the Indian Mutiny. 8vo. Lond., 1888. B 10 U 35

SIBORNE, Major-General H. T. Waterloo Letters ; edited by Major-General H. T. Siborne. 8vo. Lond., 1891. B 24 S 13

SIDDONS, Mrs. Sarah. [Life of] ; by Mrs. A. Kennard. (Eminent Women.) 8vo. Lond., 1887 C 3 R 49

SIDEN, Capt. T. Historie der Sevarambes, volkeren die een gedeelte van het dardc Vast-Land bewoonen, gemeen lijk Zuid-Land genaamd. 8vo. Amsterdam, 1702.
MJ 2 T 42

SIDGWICK, A. [*See* Æschylus.]

SIDGWICK, Mrs. Alfred. Caroline Schlegel and her Friends. 8vo. Lond., 1889. C 12 R 16

SIDGWICK, Prof. Henry. Elements of Politics. 8vo. Lond., 1891. F 8 Q 21

SIDNEY, Sir P. Astrophel and Stella; edited by A. Pollard. 8vo. Lond., 1888. H 6 Q 40

SIEGFRIED, T. Das Wirthshaus. 8vo. Basel, 1883. F 11 R 56

Die Trunksucht und ihre Bekämpfung. 8vo. Zofingen, 1884. F 11 S 39

SIEMENS, Sir Charles William. Scientific Works; a Collection of Papers and Discussions, edited by E. F. Bamber. 3 vols. 8vo. Lond., 1889.
A 29 U 10–12

Life of; by W. Pole. 8vo. Lond., 1888. C 6 S 15

SIEMENS, Werner von. Scientific and Technical Papers. Vol. 1. 8vo. Lond., 1892. A 21 S 10

SIGONIUS, C. Historiarum de Regno Italiæ Libri Viginti. Sm. Fol. Francofurti, 1591. B 13 P 7 †

SILIUS ITALICUS, C. Punicorum Libri Septemdecim; illustravit C. T. Ernesti. 2 vols. 8vo. Lipsiæ, 1791–92. H 10 R 7, 8

Punicorum Libri. XVII. 24mo. Lond., 1824. H 11 P 2

SILVÉLA, Manuel. Christmas Voices. 18mo. Sydney, 1891. MH I U 52

SILVER, S. W. [*See* York Gate Library.]

SILVERTHORNE, A. London and Provincial Water Supplies. Roy. 8vo. Lond., 1884. A 22 V 26

SILVESTRE, Armand. The Gallery of Contemporary Art; an illustrated Review. 2 vols. fol. Paris (n.d.) A 40 T 10, 11 ‡

SILVESTRE DE SACY, Baron. [*See* Sacy, Baron Silvestre de.]

SIMEON, C. [Life of]; by H. C. G. Moule. 12mo. Lond., 1892. C 14 Q 31

SIMEON, S. L. [*See* Frederick the Great, *and* Macdonald, Marshal.]

SIMKIN, R. Our Armies. Ob. 8vo. Lond., 1891. B 24 T 9

SIMMONDS, C. Our Liquor Laws: a hand-book for temperance reformers. 12mo. Lond., 1884. F 11 P 9

SIMMONDS, P. L. British Roll of Honour: a Descriptive Account of the recognised Orders of Chivalry. 8vo. Lond., 1887. K 12 V 3

SIMMS, G. R. Land of Gold, and other Poems. 12mo. Lond., 1888. H 7 S 39

SIMMS, J. Physiognomy Illustrated; or, Nature's Revelations of Character. 8th ed. Roy. 8vo. New York, 1887. A 26 U 9

SIMMS, W. G. [Life of]; by W. P. Trent (American men of Letters.) 12mo. Boston, 1892. C 17 P 3

SIMON, G. E. China: its Social, Political, and Religious Life. 8vo. Lond., 1887. D 17 Q 5

SIMON, J. Letter addressed to the President of the General Board of Health on Vaccination; abridged for the use of the Colony of New South Wales, by R. Greenup. 8vo. Sydney, 1859. MA 2 S 74

SIMON, Jules. [Life of] Victor Cousin. (Great French Writers.) 8vo. Lond., 1888. C 7 P 40

SIMPSON, Rear-Adm. F. [*See* Rood, Sir E. J.]

SIMPSON, Justin. List of the Lincolnshire Series of Tradesmen's Tokens and Town Pieces of the Seventeenth Century. 8vo. Lond., 1872. A 27 S 1

SIMPSON, M. C. M. Letters and Recollections of Julius and Mary Mohl. 8vo. Lond., 1887. C 13 T 14

SIMPSON, Capt. T. B. Statement of. [*See* Carron, W.]

SIMPSON, Sir W. G. The Art of Golf. 8vo. Edinb., 1887. A 17 W 41

SIMS, G. R. Ballads and Poems. 12mo. Lond., 1888. H 7 S 38

The Dagonet Ballads.—The Ballads of Babylon.—The Lifeboat and other Poems.

SIMS, R. Manual for the Genealogist, Topographer, Antiquary, and Legal Professor. Roy. 8vo. Lond., 1888. K 12 V 1

SIMSON, A. Travels in the Wilds of Ecuador, and the Exploration of the Putumayo River. 8vo. Lond., 1886. D 15 Q 3

SINCLAIR, F. Ballads and Poems from the Pacific. 8vo. Lond., 1889. MH 1 Q 76

SINCLAIR, Mrs. F. Indigenous Flowers of the Hawaiian Islands. 44 Plates, painted in Water-colors and described. Imp. 4to. Lond., 1885. MA 1 P 31 †

SINCLAIR, Sutherland. Guide to the Contents of the Australian Museum. [*See* Australian Museum.]

SINCLAIRS OF ENGLAND, The. 8vo. Lond., 1887. C 16 Q 6

SINDHIA, Mádhava Rao. [Life of] by H. G. Keene. (Rulers of India.) 12mo. Oxford, 1891. C 17 Q 19

SINGER, I. Simplified Grammar of the Hungarian Language. 8vo. Lond., 1882. K 20 Q 6

SINKER, Rev. Robert. The Library of Trinity College, Cambridge. Sm. 4to. Camb., 1891. B 24 S 23

Memorials of the Hon. I. Keith-Falconer. 8vo. Cambridge, 1888. C 6 P 27

SINNETT, Alfred Percy. The Rationale of Mesmerism. 8vo. Lond., 1892. A 26 Q 24

SINNETT, Mrs. Patience. Hunters and Fishers. 12mo. Lond., 1846. A 29 R 35

SIR JOHN OLDCASTLE. [Part the First]: a Tragedy. [*See* British Drama, Ancient, 1.]

SIVEWRIGHT, J. [*See* Preece, W. H.]

SKEAT, Rev. Prof. Walter William. Ælfric's Lives of the Saints. [*See* Early Eng. Text Soc.]

Principles of English Etymology. 1st and 2nd Series. 8vo. Oxford, 1887-91. K 20 R 1, 2

[*See* Mayhew, Rev. A. L.]

SKELTON, H. J. Economics of Iron and Steel. 12mo. Lond., 1891. A 11 Q 34

SKELTON, John. Maitland of Lethington, and the Scotland of Mary Stuart : a History. 2 vols. 8vo. Edinb., 1887-88. B 31 T 18, 19

Royal House of Stuart. [*See* Gibb, W.]

SKETCHES of Life in the Bush : or, Ten Years in the Interior. 12mo. Sydney, 1872. MD 2 W 14

SKINNER, Alan. The County Court Act, 1890, with Rules, Notes, and Index. Roy. 8vo. Melb., 1891. MF 3 T 39

SKINNER, J., Bishop of Aberdeen. Life and Times of ; by Rev. W. Walker. 8vo. Aberdeen, 1887. C 15 Q 21

SKINNER, Major Thomas. Fifty Years in Ceylon : an Autobiography ; edited by his daughter, Annie Skinner. 8vo. Lond., 1891. C 14 T 23

SKINNER'S NEW SOUTH WALES GAZETTER, 1883. 2 vols. 8vo. Sydney, 1883. ME 4 U

SKIRVING, William. The Trial of William Skirving, 1794, for Sedition. 8vo. Edinb., 1794. F 12 P 24

[*See* Palmer, Rev. T. F.]

SKOTTOWE, Britiffe Constable. A Short History of Parliament. 12mo. Lond., 1892. B 22 Q 22

SLADEN, Douglas B. W. Australian Poets, 1788-1888. 8vo. Lond., 1888. MH 1 U 11

Australian Ballads and Rhymes. 12mo. Lond., 1888. MH 1 P 26

Another copy. MH 1 P 30

Century of Australian Song. 8vo. Lond., 1888. MH 1 R 61

SLADEN, D. W. B., and ROBERTS, G. B. Younger American Poets, 1830-90 ; with an appendix of Younger Canadian Poets. 8vo. Lond., 1891. H 5 R 46

SLAGG, C. Water Engineering : a Practical Treatise on the Measurement, Storage, Conveyance, and Utilization of Water. 8vo. Lond., 1888. A 22 Q 27

SLATER, G. & Co. New Map of Queensland. 8vo. Brisbane, 1874. MD 5 P 5 ‡

SLATER, John Herbert. Engravings and their Value : a Guide for the Print Collector. 8vo. Lond., 1891. A 23 Q 20

Round and About the Bookstalls : a Guide for the Book-hunter. 12mo. Lond., 1891. J 5 P 44

SLATER, J. W. Sewage Treatment, Purification, and Utilization : a Practical Manual for the use of Corporations, &c. 8vo. Lond., 1888. A 6 R 37

SLINGO, W., and BROOKER, A. Electrical Engineering for Electric Light Artizans and Students. New edition. 12mo. Lond., 1890. A 21 Q 31

SLOUS, F. L. [*See* Hugo, V.]

SLY, J. D. [*See* Bean, E.]

SMALLEY, G. R. Abstract of Meteorological Observations made in New South Wales, 1865-69. Roy. 8vo. Sydney, 1869. ME 16 P

SMALLEY, George W. London Letters and some others. 2 vols. 8vo. Lond., 1890. C 15 U 19, 20

SMART, T. B. Bibliography of Matthew Arnold. 8vo. Lond., 1892. K 7 S 35

SMART, W. [*See* Böhm-Bawerk, Prof. E. V.]

SMILER. [*See* Hales, A. G.]

SMILES, Dr. Samuel. A Publisher and his Friends : Memoir and Correspondence of John Murray. 2 vols. 8vo. Lond., 1891. C 10 S 18, 19

Life of Jasmin : Barber, Poet, Philanthropist. 12mo. Lond., 1891. C 17 Q 12

Life and Labour ; or, Characteristics of Men of Industry, Culture, and Genius. 8vo. Lond., 1887. J 5 P 35

SMITH, Dr. Adam. Works of. 5 vols. 8vo. Lond., 1811-12. J 17 R 31-35

An Inquiry into the Nature and Causes of the Wealth of Nations. 6th ed., revised, with an Introduction by E. B. Bax. 2 vols. 12mo. Lond., 1887. F 5 S 42, 43

SMITH, Agnes. Through Cyprus. 8vo. Lond., 1887. D 18 U 6

SMITH, Rev. A. C. The Birds of Wiltshire ; comprising all the Periodical and Occasional Visitants, and those which are indigenous. 8vo. Lond., 1887. A 14 T 35

SMITH, A. H. Chinese Characteristics. 8vo. Lond., 1892. D 17 T 10

SMITH, Bruce. Liberty and Liberalism : a Protest against the growing tendency toward undue interference by the State, &c. 8vo. Melb., 1887.* MF 1 P 40

Strikes and their Cure. 8vo. Sydney, 1888. MF 1 T 60

SMITH, Charles. Treatise on Algebra. 8vo. Lond., 1888. A 25 Q 29

SMITH, Courtenay. Profitable Uses for Surplus Fruits and Vegetables, compiled from latest European and American Sources. 1st edition. 8vo. Sydney, 1890. MA 3 Q 16

Another copy. 2nd ed. 8vo. Sydney, 1890. MA 3 Q 17

SMITH, C. H. Natural History of the Human Species. 12mo. Lond., 1852. A 18 P 25

SMITH, C. M. On Innovations in Banking Practice by certain of the Australian Banks. 8vo. Lond., 1871. MF 1 T 59

Sheep v. Rabbits : an article on Louis Pasteur. 18mo. Sydney, 1891. MA 3 P 23

SMITH, Charles Roach. [*See* Stevenson, S. W.]

SMITH, Daniel. Ancient Ones of the Earth : being the History of the Primitive Alphabet lately discovered by the Author. 8vo. Melb., 1864. MK 1 Q 23

SMITH, David. Three Lectures on Preservation of
Light. 8vo. Lond., 1871.   A 13 P 38

SMITH, Edward. Foreign Visitors in England, and
what they have thought of us. 12mo. Lond., 1889.
D 19 P 1

SMITH, F. H. Through Abyssinia : an Envoy's Ride to
the King of Zion. 8vo. Lond., 1890.   D 14 R 4

SMITH, Dr. George. A Modern Apostle : Alexander N.
Somerville, D.D., 1813–89. 8vo. Lond., 1890. C 14 R 7

Stephen Hislop, Pioneer Missionary and Naturalist in
Central India, 1844–63. 8vo. Lond., 1888. C 15 T 17

SMITH, George Barnett. Prime Ministers of Queen Victoria. 8vo. Lond., 1888.   C 16 Q 5

William I and the German Empire : a Biographical and
Historical Sketch. 8vo. Lond., 1887.   C 12 S 26

SMITH, Dr. Goldwin. Canada and the Canadian Question.
8vo. Lond., 1891.   F 4 S 30

The Civil War in America. 8vo. Lond., 1866. B 17 Q 4

The Empire : a series of Letters published in *The Daily
News*, 1862–63. 12mo. Oxford, 1863.   F 9 U 22

Irish History and Irish Character. 8vo. Oxford, 1861.
B 29 Q 14

Lectures on Modern History, delivered in Oxford, 1859–
61. 8vo. Oxford, 1861.   B 35 T 17

Trip to England. 18mo. Lond., 1892.   D 20 P 2

SMITH, G. Gregory. Days of James IV., 1488–1513.
12mo. Lond., 1890.   B 32 P 1

SMITH, H. E. History of Conisborough Castle, with
Glimpses of Ivanhoe-land. 4to. Worksop, 1887.
B 4 U 4

SMITH, Herbert Greenhough. The Romance of History.
8vo. Lond., 1891.   C 18 Q 19

SMITH, Herbert Llewellyn. Economic Aspects of State
Socialism. 12mo. Oxford, 1887.   F 14 P 17

Modern Changes in the Mobility of Labour. 8vo. Lond.,
1891.   F 14 S 5

SMITH, H. S. Statement of the General and Particular
Average and Charges of the British Ship "Northamp-
ton." Fol. Sydney, 1884.   MF 11 Q 3 †

SMITH, I. G. Christian Monasticism, from the fourth to
the ninth centuries of the Christian Era. 8vo. Lond.,
1892.   G 13 U 41

SMITH, Mrs. James. The Booandik Tribe of South Aus-
tralian Aborigines ; a sketch of their Habits, Customs,
Legends, and Language. 12mo. Adelaide, 1880.
MA 3 P 46

SMITH, Rev. J. Frederick. [See Ewald, Dr. G. H. A.]

SMITH, Prof. John. Anniversary Address ; [delivered
to the Royal Society of N. S. W., 29th May, 1879,
mostly a Biographical Sketch of the Rev. W. B. Clarke.]
8vo. Sydney, 1879.   MA 2 T 52

Speech in Opposition to the Medical Bill. 8vo. Sydney,
1875.   MF 1 T 56

SMITH, Capt. John, President of Virginia. Adventures
and Discourses of. Newly ordered by J. Ashton. 8vo.
Lond., 1883.   C 17 Q 1

SMITH, J. Bucknall. Treatise upon Wire : its manufacture and uses. 4to. Lond., 1891.   A 25 V 4

Treatise upon Cable or Rope Traction, as applied to the
working of Street and other Railways. 4to. Lond.,
1887.   A 22 V 20

SMITH, Joseph. Short Biographical Notices of William
Bradford, Reinier Janson, Andrew Bradford, and Samuel
Keimer, early Printers in Pennsylvania. 8vo. Lond.,
1891.   C 14 P 27

SMITH, Laura Alexandrine. The Music of the Waters : a
collection of Sailors' Chanties, or Working Songs of the
Sea, Boatmen's Songs, &c. 8vo. Lond., 1888.
H 10 S 7

SMITH, Miss Lucy Toulmin. [*See* Jusserand, J. J.]

SMITH, Robert Burdett. [See Melbourne Centennial
International Exhibition.]

SMITH, Prof. R. M. Emigration and Immigration : a
study in social science. 8vo. Lond., 1890. F 14 Q 6

SMITH, Sidney. The Settler's New Home ; or, Whether
to go, and Whither ? 12mo. Lond., 1850. MD 2 W 42

Whether to Go and Whither ? 12mo. Lond., 1849.
MD 1 S 3

SMITH, Rev. Sydney. Ballot. 8vo. Lond., 1839.
G 15 R 27

SMITH, S. P. Eruption of Tarawera. Roy. 8vo. Wellington, 1887.   MA 2 R 31

Kermadec Islands : their Capabilities and Extent. Roy.
8vo. Wellington, 1887.   MD 7 P 30

SMITH, Thomas. De Republica Anglorum, libri tres ;
quibus accesserunt chorographica illius descriptio, aliique
politici tractatus. 32mo. Lug. Bat., 1630. B 21 P 25

SMITH, Prof. Thomas. Memoirs of James Begg, D.D.
2 vols. 8vo. Edinb., 1885.   C 17 T 1, 2

SMITH, Thomas. Arithmetical Tables for Junior Scholars.
18mo. Sydney, 1891.   MA 3 P 22

SMITH, Tom. C., and SHORTT, Rev. Jonathan. History
of the Parish of Ribchester, in the County of Lancaster.
8vo. Lond., 1890.   B 23 R 4

SMITH, T. E. Summary of the Law and Practice in
Admiralty. 4th edition. 8vo. Lond., 1892. F 9 T 6

SMITH, Wentworth. The Puritan or the Widow of Watt-
ling Street : a comedy. [*See* British Drama, Ancient, 1.]

SMITH, William. Old Yorkshire. Edited by Wm. Smith.
New Series. Vols. 1–3. 8vo. Lond., 1889–91.
B 22 T 6–8

Registers of Topcliffe and Morley : Baptisms, 1654–1830 ;
Burials, 1654–1888. 8vo. Lond., 1888.   B 4 S 18

SMITH, W., and WACE, H. Dictionary of Christian
Biography, &c. 4 vol. roy. 8vo. Lond., 1877–87.
C 11 R 45–48

SMITH, Dr. W. [*See* Fichte, J. G.]

SMITH, Dr. W., and HALL, T. D. Grammar of the Latin Language. 2nd edition. 8vo. Lond., 1867.
K 16 P 38

SMITH, Dr. W., WAYTE, W., and MARINDIN, G. E. Dictionary of Greek and Roman Antiquities. 3rd ed. 2 vols. roy. 8vo. Lond., 1890-91.
K 7 Q 11, 12

SMITH, W. A. Loch Creran : Notes from the West Highlands. 8vo. Paisley, 1887.
D 18 R 3

SMITH, W. H., & SONS. Hand-book No. 2 of Line of Intercolonial Steamships; with a Popular History of Australia, by P. J. Holdsworth. 4to Sydney, 1888.
MB 1 U 20

SMITH, Dr. W. R. Lectures on the Religions of the Semites. 8vo. Edinb., 1889.
G 6 S 37

SMITHSONIAN INSTITUTION. Annual Reports, 1884-86, 1888-90. 8 vols. 8vo. Washington, 1885-91.
E 2. 18
U. S. National Museum. Reports, 1887, 1888. 3 vols. 8vo. Washington, 1889-90.
E 2. 17-18

SMYLIE, A. Free Trade v. Protection ; a Question previous to Confederation. 8vo. Sydney, 1890.
MF 1 T 55

SMYTH, A. Official Newspaper Directory of Australasia. 8vo. Sydney, 1892.
ME 3 T

SMYTH, Lieut. B. History of the 20th Regiment, 1688-1888. 8vo. Lond., 1889.
B 23 U 12

SMYTH, C. P. Our Inheritance in the Great Pyramid. 5th edition. 8vo. Lond., 1890.
B 1 P 51

SMYTHE, Mrs. W. J. Ten Months in the Fiji Islands; with an Introduction and Appendix, by Col. W. J. Smythe. 8vo. Oxford, 1864.
MD 6 T 5

SMYTHIES, H. Education of Man ; by "A Member of the New Zealand Bar." 8vo. Lond., 1873.
MG 2 R 1

SNELL, H. [*See* Mouat, Dr. F. J.]

SNOWDON, J. W. Treatise on Treble Bob. 2 vols. 12mo. Leeds, 1878-79.
A 23 Q 10, 11
Standard Methods in the Art of Change-ringing, with diagrams. 12mo. Lond., 1887.
A 23 Q 12
"Grandsire" : the Method, its Peals, and History. 12mo. Lond., 1888.
A 23 Q 13
Rope-sight : an Introduction to the Art of Change-ringing. 4th edition. Lond., 1891.
A 23 Q 14

SOAMES, Laura. Introduction to Phonetics (English, French, and German) ; with Reading Lessons and Exercises. 8vo. Lond., 1891.
K 20 Q 1

SOAMES, P. Treatise on the Manufacture of Sugar from the Sugar-cane. Roy. 8vo. Lond., 1872.
A 25 V 1

SOCIAL HORIZON, The. 12mo. Lond., 1892.
F 9 U 18

2 D

SOCIAL SCIENCE. Transactions of the National Association for the Promotion of Social Science : Conference on Temperance Legislation, 1886. 8vo. Lond., 1886.
F 11 R 51

SOCIEDAD DE GEOGRAFÍCA Y ESTADISTICA DE LA REPUBLICA MEXICANA (*formerly Instituto Nacional de Geografica y Estadistica de la Republica Mexicana.*) Boletin. 21 vols. roy. 8vo. Mexico, 1861-82.
E 1. 38

SOCIETÁ ITALIANA DI SCIENZE NATURALI, Atti della. Vols. 28-32. Roy. 8vo. Milano, 1885-89.
E 1. 56

SOCIÉTÉ DE GÉOGRAPHIE. Bulletin. Tomes 7-12 8vo. Paris, 1888-91.
E 1. 26
Compte Rendu des Séances. 8vo. Paris, 1886-91. E 1. 26

SOCIÉTÉ IMPERIALE DES NATURALISTES DE MOSCOU. Bulletin. Vols. 53, 54. Roy. 8vo. Moscou, 1878-79.
E 1. 26

SOCIETY FOR PROMOTION OF MORALITY. Report, 1885-86. 8vo. Melb., 1887.
F 11 R 52

SOCIÉTÉ ROYALE DES ANTIQUAIRES DU NORD. [*See* Koneglige Nordiske Oldskrift-Selskab.]

SOCIETY OF BIBLICAL ARCHÆOLOGY. Transactions. Vols. 1-8. 8vo. Lond., 1872-85.
E 1. 46

SOCRATES SCHOLASTICUS, and HERMIAS SOZOMEN. Historia Ecclesiastica. (Gr. et Lat.) Fol. Parisiis, 1686.
C 6 R 7 ‡

SODA WATER BOTTLERS' AND CORDIAL MAKERS' BOOK OF REFERENCE AND HOTELKEEPERS' GUIDE. 8vo. Sydney, 1884.
MA 3 Q 18

SOHM, R. Institutes of Roman Law. Translated by J. C. Ledlie. 8vo. Oxford, 1892.
F 9 T 7

SOHNCKE, Prof. L. Ueber Stürme und Sturmwarnungen. 8vo. Berlin, 1875.
A 19 T 27

SOLANDER, Dr. D. [*See* Ellis, J.]

SOLOMON ISLANDS. Papers relating to the recent Operations of H.M.S. *Opal* against Natives of the Solomon Islands. Fol. Lond., 1887.
MF 1 P 33 †
Another copy. Fol. Lond., 1887.
MF 4 S 32

SOMERVILLE, Rev. A. N. A Modern Apostle, 1813-89; by G. Smith. 8vo. Lond., 1890.
C 14 R 7

SOMERVILLE, Mrs. Mary. On the Connexion of the Physical Sciences. 9th edition. 8vo. London, 1858.
A 29 S 3
[*See* Walford, L. B.]

SOMMER, H. O. [*See* Malory, Sir T., *and* Spenser, E.]

SONNENSCHEIN, A. Educational Codes of Foreign Countries. 2nd edition. 8vo. Lond., 1889. G 17 P 44

SONNENSCHEIN, W. S. The Best Books : a reader's guide to the choice of the best available books. 4to. Lond., 1887.
Libr.
Another copy. 2nd edition. [Enlarged.] 4to. Lond., 1891.
Libr.

SONNENSCHEIN, W. S., & CO. Cyclopædia of Education; edited by A. E. Fletcher. 8vo. Lond., 1889. K 4 S 19

SOPHIA, Electress of Hanover. Memoirs of : 1630–80. Trans. by H. Forester. 8vo. Lond., 1888. C 5 Q 4

SOPHOCLES. Lexicon Sophocleum. [*See* Ellendt, F.]

Œdipus Rex, Trachiniæ, Philoctetes, Œdipus Coloneus ; recensuit E. Wunderus. [Gr. text.] 4 vols. (in 1). 12mo. Lipsiæ, 1824. H 2 Q 51

Plays and Fragments ; with Notes, Commentary, and Translation, by Prof. R. C. Jebb. Parts 3–5. 8vo. Camb., 1888–92. H 1 S 24–26

Sophocles ; by C. W. Collins. (Ancient Classics for English Readers.) 12mo. Edinb., 1886. J 14 P 24

Tragœdiæ Septem, ex editione R. F. P. Brunck. 2 vols. 8vo. Oxonii, 1808. H 9 S 2, 3

Tragœdiæ Superstites et Deperditarum Fragmenta ex recensione G. Dindorfii. 8vo. Oxonii, 1849. H 4 S 32

Tragœdiæ ; edidit T. Bergk. (Greek text.) 8vo. Lipsiæ, 1858 H 4 P 37

Tragedies of ; new translation by E. H. Plumptre. 12mo. Lond., 1890. H 1 Q 38

Tragedies of ; translated by T. Francklin, M.A. 2 vols 12mo. Dublin, 1778. H 2 Q 45, 46

SOREL, Albert : Life of Madame de Staël. 12mo. Lond., 1892. C 14 Q 30

[Life of] Montesquieu. (Great French Writers.) 8vo. Lond., 1887. C 11 P 19

SORELLI, Guido. My Confessions to Silvio Pellico : the Autobiography of Guido Sorelli. 8vo. Lond., 1836. C 13 S 4

SOTHERAN, H., & CO. Catalogue of Superior Second-hand Books, in Literature, Science, and the Fine Arts. Roy. 8vo. Lond., 1888. Libr.

SOULES, F. [*See* Bligh, Lieut. G.]

SOUTH AFRICAN PHILOSOPHICAL SOCIETY : Transactions. Vols. 4–6. 8vo. Capetown, 1887–92. E 1. 43

SOUTH AUSTRALIA. Account of the Celebration of the Jubilee Year of South Australia, 1886. 8vo. Adelaide, 1887. MB 2 Q 46

Copies of all Letters and Accounts which have passed since 1st January, 1843, between the Manager of the South Australian Company and the Colonization Commissioners, or the Colonial Office ; also, of all Memorials and Letters to Sir Robert Peel and the Secretary of State for the Colonies, and of the replies to the same, on the subject of the Emigration Land Fund of South Australia ; and Extracts from the Despatches of Governor Grey on the Expediency of renewing Emigration to that Colony. Fol. Lond., 1844. MF 4 S 9

First and Second Reports from the Select Committee on South Australia. 2 vols. (in 1.) Fol. Lond., 1841. MF 4 S 13

SOUTH AUSTRALIA—*contd.*

Native Tribes of South Australia. 8vo. Adelaide, 1879. MA 1 R 15

Papers relative to South Australia. Fol. Lond., 1843. MF 4 S 13

ACTS. [*See* Statutes.]

COLONIZATION COMMISSIONERS.

First–Fourth Annual Reports of the Colonization Commissioners, 1836–39. 4 vols. (in 1.) fol. Lond., 1836–41. MF 4 S 11

FINANCE.

Correspondence of the Colonial Department explanatory of the Debts incurred by the Government ; and also an account of the Income and Expenditure of the said Colony for each year since the Act for Establishing the Colony was passed. Fol. Lond., 1841. MF 4 S 14

GOVERNMENT GAZETTE.

Government Gazette. 4 vols. 4to. Adelaide, 1887–88. ME 2. 28

PARLIAMENT.

Papers and Proceedings of Parliament for 1877, 1885–91. 28 vols., fol. Adelaide 1878–92. ME 2. 26–28

STATISTICS.

Statistics, 1845. Sm. 4to. Adelaide, 1845. MF 3 T 40

Statistics, 1845–6. Fol. Adelaide, 1846. MF 4 S 17

STATUTES.

Acts of Parliament, 1888–91. 4 vols. 4to. Adelaide, 1888–92. ME 2. 27

Alphabetical Index to Public Acts in force, or partly in force. 4to. Adelaide, 1879. MF 3 S 16

Alphabetical Index to the Acts and Ordinances; prepared by G. W. D. Beresford. 4to. Adelaide, 1879. MF 3 S 16

Certain Acts passed by the Legislatures of South Australia and New Zealand relating to the registration and transfer of Land ; together with reports and regulations relating to those Acts. Fol. Lond., 1862. MF 11 Q 17†

Second and Final Report of Commission appointed to report on the Destitute Act, 1881. Fol. Adelaide, 1885. MF 11 Q 10†

Report of Commission appointed to Inquire into the Intestacy, Real Property, and Testamentary Causes Acts. Fol. Lond., 1874. MF 4 S 18

Supreme Court Act, 1878, and the Rules of Court made thereunder. Imp. 8vo. Adelaide, 1879. MF 1 U 26

SOUTH AUSTRALIAN COMPANY. Supplement to the First Report of the Directors. 8vo. Lond., 1837. MF 1 Q 28

Second Report of the Directors. 8vo. Southwark, 1838. MF 1 R 61

SOUTH AUSTRALIAN PUBLIC LIBRARY, MUSEUM, AND ART GALLERY. Report, 1888-92. 2 vols. fol. Adelaide, 1888–92. ME

SOUTH KENSINGTON MUSEUM. Catalogue of the Third Exhibition of National Portraits, 1800-1857. Imp. 8vo. Lond., 1868.   C 17 U 16

SOUTH SEA ISLANDERS. An Act for the Prevention of Criminal Outrages upon Natives of the Islands in the Pacific Ocean. Imp. 8vo. Lond., 1879.   MF 4 S 21

Correspondence relating to the Importation of South Sea Islanders into Queensland. Fol. Lond., 1868.
MF 4 S 7

Further Correspondence relating to the Importation of South Sea Islanders into Queensland. Fol. Lond., 1871.
MF 4 S 5

Correspondence between the Governor of New South Wales and the Earl of Kimberley, respecting certain statements made by Capt. Palmer, R.N., in his book entitled Kidnapping in the South Seas. Fol. Lond., 1872.   MF 4 S 6

Report of Proceedings of H.M. Ship "Rosario," during her cruise among the South Sea Islands, 1871-72. Fol. Lond., 1872.   MF 4 S 6

Correspondence and Further Correspondence respecting the Deportation of South Sea Islanders. 4 vols. (in 1.) Fol. Lond., 1869-72.   MF 4 S 5

Correspondence respecting Outrages committed upon Natives of South Sea Islands. 2 vols. (in 1.) Fol. Lond., 1873-74.   MF 4 S 3

SOUTHAN, W. M. The Two Lawyers: a Novel. 8vo. Dunedin, 1881.   MJ 1 T 47

SOUTHERN, T. Isabella: a Tragedy. [See British Drama, Modern, 1.]

Oroonoko: a Tragedy. [See British Drama, Modern, 1.]

SOUTHEY, R. [See Knight, W.]

SOWDEN, W. J. The Northern Territory as it is. A Narrative of the South Australian Parliamentary Party's Trip. 8vo. Adelaide, 1882.   MD 1 R 25

SOWERBY, F. Forest Cantons of Switzerland. 8vo. Lond., 1892.   D 18 R 23

SOWERBY, J. English Botany. Supplement to 3rd edition. Vols. 1-4. Compiled by N. E. Brown. Imp. 8vo. Lond., 1892.   A 32 U 15

SOWERBY, Jas. The Genera of Recent and Fossil Shells. 2 vols. 8vo. Lond. (n.d.)   A 27 T 25, 26

SPAGNOLETTI, E. The Volunteer's Polka. Fol. Sydney (n.d.)   MA 11 Q 15 †

The Woolloomooloo Octave Polka. Fol. Sydney (n.d.)
MA 11 Q 15 †

The Sydney Schottische. Fol. Sydney (n.d.) MA 11 Q 15 †

SPALDING, Lieut.-Col. Henry. [Life of Count Alexander Vassilovich] Suvóroff. 8vo. Lond., 1890.   C 14 R 9

SPANISH AND ITALIAN FOLK SONGS; translated by Alma Strettel. 8vo. Lond., 1887.   H 7 Q 41

SPARKES, J. C. L. Manual of Artistic Anatomy, for the use of Students in Art. Imp. 8vo. Lond., 1888. A 36 P 7 †

SPECTATOR, The. 20 vols. fol. Lond., 1876-92.
E 2. 71, 72

SPENCE, W. Entomology. [See Kirby, Rev. W.]

SPENCER, Herbert. Essays : scientific, political, and speculative. 3 vols. 8vo. Lond., 1883-88.   J 5 R 4-6

Factors of Organic Evolution. 8vo. Lond., 1887.
A 29 U 1

Justice : being part IV. of the Principles of Ethics. 8vo. Lond., 1891.   G 12 R 35

Reasons for Dissenting from the Philosophy of M. Comte. 8vo. Lond., 1884.   G 12 R 28

The Man versus The State : containing "The New Toryism," "The Coming Slavery," "The Sins of Legislators," and "The Great Political Superstition." 8vo. Lond., 1888.   G 12 R 28

[See Ritchie, D. G., and Robertson, J. M.]

SPENCER, W. B. [See Royal Society of Victoria.]

SPENDER, J. A. The State and Pensions in Old Age. 12mo. Lond., 1892.   F 9 U 23

SPENGEL, Dr. F. W. Ein Beitrag zur Kenntniss der Polynesier-Schädel. 4to. Hamburg 1876. MA 3 Q 7 †

SPENS, W. C., and YOUNGER, R. T. Employers and Employed. 8vo. Glasgow, 1887.   F 6 S 32

SPENSER, E. The Shepheardie's Calender. Original edition of 1579 in photographic fac-simile, with an introduction by H. O. Sommer. 4to. Lond., 1890. H 7 V 22

The Faerie Queene. Imp. 8vo. Lond., 1609. H 5 V 5

SPICER, Rev. E. C. [See Bright, C.]

SPIERS, R. P. Architectural Drawing. 4to. Lond., 1887.   A 9 P 24 †

Egypt : a series of thirty-six Views of Ancient and Modern Egypt. Imp. 4to. Lond., 1887.   D 29 Q 9 ‡

SPILBERGEN, George de. Oost-en-West Indische Voyagie door de Strate Magallanes naer de Moluquos met ses schepen onder den Commandeur Joris Spilbergen ; als mede de Wonderlijcke Reyse ghedaen door Willem Cornelisz Schouten van Hoorn, en Jacob le Maire in den Jaere, 1665-17. Sm. 4to. Amstelredam, 1648.   MD 8 Q 6

SPILSBURY, W. H. [See Lincoln's Inn.]

SPIRIT OF THE AGE : a Monthly Magazine. First Series. 4to. Sydney, 1855-56.   ME 17 S

SPIRIT OF THE TWILIGHT HOUR, and other Poems, by "Dusk." 12mo. Melb., 1874.   MH 1 Q 46

SPIRITUALISM. Preliminary Report of the Commission appointed to investigate Modern Spiritualism in accordance with the request of the late Henry Seybert. 8vo. Philad., 1887.   G 16 S 34

Report on. [See London Dialectical Society.]

SPITZER, H. Hylogoismus. 8vo. Graz, 1881. G 4 S 37

SPON, E. and F. N. Engineers' and Contractors' Illustrated Book of Prices of Machines, Tools, Ironwork, and Contractors' Material, 1892-93. 4to. Lond., 1892.
A 36 S 4 ‡

Spons' Household Manual: a Treasury of Domestic Receipts, and Guide for Home Management. 8vo. Lond., 1887. K 18 Q 17

SPON, E., HALDANE, R., and LOCK, C. G. W. Workshop Receipts. [1st]-4th Series. 8vo. Lond., 1888-89.
A 25 P 2-5

SPOONER, Rev. W. A. [*See* Tacitus, C.]

SPRING, Prof. L. W. Kansas, the Prelude to the War for the Union. (American Commonwealths.) 12mo. Boston, 1890. B 17 P 14

SPRUNER, Dr. C. do. Atlas Antiquus. Fol. Gothæ, 1850. D 8 P 20 ‡

SPURGEON, C. H. Sermons delivered at the Metropolitan Tabernacle, &c., 1855-87. Vols. 1, 2. 8vo. Lond., 1887. G 2 Q 26, 27

SQUIRE, P. Companion to the latest edition of the British Pharmacopœia. 8vo. Lond., 1890. A 33 S 5

STACKELBERG, Natalie, Baronness von. Life of Carmen Sylva [Elizabeth, Queen of Roumania]; translated from the German by Baroness Hilda Deichmann. 8vo. Lond., 1890. C 15 U 15

STACKHOUSE, Rev. A. Eight Lectures on the Signs of the Times. 12mo. Launceston, 1849. MG 2 P 22

The Lord is at Hand. Four Lectures. 12mo. Launceston, 1853. MG 2 P 33

STAËL-HOLSTEIN, Anne Louise Germaine Necker, Baronne de. Madame de Staël, her Friends, and her Influence in Politics and Literature ; by Lady Blennerhassett. 3 vols. 8vo. Lond., 1889. C 13 U 16-18

[Life of] ; by A. Sorel. 12mo. Lond., 1892. C 14 Q 30

[Life of] ; by Bella Duffy. (Eminent Women.) 8vo. Lond., 1887. C 12 Q 29

STAFFORD, Millicent Fanny, Marchioness of. How I spent my Twentieth Year. 12mo. Edinb., 1889.
D 20 Q 11

STAFFORD, W. Compendious, or Briefe Examination of certayne ordinary Complaints of divers of our Countrymen. 12mo. Lond., 1581. F 9 U 16

STAFFORD HOUSE PAPERS ; edited by Lord Ronald Gower. 8vo. Lond., 1891. C 16 T 1

STAHL, J. M. [*See* Thucydides.]

STAHLSCHMIDT, J. C. L. Church Bells of Kent; their Inscriptions, Founders, Uses, and Traditions. 4to. Lond., 1887. B 21 U 17

STAIGER, K. T. Mineral Industries of Queensland. [*See* Indian and Colonial Exhibition, 1886.]

STALEY, Rt. Rev. T. N. Five Years' Church Work in the Kingdom of Hawaii. 8vo. Lond., 1868. MG 1 Q 51

STALLYBRASS, J. S. [*See* Grimm, J.]

STANDARD FREE PRESBYTERIAN MAGAZINE OF VICTORIA. June, 1859 - April, 1860. 8vo. Melb., 1859-60. ME 3 Q

STANFORD, E. [*See* Wallace, A. R.]

STANHOPE, Philip Henry, 5th Earl. Notes of Conversations with the Duke of Wellington, 1831-51. 3rd ed. Lond., 1889. C 12 Q 20

STANLEY, Very Rev. A. P. The Epistles of St. Paul to the Corinthians. 4th ed. 8vo. Lond., 1876. G 16 T 8

History of the Eastern Church. 3rd ed. 8vo. Lond., 1864. G 16 S 45

Life and Correspondence of T. Arnold. 7th ed. 8vo. Lond., 1852. C 14 U 16

Sinai and Palestine. 8vo. Lond., 1860. D 16 T 9

STANLEY, H. M. In Darkest Africa ; or, the Quest, Rescue, and Retreat of Emin. 2 vols. 8vo. Lond., 1890. D 14 U 1, 2

Nell' Africa Tenebrosa, ovvero Ricerca, Liberaziono, e Ritorno di Emin. Traduzione italiana di A. Massoni. 2 vols. 8vo. Milano, 1890. D 14 U 3, 4

His Life, Travels, and Explorations ; by the Rev. H. W. Little. 8vo. Lond., 1890. C 12 S 7

STANLEY, W. Eugenie Schottische. Fol. Sydney (n.d.) MA 11 Q 15 †

STANSFELD-HICKS. [*See* Hicks, C. S.-]

STANTON, G. K. Rambles and Researches among Worcestershire Churches. 8vo. Lond., 1886. D 10 Q 6

STANTON, R. Menology of England and Wales; or, Brief Memorials of the Ancient British and English Saints. 8vo. Lond., 1887. G 4 R 37

STAPLETON, R. J. [*See* Canning, G.]

STARCKE, C. N. The Primitive Family in its Origin and Development. 8vo. Lond., 1889. A 1 V 19

STATE INSURANCE FOR OLD AGE: Is it Needed in Scotland ? Reprint of Articles published in Glasgow Mail. Roy. 8vo. Glasgow, 1891. F 1 T 20

STATE OF MAN, On the, subsequent to the Promulgation of Christianity. 8vo. Lond., 1851. G 16 P 45

STATE TEMPERANCE CONVENTION, Proceedings of. 8vo. Lancaster, 1870. F 11 S 38

STATESMAN'S YEAR-BOOK for 1864-67, 1887-92. 10 vols. 8vo. Lond., 1864-92. E

STATIUS, P. P. [Opera.] 32mo. Amster., 1624. H 11 P 1

STATUTES, Revised. [*See* Great Britain.]

STAVORINUS, J. S. Voyage par le Cap de Bonne-Espérance à Batavia, à Bantam, et au Bengale, en 1768-71 ; traduit du Hollandois par H. J. Jansen. 8vo. Paris, 1798. D 17 R 10

STAVORINUS, J. S.—*contd.*

Voyage par le Cap de Bonne-Espérance et Batavia à Samarang, à Macassar, à Amboine, et à Surate, en 1774-78; traduit du Hollandois. 2 vols. 8vo. Paris, 1799. D 17 R 11, 12

STAYTON, G. H. Sewage Purification : Report upon the Questions of Sewage Purification and Sewer Ventilation now in use in Great Britain. Fol. Sydney, 1891. MA 11 Q 11 †

Report on the Sewerage and Drainage of the Western Suburbs of Sydney. Sm. fol. Sydney, 1888.* MA 2 Q 29 †

STEAD, R. [*See* Hug, Mrs. L.]

STEADMAN, F. Campanalogia Improved; or, the Art of Ringing made easy. 3rd ed. 18mo. Lond., 1733. A 23 P 2

STEAM COMMUNICATION. Copies of Reports of 1846, 1848, and 1850, of Committees of the Legislative Councils of New South Wales, New Zealand, and the Mauritius, on the subject of Steam Communication with Europe ; and of any resolutions passed with reference to these reports by the said Councils. Fol. Lond., 1851. MF 3 S 10

Copies of a Proposal made about 8th Sept., 1848, by the Peninsular and Oriental Steam Navigation Company to Her Majesty's Government ; and of any offers to H.M. Government by the P. & O. S.N. Co. under date 17th July and 2nd Nov., 1848, and 13th Jan., 1851, for establishing steam communication with Australia. Fol. Lond., 1851. MF 4 S 2

Copies of Despatches received at the Colonial Office from any of the Governors of the Australian Colonies and New Zealand on Steam Communication between 1846 and 1851. Fol. Lond., 1851. MF 4 S 2

STEBBING, Rev. T. R. R. The Naturalist of Cumbrae : a true Story ; being the Life of David Robertson. 8vo. Lond., 1891. C 15 Q 4

STEBBING, William. Peterborough. (English Men of Action.) 12mo. Lond., 1890. C 12 P 31

Sir Walter Raleigh : a Biography. 8vo. Oxford, 1891. C 18 Q 9

Some Verdicts of History Reviewed. 8vo. Lond., 1887. B 35 S 6

STEBLER, Dr. F. G., and SCHRÖTER, Dr. C. The Best Forage Plants fully described and figured ; translated by Prof. A. N. McAlpine. Roy. 4to. Lond., 1889. A 1 S 24 †

STEDMAN, E. C. Victorian Poets, revised and extended. 8vo. Lond., 1887. C 13 R 15

STEDMAN, E. C., and HUTCHINSON, Ellen M. Library of American Literature from the Earliest Settlement to the Present Time. 11 vols. roy. 8vo. New York, 1889-90. J 6 V 4-14

STEEGMANN, Dr. Zur Lehre von der gerichtsärztlichen Beurtheilung der Trunkenheit und der Trunkfälligkeit. 8vo. Erlangen, 1835. F 11 Q 19

STEEL, A. G., and LYTTELTON, Hon. R. H. Cricket. 8vo. Lond., 1888. A 17 U 36

STEEL, H. P. A Crown of Wattle. 8vo. Sydney, 1888.* MH 1 P 45

STEEL, Prof. J. H. Treatise on the Diseases of the Dog: a Manual of Canine Pathology. 8vo. Lond., 1888. A 1 T 33

Treatise on the Diseases of the Sheep ; being a Manual of Ovine Pathology. 8vo. Lond., 1890. A 18 T 6

STEEL, Rev. Dr. Robert. The Shorter Catechism. 8vo. Lond., 1888. G 16 R 49

The Achievements of Youth. 8vo. Lond., 1890. C 15 Q 5

Burning and Shining Lights; or, Memoirs of Eminent Ministers of Christ. 8vo. Lond., 1864. C 13 Q 1

STEELE, Sir R. The Funeral : a Comedy. [*See* British Drama, Modern, 4.]

The Tender Husband : a Comedy. [*See* British Drama, Modern, 4.]

The Conscious Lovers : a Comedy. [*See* British Drama, Modern, 4.]

STEELE, Sarah L. The Rt. Hon. Arthur Macmurrough Kavanagh : a Biography. 8vo. Lond., 1891. C 15 T 16

STEERE, Rt. Rev. E. Memoir of; by Rev. R. M. Heanley. 8vo. Lond., 1888. C 12 R 11

STEFANI, Guglielmo. [*See* Pellico, S.]

STENDHAL, De. [*See* Beyle, M. H.]

STEPHANUS, Byzantius. De Urbibus (à T. de Pinedo.) [Gr. et. Lat.] Fol. Amstel., 1678. D 42 Q 6‡

STEPHANUS, H. [*See* Estienne, H.]

STEPHEN, Sir Alfred. Address on Intemperance and the Licensing System. 12mo. Sydney, 1870. MF 2 P 59

Australian Divorce Bills: the Objections raised to them, Religious and Social, considered. 8vo. Sydney, 1888. MF 1 Q 29

Introduction to the Law Reform Commissioners' Report and Criminal Law Consolidation and Amendment Bill. 8vo. Sydney, 1876. MF 1 T 58

The Name "Port Jackson," Sydney, N.S.W. 4to. Sydney, 1890. MB 2 U 17

Speech on the Medical Bill. 8vo. Sydney, 1875. MF 1 T 57

Wives and their Friends. 8vo. Sydney, 1891. MF 1 T 73

STEPHEN, Sir A., and ROBERTSON, Sir J. Views of, on the Proposal to alter the name of New South Wales to the Colony of Australia. 8vo. Sydney, 1887. MF 3 Q 34

STEPHEN, Sir George. The Royal Pardon Vindicated, in a Review of the Case between Mr. W. H. Barber and the Incorporated Law Society. 8vo. Lond., 1851. MF 1 T 72

STEPHEN, George Milner. Essay on Magnetic Healing and some Wonderful Cures. 12mo. Dunedin, 1884.
MA 3 P 44

STEPHEN, H. W. H. The Golden Yankee: a Tale of Life and Adventure on the Diggings; to which is added Uncle Gabriel's Legacy; or, Wanted a Wife. 12mo. Sydney, 1877.
MJ 3 P 7

Lily's Fortune. 12mo. Sydney, 1886.
MJ 1 Q 58

Vagabonds and their Dupes. 8vo. Sydney, 1879.
MG 1 R 51

STEPHEN, Sir J. F. General View of the Criminal Law of England. 2nd edition. 8vo. Lond., 1890.
F 6 U 30

STEPHEN, L. Dictionary of National Biography. Vols. 10-31, CHA-LAM. Roy. 8vo. Lond., 1887-92.
C 11 Q 25-R 5

STEPHENS, F. G. Memoir of George Cruikshank; and an Essay on the Genius of G. Cruikshank, by W. M. Thackeray. 8vo. New York, 1891.
C 16 Q 15

STEPHENS, H. Book of the Farm. 4th edition, revised by James Macdonald. 3 vols. Roy. 8vo. Edinb., 1891.
A 1 T 38-40

STEPHENS, H. M. History of the French Revolution. Vol. 2. 8vo. Lond., 1891.
B 9 P 44

Portugal. (Story of the Nations Series.) 8vo. Lond., 1891.
B 34 Q 2

STEPHENS, J. B. Convict Once, and Other Poems. New edition. 8vo. Melb., 1888.
MH 1 U 16

Fayette; or Bush Revels: an Original Australian Comic Opera, in three Acts; composed by G. B. Allen. 8vo. Brisb., 1892.
MH 1 S 65

A Hundred Pounds: a Novelette, to which is added, Bailed up with a Whitewash Brush. 12mo. Melb., 1876.
MJ 1 P 31

Miscellaneous Poems. 8vo. Lond., 1880.
MH 1 P 4

STEPHENS, Prof. W. J. President's Address, Annual General Meeting of the Linnean Society of New South Wales, 1890. 8vo. Sydney, 1890.
MA 2 T 59

Literæ Humaniores: a Letter to the Chancellor of the Sydney University concerning the Literary Side of the Arts Course. 8vo. Sydney, 1887.
MG 2 Q 43

Quam Minimum: a Latin Class-book for beginners. Sm. 4to. Sydney, 1878.
MK 1 P 61

Attempt to synchronise the Australian, South African, and Indian Coal Measures. Part 1. 8vo. Sydney, 1889.
MA 3 T 44

Notes on the recent Eruptions in the Taupo Zone, New Zealand. 8vo. Sydney, 1886.
MA 3 T 43

Note on a Labyrinthodont Fossil from Cockatoo Island, Port Jackson. 8vo. Sydney, 1886.
MA 3 T 43

On some additional Labyrinthodont Fossils from the Hawkesbury Sandstones of New South Wales. 8vo. Sydney, 1886.
MA 3 T 43

President's Addresses, Annual General Meetings of the Linnean Society of N.S.W., 1888 and 1889. 8vo. Sydney, 1888-89.
MA 3 T 43

STEPHENS, W. R. W. Hildebrand and his Times. 8vo. Lond., 1888.
G 19 P 12

STEPNIAK. [*See* Dragomanoff, M.]

STERNE, S. Representative Government and Personal Representation. 12mo. Philad., 1871.
F 9 U 15

STERRETT, J. R. S. Archæological Journey made through Asia Minor in 1884. [*See* Archæological Institute of America.]

STETEFELDT, C. A. The Lixiviation of Silver-ores with Hyposulphite Solutions. 8vo. New York, 1888.
A 24 U 8

STERENI, W. B. Through Famine-Stricken Russia. 12mo. Lond., 1892.
D 18 R 15

STEVENS, B. F. [*See* Clinton, Sir H.]

STEVENS, E. T. Flint Chips: a Guide to Pre-historic Archæology. 8vo. Lond., 1870.
A 18 T 28

STEVENS, H. [*See* Schöner, J.]

STEVENS, J. W. Leather Manufacture: a treatise on the practical workings of the Leather Manufacture. Imp. 8vo. Lond., 1891.
A 11 V 20

STEVENS, R. Improvement in the Pathology and Treatment of Small-Pox. 12mo. Sydney, 1881.
MA 3 P 7

STEVENS, T. Around the World on a Bicycle, from San Francisco to Teheran. 8vo. Lond., 1887.
D 10 S 29

Around the World on a Bicycle, from Teheran to Yokohama. 8vo. Lond., 1888.
D 10 S 30

STEVENSON, Capt. G. de St. C. Military Dictionary. [*See* Voyle, Major-Gen. G. E.]

STEVENSON, James B. Seven Years in the Australian Bush. 8vo. Liverpool, 1880.
MD 7 T 44

STEVENSON, Robert Louis. Across the Plains; with other Memories and Essays. 12mo. Lond., 1892.
J 11 W 24

Ballads. 8vo. Lond., 1890.
H 5 R 45

A Footnote to History: Eight Years of Trouble in Samoa. 8vo. Lond., 1892.
MB 1 Q 43

Memories and Portraits. 12mo. Lond., 1887.
J 1 S 50

Virginibus Puerisque, and other Papers. 12mo. Lond., 1887.
J 1 S 50

[*See* Jenkin, F.]

STEVENSON, Robert L., and OSBOURNE, Lloyd. The Wrecker. 8vo. Lond., 1892.
MJ 2 T 41

STEVENSON, S. W., and MADDEN, F. W. Dictionary of Roman Coins, republican and imperial. Revised by C. R. Smith. Roy. 8vo. Lond., 1889.
A 27 V 2

STEVENSON, Dr. T. Medical Jurisprudence. [*See* Taylor, Dr. A. S.]

STEVENSON, W. The Trees of Commerce. 12mo. Lond., 1888.
A 18 P 3

STEWARDSON, H. C. The Survey of Western Palestine: a General Index to the Memoirs. Vols. 1-3. The Jerusalem Volume, the Flora and Fauna of Palestine, the Geological Survey, and the Arabic and English Name Lists. 4to. Lond., 1888. D 4 V 12

STEWART, A. [See Pfleiderer, Dr. O.]

STEWART, Rev. A. Elements of Galic Grammar. 8vo. Edinb., 1801. K 12 U 20

STEWART, Aubrey. [See Seneca, L. A.]

STEWART, Prof. B., and GEE, W. W. H. Lessons in Elementary Practical Physics. Vol. 1, General Physical Processes ; Vol. 2, Electricity and Magnetism. 2 vols. 8vo. Lond., 1885-87. A 17 T 55, 56

STEWART, C. G. Murders by Poisoning. [See Brown, G. I.]

STEWART, C. S. Visit to the South Seas in the Ship Vincennes, 1829-30. 2 vols. 12mo. New York, 1833. MD 2 P 1, 2

STEWART, D. Life of W. Robertson. [See Robertson, W.]

STEWART, J. Questions in Science and General Lessons, with Answers for State School Scholars. 12mo. Melb., 1889. MG 2 P 19

STEWART, J. L. Golfiana Miscellanea : a Collection of Monographs on the Game of Golf. 8vo. Lond., 1887. A 17 W 40

STEWART, S. A., and CORRY T. H. Flora of the North-east of Ireland. 8vo. Belfast, 1888. A 20 P 2

STIELER, A. Hand Atlas. Fol. Gotha, 1864. D 41 P 18 ‡

STIER, C. W. F. The Native Flower Polka. Fol. Sydney (n.d.) MA 11 Q 15 †
The Fitz Roy Schottische. Fol. Sydney (n.d.) MA 11 Q 15 †

STILL, Rt. Rev. John. Gammer Gurton's Needle : a Comedy. [See British Drama, Ancient, 1.]

STIMPSON, P. E. [See Taylor, Dr. J. E.]

STIMSON, F. J. American Statute Law : a Digest of the Statutes of all States and Territories relating to Persons and Property, in force Jan. 1, 1886. Imp. 8vo. Boston, 1886. G 13 P 11 †

STIMULANTS IN WORKHOUSES. 12mo. (n.p. n.d.) F 11 P 59

STINDE, Dr. J. The Buchholz Family. 2nd Part. Sketches of Berlin Life. 12mo. Lond., 1887. J 9 Q 46
The Buchholzes in Italy : Travelling Adventures of Wilhelmine Buchholz. 8vo. Lond., 1887. J 9 Q 47
Frau Wilhelmine : Sketches of Berlin Life. 12mo. Lond., 1887. J 9 Q 48

STIRLING, Earl of. Register of Royal Letters relative to the Affairs of Scotland and Nova Scotia, 1615-35 ; edited by Rev. C. Rogers. 2 vols. roy. 4to. Edinb., 1885. B 1 S 21, 22†

STIRLING-MAXWELL, Sir D. [See Maxwell, Sir W. S.]

STIRTON, J. New Genus of Lichens. 8vo. Melb., 1880. MA 3 Q 19
Additions to the Lichen Flora of Queensland. 8vo. Melb., 1880. MA 3 Q 20

STOBÆUS, J. Eclogarum Physicarum et Ethicarum Libri duo : recensuit A. Meineke. (Greek text.) Tom. 1. 8vo. Lipsiæ, 1860. G 2 V 44
Florilegium ; recognovit A. Meineke. (Greek text.) 4 vols. (in 2.) 12mo. Lipsiæ, 1855-57. J 19 R 28, 29
Sententiæ ex Thesauris Græcorum delectæ. Fol. Tiguri, 1559. J 42 Q 9 ‡

STOCKER, C. W. [See Persius Flaccus, A., and Juvenalis, D. J.]

STÖCKL, Dr. A. Hand-book to the History of Philosophy. Part 1. Pre-Scholastic Philosophy. Roy. 8vo. Dublin, 1887. G 13 V 30

STOCKWHIP, The. 4 vols. (in 3.) Fol. Sydney, 1875-76. ME 21 T

STODDARD, C. W. Summer Cruising in the South Seas. 8vo. Lond., 1873. MD 4 R 43

STÖHR, P. Histology. [See Mackendrick, Prof. J. G.]
[See Mackendrick, Prof. J. G.]

STOKES, A. View of the Constitution of the British Colonies in North America and the West Indies, at the time the Civil War broke out on the Continent of America. 8vo. Lond., 1873. F 10 Q 24

STOKES, Prof. G. G. Burnett Lectures on Light, in three courses. (Nature series.) 12mo. Lond., 1887. A 21 Q 32

STOKES, Prof. G. T. Ireland and the Anglo-Norman Church. 8vo. Lond., 1889. G 13 S 45
Mediæval History. [See Rawlinson, Prof. G.]

STOKES, Margaret. Six Months in the Apennines. Sm. 4to. Lond., 1892. D 18 S 11
Early Christian Art in Ireland. 8vo. Lond., 1887. A 23 U 1

STOKES, Wm. Historical Chronometer. 2nd edition. [With chart.] Sm. fol. Lond., 1877. G 13 P 11 †
Memory. 89th edition. Lond., 1888 G 9 U 16
Companion to Stokes's Capital Mnemonical Globe. 18th edition. Lond., 1879. G 18 P 30
Rapid Writing. 21st ed. 18mo. Lond., 1884. G 9 U 17
Memory-Aiding Pocket Key-board, Piano, Organ, and Harmonium. 18mo. Lond., 1884. G 9 U 18
Stokes's Memory Aids for England and Wales. 18mo. Lond., 1877. G 18 P 29
Stokes's Memory-aiding Extended Multiplication Table. 2nd edition. 18mo. Lond., 1879. G 18 P 29
Stokes's Rapid Plan of Teaching Music. 10th edition. 18mo. Lond., 1879. G 18 P 28
Stokes's Memory-aiding Music Scales. 2nd edition. 18mo. Lond., 1879. G 18 P 28

STOKES, Wm.—*contd.*
Stokes's Memory-aiding Music Staff. 4th edition. 18mo.
Lond., 1875. G 18 P 28
Pictorial Multiplication Table. 11th edition. 4to. Lond.,
1877. G 13 P 10 †
French Genders in Five Minutes. 2nd edition. 18mo.
Lond., 1879. G 18 P 29
German Genders Simplified : a Mnemonic Scrap. 18mo.
Lond., 1877. G 18 P 29
Memory Aids for Elocution : a Mnemonical Scrap. 18mo.
Lond., 1875. G 45 P 29

STOKES, Whitley. Lives of the Saints. [*See* Anecdota
Oxoniensia.]

STOKVIS, A. M. H. J. Manuel d'Histoire de Généalogie,
et de Chronologie de tous les Etats du Globe, depuis les
Temps les plus reculés jusqu'à nos Jours. Vol. 1.
Imp. 8vo. Leide, 1888. B 15 U 14

STOLICZKE, F. [*See* Cambridge, Rev. O. P.]

STOLZE, F. Persepolis. 2 vols. fol. Berlin, 1882.
D 41 P 16, 17‡

STONE, A. P. [*See* Law Reports.]

STONE, J. Stone's Otago and Southland Directory for
1887-90, and 1892. 6 vols. 8vo. Dunedin, 1887-92.
ME 12 R-S
Wellington Directory, 1891-92. 8vo. Dunedin, 1891.
ME 12 R-S

STONE, Olivia M. Teneriffe and its Six Satellites ; or
Canary Islands, Past and Present. 2 vols. 8vo. Lond.,
1887 D 14 U 22, 23

STONES, W. New Zealand (the Land of Promise) and its
Resources. 6th ed. 12mo. Lond., 1863. MD 2 W 41

STONOR, H. Report from the Select Committee on. Fol.
Lond., 1854. MF 11 Q 9†

STORR, F. Travel Pictures. [*See* Heine, H.]

STORY, Dr. J. Commentaries on the Constitution of the
United States. 5th ed. By Dr. M. M. Bigelow. 2 vols.
roy. 8vo. Boston, 1891. F 14 V 21, 22
Commentaries on the Conflict of Laws. 8th ed. By Dr.
M. M. Bigelow. Roy. 8vo. Boston, 1883. F 14 V 20

STOTHERD, Col. R. H. Facsimiles of Anglo-Saxon
Manuscripts. [*See* Sanders, W. B.]

STOUT, Sir Robert. Notes on the Progress of New Zealand
for Twenty Years, 1864-1884. 8vo. Wellington, 1886.
MF 1 R 73

STOW, D. The Training System of Education. 11th ed.
8vo. Lond., 1859. G 17 P 53

STOWE, Mrs. Harriet Elizabeth. La Case de l'Oncle Tom ;
traduction complète par A. Michiels. 8vo. Paris (n.d.).
J 15 S 26

STRABO. Geographica, recognovit A. Meineke. (Gr. text).
2 vols. (in 1). Lipsiæ, 1852-53. • D 11 R 22

STRACHAN, Capt. J. Explorations and Adventures in
New Guinea. 8vo. Lond., 1888.* MD 5 Q 46

STRACHEY, Sir John. [Warren] Hastings and the Rohilla
War. 8vo. Oxford, 1892. B 16 R 4

STRACHEY, J. Saint Loe. [*See* Beaumont, F.]

STRACHEY, Lieut.-Gen. R. Lectures on Geography.
8vo. Lond., 1888. D 11 R 20

STRANAHAN, C. H. History of French Painting, from
its Earliest to its Latest Practice. Roy. 8vo. Lond.,
1889. A 8 R 34

STRANGE TALES of Peril and Adventure. 8vo. Lond.,
1887. J 5 P 34

STRATFORD DE REDCLIFFE, Rt. Hon. Stratford
Canning, Viscount. Life of ; by S. Lane-Poole. 2 vols. 8vo.
Lond., 1888. C 12 T 3, 4

STRATHMORE, Patrick, 1st Earl of. Book of Record.
[*See* Scottish History Soc., 9.]

STRATMANN, F. H. Middle-English Dictionary, containing words used by English writers from 12th to 15th
century. New edition, revised by H. Bradley. 4to.
Oxford, 1891. K 13 R 26

STRATHNAIRN, Sir Hugh Rose, Baron. Clyde and
Strathnairn ; by Maj. Gen. Sir O. T. Burne. (Rulers of
India.) 8vo. Oxford, 1891. C 17 Q 7

STRAUSS, A. [*See* Brown, E.]

STRAUSS, D. F. Ulrich von Hutten, his Life and Times.
8vo. Lond., 1874. C 21 Q 20

STRAUSS, G. L. M. Dishes and Drinks ; or, Philosophy
in the Kitchen ; by "An Old Bohemian." 8vo. Lond.,
1887. A 22 Q 11
Emperor William : the Life of a Great King and Good
Man. 12mo. Lond., 1888. C 12 P 41

STREAMS OF LIFE to Refresh the Weary and Impart
Vitality to all. 8vo. Sydney, 1875. MG 2 P 26

STREET, A. E. Memoir of G. E. Street, R.A., 1824-81.
8vo. Lond., 1888. C 13 T 8

STREET, G. E. Memoir of ; by his Son, A. E. Street.
8vo. Lond., 1888. C 13 T 8

STRETCH, Rev. J. F. [*See* Church History.]

STRETTELL, Alma. [*See* Spanish and Italian Folk
Songs.]

STRETTON, C. E. Safe Railway Working: a Treatise
on Railway Accidents, their Cause and Prevention.
8vo. Lond., 1887. A 6 R 38

STRICKLAND, Miss Agnes. Tales and Stories from His-
tory. 8th ed. 12mo. Lond., 1859. B 35 Q 5
Life of ; by Jane M. Strickland. 8vo. Edinb., 1887.
C 12 R 15
Lives of the Tudor and Stuart Princesses. 8vo. Lond.,
1888. C 12 P 23

STRICKLAND, Sir E. Annual Address, Geographical
Society of Australasia, New South Wales Branch, 1887-88.
8vo. Sydney, 1889. MD 2 V 17

STRICKLAND, Rev. E. The Australian Pastor: A Record of the Remarkable Changes in Mind, &c., of Henry Elliott. 12mo. Lond., 1862. MC 1 P 65

STRICKLAND, Jane Margaret. Life of Agnes Strickland; by her Sister. 8vo. Edinb., 1887. C 12 R 15

STRONG, H. A. [*See* Juvenalis, D. J., and Paul, H.]

STRONG, Prof. H. A., LOGEMAN, W.S.,and WHEELER, Prof. D. I. Introduction to the Study of the History of Language. 8vo. Lond., 1891. K 12 U 29

STRONGBOW. [*See* Pembroke, Earl of.]

STUART, A. Speech on the Education Debate. 8vo. Sydney, 1875. MF 2 T 11

STUART, Arabella, Lady. Life of; by E. T. Bradley. 2 vols. 8vo. Lond., 1889. C 14 Q 17, 18

STUART, C. Address delivered by, at the Third Annual General Meeting of the English Church Union. 8vo. Sydney, 1881. MG 1 R 41

STUART, H. A. South Sea Dreamer. [Poems.] 4to. Sydney, 1886. MH 1 S 2

STUART, Henry Windsor Villiers. Adventures Amidst the Equatorial Forests and Rivers of South America; also in the West Indies and the Wilds of Florida; to which is added "Jamaica Revisited." Roy. 8vo. Lond., 1891. D 15 V 14

STUART, J. . [*See* Scotland.]

STUART, J. A. E. The Literary Shrines of Yorkshire. 8vo. Lond., 1892. D 18 T 19

The Brontë Country; its Topography, Antiquities, and History. 8vo. Lond., 1888. D 19 Q 1

STUART, James Montgomery. History of Free Trade in Tuscany. 12mo. Lond., 1876. F 9 U 9

STUART, J. Maitland. How "No. 1" became "1¼" in Norway. 8vo. Lond., 1890. B 19 Q 15

STUART, John Sobieski S. Vestiarium Scoticum. Fol. Edinb., 1842. A 40 Q 28 ‡

STUART, Mary. [*See* Mary Stuart, Queen of Scots.]

STUART, Prof. Thomas Peter Anderson. Catalogue of the Scientific Serial Literature; compiled under the direction of T. P. Anderson Stuart, by W. T. Dayton. Roy. 8vo. Sydney, 1889. MK 1 R 53

Intercolonial Medical Congress, Melbourne, 1869: Address. 8vo. Melb., 1889. MA 3 T 40

STUBBS, Rev. C. W. The Land and the Labourers: Facts and Experiments in Cottage Farming and Co-operative Agriculture. 2nd edition. 8vo. Lond., 1885. F 14 P 35

Another copy. Stereotyped edition. 8vo. Lond., 1891. F 14 P 36

STÜBEL, A. [*See* Reiss, W.]

STUD-BOOK OF NEW SOUTH WALES. Vols. 1, 2. 8vo. Sydney, 1859-68. MA 1 Q 45, 46

2 E

STUDER, Dr. Beilagen. Ueber Neu-Guinea; vortrag gehalten in der Sitzung vom 9 Juni, 1881. 8vo. Bern, 1883. MD 8 R 6

STUKELEY, Rev. William. Family Memoirs and Antiquarian Correspondence of. [*See* Surtees Society, 80.]

STYLES, Emma. Australian Poems. 12mo. Adelaide, 1883. MH 1 Q 74

SUETONIUS TRANQUILLUS, C. De XII. Cæsaribus, Libri VIII., ejusdem de Illustribus Grammaticis et de Claris Rhetoribus; I. Casaubonus recensuit. Roy. 8vo. Genevæ, 1611. C 17 T 16

Quae Supersunt Omnia; recensuit C. L. Roth. 12mo. Lipsiæ, 1858 C 13 Q 9

C. Suetonii Tranquilli liber VIII., sive Tres Imperatores Cæsares Vespasiani, interpretati et emendati a Theod. Marcilio. Roy. 8vo. Genevæ, 1611. C 17 T 16

SUEZ CANAL. Compagnie universelle du Canal Maritime de Suez—Notice sur la Participation de la Compagnie. Sm. Fol. Paris, 1890. F 42 P 19 ‡

SULLEY, H. Temple of Ezekiel's Prophecy; or, an Exhibition of the Building represented in the last nine chapters of Ezekiel. Roy. 4to. Nottingham, 1887. A 2 P 12 †

SULLIVAN, S., and O'BYRNE, J. Leading Questions of the Day. 12mo. Sydney (n.d.) MF 2 P 60

SULLY, Dr. J. The Human Mind. 2 vols. 8vo. Lond., 1892. G 6 S 32

SULMAN, J. The Fireproofing of City Buildings. 8vo. Sydney, 1888. MA 1 T 76

SUMNER, Chas. [*See* Bradlaugh, C.—Five Dead Men.]

SUMNER, Prof. W. G. Lectures on the History of Protection in the United States. Roy. 8vo. New York, 1888. F 4 T 3

Protectionism: the Ism which Teaches that Waste Makes Wealth. 12mo. New York, 1888. F 2 P 33

SUNDAY LABOUR IN THE COLONIES, Correspondence on the Subject of. Fol. Lond., 1891. MF 4 S 8

SURTEES SOCIETY. Publications. Vols. 79-88. 8vo. Durham, 1884-91. E 2. 41

79. Testamenta Eboracensia: a Selection of Wills from the Registry at York. Vol. 5.
80. Family Memoirs of the Rev. William Stukeley, M.D., and the Antiquarian and other Correspondence of William Stukeley, Roger and Samuel Gale, etc.
81. Memorials of the Church of SS. Peter and Wilfrid, Ripon. Vol. III.
82. Halmota Prioratus Dunelmensis, extracts from Halmote Court Rolls, 1296-1384.
83. Cartularium Abbathiæ de Rievalle.
84. Churchwardens' Accounts of Pittington, 1580-1700.
85. English Miscellanies, illustrating the History and Language of the Northern Counties of England.
86. Cartularium Prioratus de Gyseburne. Vol. 1.
87. Life of St. Cuthbert, in English Verse.
88. Three Early Assize Rolls of Northumberland, Sæc. 13.

SURVEYOR, The. Vo 1, 2. 8vo. Sydney, 1888-90. ME 7 S

SUTHERLAND, A. Thirty short Poems. 12mo. Melb., 1890.   MII 1 Q 75

Victoria and its Metropolis, Past and Present. 2 vols. 4to. Melb., 1888.   MD 8 Q 25, 26†

SUTHERLAND, Rev. Dr. Geo. Christian Psychology ; a New Exhibition of the Capacities and Faculties of the Human Spirit. Roy. 8vo. Sydney, 1874.   MG 1 T 28

Urgent Appeals to the Unsaved. 2nd edition. 12mo. Dunedin, 1869.   MG 2 P 23

SUTHERLAND, Geo. Tales of the Gold Fields. 12mo. Melb., 1880.   MB 1 P 25

SUTHERLAND, J. M. William Wordsworth: the Story of his Life ; with Critical Remarks on his Writings. 12mo. Lond., 1887.   C 2 R 32

SUTHERLAND, P. C. Journal of a Voyage in Baffin's Bay and Barrow Straits, 1850–51, by Her Majesty's ships *Lady Franklin* and *Sophia*, in search of the missing crews of Her Majesty's Ships *Erebus* and *Terror*, with maps. 2 vols. 8vo. Lond., 1852.   D 16 R 2, 3

SUTRO, T. Report of the Sutro Tunnel Company, and the Sutro Tunnel. 8vo. New York, 1887.   F 5 8 45

SUTTER, A. Per Mare, per Terras ; being a Visit to New Zealand, by Australia, during 1883–84, and America in 1885. 8vo. Lond., 1887.   MD 1 Q 7

SUTTOR, Hon. W H. Australian Stories Retold, and Sketches of Country Life. 12mo. Bathurst, 1887.*   MJ 1 P 49

SUVOROFF, Alexander Vassilovich, Count. [Life of ;] by Lieutenant-Colonel [Henry] Spalding. 8vo. Lond., 1890.   C 14 R 9

SUZOR, R. Hydrophobia : an Account of M. Pasteur's System. 8vo. Lond., 1887.   A 13 P 41

SVENSKA NYKTERHETSSÄLLSKAPETS. 8vo. Stockholm, 1881.   F 14 T 12

SWAINSON, W. Observations on the Climate of New Zealand, principally with reference to its Sanative Character. 8vo. Lond., 1840.   MA 1 T 25

SWANTON, W. E. Notes on New Zealand. 8vo. Lond., 1892.   MD 7 T 45

SWAYNE, G. C. Herodotus. (Ancient Classics for English Readers). 12mo. Edinb., 1885.   J 14 P 10

SWEDENBORG, E. The Christian Religion; containing the universal Theology of the New Church. 2 vols. 4to. Lond., 1781.   G 10 V 5, 6

Compendium of the Theological Writings of ; by Rev. S. M. Warren. 8vo. Lond., 1885.   G 6 R 40

The Consummation of the Age, the Lord's Second Coming, and the New Church. 12mo. Lond., 1888.   G 16 P 49

SWEET, H. History of English Sounds, from the earliest period ; with full Word-lists. 8vo. Oxford, 1888.   K 12 U 10

SWETTENHAM, F. A. Vocabulary of the English and Malay Languages. 2 vols. 8vo. Singapore, 1887–89.   K 12 U 27, 28

SWIFT, Very Rev. Jonathan, Dean. Gulliver's Voyage to Lilliput, printed in the corresponding style of phonography. 12mo. Lond., 1883.   J 7 R 56

The Mystery of his Life and Love ; by J. Hay. 8vo. Lond., 1891.   C 15 Q 8

Polite Conversation, with Notes by G. Saintsbury. 8vo. Lond., 1892.   J 12 Q 39

SWINBURNE, A. C. Poems and Ballads. First, second, and third series. 3 vols. 8vo. Lond., 1884–89.   H 8 T 3–5

The Sisters : a Tragedy. 8vo. Lond., 1892.   H 3 P 47

The Bibliography of. [*See* Shepherd, R. H.]

Locrine : a Tragedy. 8vo. Lond., 1887.   H 8 T 23

Song of Italy. 12mo. Lond., 1867.   H 8 T 21

William Blake : a Critical Essay. 2nd ed. 8vo. Lond., 1868.   C 8 R 17

Word for the Navy. 8vo. Lond., 1887.   H 8 T 22

SYDER, M. The Temperance Lancet. 8vo. Lond., 1842.   F 11 R 55

SYDNEY, W. C. England and the English in the 18th Century. 2 vols. 8vo. Lond., 1891.   B 8 T 35, 36

SYDNEY : Act to make Better Provision for the Construction of Buildings and for the Safety and Health of the Inhabitants within the City of Sydney. 8vo. Sydney, 1879.   MF 3 R 59

City of Sydney : General Specifications for Paving Footways. Fol. Sydney, 1880.   MA 12 P 24 †

Directory, 1855. [*See* Waugh & Cox.]

Hand-book to Sydney and Suburbs. [*See* Leigh & Co.]

Plans of the City of. 2 vols. fol. Sydney, 1888.   MD 1 P 11, 12 †

Photographs of some of the Principal Buildings in the City, 1890. 4to. Sydney, 1890.   MD 11 P 14 †

SYDNEY BARMAID, A. [*See* Life, Adventures, and Confessions of a Sydney Barmaid.]

SYDNEY BOTANIC GARDENS. Catalogue of the Botanical Museum. 8vo. Sydney, 1883.   MA 3 R 43

SYDNEY DAILY TELEGRAPH. [*See* Daily Telegraph.]

SYDNEY DIOCESAN DIRECTORY, for 1881, 1886, 1888. 3 vols. 8vo. Sydney, 1881–88.   ME 4 T

SYDNEY GUARDIAN, The : a Journal of Religious, Literary, and Scientific Information. 4to. Sydney, 1848–50.   ME 19 T

SYDNEY HOSPITAL : By-Laws, 1882. 8vo. Sydney, 1882.   MF 1 T 53

Fortieth Annual Report. 8vo. Sydney, 1885, ME 6 S

Rules and Regulations, 1882. 8vo. Sydney, 1882.   MF 1 T 54

SYDNEY INFIRMARY, Pharmacopœia of. 12mo. Sydney, 1869. MA 3 P 59

SYDNEY INTERNATIONAL EXHIBITION, 1880 : References to the Plans, showing the Space and Position occupied by the various Exhibits in the Garden Palace. Roy. 8vo. Sydney, 1880. MH 1 S 38

SYDNEY MAIL, 1860-71, 1887-92. 21 vols. fol. Sydney, 1860-92. ME

SYDNEY MECHANICS' SCHOOL OF ARTS : Catalogue of the Libraries. 8vo. Sydney, 188. MK 1 R 40
Commemorative Address on its 50th Anniversary. [*See* Windeyer, Sir W. C.*]

SYDNEY MINT : Report from the Select Committee on the Sydney Branch Mint. Fol. Lond., 1862. MF 4 S 1

SYDNEY MORNING HERALD. 32 vols. fol. Sydney, 1887-92. ME
Centennial Supplement; together with Reports of Principal Events in connection with the Celebration of the Centenary of Australian Settlement. 4to. Sydney, 1888. MB 2 U 8

SYDNEY ONCE A WEEK MAGAZINE, The. 8vo. Sydney, 1878. ME 3 Q

SYDNEY PUNCH, The, 1888. 4to. Sydney, 1888. ME 20 T

SYDNEY QUARTERLY MAGAZINE, The. Vols. 4-6, 1887-89. 8vo. Sydney, 1887-89. ME 3 R

SYDNEY TECHNICAL COLLEGE. Calendar for 1884. 8vo. Sydney, 1884. ME 6 T

SYDNEY TOTAL ABSTINENCE SOCIETY. Second Annual Report. 12mo. Sydney, 1840. ME 5 Q

SYDNEY TRADES DIRECTORY. [*See* Marcus and Andrew.]

SYDNEY UNIVERSITY. Calendars for 1857, 1888-92. 6 vols. 8vo. Sydney, 1857-92. ME 5 S
Manuals of Public Examinations, 1872, 1876, 1877, 1879-81, 1884, 1886, 1887. 9 vols. 8vo. Sydney, 1872-87. ME 5 S
Syllabus of Courses of Lectures and Laboratory Work on Elementary Biology. 8vo. Sydney, 1889. MA 2 T 68

SYDNEY UNIVERSITY MAGAZINE. 8vo. Sydney, 1878-79. ME 3 Q

SYDNEY UNIVERSITY REVIEW. Nos. 1-5. Roy. 8vo. Sydney, 1881-83. ME 3 Q

SYLBURG, F. [*See* Pausanias.]

SYME, D. Representative Government in England : its Faults and Failures. 12mo. Lond., 1882. F 9 U 27

SYME, J. Nine Years in Van Diemen's Land ; comprising an Account of its Discovery, Possession, Settlement, Progress, &c. 12mo. Dundee, 1848. MD 2 W 12

SYMONDS, J. A. Essays, speculative and suggestive. 2 vols. 8vo. Lond., 1890. J 11 S 38, 39
Introduction to the Study of Dante. 2nd edition. 8vo. Edinb., 1890. C 12 R 9
[*See* Cellini, B., Gozzi, Count C., and Webster, J.]

SYMONDS, J. D. Studies of the Greek Poets. 1st and 2nd Series. 2nd edition. 2 vols. 8vo. Lond., 1877-79. H 10 Q 10, 11

SYMONS, A. [*See* Massinger, P.; Nero and other Plays.]

SYMONS, G. J. Eruption of Krakatoa, and subsequent Phenomena : Report of the Krakatoa Committee of the Royal Society. Roy. 4to. Lond., 1888. A 3 P 18 †

SYMONS, Rev. J. C. Life of the Rev. D. J. Draper ; with historical notices of Wesleyan Methodism in Australia ; chapters also on the Aborigines and Education in Victoria. 8vo. Lond., 1870. MC 1 Q 47

SYNESIUS. De Regno ad Arcadium Imperatorem.—Dion, sive de suæ vitæ ratione.—Calvitii laudatio.—De providentia, suœægyptius.—Concio quædam panegyrica.—De insomniis, cum Nicephori Gregoræ explicatione.—Ejusdem Synesii Epistolæ. (Greek Text.) Sm. fol. Paris, 1553. G 13 P 4 †

SZCZEPAŃSKI, F. von. Bibliotheca Polytechnica : Directory of Technical Literature published in England, America, France, and Germany. 8vo. Lond., 1891. K 7R 67

T

T., E. A. [*See* Mackonochie, A. H.]

TABLEAUX HISTORIQUES DES CAMPAGNES D'ITALIE depuis l'an IV Jusqu'à la Bataille de Marengo suivis du précis des opérations de l'armée d'Orient de la campagne d'Allemange en 1805, &c. Fol. Paris, 1806. B 41 P 22 ‡

TACITUS, C. C. Annales : recognovit T. Kiessliugius. (*Bound with Manetho-Apostelesmaticorum.*) 12mo. Lipsiæ, 1829. H 10 P 24
Annals of ; edited by H. Furneaux. (Latin Text.) 2 vols. 8vo. Oxford, 1884-91. B 36 R 2, 3
[Opera], emendatus ab I. Bekkero. 2 vols. 8vo. Lipsiæ, 1831. B 30 S 5
Historiarum libri qui supersunt ; with introduction, &c., by Rev. W. A. Spooner. 8vo. Lond., 1891. B 30 U 12
Tacitus ; by W. B. Donne. (Ancient Classics for English Readers.) 12mo. Edinb., 1889. J 14 P 25

TAGART, E. Memoir of the late Captain Peter Heywood ; with Extracts from his Diaries, &c. 8vo. Lond., 1832. MC 1 R 29

TAHITI. Exposé des Faits qui ont accompagné l'Agression des Français contre l'Ile de Tahiti. 8vo. Paris, 1843. MB 1 Q 44
History of the Otaheitean Islands from their first discovery to the present time. 12mo. Edinb., 1800. MD 2 W 7

TAHITI—*contd.*
Narrative of the Mission at Otaheiti and other Islands in the South Seas. 8vo. Lond., 1818.   MG 2 Q 8

Tahiti and the Society Islands. Missionary Records. 2nd ed. 12mo. Lond. (n.d.)   MD 2 W 45

TAILOR, R. The Hog hath lost his Pearl: a Comedy. [*See* British Drama, Ancient.]

TAINE, H. Essai sur Tite Live. 8vo. Paris, 1874.
B 17 P 17

La Fontaine et ses Fables. 7° 6d. 8vo. Paris, 1879.
J 9 Q 44

Philosophie de l'Art. 3' 6d. 2 vols. 8vo. Paris, 1881.
A 23 Q 24, 25

Les Origines de la France Contemporaine. 5 vols. 8vo. Paris, 1888–91.   B 26 U 17–21
1. L'Ancien Régime.
2-4. La Révolution.
5. Le Régime Moderne, tome 1.

TAIT, Most Rev. A. C., Archbishop of Canterbury. Life of ; by Rev. R. T. Davidson and Rev. W. Benham. 2 vols. 8vo. Lond., 1891.   C 14 T 20, 21

TAIT, Rev. J. Sermon delivered in the Scots' Church, Sydney, at the opening of the Synod of Australia, in connection with the Established Church of Scotland. Roy. 8vo. Sydney, 1842.   MG 1 R 53

TAIT, Prof. P. G. [*See* Andrews, Prof. T.]

TAKEN IN; being a Sketch of New Zealand Life; by "Hopeful." 12mo. Lond., 1887.   MD 1 P 8

TALICE, S. [*See* Dante Alighieri.]

TALLACK, W. Penological and Preventive Principles. 8vo. Lond., 1889.   F 9 S 10

TALLENTS, F. View of Universal History, &c., from the Creation of the World to the Present Time. Roy. fol. Lond., 1758.   B 34 P 16 ‡

TALLEYRAND, Charles Maurice de, Prince. Memoirs of ; edited by the Duc de Broglie ; translated by R. L. de Beaufort. 5 vols. 8vo. Lond., 1891–92. C 16 S 10–14

TALMUD. The Babylonian Talmud, with Commentaries and Annotations. [Hebrew Text.] 20 vols. fol. Warsyawa, 1859–64.   G 39 T 1–20‡

The Talmud ; by J. Barclay. Roy. 8vo. Lond., 1878.
G 6 Q 37

TANCRED, Capt, G. Historical Record of Medals and Honorary Distinctions conferred on the British Navy, Army, and Auxiliary Forces, from the Earliest Period. 4to. Lond., 1891.   B 24 V 9

TAPERELL, H. J. [*See* Rodyhouse, T. R.]

TARANAKI, J. K. [*See* Whitcombe, C. D.]

TARANAKI ALMANAC and Directory, 1872. [*See* Seffern, W. H. J.]

TARBUCK, E. L. Hand-book of House Property: a Popular and Practical Guide. 8vo. Lond.,1887. F 5 R 32

TARENTUM, Duke of. [*See* Macdonald, Marshall E. J. A.]

TARIFFS OF VICTORIA AND NEW SOUTH WALES. Fol. Lond., 1879.   MF 4 S 28

TARN, E. W. Light, an Introduction to the Science of Optics. (Weale.) 12mo. Lond., 1890. A 17 R 23
The Science of Building (Weale). 3rd. ed. 12mo. Lond., 1890.   A 17 R 23

TASCHENBERG, E. O. Anatomie, Histologie, und Systematik der Cylicozoa. 8vo. Halle, 1877. A 14 T 49

TASMAN, J. [*See* Voyages and Discoveries.]

TASMANIA.

ABORIGINES.
Copies of all Correspondence between Lieutenant-Governor Arthur and His Majesty's Secretary of State for the Colonies, on the Subject of Military Operations lately carried on against the Aboriginal Inhabitants of Van Dieman's Land. Fol. Lond., 1831.   MF 3 U 51

CUSTOMS.
Copies of all Correspondence between Her Majesty's Principal Secretary of State for the Colonies and the Lieutenant-Governor of Van Dieman's Land respecting the Taxation Ordinances passed by the Legislative Council of that Colony, which were recently declared by the Supreme Court of the Colony to be illegal, &c. ; or respecting the removal of Judge Montagu, or of any Ordinance subsequently passed by that Council for giving Validity to any such Taxation Ordinances. Fol. Lond., 1849.   MF 4 S 24

Copies of Despatches and Petitions relating to the Passing and Operation of the Act to confirm an Act of the Legislature of Van Dieman's Land, for authorising the Levy of certain Duties of Customs and on Spirits : Also the names of all Applicants for Restitution of Duties levied between 1829–34, who, by the Act referred to were debarred from Appeal to the Laws of the Realm for Redress ; and all recent Petitions to Her Majesty and other Appeals for Restitution of Money arising out of that Act. Fol. Lond., 1845.   MF 4 S 25

IRRIGATION.
Papers relative to the Irrigation of Lands. 8vo. Hobart, 1855.   M A 3 Q 40

LUNATIC ASYLUMS.
Regulations for the Guidance of the Officers and Attendants in the Lunatic Asylum, New Norfolk. 8vo. Hobart, 1856.   MF 2 T 38

PARLIAMENT.
Act to Provide for the Establishment of a Legislative Council, the Division of the Colony of Van Dieman's Land into Electoral Districts, and the Election of Members to serve in such Legislative Council. 8vo. Launceston, 1851.   MF 3 T 22

Journals and Papers of Parliament. Vols. 10–24. Fol. Hobart, 1887–91.   MF 2. 55

Standing Orders of the Legislative Council of Van Dieman's Land. 8vo. Hobart (n.d.)   MF 3 T 23

TASMANIA—*contd.*

PRISON REGULATIONS.

General Prison Regulations, 1866, for the Penal Establishment situate within the Police District of Launceston. 8vo. Hobart, 1866.　　　MF 2 T 39

STATISTICS.

Statistics of the Colony for 1828 and 1886–89. 5 vols. Fol. Hobart, 1829–90.　　　ME 2. 56

STATUTES.

Acts of the Lieutenant-Governers [Col. Sir G. Arthur and Sir John Franklin] and Council of Van Diemen's Land, 1824–39. Sm. fol. Hobart, 1840.　　　ME 2. 56

Acts of Parliament, 1887–91. Sm. fol. Hobart, 1889–91.　　　ME 2. 56

Abstract of the Waste Lands Act of Tasmania, 1863. 8vo. Hobart, 1864.　　　MF 3 T 21

Electoral Act for Van Diemen's Land. 8vo. Launceston, 1851.　　　MF 2 T 40

TASMANIAN ALMANAC. [*See* Walch, J.]

TASMANIAN EXHIBITION, LAUNCESTON, 1891–92. Official Catalogue of the Exhibits. 8vo. Launceston, 1891.　　　MK 1 T 22

Report by W. H. Vivian, Executive Commis-ioner. Roy. 8vo. Sydney, 1892.　　　MK 2 R 2

TASTY DISHES, made from Tested Receipes. 12mo. Lond., 1890.　　　A 22 Q 9

TATE, Prof. Ralph. Handbook of the Flora of Extra-tropical South Australia, containing the Flowering Plants and Ferns. 12mo. Adelaide, 1890. MA 3 P 8

The Gastropods of the Older Tertiary of Australia. Part 2. 8vo. Adelaide, 1888.　　　MA 3 T 34

Supplemental Notes on the Palliobranchs of the Older Tertiary of Australia, and a description of a New Species of Rhynchonella. 8vo. Adelaide, 1885.　MA 3 T 33

The Lamellibranchs of the Older Tertiary of Australia. Part 1. 8vo. Adelaide, 1885.　　　MA 3 T 33

The Botany of Kangaroo Island. 8vo. Adelaide, 1883.　　　MA 3 T 32

Additions to the Flora of Extra-tropical South Australia, including descriptions of Two New Species. 8vo. Adelaide, 1885.　　　MA 3 T 32

Additions to the Flora of the Port Lincoln District, including brief descriptions of Two New Species. 8vo. Adelaide, 1888.　　　MA 3 T 32

Plants of the Lake Eyre Basin. 8vo. Adelaide, 1888.　　　MA 3 T 32

Census of the Fauna of the Older Tertiary of Australia. 8vo. Adelaide, 1888.　　　MA 3 T 32

Descriptions of some New Species of Marine Mollusca from South Australia and Victoria. 8vo. Adelaide, 1888.　　　MA 3 T 32

Supplement to a List of the Lamellibranch and Palliobranch Mollusca of South Australia. 8vo. Adelaide, 1888.　　　MA 3 T 32

TATE, Prof. Ralph.—*contd.*

Census of the Mollusca Fauna of Australia. 8vo. Adelaide, 1888.　　　MA 3 T 32

Census of the Mollusca of Australia. 8vo. Adelaide, 1888.　　　MA 3 T 32

List of Australian Terebridæ. 8vo. Adelaide, 1886.　　　MA 3 T 32

On the Geographical Relations of the Pulmoniferous Mollusca of Victoria. 8vo. Adelaide, 1881. MA 3 T 32

Post-miocene Climate in South Australia. 8vo. Adelaide, 1885.　　　MA 3 T 32

Rudimentary Treatise on Geology. Part 1, Physical Geology. Part 2, Historical Geology. 12mo. Lond., 1875.　　　A 24 P 7

TAUFAPULOTU, Grégoire. La Langue de l'Archipel Toga. Roy. 8vo. Paris, 1887.　　　MK 1 U 22

TAUNTON, T. H. Portraits of Celebrated Racehorses of the Past and Present Centuries, 1702–1870, with Pedigrees and Performances. 4 vols. 4to. Lond., 1887–88.　　　A 18 V 2–6

TAUSSIG, Dr. F. W. Tariff History of the United States. 8vo. New York, 1880.　　　F 6 S 35

TAVERNIER, Jean Baptiste, Baron of Aubonne. Travels in India; translated from the French by V. Ball, LL.D. 2 vols. Roy. 8vo. Lond., 1889.　　D 17 U 10, 11

TAYLOR, A. G. The Marble Man; Humours of his Life's History. 8vo. Sydney, 1889.　　　MJ 2 T 2

Law and Practice of New South Wales Letters Patent. 8vo. Sydney, 1888.　　　MF 1 R 37

TAYLOR, A. J. Advice Gratis; being Friendly Hints to Parents touching the Training and Education of their Children. 8vo. Hobart, 1885.　　　MA 2 T 51

Chat about the Aborigines of Tasmania, with some Reflections on the Subject; also, some Notes on the Shell Mounds at Little Swanport. 8vo. Hobart, 1891.　　　MA 3 Q 63

Imperial Federation *versus* Australian Independence. 8vo. Hobart, 1889.　　　MF 4 Q 1

Overpressure in Education, an inevitable consequence of Payment by Results; a Protest and Warning to Parents. 8vo. Hobart, 1885.　　　MG 1 R 42

TAYLOR, Commander Alfred D. India Directory for the Guidance of Commanders of Steamers and Sailing Vessels. Revised edition. 2 vols. Imp. 8vo. Lond., 1891.　　　D 11 V 11, 12

TAYLOR, Alice. [*See* Baernreither, J. M.]

TAYLOR, Annie. Life of G. M. Murphy. 8vo. Lond., 1888.　　　C 12 P 16

TAYLOR, Dr. Alfred Swaine. Manual of Medical Jurisprudence. 12th ed.; edited by Dr. T. Stevenson. 12mo. Lond., 1891.　　　F 7 V 1

TAYLOR, C. F. Summer Dreamings: a Poem. 8vo. Melb., 1872.　　　MH 1 Q 57

TAYLOR, E. R. Elementary Art Teaching. 8vo. Lond., 1890.　　　A 23 S 6

TAYLOR, Dr. F. Manual of the Practice of Medicine. 12mo. Lond., 1890. A 26 Q 10

TAYLOR, Hannis. Origin and Growth of the English Constitution: an Historical Treatise. Part 1. 8vo. Boston, 1889. B 3 T 20

TAYLOR, Sir Henry. Correspondence of; edited by E. Dowden. 8vo. Lond., 1888. C 9 U 53

TAYLOR, J., the Water Poet, 1583-1653. Early Prose and Poetical Works. 8vo. Lond., 1888. H 8 U 34

TAYLOR, Dr. J. E. In and about Ancient Ipswich, with illustrations by P. E. Stimpson. Imp. 8vo. Norwich, 1888. B 23 V 1

TAYLOR, Rev. James. The Great Historic Families of Scotland. 2 vols. roy. 4to. Lond., 1887. C 1 S 19, 20 †

TAYLOR, Jane. [See Walford, L. B.]

TAYLOR, Rev. Jeremy. Rule and Exercises of Holy Living. 19th ed. 8vo. Lond., 1706. G 13 Q 36
Rule and Exercises of Holy Dying. 20th ed. 8vo. Lond., 1706. G 13 Q 36

TAYLOR, Mrs. John, AUSTIN, Mrs. Sarah, and GORDON, Lady Duff. Three Generations of English-women; Memoirs and Correspondence of; by Janet Ross. 2 vols. 8vo. Lond., 1888. C 14 R 5

TAYLOR, R.: a Biography; by E. G. Parry. 8vo. Lond., 1888. C 13 S 1

TAYLOR, R. Leaf from the Natural History of New Zealand; or, a Vocabulary of its different Productions, &c., with their Native Names. 18mo. Wellington, 1848. MA 2 P 27

TAYLOR, R. W. C. The Modern Factory System. 8vo. Lond., 1891. F 14 S 4

TAYLOR, T. Euchred. [A Novel.] 12mo. Melb., 1885. MJ 1 Q 56
Buds and Blossoms. 8vo. Melb., 1885. MH 1 Q 58

TAYLOR, W. C. The Students' Manual of Modern History. New edition; revised by C. D. Yonge. 8vo. Lond., 1866. B 35 P 16

TAYLOR, W. F. England under Charles II., from the Restoration to the Treaty of Nimeguen, 1660-1678. Arranged and edited by W. F. Taylor. (English History by Contemporary Writers.) 18mo. Lond., 1889. B 22 P 5

TEALL, J. J. H. British Petrography, with special reference to the Igneous Rocks. Imp. 8vo. Lond., 1888. A 9 V 24

TEBBUTT, C. G. Skating and Bandy. [See Heathcote, J. M.]

TEBBUTT, John. Double Star Measures at Windsor, New South Wales, 1889 and 1890. 8vo. Lond. (n.d.) MA 3 Q 61
Observations of Phenomena of Jupiter's Satellites at Windsor, New South Wales, in the Year 1890. 8vo. Lond., 1891. MA 3 Q 60

TEBBUTT, John—*contd.*
Observations of the Variable Star R Carinæ, from November 1886–June 1890. 8vo. Lond. (n.d.) MA 3 Q 62
Results of Meteorological Observations, made at the Private Observatory, The Peninsular, Windsor, New South Wales, in the Years 1886-90. Sm. Fol. Sydney, 1891. MA 12 P 21 †
The Sydney Observatory, and the *Sydney Morning Herald;* a Plea for Astronomy in New South Wales. 8vo. Sydney, 1891. MA 3 Q 64

TECHNICAL OR WORKING MEN'S COLLEGE. Report from the Committee. Fol. Sydney, 1881. MG 3 Q 26 †

TECKLENBOROUGH, J. Seven Years' Cadet-life: Records of the Oxford Military College. 4to. Oxford, 1885. B 33 P 15 ‡

TEGG, J. New South Wales Pocket Almanac, 1837, 1839, and 1840. 3 vols. 18mo. Sydney, 1837-40. ME 4 Q.

TEGNER, E. Frithiofs-Sage. 18mo. Leipzig (n.d.) H 6 P 50
Frithiofs-Sage, unschrift und nebertragung in prosa. 8vo. Frankfort-on-Main, 1846. H 10 Q 18
Frithiofs-Saga: a Legend of the North; translated from the Swedish by "P. S." 8vo. Stockholm, 1839. H 6 T 22
The Frithiof-Saga: or Lay of Frithiof; translated by the Rev. W. L. Blackley. Fol. Lond., 1880. H 39 P 14 ‡

TEICHELMANN, C. G., and SCHÜRMANN, C. W. Outlines of a Grammar Vocabulary, and Phrasoology of the Aboriginal Language of South Australia. 8vo. Adelaide, 1840. MK 1 Q 33

TELANG, K. T. [See Müller, F. Max, Sacred Books, 8.]

TELL EL-AMARNA TABLETS, in the British Museum; with Autotype Facsimiles. Imp. 8vo. Lond., 1892. B 21 V 10

TEMPERANCE. Voice of Science on Temperance; by various authors. 3rd ed. 12mo. Lond. (n.d.) F 11 P 44
Religious and Educational Aspects of Temperance: by various authors. 2nd edition. Lond. (n.d.) F 11 P 58
Temperance Congress of 1862. 8vo. Lond., 1862. F 11 R 58

TEMPLE, Dorothy Osborne, Lady. Letters from Dorothy Osborne to Sir William Temple, 1652-54; edited by E. A. Parry. Lond., 1888. C 15 U 4

TEMPLE, Rt. Hon. Frederick. [See Dufferin, Earl of.]

TEMPLE, Sir Richard. Asia. [See Keane, A. H.]
Lord Lawrence: (English Men of Action.) 8vo. Lond., 1889. C 12 R 28
Journals kept in Hyderabad, Kashmir, Sikkim, and Nepal; edited by his Son. 2 vols. 8vo. Lond., 1887. D 17 U 1, 2
Palestine Illustrated. Roy. 4to. Lond., 1888. D 4 S 9 †

TEMPLE, Sir William. Works of. 4 vols. 8vo. Lond., 1770. B 36 T 20–23
[*See* Temple, Lady.]

TENISON-WOODS, Rev. J. E. North Australia; its Physical Geography, and Natural History. 8vo. Adelaide, 1864. MA 2 T 54
On the Fossil Flora of the Coal Deposits of Australia. 8vo. Sydney (n.d.) MA 2 T 53
On the Natural History of New South Wales. 8vo. Sydney, 1882. MA 3 R 45
Palæontology of New Zealand. Part 4. Corals and Bryozoa of the Neozoic Period in New Zealand. Roy. 8vo. Wellington, 1880. MA 2 R 34

TENNANT, Charles. The People's Blue Book : Taxation as it is, and as it ought to be. 4th ed. 8vo. Lond., 1872. F 11 Q 21

TENNANT, Prof. James. Geology. [*See* Ansted, Prof. D. T.]

TENNIS, by J. M. Heathcote. Lawn Tennis; by C. G. Heathcote. Rackets; by E. O. P. Bouverie. Fives; by A. C. Ainger. (Badminton Library.) 12mo. Lond., 1890. A 17 U 44

TENNYSON, Alfred, Baron. Demeter, and other Poems. 12mo. Lond., 1889. H 8 T 34
The Foresters. 12mo. Lond., 1892. H 3 P 42
Illustrations of. [*See* Collins, J. C.]
Poetry of. [*See* Van Dyke, H.]
[*See* Powning, W.]

TEPPER, J. G. O. Common Native Insects of South Australia. Part 1. Coleoptera, or Beetles. Sm. 4to. Adelaide, 1887. MA 2 U 30
Descriptive List of Tokens in the Museum Collection, Numismatical Department, Public Library, Museum and Art Gallery of South Australia. 4to. Adelaide, 1890. MA 2 U 54
List of named Insects in the South Australian Museum, Adelaide. 3rd and 4th Series. 2 vols. (in 1). sm. 4to. Adelaide, 1891. MA 2 U 45

TERENTIUS, P. Comœdiæ Sex; ed. J. A. Giles. 8vo. Lond., 1837. H 4 U 24
Comœdiæ; recensuit A. Fleckeisen. 12mo. Lipsiæ, 1857. H 2 Q 40
Œuvres de [*See* Nisard, D.]
Terence. [*See* Collins, Rev. W. L.]

TERREIN DE LACOUPERIE, Prof. A.E.J.B. Languages of China before the Chinese. 8vo. Lond., 1887. K 12 U 8

TERTULLIANUS, Q. S. F. Quæ Supersunt Omnia; edidit F. Oehler. 3 vols. 8vo. Lipsiæ, 1853. G 4 T 22–24

TEUFFEL, W. S. History of Roman Literature; translated from the German by G. C. W. Warr. 2 vols. 8vo. Lond., 1891. B 30 U 18, 19

THACKERAY, Anne. [*See* Aulnoy, Marie C. J. d']

THACKERAY, Rev. J. R. Revival of the Spanish Inquisition in the Diocese of Newcastle : an Address. 8vo. Wallsend, 1875. MG 1 R 52

THACKERAY, W. M. Essay on Genius of Cruickshank. [*See* Stephens, F. G.]
Collection of Letters of, 1847–55; with Portraits and Reproductions of Letters and Drawings. Imp. 8vo. Lond., 1887. C 17 U 13
Early Writings. [*See* Johnson, C. P.]

THEAL, G. McCall. History of South Africa, 1486–1872. vols. 1–4 8vo. Lond., 1888–89. B 16 S 26–29
History of the Boers in South Africa. 8vo. Lond., 1887. B 16 S 25

THEMIS, regtskundig tijdschrift. 8vo. 's Gravenhage, 1880. F 11 S 40

THEOBALD, M. Spirit Workers in the Home Circle: an Autobiographic Narrative of Psychic Phenomena for Twenty Years. 8vo. Lond., 1887. G 12 P 34

THEOCRITUS. Scholia in Theocritum, Nicandrum, et Oppianum. (Gr. text.) Imp. 8vo. Parisiis, 1849. H 7 V 25
Theocritus, Bion, et Moschus. [*Opera.*] (Gr. et Lat.) 2 vols. 8vo. Lond., 1829. H 6 T 23, 24

THEODOSIA ERNEST; or the Heroine of Faith; with an Outline of the Baptist Churches from the Great Founder. 8vo. Sydney, 1861. MG 2 P 34

THEOGNIS. [*See* Davies, Rev. J.]

THEOPHRASTUS. Theophrasti Charactere, Marci Antonini Commentarii, Epicteti Dissertationes ab Arriano Literis Mandatæ, Fragmenta, etc., Simplicii, Cebetis Tabula, Maximi Tyrii Dissertationes; (Gr. et Lat.) emendavit F. Dübner. Imp. 8vo. Parisiis, 1840. J 18 V 23
Characteres; edidit H. E. Foss (Greek text). 12mo. Lipsiæ, 1858. G 13 T 44
Historia Plantarum (Greek text). 2 vols. (in 1). 12mo. Lipsiæ, 1854. A 20 P 16
Quæ supersunt Opera; ed. J. G. Schneider. 5 vols. 8vo. Lipsiæ, 1818–21. J 17 Q 4–8

THERRY, Sir R. An Appeal on behalf of the Roman Catholics of New South Wales. 8vo. Sydney, 1833. MG 1 R 16

THEVINOT, M. Relations de divers Voyages Curieux. 3 vols. (in 2.) fol. Paris, 1663–64. D 40 S 16, 17 ‡

THESAURUS MUSICUS : a Collection of two, three, and four, part songs, set to music by the most Eminent Masters. Fol. Lond. (n.d.) H 36 S 10 ‡

THEURIET, A. Jules B. Lepage, and his Art. Roy. 8vo. Lond., 1892. C 19 U 12

THIBAUT, G. The Vedanta-Sutras. [*See* Müller, F. M.]

THIERFELDER, Dr. Der Wein als Heilmittel im Alterthum und in der Neuzeit. 8vo. (n.p.n.d.) F 11 Q 40

THIERRY, Augustin. Essai sur l' Histoire de la formation et des progres du Tiers Etat. Roy. 8vo. Paris, 1853.
B 26 V 5

Récits des Temps Mérovingiens ; précédés de considérations sur l' histoire de France. Roy. 8vo. Paris, 1840.
B 26 V 6

Lettres sur l' histoire de France : dix ans d'études historiques. Roy. 8vo. Paris, 1830. B 26 V 7

Histoire de la Conquête de l'Angleterre par les Normands. 2 vols. Roy. 8vo. Paris, 1830. B 26 V 8, 9

Nouveaux éloges historiques. [See Mignet, F. A. M.]

Tableau de l'Empire Romain depuis la fondation de Rome jusqu' à la fin du gouvernement impérial en Occident. 8vo. Paris, 1876. B 30 Q 3

THIERS, L. A. Histoire de la Révolution Française : 13ᵉ éd. 10 vols. 8vo. Paris, 1880. B 16 Q 24-33

Atlas pour servir à l'intelligence des Campagnes de la Révolution Française. Fol. Paris (n.d.) B 44 P 7 ‡

Histoire du Consulat et de l'Empire. 21 vols. 8vo. Paris, 1884. B 16 Q 3-23

Atlas de l'Histoire du Consulat et de l'Empire. Fol. Paris, 1864. B 44 P 8 ‡

Life of ; by P. de Remusat. 12mo. Lond., 1892.
C 17 Q 22

THIMM, Carl A. Complete Bibliography of the Art of Fence. 12mo. Lond., 1891. A 29 P 18

THISTLEWOOD, A. The Trials of Arthur Thistlewood, and others for High Treason ; taken in Shorthand by J. Byrom. 8vo. Lond., 1820. F 12 R 11

THOM, A. Thom's Official Directory of the United Kingdom, 1884, 1887-90. 5 vols. 8vo. Dublin, 1884-90. E 2.81

THOMAS, A. P. W. Report on the Eruption of Tarawera and Rotomahana: New Zealand. 8vo. Wellington, 1888. MA 2 R 39

THOMAS, E. C. [See Bury, R. de.]

THOMAS, F. S. Hand-book to the Public Records. (Record Commissioners' Pubs.) Roy. 8vo. Lond., 1853.
B 15 T 31

Historical Notes, 1509-1714. (Record Commissioners' Pubs.) 3 vols. Roy. 8vo. Lond., 1856. B 15 T 33-35

THOMAS, H. Guide to Excursionists between Australia and Tasmania. 12mo. Melb., 1883. MD 1 T 58

THOMAS, John D. Hydatid Disease, with special reference to its Prevalence in Australia. 8vo. Adelaide, 1884. MA 2 Q 65

Hydatid Disease of the Lungs. 8vo. Adelaide, 1884.
MA 3 T 1

THOMAS, Julian. South Sea Massacres. Roy. 8vo. Sydney, 1881. MF 2 T 12

The "Vagabond" Annual, Christmas, 1877. 8vo. Sydney, 1877. MJ 2 S 17

THOMAS, Margaret. A Scamper through Spain and Tangier. 8vo. Lond., 1892. D 18 S 10

THOMAS, Sidney G. Memoir and Letters of ; edited by R. W. Burnie. 8vo. Lond., 1891. C 15 Q 14

THOMAS, W. M. [See Montagu, Lady M. W.]

THOMAS, W. W. Sweden and the Swedes. Roy. 8vo. Chicago, 1892. D 18 V 11

THOMES, W. H. A Gold Hunter's Adventures between Melbourne and Ballarat. 8vo. Lond. (n.d.) MJ 1 S 58

THOMPSON, C. W. Manual of the Sextant. 8vo. Lond., 1887. A 19 S 25

THOMPSON, D. G. The Problem of Evil: an Introduction to the Practical Sciences. 8vo. Lond., 1887. G 12 P 33

THOMPSON, D. W. Day Dreams of a School Master. 2nd ed. 12mo. Edinb., 1864. G 17 P 50

THOMPSON, E. P. Life in Russia; or, the Discipline of Despotism. 8vo. Lond., 1848. D 8 R 48

THOMPSON, G. Slavery and Famine, Punishments for Sedition, or an account of the Miseries and Starvation at Botany Bay. 8vo. Lond., 1794. MB 1 Q 40

THOMPSON, H. A. Notes on the Reduction of Gold Ores. 8vo. Melb., 1867. MA 3 P 25

THOMPSON, H. M. The Purse and the Conscience : an attempt to show the connection between Economics and Ethics. 8vo. Lond., 1891. F 14 P 37

THOMPSON, J. Owens College : its Foundation and Growth, and its connection with Victoria University, Manchester. 8vo. Manchester, 1886. B 22 U 12

THOMPSON, J. A. Report upon an outbreak of Typhoid Fever in the Municipal District of Leichhardt, due to Polluted Milk. Fol. Sydney, 1886. MA 3 Q 17 †

THOMPSON, J. A., and STAYTON, G. H. Report upon an outbreak of Typhoid Fever in the Municipalities of Newtown and Macdonaldtown. Fol. Sydney, 1889.
MA 3 Q 18 †

THOMPSON, R. A. Thomas Becket, martyr, patriot. 8vo. Lond., 1889. C 12 R 10

THOMPSON, Prof. S. P. [See Guillemin, A.]

THOMSON, A. [See Suetonius Tranquillus, C.]

THOMSON, Sir C. W., and MURRAY, J. Reports of the Scientific Results of Voyage of H.M.S. Challenger during the years 1873-76. Zoology, vols. 17-26. 10 vols. (in 14) roy. 4to. Lond., 1886-88. A 6 Q 3-R 1 †

Botany, vol. 2. Roy. 4to. Lond., 1886. A 6 R 6 †

THOMSON, D. C. The Barbizon School of Painters. 4to. Lond., 1891. A 8 T 34

THOMSON, Sir E. Deas. Letter respecting compensations. [See New South Wales-Crown Lands.]

Suggestions for the Division of the Cabinet or Administration, under Responsible Government, into different Ministerial Departments. Fol. Sydney, 1856.
MF 3 U 50

THOMSON, George M. Introductory Class Book of Botany for use in New Zealand Schools ; Part 1, Structural ; Part 2, Systematic. 8vo. Wellington, 1891. MA 3 T 2

THOMSON, J. [*See* Victoria.]

THOMSON, Prof. J. J. Applications of Dynamics to Physics and Chemistry. 8vo. Lond., 1888. A 29 R 1

THOMSON, James. "B.V." Life of ; by H. S. Salt. 8vo. Lond., 1889. C 14 S 1

Essays and Phantasies. 12mo. Lond., 1881. J 11 W 17

The City of Dreadful Night and other poems. 2nd ed. 12mo. Lond., 1888. H 8 T 53

A Voice from the Nile and other poems ; with Memoir of the Author by B. Dobell. 12mo. Lond., 1884. H 8 T 52

THOMSON, James. The Seasons. 18mo. Lond., 1805. H 6 P 47

Tancred and Sigismunda : a Tragedy. [*See* British Drama, Modern.]

THOMSON, J. A. Study of Animal Life. 8vo. Lond., 1892. A 28 Q 27

Outlines of Zoology. 8vo. Edinb., 1892. A 28 Q 28

THOMSON, Jos. Travels in the Atlas and Southern Morocco. 8vo. London, 1889. D 14 Q 2

Mungo Park and the Niger. 8vo. Lond., 1890. D 14 Q 6

THOMSON, R. Australian Nationalism ; an earnest appeal to the Sons of Australia in favour of Federation and Independence of the States of our Country. 12mo. Burwood (near Sydney), 1888. MF 1 P 36

THOMSON, Dr. Robert D. Digestion ; the influence of alcoholic fluids on that function. 8vo. Lond., 1841. F 11 R 59

THOMSON, Dr. Spencer. Temperance and Total Abstinence. 8vo. Lond., 1850. F 11 Q 41

THOMSON, W. Remarks on the Introduction of Diphtheria into Victoria. 8vo. Melb., 1872. MA 3 Q 65

THOMSON, Most Rev. Wm. Laws of Thought. 4th ed. 12mo. Lond., 1857. G 13 T 46

THOMSON, Prof. Sir Wm. Mathematical and Physical Papers. Vols. 1–3. Camb., 1882-90. A 25 T 29–31

Popular Lectures and Addresses. Vols. 1 and 3. 2 vols. 8vo. Lond., 1889-91. A 29 R 1, 3

1. Constitution of Matter.
3. Navigational Affairs.

[*See* Newton, Sir I.]

THOMSON, W. M. [*See* Renan, E.]

THOREAU, Henry David. Anti-Slavery and Reform Papers. 8vo. Lond., 1890. F 6 P 41

Life of ; by H. S. Salt. 8vo. Lond., 1890. C 14 T 16

THORESBY, R., the Topographer: his Town and Times, by D. H. Atkinson. 2 vols. roy. 8vo. Leeds, 1885-87. C 12 T 15, 16

2 F

THOREZA, Adelaide de la : a Chequered Career ; by the Rev. J. Cameron. 12mo. Sydney, 1878. MC 1 P 62

THORNTON, P. M. The Brunswick Accession. 8vo. Lond., 1887. B 24 T 1

The Stuart Dynasty : short studies of its Rise, Course, and Early Exile. Roy. 8vo. Lond., 1890. B 13 S 18

THORNTON, Dr. R. J. Botanical Extracts : or, Philosophy of Botany. 3 vols. fol. Lond., 1810. A 41 P 9-11 ‡

THORPE, B. Anglo-Saxon Grammar. [*See* Rask, E.] History of England. [*See* Lappenberg, J. M.]

THORPE, Mrs. Mary. The Balkan Peninsula. [*See* Laveleye, E. de.]

THORPE, Prof. T. E. Dictionary of Applied Chemistry. Vols. 1 and 2. R. 8vo. Lond., 1890-91. K 9 R 11, 12

THORPE, W. G. The Still Life of the Middle Temple. 8vo. Lond., 1892. C 18 Q 7

THREE FRIENDS. Poems by. [*See* MacDonald, G.]

THRELKELD, C. Synopsis Stirpium Hibernicarum alphabetice depositarum sive Commentatio de Plantis Indigenis præsertim Dublinensibus instituta. 12mo. Dublin, 1727. A 20 P 6

THRUPP, J. G. [*See* James, F. L.]

THUCYDIDES. De Bello Peloponnesiaco libri octo ; [edidit] Franciscus Goeller. 2 vols. 8vo. Lipsiæ, 1826. B 27 S 19, 20

History of the Peloponnesian War, with notes by T. Arnold. 2nd ed. 3 vols. 8vo. Oxford, 1840-42. B 27 S 16-18

History of the Grecian War ; trans. by T. Hobbs. 3rd ed. 2 vols. 8vo. Lond., 1723. B 27 Q 24, 25

Historia Belli Peloponnesiaci ; edidit Ioannes Matthias Stahl. 2 vols. (in 1.) 8vo. Lipsiæ, 1873-74. B 27 Q 22

Thucydides ; by Rev. W. L. Collins. (Ancient Classics for English Readers.) 12mo. Edinb., 1887. J 14 P 26

The Fourth Book of. A revision of the text ; by Dr. W. G. Rutherford. 8vo. Lond., 1889. B 27 U 19

THUDICHUM, Dr. J. L. W. Alcoholic Drinks. 8vo. Lond., 1884. F 11 R 61

THURBER, Dr. G. Silos and Ensilage. 12mo. New York, 1886. A 1 U 28

THURSFIELD, J. R. [Life of] Peel. (English Statesmen.) 8vo. Lond., 1891. C 16 Q 21

THURSTON, R. H. Heat as a form of Energy. 12mo. Lond., 1890. A 21 P 9

Steam-boiler Explosions in Theory and Practice. 8vo. New York, 1887. A 6 R 39

THWAITES, R. G. The Colonies, 1492-1750. (Epochs of American History.) 12mo. Lond., 1891. B 19 P 1

THWING, C. F. and Carrie F. B. The Family: an Historical and Social Study. 8vo. Boston, 1887. G 16 S 35

TIBULLUS, A. [*See* Catullus, C. V., *and* Davies, Rev. J.]

TIETKENS, W. H. Journal of the Central Australian
Exploring and Prospecting Association's Expedition,
1889, under command of W. H. Tietkins. Fol. Adelaide, 1890.   MD 12 P 22 †
Another copy.   8vo. Adelaide, 1891.   MD 7 S 33

TIKHOMIROV, L. Russia, Political and Social; translated
from the French by E. Aveling. 2 vols. 8vo. Lond.,
1888.   F 14 S 19, 20

TILDEN, W. A. Introduction to the Study of Chemical
Philosophy : Principles of Theoretical and Systematic
Chemistry. 12mo. Lond., 1888.   A 21 P 2

TILLEY, W. The Wild West of Tasmania, being a description of the Silver Fields of Zeehan and Dundas. 8vo.
Zeehan, 1891.   MD 8 R 7

TIMBS, J.   Curiosities of London. Roy. 8vo. Lond.,
1885.   D 18 V 10

TIMES, The.   Index to, 1840-1852, 1866, 1886-91.
Sm. 4to. Lond., 1876-92.   E
Register of Events, 1886-89. 2 vols. 8vo. Lond.,
1887-90.   E 2.21
The Times ; weekly edition. Vols. 10-15. Fol. Lond.,
1886-92.   E

TIMMINS, S. History of Warwickshire. 8vo. Lond.,
1889.   B 5 T 31

TIRARD, H. M. and N. Sketches from a Nile steamer,
for the use of travellers in Egypt. 8vo. Lond., 1891.
                                                D 14 Q 3

TIREBUCK, W. Great Minds in Art ; with an Introduction on Art and Artists. 8vo. Lond., 1888.   C 13 R 1

TIROSH LO YAYIN ; or, the Wine Question Considered.
12mo. Lond., 1841.   F 11 P 39

TISCHENDORF, C. Vetus Testamentum Greece. [*See*
Bibles.]

TISDALL, H. T. State School Examination Papers, in
sets as given by inspectors during 1889. 12mo. Melb.,
1890.   ME 5 T

TISDALL, Rev. W. St. C. Simplified Grammar and
Reading Book of the Panjábí Language. 8vo. Lond.,
1889.   K 20 Q 22
Simplified Grammar of the Gujaráti Language, together
with a short reading book and vocabulary. 8vo. Lond.,
1892.   K 20 Q 26

TISSANDIER, G. Royal Treasure House of Knowledge :
a Book of Pleasing Experiments and Attractive Pastimes. Roy. 8vo. Lond., 1887.*   MA 2 V 19

TIT-BITS. Vols. 1-21. Lond., 1881-92.   E 1.57

TOBACCO, SUGAR, SPIRITS, &c. Reports respecting
the Growth and Manufacture of. 8vo. Lond., 1866.
                                                F 11 S 41

TOCQUEVILLE, A. de. Nouveaux éloges historiques.
[*See* Mignet, F. A. M.]

TODD, A. On Parliamentary Government in England :
its Origin, Development, and Practical Operation.
2 vols. 8vo. Lond., 1887-89.   F 4 P 20, 21

TODD, John, and WHALL, W. B. Practical Seamanship
for use in the Merchant Service. Roy. 8vo. Lond.,
1890.   A 19 U 1

TOLLER, T. N. Correspondence of Edward, Third Earl
of Derby. [*See* Chetham Soc., N.S. 19.]

TOLLINS, J. [*See* Longinus.]

TOMKIS, Mr. Albamazar. [*See* British Drama, Ancient.]

TONER, J. M. [*See* Washington, G.]

TOOKE, J. H. Diversions of Purley. 8vo. Lond., 1860.
                                                 J 10 V 28

TOPINARD, Dr. Paul. Anthropology. 8vo. Lond.,
1878.   A 18 R 26
Etude sur les Races Indigènes de l'Australie. 8vo. Paris,
1872.   MA 3 T 3

TORCEANU, R. Simplified Grammar of the Roumanian
Language. 8vo. Lond., 1883.   K 20 Q 10

TORCH, THE, AND COLONIAL BOOK CIRCULAR.
Vols. 1-4. 4to. Lond., 1887-91.   E 1.40

TORONTO PUBLIC LIBRARY. Subject Catalogue of
Books in the Reference Library, with an Index of Subjects and Personal Names, 1889. 8vo. Toronto, 1889.
                                                 K 7 R 47

TORR, C. Rhodes in Modern Times. 8vo. Cambridge,
1887.   B 34 T 12

TORRENS, Sir R. An Essay on the Transfer of Land,
by Registration. 8vo. Lond., 1882.   F 5 R 33

TORRINGTON, George Byng, Viscount. Memoirs of.
[*See* Camden Soc.]

TOURNEUR, C. The Revenger's Tragedy. [*See* British
Drama, Ancient.]
[*See* Webster, J.]

TOVEY, D. C. [*See* Gray, Thos.]

TOWLE, Mrs. E. A. Alexander Heriot Mackonochie : a
Memoir ; edited by Edward Francis Russel, M.A. 8vo.
Lond., 1890.   C 12 R 12

TOWN AND COUNTRY JOURNAL. 48 vols. Fol.
Sydney, 1870-92.   ME

TOWN AND COUNTRY MAGAZINE. Vol. 21. 8vo.
Lond., 1789.   E

TOWN-HOLDINGS : a Digest of Evidence as to England and Wales, given before the Select Committee of
the House of Commons, 1886-87. Roy. 8vo. Lond.,
1888.   F 10 T 21

TOWNS, R. South Sea Island Immigration for Cotton
Culture. 8vo. Sydney, 1864.   MF 2 T 14

TOWNSEND, G. W. Floods and Droughts, and How to
cure both these Evils. 8vo. Parramatta, 1882.
                                                MA 3 Q 5

TOZER, Rev. H. F. The Church and the Eastern Empire. 12mo. Lond., 1888. G 19 P 14

TRACY, A. [*See* Leffingwell, A. T.]

TRADE PROTECTIVE INSTITUTE. Reports, 1882-87 and 1889. 3 vols. 4to. Sydney, 1882-89 ME 19 T
Index to Trade Report. Vol. 22. 8vo. Sydney, 1890. ME 19 T

TRADES DIRECTORY OF SYDNEY. [*See* Marcus and Andrew.]

TRAILL, H. D. [Life of] The Marquis of Salisbury. 12mo. Lond., 1891. C 16 P 23
[Life of] William III. 8vo. Lond., 1888. C 3 R 3

TRAILL, T. W. Boilers : their Construction and Strength. 8vo. Lond., 1888. A 22 R 25

TRAMP, A. [*See* Ramblings.]

TRANSPORTATION, Report from the Select Committee. Fol. Lond., 1861. MF 4 S 26
Copies of any Memorials in favour of, or against Transportation to any part of Australia; and of addresses and resolutions on the same subject adopted by the Conference of Delegates from New South Wales, Victoria, South Australia, and Tasmania. Fol. Lond., 1863. MF 4 S 27
Correspondence relative to discontinuance of Transportation. Fol. Lond., 1865. MF 4 S 27
Report from the Select Committee on Transportation. Fol. Lond., 1812. MF 8 P 30 †
Report from the Select Committee of the House of Lords appointed to Inquire into the Provisions and Operation of the Act 16 and 17 Vict., cap. 99, intituled "An Act to Substitute, in certain Cases, other Punishment in lieu of Transportation." Fol. Lond., 1856. MF 8 P 31 †
First Report from the Select Committee, together with the Minutes of Evidence. Fol. Lond., 1856. MF 8 Q 27 †
Transportation and Penal Servitude. Report of Commissioners on the Operation of the Acts relating to. 2 vols. roy. 8vo. Lond., 1863. MF 2 S 9, 10
[*See* Convicts.]

TRANSVAAL INDEPENDENCE COMMITTEE.
Annexation of the Transvaal; by G. P. Moodie. 8vo. Lond., 1881. F 8 S 26
Annexation of the Transvaal. Correspondence between Sir M. Hicks-Beach and the Transvaal Delegates. 8vo. Lond., 1881. F 8 S 26
Balance-Sheet. 8vo. Lond., 1882. F 8 S 26
British Policy towards the Boers; by G. B. Clark. 8vo. Lond., 1881. F 8 S 26.
Capt. Elliott's Murder and the Transvaal Government. (Folded sheet.) 8vo. Utrecht, 1881. F 8 S 26
Case of the Boers in the Transvaal; by C. F. Davison. 2nd ed. 8vo. Lond., 1881. F 8 S 26
Extract from *Daily News*, January 25, on the Intentions of the Boers. 8vo. Lond., 1881. F 8 S 26

TRANSVAAL INDEPENDENCE COMMITTEE—*contd.*
Four Years of Protest in the Transvaal; by Capt. E. H. Verney. 8vo. Lond., 1881. F 8 S 26
Another copy. 2nd ed. 8vo. Lond., 1881. F 8 S 26
History of English Rule and Policy in South Africa: a Lecture; by R. S. Watson. 8vo. Newcastle, 1881. F 8 S 26
Imperialism in South Africa; by J. E. Ritchie. 8vo. Lond., 1879. F 8 S 26
Independence or Destruction. (Folded sheet.) 8vo. Utrecht (n.d.) F 8 S 26
Interview between Sir B. Frere and the Deputation from the Boer Committee. 8vo. Lond., 1879. F 8 S 26
Invasion of the Transvaal ; Extracts from Mr. Gladstone's Midlothian Speeches, 1879-80. 8vo. Lond., 1881. F 8 S 26
John Bright's Answer to the International Memorial on the Transvaal Question. (Folded sheet.) 8vo. Lond., 1881. F 8 S 26
Letter from Field-Cornet H. P. N. Pretorius to Col. O. Lanyon, on the Subject of Probable Hostilities. 8vo. Lond., 1880. F 8 S 26
Materials for a Speech in Defence of the Policy of Abandoning the Orange River Territory. 8vo. Lond., 1878. F 8 S 26
Objects of the Association. 8vo. Lond., 1881. F 8 S 26
Petition for Peace in Transvaal. (Folded sheet.) 8vo. Lond., 1881. F 8 S 26
Proclamation of the Triumvirate. (Folded sheet.) 8vo. Utrecht, 1880. F 8 S 26
Reader! we must try to stop this unjust war at once. 8vo. (n.p.n.d.) F 8 S 26
Short Summary of Chief Facts relating to the Transvaal War. (Folded sheet.) 8vo. Lond., 1881. F 8 S 26
Slavery in the Transvaal; by J. C. M. Weale. 8vo. Lond., 1881. F 8 S 26
South Africa : its difficulties and present state ; by A. R. Campbell-Johnston. 8vo. Lond., 1877. F 8 S 26
The Transvaal; by F. Harrison. 8vo. Lond. (n.d.) F 8 S 26
War Map of the Transvaal and Adjoining Countries in South Africa. (Folded sheet.) 8vo. Lond., 1881. F 8 S 26
Word from Holland on the Transvaal Question; by Prof. R. Fruin. 8vo. Utrecht, 1881. F 8 S 26

TRANT, W. Trade Unions: their origin and objects, influence, and efficacy. 12mo. Lond., 1884. F 14 P 38

TRAQUAIR, Phoebe A. Illustrations of Dante. [*See* Dante Alighieri.]

TRAVIS, J. Law Treatise on the Constitutional Powers of Parliament, and of the Local Legislatures, under the British North America Act, 1867. Roy. 8vo. Saint John, N.B., 1884. F 1 V 4

TREGARTHEN, G. New South Wales, 1860-89 : a Statistical Sketch. 8vo. Sydney, 1890. MF 2 T 15

TREGEAR, E. The Maori-Polynesian Comparative Dictionary. Roy. 8vo. Wellington, 1891. MK 1 U 6

Southern Parables [New Zealand]. 12mo. New Plymouth, 1884. MJ 1 Q 57

TRELAWNY, E. J. Adventures of a Younger Son. New edition. 8vo. Lond., 1890. C 14 S 5

TRENCH, Most Rev. Richard Chenevix. English, Past and Present. 3rd edition. 12mo. Lond., 1856. K 16 P 26

Notes on the Miracles of our Lord. 6th ed. 8vo. Lond., 1858. G 16 T 22

Notes on the Parables of our Lord. 8vo. Lond., 1867. G 12 Q 9

Letters and Memorials; edited by Miss Mary Trench. 2 vols. 8vo. Lond., 1888. C 13 T 19, 20

TRENCH, Miss Mary. [*See* Trench, Most Rev. R. C.]

TRENDELENBURG, F. A. [*See* Aristoteles.]

TRENT, W. P. [Life of] W. G. Simms. (Am. Men of Letters). 12mo. Boston, 1892. C 17 P 3

TREVELYAN, G. O. Early History of Charles James Fox. 8vo. Lond., 1880. C 11 P 36

TRIALS AND TRAVELS OF A DOMINIE at Home and Abroad; by "Amnema." 8vo. Lond., 1874. MJ 3 P 31

TRIBU DE WAGAP, La, (Nouvelle-Calédonie) ses Mœurs et sa Langue d'apres les Notes d'un Missionnaire Mariste, coordonnées par le P.A.C. Imp. 8vo. Paris, 1890. MK 1 U 25

TRIBUNE, THE, and News of the Week, Jan. 1887–June 1889. 6 vols Fol. Sydney, 1887–89. ME, Fol. 6

TRIMEN, R., and BOWKER, J. H. South African Butterflies. 3 vols. imp. 8vo. Lond., 1887–89. A 15 S 18–20

1. Nymphalidæ.
2. Erycinidæ and Lycænidæ.
3. Papilionidæ and Hesperidæ.

TRIPPLIN, J. [*See* Saunier, C.]

TROLLOPE, Anthony. Commentaries of Cæsar. (Ancient Classics for English Readers.) 8vo. Edinb., 1887. J 14 P 4

Australia and New Zealand. Division 2, New South Wales. 8vo. Melb., 1873. MD 8 R 21

New South Wales and Queensland. 12mo. Lond., 1875. MD 1 S 17

TROLLOPE, Thomas Adolphus. What I Remember. 2 vols. 8vo. Lond., 1887. C 6 S 13, 14

TROPICAL AGRICULTURIST, The: a Monthly Record of Information for Planters in the Tropics; compiled by A. M. and J. Ferguson, 1881–87. Vols. 1–6. Roy. 8vo. Colombo, 1882–87. E 2. 8

TROTTER, Rev. E. B. The Church of England: her Early History, her Property, and her Mission. 12mo Lond., 1887. G 19 P 2

TROTTER, Capt. L. J. History of India, from the earliest times to the present day. 8vo. Lond., 1889. B 10 Q 41

Life of the Marquis of Dalhousie. (Statesmen Series.) 8vo. Lond., 1889. C 12 Q 37

Warren Hastings. (Rulers of India.) 12mo. Oxford 1890. C 12 P 36

TROTTER, Thomas. Medical and Chemical Essays, containing Communications from New South Wales on Scurvy and other interesting subjects, by Edward Laing. 8vo. Lond., 1795. MA 3 T 4

TROUP, J. R. With Stanley's Rear Column. 8vo. Lond., 1890. D 14 U 6

TROYTE, C. A. W. Change Ringing: an introduction to the early stages of Church or Hand Bell-ringing. 4th edition. Lond. (n.d.) A 23 Q 15

TRUBNER, C. [*See* Martin, L. C.]

TRUMBULL, Rev. H. C. The Blood Covenant: a Primitive Rite, and its Bearings on Scripture. 8vo. Lond., 1887. G 16 S 36

TRYON, G. W., Jr. Manual of Conchology, structural and systematic, with Illustrations of the Species. Continued by H. A. Pilsbry. (First Series.) Vols. 1-14. Roy. 8vo. Philad., 1879–92. A 32 P 1-14

Manual of Conchology, structural and systematic, with Illustrations of the Species. Second Series. Vols. 1-8. Roy. 8vo. Philad., 1885-92. A 32 Q 1-8

Biographical Notice of; by W. S. W. Ruschenberger. Roy. 8vo. Philad., 1888. C 16 U 2

TRYON, H. Report on Insect and Fungus Pests, No. 1. 8vo. Brisb., 1889. MA 3 Q 22

TUCKER, Rev. H. W. Memoir of the Life and Episcopate of G. A. Selwyn, D.D., Bishop of New Zealand, 1841–69, Bishop of Lichfield, 1867–1878. 2 vols. 8vo. Lond., 1879. MC 1 R 55, 56

TUCKER, Col. J. M. Life and Naval Memoirs of Lord Nelson. 8vo. Lond. (n.d.) C 18 R 15

Life of the Duke of Wellington. 8vo. Lond. (n.d.) C 18 Q 22

TUCKER, J. O. Golden Spring: a Tale of Tasmania; and other Poems. 12mo. Melb., 1865. MH 1 P 33

TUER, A. W., and FAGAN, C. E. First Year of a Silken Reign, 1837–38. 8vo. Lond., 1887. B 37 U 7

TUKE, Sir S. Adventures of Five Hours. [*See* British Drama, Ancient, 3.]

TULLOCH, Principal John. Memoir of the Life of; by Mrs. Oliphant. 8vo. Edinb., 1888. C 13 T 22

TULOU, F. Enfants Célèbres. 2 vols. 8vo. Paris, 1890. C 18 S 12, 13

Les Généraux de Vingt Ans : Hoche—Marceau—Joubert ―Desaix. 2ᵉ ed. 8vo. Paris, 1891. C 18 S 14

TURCICI IMPERII STATUS; accedit De Regn. Algeriano atque Tunetano Commentarius. 32mo. Lugd. Bat., 1634. B 34 P 12

TURGOT, A. R. J. [Life of]; by L. Say. (Great French Writers.) 8vo. Lond., 1888.   C 14 U 1

TURNBULL, John. Voyage fait autour du Monde, 1801-4. Suivi d'un extrait du voyage de James Grant à la Nouvelle Hollande, 1801-2. 8vo. Paris, 1807. MD 7 T 47

Voyage Round the World in the years 1800-4. 2nd ed. 4to. Lond., 1813.   MD 7 P 24 †

TURNER, D. W. Grammar of the German Language. [See Ahn, Dr. F.]

TURNER, F. General Boulanger: a biography. 8vo. Lond., 1889.   C 15 U 5

TURNER, F. Census of the Grasses of New South Wales, together with a popular description of each species. Roy. 8vo. Sydney, 1890.   MA 3 R 5

Forage Plants of Australia (with Illustrations). Roy. 8vo. Sydney, 1891.   M A 3 R 30

TURNER, Rev. J. G. Life of the Rev. N. Turner, the Pioneer Missionary. 8vo. Melb., 1872.   MC 1 Q 56

TURNER, C. J. Ribton-. History of Vagrants and Vagrancy, and Beggars and Begging. 8vo. Lond., 1887.   F 5 P 12

TURNER, J. M. W., and RITCHIE, L. Wanderings by the Seine, from Rouen to the Source. Roy. 8vo. Lond., 1835.   D 18 V 3
[See Milton, J.]

TURNER, Rev. N. Life of the Pioneer Missionary; by his Son, Rev. J. G. Turner. 8vo. Melb., 1872.   MC 1 Q 56

TURNER, R. S. Catalogue of the second and remaining portion of the Library of the late R. S. Turner. Roy. 8vo. Lond., 1888.   K 8 R 9

TURNER, T. A. Argentina and the Argentines. 8vo. Lond., 1892.   D 15 S 18

TURRI, G. G., & Co. The Inventor's Guide to Obtaining and Selling Patents. 8vo. Melb., 1890. MF 2 T 13

TURTON, W. Conchylia dithyra Insularum Britannicarum : the Bivalve Shells of the British Islands. 4to. Lond., 1848.   A 15 T 15

TUSON, E. W. A. The British Consul's Manual. 8vo. Lond., 1856.   F 9 S 29

TUTTLE, Prof. H. History of Prussia, 1134-1756. 3 vols. 8vo. Boston and London, 1884-88. B 27 R 2-4

TWAIN, Mark. [See Clemens, Samuel Langhorne.]

TWEED, Isa. Cow-keeping in India. 8vo. Calcutta, 1891.   A 1 U 30

TWEMLOW, Fanny. [See Coignet, Clarisse.]

TWO OBADIAS, The. [See Bars and Barmaids.]

TYERMAN, Rev. L. Life and Times of Rev. John Wesley, Founder of the Methodists. 6th ed. 3 vols. 8vo. Lond., 1890.   C 17 T 3-5

TYLER, M. C. Patrick Henry. (American Statesmen.) 12mo. Boston, 1887.   C 12 P 25

TYLER, T. [See Shakespeare, Wm.]

TYLOR, C. [See Backhouse, E.]

TYNDALL, Prof. John. New Fragments. 8vo. Lond., 1892.   J 12 Q 34

Researches on Diamagnetism and Magne-crystallic Action. 8vo. Lond., 1888.   A 21 Q 6

TYRRELL, Prof. R. Y., and PURSER, C. L. Correspondence of M. Tullius Cicero; with a revision of the text, a commentary, and introductory essays. Vols. 1-3. (Vols. 1 and 2, by Tyrrell; vol. 3, by Tyrrell and Purser.) 3 vols. 8vo. Dublin, 1885-90.   C 14 U 6-8

TYRWHITT, Rev. R. St. J. Our Sketching Club. 8vo. Lond., 1874.   A 29 Q 42

TYRWHITT, W. S. S. The New Chum in the Queensland Bush. 8vo. Oxford, 1887.   MD 1 Q 26

U.

UBIQUE. [See Gillmore, P.]

UDALL, N. Apophthegmes of Erasmus. [See Erasmus.]

UHLIG, Theodor. Wagner's Letters to. [See Wagner, R.]

ULESPIÈGLE, T. Les Aventures de. (Collection Jannet–Picard.) 12mo. Paris (n.d.)   J 15 Q 20

ULLATHORNE, Most Rev. W. B. Ceremony of Blessing and Laying the Foundation Stone of a New Church. Translated from the Pontifical with a Preliminary Instruction. 8vo. Sydney (n.d.)   MG 1 Q 63

Memoir of Bishop Willson, First Bishop of Hobart, Tasmania. 8vo. Lond., 1887.   MC 1 Q 49

Letters of. Roy. 8vo. Lond., 1892.   MC 1 R 51

ULPIANUS. Fragmenta, sive Excerpta ex Ulpiani libro singulari regularum, accedunt ejusdem Institutionum aliaque Veteris Juris Romani Fragmenta ; emendavit E. Böcking. 12mo. Bonnæ, 1845.   F 2 U 32

UNFORTUNATE CAREER OF JOHNSON, The ; by "An Australian." 12 mo. Sydney, 1873. MJ 2 T 14

UNITED AUSTRALIA : Public Opinion in England as expressed in the Leading Journals of the United Kingdom. Roy. 8vo. Sydney, 1890.   MF 3 T 20

UNITED SERVICE INSTITUTION OF NEW SOUTH WALES. Journal and Proceedings for 1889 and 1891. 2 vols. 8vo. Sydney, 1890-92.   ME 6 R

[Rules, List of Members, and By-laws.] 8vo. Sydney, 1889.   MF 1 T 5

UNITED SERVICE MAGAZINE. [See Colburn's United Service Magazine.]

UNITED STATES.

AGRICULTURE.

Commissioner of Agriculture. Reports, 1886-91. 5 vols.
8vo. Washington, 1887-92.　　　　　　　E 1. 38

Department of Agriculture. Report of Diseases of Swine,
&c. Roy. 8vo. Wash., 1879.　　　　　A 18 V 7

Sorghum Sugar, Letters on; by the Commissioner of Agriculture. 8vo. Wash., 1880.　　　　　A 18 V 6

ARMY.

Report upon a Pattern of Ambulance Waggon for
Army Use. 8vo. Washington, 1878.　A 29 V 11

CONSTITUTION.

Constitution of the United States of America, with the
Amendments thereto ; to which are added Jefferson's
Manual of Parliamentary Practice and the Standing
Rules and Orders for Conducting Business in the
House of Representatives. 8vo. Washington (n.d.)
　　　　　　　　　　　　　　　　　　F 14 T 26

CONSULAR REPORTS.

Consular Reports. Vols. 18-38. 8vo. Washington,
1888-91.　　　　　　　　　　　　　E 2. 17

Index to the Consular Reports, No. 1 to No. 59.
1880-85. 8vo. Washington, 1887.　　E 2. 17

Consular Reports : Forestry in Europe. 8vo. Washington, 1887.　　　　　　　　　　　　E 2. 17

Consular Reports : Emigration and Immigration. 8vo.
Washington, 1887.　　　　　　　　E 2. 17

Consular Reports : Cattle and Dairy Farming. 2 vols.
8vo. Washington, 1887.　　　　　　E 2. 17

Consular Reports, Special. Vols. 1-4, 6. 8vo. Washington, 1890-92.　　　　　　　　　E 2. 17

CURRENCY.

Annual Reports of the Comptroller, 1887-88. 2 vols.
roy. 8vo. Washington, 1887-88.　　　E 2. 18

ETHNOLOGY, BUREAU OF.

2nd to 6th Annual Reports. 6 vols. imp. 8vo. Washington, 1883-88.　　　　　　　　　E 2. 24

EXPLORATIONS AND SURVEYS.

Geological Exploration of the 40th parallel, C. King, Geolo-
gist, in charge. Vols. 1-4. Roy. 4to. Wash., 1870-78.
　　　　　　　　　　　　　　　　　A 11 Q 8-11
　　1. Systematic Geology; by C. King.
　　2. Descriptive Geology; by A. Hague and S. F. Emmons.
　　3. Mining Industry; by J. D. Hague. With Geological Contri-
　　butions by C. King.
　　4. Palæontology; by F. B. Meek, J. Hall, and R. P. Whitfield.
　　Ornithology; by R. Ridgway.

Reports on Survey of Boundary between the Territory of
United States and Possessions of Great Britain. Roy.
4to. Wash., 1878.　　　　　　　　A 11 Q 7 †

FINANCE.

Digest of Appropriations for Support of the Government, 1884. 4to. Washington, 1883.　E 2. 18

UNITED STATES—*contd.*

LABOR.

Bureau of Statistics of Labor. Annual Report for 1887.
Roy. 8vo. Wash., 1888.　　　　　　　　E

1st, 2nd, and 4th—6th Annual Reports of the Commissioner of. Roy. 8vo. Washington, 1886-91.
　　　　　　　　　　　　　　　　　E 2. 17-18

NAVY.

Report of the Chief Engineer, J. W. King, U.S. Navy, on
European Ships of War and their Armaments, &c.
2nd ed. Roy. 8vo. Wash., 1878.　　　A 19 T 6

PATENTS.

Commissioner of Patents. Decisions for 1877-78. 2 vols.
roy. 8vo. Wash., 1878-79.　　　　　　　E

Official Gazette. Vols. 35-57. Imp. 8vo. Washington,
1886-91.　　　　　　　　　　　　　E

Report of Commissioner of Patents, 1886-90. 4to.
Washington, 1887-91.　　　　　　　　E

SURGEON-GENERAL'S LIBRARY.

Index-Catalogue. Vols. 8-12. Imp. 8vo. Washington,
1887-91.　　　　　　　　　　　　K 8 S 9-13†

CALIFORNIA.

7th—10th Annual Reports of the State Mineralogist ;
with maps. 5 vols. 8vo. Sacramento, 1888-90.
　　　　　　　　　　　　　　　　　E 2. 17-18

CONNECTICUT.

Public Acts of, 1882. Roy. 8vo. New Haven, 1882.
　　　　　　　　　　　　　　　　　F 11 T 11

ILLINOIS.

Annual Reports of Trade and Commerce of Chicago.
Roy. 8vo. Chicago, 1889-92.　　　E 2. 17-18

Chicago Board of Trade. Act of Incorporation, Rules,
&c. Roy. 8vo. Chicago, 1891.　　F 14 V 23

Journal of House of Representatives. 8vo. Spring-
field, 1885.　　　　　　　　　　　F 11 S 48

Revised Statutes. Edited by G. W. Cochran. 8 vo.
Chicago, 1884.　　　　　　　　　　F 11 S 47

IOWA.

Proceedings at the 5th Annual Session of National Convention of Bureaus of Statistics of Labor. 8vo.
Des Moines, 1887.　　　　　　　　F 12 Q 40

Weather Service : Report for 1884 ; by Dr. G. Hinrichs.
8vo. Des Moines, 1889.　　　　　E 2. 17-19

MAINE.

First Annual Report of the State Board of Health, 1885.
Roy. 8vo. Augusta, 1886.　　　　　F 11 T 10

Revised Statutes of. Imp. 8vo. Portland, 1864.
　　　　　　　　　　　　　　　　　F 11 V 2

MASSACHUSETTS.

Annual Statistics of Manufactures, 1886-91. 4 vols.
8vo. Boston, 1889-92.　　　　　　E 2. 17-18

Bureau of Statistics of Labor. Reports. 4 vols. 8vo.
Boston, 1887-89, 1892.　　　　　　E 2. 15-18

Bureau of Statistics of Labor. Index to Reports. 8vo.
Boston, 1890.　　　　　　　　　　E 2. 15-18

Census, 1885. 4 vols. 8vo. Boston, 1887-88. E 2. 15-18

UNITED STATES—*contd.*

MINNESOTA.

Geological and Natural History Survey. Reports, 1886–87, 1889, 1891, 1892. 5 vols. 8vo. Minneapolis, 1886–92. · E 2. 15–18

[*See* Arthur, J. C.; Oestlund, O. W.; and Wadsworth, M. E.]

MONTANA.

Revised Statutes of. 8vo. Helena, 1881. F 11 S 49

NEW HAMPSHIRE.

General Laws of. Roy. 8vo. Manchester, 1878.
F 11 T 12

State Librarian's Report. 8vo. Concord, 1891. E 2. 18

NEW YORK.

Bureau of Labour. 4th–8th Annual Reports. 8vo. Albany, 1887–92. E 2. 15–18

Documents of the Assembly. 30 vols. roy. 8vo. Albany, 1882–85. E 2. 15–18

Documents of the Senate. 27 vols. roy. 8vo. Albany, 1882–85. E 2. 15–18

Journal of the Assembly. 8 vols. roy. 8vo. Albany, 1882–85. E 2. 15–18

Journal of the Senate. 4 vols. roy. 8vo. Albany, 1882–85. E 2. 15–18

Laws of the State. 17 vols. roy. 8vo. Albany, 1875–83. E 2. 15–18

PENNSYLVANIA.

Adjutant-General's Report, 1890. 8vo. Harrisburg, 1891. E 2. 18

Agriculture, State Board of. Report, 1890. 8vo. Harrisburg, 1891. E 2. 15–18

Attorney-General's Report, 1889–90. 8vo. Harrisburg, 1891. E 2. 18

Flood Relief Commission : Report. 8vo. Harrisburg, 1890. E 2. 18

Industrial Education : Report. 8vo. Harrisburg, 1889. E 2. 18

Internal Affairs, Secretary of : Report, 1890. 2 vols. 8vo. Harrisburg, 1891. E 2. 18

Oil and Gas Fields : Report. 8vo. Harrisburg, 1890. E 2. 18

Public Instruction : Report, 1890. 8vo. Harrisburg, 1890. E 2. 18

Sinking Fund : Report, 1890. 8vo. Harrisburg, 1891. F. 2. 18

Soldiers' Orphan Schools : Report, 1890. 8vo. Harrisburg, 1890. E 2. 18

State Treasurer : Report, 1890. 8vo. Harrisburg, 1891. E 2. 18

RHODE ISLAND.

Act for the Suppression of Intemperance. 8vo. Providence, 1886. F 11 S 45

District Courts : their Civil and Criminal Jurisdiction. 8vo. Providence, 1886. F 11 S 46

UNITED STATES—*contd.*

UTAH.

Laws of the Territory of Utah, 1884 and 1886. 2 vols. 8vo. Salt Lake, 1886. F 11 S 43, 44

VERMONT.

Laws relating to the Illegal Sale and Use of Intoxicating Liquor. 8vo. Rutland, 1885. F 11 S 42

VIRGINIA.

Acts of, 1885–86. 8vo. Richmond, 1886. F 11 S 50

UNITED STATES EXPLORING EXPEDITION (1839–42). Gray's Botany. Vol. 1. 4to. New York, 1854. A 31 Q 2 ‡
Plates [to the above]. Imp. fol. New York, 1857.
A 31 R 8 ‡

UNIVERSAL LIBRARY, The. Essays. Vol. 1. Containing Alison's Essay on Taste ; Locke and Bacon's Essays ; Emerson's Essays and Orations ; Goldsmith's Essays ; Michelet's Life of Luther. Roy. 8vo. Lond., 1854. J 10 V 31

UNIVERSAL REVIEW. Vols 1–8. Imp. 8vo. Lond., 1888–90. E 1. 72

UNWIN, Prof. W. C. Elements of Machine Design. Pt. 2. (Text-books of Science.) 11th edition. 12mo. Lond., 1891. A 17 S 43
Exercises on Wood-working for Handicraft Classes in Elementary and Technical Schools. Sm. fol. Lond., 1887. A 36 Q 21 ‡
Testing of Materials of Construction : a Text-book for the Engineering Laboratory. 8vo. Lond., 1888. A 6 T 28

UPCOTT, L. E. Introduction to Greek Sculpture. 8vo. Oxford, 1887. A 23 Q 40

URE, A. Cotton Manufacture of Great Britain. 2 vols. 8vo. Lond., 1836. A 11 R 17, 18

URQUHART, F. C. Camp Canzonettes ; being Rhymes of the Bush and other Things. 8vo. Brisb., 1891.
MH 1 U 37

URQUHART, J. W. Dynamo Construction. 8vo. Lond., 1891. A 21 P 36
Electric Light Fitting, embodying Practical Notes on Installation Management. 8vo. Lond., 1890. A 21 Q 29
Electro-plating : a Practical Hand-book. 2nd edition. 12mo. Lond., 1888. A 11 Q 36
Electro-typing : a Practical Manual. 12mo. Lond., 1881. A 11 Q 35

USILL, G. W. Practical Surveying : a Text-book for Students preparing for Examinations, or for Survey Work in the Colonies. 8vo. Lond., 1889. A 22 Q 26

UZANNE, O. The Frenchwoman of the Century. Fashions, Manners, Usages. Imp. 8vo. Lond., 1886. B 26 V 1

UZIELLI, M. Catalogue of the various Works of Art forming the Collection of M. Uzielli. 8vo. Lond., 1861. K 8 Q 40

V.

V., B. [*See* Thomson, Jas.]

VACCINATION QUESTION, The. Lymph or Liberty? 8vo. Hobart (n.d.) MA 3 Q 66

VAGABOND ANNUAL, The. Christmas, 1877. 8vo. Sydney, 1877. MJ 2 S 17

VALENCIENNES, M. [*See* Cuvier, Baron G.]

VALENTYN, Franz. [*See* La Pérouse, J. F. G. Comte de.]
Oud en Nieuw Oost-Indiën, vervattende een Naaukeurige en Uitvoerige Verhandelinge van Nederlands Mogentheyd in die Gewesten. 5 vols. (in 8) sm. fol. Dordrecht, 1724–26. D 7 S 7–14 †

VALERIUS FACCUS, C. Argonauticon libri octo. 8vo. Biponti, 1786. H 10 R 9

VALERIUS MAXIMUS. Factorum et Dictorum Memorabilium libri novem ; recensuit C. Kempfius. 8vo. Berolini, 1854. J 17 P 39
Noviter Recognitus. Fol. Venetiis, 1518. J 42 Q 1‡

VALLACK, Dr. A. Statement of. [*See* Carron, W.]

VALLÉE, L. Bibliographie des Bibliographies. 2 parts, with supplement. 2 vols. roy. 8vo. Paris, 1883–87. K 19 V 1, 2

VAMBÉRY, Prof. A. Hungary in Ancient, Mediæval, and Modern Times. 8vo. Lond., 1887. B 7 S 54

VANBURGH, Sir J. The Confederacy : a Comedy. [*See* British Drama, Modern, 3.]
The Mistake : a Comedy. [*See* British Drama, Modern, 3.]
The Provoked Wife : a Comedy. [*See* British Drama, Modern, 3.]

VANBURGH, Sir J., and CIBBER, C. The Provoked Husband : a Comedy. [*See* British Drama, Modern, 3.]

VAN BUREN, M. [Life of]; by E. M. Shepard. (American Statesmen.) 12mo. Boston, 1888. C 13 Q 3

VANCOUVER, Capt. G. Voyage of Discovery to the North Pacific Ocean, and Round the World, in the years 1790–95. 3 vols. 4to. Lond., 1798. MD 3 P 17–19†
Georg Vancouver's Reisen nach dem nordlichen Theile der Sudsee wahrend der Jahre, 1790–95. 2 vols. 8vo. Berlin, 1799–1800. MD 7 S 61, 62

VANDAM, A. D. [*See* Huet, C. B.]

VAN DER CRAB, P. Reis naar de Zuidwestkust van Nieuw-Guinea, de Goram-en Ceram-Laut Eilanden en Oostelijk Ceram. 8vo. Batavia, 1864. MD 8 R 8

VAN DER WAALS, J. D. Over de Continuiteit van den Gas- en Vloeistoftoestand. Roy. 8vo. Leiden, 1873. A 21 V 1

VAN DE VELDE Nieuwe nederduitsch-fransch Zakwoordenboek. 18mo. Bruxelles, 1850. K 16 P 18

VAN DYKE, H. Poetry of Tennyson. 2nd ed. 8vo. Lond., 1892. H 9 P 7

VANE, Sir Henry. Life of ; with a consideration of the English Commonwealth as a forecast of America ; by Prof. J. K. Hosmer. 8vo. Lond., 1888. C 12 S 29

VAN EYS, W. J. Outlines of Basque Grammar. 12mo. Lond., 1883. K 14 P 27

VAN HARE, G. Fifty Years of a Showman's Life ; by himself. 8vo. Lond., 1888. C 12 Q 31

VAN KERKWYK, L. C. Sketch of the Public Works in the Netherlands. Imp. 8vo. Haarlem, 1876. A 22 V 27

VAN RENSSELAER, Mrs. J. K. The Devil's Picture Books : a History of Playing-cards. Roy. 8vo. Lond., 1892. A 30 V 5

VANSLEB, J. M. Sa Vie, sa Disgrace, ses Œuvres; par l'Abbé A. Pougeois. Roy. 8vo. Paris, 1869. C 13 V 3

VAN'T HOFF, Prof. J. H. Chemistry in Space ; translated by J. E. Marsh, B.A. (Clar. Press) 12mo. Oxford, 1891. A 21 Q 27

VAPEREAU, G. Dictionnaire universal des Littératures. Roy. 8vo. Paris, 1876. Libr.

VARIGNY, C. de. L'Ocean Pacifique. 8vo. Paris, 1888. MD 1 Q 27

VARRO, M. T. De Lingua Latina, accedunt notæ. 8vo. Biponti, 1788. K 16 P 40
De Lingua Latina, emendata et annotata a C. O. Muellero. 8vo. Lipsiæ, 1833. K 16 T 25
Saturarum Menippearum Reliquiæ, edidit F. Oehler. 8vo. Quedlinburgi, &c., 1844. J 15 S 22
[*See* Agronomes Latins, Les.]

VASON, George. Life of, with a Preliminary Essay on the South Sea Islands ; by the Rev. J. Orange. 12mo. Lond., 1840. MC 1 Q 55

VAUGHAN, Most Rev. Roger William Bede. Arguments for Christianity, delivered in St. Mary's Pro-Cathedral, Sydney. Lent, 1879. 8vo. Sydney, 1879. MG 1 S 70
Hidden Springs, or Perils of the Future and How to Meet Them. 8vo. Sydney, 1891. MG 1 S 71
Higher Education. Inaugural Address at St. John's College. 8vo. Sydney, 1875. MG 1 R 54
Life and Labours of ; containing an account of his career from opening to close ; a Review of his Writings, Speeches and Ecclesiastical Work, together with some Personal Sketches never before published. 8vo. Sydney, 1883. MC 1 T 17
"Second Advent" Conference. The Church of Christ and the Bible. 8vo. Sydney, 1876. MG 1 R 55
"Third Advent" Conference. Is the Protestant Church the Church of Christ? 8vo. Sydney, 1876. MG 1 S 72
Fourth Advent Conference : the Church of Christ the Catholic Church. 8vo. Sydney, 1876. MG 1 Q 41
Lenten Exercises, given in St. Mary's Pro-Cathedral. 8vo. Sydney 1877 MG 1 Q 42

VAUGHAN, T. The Magical Writings of Thomas Vaughan (Eugenius Philalethes) with the Latin passages translated by A. E. Waite. Sm. 4to. Lond., 1888. A 24 R 25

VEGETIUS, Flavius Renatus. Oeuvres de. [*See* Nissard, D.]

VEITCH, Prof. J. The Feeling for Nature in Scottish Poetry. 2 vols. 8vo. Edinb., 1887. H 8 R 40, 41

VELAZQUEZ, Diego, and his Times ; by Prof. C. Justi ; translated by Prof. A. H. Keane. Imp. 8vo. Lond., 1889. C 18 U 4

VELLEIUS PATERCULUS, C. Quæ supersunt ex Historiæ Romanæ libris duobus. 8 vo. Argentorati, 1811. B 30 R 6

VELSCHOW, F. A. The Natural Law of Relations between Rainfall and Vegetable Life, and its application to Australia. 8vo. Lond., 1888. MA 1 T 10

VELUDO, G. The Pala d' Oro of the Basilica of S. Mark, Venice. 4to. Venice, 1887. B 30 V 6

VENI. [*See* Brothers, B.]

VENN, Rev. H. The Complete Duty of Man. 8vo. Lond., 1828. G 16 P 40

VENN, Dr. J. Principles of Empirical or Inductive Logic. 8vo. Lond., 1889. G 6 Q 30

The Logic of Chance: an Essay on the Theory of Probability as applied to Moral and Social Science and Statistics. 8vo. Lond., 1888. G 8 Q 30

VENN, J. and S. C. Admissions to Gonville and Caius College, in the University of Cambridge, 1558-1679. 8vo. Lond., 1887. B 23 U 15

VERDI, G. Verdi: an Anecdotic History of his Life and Works; by A. Pougin. 8vo. Lond., 1887. C 13 R 2

VERDY DU VERNOIS, Col. I. Von. Studies in Troop Leading ; translated from the German by H. J. T. Hildyard. 8vo. Lond., 1872. A 29 T 26

VERE, Sir F. and Sir H., "The Fighting Veres." Lives of; by C. R. Markham. Roy. 8vo. Lond., 1888. C 11 P 42

VERESTCHAGIN, V., Painter, Soldier, Traveller: Autobiographical Sketches; translated by F. H. Peters. 2 vols. 8vo. Lond., 1887. C 5 Q 5, 6

VERGUET, C. M. L. Histoire de la Première Mission Catholique au Vicariat de Mélanésie. 8vo. Carcassonne, 1854. MD 8 Q 10

VERITAS VINCIT. [*See* Burgess, Rev. H. T., and Milne, Rev.]

VERITY, A. W. [*See* Etheredge, Sir G.; Heywood, T.; Nero; and other Plays.]

VERNEY, Frances Parthenope, Lady. How the Peasant Owner Lives in parts of France, Germany, Italy, Russia. 8vo. Lond., 1888. F 5 R 34

VERNER, Capt. W. Rapid Field-Sketching and Reconnaissance. Roy. 8vo. Lond., 1889. A 22 V 21

2 G

VERNEY, Capt. E. H. Four years of Protest in the Transvaal. 8vo. Lond., 1881. F 8 S 26

Another copy. 2nd ed. 8 vo. Lond., 1881. F 8 S 26

VERNON, R. James Calvert ; or, From Dark to Dawn in Fiji. 8vo. Lond., 1890. MC 1 Q 41

VERNON, Hon. W. W. Readings on the Purgatorio of Dante. 2 vols. 8vo. Lond., 1889. H 8 Q 42, 43

VERRAL, J. M. The Stockwhip. Address to the Ashley Electors. 8vo. Christchurch, 1887. MF 1 T 28

VERRALL, A. W. [*See* Æschylus.]

VERRALL, Margaret de G. Mythology and Monuments of Ancient Athens, with introductory essay, &c., by Jane E. Harrison. 8vo. Lond., 1890. B 27 Q 17

VERSCHOYLE, Rev. J. History of Ancient Civilization. Edited by the Rev. J. Verschoyle. 8vo. Lond, 1889. B 14 Q 33

VERSCHUUR, G. Aux Antipodes : Voyage en Australie, à la Nouvelle-Zélande, aux Fidji, à la Nouvelle-Calédonie, aux Nouvelles-Hébrides et dans l'Amérique du Sud, 1888-89. 8vo. Paris, 1891. MD 7 T 48

At the Antipodes : Travels in Australia, New Zealand, &c., 1888-89. 8vo. Lond., 1891. MD 7 T 49

VETERINARIAN, The. Vols. 52, 59-64. 8vo. Lond., 1879-91. E 1. 50

VETTORI, P. Aristotelis Ethicorum Libri. [*See* Aristoteles.]

VEZZANI, G. de. [*See* Rimini, Baron de.]

VIAGGIO PITTORICO DELLA TOSCANA. 3 vols. fol. Firenze, 1801-3. D 8 Q 2-4 ‡

VIBERT, J. G. Science of Painting. 8vo. Lond., 1892. A 23 Q 26

VICARY, J. F. Olav the King, and Olav King and Martyr. 8vo. Lond., 1886. B 20 Q 13

Saga Time. 8vo. Lond., 1887. B 20 Q 14

VICTORIA, H. M. Queen. Her Life and Reign ; by Dr. Macaulay. Roy. 8vo. Lond., 1887. C 12 V 7

VICTORIA.

How to Settle in Victoria ; or, Instructions on the Purchase and Occupation of the Land ; with observations on Gardening and Farming ; the growth of the Vine, and other fruit trees ; the Nature and Quality of the Australian Soils ; and on the use of Manures. To which is added a Rural Calendar, Description of the Climate, and other useful information, by "Rusticus." 12mo. Melb., 1855. MA 3 U 9

Black Thursday. [No title page.] 12mo. Adelaide (n.d.) MB 1 P 31

Illustrated Hand-book, specially prepared for the Colonial and Indian Exhibition, London, 1886; edited by J. Thomson. Imp. 8vo. Melb., 1886. MD 6 U 20

VICTORIA—contd.

AGRICULTURE.

Bill to encourage Village Settlements of Agricultural and other Labourers in Agricultural Districts. 4to. Melb., 1892.　　　　　MF 4 S 43

Journal of the Board of Viticulture. 8vo. Melb., 1888.　　　　　MA

Royal Commission on Vegetable Products. 1st–6th Progress Reports, with Minutes of Evidence. 3 vols. 8vo. Melb., 1886–88.　　　　　ME 8 Q

Report of Council of Agricultural Education for 1884–87. 8vo. Melb., 1888.　　　　　ME 8 Q

Department of Lands and Agriculture. Third Annual Report of the Secretary for Agriculture. 8vo. Melb., 1875.　　　　　ME 1 T

CONSTITUTION.

Act to enable Her Majesty to assent to a Bill, as amended, of the Legislature of Victoria, to establish a Constitution in and for the Colony of Victoria. Fol. Lond., 1855.　　　　　MF 4 S 23

EDUCATION.

Royal Commission on Education, Report. Fol. Melb., 1884.　　　　　MG 3 Q 32 †

Minister for Public Instruction: Report for 1886–87. Sm. fol. Melb., 1887.　　　　　ME 10 Q 8 †

GOLDFIELDS.

Reports of the Mining Registrars, 1887–89. 7 vols. fol. Melb., 1887–89.　　　　　ME 2. 54

Mineral Statistics of Victoria for 1886 and 1888. 2 vols. fol. Melb., 1886–89.　　　　　ME 2. 54

LEGISLATIVE ASSEMBLY.

Votes and Proceedings of the Legislative Assembly, 1886–91. 23 vols. fol. Melb., 1886–91. ME 2. 47–54

MINES AND WATER SUPPLY.

Secretary for Mines and Water Supply: Annual Report for 1886–87. Sm. fol. Melb., 1887–88.　　ME 2. 54

PUBLIC SERVICE.

Regulations from Public Service Act, 1883, together with the Examination Papers, 1885–86. 12mo. Melb., 1886.　　　　　ME 5 S

REGISTRAR-GENERAL.

Report of Board appointed to Inquire into the Registrar-General's Office in relation to Management, Distribution, and Cancellation of Stamps, &c. Fol. Melb., 1889.　　　　　MF 3 Q 31 †

SANITATION.

Sanitary Condition of Melbourne : Progress Reports of Royal Commission. Fol. Melb., 1889–90.　　　　MA 3 Q 29 †

STATISTICS.

Statistical Registers, 1886 and 1889–90. 3 vols. fol. Melb., 1886–91.　　　　　ME 2. 54

VICTORIA—contd.

STATUTES.

Acts of Parliament, Session, 1887. 4to. Melb., 1887.　　　　　ME 2. 49

Acts of Parliament, 1889–91. 8m. fol. Melb. 1890–92.　　　　　ME 2. 49

SUPREME COURT.

Digest of Cases, 1846–71; by G. B Kerford and J. B. Box. Roy. 8vo. Melb., 1871.　　ME 21 P–R

The Judicature Act, 1883 : Rules of the Supreme Court, 1884. Fol. Melb., 1884.　　　　MF 3 Q 30 †

WATER SUPPLY.

Royal Commission on, 1st and 4th Reports by the Hon. A. Deakin. 2 vols. 8vo. Melb., 1885–87. ME 8 Q

VICTORIA INSTITUTE. Journal of Transactions. Vols. 23–24. 8vo. Lond., 1890.　　　　　E 1. 46

VICTORIA POST OFFICE DIRECTORY. [See Wise, H. and Co.]

VICTORIAN REVIEW, The. Nos. 1 and 2, November and December, 1879. Roy. 8vo. Melb., 1879. ME 18 R

VICTORIAN YEAR-BOOK. [See Hayter, H. H.]

VICTORIUS, P. [See Vettori, P.]

VICUÑA MACKENNA, B. Miscellanea : Collection de Articulos, Discursos, &c. 2 vols. 8vo. Santiago, 1872.　　　　　J 7 S 20, 21

VIDAL, Mrs. Frances. Bengala ; or, Some Time Ago. 2 vols. 12mo. Lond., 1860.　　　　MJ 3 P 13, 14

Tales for the Bush. 12mo. Lond., 1852.　　MJ 1 P 19

VIEILLARD, Mons., and DEPLANCHE, E. Essais sur la Nouvelle-Calédonie. Roy. 8vo. Paris, 1863. MD 5 V 49

VIEILLEVILLE, Sire de. [See Scépeaux, F. de.]

VIEL CASTEL, Count H. de. Memoirs of : a Chronicle of the Principal Events during the Reign of Napoleon III, 1851–64; translated and edited by C. Bousfield. 2 vols. 8vo. Lond., 1888.　　　　　C 13 U 1, 2

VIGNOLES, Charles Blacker. Life of : a Reminiscence of Early Railway History ; by O. J. Vignoles. 8vo. Lond., 1889.　　　　　C 10 P 34

VILLA-LOBOS, Prof. R. Compendio Elementar de Chorographia do Brasil. 2nd edition. 12mo. Rio de Janeiro, 1890.　　　　　D 15 Q 10

VILLARI, Prof. Pasquale. Life and Times of Girolamo Savonarola. 2 vols. 8vo. Lond., 1888.　C 8 Q 17, 18

VILLEMAIN, A. F. Choix d'études sur la Littérature Contemporaine. 12mo. Paris, 1878.　　B 34 P 25

Cours de Littérature Française : Tableau de la Littérature au moyen âge. 2 vols. 12mo. Paris, 1890.　B 34 P 15, 16

Cours de Littérature Française : Tableau de la Littérature au 18e siècle. 4 vols. 12mo. Paris, 1891. B 34 P 17–20

Discours et Mélanges. 12mo. Paris, 1888.　J 16 R 34

Études de Littérature ancienne et étrangère. 8 vo. Paris, 1877.　　　　　B 36 T 2

VILLEMAIN, A. F.—*contd.*
Another copy. 12mo. Paris, 1884. B 34 P 23

Études d'histoire moderne. 12mo. Paris, 1878. B34 P24

Histoire de Grégoire VII ; précédée d'un discours sur l'histoire de la papauté jusqu'au 11e Siècle. 2e éd. 2 vols. 8vo. Paris, 1874. G 11 U 1, 2

La République de Cicéron. [*See* Cicero.]

Souvenirs Contemporains d'histoire et de littérature. 2 vols. 12mo. Paris, 1874. B 34 P 21, 22

Tableau de l'éloquence chrétienne au 4o Siècle. 12mo. Paris, 1891. G 2 V 24

Vie au Chancelier de L'Hôpital. 12mo. Paris, 1874. B 34 P 26

VILLON, F. Œuvres complètes. (Collection Jannet-Picard.) 12mo. Paris (n.d.) H 1 P 46

Œuvres complètes de; precedée d'une étude sur Villon, par T. Gautier. 8vo. Paris (n.d.) H 8 R 39

VINCENDON-DUMOULIN, C. A., et DESGRAZ, C. Iles Taiti : Esquisse Historique et Géographique. 2 vols. 8vo. Paris, 1844. MD 7 S 15, 16

VINCENT, F. Around and About South America ; Twenty Months of Quest and Query. 8vo. New York, 1890. D 3 U 38

VINCENT, Mrs. H. 40,000 Miles over Land and Water : the Journal of a Tour through the British Empire and America. 2 vols. 8vo. Lond., 1885. MD 3 Q 26, 27

VINCENT, J. E. M. Australian Irrigation Colonies on the River Murray in Victoria and South Australia. Roy. 8vo. Melb., 1887. MA 1 Q 14

VINCK, Nicolaes. Voyage à la Nouvelle Guinée en 1663. (Prévost, A. F., Suite de l'Histoire Générale des Voyages. Tome 17.) Amsterdam, 1761. MD 11 P 16 †

VINE, Rev. F. T. Cæsar in Kent : an Account of the Landing of Julius Cæsar, and his Battles with the Ancient Britons. 2nd ed. 8vo. Lond., 1887. B 4 P 20

VINES, S. H. [*See* Bower, F. O.]

VINNIUS, A. Institutionum Imperialium Commentarius. Sm. 4to. Amst., 1655. F 2 T 22

VINSON, A. Aranéides des Isles de La Réunion, Maurice, et Madagascar. Roy. 8vo. Paris, 1863. A 28 V 11

VIOLETTE, P. L. Dictionnaire Samoa-Français-Anglais et Français-Samoa-Anglais, précédé d'une grammaire de la langue Samoa. 8vo. Paris, 1879. MK 1 T 23

VIOLLET-LE-DUC, E. E. Dictionnaire raisonné du Mobilier français. 6 vols. roy 8vo. Paris, 1858-75. A 19 U 2-7

VIRCHOW, R. Ueber die Heilkrafte des Organismus. 8vo. Berlin, 1875. A 26 8 5

Die Freiheit' der Wissenschaft im modernen Staat. 8vo. Berlin, 1877. A 30 U 2

VIRGILIUS MARO, Publius. Æneids of Virgil done into English Verse, by W. Morris. 2nd edition. 8vo. Lond., 1889. H 8 Q 23

Bucolics and Georgics. Edited by T. L. Papillon and A. E. Haigh. 8vo. Oxford, 1891. H 8 Q 33

De Rerum Inventoribus Libri VIII, et de Prodigiis Libri III. 18mo. Lugd. Batav., 1644. B 35 P 12

Opera : recensuit P. Masvisius. 2 vols. sm. 4to. 1717. H 5 V 3, 4

Codex Virgilianus qui nuper ex Bibliotheca canonici abbatis venetiani Bodleianæ accessit studio et opera Georgii Butler, A.M. 8vo. Oxoniæ, 1854. K 15 R 37

Opera. Works of Virgil, with a Commentary by Prof. J. Conington. 3rd edition. 3 vols. 8vo. Lond., 1872-75. H 4 U 19-21

Virgil ; by Rev. W. L. Collins. (Ancient Classics for English Readers.) 12mo. Edinb., 1882. J 14 P 27

Virgil in English Verse : Eclogues and Æneid I-VI ; by Sir C. Bowen. Roy. 8vo. Lond., 1887. H 6 S 31

VIRTUE, P. Some Remarks on the Pulpit. 8vo. Maryborough. 8vo. Maryborough, 1884. MG 1 R 57

The Churches of Maryborough. 8vo. Maryborough, 1889. MG 1 R 56

Address on Ignorance of the Scriptures and of the Power of God, the True Cause of Religious Error ; also two Letters on Rationalism and Christianity, by "A Layman." 8vo. Melb., 1873. MG 1 R 58

VISCONTI, P. E. Rime di Vittoria Colonna. [*See* Colonna, V.]

VISRAM, F. A Khoja's Tour in Australia. (Reprinted from *The Times of India.*) 12mo. Bombay, 1885. MD 1 P 19

VITRUVIUS, M. P. De Architectura libri decem. 4 vols. Fol. Romæ, 1836. A 37 Q 13-16 ‡

VITZTHUM, Count C. F. St. Petersburg and London in 1852-64 ; edited by H. Reeve. 2 vols. 8vo. Lond., 1887. B 7 T 39, 40

VIVIAN, F. Anarchy ; the Dance of Death in the Goal Yard. Melb., 1888. MF 1 T 12

VIVIAN, Lieut.-Col. J. L. The Visitations of Cornwall ; comprising the Heralds' Visitations of Cornwall, 1530, 1573, and 1620. 4to. Exeter, 1887. K 4 Q 20 †

VIVIAN, W. H. Report for the Tasmanian Exhibition, Launceston. [*See* Tasmanian Exhibition, Launceston, 1891-92.]

VIZETELLY, Henry. Wines of the World Characterized and Classed. 12mo. Lond., 1875. A 1 U 22

Facts about Sherry. 12mo. Lond., 1876. A 18 Q 19

VLACHOS, Dr. A. Neugriechische Chrestomathie. 8vo. Leipzig, 1870. K 16 P 34

VLAMING, Wm. de. Journaal Wegens een Voyagie, Gedaan op order der Hollandiche Oost-Indische Maatschappy in de Jaaren, 1696-97. Sm. 4to. Amsterdam, 1701. MD 7 T 50

VLAMING, Wm. de.—*contd.*
Voyage aux Terres Australes en 1696. (Prévost, A. F.
Suite de l'Histoire générale des Voyages, tome 17.) 4to.
Amsterdam, 1761.   MD 11 P 16 †

VOCABULARY OF DIALECTS spoken by Aboriginal
Natives of Australia. 8vo. Melb., 1867.   MK 1 T 24

VŒMEL, Dr. J. T. [*See* Demosthenes.]

VOGLENO, P. [*See* Saccardo, P. A.]

VOLTAIRE, F. M. A. de. Dialogues et Entretiens Philo-
sophiques. (Collection Jannet–Picard.) 3 vols. 12mo.
Paris (n.d.)   G 4 V 7–9
The Maid of Orleans; translated by W. H. Ireland. 2
vols. 8vo. Lond., 1882.   H 3 R 24, 25
Siècle de Louis XIV. 8vo. Paris, 1881.   B 26 Q 9
Zadec, and other Tales; a new translation by R. B. Bos-
well. 12mo. Lond., 1891.   J 11 W 21

VOLUNTEER SERVICE GAZETTE. Vols. 28–32.
Fol. Lond., 1887–91.   E

VONDEL, J. van. Al de Dichtwerken. 2 vols. imp.
8vo. Schiedam, 1864–66.   H 6 V 31, 32

VOSMAER, Dr. G. C. J. [*See* Bronn, Dr. H. G.]

VOYAGES AND DISCOVERIES: an Account of several
Late Voyages and Discoveries to the South and North,
by Sir J. Narborough, Capt. J. Tasman, Capt. J. Wood,
and others. 8vo. Lond., 1694.   MD 1 R 19

VOYLE, G. E., and STEVENSON, Capt. G. de St. C.
A Military Dictionary, comprising Terms, Scientific and
otherwise, connected with the Science of War. 8vo.
Lond., 1876.   A 29 Q 16

W

W., H.C. [*See* Wild Flowers of Switzerland.]

W., P. [*See* Albanian Language.]

WAAGER, Wm. Productus Limestone Fossils. [*See*
India—Palæontologia Indica.]

WACE, H [*See* Smith, Wm.]

WACHSMUTH, C [*See* Leipziger Studien.]

WADDINGTON, Rev. G. History of the Church. 8vo.
Lond., 1833.   G 16 T 25

WADDINGTON, R. Notes of a Tour in the England of
the Antipodes and Brighter Britain. 8vo. Lond.,
1887.   MD 1 Q 30

WADE, C. G. Treatise upon the Employers' Liability
Act of New South Wales. 8vo. Sydney, 1891.
                                          MF 2 R 59.

WADLIN, H. G. Abandoned Farms in Massachusetts.
8vo. Boston, 1891.   F 14 T 6
Citizens and Aliens. Roy. 8vo. Boston, 1889. F 12 R 15
Classified Weekly Wages. 8vo. Boston, 1890.   F 14 T 7

WADLIN, H. G.—*contd.*
Condition of Employés. 8vo. Boston, 1890.   F 14 T 5
Daily Working Time. 8vo. Boston, 1890.   F 14 T 8
Growth of Manufactures. Roy. 8vo. Boston, 1890.
                                            F 12 R 14
Index to Reports, 1870–90, Massachusetts Bureau of
Statistics of Labor. 8vo. Boston, 1890.   E 2. 15-18
Markets, Transportation, Imports, Exports, and Competi-
tion. Roy. 8vo. Boston, 1890.   F 12 R 13
Relation of Wages to Cost of Production. 8vo. Boston,
1890.   F 14 T 4
Strikes and Lockouts, 1881–86. 8vo. Boston, 1886.
                                          F 14 T 3
Women in Industry. 8vo. Boston, 1890.   F 14 T 9

WADSWORTH, M. E. Preliminary Description of Peri-
dotytes, Gabbros, Diabases, and Andesytes of Minnesota.
(Geol. and Nat. Hist. Survey of Minnesota.) Roy. 8vo.
St. Paul, 1887.   E 2. 15-18

WAECHTER, Harriet. The Chaucer Birthday Book.
8vo. Lond., 1889.   H 7 S 40

WAFER, L. New Voyage and Description of the Isthmus
of America. 12mo. Lond., 1699.   D 15 Q 16

WAGNER, F. G. [*See* Euripides.]

WAGNER, Richard. Letters to his Dresden Friends,
Theodor Uhlig, Wilhelm Fischer, and Ferdinand Heine:
translated by J. S. Shedlock. 8vo. Lond., 1890.
                                          C 14 R 4
Sa Vie et ses Œuvres; par A. Jullien. 4to. Paris, 1886.
                                          C 13 P 8†

[*See* Praeger, F.]

WAGNER, R., and LISZT, F. Correspondence of,
1841–61; translated by F. Hueffer. 2 vols. 8vo. Lond.,
1888.   C 14 R 2, 3

WAITE, A. E. Real History of the Rosicrucians. 8vo.
Lond., 1887,   G 16 R 45

[*See* Vaughan, T.]

WAKE, C. S. Development of Marriage and Kinship.
8vo. Lond., 1889.   A 1 W 40
Serpent-Worship, and other Essays; with a Chapter on
Totemism. 8vo. Lond., 1888.   G 12 P 36

WAKEFIELD, E. G. New Zealand after Fifty Years.
8vo. Lond. (n.d.)   MD 7 Q 57
[*See* Horton, Rt. Hon. Sir R. W.]

WAKELIN, T. Mechanical Principles of a Theory of
Gravitation briefly indicated. 12mo. Wellington, 1889.
                                          MA 3 P 27

WAKEMAN, H. O. Life of Charles James Fox. (Statesmen Series.) 8vo. Lond., 1890.   C 12 R 33
The Church and the Puritans, 1570–1660. 12mo. Lond.,
1887.   G 19 P 8

WALCH, G. The "Fireflash," four oars and a coxswain : Where they went—How they went—and why they went; and the stories they told last Christmas Eve. 8vo. Melb., 1878. MJ 2 S 58

Australasia : an Intercolonial Christmas Annual. 8vo. Melb., 1878. MJ 2 S 59

"Hash " : a mixed dish for Christmas. 8vo. Melb., 1877. MJ 2 S 55

Head over Heels : a Christmas Book of Fun and Fancy. 8vo. Melb., 1874. MH 1 R 17

On the Cards ; or a Motley Pack. 8vo. Melb., 1875. MJ 2 R 28

WALCH, J. Walch's Tasmanian Almanac and Guide to Tasmania for 1864-65, and 1882. 12mo. Hobart, 1864-82. ME 4 P

Walch's Tasmanian Almanac for 1878 and 1891. 2 vols. 12mo. Hobart, 1878-91. ME P 4

WALCKENAER, Baron Charles A. Le Monde Maritime, ou Histoire des Peuples en descriptions de toutes les Iles du Grand Océan et du Continent de la Nouvelle-Holland. 4 vols. (in 2). 18mo. Paris, 1819. MD 2 W 36, 37

WALD, A. De Vini Natura, præcipue de ejus principio inebriante. 8vo. Berolini, 1842. F 11 Q 22

WALDMEIER, T. Autobiography of; being an Account of Ten Years' Life in Abyssinia and Sixteen Years in Syria. 8vo. Lond., 1886. C 10 S 1

WALDOW, C. O. Present Depression in Trade, its Cause and Remedy. 12mo. Sydney, 1887. MF 2 P 61

WALDUCK, W. W. Constitutionalism in Victoria. 8vo. Melb., 1873. MF 2 T 41

WALES, W., and BAYLY, W. Original Astronomical Observations made in the course of a Voyage towards the South Pole and Round the World in His Majesty's ships Resolution and Adventure in the years 1772-75. 4to. Lond., 1777. MA 3 P 16 †

WALFORD, C. Gilds : their Origin, Constitution, Objects, and later History. 8vo. Lond., 1888. F 14 T 30

WALFORD, E. County Families of the United Kingdom, 1887-92. 6 vols. roy. 8vo. Lond., 1891. E

Windsor Peerage for 1892. 8vo. Lond., 1891. E

Juvenal. (Ancient Classics for English Readers.) 12mo. Edinb., 1880. J 14 P 15

Tales of our Great Families. 2nd. Series. 2 vols. 12mo. Lond., 1880. B 35 Q 6, 7

WALFORD, L. B. Four Biographies from " Blackwood" : Jane Taylor, Hannah More, Elizabeth Fry, and Mary Somerville. 8vo. Edinb., 1888. C 15 Q 15

WALKER. [See Jones v. Jenkins.]

WALKER, Bettina. My Musical Experiences. 8vo. Lond., 1890. C 12 T 33

WALKER, F. Catalogue of Specimens of Neuropterous Insects in the British Museum. (Pts. 1-4.) Lond., 1852-53. A 27 P 25

WALKER, G. Idiomatologia Anglo-Latina. Quinta editio. 12mo. Lond., 1690. K 16 P 22

WALKER, G. W. Life and Labours of G. W. Walker, of Hobart Town, Tasmania, by J. Backhouse and C. Tylor. 8vo. Lond., 1862. MC 1 R 32

WALKER, J. B. Discovery and Occupation of Port Dalrymple. 8vo. Hobart, 1890. MB 2 R 39

The French in Van Dieman's Land and the First Settlement on the Derwent. 8vo. Hobart, 1889. MB 2 R 17

The Settlement of Tasmania. [Papers read before the Royal Society of Tasmania.] 8vo. Hobart, 1890. MB 2 R 25

WALKER, Capt. J. H. The Wreck, the Rescue, and the Massacre : an Account of the loss of the barque *Thomas King*, in 1852. 18mo. Lond.,1853. MD 2 P 44

WALKER, R. The Five Threes—33,333 Miles by Land and Sea : Holiday Notes. 8vo. Lond., 1884. MD 2 S 28

WALKER, Rev. S. The Covenant of Grace. 8vo. Lond., 1847. G 16 P 47

WALKER, Thomas. Letter on the Subject of Land Laws of the Colony. 8vo. Sydney (n.d.) MF 1 T 61

WALKER, Thomas. Bush Pilgrims, and other Poems. 12mo. Sydney, 1885. MH 1 U 1

Felonry of New South Wales, by "An Old Identity." 12mo. Sydney, 1891. MJ 3 P 22

Oration on Mr. Dalley's offer of Troops for the Soudan Campaign. 8vo. Sydney, 1885. MF 4 Q 7

Treatise upon the Immortality of the Soul : an Answer to Popular Arguments and a Defence of Materialism. 18mo. Sydney, 1886. MG 2 P 35

WALKER, T. A. The Severn Tunnel : its Construction and Difficulties, 1872-87. Roy. 8vo. Lond., 1888. A 6 U 21

WALKER, W. Bards of Bon Accord, 1375 1860. Roy. 8vo. Aberdeen, 1887. H 6 S 37

WALKER, Rev. W. Life and Times of John Skinner, Bishop of Aberdeen. 8vo. Aberdeen, 1887. C 15 Q 21

WALKER, Wm. Account of the Great Flood on the Hawkesbury of June, 1864, and the Lesser Flood of July following. 8vo. Parramatta, 1864. MB 2 R 23

Reminiscences (Personal, Social, and Political) of a Fifty Years' Residence at Windsor, on the Hawkesbury : a Lecture. 8vo. Sydney, 1890. MC 1 Q 50

WALKER, W. G. The Practice in Equity being the Equity Act of 1880, and the Rules of Court issued thereunder. 8vo. Sydney, 1884. MF 1 T 16

WALKER, W. G., and RICH, G. E. The Practice in Equity being the Equity Act of 1880, and the Rules of Court issued thereunder. 2nd edition. 8vo. Sydney, 1891. MF 2 R 61

WALL, A. H. Shakespeare's Face : a Monologue on the Various Portraits of Shakespeare in comparison with the Death Mask. Roy. 8vo. Stratford-upon-Avon. 1890. J 4 U 6

WALL, G. Natural History of Thought in its Practical
· Aspect. 8vo. Lond., 1887.   G 12 P 28

WALL, W. S. History and Description of Skeleton of a
New Sperm Whale, lately set up in the Australian
Museum, together with some Account of a new genus of
Sperm Whales called Euphysetes. 8vo. (Sydney, 1851,
reprinted.) Sydney, 1890.   MA 3 S 2

WALLACE, A. R. Australasia. (Stanford's Compendium of Geography and Travel.) 8vo. Lond., 1888.
                                               MD 1 R 20

Darwinism, an Exposition of the Theory of Natural
Selection, with some of its Applications. 2nd edition.
8vo. Lond., 1889.   A 29 S 2

Natural Selection and Tropical Nature : essays on Descriptive and Theoretical Biology. 8vo. Lond., 1891.
                                               A 27 R 26

WALLACE, J. H. Manual of New Zealand History.
8vo. Wellington, 1886.   MB 1 R 36

Another copy.   MB 2 R 33
[*See* Sherrin, R. A. A.]

WALLACE, Professor Robert. The Rural Economy and
Agriculture of Australia and New Zealand. 8vo.
Lond., 1891.   MA 3 S 2

India in 1887. 8vo. Edinb., 1888.   A 1 T 31

WALLACE, Sir Wm. Actis and Deidis of. [*See* Scottish
Text Soc.]

WALLEY, Prof. T. Practical Guide to Meat Inspection.
12mo. Edinb., 1890.   A 26 Q 7

.Another Copy. 2nd ed. 8vo. Edinb., 1891.   A 18 R 9

WALLIS, A. Examples of the Bookbinders' Art of the
16th and 17th Centuries. 4to. Exeter, 1890.
                                               A 40 P 12 ‡

WALLIS, H. W. The Cosmology of the Rigveda : an
Essay. 8vo. Lond., 1887.   G 10 T 29

WALLIS, Sir Provo W. P. Admiral of the Fleet. A
Memoir ; by Dr. J. G. Brighton. 8vo. Lond., 1892.
                                               C 18 S 5

WALMISLEY, A. T. Iron Roofs ; illustrated with Working Drawings. 2nd edition. 4to. Lond., 1888.
                                               A 40 Q 5 ‡

WALPOLE, C. G. Short History of the Kingdom of
Ireland. 2nd edition. 8vo. Lond., 1885.   B 29 Q 13

WALPOLE, Horace, Earl of Oxford. Letters of. Selected
and Edited by C. D. Yonge. 2 vols. 8vo. Lond.,
1890.   C 14 T 17, 18

The Mysterious Mother : a Tragedy. [*See* British Drama,
Modern, 2.]

WALPOLE, Sir Robert. [Life of] ; by John Morley. 8vo.
Lond., 1889.   C 12 R 34

WALPOLE, Spenser. The Electorate and the Legislature.
12mo. Lond., 1881.   F 9 U 38

Life of Lord John Russell. 2 vols. 8vo. Lond., 1889.
                                               C 14 T 5, 6

WALSH, J. H. The Horse in the Stable and in the
Field. 12th edition. 8vo. Lond., 1888.   A 18 T 7

Manual of Domestic Economy, suited to Families spending
from £150 to £1,500 a year. 8vo. Lond., 1890.
                                               A 22 R 1

The Modern Sportsman's Gun and Rifle. 2 vols. 8vo.
Lond., 1882–84.   A 11 U 19, 20

WALSH, R. Fingal and its Churches : a Historical
Sketch of the Foundation and Struggles of the Church
of Ireland. 8vo. Dublin, 1888.   G 16 R 27

WALTER, Jas. Shakespeare's True Life. Illustrated.
Imp. 8vo. Lond., 1890.   C 36 S 14 ‡

WALTERS, A. Palms and Pearls ; or, Scenes in Ceylon.
8vo. Lond., 1892.   D 17 U 21

WALTON, A. Eldorado : the South African Diamond and
Gold Fields, and how to get there. 8vo. Sydney, 1889.
                                               MD 7 S 34

WALTON, William. The Alpaca : its Naturalization in
the British Isles, &c. 12mo. Edinb., 1844.   A 18 P 2

WANDERER. [*See* D'Avigdon, E. H.]

WANGANUI. Interesting Chapters from the Early
History of Wanganui, and Wanganui in 1856. 8vo.
Wanganui, 1887.   MB 2 R 18

WANKLYN, J. A., and COOPER, W. J. Air Analysis:
a Practical Treatise on the Examination of Air, with an
Appendix on Illuminating Gas. 12mo. Lond., 1890.
                                               A 21 P 11

WARBURTON, Lieut. Col. R. The Race Horse : how to
Buy, Train, and Run him. 12mo. Lond., 1892.
                                               A 1 U 29

WARD, Prof. A. W. The Counter-Reformation. 12mo.
Lond., 1889.   G 19 P 10

WARD, Herbert. Five Years with the Congo Cannibals.
4to. Lond., 1890.   D 2 U 15

WARD, Prof. H. Marshall. The Oak : a popular Introduction to Forest Botany. 8vo. Lond., 1892.   A 20 P 7

Timber and some of its Diseases. 12mo. Lond., 1889.
                                               A 1 U 27
[*See* Sachs, J. von.]

WARD, J. Information relative to New Zealand. 2nd
edition. 12mo. Lond., 1840.   MD 1 P 56

WARD, T. H. The Reign of Queen Victoria : a Survey
of Fifty Years of Progress. 2 vols. 8vo. Lond., 1887.
                                               B 22 U 2, 3
[*See* Men of the Time.]

WARD, Wilfred. William George Ward and the Oxford
Movement. 8vo. Lond., 1889.   C 12 S 27

WARD, William George, and the Oxford Movement ; by
W. Ward. 8vo. Lond., 1889.   C 12 S 27

WARD, W. C. [*See* Wycherley, W.]

WARDEN, W. [*See* Napoleon Buonaparte.]

WARDEN, A. J. Angus; or, Forfarshire, the Land and the People, Descriptive and Historical. 5 vols. 4to. Dundee, 1880-85. B 31 U 13-17

WARDLE, T. Royal Jubilee Exhibition, Manchester, 1887 : Descriptive Catalogue of the Silk Section. Manchester, 1887. K 7 R 6

WARE, L. S. The Sugar Beet : including a History of the Beet Sugar Industry in Europe. Roy. 8vo. Philad., 1880. A 18 U 13

WARING, C. State-Purchase of Railways. 8vo. Lond., 1887. F 10 R 21

WARNER, Dr. F. Lectures on Growth and Means of Training the Mental Faculty. 12mo. Camb., 1890. G 16 Q 44

WARNER, R., and WILLIAMS, B. S. Orchid Album. Vols. 1-10. 4to. Lond., 1882-93. A 14 P 1-10 †

WARR, G. C. W. [*See* Teuffel, W. S.]

WARREN, S. Select Extracts from Blackstone's Commentaries. 8vo. Lond., 1837. F 14 Q 10

WARREN, Rev. S. M. [*See* Swedenborg, E.]

WARRIGAL CLUB, The. Rules [and] List of Members. 12mo. Sydney, 1885. MF 3 P 38

WARRINGTON AND BEWSEY, Lords of. [*See* Beamont, W.]

WARTER, Rev. J. W. An Old Shropshire Oak ; edited by Dr. R. Garnett. 4 vols. 8vo. Lond., 1886-91. B 24 S 2-5

WARUNG, Price. [*See* Astley, Wm.]

WARWICK, Richard Neville, Earl of. Warwick, the King-Maker ; by C. W. Oman. (English Men of Action.) 8vo. Lond., 1891. C 15 Q 12

WASHBURNE, E. B. Recollections of a Minister to France, 1869-77. 2 vols. roy. 8vo. Lond., 1887. C 12 U 27, 28

WASHINGTON, George. Life of ; by H. C. Lodge. (American Statesmen.) 2 vols. 12mo. Boston, 1889. C 13 Q 5, 6

Cromwell and Washington : a Contrast ; by C. Bradlaugh. 12mo. Lond., 1883. F 7 V 21

Histoire de Washington ; par C. de Witt. 12mo. Paris, 1876. C 17 Q 28

Daily Journal of. Kept on a tour from Virginia to Barbadoes, 1751-52 ; edited, with notes, by J. M. Toner. Sm. 4to. Albany, N.Y., 1892. D 15 S 16

Journal of my Journey over the Mountains, 1747-8 ; edited, with notes, by J. Toner. Sm. 4to. Albany, N.Y., 1892. D 15 S 20

Life of, studied anew ; by E. E. Hale. 8vo. New York, 1888. C 4 V 37

WATER DRINKER, A. [*See* Montagu, B.]

WATERHOUSE, C. H. Signification and Principles of Art : a Critical Essay for General Readers. 8vo. Lond., 1886. A 23 T 2

WATERHOUSE, F. H. Index Generum Avium : a List of the Genera and Subgenera of Birds. 8vo. Lond., 1889. A 14 T 38

WATERHOUSE, G. W., and EDMONDSON, F. W. Digest of Reported Cases in the Supreme Court, Court of Insolvency, &c., of Victoria. 8vo. Melb., 1886. MF 2 S 50

WATERHOUSE, Col. J. Practical Notes on the Preparation of Drawings for Photographic Reproduction. 12mo. Lond., 1890. A 25 Q 23

WATERHOUSE, Rev. Joseph. Vah-Ta-Ah, the Feejeean Princess ; with occasional allusions to Feejeean customs, &c. 18mo. Lond., 1857. MG 2 P 36

The King and People of Fiji ; containing a Life of Thakombau, with notices of the Fijians, their Manners, Customs, and Superstitions previous to the great Religious Reformation in 1854. 12mo. Lond., 1866. M D 2 W 46

WATKIN, Sir E. W. Canada and the States : Recollections, 1851-86. 8vo. Lond., 1887. D 15 Q 2

WATKINS, John L. Collection of the Statutes relating to the Title and Transfer of Real Estate in force in the Colony of New South Wales ; with Notes. Roy. 8vo. Sydney, 1892. MF 3 R 52

WATKINS, J. L., O'CONNOR, R. E., NASH, A., and BROWNING, R. J. Digest of Reported Cases, decided in the Supreme Court of New South Wales, 1860-84. 8vo. Sydney, 1885. MF 3 T 11

WATSON, A. F. Diary of a Voyage from London to Sydney on board the S.S. Austral. Sq. 8vo. Lond., 1885. MD 8 R 12

WATSON, H. Lecture on South Australia. 8vo. Lond., 1838. MF 1 R 60

WATSON, H. B. M. [*See* Mennell, P.]

WATSON, John. Tenancy and Ownership. 12mo. Lond., 1891. F 6 P 46

WATSON, Joshua. [Memoir of] ; edited by Rev. E. Churton. 2 vols. 8vo. Oxford, 1861. C 16 R 5, 6

WATSON, R. H. L. Let There Be Light. [Song.] Words by E. B. Parnell. Fol. Sydney (n.d.) MA 11 Q 15 †

WATSON, R. S. History of English Rule and Policy in South Africa. 8vo. Newcastle, 1881. F 8 S 26

WATSON, S. G. Spiritual Communications, &c., through the Mediumship of Elizabeth Armstrong. 8vo. Melb., 1869. MG 2 Q 12

WATSON, S. J. The Constitutional History of Canada. Vol. 1. 12mo. Toronto, 1874. B 19 Q 2

WATSON, W. Adventures of a Blockade Runner. 8vo. Lond., 1892. D 15 S 14

Life in the Confederate Army ; being Observations of an Alien during the American Civil War. 8vo. Lond., 1887. B 17 Q 2

WATSON, W. [*See* Agriculture, Dept. of, Queensland.]

WATT, A. Art of Paper-making. 12mo. Lond., 1890.
A 11 Q 32

WATT, F. Pictorial Chronicles of the Mighty Deep; or, the Sea, its Ships and Sailors. Roy. 8vo. Lond., 1887.
B 35 T 1

WATTS, Henry. Dictionary of Chemistry; revised, &c., by M. M. P. Muir and H. F. Morley. Vols. 1–3. Roy. 8vo. Lond., 1887–92.
K 9 R 5–7

WATTS, Henry E. [*See* Cervantes Saavedra, M. de.]

WAUGH, Edwin. Poems and Songs. 1st series. 8vo. Manchester, 1883.
H 10 Q 12

Poems and Songs. 2nd series. 8vo. Liverpool, 1889.
H 10 Q 13

WAUGH, James. Three Years' Practical Experience of a Settler in New South Wales. 8th edition. 12mo. Edinb., 1838.
MD 2 W 28

WAUGH and COX. Australian Almanac for 1856. 8vo. Sydney, 1856.
ME 4 R
Sydney Directory, 1855. 8vo. Sydney, 1855.
ME 4 R

WAURIN, J. de. Chroniques de la Grant Bretaigne. [*See* Chronicles and Memorials of Great Britain, &c.]

WAY, A. S. [*See* Homer.]

WAYTE, G. H. Prospecting; or, Eighteen Months in Australia and New Zealand. 12mo. Lond., 1879.
MD 1 Q 6

WAYTE, W. [*See* Smith, Dr. W.]

WEALE, J. C. M. Slavery in the Transvaal. 8vo. Lond., 1881.
F 8 S 26

WEATHERLEY, W. S. [*See* Brindley, W.]

WEBB, S. Socialism in England. 8vo. Lond., 1890.
F 14 P 18

WEBB, Thomas P. Compendium of the Imperial Law and Statutes in force in the Colony of Victoria, together with a Table of the Sections of Imperial Statutes transcribed into Victorian Statutes. 2nd edition. 8vo. Melb., 1892.
MF 3 T 41

WEBER, Georg. Allgemeine Weltgeschichte Zweite Auflage. Bande 1–15 (in 16). Roy. 8vo. Leipzig, 1882–89.
B 35 U 1–16

Register zu G. Weber's Allgemeine Weltgeschichte. 4 vols. Roy. 8vo. Leipzig, 1883–90.
B 35 U 17–V 1

WEBSTER, J. The White Devil: a Tragedy. [*See* British Drama, Ancient, 3.]
Dutchesse of Malfy: a Tragedy. [*See* British Drama, Ancient, 3.]

WEBSTER, J., and TOURNEUR, C. Best Plays; with Notes by J. A. Symonds. (Mermaid Series; edited by H. Ellis.) 8vo. Lond., 1888.
H 4 Q 26
The White Devil.—The Duchess of Malfi.—The Atheist's Tragedy. — The Revenger's Tragedy.

WEBSTER, W. Proceedings of a Court of Inquiry and General Courts-martial, together with action taken in the Supreme Court in the case of Brigade Quarter-master-Sergeant (now Gunner) W. Webster. Fol. Sydney, 1889.
MF 2 U 50

WEBSTER'S Royal Red Book. 12 vols. 12mo. Lond., 1887–92.
F 2. 4

WEDDELL, G. Arcana Fairfaxiana. [*See* Arcana.]

WEEK, The. 1889. Fol. Brisbane, 1889. ME Fol. 6

WEGG-PROSSER, F. R. [*See* Prosser, F. R. Wegg.]

WEIGEL, C. Ethica Naturalis. Sm. 4to. Norimbergæ (n.d.)
H 7 V 27

WEINMANN, F. W. Grammar of the German Language. [*See* Ahn, Dr. F.]

WEINRITTER, G. M. The Kangaroo Hunt Polka. Fol. Melb. (n.d.)
MA 11Q 15‡

WEIR, Capt. R., and BROWN, J. M. Riding. Polo. (Badminton Library.) 12mo. Lond., 1891. A 17 U 45

WEISE, C. H, [*See* Hesiod, *and* Plautus, M. A.]

WEISMANN, Dr. A. Essays upon Heredity and kindred Biological Problems. Roy. 8vo. Oxford, 1889. A 2 P 26

WEITEMEYER, H. Denmark : its History and Topography, Language, Literature, Fine Arts, Social Life, and Finance. Edited by H. Weitmeyer. 8vo. Lond., 1891.
B 2 R 3

WELD, F. A. Hints to Intending Sheep Farmers in New Zealand. 2nd. ed. Lond., 1853. MD 6 T 2

WELLAUER, A. Lexicon Æschyleum. 2 vols. (in 1). 8vo. Lipsiæ, 1830–31.
K 16 T 24
[*See* Æschylus.]

WELLBANK, J. The Australasian Ship Owner's and Master's Assistant. 8vo. Lond. MF 1 T 75
Australian Nautical Almanac and Coaster's Guide for the Southern and Eastern Coasts of New Holland, for 1874. 8vo. Sydney, 1873.
ME 2 U

WELLES, A. Genealogical Chronology of the World before Christ, giving the Origin, &c., of the Earliest Races of Mankind. 4to. Lond., 1889. G 9 R 28†

WELLESLEY, Richard Cowley, Marquess. Life of; by Colonel G. B. Malleson. 8vo. Lond., 1889. C 12 Q 21

WELLINGTON, Arthur Wellesley, Duke of. [Life of] by G. Hooper. 8vo. Lond., 1889. C 12 Q 19
Notes of Conversations with, 1831–51. By Philip Henry, Fifth Earl Stanhope. 3rd edition. 8vo. Lond., 1889.
C 12 Q 20
Public and Private Life of; by G. L. Browne. 8vo. Lond., 1888.
C 17 Q 4
Words on Wellington, the Duke—Waterloo—the Ball; by Sir W. Fraser. 8vo. Lond., 1889. C 13 R 12
Life of. [*See* Yonge, C. D.]
Life of; by Col. J. M. Tucker. 8vo. Lond. (n.d.)
C 18 Q 22
[*See* Raikes, Harriet.]

WELLS, B. History of Taranaki. 8vo. New Plymouth, 1878. MB 2 R 28

WELLS, Dr. D. A. Free Trade and Free Enterprise. 12mo. Lond., 1873. F 12 S 3

Recent Economic Changes and their Effect on the Production and Distribution of Wealth and the Well-being of Society. 8vo. Lond., 1890. F 6 S 36

WELLS, Robert. The Bread and Biscuit Baker's and Sugar Boiler's Assistant. 2nd ed. 8vo. Lond., 1890. A 22 Q 5

The Pastrycook and Confectioner's Guide. 8vo. Lond., 1889. A 22 Q 4

WELLS, W. H. In Memoriam. 8vo. Chicago, 1887. C 18 T 5

WELSH TEXT SOCIETY. Publications. Roy. 8vo. Oxford, 1890. E 1 . 73

Text of the Bruts, from the Red Book of Hergest.

WENDEL, R. New South Wales Album. Ob. fol. Sydney, 1888. MD 8 P 8 †

WENTWORTH, W. C. Australasia : a Poem. 12mo. Lond., 1873. MH 1 Q 78

WERNER, A. [*See* Garibaldi, G.]

WERNER, J. R. Visit to Stanley's Rear-Guard at Major Barttelot's Camp on the Aruhwimi. 8vo. Edinb., 1889. D 14 S 3

WESLEY, Rev. John. Life and Times of ; by Rev. L. Tyerman. 6th ed. 3 vols. 8vo. Lond., 1890. C 17 T 3–5

[Life of] ; by J. H. Overton. 8vo. Lond., 1891. C 15 Q 10

WESLEYAN MISSIONARY SOCIETY. Thirty-third Report, 1853-54. 12mo. Sydney, 1855. ME 5 Q

WEST, A. Views in New South Wales. Imp. 4to. Sydney, 1813-14. MD 7 Q 2 †

WEST, E. W. [*See* Müller, F. Max ; Sacred Books.]

WEST, J. Horticulture, principally with Irrigation : an Address. 12mo. Adelaide, 1891. MA 3 P 54

WESTALL, W. Views of Australian Scenery. Ob. imp. 8vo. Lond., 1814. MD 3 P 14 ‡

WESTBURY, Richard Lord. Life of ; by T. A. Nash. 2 vols. 8vo. Lond., 1888. C 12 T 26, 27

WESTBY-GIBSON. [*See* Gibson, J. Westby-.]

WESTCOTT, B. F. From Strength to Strength : three Sermons. 12mo. Lond., 1890. G 16 Q 43

WESTERBY, Rev. W. M. Has, or Is, Man a Soul ? Verbatim Report of a two nights' Debate between the Rev. W. M. Westerby and C. Bradlaugh. 12mo. Lond. (n.d.) G 2 V 27

WESTERMARCK, Edward. History of Human Marriage. 8vo. Lond., 1891. A 18 T 24

2 H

WESTERN AUSTRALIA.

Correspondence of the Colonial Department with certain Gentlemen proposing to form a Settlement in the Neighbourhood of the Swan River. Fol. Lond., 1829. MF 4 S 15

Notes on. 12mo. Lond., 1890. MD 2 W 29

Regulations for the Guidance of those who may purpose to Embark, as Settlers for the New Settlement on the Western Coast of New Holland. 8vo. Lond., 1829. MD 8 R 14

BLUE BOOK.

Blue Books for 1878, 1883-84, 1887-89. 6 vols. fol. Perth, 1879-90. ME 2 . 61

CONSTITUTION.

A Bill intituled An Act to enable Her Majesty to assent to a bill for conferring a Constitution on Western Australia. Fol. Lond., 1890. MF 3 Q 33 †

A Bill [As Amended by the Select Committee]. Fol. Lond., 1890. MF 3 Q 33 †

Index to Report from Select Committee on. Fol. Lond., 1890. MF 3 Q 33 †

Constitution Act, 1890. Imp. 8vo. Lond., 1880. MF 4 S 36

Constitution Bill, from the Debates in the Times. Roy. 8vo. Sydney, 1889. MF 2 S 21

Correspondence and Further Correspondence respecting the proposed Introduction of Responsible Government into Western Australia. 2 vols. (in 1.) Fol. Lond., 1889. MF 4 S 35

Correspondence between the Secretary of State for the Colonies and the Governor of Western Australia upon the subject of proposed Changes in the Constitution of the Legislative Council of that Colony. Fol. Lond., 1867. MF 4 S 34

Correspondence respecting the Proposed Introduction of Responsible Government. Fol. Lond., 1889. MF 8 Q 28 †

The New Constitution for Western Australia : Debate in the Legislative Assembly of New South Wales. Roy. 8vo. Sydney, 1889. MF 2 S 20

Report from the Select Committee on the Western Australia Constitution Bill. Fol. Lond., 1890. MF 4 S 37

CROWN LANDS.

Return of all Land Grants, Sales, or Leases made by the Government during the last ten years, including concessions to Syndicates or Companies. Fol. Lond., 1889. MF 4 S 33

ELECTORAL ACT.

Electoral Act, 1889. Fol. Lond., 1890. MF 4 S 31

GOVERNMENT GAZETTE.

Government Gazette. Fol. Perth, 1887-88. ME 2 . 62

LEGISLATIVE COUNCIL.

Votes and Proceedings, 1885-89. 8 vols. Fol. Perth, 1885-89. ME 2 . 62

WESTERN AUSTRALIA—*contd.*

STATUTES.

Acts of Council. 4to. Perth, 1888. ME 2 . 62

TRANSPORTATION.

British Convict in Western Australia : a Visit to the Swan River Settlements ; by the Special Correspondent of the Melbourne *Argus* [W.] 8vo. Lond., 1865. MF 1 Q 30

WESTERN PACIFIC.

Correspondence respecting the Natives of the Western Pacific and the Labour Traffic. Fol. Lond., 1883. MF 4 S 40

Correspondence relating to proposals for an International Agreement regulating the Supply of Arms, Ammunition, Alcohol, and Dynamite to Natives of the Western Pacific. Fol. Lond., 1887. MF 4 S 38

Papers relative to Armed Reprisals inflicted upon Natives of Various Islands of the Western Pacific, by H.M.S. "Diamond." Fol. Lond., 1886. MF 4 S 32

Report of a Commission appointed to inquire into the Working of the Western Pacific Orders in Council. Fol. Lond., 1884. MF 4 S 39

Report concerning the State of Affairs in the Western Pacific, received from Deputy Commissioner Romilly, during 1883. Fol. Lond., 1884. MF 4 S 39

WESTGATH, W. Half a Century of Australasian Progress : a Personal Retrospect. 8vo. Lond., 1889. MD 7 Q 4

Personal Recollections of Early Melbourne and Victoria. 8vo. Melb., 1888. MB 1 Q 37

WESTMINSTER REVIEW. July, 1886–June, 1892. 12 vols. Roy. 8vo. Lond., 1886–92. E 2. 9

WESTWOOD, J. O. Modern Classification of Insects. 2 vols. 8vo. Lond., 1839-40. A 27 U 3, 4

The Butterflies of Great Britain, with their Transformations delineated and described. Roy. 8vo. Lond., 1887. A 27 V 22

WETHERSPOON, J. Warblings from the Bush. 12mo. Sydney, 1890. MH 1 Q 80

WEYLAND, Jacob. Geschied en Zeevaartkundige Foelichting Betreffende Eene Kaart van de Geelvinkstaai op de Noordkust van Nieuw-Guinea. 8vo. 's Gravenhage, 1866. MD 7 R 50

WHALL, W. B. [*See* Todd, J.]

WHARNCLIFF, Lord. [*See* Montagu, Lady M. W.]

WHARTON, H T. [*See* Sappho.]

WHARTON, J. S. Wharton's Law Lexicon. 9th edition, by J. M. Lely. Roy. 8vo. Lond., 1892. K 11 R 10

WHATELY, Rev. R. Bacon's Essays. [*See* Bacon, Sir F.]

WHATTON, W. R. [*See* Baines, E.]

WHEATER, W. Some Historic Mansions of Yorkshire, and their associations, 1st and 2nd Series. 4to. Leeds, 1888–89. B 23 V 4, 5

WHEATLEY, H. B. Bibliography of Domesday Book. [*See* Dove, P. E.]

Dedication of Books to Patron and Friend : a Chapter in Literary History. 12mo. Lond., 1887. J 7 P 42

How to Catalogue a Library. 12mo. Lond., 1889. J 7 R 47

London, past and present, its history, associations, and traditions. 3 vols. Roy. 8vo. Lond., 1891. B 21 V 15–17

Remarkable Bindings in the British Museum, selected for their Beauty, or Historic Interest. 4to. Lond., 1889 A 42 R 6 ‡

[*See* Wraxall, Sir N. W.]

WHEATON, Dr. H. Elements of International Law. 3rd edition. Edited with Notes by Dr. A. C. Boyd. Roy. 8vo. Lond., 1889. F 14 V 15

Elements of International Law ; 2nd edition. By W. B. Lawrence. Roy. 8vo. Boston, 1863. F 14 V 14

WHEELER, Prof. B. I. [*See* Strong, Prof. H. A.]

WHEELER, J. C. Report and Narrative of the Trial of Thomas Hall, and Margaret G. Houston, charged with attempting to murder Kate E. Hall. Roy. 8vo. Christchurch, 1886. MF 3 R 38

WHEELER, O. S. [*See* Fisher, J. C.]

WHEELER, W. A. [*See* Pierce, G. A.]

WHEWELL, Rev. Dr. Wm. Of the Plurality of Worlds. 8vo. Lond., 1853. A 19 U 30

History of Moral Philosophy in England. 8vo. Lond., 1852. G 12 Q 36

[*See* Grotius, H.]

WHIBLEY, L. Political Parties in Athens during the Peloponnesian War. (Cambridge Historical Essays.) 8vo. Camb., 1889. B 27 Q 12

WHINFIELD, E. H. [*See* Jalálu-d-Dín.]

WHIPPLE, E. P. American Literature and other Papers, with Introductory Note, by J. G. Whittier. 8vo. Boston, 1887. J 12 Q 28

WHISHAW, B. [*See* Sargeaunt, E. B.]

WHISTLER, J. McNeill. The Gentle Art of Making Enemies. 8vo. Lond., 1890. A 23 S 7

"Ten O'Clock." 8vo. Lond., 1888. A 23 Q 2

WHISTON, Rev. R. [*See* Demosthenes.]

WHISTON, Wm. Historical Memoirs of the Life of Dr. S. Clarke. 8vo. Lond., 1730. C 4 T 4

[*See* Josephus, F.]

WHITAKER, J. Almanacs. 5 vols. 8vo. Lond., 1888-92. E

Reference Catalogue of Current Literature, 1889. 8vo Lond., 1889. Libr.

WHITAKER, Rev. T. D. History and Antiquities of the Deanery of Craven, in County of York. 2nd ed Imp. 4to. Lond., 1812. B 1 S 23 †
History of Parish of Whalley, and Honor of Clitheroe, in the Counties of Lancaster and York. 3rd ed. Roy. 4to. Lond., 1818. B 3 P 19 †

WHITCOMBE, C. D., and TARANAKI, J. K. Conciliation and Arbitration between Capital and Labour: a Plea and a Suggestion for Industrial Union. 8vo. Sydney, 1890. MF 4 Q 6

WHITCOMBE, S. Five Letters to the Prince Regent; containing a View of the Three Branches of the Legislature, the Influence of the Crown, and Observations on Parliamentary Reform. 4to. Lond., 1882. F 33 P 16 ‡

WHITE, Arnold. The Destitute Alien in Great Britain: a Series of Papers dealing with the subject of Foreign Pauper Immigration; arranged and edited by A. White. 12mo. Lond., 1892. F 9 U 8
Tries at Truth. [Socialism, Strikes, Drink, &c.] 8vo. Lond., 1891. F 14 P 39
Letters of S. G. O. [*See* Osborne, Rev. Lord S. G.]

WHITE, Arthur Silva. The Development of Africa. 8vo. Lond., 1890. D 14 T 1
[*See* Britannic Confederation.]

WHITE, C. Early Australian History. Convict Life in New South Wales and Van Diemen's Land. Pts. 1 and 2. 8vo. Bathurst, 1889. MB 1 Q 38

WHITE, C. A., and NICHOLSON, H. A. Bibliography of North American Invertebrate Palæontology. (U.S. Geological Survey.) Roy. 8vo. Wash., 1878. A 24 V 8

WHITE, H. History of the Reformation. [*See* Merle d'Aubigné, J. H.]

WHITE, H. A. Crime and Criminals; or, Reminiscences of the Penal Department in Victoria. 8vo. Ballarat, 1890. MF 2 R 58

WHITE, H. J. Australia, Old Associations, the Bush, and other Poems. 8vo. Port Augusta, 1888. MH 1 S 59
Recreations of Toil. 12mo. Port Augusta, 1888. MH 1 U 2

WHITE, J. Memoirs of the Professional Life of Lord Nelson. 3rd edition. 12mo. Lond., 1806. C 14 P 10

WHITE, Rt. Rev. James S. Address delivered from the chair of the General Assembly of the Presbyterian Church of New South Wales, March, 1892. 12mo. Sydney, 1892. MG 2 R 22

WHITE, John. Ancient History of the Maori, his Mythology, and Traditions. [In English and Maori.] 5 vols. 8vo. Wellington, 1887-88. MB 1 S 32-36

WHITE, Maude Valerie. Letters from a Mourning City. [*See* Munthe, A.]

WHITE, T. W. Our English Homer; or, Shakespeare historically considered. 12mo. Lond., 1892. C 17 Q 13

WHITEAVES, J. F. Canadian Palæontology. [*See* Canada—Geological Survey.]

WHITEHEAD, C. A Forgotten Genius: C. Whitehead; by H. T. M. Bell. 8vo. Lond., 1884. C 14 S 11

WHITEHEAD, W. The Roman Father: a Tragedy. [*See* British Drama, Modern, 2.]

WHITEHOUSE, Rev. O. C. Cuneiform Inscriptions. [*See* Schrader, E.]

WHITELEGGE, T. List of the Marine and Fresh-Water Invertebrate Fauna of Port Jackson and Neighbourhood. 8vo. Sydney, 1889. MA 2 U 53
Report on the Worm Disease affecting the Oysters on the Coast of New South Wales. Roy. 8vo. Sydney, 1890. MA 3 R 6

WHITELOCKE, N. B. P. Etchings taken from the Works of Charles Dickens. 4to. Sydney, 1884. MA 2 P 26 ‡

WHITELY, J. Centennial Geography of New South Wales. 12mo. Sydney, 1888. MD 1 T 43

WHITFIELD, R. P. [*See* United States of America.]

WHITINGTON, F. T. Augustus Short, First Bishop of Adelaide: the Story of a Thirty-four Years' Episcopate. 8vo. Lond., 1888. MC 1 Q 35
[*See* Robinson, Rev. W. G.]

WHITMAN, Walt. Leaves of Grass. 8vo. Philad., 1891-92. H 7 T 39
[Life of]; by W. Clarke. 12mo. Lond., 1892. C 17 P 2
November Boughs. 8vo. Paisley, 1889. J 3 V 26

WHITNEY, H. M. The Tourists' Guide through the Hawaiian Islands, descriptive of their Scenes and Scenery. 8vo. Honolulu, 1890. MD 7 Q 58

WHITNEY, Prof. W. D. [*See* Century Dictionary.]

WHITTIER, J. G. [*See* Whipple, E. P.]

WHITTON, Henry W. A New Ready Reckoner, calculated on the Decimal System. Fol. Melb., 1873. MA 9 Q 1†

WHITTON, John. New South Wales Railways—Cootamundra to Gundagai, Contract No. 1. Fol. Sydney, 1883. MA 6 P 9 ‡
New South Wales Railways—Goulburn to Cooma, Contracts 2 and 3; Bungendore to Michelago River; Michelago River to Cooma. 2 vols. fol. Sydney, 1884. MA 6 P 7, 8 ‡
New South Wales Railways—Homebush to Waratah, Contracts 1 and 3; Homebush to the Hawkesbury; Hawkesbury River to Gosford. 2 vols. el. fol. Sydney, 1883. MA 6 P 10, 11 ‡
New South Wales Railways—Murrumburrah to Blayney, Contracts 2 and 3; Young to Cowra; Blayney to Cowra. 2 vols. el. fol. Sydney, 1884. MA 6 P 1, 2 ‡
New South Wales Railways—Narrandera to Jerilderie, Contract No. 1. El. fol. Sydney, 1882. MA 6 P 4 ‡

WHITTON, John—*contd.*

New South Wales Railways—Orange to Forbes, Contract No. 1 ; Orange to Molong. El. Fol. Sydney, 1884.
MA 6 P 5 ‡

New South Wales Railways—Sydney to Wollongong and Kiama, Contract No. 4. El. fol. Sydney, 1885.
MA 6 P 3 ‡

New South Wales Railways—Great Northern Railway Extension, Tenterfield to Queensland Border. Fol. Sydney, 1885.
MA 6 P 6 ‡

WHITWORTH, Charles, Lord. [*See* Browning, O.]

WHYMPER, E. Travels amongst the Great Andes of the Equator ; Maps and Illustrations. 2 vols. 8vo. Lond., 1891-92.
D 15 T 8, 9

WICHMANN, A. [*See* Martin, K.]

WICKEN, Mrs. H. F. The Australian Home : a Handbook of Domestic Economy. 8vo. Sydney, 1891.
MA 3 P 26

The Kingswood Cookery Book. 3rd edition. 8vo. Sydney, 1891.
MA 3 P 58

WICKES, C. Illustrations of the Spires and Towers of the Medieval Churches of England. 3 vols. (in 1). Fol. Lond., 1858-59.
A 8 Q 12 ‡

WICLIF, John. Sermons ; edited by Dr. J. Loserth. 4 vols. 8vo. Lond., 1887-90.
G 8 U 21-24

Tractatus de Officio Regis ; edited by A. W. Pollard and C. Sayle. 8vo. Lond., 1887.
G 8 U 25

Tractatus de Apostasia ; edited by M. H. Dzilwicki. 8vo. Lond., 1889.
G 8 U 26

Tractatus de Benedicta Incarnacione ; edited by E. Harris. 8vo. Lond., 1886.
G 8 U 27

[*See* Poole, R. L.]

WIDNEY, J. P. [*See* Lindley, W.]

WIESELGREN, S. Fran Striderna om Svenska Bränvinslagstiftningen, 1835-85. 8vo. Götenborg, 1885.
F 11 R 64

WIGHT, G. Congregational Independency ; its Introduction to Queensland, &c. 12mo. Brisbane, 1887. MG 1 P53

WIGMORE, J. H. The Australian Ballot System as embodied in the Legislation of the Various Countries. Roy. 8vo. Boston, 1889.
MF 3 R 41

WIGRAM, Rev. W. Change-ringing Disentangled : with Hints on the Direction of Belfries, on the management of Bells, &c. 2nd ed. 12mo. Lond., 1880. A 23 Q 17

WIGSTON, W. F. C. The Columbus of Literature ; or, Bacon's New World of Sciences. 8vo. Chicago, 1892.
J 2 S 29

Francis Bacon, poet, prophet, and philosopher, *versus* Phantom Captain Shakespeare. 8vo. Lond., 1891.
J 3 S 29

WIJESINHA, L. C. The Mahávansa. [*See* Mahávansa.]

WILBERFORCE, Rt. Rev. Samuel. [Life of] ; by Very Rev. J. W. Burgon. (Lives of Twelve Good Men.) 2 vols. 8vo. Lond., 1888.
C 13 R 10, 11

Bishop Wilberforce ; by G. W. Daniell. 8vo. Lond., 1891.
C 15 Q 9

WILBERFORCE, W. The Prevailing Religious System of Professed Christian. 18mo. Lond. (n.d.) G 9 U 8

WILCANNIA PASTORAL PROTECTION ASSOCIATION, Western Division. The Land Act and the Rabbits. 1st edition. Sydney, 1886. MF 1 T 39

Another Copy. 2nd edition. Sydney, 1887. MF 1 T 40

WILD FLOWERS of Switzerland ; by H. C. W. 4to. Lond., 1883.
A 40 Q 3 ‡

WILDER, A. Symbolical Language. [*See* Knight, R.P.]

WILHELM, F. Military Dictionary and Gazetteer. Revised ed. Roy. 8vo. Philad., 1881. A 29 V 12

WILHELMINE, Margravine of Baireuth. Memoirs of ; translated and edited by H.R.H. Princess Christian. 8vo. Lond., 1887.
C 8 P 11

WILKES, J. Life and Times of ; by P. Fitzgerald. 2 vols. 8vo. Lond., 1888.
C 15 Q 1, 2

WILKINS, Rev. H. W. Olynthiacs of Demosthenes. [*See* Demosthenes.]

WILKINS, G. The Miseries of Inforced Marriage : a Comedy. [*See* British Drama, Ancient, 2.]

WILKINS, J. Essay towards a Real Character and a Philosophical Language, with alphabetical dictionary. Sm. fol. Lond., 1668.
K 39 R 10‡

WILKINS, W. National Education ; an Exposition of the National System of New South Wales. 8vo. Sydney, 1865.
MG 1 R 59

Australasia : a Descriptive and Pictorial Account of the Australasian Colonies. 8vo. Lond., 1888.* MD 1 R 1

WILKINS, W. H. The Alien Invasion. 12mo. Lond., 1892.
F 7 V 28

WILKINS, Rev. W. J. Hindu Mythology, Vedic and Purānic. Illustrated. 8vo. Calcutta, 1882.
B 17 P 26

Modern Hinduism : an Account of the Religion and Life of the Hindus in Northern India. 8vo. Lond., 1887.
G 6 P 34

WILKINSON, C. S. The Church and Modern Thought : Paper read at Church Congress, Sydney, 1889. Revelation and Science. 8vo. Sydney, 1889. MG 2 Q 41

WILKINSON, Rev. J. F. Pensions and Pauperism ; with notes by T. E. Young. 12mo. Lond., 1892. F 9 U 7

Mutual Thrift. 8vo. Lond., 1891. F 14 P 24

WILKINSON, Sir J. G. Popular Account of the Ancient Egyptians. 2 vols. 8vo. Lond., 1854. A 21 R 1, 2

WILKINSON, S. The Brain of an Army : a popular account of the German General Staff. 12mo. Lond., 1890.
A 29 Q 14

[*See* Dilke, Sir C. W.]

WILKINSON, W. C. The Epic of Saul. 8vo. New York, 1891. H 7 T 38

WILKINSON, W. H. The Queensland Magistrate. 2nd edition. 8vo. Brisb., 1879. MF 1 Q 64

Another Copy. 2nd ed. 8vo. Brisb., 1891. MF 1 Q 65

WILKS, M. Tahiti, containing a review of the Origin, Character, and Progress of French Roman Catholic Efforts for the Destruction of English Protestant Missions in South Seas. Roy. 8vo. Lond., 1844. MB 2 Q 43

WILL, J. S. [*See* Michael, W. H.]

WILLCOCKS, W. Egyptian Irrigation. Roy. 8vo. New York, 1889. A 22 V 22

WILLIAM I, of Germany: a succinct Biography of; by A. Forbes. 8vo. Lond., 1888. C 14 Q 22

Emperor William: Life of a Great King and Good Man; by G. L. M. Strauss. 12mo. Lond., 1888. C 12 P 41

William I, and the German Empire: a Biographical and Historical Sketch; by G. B. Smith. 8vo. Lond., 1887. C 12 S 26

WILLIAM III [Life of]; by H. D. Traill. (Twelve English Statesmen.) 8vo. Lond., 1888. C 3 R 3

WILLIAM OF MALMESBURY. De Regum Gestis Anglorum. [*See* Chronicles and Memorials of Great Britain, &c.]

WILLIAM THE CONQUEROR. Life of; by Prof. E. A. Freeman. 8vo. Lond., 1888. C 3 R 17

WILLIAMS, B. S. Orchid Album. [*See* Warner, R.]

WILLIAMS, C. The Life of Sir Henry Evelyn Wood. 8vo. Lond., 1892. C 18 Q 15

WILLIAMS, E. De Buckley; or, Incidents of Australian Life. 8vo Birmingham, 1887. MH 1 S 30

The Merlin: Tales in Verse about the Land and Sea. 8vo. Birmingham, 1888. MH 1 S 29

WILLIAMS, Frederick Wells. Life and Letters of Samuel Wells Williams, Missionary Diplomatist, Sinologue. 8vo. New York, 1889. C 10 P 33

WILLIAMS, Prof. George Huntingdon. Elements of Crystallography. 2nd edition. 12mo. Lond., 1890. A 24 Q 8

WILLIAMS, G. P., and REEVES, W. P. Colonial Couplets: being Poems in Partnership. 12mo. Christchurch, 1889. MH 1 U 3

WILLIAMS, H. [*See* Lucian.]

WILLIAMS, Isaac. Autobiography of; edited by the Ven. Sir G. Prevost. 12mo. Lond., 1892. C 13 Q 17

WILLIAMS, Jane. Autobiography of Elizabeth Davis. 2 vols. 8vo. Lond., 1857. C 16 R 7, 8

WILLIAMS, Rev. J. [*See* Campbell, J.]

WILLIAMS, J. F. The Geography of Australasia and Polynesia. 12mo. Lond., 1892. MD 7 T 54

WILLIAMS, Sir Monier Monier-. Buddhism, in its connexion with Bráhmanism and Hindúism, and in its contrast with Christianity. 8vo. Lond., 1889. G 6 P 33

Grammar of the Sanskrit Language. 4th edition. Imp. 8vo. Oxford, 1877. K 14 Q 3

WILLIAMS, Montague. Leaves of a Life. 2 vols. 8vo. Lond., 1890. C 12 T 31, 32

Later Leaves, being Further Reminiscences. 8vo. Lond., 1891. C 12 T 33

WILLIAMS, R. F. Shakspeare and his Friends; or, the "Golden Age" of Merry England. 3 vols. 8vo. Lond., 1838. J 4 R 24-26

Youth of Shakspeare. 3 vols. 8vo. Lond., 1839. C 13 R 16, 18

WILLIAMS, Samuel Wells. Life and Letters of; by F. W. Williams. 8vo. New York, 1889. C 10 P 33

WILLIAMS, T. Ostriches and Ostrich Farming in Australia. 8vo. Adelaide, 1887. MA 3 Q 23

WILLIAMS, T. [*See* Wood, J.]

WILLIAMS, T., and CALVERT, J. Fiji and the Fijians; and Missionary Labours among the Cannibals. Edited by G. S. Rowe. 8vo. Lond., 1870. MD 3 Q 54

WILLIAMS, Prof. W. Carleton. Outlines of Theoretical Chemistry. [*See* Meyer, Prof. Lothair.]

WILLIAMS, Ven. Archdeacon W. L. Lessons in the English Language for Maori Schools. 8vo. Wellington 1875. MK 1 P 37

WILLIAMS, W. M. Chemistry of Cookery. 8vo. Lond., 1885. A 22 Q 1

WILLIAMSON, Rev. A. Missionary Heroes in the Islands of the Pacific. 8vo. Edinb., 1888. MD 1 Q 28

WILLIAMSON, T. M. Small Debts Recovery Acts and other Statutes, together with Supreme Court Decisions affecting Petty Sessions Court. 2nd edition. 8vo. Sydney, 1891. MF 2 R 60

WILLIE'S First English Book, written for young Maoris who wish to learn the English Language. Part 1. 12mo. Wellington, 1872. MK 1 P 35

WILLIS, J. A. C. Pocket Map of Port Jackson and City of Sydney. 12mo. Sydney, 1867. MD 6 P 24

WILLIS, GANN & CO. New Zealand Hand-book; or, Guide to the Britain of the South. 8th ed. 12mo. Lond., 1862. MD 1 P 16

WILLIS, R. Remarks on the Architecture of the Middle Ages, especially of Italy. 8vo. Camb., 1835. A 3 P 23

WILLMORE, F. W. History of Walsall and its Neighborhood. 8vo. Walsall, 1887. B 23 U 6

WILLOCK, J. Legal Facetiæ, Satirical and Humorous. 8vo. Lond., 1887. J 2 S 28

WILLOUGHBY, H. Australian Federation, its Aims and its Possibilities. 8vo. Melb., 1891. MF 4 P 2

WILLOUGHBY, Capt. Sir J. C. East Africa and its Big Game : the narrative of a sporting trip from Zanzibar to the borders of the Masai. 8vo. Lond., 1889.
                                     D 14 U 14

WILLS, W. J. [*See* Burke, R. O'H.]

WILLS, W. R. A Bunch of Wild Pansies. 12mo. Auckland, 1885.   MH 1 Q 59

WILLSON, Rt. Rev. R. W. Memoir of Bishop Willson, first Bishop of Hobart, Tasmania ; by Bishop Ullathorne. 8vo. Lond., 1887.   MC 1 Q 49

WILLYAMS, Rev. C. A Voyage up the Mediterranean, with a Description of the Battle of the Nile. Fol. Lond., 1802.   D 44 Q 6 ‡

WILMER FAMILY, History of the ; by C. W. Foster and J. J. Green. 4to. Leeds, 1888.   C 12 V 8

WILMOT, Sir Eardley. Correspondence between the Secretary of State and Sir Eardley Wilmot relative to the recall of the latter from the government of Van Diemen's Land. 2 vols. (in 1). Fol. Lond., 1847.
                                     MF 4 S 41

WILMOT, Lieut. S. E. Our Journal in the Pacific ; by the officers of H.M.S. Zealous. 8vo. Lond., 1873.
                                       D 20 S 4

WILSHIRE, W. J. Lady Cordelia ; or Federation, Aristocracy, and Democracy, Australia in London. An Australian Novel. 8vo. Sydney, 1890.   MJ 2 T 3

WILSON, Col. Sir Charles. Lord Clive. (English Men of Action.) 12mo. Lond., 1890.   C 12 P 33

WILSON, Col. Sir Charles William. [*See* Armstrong, G.]

WILSON, Dr. C. Pathology of Drunkenness. 12mo. Edinb., 1855.   F 11 P 18

WILSON, Sir Daniel. Prehistoric Man. 2 vols. 8vo. Cambridge, 1862.   A 18 T 29, 30

The Right Hand : Left-handedness. (Nature Series.) 12mo. Lond., 1891.   A 26 Q 9

WILSON, E. The Anatomist's Vademecum : a System of Human Anatomy. 7th edition. 12mo. Lond., 1857.
                                     A 26 P 2

WILSON, E. L. Quarter of a Century in Photography : a Collection of Hints on Practical Photography. Sm. 4to. New York, 1887.   A 7 T 21

WILSON, F. J. F., and **GREY, D.** Practical Treatise upon Modern Printing Machinery and Letterpress Printing. Roy. 8vo. Lond., 1888.   A 11 V 15

WILSON, H. [*See* Dunlop, J. C.]

WILSON, Capt. J. Memoirs of ; by John Griflin. 2nd edition revised. 8vo. Lond. (n.d.)   MC 1 R 1

WILSON, J. E. [*See* Couche, C.]

WILSON, J. G. [*See* Appleton, D., and Co.]

WILSON, Mrs. J. G. "Austral." Themes and Variations. 12mo. Lond., 1889.   MH 1 Q 77

WILSON, J. H. China. Travels and Investigations in the Middle Kingdom, &c. ; with a Glance at Japan. 8vo. New York, 1887.   D 17 Q 11

WILSON, J. M., and **FOWLER, T.** The Principles of Morals. 8vo. Oxford, 1886.   G 8 T 24

WILSON, J. T. Observations on the Innervation of Axillary Muscular Arches (Achselbogen) in Man with remarks on their Homology suggested by comparative considerations. 8vo. Lond. (n.d.)
                                     MA 3 T 38

WILSON, Gen. Sir R. Life of ; by the Rev. H. Randolph. 2 vols. 8vo. Lond., 1862.   C 18 R 1, 2

Private Diary of Travels, Personal Services, and Public Events, 1812–14. 2 vols. 8vo. Lond., 1861.
                              C 18 R 13, 14

WILSON, Sir Samuel. The Californian Salmon, with an Account of its Introduction into Victoria. 8vo. Melb., 1878.   MA 3 R 32

WINCHESTER, B. The Swiss Republic. 8vo. Philad., 1891.   F 9 S 9

WINCHESTER COLLEGE SHAKESPERE SOCIETY. Noctes Shaksperianæ ; edited by Rev. C. H. Hawkins. 8vo. Winchester, 1887.   C 10 T 2

WINDEYER, Sir W. C. Commemorative Address on the 50th Anniversary of the Sydney Mechanics' School of Arts, March 22nd, 1883. Roy. 8vo. Sydney, 1883.
                                     MJ 2 S 35

WINDT, H. de. From Pekin to Calais by Land. Roy. 8vo. Lond., 1889.   D 17 U 8

A Ride to India across Persia and Baluchistan. Roy. 8vo. Lond., 1891.   D 17 U 9

Siberia as it is. 8vo. Lond., 1892.   D 17 V 9

WINGATE, Major F. R. Mahdism and the Egyptian Sudan. 8vo. Lond., 1891.   B 16 R 2

WINGFIELD, Hon. Lewis. Wanderings of a Globe Trotter in the Far East. 2 vols. 8vo. Lond., 1889.
                                 D 17 S 1, 2

WINSLOW, Dr. F. On Uncontrollable Drunkenness considered as a form of mental disorder. 12mo. Lond., 1866.   F 11 P 13

WINSOR, J. Narrative and Critical History of America ; edited by J. Winsor. Vols. 1–8. Imp. 8vo. Lond., 1886–89.   B 17 U 1–8

WINT, Peter de. [Life of ;] by G. R. Redgrave. (Great Artists.) 8vo. Lond., 1891.   C 17 Q 6

WINTER, A. The New York State Reformatory in Elmira. 8vo. Lond., 1891.   F 6 R 40

WINTERBOTTOM, J. The Lady Don Waltz. Fol. Sydney (n.d.)   MA 11 Q 15†

WINTERBOTTOM, M. Hermione, Waltz. Fol. Sydney (n.d.)   MA 11 Q 15†

WINTRINGHAM, W. H. The Birds of Wordsworth. 8vo. Lond., 1892.   A 27 T 38

WINZET, N. Tractates of Vincentius Lirinensis. [*See* Scottish Text Soc.]

WISCHNEWETZKY, Florence K. [*See* Engels, F.]

WISE, B. R. Industrial Freedom : a Study in Politics.
8vo. Lond., 1892. MF 4 P 1

The Influence of Free Trade on Wages; or, Why Working
Men should be Free Traders. 8vo. Sydney, 1884.
MF 4 Q 4

Position of the Liberal Party ; a speech. 8vo. Sydney,
1888. MF 1 T 13

Australian Economic Association. Papers No. 1. Mutual
Relations of Imports and Exports. 8vo. Sydney,
1887. MF 3 Q 35

WISE, B. R., and DAVIES, H. Bankruptcy Act, 1887 :
Rules and Forms; with Notes of Cases, and Index.
8vo. Sydney, 1888.* MF 3 Q 12

WISE, C. Puritanism in Power. 8vo. Lond., 1890.
G 6 P 39

WISE, H., & Co. New South Wales Post Office Directory,
1889-90, 1892-93. 2 vols. roy. 8vo. Sydney, 1889-92.
ME

New Zealand Directory, 1892-93. Imp. 8vo. Dunedin,
1892. ME

Queensland Official Directory, 1890, 1892-93. 2 vols. roy.
8vo. Brisbane, 1889-93. ME

Tasmanian Post-Office Directory, 1892-93. Imp. 8vo.
Hobart, 1892. ME

Victoria Post-Office Directory, 1888-89. Imp. 8vo.
Melb., 1888. ME

WISE, H. A. Los Gringos ; or, An Inside View of
Mexico and Californa, with Wanderings in Peru, Chili,
and Polynesia. 12mo. New York, 1849. D 4 P 55

WISEMAN, R. Biographical Study of ; by Sir T. Longmore. 8vo. Lond., 1891. C 17 T 20

WISTRAND, Dr. A. T. Zur gerichtsärztlichen Beurtheilung der körperlichen Verletzung berauschter Personen.
8vo. Erlangen, 1866. F 11 Q 42

WITHAM, T. M. [*See* Heathcote, J. M.]

WITHERS, W. B. History of Ballarat, from the First
Pastoral Settlement to the Present Time. 8vo. Bal-
larat, 1870. MB 2 Q 33
Another copy. 2nd ed. 8vo. Ballarat, 1887. MB 2 Q 34

WITT, C. DE. Histoire de Washington ; précédée d'une
Etude Historique sur Washington, par M. Guizot. 12mo.
Paris, 1876. C 17 Q 28

WOELFFLIN, E. [*See* Polyænus.]

WOFFINGTON, Mary [Peg]. A Tribute to the Actress
and the Woman ; by A. Daly. 2nd ed. 4to. New
York, 1890. C 17 U 15

WOIIL, J. François Liszt : Recollections of a Compatriot. 8vo. Lond., 1887. C 15 Q 22

WOLF, J. Die Branntweinsteuer. 8vo. Tübingen, 1884.
F 11 S 51

WOLF, L. [*See* Anglo-Jewish Historical Exhibition.]

WOLFF, Sir H. D. [*See* Egypt.]

WOLFF, H. W. The Country of the Vosges. 8vo.
Lond., 1891. D 18 S 8

The Watering Places of the Vosges. 8vo. Lond., 1891.
D 19 Q 13

WOLSELEY, Gen. Sir Garnet Joseph, Viscount. The
Soldier's Pocket-book, for Field Service. 5th ed. Sq.
18mo. Lond., 1886. A 29 P 47

Memoir of ; by C. R. Low. 2 vols. 8vo. Lond., 1878.
C 12 Q 22, 23

WOLSEY, Cardinal Thos. [Life of]; by M. Creighton.
8vo. Lond., 1888. C 3 R 1

WOMAN'S JOURNAL. Fol. Boston, 1888-90. E

WOOD, Dr. G. B. Household Practice of Medicine, Hygiene, and Surgery. Edited by F. A. Castle. 2 vols.
roy. 8vo. Lond., 1884. A 12 V 7, 8

WOOD, Dr. G. B., & BACHE, Dr. F. The Dispensatory
of the United States of America. 16th ed. Roy. 8vo.
Philad., 1889. A 26 V 3

WOOD, H. Mineral Products of New South Wales.
Notes on the Geology of New South Wales, by C. S.
Wilkinson ; and Descriptions of Seams of Coal worked
in New South Wales, by J. Mackenzie. (Department
of Mines.) Roy. 4to. Sydney, 1887.* MA 1 Q 36 †

WOOD, Lt.-Gen. Sir H. E. Life of ; by C. Williams.
8vo. Lond., 1892. C 18 Q 15

WOOD, H. T. Modern Methods of Illustrating Books.
12mo. Lond., 1887. A 23 P 1
[*See* Colonial and Indian Exhibition.]

WOOD, Capt. J. [*See* Voyages and Discoveries.]

WOOD, James. Wood's Tasmanian Almanack for 1852
and 1854. 2 vols. 12mo. Launceston, 1852-54.
ME 4 P

WOOD, James. Memoir of ; including Notices of other
Members of his Family, by T. Williams. 12mo. Geelong,
1883. MC 1 Q 51

WOOD, Lady M. [*See* Edgcumbe, Lady E.]

WOOD, Mrs. N., and LAPHAM, H. Waiting for the
Mail, and other Sketches and Poems. 12mo. Melb.,
1875. MJ 1 Q 60

WOOD, R. Ruins of Balbec, otherwise Heliopolis, in
Cœlosyria. Imp. fol. Lond., 1757. B 20 P 8 †

WOODBURY, Charles J. Talks with Ralph Waldo
Emerson. 12mo. Lond., 1890. C 12 P 24

WOODFORD, C. M. A Naturalist among the Head-
Hunters, being an Account of Three Visits to the
Solomon Islands, 1886-88. 8vo. Lond., 1890.
MD 7 P 41

WOODGATE, W. B. Boating; with a Chapter on Rowing
at Eton, by R. H. Mason. 8vo. Lond., 1888. A 17 U 38

WOODS, J. The Tourist's Flora : a descriptive catalogue
of the flowering plants and ferns of the British Islands,
France, Germany, Switzerland, Italy, and the Italian
Islands. 8vo. Lond., 1850. A 4 S 24

WOODS, R. A. English Social Movements. 12mo. Lond., 1892. F 9 U 17

WOODS, W. J. Visit to Victoria. 8vo. Lond., 1886. MD 1 Q 29

WOODWARD, Dr. C. M. Manual Training in Education. 8vo. Lond., 1890. G 18 Q 13

WOODWARD, G. P. M., M.D., &c. New South Wales Ambulance Hand-book. Enlarged ed. 12mo. Sydney, 1887. MA 2 S 21

WOODWARD, H. B. Geology of England and Wales. 2nd ed. 8vo. Lond., 1887. A 24 U 1

WOOLCOCK, J. L. Queensland Justices Act of 1886 and Offenders Probation Act of 1886. 8vo. Brisb., 1887. MF 1 T 5

WOOLCOTT, W. C. Tourist's Pocket Guide to the Blue Mountains, Jenolan Caves, &c. 18mo. Sydney, 1888. MD 1 P 20

WOOLER, W. M. On the Philosophy of Temperance, and the Physical Causes of Moral Sadness. Part 1. 8vo. Lond., 1840. F 11 R 62

WOOLLEY, T. Reminiscences of the Life of a Bushman in Australia. 8vo. Lond., 1850. MD 3 Q 28

WOOLLS, Rev. William. The Progress of Botanical Discovery in Australia ; a Lecture. 18mo. Sydney, 1869. MA 2 P 68

Plants Indigenous and Naturalised in the Neighborhood of Sydney. 8vo. Sydney, 1891. MA 3 S 1

Lectures on the Vegetable Kingdom ; with special reference to the Flora of Australia. 8vo. Sydney, 1879. MA 1 T 43

WOOLSEY, T. D. Communism and Socialism in their History and Theory. 8vo. Lond., 1879. F 14 P 19

WORDSWORTH, Rev. C. Rutland Words. [*See* English Dialect Soc.]

Social Life at the English Universities in the 18th Century. 8vo. Cambridge, 1874. B 21 R 21

WORDSWORTH, Rt. Rev. Charles. Annals of My Early Life, 1806–46. 8vo. Lond., 1891. C 17 T 12

[Life of] ; by J. H. Overton, and Elizabeth Wordsworth. 8vo. Lond., 1888. C 12 S 28

WORDSWORTH, Elizabeth. [*See* Overton, J. H.]

WORDSWORTH, William. The Birds of. [*See* Wintringham, W. H.]

Wordsworthiana : a Selection from Papers read to the Wordsworth Society ; edited by W. Knight. 8vo. Lond., 1889. C 12 Q 18

Life of ; by Prof. W. Knight. 3 vols. 8vo. Edinb., 1889. C 17 T 9–11

[Life of] by F. W. H. Myers. (English Men of Letters.) 12mo. Lond., 1888. C 1 U 40

WORDSWORTH, William—*contd.*
The Story of his Life ; with critical Remarks on his Writings, by J. M. Sutherland. 12mo. Lond., 1887. C 2 R 32

WORDSWORTH SOCIETY. Transactions. Vols. 2, 5–8. 8vo. Edinb., 1882–86. E

WORLD'S TEMPERANCE CONVENTION. Proceedings. 8vo. Lond., 1846. F 11 R 63

WORMS, Baron H. de. [*See* Beust, Count F. F. von.]

WORSNOP, Thomas. Jubilee of Municipal Institutions in Australasia, October 31st, 1890. 8vo. Adelaide, 1890. MF 4 Q 5

WORT AN DAS SCHWEIZERVOLK, Ein. 12mo. Basel, 1885. F 11 P 68

WORTHINGTON, Dr. J. Bibliography of Works by. [*See* Chetham Soc., N.S., 13.]

WOTHERSPOON, A. Maid of Erin, and other Poems. 18mo. Sydney, 1859. MH 1 P 73

WOTTON, Mabel E. Word Portraits of Famous Writers. 8vo. Lond., 1887. C 6 P 28

WRAXALL, Sir N. W. Historical and Posthumous Memoirs of, 1772–84. Edited by H. B. Wheatley. 5 vols. 8vo. Lond., 1884. C 12 U 20–24

WRAYS OF GLENTWORTH, History of the, 1523–1852 ; by C. Dalton. 2 vols. 8vo. Lond., 1880–81. C 10 U 35, 36

WRIGHT, Dr. A. Te Aroha, New Zealand : a Guide for Invalids and Visitors to the Thermal Springs and Baths. 12mo. Te Aroha, 1887. MD 1 P 57

WRIGHT, B. Description of the Collection of Gold Ornaments from the Graves of some Aboriginal Races of the North-western Provinces of South America, belonging to Lady Brassey. 8vo. Lond., 1885. A 23 T 4

WRIGHT, C. D. Fisheries of Massachusetts. Roy. 8vo. Boston, 1887. F 8 T 17

Manual of Distributive Co-operation. 8vo. Boston, 1885. F 14 T 1

Profit Sharing. 2nd ed. 8vo. Boston, 1886. F 14 T 2

Report on Marriage and Divorce in the United States, 1867–86. 8vo. Washington, 1889. E

Industrial Conciliation and Arbitration. 8vo. Boston, 1881. F 12 R 31

WRIGHT, F. Horticulture. [*See* Indian and Colonial Exhibition, 1886.]

WRIGHT, L. Practical Poultry Keeper. 23rd ed. 8vo. Lond., 1890. A 18 Q 15

WRIGHT, T. History of Domestic Manners and Sentiments in England during the Middle Ages. Illustrated by F. W. Fairholt. 8vo. Lond., 1862. B 22 U 19

WRIGHT, W. A. Letters, &c., of E. Fitzgerald. [*See* Fitzgerald, E.]

[*See* Shakespeare, W.]

WRIGHTSON, J. Principles of Agricultural Practice. 8vo. Lond., 1888. A 18 R 1

WÜLLERSTORF-URBAIR, B. von. Reise der Oesterreichischen Fregatte Novara um die Erde, in den Jahren 1857-59. 3 vols. roy. 8vo. Wien, 1861-62.
MD 7 U 2-4

WUNDER, E. [*See* Sophocles.]

WUNDT, W. Philosophische Studien. Bande 1-7. Roy. 8vo. Leip., 1883-92. G 6 T 1-7

WURZBACH, A. von. [*See* Rembrandt-Galerie.]

WURZER, F. J. R. De Alcohole. 8vo. Marburgi-Cattorum, 1826. F 11 Q 23

WYCHERLEY, W. Best Plays; edited by W. C. Ward. 8vo. Lond., 1888. H 4 Q 27

Love in a Wood; or, St. James's Park.—The Gentleman Dancing Master.—The Country Wife.—The Plain Dealer.

The Country Girl : a Comedy. [*See* British Drama, Modern.]

The Plain Dealer : a Comedy. [*See* British Drama, Modern.]

WYCLIFFE, J. [*See* Wiclif, J.]

WYLD, James. Map of South Australia, New South Wales, Van Dieman's Land, and settled parts of Australia. (Folded.) 8vo. Lond. (n.d.) MD 8 R 13

Map of the Province of Queensland. 8vo. Lond. (n.d.)
MD 5 P 16 ‡

WYLIE, Dr. W. G. Hospitals : their History, Organization, and Construction. 8vo. New York, 1877.
A 19 T 1

WYNDHAM, H. T. [*See* Bubb-Dodington, G.]

WYSS, Dr. H. von. [*See* Ranvier, L.]

X

XENOPHON. Cyropædia ; recensuit J. C. Zeunius. 8vo. Lipsiæ, 1780. B 27 S 15

Scripta Quæ Supersunt. (Græce et Latine.) Roy. 8vo. Paris, 1853. B 39 S 11 ‡

Xenophontis Philosophi et Imperatoris Clarissimi Opera. (Gr. et Lat.) Fol. Paris, 1625. B 39 S 11 ‡

Works of. Translated by H. G. Dakyns. 8vo. Lond., 1890. J 11 S 40

Xenophon ; by Sir A. Grant. (Ancient Classics for English Readers.) 12mo. Edinb., 1889. J 14 P 28

XYLANDER, G. [*See* Pausanias.]

2 ı

Y .

YACHT RACING CALENDAR AND REVIEW. 4 vols. 8vo. Lond., 1888-92. E 1. 78

YARRINGTON, Rev. W. H. H. University Prize Poem, and other Verses. 12mo. West Maitland, 1880.
MH 1 U 4

Cœlestia : a Religious and Philosophic Poem. 12mo. Sydney, 1882. MH 1 U 5

YATE, Major C. E. Northern Afghanistan; or, Letters from the Afghan Boundary Commission. 8vo. Edinb., 1888. D 17 U 4

YATES, Dr. J. Golden Gates of Trade with Our Home Industries. 8vo., Lond., 1890. F 6 P 48

Map Studies of the Mercantile World. 8vo. Lond., 1890.
F 6 P 49

YEAR-BOOK OF SCIENCE. 8vo. Lond., 1892. E 1. 78

YEAR-BOOK OF SCIENTIFIC AND LEARNED SOCIETIES of Great Britain and Ireland. 5 vols. 8vo. Lond., 1888-92. E 1. 59

YEAR-BOOK OF AUSTRALIA. [*See* Greville, E.]

YEAR'S ART, The. [*See* Huish, M. B.]

YEATS, J. Growth and Vicissitudes of Commerce in all Ages. 3rd ed. 8vo. Lond., 1887. F 5 R 35

Natural History of the Raw Materials of Commerce. 3rd ed. 8vo. Lond., 1887. F 5 R 36

Recent and Existing Commerce. 3rd ed. 8vo. Lond., 1887. F 5 R 37

Technical History of Commerce ; or, Progress of the Useful Arts. 3rd ed. 8vo. Lond., 1887. F 5 R 38

YELLAND, Rev. C. M. : Life of. Mission Work in Collingwood, and the History of St. Saviour's Church, Collingwood. 8vo. Melb., 1891. MC 1 Q 57

YEN-TSUNG. [*See* Hwui Li.]

YONGE, C. D. Modern History. [*See* Taylor, W. C.]

Our Great Military Commanders : Sketches of the Lives of Marlborough, Clive, Wellington, Napier, Gough, and Clyde. 12mo. Lond., 1892. C 17 Q 11

[*See* Walpole, H.]

YONGE, Miss Charlotte M. Cameos from English History. Seventh Series. The Rebellion and Restoration (1642-1678.) 12mo. Lond., 1890. B 23 P 13

Deacon's Book of Dates : an Outline of Universal History. 8vo. Lond., 1888. B 35 P 8

Hannah More. (Eminent Women.) 8vo. Lond., 1888. C 12 Q 28

YONGE, Miss Charlotte M.—*contd.*
History of Christian Names. New edition. 8vo. Lond.,
1884.   K 19 Q 12

Life of H.R.H. the Prince Consort. (Statesmen Series.)
8vo. Lond., 1890.   C 12 R 40

The Victorian Half Century : a Jubilee Book. 8vo.
Lond., 1886.   B 22 Q 1

Yorkshire Tragedy, A. [*See* British Drama, Ancient.]

YORK GATE LIBRARY. Catalogue of the York Gate
Library [formed by S. W. Silver]; compiled by E. A.
Petherick. 2nd ed. Imp.8vo. Lond.,1886. MK 1 U 21

YOUMANS, Eliza A. The First Book of Botany. 12mo.
Lond., 1872.   A 20 P 15

YOUNG, A. Travels in France, 1787–89. 8vo. Lond.,
1889.   C 18 P 22

YOUNG, Surg.-Gen. A. G. Story of Active Service in
South Africa, India, and China, 1856–82. 8vo. Edinb.,
1888.   D 20 Q 3

YOUNG, C. Every Day Heroes, and other Poems. 8vo.
Sydney, 1891.   MH 1 U 19

YOUNG, E. The Brothers : a Tragedy. [*See* British
Drama, Modern.]

The Revenge : a Tragedy. [*See* British Drama, Modern.]

YOUNG, E. D. Nyassa : a Journal of Adventure. 8vo.
Lond., 1877.   D 1 R 15

YOUNG, Sir G. Fac-simile of a Proposal for a Settlement on the Coast of New South Wales, 1785. Sm. fol.
Sydney, 1888.*   MB 3 P 6†

YOUNG, Prof. J. R. On the General Principles of
Analysis. Part 1. Analysis of Numerical Equations.
8vo. Lond., 1850.   A 25 T 25

YOUNG, Dr. T. Life of ; by G. Peacock. 8vo. Lond.,
1855.   C 14 U 17

Miscellaneous Works of. 3 vols. 8vo. Lond., 1855.
     J 17 P 35–37

YOUNG, T. E. [*See* Wilkinson, J. F.]

YOUNG AUSTRALIA, the Journal of the Naval and
Military Forces, &c., in Australia. Fol. Melb., 1889.
     ME 1.88

YOUNGER, R. T. [*See* Spens, W. C.]

YUILLE, Archibald. The Australian Stud Book. Vols.
2–4. 8vo. Melb., 1882–89.   MA 3 W 1–4.

Z

ZEITSCHRIFT FÜR ETHNOLOGIE. Organ der
Berliner Gesellschaft fur Anthropologie, Ethnologie und
Urgeschichte. Bande 1–20. 20 vols. roy. 8vo. Berlin,
1869–88.   E

Supplements, 1871–85. 8 vols. roy. 8vo. Berlin,
1871–85.   E

ZEITSCHRIFT FÜR WISSENSCHAFTLICHE ZOO-
LOGIE. Bande 44–53. 8vo. Leip., 1886–92. E 1.37
Register. Bande 31–45. 8vo. Leip., 1888.   E 1.37

ZELLER, Dr. E. The Contents and Origin of the Acts of
the Apostles, critically investigated. 2 vols. 8vo. Lond.,
1875–76.   G 4 U 16, 17

ZERFFI, Prof. G. G. [*See* Goethe, J. W. von.]

ZEUNE, J. G. [*See* Xenophon.]

ZILLMANN, Rev. J. H. L. Past and Present Australian
Life. 8vo. Lond., 1889.   MD 1 P 55

ZIMMERN, Helen. The Hansa Towns. 8vo. Lond.,
1889.   B 27 R 1

ZITTEL, Karl A. Handbuch der Palæontologie. 4 vols.
roy. 8vo. München, 1876–90.   A 24 V 12–15

ZÖLLER, Hugo. Deutsch-Neuguinea und meine Erstei-
gung des Finisterre-Gebirges. Roy.8vo. Stuttgart, 1891.
     MD 7 U 14

ZOOLOGICAL AND ACCLIMATISATION SOCIETY
OF VICTORIA. Proceedings. Vol. 3. 8vo. Melb.,
1874.   ME 1 Q

ZOOLOGICAL RECORD for 1886–90. 5 vols. 8vo.
Lond., 1887–92.   E

ZOOLOGICAL SOCIETY OF LONDON. Proceedings.
Vols. 9–14. Roy. 8vo. Lond., 1887–91.   E 1.47
Index to Proceedings, 1881–90. 8vo. Lond., 1892. E

ZOOLOGISCHEN INSTITUTE, WIEN. Arbeiten.
Bande 1–5. 8vo. Wien, 1878–84.   E 2.6

ZOOLOGISCHEN STATION, NEAPEL, Mittheilungen.
Bande 1–6. 8vo. Leip., 1879–85.   E
Monographie, 13–16. Imp. 4to. Berlin, 1885–87. E 1.79

ZOOLOGISCHER ANZEIGER. Bande 1–8. 8vo. Leip.,
1878–85.   E

ZOOLOGISCHER JAHRESBERICHT, 1885–90.   G
vols. 8vo. Berlin, 1886–92.   E

ZURCHER, F., and MARGOLLÉ, Lieut. E. Volcanoes
and Earthquakes. 8vo. Lond., 1874.   A 24 Q 15